Southern Living® GARDEN PROBLEM SOLVER

Edited by Steve Bender, Senior Writer, *Southern Living*

Oxmoor House®

Southern Living® Garden Problem Solver

Editor: Steve Bender
Managing Editor: Pamela Cornelison
Art Director: Alice Rogers
Consulting Art Director: James Boone
Consulting Editor: Bob Doyle
Associate Editors: Marianne Lipanovich, Tom Wilhite
Writers: L. Patricia Kite, Bob Polomski, Robert Bowden, Walter Reeves,
    Jack Siebenthaler, Jean Williams-Woodward
Photo Researcher: Tishana Peebles
Researcher: Barbara Brown
Editorial Assistants: Virginia Cochrane, Jackie Osborn
Production Coordinator: Patricia S. Williams
Copy Editors: Carolyn McGovern, Judith Dunham, Fran Haselsteiner,
    Christine Miklas, Jan deProsse
Proofreaders: Desne Border, Alicia Eckley, Margaret E. Hines,
    David Sweet, Judy Weiss, Carol Whiteley
Indexer: Thérèse Shere
Computer Production: Linda M. Bouchard (Manager), Joan Olson,
    David Van Ness
Botanical Illustrators: Jenny Speckels, Mimi Osborne, Margaret Robinson
Map Design and Cartography: Reineck & Reineck, San Francisco

Southern Living®

Editor: John Alex Floyd, Jr.
Executive Editor: Eleanor Griffin
Garden Editor: Linda C. Askey
Assistant Garden Design Editors: Rebecca Bull Reed, Troy Black
Assistant Garden Editors: Ellen Riley, Charles Thigpen
Senior Garden Photographer: Van Chaplin
Photographers: Jean Allsopp, Gary Clark, Tina Cornett, J. Savage Gibson,
    Sylvia Martin, Allen Rokach, Meg McKinney Simle

Copyright 1999 by Oxmoor House, Inc.
Book Division of Southern Progress Corporation
P.O. Box 2463, Birmingham, Alabama 35201

Southern Living® is a federally registered trademark of
Southern Living, Inc.

    5 6 7 8 9 QPD QPD   0
Library of Congress Catalog Card Number: 98-87557. Hardcover
edition: ISBN 0-376-03872-1. Softcover edition: 0-376-03873-X

For additional copies of the *Southern Living Garden Problem Solver* or
other Southern Living books, call our distribution partners at Leisure Arts,
1-800-526-5111.

Printed in the United States.

Cover photograph: *Insects can be a blessing or a curse. There's no
denying the beauty of a monarch butterfly on a butterfly bush, but
you may also find its caterpillars munching on your plants.*

Title page photograph: *George L. Taber azaleas*

Copyright page photograph: *Bearded iris and blue phlox, Bill Smith
garden, Atlanta*

Photographs by Van Chaplin

Getting It Right

In the garden, a little knowledge can be very dangerous indeed. I vividly remember the day our neighbor complained that his vegetable plants mysteriously started shriveling soon after he sprayed them for bugs. I asked when he'd used that sprayer before. "Oh, it was about a week ago," he replied. "I sprayed the grass for weeds."

Well, it didn't take Isaac Newton to surmise what had happened. Our neighbor neglected to clean out his sprayer. Now the same chemical he'd used to hammer his dandelions was stir-frying his tomatoes.

All of which goes to show that when it comes to dealing with bugs, weeds, fungi, and critters, it's not enough to get most things right. You have to get them *all* right. And that's exactly what this book will help you do.

The *Southern Living Garden Problem Solver* addresses the most common dilemmas Southerners face when a pest or malady plagues their gardens. We've designed it to provide quick answers when you're in a hurry and want a solution immediately. But it's also jam-packed with interesting facts, tips, and humorous observations you'll appreciate during a more leisurely read. Most important, it helps you prevent problems before they occur, so you can spend more time doing the things you like.

Please note that we haven't shied away from recommending chemical as well as natural (organic), cultural, and biological solutions. Rather than promoting a single approach, we believe in presenting all the pertinent information and choices and letting you make the decision.

But if you choose chemicals, do yourself and your plants a favor. Read the label and follow directions carefully—unless, of course, you prefer your watermelons and collard greens to glow in the dark.

Steve Bender

CONTENTS

1

GARDENING DOWN SOUTH

6

The Never-Ending Challenges of Southern Gardening
Success by Climate Zone • The Highs, Lows, and
In-Betweens of Southern Weather

2

AN OUNCE OF PREVENTION

18

Choosing the Right Plants • Building Good Soil • Compost and
Mulches • Watering and Garden Hygiene • Managing Pests
Easy Solutions for Tough Problems

3

A POUND OF CURE

60

Applying Pesticides Safely and Effectively • Working Around
Allergenic Plants • Quick Reference Guide to Synthetic and
Natural Pesticides • Beneficial Creatures

4

SOLVING PLANT PROBLEMS

80

Illustrated Guide for Quick Diagnosis of
Common Plant Problems • Prevention Methods and
Practical Solutions

Gardening
DOWN SOUTH

*G*ardening in the South is great fun. Our long growing season means that most of us can be out working in the yard practically year-round. And thanks to our climate, we can grow thousands of wonderful plants from all over the world.

But gardening here also poses special challenges. For one thing, many Southerners find themselves saddled with clay soil, which is better for making bricks than growing things. Others living along the coast must overcome sandy soil, constant wind, and salt spray.

Heaven is under our feet as well as over our heads.

–Henry David Thoreau

Our weather tests us as well. Rather than charting a steady course, it seems to bounce between extremes. For example, Lubbock, Texas, has been as hot as 114 degrees F and as cold as −16 degrees F (see "Hot and Cold," page 17). Withering droughts, scorching heat waves, torrential downpours, pummeling hailstorms, paralyzing ice storms, and oppressive humidity are all par for the course. Oh yes, it snows here, too— and not just in West Virginia, Kentucky, and the Appalachians, but occasionally as far south as Florida. What this means is that most days are fine for gardening, but you have to be prepared for anything.

People and plants aren't the only ones who love it here; so do bugs, fungi, weeds, and critters. Our long, hot summers and short, mild winters mean a continuous party for many of them. Bugs that produce one generation a year up north produce two or three down here. And is there a pest from outside the South that hasn't found our region to its liking? Such exotic troublemakers as fire ants, Japanese beetles, armadillos, Dutch elm disease, Asian tiger mosquitoes, and Chinese privet have taken up residence and spread throughout our land.

Learning to deal with these pests, and the sundry other conundrums that inevitably arise, is part of the challenge—and fun—of gardening here. This book, a companion to the best-selling *Southern Living Garden Book,* will help you cope.

Catherine Sims,
Homewood, Alabama

Handled with care: In Maryland, well-prepared soil and attentive care result in a rich tapestry of plants including Japanese maple, golden Hinoki false cypress, blue fescue, and rosy 'Gumpo Pink' azaleas.

HOW TO USE THIS BOOK

Let's assume you're a beginning gardener. You've just come from your garden, something looks amiss, and you're upset. "The leaves of my camellia are turning black," you say. "I wonder what's causing it?"

Turn to Chapter 4, "Solving Plant Problems." There you'll find, in alphabetical order, about 140 of the South's most popular trees, shrubs, annuals, perennials, vegetables, fruits, and ground covers. Color illustrations help you identify the most common problems of each plant. And for each problem you'll find a practical solution.

But perhaps you're an experienced gardener who knows a common pest when you see it. What you want now is detailed information about the pest's favorite targets, its life cycle, the kind of damage it does, and how to control it. Depending on the kind of pest, turn to Chapter 5, "Bugs and Other Critters"; Chapter 6, "Plant Diseases and Ailments"; or Chapter 7, "Weeds and Other Pesky Plants." Color photographs clearly identify 375 gardening problems you've probably encountered before.

BUT WAIT, THERE'S MORE

Half the battle in growing a beautiful garden is keeping problems from cropping up in the first place. So when you have a few minutes, sit down and read Chapter 2, "An Ounce of Prevention." You'll find a slew of information about how to keep your plants healthy and trouble-free through proper watering, fertilization, mulching, and soil preparation; crop rotation; soil solarization; using disease-resistant selections; and practicing good garden sanitation.

Most important, you'll learn how to choose the right plant for the right spot. To that end, beginning on page 39, we've included detailed lists of plants suited to specific situations, such as plants for wet soil, plants for alkaline soil, plants for the beach, and so on.

Next, turn to Chapter 3, "A Pound of Cure." Here you'll see listings of commonly available insecticides, fungicides, herbicides, and other pest-related products. You'll learn the proper use of each and how to apply it safely and effectively. You'll also be introduced to natural and biological controls that are often easier on the environment than synthetic pesticides.

Finally, check out Chapter 8, "Suppliers and Expert Resources." Wondering where in the world you can find the beneficial insects, natural pesticides, and biological controls mentioned elsewhere in the book? This chapter includes a handy list of mail-order suppliers. And just in case there's a pest in your garden that's not in this book, we've also listed telephone numbers of cooperative extension services throughout the South. Your county agent is there to help you solve your garden problem.

A Matter of Pride

No matter the type of gardening, we Southerners aim to finish on top. In Atlanta, Annabelle hydrangeas and a walk laced with mondo grass (left) make Sharon Abroms's garden a winner. And we always take pride in the harvest, whether it's a champion pumpkin hauled from the field by Scott Blair and his son in Allardt, Tennessee (above), or fresh asparagus (right) picked just in time for dinner.

SOUTHERN LIVING'S
CLIMATE ZONES

Nothing affects the success of a garden more than the climate. So some garden books try to predict precisely how the climate will affect your garden by providing climate zone maps. Some maps feature ten or eleven zones. Others offer many more.

Southern Living *believes in keeping things simple. Growing conditions vary from one side of town to another or even between gardens on opposite sides of the street. There's no way a map smaller than the planet Jupiter can track this jigsaw puzzle of microclimates.*

So, we divide the South into just five zones—the Upper South, Middle South, Lower South, Coastal South, and Tropical South (see map, pages 12–13). Then for every plant featured in this book we specify the zone or zones where we think it grows best. Pests have zone ratings too, so we tell you where a particular pest is prevalent.

Remember, though, that these climate zones offer general guidelines, not guarantees. Many other factors besides heat and cold influence a garden's success, including elevation, topography, prevailing winds, sun exposure, humidity, soil, and proximity to water. Annual fluctuations in weather may kill plants normally hardy in your area or exacerbate pest problems that usually aren't serious.

If you've just moved into a new area, ask veteran gardeners in the neighborhood what challenges they face. They might just give you the answers you seek.

Blue phlox and wild pinks (Silene caroliniana) *highlight a colorful spring in this Annapolis, Maryland, garden.*

UPPER SOUTH

The Upper South experiences the longest winters and shortest summers in our region. But summers are still hot and sticky, with temperatures occasionally exceeding 100 degrees F in July and August. Fortunately, such summer scorchers rarely persist for more than a few days. Summer nights usually cool off into the 60s, a necessity for many northern plants that grow there. Winter lows range from 0 to –10 degrees F, but frigid arctic air masses sometimes send the mercury plunging to –20 degrees F in Missouri, Kentucky, West Virginia, and the Appalachians.

Lawns consist primarily of Kentucky bluegrass, perennial ryegrass, and fescue, although there always seem to be a few radicals in town who insist on trying zoysia. Cabbage, broccoli, kale, asparagus, raspberries, and rhubarb produce better here than farther south. So do bunch grapes, highbush blueberries, apricots, and cherries.

However, cold winters do exact a price. The soil often freezes from mid-December until March. Dahlias, cannas, gladiolus, and other summer-flowering bulbs must be dug in autumn and stored indoors. Crepe myrtles, figs, camellias, and Southern magnolias may die back in some areas.

MIDDLE SOUTH

The Middle South marks the dividing line between warm-weather and cool-weather growing areas. Here you often encounter plants from the Northeast, Northwest, and Great

Plains growing side-by-side with those from the Old South. Summers are hot and, in most places, humid, though nights cool off in the mountain areas. Most perennials and bulbs flourish, but you still have to dig and store cannas, dahlias, and gladiolus. Winter lows seldom hit the zero mark, but temperatures of −15 degrees F do occur.

Vegetables grown in the old way flourish at Old Salem, a restored Moravian village in the Middle South city of Winston-Salem, North Carolina.

When the rose of Sharon blooms in Georgia, you know it's the dog days of summer in the Lower South.

LOWER SOUTH

Spring comes early to the Lower South. Daffodils, star magnolia, flowering quince, and forsythia open in February. Flowering dogwood, flowering cherry, and Bradford pear put on a glorious show in March. Summer is hot and sultry. Torrential downpours punctuate long stretches of drought in July and August. Nighttime temperatures in summer usually remain in the mid-70s or higher. The short winter seldom sees more than a few nights with temperatures dropping into the upper teens.

Lush gardens show the benefits of mild temperatures and high humidity of the Coastal South.

COASTAL SOUTH

Water rules the Coastal South. The close proximity of the Atlantic Ocean and the Gulf of Mexico ensures that winters are mild and brief, while summers are long, hot, and unmercifully humid. Although winter lows can drop into the low 20s or upper teens at the northern limit of this zone, this is rare. Many winters are frost-free, turning impatiens, coleus, geraniums, and caladiums into temporary perennials. Spring commences in January, when oriental magnolias, evergreen viburnums, and 'Okame' cherries bloom. Fall color is mostly just a dream, but Chinese tallow trees turn brilliant shades of red, orange, and yellow in early December.

TROPICAL SOUTH

The Tropical South is its own gardening world. Because it rarely, if ever, feels frost, gardens here enjoy an exotic, tropical look. Rainfall averages about 25 inches a year in the southernmost tip of Texas and more than twice that over the lower Florida peninsula. While most of the South deals with dry summers and wet winters, the Tropical South reverses that.

The lack of winter chilling takes its toll, however. While you can grow citruses (and in the lower Tropical South, mangoes, bananas, and avocados), apples, peaches, pears, blueberries, grapes, and other popular fruits flounder. So do many traditional flowering shrubs of the South, including forsythia, spiraea, quince, and azaleas.

The lack of frost makes exotic tree ferns dependable outdoor plants in south Florida.

THE SOUTH'S CLIMATE ZONES

As charted by the garden editors of *Southern Living*

IOWA

Des Moines

NEBRASKA

Denver

COLORADO

Arkansas River

KANSAS

Kansas City

Missouri River

MIS

Wichita

Springfield

Santa Fe

Rio Grande

Albuquerque

NEW MEXICO

Roswell

Alamogordo

El Paso

Rio Grande

Davis Mountains

MEXICO

TEXAS

Amarillo

Lubbock

Midland

Odessa

Abilene

San Antonio

Upper South

OKLAHOMA

Tulsa

Oklahoma City

Fort Smith

Wichita Falls

Fort Worth

Dallas

Middle South

TEXAS

Waco

Austin

Houston

Lower South

Corpus Christi

Coastal South

Rio Grande

Tropical South

Brownsville

Boston Mountain

Ouachita Mountain

ARKA

Ouachita Mountains

Lake Texoma

Arkansas River

Shrevepo

Lower South

Lake Charles

LO

Gulf of Mexico

LONG SUMMERS, SHORT WINTERS

It never stays cold for very long in the South. Long growing seasons give many Southerners the chance to garden outdoors nearly year-round.

CITY & ZONE*	Days per Year with Maximum Temperature Above 90°F	Days per Year with Maximum Temperature Below 32°F
Atlanta, Ga. (LS)	33	3
Charlotte, N.C. (LS)	37	3
Houston, Tex. (CS)	96	1
Little Rock, Ark. (MS)	73	6
Louisville, Ky. (US)	30	20
Miami, Fla. (TS)	52	0
Nashville, Tenn. (MS)	46	10
New Orleans, La. (CS)	68	0

* US = Upper South, MS = Middle South, LS = Lower South
CS = Coastal South, TS = Tropical South

We're Always Growing

A long growing season blesses most of the South. Bobby Rackley of Rocky Mount, North Carolina (left), says one of his secrets to growing the world's largest collards is leaving the plants in the ground until December. Meanwhile in Birmingham, Alabama, perennials bloom from summer into fall (above), including red Texas star, pink Joe-Pye weed, yellow cutleaf coneflower, and purple verbena.

STORMY WEATHER

Gray skies are gonna clear up—after the thunderstorm. Here's how some Southern cities stack up for stormy and sunny weather.

CITY & ZONE	Annual Number of Thunderstorms	Annual Percentage of Clear Skies
Baltimore, Md. (US)	28	57
Charlotte, N.C. (LS)	41	62
Houston, Tex. (CS)	64	59
Jackson, Miss. (LS)	68	61
Miami, Fla. (TS)	74	70
Nashville, Tenn. (MS)	52	56
New Orleans, La. (CS)	69	57
Richmond, Va. (MS)	36	62
Tulsa, Okla. (US)	51	62

SNOW OR NO

Yes, it does snow in the South, though not very often. Take a look at the chart below to see which towns near you are the flakiest in winter.

CITY & ZONE	Average Annual Snowfall (in.)	Greatest 1-Day Snowfall (in.)
Baltimore, Md. (US)	21.8	22.8 (Feb. 1998)
Birmingham, Ala. (LS)	1.4	13.0 (Mar. 1993)
Charleston, S.C. (CS)	1.0	6.6 (Dec. 1989)
Little Rock, Ark. (MS)	5.7	12.1 (Jan. 1998)
Louisville, Ky. (US)	17.4	15.9 (Jan. 1994)
Lubbock, Tex. (MS)	11.3	16.3 (Jan. 1993)
New Orleans, La. (CS)	0.1	2.7 (Dec. 1993)
Richmond, Va. (MS)	16.3	21.6 (Jan. 1940)
Tallahassee, Fla. (CS)	0.0	1.0 (Dec. 1989)

SINGING IN THE RAIN

No climatic factor exerts more influence over what you can grow in your garden than precipitation. As you can see from the following statistics, the South varies from nearly bone-dry to soupy-wet.

CITY & ZONE	Annual Rainfall (in.)	Days with Rain per Year
Baltimore, Md. (US)	41	112
Birmingham, Ala. (LS)	53	116
Charleston, S.C. (CS)	56	111
Jackson, Miss. (LS)	55	108
Lubbock, Tex. (MS)	19	64
Nashville, Tenn. (MS)	47	118
Richmond, Va. (MS)	43	110
Tallahassee, Fla. (CS)	66	115

Season's Bounty

Many fruits need both chill (cool winter weather) to set flower buds and heat (warm summer weather) to ripen the fruit. Each September, folks gather in Canton, Mississippi (above), to pick muscadines and enjoy each other's company. In Pittsboro, North Carolina, Lee and Edith Calhoun (below) harvest heirloom apples from their orchard. Piedmont azaleas (left) brighten a rainy day in Mountain Brook, Alabama.

HOT AND COLD

Southern weather is known for extremes. These are the hottest and coldest days ever recorded in these cities.

CITY & ZONE	Hottest Temperature	Coldest Temperature
Atlanta, Ga. (LS)	105 (July 1980)	−8 (Jan. 1985)
Baltimore, Md. (US)	105 (Aug. 1983)	−7 (Jan. 1984)
Houston, Tex. (CS)	107 (Aug. 1980)	7 (Dec. 1989)
Little Rock, Ark. (MS)	112 (July 1986)	−5 (Feb. 1951)
Louisville, Ky. (US)	105 (July 1954)	−22 (Jan. 1994)
Lubbock, Tex. (MS)	114 (June 1994)	−16 (Jan. 1963)
Miami, Fla. (TS)	98 (Aug. 1990)	30 (Dec. 1989)
Nashville, Tenn. (MS)	107 (July 1952)	−17 (Jan. 1985)
Tulsa, Okla. (US)	112 (July 1954)	−11 (Feb. 1996)

An Ounce
OF PREVENTION

*M*ost fires begin as sparks, not explosions. It's only by ignoring or overlooking the sparks that folks give them a chance to blaze out of control. Plant pests and ailments are like that too. It's better to catch them early in the game than to sound the alarm once hope appears lost.

At *Southern Living*, we believe that dusting roses, rooting out dandelions, and plotting revenge on unrepentant armadillos are not high on the average gardener's list of exciting weekend activities. But by carefully planning what you grow, keeping a close watch, and anticipating problems before they occur, you can have a nice garden and still spend your free time doing the things you like.

> *Before everything else, getting ready is the secret of success.*
>
> —Henry Ford

This chapter deals with preventing garden problems and managing small headaches so they don't become major ones. Of course, sometimes things get out of hand—then it's time to call in the big guns. You'll find guidelines for using pesticides in Chapter 3, "A Pound of Cure." Keep in mind, though, that chemical pesticides should really be used as a last resort. Applied improperly, they can injure desirable plants and wildlife, contaminate streams and groundwater, promote chemically resistant pests, and make your gardening job a whole lot harder.

CHOOSE THE RIGHT PLANT

If you've ever viewed lions hunting, you know that they inevitably seek out the weakest animal in the herd. Garden pests do this too. Plants that are stressed often fall victim to opportunistic insects and fungi. But healthy, vigorous plants fend off adversaries with little or no help from you.

The best way to keep your plants healthy is to plant them where the growing conditions naturally meet their needs. For example, a prime consideration for any outdoor plant is its tolerance of winter cold. While you can sometimes nurse a tender plant through winter by mulching heavily or covering it with leaves, this rarely succeeds indefinitely. Eventually, you'll be left with a plant that is either dead or so weak that the first pest that comes along will do it in.

Here in the South, heat tolerance is just as important as cold-hardiness. Plants that flourish in northern climates often scream in agony when exposed to our long, sultry summers. Just try growing fuchsias in New Orleans or Concord grapes in San Antonio. You'd have better luck teaching a turtle to fetch.

So how can you tell which plants are adapted to your climate? One way is to check out what your neighbors are growing. If the same plants show up in several gardens, chances are they like the local weather. Read the gardening column in your city's newspaper too. And if there's a botanical garden nearby (see Chapter 8, "Suppliers and Expert Resources"), pay a visit. You'll probably find demonstration gardens that showcase plants for your area.

Muscadines by the bucket

At the risk of tooting our own horn, we also suggest that you pick up a copy of the *Southern Living Garden Book*. This comprehensive, 512-page reference book describes more than 5,000 plants commonly grown in the South. Each plant is rated according to which of

As these young Southern gardeners (upper left) can attest, it's better to head off trouble before it occurs. Careful planning produces (clockwise from upper right) pest-free golden irises, prize-winning chard, and a vibrant mixed border.

Location, Location, Location

Choosing the right spot for a plant is critical to its health, but it isn't everything. Adequate watering is important, too. Failure to attend to the water needs of these beans (top, left) has stunted them and left them susceptible to spider mites. Compare these beans to their well-watered counterparts (top, right). The shade-loving rhododendron (middle), planted in a sunny spot, suffers from sunscald. Sheltered from direct sun, another rhododendron (bottom) thrives.

ARE NATIVES REALLY TOUGHER?

I f you've ever discussed trouble-free plants with another gardener, you've probably heard this: "Choose native plants rather than exotics, because natives are adapted to local conditions and have fewer problems." Sounds logical. But is it true? Not always.

The trouble is, few plants are native to the entire South. Just because a plant is native to the Southwest doesn't mean it will grow in the Southeast. The climates and soils of those two areas are completely different. So if you want to focus on native plants, concentrate on plants indigenous to an area no larger than your state.

That brings us to another point. Not all native plants are easy to grow. For example, lady's-slipper (*Cypripedium*) orchids are harder than a stale fruitcake to grow in home gardens. Franklin tree (*Franklinia alatamaha*), another native, is extremely temperamental and prone to root rot in hot, wet weather. On the other hand, exotic plants such as ginkgo, nandina, and daylily (*Hemerocallis*) are quite carefree. So here again, choosing the right plant for the right spot is the key. If an exotic plant fills the bill, so be it.

the five *Southern Living* climate zones—Upper, Middle, Lower, Coastal, and Tropical South—it does well in. Take your copy with you when you visit the garden center. Ask for the center's recommendations; then check out the advice against that in the book. But don't stop at merely considering the climate. More questions need asking before you settle on a plant. Does it need sun or shade? Flowering and fruiting plants generally need sun to perform well. But remember, the sun grows more intense the farther south you are. Plants that like all-day sun in the Upper South often prefer light afternoon shade in other Southern zones.

Does the plant like acid or alkaline soil? Whether the soil is acid or alkaline determines availability of certain nutrients to the plant. For example, iron is largely unavailable to plants growing in alkaline

Harvesting muscadines

soil. Plants that need iron, such as azalea, gardenia, camellia, and pin oak (*Quercus palustris*), will develop chlorosis (an iron deficiency that produces yellow leaves with green veins) and slowly die in alkaline soil. (See "Soil pH—The Acid Test," page 23.)

(Clockwise from upper left) cardinal flower, goldenrod; purple coneflower; black-eyed Susans; serviceberry

Book or another good gardening reference. Many pest-resistant selections will be noted and described.

Finding resistant vegetable selections is a bit easier. Often several letters printed on a seed pack indicate that selection's level of resistance. For example, 'Celebrity' VFTN is a main-season tomato that resists four major tomato pests: verticillium wilt (V), fusarium wilt (F), tobacco mosaic virus (T), and

DISEASE RESISTANCE BY THE LETTER

Look for the following abbreviations on seed packets, in catalogs, and in garden centers. They indicate diseases to which certain vegetables are resistant. (This list also includes nematodes, which are microscopic worms.)

Letter	Disease	Vegetables Affected
A	Alternaria or early blight	Tomato
ALS	Angular leaf spot	Cucumber
AN	Anthracnose	Beans, cucumber, melons, peppers
BMV	Bean mosaic virus	Beans
BV	Black rot	Broccoli, cabbage
BW	Bacterial wilt	Cucumber
C	Cercospora leaf spot	Beets, carrot, peppers
CMV	Cucumber mosaic virus	Cucumber
DM	Downy mildew	Beans, cabbage, cauliflower, lettuce, melons, peas, spinach
F	Fusarium wilt	Tomato
HB	Halo blight	Cucumber
L	Leaf spot (Septoria)	Tomato
LB	Late blight	Tomato
LMV	Lettuce mosaic virus	Lettuce
N	Nematodes	Tomato
PM	Powdery mildew	Cucumber, melons, peas
PVY	Potato virus Y	Beans, peppers, potato
S	Scab	Potato
SW	Stewart's wilt	Corn
T (or TMV)	Tobacco mosaic virus	Tomato, eggplant, peppers
V	Verticillium wilt	Tomato, eggplant, peppers

How much water does the plant need? Some plants are picky. For instance, a French hydrangea *(Hydrangea macrophylla)* planted in dry, rocky soil will give new meaning to the word "wilt." Or, plant showy sedum *(Sedum spectabile)* in boggy ground and before you can say "rot," it will.

How fast does the plant grow? Plants you must repeatedly hack back to keep in bounds are prone to pests. So don't plant rampant firethorn *(Pyracantha)* under your windows unless you need to keep burglars out or your teenagers in.

PLANTS THAT FEND FOR THEMSELVES

Back in the days before mass hybridization, gardeners had a simple choice. Either accept plants with all their faults or discard pest-prone plants altogether. But today, many popular plants have pest resistance built right in. You can buy crepe myrtles *(Lagerstroemia indica)* that don't get mildew, St. Augustine grass that doesn't get chinch bugs, apples and pears that don't get fireblight, and roses that don't get black spot. (See "Trouble-Free Roses," page 48; Chapter 6, "Plant Diseases and Ailments," Black spot.)

To find out which ornamental plants are pest resistant, read the plant labels at the garden center. If a plant resists a serious and widespread insect or disease, the label should say so. Also, look up the plant in the *Southern Living Garden*

nematodes (N). All things being equal, a tomato like 'Celebrity' should prove more reliable than one with no resistance.

Take pest resistance into account when considering heirloom selections. Heirlooms may indeed possess superior flavor and unique shapes and colors, but few resist pests as well as modern hybrids.

SOIL SUPPORT

Nothing contributes to plant health more than good soil. Good soil retains sufficient moisture, while letting excess water drain away. It permits the free passage of oxygen and other gases. It contains and releases essential nutrients. It promotes the growth of beneficial microorganisms, which break down organic matter and help keep soilborne diseases in check. And by increasing a plant's vigor, it boosts the plant's natural resistance to attack.

SOIL TYPES

Soil is a complex biological stew consisting of mineral particles mixed together with living and dead organic materials. There are three principal kinds of soil: clay, sand, and loam. Clay particles are extremely small, while sand particles are relatively large. Loam, a mixture of clay, sand, and silt, has midsize particles. Loam—what you are hoping to get when you buy a truckload of topsoil—is the best soil for most plants, because it's rich in nutrients as well as easy to work. Unfortunately, most gardeners start out with either clay or sandy soil.

The Right Stuff

These key ingredients make the difference between boom and bust soil. Sand (front bucket) loosens clay; sulfur (yellow material) acidifies alkaline soil; lime (upper right) improves overly acidic soil; compost (front left) and aged cow manure (dark brown material) loosens clay and adds valuable organic matter.

Clay, which ranges in color from classic red to near black, white, and even blue, is the bane of many gardens. When wet, its tiny particles stick tighter together than members of a labor union. Squeeze a handful together and you'll get a gummy mass that's sticky as taffy. Let it dry and it turns hard enough to deflect a howitzer shell. Because clay is dense and compacts readily, it drains poorly and restricts the movement of air and roots through the soil. On the plus side, it stores a wellspring of nutrients.

Start with the Soil

The original soil in this new border contained lots of clay. So the gardener tilled in generous amounts of topsoil, sphagnum peat moss, and builder's sand (right). He then used a rake to smooth and shape the bed from front to back (far right). The result? A beautiful border of annuals and perennials by summer. (In case you're wondering, the copper tubing on the fence serves as support for vines.)

In most ways, sand acts the opposite of clay. Water and nutrients pass right through it, so you need to replenish them frequently. But sand doesn't compact, leaving plenty of room for water, air, and roots.

ORGANIC MATTER

The best way to improve soils, especially clay and sand, is by adding large amounts of organic matter. Put simply, organic matter consists of the decaying remains of once-living plants and animals. As it decomposes, it releases nutrients that add to soil fertility. What's left at the end of this process is humus, a soft, crumbly material that binds with clay or sand particles. Clay becomes more porous; sand becomes less so.

Organic matter comes in many different forms, including peat moss, manure, ground bark, chopped leaves, sawdust, and homemade compost. The easiest way to incorporate it into a new planting bed is to spread it evenly over the soil surface, then use a garden fork or rotary tiller to mix it in thoroughly to a depth of 10 to 15 inches. If your soil is primarily clay or sand, the finished mix should contain about at least 1 part organic matter to 2 parts soil. (A half-and-half mix is, of course, better.) If your soil is loam or it's been amended in the past, add 1 part organic matter to 4 parts soil.

Before you settle on a particular type of organic matter, consider these points: If you're going to use peat moss, choose sphagnum peat moss. It conditions the soil much better than products labeled either "peat humus," or just plain "peat moss." Never use fresh manure. It can burn plants. It's also likely filled with a billion weed seeds, all chomping at the bit to sprout in your garden. Instead, choose bagged or composted manure. Don't use fresh sawdust either. As microbes break it down, they suck all of the nitrogen out of the soil, turning plants yellow. Only use sawdust that has composted for a year.

SOIL pH—THE ACID TEST

E ven in gardening, simple terminology has the power to intimidate. Take the term "pH," for example. Folks can listen to television commercials touting pH-balanced deodorants and shampoos without batting an eye. But say "soil pH," and their eyes glass over.

It's really not that frightening. In gardening, the term "pH" refers to the soil's relative acidity or alkalinity. It's measured on a scale from 0 to 14. A pH less than 7 is acid, while one greater than 7 is alkaline. A pH of 7 is neutral. Most garden plants prefer a pH range between 6.0 and 6.8, though exceptions abound. Having the proper degree of soil acidity or alkalinity enables plants accustomed to those soil conditions to extract the nutrients that they require from the soil. Therefore, if you plant an acid-loving blueberry in highly alkaline soil, it won't survive even if you meet all its other needs. Other than prayer, the only way to make it flourish is to make the soil acidic.

Annual rainfall is one of the greatest determinants of soil pH. High-rainfall areas tend to have acid soils; low-rainfall areas tend toward alkaline soils. Some gardening books consider the Mississippi River a good dividing line between the acid soils of the Southeast and the alkaline soils of the Southwest. But this fails to consider vast deposits of limestone that lie just beneath the surface in Kentucky, Tennessee, Florida, Alabama, Georgia, and the Carolinas. Soils in these places are alkaline. Moreover, almost all of Louisiana lies west of the Mississippi, yet most of its soil is acid.

To provide the proper soil pH for your plants, you first have to know what your soil is. You can have it tested by your cooperative extension service. You'll probably have to pay a fee, but you'll get a detailed analysis showing nutrient amounts in addition to pH. For less money, you can buy a soil-testing kit from a garden center. The results will be less precise but informative enough to give you a good idea of what you're dealing with.

How do you alter soil pH? Add soil amendments according to the recommendations of a detailed soil test. To make soil more acid, add garden sulfur, aluminum sulfate, iron sulfate, or sphagnum peat moss. To make it more alkaline, add lime.

Of course, it's a whole lot easier just to select plants well adapted to acid or alkaline soil. Acid-loving plants include American holly *(Ilex opaca),* azalea, blueberry, camellia, centipede grass *(Eremochloa ophiuroides),* dogwood *(Cornus),* eastern red cedar *(Juniperus virginiana),* gardenia, Japanese andromeda *(Pieris japonica),* ixora, pin oak, and rhododendron. Alkaline-loving plants include bottlebrush *(Callistemon),* Chinese pistache *(Pistacia chinensis),* cinquefoil *(Potentilla),* Indian hawthorn *(Raphiolepis indica),* lilac *(Syringa),* mesquite *(Prosopis glandulosa),* Texas mountain laurel *(Sophora secundiflora),* and thyme *(Thymus).*

A test kit from your cooperative extension service can supply a detailed soil analysis.

Lawns in areas with acid soil need periodic applications of lime.

pH Particular Plants

Many plants are fussy about soil pH, such as rhododendrons (top, left) and camellias (top, right), which need moderately acid soil. Others like thyme (Thymus) and cinquefoil (Potentilla) prefer neutral or alkaline soil (at or above a pH of 7).

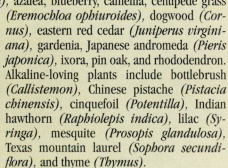

COMPOST BINS: CHOOSING THE RIGHT SPEED

Plant debris placed in a simple bin (left) takes its time turning into compost. A compost container (right) speeds up decomposition by heating up plant materials.

COMPOST WITH THE MOST

Compost—decomposed organic matter from your lawn, garden, and kitchen—is probably the top all-around soil amendment. It's easy to make, although it takes time and space. If you don't have either, check to see whether any public agency supplies compost. Many cities now compost leaves, grass clippings, and other yard waste left by the curb, then sell it to the public.

A simple (though not the most efficient) way to make compost is by building an old-fashioned compost heap. Pile up garden debris, mix it with vegetable and fruit scraps from the kitchen, and let it sit. After about 6 months, depending on temperature, rainfall, and size of materials, the compost will have broken down enough to be used. Compost decomposes more rapidly if you confine it in a container that has vents to allow air circulation (see illustration above), and if you turn it frequently. You'll find a number of different composters available for purchase at garden supply stores and through catalogs.

The compost material in the middle "cooks" at the hottest temperature and decomposes most quickly; it's hot enough to kill most diseases, insects, and weeds. Still, if you choose this method, don't add any diseased leaves or weed seeds to the compost, as the temperature generated during the decomposition process won't be high enough to kill bacteria, fungi, or seeds.

It's best to play it safe and consign weeds and infested plants to the garbage instead of the compost bin. Never compost diseased rose leaves and stems. The bacterial diseases found on them aren't always killed during composting, so you risk reintroducing them to your garden when you distribute finished compost.

They Need to Breathe

The microorganisms that break down garden debris into compost need oxygen to do their job. Here, PVC pipes with holes drilled into them are inserted into the compost pile, keeping the oxygen flowing.

THE WORM REALLY DOES TURN

There's a new kind of composting suited to small gardens, such as container gardens on decks and patios. It's called a worm box. You fill a small wooden box with red worms you get through mail-order suppliers; then watch them turn newspaper and kitchen scrap into rich compost in just a few weeks. It's fun for kids, but heed this warning—never put fruit scraps in the worm box, lest you spawn a fruit fly invasion. Ignore this advice at your peril.

MULCH MADNESS

No single weed-prevention technique works better than applying a thick layer of mulch over exposed soil. It smothers many weed seeds as they germinate and makes it easier to pull up any weed seedlings that manage to survive the mulch.

Mulch serves many other useful purposes. It cools the soil—an important consideration if you're growing plants such as clematis that like cool roots. It reduces soil compaction and

MURDER BY MULCH

Mulch can be a great boon to plants and the garden, but like anything else, too much is bad. Some people replenish mulch every spring and autumn, no matter if the previous layer has decomposed or not. The result is a smothering blanket 6 to 8 inches thick that retards the passage of air and water and can

Yes, it is possible to overdo it on the mulch and cause damage to plants.

even produce harmful chemical compounds. If that's not bad enough, mulch piled up against the trunks of trees and shrubs also provides perfect cover for mice and insects that may damage the bark. Shredded bark and wood chips are the mulches most often overapplied. Use them and other mulches as often as you need them, but don't let them build up to more than 3 inches deep.

keeps the soil from crusting over. It conserves soil moisture and reduces runoff. It insulates the ground during cold winters, helping tender plants survive. It adds organic matter to the soil as it decays. It also covers disease spores on the ground and keeps them from infecting nearby plants.

Finally, mulch spiffs up a garden. A fresh layer of mulch atop planting beds unifies the garden visually and gives it a finished look.

Straw Bed

A thick mulch of straw keeps the soil surface from drying out and also smothers weeds. An added benefit: The pumpkin rests on a nice, clean bed.

A QUICK LOOK AT MULCHES

You'll find a number of different mulches available around the South. Here are some pros and cons of the most popular kinds.

Cocoa hulls. *Pro*—Mouthwatering odor when fresh; smells like chocolate cake right out of the oven; very good source of potassium. *Con*—Expensive; hard to find; grows a disgusting mold if kept too wet.

Dead leaves. *Pro*—Free; decompose rapidly to add nutrients to the soil. *Con*—Must be shredded first; unshredded leaves can form a mat nearly impenetrable to water.

Pine bark and pine straw are common mulches.

Grass clippings. *Pro*—Free; decompose very rapidly adding organic matter to the soil. *Con*—Can burn plants; need frequent replenishing; malodorous if piled too thickly; clippings from lawns treated with herbicide could harm mulched plants.

Peat moss. *Pro*—Looks nice; adds organic matter to soil as it decomposes. *Con*—Can blow away; once completely dry, becomes impenetrable to water.

Pine straw. *Pro*—Free if you have pine trees; perfect for acid-loving plants, such as azaleas, rhododendrons, and camellias; one application usually lasts a season; won't wash off slopes; has a natural look; enriches soil as it decomposes. *Con*—None.

Shredded bark. *Pro*—Attractive; one application lasts a season. *Con*—Floats away in heavy rains; may attract termites.

Wheat straw. *Pro*—Readily available and inexpensive; lasts several months. *Con*—Often contains weed seeds; floats away in heavy rains.

Wood chips. *Pro*—Often free from tree-trimming companies; decompose slowly; stay in place. *Con*—May be infested with insects; may attract termites; can cause nitrogen deficiency in soil.

MAINTAINING A HEALTHY DIET

Growing plants need food. In addition to water, air, and soil, they require 13 different nutrients in order to thrive. Lacking these nutrients, plants not only falter, but also become more susceptible to pests.

Plants need large amounts of nitrogen (N), phosphorus (P), and potassium (K). These are called macronutrients. The remaining elements, including iron, magnesium, sulfur, manganese, aluminum, and zinc, are called micronutrients. They're just as vital, but needed in smaller doses.

Nitrogen promotes healthy leaves and stems; phosphorus facilitates flowering and root growth; and potassium boosts the plant's overall vigor and disease resistance. Nitrogen and potassium leach readily from soil, especially in high-rainfall areas. Phosphorus stays put, but may be unavailable to plants growing in cold or highly acidic soils. To replenish or supplement these nutrients, you need to add fertilizer, which comes from either organic or inorganic sources.

ORGANIC VS. INORGANIC—THIS TIME IT'S WAR

Don't expect terms of endearment when proponents of organic and inorganic fertilizers meet. Both think their products are best for your garden and the opinions of the other side are full of, well, fertilizer.

Organic fertilizers are most often recycled, natural by-products. They include compost, manure, bat guano, blood meal, bonemeal, cottonseed meal, fish emulsion, fish meal, kelp, alfalfa meal, and composted sewage sludge. Most come in powdered or granular form. Fish emulsion is a liquid.

Inorganic fertilizers are manufactured from different chemical compounds. You'll find them either in granular form or as liquid concentrates that you mix with water.

As a plant absorbs nutrients through its roots, it can't distinguish between an organic and inorganic fertilizer. However, there are differences between these two types that may make one preferable to a particular gardener. For one thing, many organic fertilizers have soil-building qualities. They bind soil particles while also adding organic matter, thus promoting the good work of earthworms and soil microbes. Their nutrients tend to be slow releasing and stored in the soil until needed by the plant. They generally have low nutrient-grade levels (5-2-2, for example), so they're less likely to burn roots or leach into groundwater. And they usually contain micronutrients. On the downside, they cost more per pound and work more slowly than inorganic fertilizers. And it takes more to correct a serious mineral deficiency.

Inorganic fertilizers are the gardener's hired guns, providing major amounts of macronutrients. Lawn fertilizers, for example, typically sport analyses like 30-3-8. (For information on nutrient analyses, see "Deciphering the Label," opposite page.) Inorganic fertilizers act fast, which can be useful if a plant is stressed due to a nutrient deficiency, physical injury, or pest infestation.

Dinnertime for Plants

Cottonseed meal (being applied, left) is a popular, slow-release, organic fertilizer that feeds both plants and beneficial soil microorganisms. Soil rich in organic matter (center) not only provides healthy nutrients for plants, but also is lighter, better drained, and easier to work. Water-soluble fertilizers (right) can be applied through a hose.

DECIPHERING THE LABEL

The three major nutrients—nitrogen (N), phosphorus (P), and potassium (K)—are always listed on a fertilizer label in that order. The numbers you find on the bag or container stand for the percentage of each element. A formula of 18-6-12 means the product contains 18 percent total nitrogen, 6 percent phosphorus, and 12 percent potassium. Any fertilizer that contains any amount of these three nutrients is deemed a balanced fertilizer.

The relative percentages of these three elements indicate the fertilizer's primary use. For example, a formula of 31-3-7 is considered a high-nitrogen fertilizer because it contains many times more nitrogen than phosphorus or potassium. High-nitrogen fertilizers spur fast growth of leaves and stems. They're used mostly on lawns.

Bloom-booster fertilizers, such as those with formulas of 11-40-6, contain higher amounts of phosphorus than nitrogen or potassium. They increase flowering and bud set for annuals and perennials.

High-potassium fertilizers, such as a formula of 8-8-25, are commonly used for winterizing warm-season grasses because potassium aids vigor and winter hardiness.

Lawn fertilizers typically contain high amounts of nitrogen.

Many fertilizers also contain micronutrients, such as sulfur, boron, copper, iron, manganese, and zinc. You'll find these listed in the "guaranteed analysis" on the label. While plants need only small amounts of these elements, many gardeners feel that a balanced fertilizer replete with micronutrients is best for general garden use.

However, plants can't absorb excess nutrients. Thus, these chemicals may end up poisoning earthworms and soil microorganisms or contaminating groundwater and streams. For this reason, *Southern Living* recommends that if you use inorganic fertilizers, especially lawn fertilizer, check the bag to see that at least 33 percent of the nitrogen (the most readily leachable nutrient) is in a slow-release or controlled-release form. Such products release nitrogen over many weeks, so most of it goes into plants.

WATER, WATER EVERYWHERE

Water is the stuff of life. But too much or too little causes problems for plants that you might mistakenly blame on diseases or insects. More plants have been killed by improper watering than by just about anything else.

The basic problem is, of course, that no two plants have exactly the same water requirements. So you can't put your irrigation system on automatic and give all your plants the optimum amount at once. Moreover, soil types differ in how much water they hold and how long they hold it. Sand holds little water and dries out quickly. Clay holds lots of water and dries out slowly. Loam reacts somewhere in between.

There's no magic rule of watering that covers all plants. Our advice is to learn as much as you can about the water needs of individual plants, then group together plants based on those needs. For example, plant impatiens, cardinal flower (*Lobelia cardinalis*), astilbe, and other moisture-loving plants in one spot. Then plant junipers (*Juniperus*), sedums, yuccas, and other dry-soil plants elsewhere.

Baby That New Lawn

Whether seeded or sodded, all new lawns need lots of water until they become established. A good rule of thumb is to water them on every rainless day for at least 3 weeks after the sod is down or the seed has germinated. This promotes vigorous root systems that will better tolerate drought in the future.

TELLTALE WATER SIGNS

Here are some common ways plants tell you they're getting too little or too much water.

Too Little
- Wilting throughout the day
- Leaf scorch on the edges of leaves
- Leaves that curl or drop prematurely
- Leaves that lose their bright green color
- Flowers that drop prematurely
- Fruit that shrivels and drops before maturing
- A lawn that shows footprints 10 minutes after you've walked across it

Too Much
- Wilting in bright sunlight
- Yellowing leaves
- Leaves that drop while green
- Sudden collapse of plant
- Rotting roots
- Malodorous soil
- Edema (blisters that form on leaves)

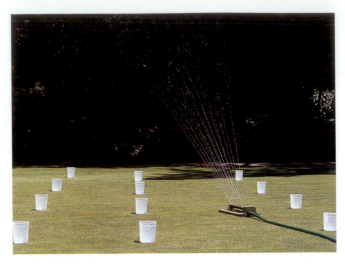

Measuring Up

To gauge how evenly sprinklers distribute water over your lawn, set out same-size containers in a grid as shown above. Turn on your sprinkler or irrigation system for about 15 minutes; then measure the water in each container. More than a ¼-inch difference between the levels in the containers means that you need to adjust your sprinkling system.

Always give potted plants a drink before you set them in the planting hole.

WATERING CANS AND CAN'TS

There's no substitute for experience when watering a wide variety of plants. But the following tips will speed your education along.

- You *can* harm your lawn by watering too often. Many people water their lawns for a few minutes each day, so that water penetrates only the top inch or so of soil. As a result, grass roots crowd near the surface. Then if folks forget to water for a few days and the soil dries out, the lawn dies of thirst. Therefore, it is important that you water your lawn infrequently, but deeply.

How deeply? Wet the soil to about 18 inches to encourage deep roots. Note: An inch of rain penetrates to about 12 inches in sandy soil, 7 inches in loam, and 4 to 5 inches in clay. Leave your sprinklers on long enough to do the job. Check their coverage pattern and distribution rate by placing cans, all the same size, in a grid pattern across the lawn. Thoroughly water the lawn about once a week in dry weather.

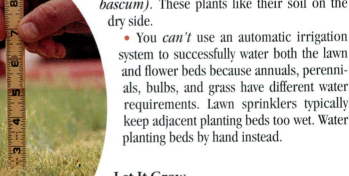

- You *can* reduce your watering bills by cutting your lawn a little higher in summer; reducing the size of your lawn; using hoses and sprinklers to water the lawn instead of an automatic irrigation system; applying a 2–3-inch layer of mulch over planting beds; and choosing drought-tolerant plants for your garden (for an extensive list, see the *Southern Living Garden Book*).

- You *can't* be too careful when watering succulents, such as sedums, yuccas, and hen and chickens (*Sempervivum tectorum*). These plants store water in thick leaves and stems and quickly rot if overwatered. Also be careful not to overwater plants with gray, silvery, or woolly leaves, such as lamb's ears (*Stachys byzantina*), artemisia, rose campion (*Lychnis coronaria*), or mullein (*Verbascum*). These plants like their soil on the dry side.

- You *can't* use an automatic irrigation system to successfully water both the lawn and flower beds because annuals, perennials, bulbs, and grass have different water requirements. Lawn sprinklers typically keep adjacent planting beds too wet. Water planting beds by hand instead.

Let It Grow

The simplest way to reduce the amount of water your lawn needs in summer is to let the grass grow taller in dry weather. Taller grass stays green much longer between waterings than freshly cut grass.

KEEP IT CLEAN

There's no point in worrying about new pests until you're certain you've dispatched the old. Proper sanitation practices will keep diseases, weeds, and bugs of the past from coming back to haunt you.

Whack those weeds. Weeds do more than make your garden a mess. They also harbor millions of insects, mites, and diseases. Tall weed patches near your garden virtually guarantee some sort of invasion. So cut the weeds and save the peace.

Inspect all newcomers. How many times have you heard that the worst place to go if you want to stay healthy is the hospital? That's because it's filled to the gills with sick people. When it comes to plants, a garden center is pretty much the same way. With so many plants growing so close together, it's nearly impossible to keep them pest free. So check new plants for unwelcome hitchhikers as soon as you get them home. Remove and destroy diseased leaves.

A Clean Bug Is a Dead Bug, Sometimes

Insecticidal soaps devastate soft-bodied pests, such as aphids (top), by causing their cell membranes to burst. However, a good wash with insecticidal soap won't affect hard-bodied insects like the striped cucumber beetle pictured above.

Spray insect- or mite-laden plants with insecticidal soap or horticultural oil.

Bury the fallen. Don't allow infested leaves, fruits, or flowers that fall to the ground to remain there. The pests and problems they harbor may reinfest your plants. Instead, gather them immediately and burn them, put them in the trash, or bury them away from your garden. Don't compost them—this process may not kill the little beasts. And don't fool yourself into thinking winter cold will kill them either. Many pests overwinter on plant debris and emerge the next spring meaner than ever.

Strip your roses. Only in the Upper South do roses lose all of their leaves in autumn. Elsewhere, they hold onto much of their foliage throughout winter. These leaves often carry black spot and other diseases that infect new leaves the following spring. So strip off and destroy all rose foliage in late autumn. (No, this won't affect future blooming.)

Shower your plants. Buy a hose nozzle you can set to a sharp stream. Use it to blast aphids, mealybugs, spittlebugs, and other insects from your plants. Once these pests hit the ground, they'll likely either die or make a fine meal for a predator. The key here is to spray regularly with water and to thoroughly wet all leaf surfaces. Water spraying controls spider mites as well, because mites like dusty leaves and low humidity.

Nip It in the Bud

You can prevent many plant problems by following a few simple steps. For example, to control camellia petal blight, shown far left, immediately pick up fallen petals and flowers. To remove sooty mold, like that shown at left on Carolina jessamine *(Gelsemium sempervirens)*, spray the leaves with a jet of water. The water also removes aphids and other insects that secrete honeydew on which the mold grows.

Tipping the Scales

Orange growers have to contend with outbreaks of scale (shown here on an orange, greatly magnified). Spraying trees with horticultural oil can minimize infestations. Using oil instead of other insecticides helps to maintain a healthy population of beneficial insects, which keeps scales in check.

Change your oil. Modern horticultural oil sprays are great garden tools, because they're nontoxic and easy to apply, and they destroy a wide range of pests, including mites, scales, and aphids. They do so by coating leaves, stems, and trunks, thereby smothering the pest. Oils come in two main types: summer oils, which are lighter and can be applied during the growing season; and dormant oils, which are applied only in late autumn and winter when plants are dormant. Dormant oil is a must if you want to grow healthy fruit trees.

GARDENING—A MOVING EXPERIENCE

One of the best ways to prevent the same pests from decimating your vegetables each year is by practicing crop rotation. Simply put, crop rotation means that you don't grow the same plant in the same spot year after year. By planting in a new location, you interrupt the life cycle of an insect or a disease. For example, onion maggots living in the soil die out if they don't have new onions to eat each year. But fewer pests aren't the only benefit. By rotating plants annually, you're also less likely to deplete a particular nutrient in the soil.

While it's wise to rotate all of the plants in your vegetable garden, it's especially important to do so for members of the tomato family *(Solanaceae)*—tomato, potato, pepper, and eggplant. These plants fall victim to soilborne diseases if planted in the same soil year after year. The same problem also besets most members of the cabbage family *(Brassicaceae)*—cabbage, broccoli, brussels sprouts, and cauliflower.

Willing to Relocate

A healthy, productive vegetable garden depends on your willingness to move things around periodically, so that pests don't build up in the soil. This is especially important for tomatoes, which often fall victim to soilborne diseases. If you can't move your garden, be sure to plant disease-resistant selections.

GROUND CONTROL: ROTATE CROPS TO BEWILDER PESTS

Year 1

Year 2

Year 3

Year 4

Garden pests have a hard time hitting a moving target. That's why it's important to rotate your vegetable plantings every year. In this crop rotation scheme, each of the plant types moves on a 4-year schedule, making it less likely for a plant to pick up a soilborne disease.

Crop rotation can also help annual flowers plagued by soil-borne diseases. For example, a number of different soil fungi attack snapdragons *(Antirrhinum majus)*, causing them to suddenly wilt and die. One solution is to apply a soil sterilant. But it's much easier for most people to simply plant a different annual. The illustration above shows an easy way to rotate crops on a 4-year cycle. Members of the same vegetable family are moved to a different spot each year. One of the four groups always consists of a member of the pea family *(Fabaceae)*, such as beans or peas, because these vegetables can take nitrogen from the air and help replenish depleted soil. Instead of planting peas or beans, you may want to set aside a quarter of the garden for a green-manure crop. Or you may want to plant green manure throughout the entire garden from time to time. Green manure is a crop grown solely for the purpose of tilling it back into the ground to improve the soil. Commonly grown green-manure plants include buckwheat *(Fagopyrum)*, clover *(Trifolium)*, fava beans, field peas, and annual ryegrass *(Lolium multiflorum)*. In most areas of the South, you can plant a green-manure crop in autumn or winter, till it under in late spring, and still have time to plant a main-season crop. Always till in

A buckwheat cover crop

a cover crop when it's green, because that's when it contains the most nutrients.

Unfortunately, crop rotation isn't a panacea. It works better in large gardens. In small gardens, rotating a crop only a few feet away isn't enough to keep pests from finding it the next season. If pests become a real pain, skip a problem vegetable for a season or two. Or change your timing to evade the pests. For example, you'll have fewer problems with cabbage worms by planting cabbage and broccoli as autumn crops rather than as spring ones.

GOING SOLAR

Here's a bright idea: Use the sun's rays to kill weed seeds, insects, and diseases in the soil. It's called solarization.

This technique involves covering the ground with clear plastic to trap solar energy and literally cook the soil. While solarization isn't foolproof (it probably won't kill Bermuda grass, red clover, nutsedges, or Texas root rot), it's an inexpensive and simple way to kill many pests without resorting to toxic soil sterilants. Here's how to do it.

• Pick an area that's at least 2 feet wide (it's hard to retain heat in beds narrower than this). Clean the bed of all weeds

SOLARIZING THE SOIL: HARNESS THE SUN TO KILL WEEDS AND DISEASES

Edges buried in soil

1–4-mil plastic sheet

Soda-can spacers between two plastic sheets

and rocks. If you plan to install an irrigation system, do it now. Then thoroughly wet the soil to a depth of 8 to 12 inches.

• Buy enough 1–4-mil clear plastic sheeting to cover the bed twice. Place the first layer of plastic on the ground. Place the second layer over the first, raising it a few inches by placing bricks or cans between the layers. Leave enough loose plastic around the edges so that you can bury the ends a couple of inches deep in the soil.

• Wait 4 to 8 weeks before removing the plastic. Now you're ready to plant.

One Humongous Tomato

Gordon Graham of Edmond, Oklahoma, set a world record when he grew this monstrous tomato (7 pounds 12 ounces) in his backyard. He credits his record to solarizing the soil, planting early, fertilizing with Miracle-Gro and rabbit manure, letting only one tomato form per plant, and letting his plants listen to CB radio.

BLOCK THAT PEST!

Bugs and critters can't attack your plants if they can't get to them. Many garden products now on the market are dedicated to the proposition that pests and plants should forever remain apart.

For example, vegetable gardeners worth their hoes should never be without floating row cover. This material, made from spun-bonded polyester, is so light you can lay it atop your plants. It lets in sunlight, air, and rainfall or watering, but keeps out insects. Keep two things in mind if you use it, though. First, look to see no bugs accompany your plants when you cover them or you will trap hungry insects inside. Second, remove the row cover from vegetables that require insect pollination, such as squash and cucumber, once they begin to flower.

To discourage slugs and snails, try placing copper banding around their favorite plants. When these mollusks touch the copper, they receive a mild electrical shock, then beat a hasty

Protecting the Young

Many opportunistic pests present the biggest threat in the garden when plants are young and tender. Limit their marauding by covering garden beds with floating row covers during this critical time. The gauzelike material keeps out flying and crawling pests while letting in light and air.

retreat. To be effective, the copper banding must be at least 3 inches high. Make sure, too, that no foliage hangs over the edge of the banding, forming a bridge to the planting bed. Copper banding can be expensive initially, but lasts for years.

Diatomaceous earth makes a good slug and snail barrier too. This powdery product consists of the skeletal remains of diatoms, which are single-celled marine algae. When soft-bodied pests pass over it, diatomaceous earth lacerates their bodies, causing them to dehydrate and die. For this product to be effective, you need to surround individual plants or the entire planting bed with a band of it that's 3 to 4 inches wide. And you have to reapply it following heavy rains. Wood ashes and lime are cheaper, if less effective, alternatives. They repel, but don't kill, slugs and snails.

Sticky barriers work like flypaper. They consist of materials such as castor oil, natural gum resins, and vegetable wax. ("Tanglefoot" is the most widely known.) You "paint" these materials onto the tree trunks and stop crawling pests, such as cankerworms, gypsy moth caterpillars, climbing cutworms, and ants dead in their tracks. Sticky barriers also come in spray form, which you can use to coat yellow cardboard squares that you place throughout the garden. Why do this? Well, for some reason, many harmful insects, such as whiteflies, find yellow

Less-Toxic Alternatives

Here are several options for folks concerned about using strong chemicals in the garden. Sprinkling diatomaceous earth around young seedlings (above, left) protects them from slugs and snails. Plastic cartons (right) keep cutworms from nibbling vegetable seedlings. Yellow sticky cards (far right) trap whiteflies and other small, flying insects attracted to the color.

irresistible. An insect that lands on a yellow sticky card won't be taking off again.

Pheromone traps contain secreted chemicals of a particular pest that help regulate the behavior of insects and other creatures. In the garden, these traps typically employ sex pheromones to attract and catch male insects. Because pheromones are insect specific, these traps control only a single pest type. The most common traps include those for Japanese beetles, cabbage loopers, codling moths, corn earworms, and peach tree borers. They're more effective when used in large numbers in farms and orchards. At your home, one or two traps will probably attract many more insects to your yard than before.

You can also try the old overturned-grapefruit trick. Place empty grapefruit halves, rind side up, in the garden. Slugs, snails, and earwigs will crawl under these citrus motels at night. In the morning, pick up the grapefruit halves, scoop out the pests, and destroy them. (See what happens when you don't check out by 11 A.M.?)

CRITTER CONTROL

When the Lord gave people dominion over the beasts of the world, He apparently forgot to tell the animals. Most think they have just as much of a right to your garden as you do. Discouraging them requires constant vigilance and much patience. For suggestions regarding individual animal pests, see Chapter 5, "Bugs and Other Critters." But here are some quick tips as well.

Deer. As ever-expanding neighborhoods conquer former deer habitat, cute little Bambi is becoming cursed big Bambi. Hungry deer will eat almost anything, including the tires off of your pickup. A sturdy fence, at least 8 feet high, remains the best control. If that's too expensive, spray ornamental plants with a deer repellant, such as Deer Away, Hinder, and Deer-Off. You can also apply bobcat, wolf, or lion urine, if you don't have too many close neighbors.

Moles and gophers. These sneak thieves do their dirty work underground, digging tunnels that deface lawns and garden beds. Moles eat insects and grubs; gophers chomp plants. Controlling either is very difficult. One way is to place traps in active tunnels. Probably the surest methods are planting plants inside wire cages or lining the sides and bottom of entire planting beds with chicken wire.

Birds. Although birds occasionally pull up seedlings, mistaking them for bugs and worms, our feathered friends

Permanent Protection

Permanently protect plant roots from gopher damage by lining the sides and bottom of raised beds with aviary wire.

Don't Be Rattled

Don't worry, this is Ralphie, a very friendly, inflatable plastic snake placed in this garden to scare away birds. Ralphie works too, as long as you remember to relocate him from time to time, so the birds don't catch on.

mainly pester growers of fruit trees and bushes. Covering the ripening fruit with netting is your best bet. Reflective mylar tape scares away flocking birds. Inflatable plastic snakes and owls work too, but you need to move them around from time to time. Birds may have bird brains, but they're not that dumb!

Rabbits. Controlling rabbits is easy, once you master this simple concept: Rabbits can't climb. A chicken-wire fence, 3 feet high, around the vegetable garden sends these furry pests over to your neighbor's plot. Just make sure you anchor the fence 6 inches deep in the ground, because rabbits can dig.

Squirrels. Although squirrels are best known as pillagers of bird feeders, they also enrage gardeners by picking fruit or tomatoes, taking a tiny bite, then going to get more. Netting is the best control. You can also trap squirrels and release them in the wild.

Armadillos. Armadillos, a common sight lying belly-up along Southern interstates, have become frequent garden pests in recent years. They use powerful claws to tear up lawns in search of grubs and other food. One answer is to treat the lawn with insecticide, removing the food source. Or you can trap the offending animal. If all else fails, consider building an interstate through your yard.

SEVEN EASY WAYS TO MAKE PROBLEMS WORSE

You can't blame everything that goes wrong in your garden on a bug, blight, or critter. Some things may be your fault.

Crowding plants. Jamming plants together may give your garden a mature look initially, but it reduces air circulation around leaves and stems, promoting disease. And it weakens plants by forcing them to compete for sunlight, water, and nutrients.

Improper watering. If you really want to kill a plant, giving it too much or too little water is a great way to do it.

Nicking the bark. Bark works like your skin: It keeps good things in and bad things out. Accidentally wounding the bark of a shrub or tree with a string trimmer, lawn mower, saw, or hockey stick promotes ready access for insects, fungi, bacteria, and viruses.

Monoculture. This term means planting large numbers of the same plant close together. All of the plants have the same susceptibility to certain pests. So if those pests show up, instead of one or two plants dying, all do.

Overfeeding. Giving a plant too much food, particularly nitrogen, encourages lush, soft growth that insects and diseases relish.

Topping trees. Read our lips. Topping trees is *always* a bad idea. It not only ruins their appearance, but also makes them prone to insect and fungi attack, as well as storm damage.

Scalping the lawn. So you think cutting the grass down to the soil line means you won't have to mow it as often? Well, you're right, because doing so repeatedly weakens the grass so much it might die. Unfortunately, the weeds that soon replace it like close cutting. So you'll end up mowing those instead.

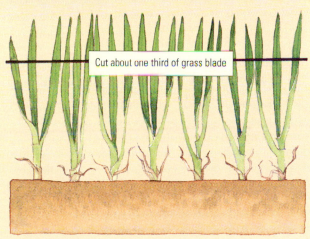

Cut about one third of grass blade

Scalping your grass is a big no-no. Cutting it at the correct height helps to keep it happy and healthy.

THE AIR DOWN THERE

Most people know how important it is to water and fertilize plants. But it's just as important to get oxygen down to the roots. If the roots can't "breathe," they can't take up water and flourish.

Well-oxygenated soil is also essential to many soil microorganisms that break down minerals and organic matter to provide food for plants.

So how can you get more air down there? For flower and vegetable gardens, thorough tilling usually does the job. To

oxygenate lawns, use a core aerator. (These machines are usually available for rent.) Core aerators extract small soil plugs and drop them on the lawn to disintegrate. Early spring is an excellent time to aerate your lawn.

A Breath of Fresh Air

Grass roots, like the roots of any plant, need sufficient air to keep the plants healthy. Core aerators, such as the one pictured here, increase airflow by creating holes in the lawn that reduce compaction and bring oxygen to the roots.

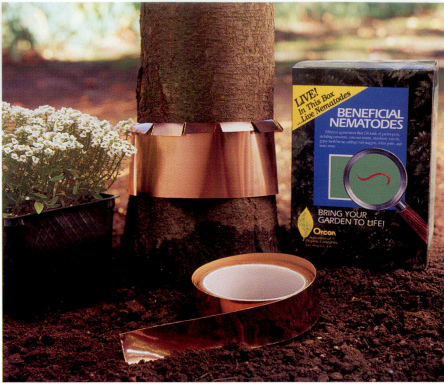

Under New Management

Neem-based pesticides, which dissipate rapidly and are safe to use on food crops, manage stubborn pests like the leafhoppers pictured above. Basic tools of integrated pest management (IPM), shown at right, include sweet alyssum, which hosts beneficial insects; beneficial nematodes, which kill grubs; and copper strips, which keep slugs and snails away.

A LITTLE COMMON SENSE

Anytime you see an insect or a fungus attacking a favorite plant, it's tempting to "nuke" the entire garden with pesticide and feel you've solved the problem for good. Unfortunately, it doesn't work that way.

Insects are resilient. Most carry enzymes that help them overcome naturally occurring toxins in the food they eat. These same compounds enable a few insects in a population to metabolize and disarm the poison in a particular pesticide. So even though the poison kills most of the pests, a few survive to pass their genetic resistance on to their offspring. Before long, the entire population is resistant.

We first learned this lesson in the 1940s, after large areas were sprayed with DDT. At first, DDT seemed a miracle cure, because it rapidly eliminated typhus-causing fleas and malaria-causing mosquitoes. Yet within a few years, DDT failed to control these very same insects.

Indiscriminate use of pesticides had other harmful consequences. For example, some pests that were not a serious problem prior to spraying became so afterward. Pesticides eliminated their natural predators, allowing these pests to multiply unchecked.

Persistence in the environment proved particularly worrisome. Many pesticides, such as DDT, lasted so long that they built up to dangerous levels in the tissues of plants, fish, and animals. DDT nearly wiped out entire eagle and falcon populations because it weakened eggshells and prevented reproduction.

INTEGRATED PEST MANAGEMENT

Over the past 40 years, increasing numbers of gardeners have moved away from the notion of eradicating pests and focused instead on the idea of managing them. Key to such management is minimizing problems by choosing appropriate plants, providing good growing conditions, and minimizing pests rather than annihilating them. This approach has a formal name—"integrated pest management," commonly known as IPM.

Bluebird house

When pest damage warrants action, according to IPM you first use physical and biological controls. Physical controls suppress a pest by mechanical means, such as traps and barriers. Biological controls involve releasing natural enemies and disease-causing microbes that attack pests. Biological controls include ladybugs that eat aphids; lacewings that consume mites, thrips, mealybugs, and whiteflies; wasps that hunt and parasitize caterpillars; beneficial nematodes that destroy grubs and harmful nematodes; and *Bacillus thuringiensis,* a bacterium that in various forms kills caterpillars, Colorado potato beetle larvae, and mosquito larvae. You'll find more information about these and other biological good guys in Chapter 3, "A Pound of Cure," and Chapter 5, "Bugs and Other Critters." Pesticides are considered a last resort.

Home Tweet Home

There's no place like home, especially when it's built to suit your preferences and exact body dimensions. The chickadee house (left) mimics the bird's favorite hangout—a hollowed-out conifer. The house on the right has a 1⅛-inch entryway that's just right for wrens. Bluebirds prefer houses mounted on a pole or fence (opposite page) at the edge of an open lawn or field. The entry holes should be exactly 1½ inches wide.

BE TOLERANT

No garden is free of insects, fungi, weeds, or critters. So don't expect yours to be either. Be willing to accept a little damage—a chewed leaf, a gnawed fruit, or a mildewed flower bud. It won't kill you. Never spray pesticides to prevent problems that aren't there yet. You'll only guarantee problems later on. Instead, accurately identify the cause of damage that's occurring now. Try first to control it through the nonpesticide means you've just finished reading about. If that doesn't work, use an appropriate pesticide.

Frequent inspection of plants can keep problems from taking root.

FIGHT BUGS WITH BUGS

Certain flowers and herbs do more than beautify. They also attract the insect enemies of common insect pests. Look for seed mixtures containing many of the following plants from mail-order companies (see Chapter 8) specializing in beneficial insects, biological controls, and wildflower seed.

Annuals

Baby blue eyes *(Nemophila menziesii)*. Blue flowers on plants 6–10 in. tall; blooms March to May. Attracts parasitoid wasps.

Common cosmos *(Cosmos bipinnatus)*. Grows 1–4 ft. tall; white, pink, rose, or lavender flowers; fernlike foliage; blooms spring to autumn. Attracts lacewings, ladybugs.

Coriander *(Coriandrum sativum)*. Small white flowers on fine-textured, 12–15-in. plants; blooms May and June. Attracts parasitoid wasps.

Crimson clover *(Trifolium incarnatum)*. To 6–12 in. tall with showy crimson flowers in spring. Attracts ladybugs, big-eyed bugs, parasitoid wasps.

Nasturtium *(Tropaeolum majus)*. Showy red, orange, yellow, or creamy white flowers appear among rounded leaves; grows 6–15 in. tall; some forms climb; blooms in cool weather. Attracts ladybugs, parasitoid wasps.

Sweet alyssum *(Lobularia maritima)*. Tiny white, pink, red, or purple flowers on 6–8-in. plants; blooms in cool weather. Attracts lacewings, parasitoid wasps.

Perennials

Bishop's weed *(Aegopodium podagraria)*. Ground cover, 6–15 in. tall, fast spreading, good for shady areas; white flowers, similar to Queen Anne's lace, in summer. Attracts parasitoid wasps, syrphid flies.

Common fennel *(Foeniculum vulgare)*. Soft, fernlike foliage and yellow, flat flower clusters on 3–5-ft. plants; blooms April to autumn. Attracts lacewings, ladybugs, soldier bugs, parasitoid wasps.

Coreopsis. Yellow flowers on 1–3-ft. plants; blooms May to September. Attracts lacewings, ladybugs, parasitoid wasps.

Goldenrod *(Solidago)*. Showy yellow flowers on plants 3–6 ft. tall from August to October. Attracts ladybugs, parasitoid wasps.

Rose campion *(Lychnis coronaria)*. Showy magenta or white flowers atop 2–3-ft. plants; soft, whitish gray foliage; blooms April to August. Attracts parasitoid wasps.

Rue *(Ruta graveolens)*. Blue-gray foliage and small yellow flowers on 2–3-ft. plants; blooms in early summer. Attracts parasitoid wasps.

Tansy *(Tanacetum vulgare)*. Yellow flowers and fernlike foliage on 2–3-ft. plants; blooms June and July. Attracts lacewings, ladybugs, parasitoid wasps, pirate bugs.

EASY SOLUTIONS

FOR TOUGH

PROBLEMS

*I*n all of human existence, only one garden has ever been perfect. And Adam and Eve managed to mess it up. Ever since then, people have sought to produce beauty and bounty from imperfection. Is your soil less than perfect? Does it hold water like a sponge, burn plants with caustic salts, or let rainfall rush through it? Well, congratulations, and join the crowd. We know how it feels. And what about the light in your garden? Chances are, you have either too much sun or too much shade. The former means that gardens fry. The latter means that lawns die.

Trouble is only opportunity in work clothes.

–Henry J. Kaiser, Industrialist

If these comments make gardening seem daunting, they shouldn't. Facing common challenges and finding solutions are two things that make gardening so rewarding.

Nevertheless, it's better to prevent problems than to solve them. And nothing aids prevention more than choosing the right plant for the right spot and following some good, basic horticultural principles.

That's what this section, "Easy Solutions for Tough Problems," is about. We've selected ten common problem situations Southern gardeners face. Then we've suggested appropriate plants for each situation and some easy guidelines for you to follow.

Wet Soil

BEAUTY

AND THE BOG

*I*t's true. Most garden plants like well-drained soil. So what do you do if your soil consists of red clay that clutches water molecules in a death grip? What if your garden sits in a low spot that fills with water from runoff or seepage? Are there any desirable plants you can grow without constructing raised beds or putting your garden up on stilts?

Sure there are. And we've listed them for you on the opposite page.

Keep in mind, though, that some plants like it wetter than others. Some will even grow with their roots underwater for months at a time. Bald cypress, winterberry, cardinal flower, yellow flag, and canna are good examples. Other plants prefer soil that's constantly moist, but not saturated or

If wet soil has your garden treading water, try these plants. As far as they're concerned, wetter is better.

Wet and Styled

Japanese primrose (above) is a great choice for Upper South gardens with wet soil. Each spring, it produces spectacular candelabras of red, pink, or white blooms. Good choices for gardens in other areas include Louisiana iris (below) and Texas star (above, right).

inundated for long stretches. These include red maple, sweet bay, red chokeberry, Texas star, Japanese primrose, cinnamon fern, summersweet, and weeping willow.

Gardeners blessed with well-drained soil will find useful information in the following plant list too. Although all of the plants tolerate poorly drained, oxygen-starved soil, most grow just fine in average, well-drained garden soil. To help you determine the needs of individual plants, look for the letters S, M, or WD after the name. S means the plant tolerates saturated or inundated soil; M means it takes constantly moist but not inundated soil; and WD means it thrives in drier, well-drained soil.

PLANTS FOR WET SOIL

Trees

Bald cypress (*Taxodium distichum*)	S, M, WD
Black gum (*Nyssa sylvatica*)	M, WD
Loblolly bay (*Gordonia lasianthus*)	M, WD
Red maple (*Acer rubrum*)	M, WD
River birch (*Betula nigra*)	S, M, WD
Sweet bay (*Magnolia virginiana*)	M, WD
Sweet gum (*Liquidambar styraciflua*)	M, WD
Water oak (*Quercus nigra*)	M, WD
Weeping willow (*Salix babylonica*)	M

Shrubs

Bottlebrush buckeye (*Aesculus parviflora*)	M, WD
Buttonbush (*Cephalanthus occidentalis*)	S, M
Dwarf palmetto (*Sabal minor*)	M, WD
Inkberry (*Ilex glabra*)	M, WD
Red chokeberry (*Aronia arbutifolia*)	M, WD
Redtwig dogwood (*Cornus stolonifera*)	S, M, WD
Summersweet (*Clethra alnifolia*)	M, WD
Winterberry (*Ilex verticillata*)	S, M, WD

Bulbs

Canna	S, M, WD
Common calla (*Zantedeschia aethiopica*)	M
Elephant's ear (*Colocasia esculenta*)	S, M, WD
Japanese iris (*Iris ensata*)	S, M, WD
Louisiana iris (*I.* hybrid)	S, M, WD
Yellow flag (*I. pseudacorus*)	S, M

Perennials

Cardinal flower (*Lobelia cardinalis*)	S, M
Chameleon plant (*Houttuynia cordata*)	S, M
Cinnamon fern (*Osmunda cinnamomea*)	M
Japanese primrose (*Primula japonica*)	M
Royal fern (*Osmunda regalis*)	S, M
Texas star (*Hibiscus coccineus*)	M, WD

Growing a Great Lawn

THE GREEN, GREEN GRASS OF HOME

Nothing puffs out a homeowner's chest more than a thick, emerald lawn. Maybe it's smelling the freshly cut grass on a Saturday afternoon. Or maybe it's knowing that the neighbor's lawn pales in comparison.

Growing a great lawn isn't hard if you start with the right grass. You'll find descriptions of major Southern lawn grasses in "A Quick Look at Grasses" on the opposite page.

Lawn grasses are classified as warm season or cool season. *Warm-season grasses*—Bahia grass, Bermuda grass, buffalo grass, carpet grass, centipede grass, St. Augustine grass, and zoysia—thrive where summers are hot and winters are short and mild. They turn brown in winter. *Cool-season grasses*—Kentucky bluegrass, perennial ryegrass, and tall fescue—prefer the cooler summers of the Upper or Middle South. They stay green in winter. Tall fescue is sometimes called a transition grass because with sufficient water and afternoon shade, it grows well in the upper half of the Lower South.

A lush lawn is a source of pride. Here's how to have the prettiest lawn on the block.

Grasses can also be either clumping or spreading. *Clumping grasses*—perennial ryegrass, tall fescue—don't fill in bare spots. To get a thick lawn, you must overseed them every year. *Spreading grasses* (all the others) spread by rhizomes, stolons, or both (see illustration, "How Grasses Grow," page 42). They form thicker lawns and crowd out weeds better than clumping grasses. However, they're also more prone to thatch—a spongy layer of stems, roots, and dead leaf blades atop the soil that can harbor pests (see page 35).

STARTING A LAWN

Depending on the grass you choose, you can start a lawn from seed, sod, or plugs. Seed is relatively inexpensive, but takes longer to produce a thick lawn. Sod costs much more, but produces an instant lawn. Plugs are cheaper than sod, but take 1 to 2 years to fill in. Seed, sod, or plug cool-season grasses in early autumn (the best time) or spring. Sod or plug warm-season grasses in spring or summer. Be sure to thoroughly water a new lawn every rainless day for at least 3 weeks, until the grass is firmly established.

INSECT PESTS

Many insects inhabit the lawn without causing any harm. They get out of hand only when improper care, such as overfertilizing, mowing too low, or simple neglect, puts the lawn under stress. Fortunately, products to control lawn insects are widely available and work well.

Three of the most common pests affecting Southern lawn grasses are chinch bugs, white grubs, and mole crickets. Chinch bugs primarily attack

The Green Carpet Treatment

Growing a beautiful lawn depends on mowing properly, watering and fertilizing regularly, watching out for pests, and choosing the right grass for your area. Tall fescue (left) stays green in winter and is a good choice for the Upper and Middle South. Buffalo grass (below, left) likes the dry Southwest, while St. Augustine grass (below, right) thrives near the coast.

A QUICK LOOK AT GRASSES

Bahia *(Paspalum notatum)* — Zones CS, TS. Drought-tolerant, durable grass. Thrives in sun. Takes dry, acid soil, little fertilizing. Start from seed, sod. Mow at 3 to 4 inches.

Bermuda (Common) *(Cynodon dactylon)* — Zones MS, LS, CS, TS. The South's most widely used grass. Tolerates drought and most soils. Spreads rapidly and takes a lot of wear. Requires full sun and moderate fertilizing. Start from seed, sod, or plugs. Mow at ½ to 1½ inches.

Bermuda (Hybrid) *(C. dactylon)* — Zones MS, LS, CS, TS. Has finer appearance than common Bermuda, but needs more water and fertilizer. Does not tolerate shade. Start from seed, sod, or plugs. Mow at ½ to 1½ inches.

Buffalo *(Buchloe dactyloides)* — Zones US, MS, LS. Low-maintenance, drought-tolerant grass with good wear resistance. Needs little fertilizing. Will not grow in shade. Start from seed, sod, or plugs. Mow from 1 to 6 inches.

Carpet *(Axonopus affinis)* — Zones CS, TS. Grass of last resort for wet, acid soil. Needs little fertilizing. Takes some shade. Start from seed, sod. Mow at 1 to 2 inches.

Centipede *(Eremochloa ophiuroides)* — Zones LS, CS. Prefers poor, acid soil. Needs little fertilizing. Takes moderate shade and wear. Start from seed, sod, or plugs. Mow at 1 to 2 inches.

Kentucky bluegrass *(Poa pratensis)* — Zone US. Beautiful, high-maintenance grass. Needs plenty of water and fertilizer. Takes moderate amounts of shade and wear. Start from seed, sod, or plugs. Mow at 2 to 3 inches.

Perennial ryegrass *(Lolium perenne)* — Zone US. Newer selections tolerate wear, drought, shade. Moderate feeder. Start from seed. Mow at 1½ to 2½ inches.

St. Augustine *(Stenotaphrum secundatum)* — Zones LS, CS, TS. Tolerates light shade, salt spray. Spreads fast in warm, rainy weather. Needs moderate fertilizing; takes some drought. Start from sod, plugs. Mow at 2 to 4 inches.

Tall fescue *(Festuca elatior)* — Zones US, MS, LS (upper half). Will grow in light shade. Tolerates moderate wear and drought. Medium feeder. Start from seed. Mow at 2 to 3 inches.

Zoysia — Zones MS, LS, CS, TS. Dense, drought tolerant. Takes light shade. Medium feeder. Wear resistant. Start from sod, plugs. Mow at 1 to 2 inches.

St. Augustine grass, sucking the juices from the blades, turning patches of lawn yellow and brown. White grubs, the larvae of Japanese beetles, June beetles, and chafers, devour grass roots, killing large patches of sod. Mole crickets, a plague on Bermuda, centipede, and St. Augustine grasses, tunnel through the grass, eating the roots. For detailed information about these pests and how to handle them, see Chapter 5, "Bugs and Other Critters."

CONTROLLING DISEASES

When it comes to lawn diseases, there's good news and bad news. First, the bad news: To the untrained eye, they all look alike. Now, the good news: By selecting a grass well adapted to your area and giving it proper care, you can minimize disease problems.

What constitutes proper care? Well, for starters, water in the morning, not at night. Grass that stays wet all night encourages all sorts of evil fungi. Don't scalp your grass. Scalped grass has a harder time defending itself against pathogens. And don't overfertilize, especially with heavy doses of nitrogen. True, extra nitrogen turns the grass deep green, but it also produces lush, succulent blades that leave fungi foaming at the mouth.

WHAT ABOUT WEEDS?

Weeds in the lawn are warning signs. They're telling you that some aspect of your lawn care isn't quite right. Healthy, thick lawns don't have many weeds. There simply isn't any room for weeds to grow.

The most common causes of weedy lawns are

- Wrong grass for the area
- Compacted soil
- Overly acidic or alkaline soil
- Too little water
- Too much water
- Not enough sunlight
- Not enough fertilizer
- Mowing too low

You can easily control most lawn weeds by applying lawn herbicides according to label directions. These products are either *pre-emergence herbicides,* which keep weed seeds from sprouting, or *postemergence herbicides,* which kill weeds that already have sprouted. For more information about specific lawn weeds, see Chapter 7, "Weeds and Other Pesky Plants." You'll also find useful descriptions of specific herbicides in Chapter 3, "A Pound of Cure."

WATERING

Different grasses have different watering requirements: Carpet grass and Kentucky bluegrass need a lot; Bermuda grass, Bahia grass, and zoysia need much less; buffalo grass, the most drought tolerant of all, prefers dry soil. But no matter which grass you have, one rule holds—when you water, water deeply.

Your aim is to wet the soil to a depth of 6 to 8 inches. This encourages deep rooting that toughens the grass. Frequent, light watering does just the opposite.

FERTILIZING

Lawns benefit from steady nutrition, not a gluttonous feast that lasts 2 or 3 days. So use slow-release lawn fertilizer that feeds over a period of weeks. In most cases, you'll want a product with a nitrogen-phosphorus-potassium ratio of 3-1-1 or 4-1-1, such as 21-7-7 or 32-8-8. However, the desired ratio varies according to the type of grass and the time of year. Look for a fertilizer specifically labeled for your type of grass and apply according to directions on the bag.

Don't overfertilize. As we said before, this practically guarantees pest problems. (Giving too much nitrogen to centipede grass will kill it.) One way you can reduce the amount of fertilizer you use is by leaving clippings on the lawn. These return vital nutrients to the soil. Mulching mowers make this easy.

HOW GRASSES GROW

Clump-forming bunchgrasses and spreading grasses produce primary shoots of sheathed grass blades, or leaves, and secondary side shoots, or tillers. Bunchgrasses form an abundance of tillers close to the primary shoots in slow-growing, expanding clumps. Spreading grasses develop secondary shoots along horizontal stems, either from underground stems (rhizomes) or from low-lying aboveground stems (stolons).

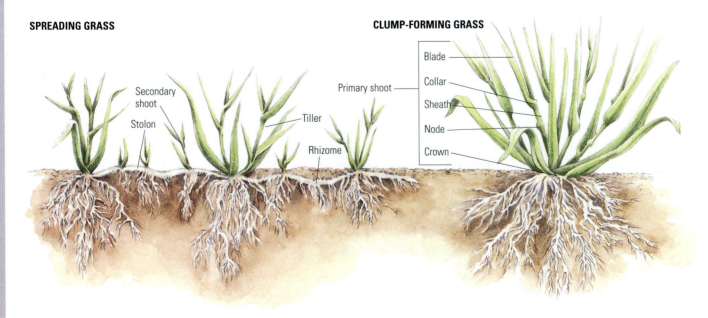

SPREADING GRASS

Secondary shoot
Stolon
Tiller
Rhizome

CLUMP-FORMING GRASS

Primary shoot
Blade
Collar
Sheath
Node
Crown

Tough to Beat

It's hard to beat zoysia grass (below) for wear resistance and drought tolerance. It grows so thickly, it chokes out weeds. And it turns an attractive shade of beige in winter. But it does cost more than other grasses, so installing a spacious zoysia lawn can be expensive.

MOWING

Proper mowing is essential to the health of your lawn. Each type of grass has recommended minimum and maximum mowing heights. Mowing at the minimum height in spring greens up dormant grass earlier and gets it going. In summer, mowing at the maximum height helps grass withstand summer heat and drought. Mowing at the maximum height in autumn strengthens the grass and prepares it for winter.

Never cut off more than one-third of the grass blades in any one cutting. For example, if the grass is 1½ inches tall, don't cut it shorter than 1 inch. Doing so weakens the grass. This means you need to cut your grass fairly often when it's growing rapidly, so that it doesn't get too tall.

DETHATCHING AND AERATING

Heavy thatch buildup and compacted soil result in thin, pest-prone lawns. Both conditions inhibit the penetration of water and oxygen that roots and beneficial soil microbes need to grow. To remove thatch, use a dethatching rake or rent a power dethatcher. To reduce compaction, rent a core aerator every spring. It lifts out plugs and deposits them on the lawn surface. You can let the plugs disintegrate by themselves or pulverize them with your lawn mower.

Hot Spots

GOOD TREES FOR QUICK SHADE

When you're sweltering in a treeless yard on a hot and sticky August day, patience is a virtue that's in pretty short supply. You don't want a shade tree that will comfort your grandchildren in 50 years; you want shade for yourself right now. Naturally, you'd like to plant the fastest-growing tree possible. But stop and think before you plant—or you could wind up with one big headache.

Fact is, fast growth is only one of several important factors to consider before planting a shade tree. You should also research the ultimate size of the tree; whether it's strong wooded, long lived, insect or disease prone, messy, or weedy; whether it has invasive roots; and what ornamental traits it offers, such as autumn color. By taking into account each of these aspects, you can assure yourself of having a tree that you will be happy with tomorrow, next year, and 20 years from now.

The chart (see opposite page) lists shade trees that grow rapidly (upwards of 2 feet a year) and make attractive, long-lived ornamentals. When selecting a tree, always buy from an established, well-respected garden center that employs trained salespeople who can answer your questions. Don't buy on price alone. A 7-foot tree that costs $1.99 is probably worth $1.99. Look for a sturdy, straight trunk, well-spaced branches, and plenty of healthy roots. And

Yes, you can choose a shade tree that's long lived, fuss-free, attractive, and fast growing. Select from the top picks listed here.

You Need More Than Speed

Look for more than quick growth when selecting a shade tree. Many trees, such as Chinese pistache (above) and red maple (left), boast superior autumn color. Willow oaks (below), like these along Queens Road in Charlotte, North Carolina, make excellent street trees due to their form and hardiness.

always check the botanical name as well as the common name on the tag or sign. This will ensure you are truly getting the tree you have in mind.

Here are some other points to remember when choosing and siting a shade tree.

• Beware of trees touted in advertisements as providing instant shade. Typically, such trees break up in storms, seed themselves like crazy, and grow surface roots that crack and lift pavement and damage water lines. Among the trees in the "Shade Tree Hall of Shame," those to avoid are silver maple (*Acer saccharinum*), box elder (*A. negundo*), white mulberry (*Morus alba*), hybrid poplar (*Populus* hybrid), eastern cottonwood (*P. deltoides*), mimosa (*Albizia julibrissin*), Siberian elm (*Ulmus pumila*), Arizona ash (*Fraxinus velutina*), and weeping willow (*Salix babylonica*).

• Match the mature height and spread of the tree to its site. Place large trees, such as maples, oaks, and tulip poplars, at least 20 to 30 feet away from the house. Use small- or medium-size trees, such as Chinese pistache (*Pistacia chi-nensis*), Chinese elm (*Ulmus parvifolia*), or crepe myrtle to shade courtyards and decks.

• Don't plant trees that drop messy fruits or seeds—mulberry, chinaberry (*Melia azedarach*), persimmon (*Diospyros virginiana* or *D. kaki*), ginkgo, black cherry (*Prunus serotina*), mimosa—near decks, terraces, walks, or parking areas.

• Consider the degree of shade a tree provides. Red maple (*Acer rubrum*) and Shumard red oak (*Quercus shumardii*) cast moderate to heavy shade that may hinder sun-loving grasses, flowers, and shrubs beneath them. Thornless honey locust (*Gleditsia triacanthos inermis*) and crepe myrtle, however, produce light, filtered shade that's better for grass and flowers, but isn't as cooling.

• Plant for shape as well as shade. Trees with ascending branches, such as Japanese zelkova (*Zelkova serrata*) and Chinese elm, are great for shading sitting and parking areas, because they provide plenty of headroom beneath. Crepe myrtles and other upright growers work well in restricted spaces, such as narrow side yards.

FAST-GROWING SHADE TREES

NAME	HEIGHT AFTER 10 YEARS*	SPREAD AFTER 10 YEARS*	SHADE DENSITY; FORM
BALD CYPRESS *Taxodium distichum*	25–30 ft.	10–15 ft.	Light to moderate; conical, pyramidal
CHINESE ELM *Ulmus parvifolia*	30–40 ft.	20–25 ft.	Light to moderate; rounded, spreading
CHINESE PISTACHE *Pistacia chinensis*	25–30 ft.	20–25 ft.	Moderate; rounded
CREPE MYRTLE *Lagerstroemia indica*	15–25 ft.	10–15 ft.	Light; upright, spreading
JAPANESE ZELKOVA *Zelkova serrata*	30–35 ft.	20–30 ft.	Light to moderate; vase shaped, spreading
PIN OAK *Quercus palustris*	30–35 ft.	15–20 ft.	Moderate to heavy; pyramidal
RED MAPLE *Acer rubrum*	30–35 ft.	15–20 ft.	Moderate to heavy; pyramidal, oval
SHUMARD RED OAK *Quercus shumardii*	30–35 ft.	20–25 ft.	Moderate to heavy; rounded
THORNLESS HONEY LOCUST *Gleditsia triacanthos inermis*	30–35 ft.	20–25 ft.	Light to moderate; spreading
TULIP POPLAR *Liriodendron tulipifera*	35–40 ft.	15–20 ft.	Light to moderate; oval
WILLOW OAK *Quercus phellos*	30–35 ft.	20–25 ft.	Moderate to heavy; rounded

* Assumes trees were 8–10 ft. tall, 5–6 ft. wide at planting.

Crepe myrtle

Shumard red oak

Too Much Shade

COVERING GROUND

Grass will do a lot of things, but growing in shade isn't one of them. So try a shade-loving ground cover instead. You'll have less maintenance and a prettier garden.

It's a simple, unalterable fact—grass needs sun. It won't grow in deep shade, no matter what. So if you need to blanket the earth beneath densely branched trees, give yourself a break. Plant a ground cover that *likes* the shade. You have lots of choices of plants that not only stay green all year, but also need relatively little care.

English ivy *(Hedera helix)* is probably the South's most popular ground cover for the shade. Once established, it fills in quickly to form a lush carpet that chokes out weeds. Algerian ivy *(H. canariensis)*, a close cousin with somewhat larger leaves, is a common sight in the Coastal and Tropical South. Both ivies climb trees and walls, so you need to clip them now and again to keep them in bounds.

Common periwinkle *(Vinca minor)* is another fast spreader. It's ideal for holding the soil on steep, shady banks. Blue, purple, or white flowers appear

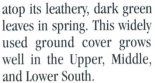

Don't Fight Mother Nature

If you can't grow grass beneath trees, try a shade-tolerant ground cover. Choices include English ivy (left), Asian star jasmine (right), wedelia (bottom), and Algerian ivy (opposite page).

atop its leathery, dark green leaves in spring. This widely used ground cover grows well in the Upper, Middle, and Lower South.

For the Lower, Coastal, and Tropical South, Asian star jasmine *(Trachelospermum asiaticum)* is practically foolproof. It's drought tolerant, tough as nails, and fills in quickly. It has no serious insect or disease problems and grows in sun or shade. If you use it to border a lawn, you'll find its dark green color contrasts nicely with the lighter greens of St. Augustine, zoysia, Bermuda, and centipede grasses. Periodic trimming keeps it off walks and from climbing walls and trees.

Gardeners in Florida and elsewhere in the Coastal and Tropical South should consider wedelia *(Wedelia trilobata)*. This fast-spreading ground cover thrives in sun or light shade; produces showy, yellow flowers continuously in warm weather; and tolerates almost any well-drained soil. However, it can be invasive, so you should plant it in confined beds or natural areas.

You'll find these and other shade-tolerant ground covers described in the following chart. Give them a try. And save the grass for the sun.

MADE FOR THE SHADE

NAME	HEIGHT	GROWTH RATE	ZONES ADAPTED	COMMENTS
ALGERIAN IVY *Hedera canariensis*	8–10 in.	Rapid	CS, TS	Larger leaves than English ivy; more open in habit; will climb
ASIAN STAR JASMINE *Trachelospermum asiaticum*	10–14 in.	Rapid	LS, CS, TS	Tough, easy to grow; will climb
COMMON PERIWINKLE *Vinca minor*	3–6 in.	Moderate to rapid	US, MS, LS	Attractive blue, purple, or white spring flowers
ENGLISH IVY *Hedera helix*	6–10 in.	Rapid once established	US, MS, LS, CS	Will climb; susceptible to leaf spot if kept too wet
JAPANESE PACHYSANDRA *Pachysandra terminalis*	6–12 in.	Slow	US, MS, LS	Needs well-drained, rich, moist, acid soil
LIRIOPE	1–2 ft.	Moderate	All	Tough, easy to grow; blue, purple, or white summer flowers
MONDO GRASS *Ophiopogon japonicus*	3–10 in.	Moderate	MS, LS, CS, TS	Carefree; looks like dark green grass; fine texture
WEDELIA *Wedelia trilobata*	1–1½ ft.	Rapid	CS, TS	Yellow, daisy-like blooms appear continuously in warm weather

Why Spray?

TROUBLE-FREE ROSES

Y ou can't pay for the real luxuries in life—watching your child take his first step, enjoying a quiet sunrise along the beach, or having roses cascade around your door, atop your fence, and out of your vase. But if you have to spray those roses every week, you feel you're earning every bloom. Roses should be as effortless as sunshine and just as plentiful.

Why work like a dog just to have roses? Many tried-and-true selections seldom need spraying and bloom without fuss.

Fortunately, even in a sultry climate that recruits diseases and insects, Southerners can grow roses without spraying them with pesticides. Wonderful roses. The secret is in the selection.

Gardeners from Texas to Virginia to Florida agree that the best all-around roses for the South are the groups called China, Noisette, and tea (not to be confused with hybrid tea). Other easy-to-grow favorites include polyanthas, floribundas, and species roses.

To increase your chances of success, select a rose from one of these groups. But don't let these categories overwhelm you. Use them as guides, like the signs above the grocery store aisles, when you shop from rose catalogs. To simplify the process, we've distilled the hundreds of roses available into a brief list of roses that folks across the South swear by (see opposite page).

Keep in mind that while the roses pictured and listed here resist leaf diseases, not all of them are immune. However, when black spot or mildew appears, these roses persevere. More vulnerable plants drop their leaves, stop blooming, weaken, and die. But should these stalwarts drop any leaves, they just sprout new ones and keep growing.

Of course, all roses crave the same basic necessities. Plant them where they'll receive at least 6 hours of sun a day, preferably more. Give them rich, fertile, well-drained soil that contains plenty of organic matter, such as sphagnum peat moss, compost, or rotted manure. Feed them at least twice a year—once in spring and again in late summer—with a balanced, slow-release, rose fertilizer. And water regularly, especially during summer droughts.

Blooms Without Bother

Not all roses cry out for attention. Easy-care choices for the South include 'Margo Koster' (top of page), 'Bonica' (left), and Lady Banks's rose (above).

NO-FUSS ROSES BY THE DOZENS

NAME	TYPE	FLOWER COLOR	COMMENTS
'ABRAHAM DARBY'	English	Pink-yellow-apricot blend	Will climb
'BALLERINA'	Hybrid musk	Small, light pink blooms	Will climb
'BETTY PRIOR'	Floribunda	Bright pink	Heavy bloomer
'BONICA'	Shrub	Pink	Blooms continuously; makes nice informal hedge
'BUFF BEAUTY'	Hybrid musk	Apricot	Will climb
'CAREFREE BEAUTY'	Shrub	Pink	Blooms continuously
'DR. W. VAN FLEET'	Rambler	Soft pink	Fragrant; very vigorous
'DUCHESSE DE BRABANT'	Tea	Pink	Fragrant; blooms continuously
'ENCHANTRESS'	Tea	Rose red	Fragrant
'FLOWER CARPET'	Shrub	Pink, rose, or white	Makes a low ground cover
LADY BANKS'S ROSE	Species	Light yellow or white	Climbs; very vigorous; thornless
'LAMARQUE'	Climbing Noisette	Yellow-white blend	Fragrant
'MARGO KOSTER'	Polyantha	Coral orange	Will climb; unusual cupped blooms
'MARIE VAN HOUTTE'	Tea	Pink-yellow blend	Sumptuous blooms
'MISTER LINCOLN'	Hybrid tea	Deep red	Fragrant
'MRS. B. R. CANT'	Tea	Silvery pink	Steady bloomer
'NEARLY WILD'	Shrub	Pink	Single flowers; blooms continuously; low grower
'NEW DAWN'	Climber	Light pink	Blooms repeatedly; very vigorous
'OLD BLUSH'	China	Pink	Heavy bloomer
'PERLE D'OR'	Polyantha	Apricot orange	Fragrant; blooms repeatedly
'SIMPLICITY'	Shrub	Pink, white, or red	Good hedge rose
'SOUVENIR DE LA MALMAISON'	Bourbon	Flesh pink	Fragrant
'THE FAIRY'	Polyantha	Pink	Blooms continuously
'ZÉPHIRINE DROUHIN'	Bourbon	Deep pink	Fragrant; will climb; thornless

'Ballerina'

'Bonica'

'Margo Koster'

'Zéphirine Drouhin'

Coping with High pH

CHALK UP A WIN OVER ALKALINE SOIL

Not all soils in the South pass the acid test. Some turn oak trees yellow and cause the leaves of azaleas and gardenias to become yellow between the veins. These soils do this because they're alkaline.

What is alkaline soil? It's soil with a pH above the neutral point of 7 (a pH below 7 is considered acid). It typically occurs in regions with sparse rainfall, such as West and North Texas and western Oklahoma. But it also occurs where beds of ancient limestone lie just beneath the surface. This is why people often refer to alkaline soil as "limy" or "chalky." Limestone deposits occur in every Southern state except Louisiana; the soil in many parts of Missouri, Texas, Kentucky, Tennessee, and Florida is alkaline.

Alkaline soil affects plants by increasing the availability of some soil nutrients while holding back on others. For example, alkaline soil supplies plants with plenty of calcium and magnesium. But it's stingy with zinc, manganese, and sulfur. These shortfalls can stunt certain plants. The major nutrient most commonly deficient in high pH soil is iron. Lack of iron causes *chlorosis* (yellow leaves with green veins). Severe chlorosis eventually kills plants.

To determine for sure whether your soil is alkaline, have it tested. You'll find simple soil-test kits at garden centers, nurseries, and home supply stores. If you discover your soil is indeed alkaline, you have two

If the leaves of your plants are turning yellow, the cause could be limy, alkaline soil. Fortunately, there's an easy answer— choose plants that like the lime.

In the Limelight

Many plants thrive in limy soil. If you need a small tree with showy summer blooms, try crepe myrtle (above) or chaste tree (left). Both tolerate drought and are easy to grow.

options. The first is to completely replace the existing soil with acid soil, so you can grow acid-loving plants. But this is laborious and expensive and seldom succeeds over time. A far better solution is simply to select plants that like alkaline soil. There are lots to choose from and many are carefree, drought-tolerant native plants.

THEY DIE IN ALKALI

The following popular plants should never be planted in alkaline soil.

American holly (*Ilex opaca*)

Azalea

Blueberry

Camellia

Flowering dogwood (*Cornus florida*)

Flowering dogwood

Gardenia

Ixora

Japanese andromeda (*Pieris japonica*)

Mountain laurel (*Kalmia latifolia*)

Pin oak (*Quercus palustris*)

Red oak (*Q. rubra*)

Rhododendron

Willow oak (*Q. phellos*)

PLANTS FOR ALKALINE SOIL

NAME	ZONES ADAPTED	HEIGHT	COMMENTS
TREES			
CADDO MAPLE *Acer saccharum* 'Caddo'	US, MS, LS	40–50 ft.	Brilliant orange-red fall color; originates in Oklahoma; performs best in Southwest
CHASTE TREE *Vitex agnus-castus*	US, MS, LS, CS	10–15 ft.	Showy blue flowers in June and July; tolerates drought; pest free
CHINESE PISTACHE *Pistacia chinensis*	US, MS, LS, CS	30–40 ft.	Excellent yellow, orange, and red fall color; tolerates drought; few pests
CREPE MYRTLE *Lagerstroemia indica*	US, MS, LS, CS	6–35 ft., depending on selection	Showy flowers, fall foliage, and bark; choose a mildew-resistant selection
EASTERN REDBUD *Cercis canadensis*	US, MS, LS, CS	25–35 ft.	Beautiful spring flowers in pink, lavender, rose purple, or white
EASTERN RED CEDAR *Juniperus virginiana*	US, MS, LS, CS	40–50 ft. or more	Aromatic needles and wood; good for lining streets, driveways, and country lanes
LIVE OAK *Quercus virginiana*	LS, CS, TS	40–80 ft., with a much wider spread	The classic tree of the Deep South
SHUMARD RED OAK *Q. shumardii*	US, MS, LS, CS	40–60 ft.	Leaves turn red in fall; good substitute for pin, red, and willow oaks
TEXAS MOUNTAIN LAUREL *Sophora secundiflora*	LS, CS	10–25 ft.	Fragrant, deep purple flowers in spring; tolerates drought; evergreen
TEXAS RED OAK *Quercus texana*	US, MS, LS, CS	15–30 ft.	Makes a nice, multitrunked, small tree
SHRUBS			
FIRETHORN *Pyracantha*	US, MS, LS, CS	3–12 ft.	Showy red, orange, or yellow berries in fall; responds well to pruning
FLOWERING QUINCE *Chaenomeles*	US, MS, LS	4–10 ft.	Spectacular red, pink, white, orange, or salmon flowers in winter or spring
INDIAN HAWTHORN *Raphiolepis indica*	LS, CS, TS	4–6 ft.	Evergreen foliage, showy spring flowers; tolerates salt spray
JAPANESE PITTOSPORUM *Pittosporum tobira*	LS, CS, TS	3–15 ft.	Handsome, evergreen foliage; tolerates salt spray
LILAC *Syringa*	US, MS	6–20 ft.	Fragrant spring flowers in lavender, blue, purple, pink, white, or red; a few types also bloom well in the Lower South
MOCK ORANGE *Philadelphus*	US, MS, LS	8–12 ft.	Fragrant, white spring flowers; also called English dogwood
NANDINA *Nandina domestica*	US, MS, LS, CS	3–8 ft.	Showy, bright red berries and handsome, evergreen foliage; tough as they come
SPIRAEA	US, MS, LS, CS	3–10 ft.	Showy flowers in either spring or summer; many different species
THORNY ELAEAGNUS *Elaeagnus pungens*	US, MS, LS, CS	10–15 ft.	Glossy, evergreen foliage; often used for tall screens; can be sheared into hedge
YAUPON *Ilex vomitoria*	MS, LS, CS	10–20 ft.	Bears huge amounts of shiny, red berries; small, evergreen leaves

officinalis), and snapdragons (*Antirrhinum majus*). Gardeners in the Lower South generally plant cool-weather flowers in autumn. These plants often bloom during midwinter mild spells.

In the Coastal and Tropical South, cool-weather annuals bloom all winter. Gardeners there rely on snapdragons, petunias, pansies, violas, flowering kale and cabbage, sweet alyssum (*Lobularia maritima*), pot marigolds, candytuft (*Iberis*), lobelia, and sweet pea (*Lathyrus*). This means sowing seeds or setting out transplants in October and November. In the Tropical South, you can continue planting through January. However, in the Coastal South where plants will be exposed to an occasional frost, you should plant about a month before cold weather, so your annuals can get established.

Cool-Weather Blooms

FLOWERS OF THE FROST

In the South, the garden never rests. Even in winter, you can enjoy cool-weather annuals that bloom in the chill and continue through the spring. Of course, this takes a little extra planning, but those early blossoms are well worth it.

Some annuals look their best during cool weather. These flowers of winter and early spring give your garden a headstart on the bloom season.

These hardy flowers provide the perfect remedy for the sudden itch to get outdoors. You have your seeds or transplants in hand and your tools await. Then a pretty day tempts you to plant, even though you know more frosts are on the way. But no matter—cool-weather annuals will survive and thrive.

Your choices are many. Depending on which flowers you select, planting can be as simple as scattering seeds in the garden or setting out a few transplants. However, success depends on planting in the right season.

In the Upper South, early spring planting is best. In an average year that means some time between March 1 and March 20. Middle South gardeners should set out most cool-weather annuals about a month earlier; however, some can be planted in autumn. These include pansies (*Viola wittrockiana*), violas (*V. cornuta*), English daisies (*Bellis perennis*), pot marigolds (*Calendula*

Early Favorites

If you're one of those gardeners who can't wait for spring to start each year, give your border a head start by planting frost-tolerant annuals, such as forget-me-nots (top, left) and English daisies (above, with tulips).

Now Warming Up

One cool-weather annual that deserves wider use is the pot marigold (right), also known as calendula. Its warm colors brighten early borders and its daisy-like blooms are great for cutting.

COOL-SEASON ANNUALS

NAME	HEIGHT	LIGHT REQUIREMENTS	FLOWER COLOR; BEST STARTED FROM
CANDYTUFT *Iberis*	9–18 in.	Sun	White, pink, lilac, maroon, carmine; seed or transplants
ENGLISH DAISY *Bellis perennis*	4–8 in.	Sun or light shade	Red, pink, salmon, white; seed or transplants
FLOWERING CABBAGE AND KALE	1¼–1½ ft.	Sun	White, pink, rose; transplants
FORGET-ME-NOT *Myosotis sylvatica*	6–12 in.	Light shade	Blue; seed
LOBELIA *Lobelia erinus*	4–6 in.	Partial to full shade	Blue, white, rose, red; seed or transplants
PANSY *Viola wittrockiana*	6–10 in.	Sun or light shade	Nearly every color; transplants
PETUNIA	9–12 in.	Sun	Nearly every color; transplants
POT MARIGOLD *Calendula officinalis*	1–2 ft.	Sun	Yellow, orange, apricot, cream; seed or transplants
SNAPDRAGON *Antirrhinum majus*	1–3 ft.	Sun	Red, orange, pink, yellow, white, lavender; seed or transplants
SWEET ALYSSUM *Lobularia maritima*	4–6 in.	Sun or light shade	White, pink, lavender, purple; seed or transplants
SWEET PEA *Lathyrus odoratus*	1–5 ft.	Sun	Nearly every color; seed
VIOLA *Viola cornuta*	6–8 in.	Sun or light shade	Blue, purple, yellow, white, red; seed or transplants

Three Cool Customers

Violas (right) look like miniature pansies, but they're tougher and more weather resistant. They also reseed. Use them for edging and in containers. Petunias (above, middle) bloom all winter in the Coastal and Tropical South and flourish in autumn in other Southern climate zones. Snapdragons (left) are among the cool-season garden's showiest bloomers. By removing spent flowers before they have a chance to form seed, you can keep new flowers coming continuously.

No Grass, No Way

Steep slopes are no place for a lawn. Mowing is too difficult and dangerous. But rejecting grass doesn't mean leaving slopes bare. You can blanket them with ground covers, such as Asian star jasmine (left) or massed plantings of perennials, such as Mexican petunia (below) or daylilies and ornamental grasses (top, opposite page).

Planting Slopes

QUOTH THE GARDENER, NEVER MOW

Tired of taking your life in your hands every time you mow that hillside? Replace that grass with shrubs or ground covers and live to a ripe old age.

There's one good thing about having to mow a steep slope out front every week. Every insurance agent in town will want to be your friend.

"But what choice do I have?" you ask. "Building terraces and retaining walls costs too much money. And if I turn the hillside over to weeds, my neighbors will turn me over to the authorities."

Answer: Plant something other than grass that looks good, covers and holds the soil, and doesn't need mowing. Plenty of ground covers, low shrubs, and perennials fill the bill (see "Plants You Can Bank On,"

opposite page). Of course, these plants may take a few years to cover the incline completely, but eventually the upkeep on your slope will be minimal.

Before you yank out the grass, however, measure the hillside to estimate its steepness. A slope with a grade of 25 percent or less—that is, a 1-foot rise for every 4 feet the slope goes back—is fine for grass and mowing. A 30 percent grade is borderline. And a 33 percent grade—a 1-foot rise for every 3 feet of slope—and higher is too steep to mow. You stand a good chance of slipping, turning over the mower, and losing some of your body's original equipment.

If you determine your slope is too steep to mow, you'll need to get rid of the grass. You can do this by spraying it with glyphosate (Roundup) or glufosinate-ammonium (Finale), according to label directions. Trouble is, bare slopes have a nasty habit of eroding during heavy rain. And whatever you plant won't hold the soil completely for a year or two.

Here's a solution. Put down a 3–4-inch layer of pine straw. Then cover the pine straw with chicken wire and stake it down. Next, use wire cutters to cut holes in the wire where you need to dig holes for the plants. Plant the plants. Eventually, the plants will cover the slope and the chicken wire will rust away. If you're worried about children scratching themselves on the wire, substitute jute mesh.

Pine straw is the best mulch for a slope, because it doesn't wash off during heavy rain. Shredded bark works too, but not as well. Don't use pine-bark chips; they wash right off.

Keeping plants watered on a hillside can be difficult because much of the water runs off. You can get around this by using soaker hoses or "leaky" hoses that water slowly and gently.

PLANTS YOU CAN BANK ON

NAME	TYPE OF PLANT	LIGHT REQUIREMENTS	ZONES ADAPTED
ALGERIAN IVY *Hedera canariensis*	Ground cover	Shade	CS, TS
ASIAN STAR JASMINE *Trachelospermum asiaticum*	Ground cover	Sun or shade	LS, CS, TS
CAPE HONEYSUCKLE *Tecomaria capensis*	Shrub	Sun	CS, TS
COMMON PERIWINKLE *Vinca minor*	Ground cover	Shade	US, MS, LS, CS
DAYLILY *Hemerocallis*	Perennial	Sun	All
ENGLISH IVY *Hedera helix*	Ground cover	Shade	US, MS, LS, CS
HOLLY FERN *Cyrtomium falcatum*	Perennial	Shade	LS, CS, TS
JUNIPER *Juniperus*	Ground cover, shrub	Sun	All
LIRIOPE	Ground cover	Sun or shade	All
MEXICAN PETUNIA *Ruellia brittoniana*	Perennial	Sun or light shade	MS, LS, CS
MONDO GRASS *Ophiopogon japonicus*	Ground cover	Shade	MS, LS, CS, TS
ORNAMENTAL GRASSES	Perennials	Sun	All
SPREADING ENGLISH YEW *Taxus baccata* 'Repandens'	Shrub	Sun or shade	US, MS
WEDELIA *Wedelia trilobata*	Ground cover	Sun or light shade	CS, TS
WEEPING FORSYTHIA *Forsythia suspensa*	Shrub	Sun	US, MS, LS
WILLOWLEAF COTONEASTER *Cotoneaster salicifolius*	Shrub	Sun	US, MS, LS
WINTERCREEPER EUONYMUS *Euonymus fortunei*	Ground cover	Sun or shade	US, MS, LS
WINTER JASMINE *Jasminum nudiflorum*	Shrub	Sun	US, MS, LS, CS

Daylily

Liriope

Winter jasmine

Coastal Winds, Salt Air
SURF'S UP
FOR BEACH PLANTS

For plants that endure seaside conditions, life is no walk on the beach. Given the challenges they face, it's tough enough just to survive.

The main obstacle is the nearly constant, salt-laden wind that robs moisture from plants and fries their foliage. This desiccating effect worsens in winter, when nearly dormant and dormant plants have a rough time dealing with stress.

A beach's frontline dunes are truly a no-plant's-land. Very few plants survive the unbuffered wind by themselves (we've marked the ones that do with an asterisk in the chart that follows). But cluster certain plants together and they provide each other with sufficient shelter to become established. These plants include live oak, oleander (*Nerium oleander*), yaupon (*Ilex vomitoria*), Southern magnolia (*Magnolia grandiflora*), and wax myrtle (*Myrica cerifera*). Such grouping can then provide shelter for other plants situated on the group's leeward side (the side out of the wind).

Another way to mitigate the wind is by planting behind dunes, berms, or walls that deflect wind over or around a planting. For example, a retaining wall that's 2 feet tall can shield many low-growing plants whose foliage doesn't reach the top of the wall. In addition, many plants that struggle on the windward side of a dune often flourish when planted behind it.

The leeward side of a house provides excellent shelter as well. Remember, though, that wind acts like a wave rolling over a barrier. The farther behind a barrier you place your plants, the less protection they'll have.

Wind and salt aren't the only obstacles. Sandy soil drains quickly, retaining little moisture. You can improve the soil before you plant by amending it with lots of organic matter, such as sphagnum peat moss, pine straw, and ground bark. Still, you'll likely have to water more often than you would elsewhere. If that isn't your style, choose drought-tolerant plants, such as yucca, prickly pear (*Opuntia humifusa*), oleander, juniper, eastern red cedar, lantana, century plant (*Agave americana*), and Indian blanket (*Gaillardia pulchella*).

Don't forget to stake large trees for the first year after you plant them. Trees growing in sandy soil need this time to anchor themselves against the wind.

Select the right plants for your coastal garden and you'll ride the wave to success.

Life Is a Breeze

Constant salt-laden breezes near the South Atlantic and Gulf coasts make life hard for most plants. But three that succeed where others fail are prickly pear (inset, left), sea grape (left), and oleander (top). Prickly pear and sea grape will grow right on the dunes.

SURE SHOTS FOR THE SEASHORE

Trees

American holly (*Ilex opaca*)	US, MS, LS, CS
Cabbage palm (*Sabal palmetto*)	LS, CS, TS*
Coconut palm (*Cocos nucifera*)	TS*
Eastern red cedar (*Juniperus virginiana*)	All
Japanese black pine (*Pinus thunbergiana*)	US, MS, LS, CS
Live oak (*Quercus virginiana*)	LS, CS, TS
Sea grape (*Coccoloba uvifera*)	TS*
Southern magnolia (*Magnolia grandiflora*)	US, MS, LS, CS
Yaupon (*Ilex vomitoria*)	MS, LS, TS

Shrubs

Cape plumbago (*Plumbago auriculata*)	CS, TS
Coontie (*Zamia pumila*)	CS, TS*
Indian hawthorn (*Raphiolepis indica*)	LS, CS, TS*
Inkberry (*Ilex glabra*)	US, MS, LS, CS
Japanese pittosporum (*Pittosporum tobira*)	LS, CS, TS*
Natal plum (*Carissa macrocarpa*)	CS, TS
Oleander (*Nerium oleander*)	LS, CS, TS
Sea buckthorn (*Hippophae rhamnoides*)	US*
Shore juniper (*Juniperus conferta*)	US, MS, LS, CS
Thorny elaeagnus (*Elaeagnus pungens*)	US, MS, LS, CS*
Wax myrtle (*Myrica cerifera*)	MS, LS, CS

Cabbage palms

Vines

Beach morning glory (*Ipomoea pes-caprae*)	CS, TS*
Bougainvillea	CS, TS
Cape honeysuckle (*Tecomaria capensis*)	CS, TS
Common allamanda (*Allamanda cathartica*)	TS
Confederate jasmine (*Trachelospermum jasminoides*)	LS, CS, TS

Annuals and Perennials

Century plant (*Agave americana*)	CS, TS*
Daylily (*Hemerocallis*)	All
Indian blanket (*Gaillardia pulchella*)	US, MS, LS, CS, TS*
Lantana	All
Lily-of-the-Nile (*Agapanthus africanus*)	LS, CS, TS
Liriope	All
Prickly pear (*Opuntia humifusa*)	MS, LS, CS, TS*
Purple heart (*Setcreasea pallida*)	MS, LS, CS, TS
Yucca	US, MS, LS, CS, TS*

*Will grow on frontline dunes unshielded from wind.

Indian blanket

Pruning
THE KINDEST CUT

No task terrifies a beginning gardener more than pruning. Suddenly, the pulse races, the palms sweat, and the eyes take on a faraway look. But pruning correctly is not that difficult. You just have to follow a few rules.

Before pruning a plant, you should have a good idea of why you're doing it. There are six basic reasons for pruning:

- To remove unwanted growth, such as dead, broken, or wayward branches
- To stimulate new growth
- To rejuvenate an overgrown or neglected plant
- To train a plant into a specific shape
- To control size
- To remove seed heads and spent flowers

In most cases, you should try to preserve the natural form of the plant, because this saves you work and it looks better. The exception is if you're shaping plants for specific purposes, such as creating espaliers or hedges.

You can't do a good job of pruning without the right tools. These include hand pruners for branches ½ inch or less in diameter; loppers for branches ½ to 2 inches; and a pruning saw for branches larger than 2 inches. Trimming branches high up in a tree calls for pole pruners. For maintaining a formal hedge, you'll need hedge trimmers.

Pruning with Purpose

In most cases, the object in pruning is to reduce the size of the plant while maintaining its natural form. The fountainlike forsythia (above) shows the results of proper pruning. But with the boxwood hedge (below, left) the goal is screening, not natural form. Correct, periodic shearing results in a dense, formal shape.

TIMING IS KEY

Prune spring-flowering plants immediately after they finish blooming. If you prune them in summer, autumn, or winter, you'll cut off flower buds and reduce flowering. Prune summer-flowering plants in late winter or spring. Don't prune woody plants in late summer or early autumn, except to groom. You may encourage new growth that won't harden off before winter.

How you prune is also important. Always cut back to within ¼ inch of a bud. If you leave more stem than this above the bud, the stem will probably rot. Slightly angle the cut so that rainwater runs off. Because a new branch grows in the direction the bud points, always prune to an outward-facing bud. This will open up the center of the plant and help prevent crossing or rubbing branches.

When pruning a shrub to control its size, remember two things. First, retain the shrub's natural shape. Second, prune a

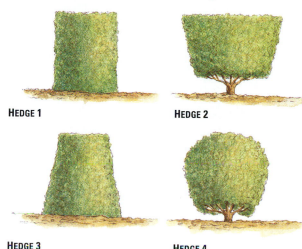

SHEAR TECHNIQUE

HEDGE 1

HEDGE 2

HEDGE 3

HEDGE 4

Hedge 1 has been sheared straight up and down. Eventually, the lower branches die like those of Hedge 2. Hedge 3 stays healthy and thick because the bottom is slightly wider than its top. Hedge 4 serves as an informal screen.

little bit every year. Don't neglect a plant for 4 or 5 years until it requires major surgery. In the case of a 4-foot evergreen azalea, for example, use hand pruners to shorten individual branches by 12 to 15 inches. Don't cut all branches to the same length. By the end of summer, the shrub will reclaim its original size. Repeat the procedure in following years.

What if you inherit a grossly overgrown plant that moderate pruning won't help? You can restore most deciduous and broad-leafed evergreen shrubs to their former beauty through a process called renewal pruning (see illustration, at right). Remove one-third of the plant's oldest canes or trunks each year over a 3-year period. Cut them at or near ground level. Fresh, vigorous growth will soon sprout, and the plant won't look disfigured. You can use this technique on overgrown forsythia, spiraea, weigela, lilac, mock orange, flowering quince, nandina, oleander, and many other shrubs.

HEDGING YOUR BETS

Maintaining a formal hedge takes more than constant shearing; it also demands correct technique. Many gardeners make the mistake of trimming the hedge either so that its sides are straight up and down or so that it's wider at the top than at the bottom (see illustration above). Both errors cause the hedge's lower branches to be shaded. When this happens, the bottom branches thin and die, leaving the hedge leggy and bare. To prevent this, shear the hedge so that it's slightly wider at the bottom than the top.

RENEWAL PRUNING

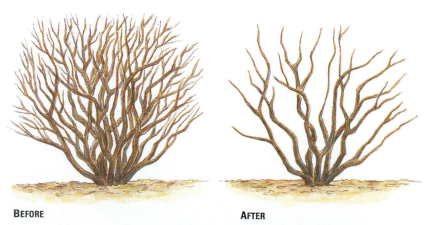

BEFORE

AFTER

Begin rejuvenating an overgrown shrub by removing one-third of the oldest trunks at or near ground level. Vigorous new growth will soon emerge.

A Pound
OF CURE

I t's a rare book today that acknowledges the use of pesticides. And while this one doesn't support their wholesale use for every problem you may encounter, we do recognize that for some pests and stages of infestation, pesticides provide an effective and logical answer. The key, as we've said before, is applying them safely, properly, and judiciously.

Many people think "pesticide" and "insecticide" are synonymous. But a pesticide is simply an agent that controls a specific pest, whether that pest is an insect, a mite, a fungus, a bacterium, a parasite, a weed, or an animal. (For an explanation of types of pesticides, see "What's in a Name?" on page 62.) All insecticides are pesticides, but not vice versa.

Gardeners usually label pesticides as either chemical or organic. And you can sum up most gardeners' feelings toward these classifications this way: Chemicals are bad; organics are good. If only it were that simple.

A major headache arises when you start defining terms. For example, when folks talk about chemical pesticides, they think of foul-smelling poisons that come in bottles decorated with a skull and crossbones. But strictly defined, a chemical is any substance consisting of a single element or a combination of elements. By that definition water, sulfur, lime, salt, oxygen, chlorophyll, and alcohol are chemicals. And pesticides are just collections of chemicals.

The organic label is nebulous, too. When people say "organic," they generally mean a pesticide made from substances occurring in nature. But the strict definition of "organic" is any compound that contains carbon. Diazinon contains carbon. So does chlordane, malathion, carbaryl, paraquat, and 2,4-D. We doubt many people consider these products organic.

> *A true conservationist is a man who knows that the world is not given by his fathers, but borrowed from his children.*
>
> —John Madson, Writer

Thus, what we've done on the following pages is label pesticides so that they make more sense to gardeners. *Synthetic pesticides* are manufactured compounds that don't normally occur in nature. *Natural pesticides* are products whose active ingredients originate in a plant, an animal, or a mineral, or whose actions result from biological processes.

Both groups have their good and bad points. Synthetics offer quick, long-lasting control of a wide variety of pests and problems. But they're often quite toxic to people and pets. If used improperly, they can also leach into streams and groundwater or build up in the environment. Natural pesticides, on the other hand, break down quickly. They're less of a pollution threat, but you typically have to apply them more often. Most are less toxic and control a narrower range of pests than synthetics.

Of course, certain products defy easy classification. Refined horticultural oils are a good example. Supremely effective and useful insecticides, they're commonly sold in natural gardening catalogs, even though some are made from petroleum. Nonetheless, we've placed them among the natural pesticides, because when used properly, they're safe for children and pets to be around and don't persist in the environment.

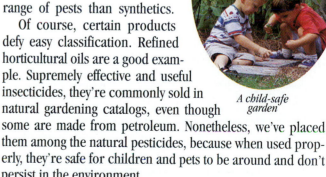

A child-safe garden

Any pesticide works even better when it allows a pest's natural enemies to flourish. So after you've read up on the various types of pesticides, turn to "Beneficial Creatures—

Native and naturalized plants, such as chicory and Queen Anne's lace (lower left), do well on their own. But growing (clockwise from upper left) man-sized watermelons, flawless apples, and prize-winning roses usually requires the use of natural or synthetic pesticides.

CHOOSING THE RIGHT -CIDE

There's more than one way to squash a bug. And there's more than one kind of pesticide to handle the job. In case you're wondering whether you need to use an insecticide, a fungicide, or a nematicide to cure a sick plant, here's a listing of pesticide types and what they do to help you make your choice.

Bactericides. Kill bacteria that cause plant diseases, such as fireblight.

Fumigants. Produce gas or vapor that kills insects, mites, fungi, weed seeds, bacteria, or even rodents. These are used to control infestations in buildings and to partially sterilize soil before planting.

Fungicides. Kill fungi (leaf spots, rusts, rots, mildews, blights, wilts, cankers, and molds) that cause plant diseases.

Herbicides. Destroy undesirable plants.

Insecticides. Kill insects.

Microbials. Microorganisms that kill, overwhelm, or inhibit the spread of pests, including insects or other microorganisms.

Miticides. Kill mites that feed on plants and animals.

Molluscicides. Destroy snails and slugs.

Nematicides. Kill nematodes (microscopic, wormlike creatures that feed on roots).

Ovicides. Destroy the eggs of insects and mites.

Repellents. Repel pests, such as mosquitoes, flies, fleas, and ticks.

Rodenticides. Kill mice, rats, and other rodents.

The term "pesticide" also includes related substances, such as the following:

Defoliants. Cause leaves or foliage to drop from a plant, usually to facilitate harvest.

Desiccants. Cause plants, insects, or other pests to dehydrate and die.

Insect growth regulators. Keep insects from reproducing or developing normally by disrupting normal hormonal processes.

Plant growth regulators. Substances that affect or disrupt the normal growth, development, and reproduction cycles of plants.

Your Garden's Best Friends," page 78. There you'll find a summary of beneficial predators that protect your garden from caterpillars, grubs, aphids, mites, nematodes, scales, and other pests.

Remember that when to spray is just as important a consideration as what to spray. While insecticides often control pests that are already present, most fungicides and bactericides must be applied before damage occurs.

SAFETY FIRST

Pesticides are powerful substances. Used properly, they can effectively defend your garden. Used improperly, synthetic and even some natural products can kill plants, sicken people and animals, and cause harm to the environment. So every time you use one, resolve to do this first: No matter how tedious or boring it may be, *read the label, completely!* Not only is this common sense, but it's also the law.

A pesticide label provides valuable information, such as how much product to use, how to apply it, what problems it controls, and what plants to use it on. For an example of the type of information carried on a pesticide label, see "Reading a Pesticide Label," opposite page.

WHAT'S IN A NAME?

Deciphering a label, we're sorry to say, isn't always easy. One reason is that it often lists a single product by chemical name (multisyllabic terms that only a chemist could love), common name, and brand or trade name. Here's one example. A popular systemic insecticide carries the chemical name O,S-dimethyl acetylphosphor-amidothioate. Never heard of it, have you? But if you read on, you may be familiar with its common name, acephate, and one of its brand names, Orthene.

When buying a particular pesticide, look for the common name first. This is because the same common name may be available under several brand names. If you insist on one brand name only, you may find yourself buying much more pesticide than you need. (See "Buy Less and Save," opposite page.)

Precautionary statements. The terms *Caution, Warning,* and *Danger/Poison* may seem to be just part of the manufacturer's standard wording. But, in fact, each carries a legal definition and a specific meaning.

These terms are signal words—they signal to you the product's potential dangers to people and animals. *Caution* denotes a product that is slightly toxic. It doesn't pose a serious hazard unless it's grossly misused. Insecticidal soap, *Bacillus thuringiensis (Bt),* chlorpyrifos (Dursban), and garden sulfur are examples. *Warning* signifies that the product is moderately toxic and must be applied carefully. Acephate (Orthene), chlorothalonil (Daconil), and malathion carry warning labels. *Danger/Poison* means just that—misuse could cause irreversible injury or even death. Triforine

READING A PESTICIDE LABEL

Precautionary statements: This section may start with the headline "Precautionary statements" or with a repeat of the *signal word* found on the front of the label. Information is customized for product type and its associated toxicity-level category. It tells you of known hazards to humans and domestic animals and to the environment.

First aid instructions: Indicates the immediate action required if the product is ingested or inhaled or comes into contact with the skin or eyes.

Directions for use: Indicates how much of the product to use, and how to mix and apply it.

Plants: Lists the plants that can safely be treated by the pesticide. If it can be used on food crops, also tells you how many days before harvest the product can be applied.

Note to physicians: Specifies the action a physician should take in the event the product is ingested or inhaled or comes into contact with the skin or eyes.

Controls: Lists the pests that the product is formulated to control.

Storage & disposal: Specifies how to safely store and dispose of the product.

Product code identification: Provides the number assigned to the product by the manufacturer and the Environmental Protection Agency (EPA) to identify it; use the number when contacting the manufacturer or EPA about the pesticide.

Product name: Provides the pesticide's brand name, may include manufacturer's trade name, often includes marketing information that positions the product against its competitors and attracts the eye of potential buyer. Sometimes the pesticide's official common name is included as part of the brand name, especially if that name has become familiar to the public.

Active ingredients: Lists the common name of the pesticide. Learn to identify pesticides by their common names and look here first to find out exactly what is in the pesticide before purchasing it. The chemical name of the pesticide may also be included in this section.

Signal word: Look for words such as *Caution, Warning, Danger,* or *Poison.* These words signal the toxicity-level category associated with the pesticide. Additional information will be found on the back of the container, under the section called "Precautionary statements."

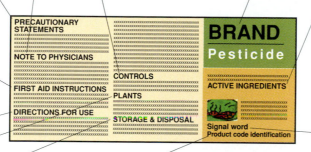

(Funginex), oxyfluorfen (Triox), lindane, and rodenticides fall into this category.

Signal words always appear on the front of a label, accompanied by a brief description, such as "CAUTION: Harmful if swallowed. Avoid contact with eyes or skin." Often you'll be directed to a side or back panel for details and additional precautionary information.

Other risk factors. In addition to precautionary statements, you need to investigate risk factors before choosing one pesticide over another. You'll find information about these on the label as well. Possible risk factors include the following:

Off-site movement. Some pesticides may move through the water or air beyond their original application site, adversely affecting animals and vegetation. For example, diazinon granules applied to kill lawn insects may wash into ponds after a heavy rain, poisoning fish. Soil sterilants, such as Triox, may leach through the soil into root zones of shade trees some distance away and kill them.

Soil contamination. Most pesticides break down in the soil relatively quickly. Others that don't, such as DDT, parathion, toxaphene, and chlordane, have been banned in the United States or their use is severely restricted. Notable exceptions include various arsenic compounds used to kill crabgrass, such as monosodium methanearsonate (MSMA) and calcium acid

BUY LESS AND SAVE

Try not to buy more of a particular pesticide than you'll use in a single year. For one thing, all pesticides lose effectiveness over time. And in these days of heightened environmental awareness, you don't want the headache of trying to properly dispose of bottles of unused, out-of-date chemicals.

methanearsonate (CAMA). Repeated use of crabgrass killers can cause a buildup of arsenic in the soil that's toxic to grass.

Phytotoxicity. This term indicates that, under certain conditions, a pesticide can harm or kill the plant it was supposed to protect. For example, many lawn weed killers injure grass if applied on an extremely hot day. And such normally benign products as insecticidal soap and horticultural oil may also harm plants if applied when temperatures exceed 85 degrees F.

Effectiveness. Some pesticides are more toxic than others but solve the problem with a single application. Thus, you may prefer using the more toxic product if it requires fewer applications. Many newer products are relatively nontoxic to mammals, but highly effective against the target pest.

PROTECTIVE GEAR

Pesticides have more ways to enter your body than a carpenter has nails. You can ingest these compounds, breathe them in, get them in your eyes, or absorb them through your skin. Common sense tells you this isn't healthy. Therefore, you need to wear protective gear when applying pesticides.

Basic protective gear includes goggles, a breathing mask, rubber gloves, nonabsorbent shoes or boots, long pants,

Safety is paramount when applying pesticides. Always wear protective clothing and gear to avoid breathing pesticides or getting them in your eyes or on your skin. In addition to a long-sleeved shirt and pants, wear goggles and rubber gloves. Also wear a hat if you'll be spraying above head level.

amount of pesticide. This chart is useful whether you're starting out with a liquid concentrate or a wettable powder.

Avoid these common mistakes. Don't fall into the trap of thinking, "Well, if the label says 2 tablespoons per gallon will kill those weeds, twice as much will really nuke 'em." Not only is using more pesticide than recommended illegal, but it may also cause considerable damage (for which you may be held legally liable). And believe it or not, it may not work as well. For example, using twice the recommended amount of a translocated weed killer (one that interferes with a plant's metabolism) may kill the top growth before the chemical has a chance to reach the roots. So the weed just grows back.

Also, never mix two pesticides together into a combination spray unless the label says this is okay. Some pesticides chemically react with others and could gum up your sprayer or harm your plants.

Safely dispose of pesticides. It's better to mix up only as much pesticide as you think you'll need for a single application. Sooner or later, however, you'll have product left over. What should you do with it? Don't store it in the sprayer—it may corrode the tank or clog the nozzle. Besides, mixed spray degrades quickly. And never pour it down any type of drain, including a storm drain. It could pollute the water supply and harm the environment.

No Dumping!

Don't dispose of unused pesticides by pouring them down a storm drain. You could pollute the local water supply.

Instead, ask a local recycler or waste disposal company where you can drop off pesticides. It may be the same place where you take leftover paint, used motor oil, and the like. These centers often accept both undiluted pesticides in their original containers and diluted solutions that you've mixed. When disposing of diluted mixtures, carefully pour the leftover portion into a glass or plastic container with a secure lid. Write the product name (common name and brand name) and its dilution ratio on the container. If you are disposing of granular or powdered pesticides, empty them into separate heavy-duty garbage bags; then seal and label each.

long-sleeved shirt, and a hat if you'll be spraying at eye level or above. Be sure to wash your clothing following each application of a pesticide.

MIXING, STORING, AND DISPOSING OF PESTICIDES

Many pesticide manufacturers don't make label directions very easy to read. They try to squeeze all of the information required by the Environmental Protection Agency onto an itty-bitty label, using type so small you have to use a magnifying glass to make sense of it. Others attach a small, folded booklet to the container. It has more space and typically is easier to read. However, once you detach it from the container to read it, it can get lost, and then you're on your own.

Probably the hardest thing for gardeners to figure out is exactly how much pesticide to use. If only every set of instructions would state something practical, such as, "Mix 1 tablespoon in a gallon of water"! Alas, some labels do their best to drive you batty, befuddling you with instructions like, "Mix 2 fluid ounces in 5 gallons of water." If you're among the millions who can't instantly convert fluid ounces to tablespoons or who doesn't have professional-level equipment, you're in trouble. But don't despair. We've included a handy conversion chart on the opposite page to help you add just the right

MEASUREMENTS CHART

Directions on pesticide labels often call for mixing large amounts of a product. While 5-gallon—or even 1-gallon—amounts may be applicable in some situations, home gardeners generally need smaller amounts, for which there are no directions. This chart will help you calculate amounts for various quantities of pesticides.

1 gallon (gal.)	=	16 cups	=	8 pints	=	4 quarts	=	128 fluid ounces (fl. oz.)
1 quart (qt.)	=	4 cups	=	2 pints			=	32 fl. oz.
1 pint (pt.)	=	2 cups					=	16 fl. oz.
1 cup							=	8 fl. oz.
1 tablespoon	=	3 teaspoons					=	½ fl. oz.
1 teaspoon							=	⅙ fl. oz.

A Gardener's Tools

Suppliers are making it easier for you to apply just the right amount of pesticide: large applicators made of lightweight but durable plastic are easier to carry, small applicators are handy for mixing and applying small amounts, and premixed solutions are simplest of all. To ensure accuracy, keep a set of measuring spoons with your applicators. Use them only for pesticides; don't mix them with your kitchen utensils.

Storing pesticides. It goes without saying, but we'll say it anyway: Keep all pesticides away from children and pets. The most secure place is in a locked cabinet. If that isn't possible, store pesticides on high shelves out of the reach of children and pets.

Store pesticides in a cool, dry place away from heat or open flame. Temperatures should stay between 40 and 85 degrees F. Keep products in their original containers. Remember that pesticides lose potency over time, so don't store them for longer than 2 years.

TOOLS OF THE TRADE

Using the proper equipment is essential to the safe and effective application of pesticides. The kind of applicator you'll need depends on whether you're using liquids, granules, or dusts.

Liquid applicators. Sprayers come in many sizes and types. The correct type depends on the nature of the job and how much spray you need. Spraying a home orchard, for example, might require a backpack sprayer that holds 4 to 5 gallons of spray. Smaller jobs call for tank sprayers that range in capacity from ½ to 2 gallons.

Large-capacity tank sprayers used to be heavy, cumbersome contraptions made of steel. They took considerable wear and tear but corroded over time. Today, most tank sprayers are plastic. Their light weight makes them easy to use, and they don't rust. They tend to wear out after several years of hard use, but replacement parts are usually easy to get.

Some folks just don't like tank sprayers. For them, simple, small pressure-pump applicators may be the answer. These generally hold from 24 to 40 fluid ounces. Their pump mechanisms allow you to pressurize the mixture, producing a fine spray that evenly coats an infested plant.

Don't substitute an ordinary spray bottle that isn't specially made for applying pesticides. Pesticide applicators are made of heavy-duty materials and come with printed instructions on how to use them safely.

Ready-to-go applicators filled by the manufacturer with premixed pesticides are becoming increasingly popular. Premixed pesticides cost more per use than concentrates you mix yourself, but they eliminate the need to measure and mix. Plus, you can store them just as you would the concentrates, and you don't have to clean the applicators after each use. With the exception of ready-to-go sprayers, you should promptly and thoroughly clean your spray applicator after using it. Fill it with a quart or two of water, swish it around, and dump the water onto bare soil away from streams or ponds. Then add another quart of water and spray it out to make sure no pesticide lingers in the wand or nozzle. Keep a separate sprayer just for herbicides. This ensures you won't accidentally injure desirable plants should traces of herbicide remain in the sprayer.

Granule applicators. Granule applicators are usually broadcast, rotary, or drop spreaders used to dispense fertilizer or pesticides on lawns. The biggest difficulty in using these devices is getting equal coverage of the area. And with broadcast or rotary spreaders, you must be especially careful that the granules don't travel beyond the intended area. If herbicide granules land on the leaves of your perennials, you could lose those plants.

Dust applicators. Dusts are the trickiest pesticide types to use. They drift through the air, often landing on your skin or ending up in your lungs. For this reason, you should always wear protective clothing and a breathing mask when applying them. Most dusts come in plastic containers you either shake or squeeze. Holes or a nozzle at the top spew a cloud of powdery pesticide that settles on stems and leaves. Dusts aren't very efficient—you have to use a lot to get thorough coverage, and they wash off when it rains or you have to water. We suggest using liquids or granules whenever possible.

Insecticidal soaps safely control soft-bodied insects like these yellow aphids.

A KINDER, GENTLER APPROACH

On pages 73 to 77 you'll find a comprehensive listing of commonly available pesticides, telling you how they work, what problems they control, and how toxic they are. Although this listing includes natural controls, most Southerners aren't as familiar with them as they are with synthetic insecticides, miticides, fungicides, and herbicides. So before we get to the list, let's introduce you to some of the better natural pesticides.

Insecticidal soaps. Insecticidal soaps are great for two reasons. First, they kill a multitude of soft-bodied pests, such as aphids, thrips, and mites. Second, they pose little hazard to you, your pets, or the environment. They're among the few insecticides you can safely apply indoors. However, they do carry the "Caution" signal word on their labels because they can irritate the eyes and also kill fish.

Commercial insecticidal soaps are made from potassium salts of fatty acids of plants and animals. They kill by penetrating cell membranes of soft-bodied pests. Soaps don't work against pests with hard body coverings, such as ants, armored scales, and beetles. Nor are they effective against fast-moving insects that can evade the spray. Insecticidal soap works best if sprayed rapidly on all parts of an infested plant to catch insects before they escape. It kills on contact but has no residual action once it dries.

You can make your own "insecticidal soap" by mixing 5 or 6 drops of liquid detergent into a quart of water; then apply this solution through a spray bottle. Some plants are soap sensitive, so test the mix on a small part of the plant first or wash it off after 30 minutes.

Soap sprays can also fight plant diseases. Fixed-copper fungicidal soaps, such as Soap Shield, control a host of leaf spots, mildews, blights, and molds. Once in the soil, the soap's components eventually biodegrade. Other soaps kill weeds.

Horticultural oils. Made from petroleum or paraffinic, citrus, or vegetable oils, horticultural oils kill insects, mites, larvae, and eggs by covering and smothering them. They also coat the bark of limbs and trunks, preventing disease spores from infecting the plant.

You can buy either "heavy" or "light" oils. Heavy oils are usually petroleum-based. Often called dormant oils, they're applied in autumn and winter, when the plant is dormant, to control tough overwintering insects and diseases. You must never use them during periods of active growth lest you severely injure the plant. Light oils—usually referred to as refined, ultra-fine, or summer oils—may be made from a petroleum, paraffin, citrus, or vegetable base. You can use them year-round.

Oils and (Pond) Water Don't Mix

Even environmentally benign pesticides can cause harm if used improperly. For example, horticultural oil can kill fish if it gets into the water. So can insecticidal soap.

DORMANT SPRAY OR DORMANT OIL?

Just because the label says "dormant" doesn't mean the product is an oil spray. Probably the most popular dormant spray is lime sulfur (calcium polysulfide). It's effective against overwintering diseases and insects on fruit trees, roses, and ornamental shrubs. But it also carries a "Danger" label because it's irritating to the skin and poisonous if swallowed and can cause irreversible eye damage. Thus, in most cases, you're better off sticking with oils.

Sometimes controlling a plant problem requires spraying with both oil and another pesticide. If so, be sure to read the pesticide product label carefully before spraying. Some pesticides should not be applied to a plant that has been first sprayed with an oil.

Combining insecticidal soaps with horticultural oils can be effective for combating a wide variety of insects. An easy way to do this at home is by mixing 1 cup of vegetable oil with 1 tablespoon of liquid dishwashing detergent. Then add 1½ teaspoons of this mixture to a quart of water and spray on infested plants. Coat all plant surfaces thoroughly. You may have to spray again in 7 to 10 days.

Keep in mind that while commercial and homemade oil sprays are quite safe, they can kill fish if they get into streams and ponds, so handle them carefully. Also, keep them away from your eyes and off of your skin.

Garden sulfur. For centuries, sulfur has provided the answer to diseases in plants as well as people. In the garden it prevents powdery mildew, apple scab, brown rot, and black spot. It also controls mites. As an added bonus, it's an essential plant nutrient and helpful in acidifying alkaline soils.

Sulfur is available in dust and liquid forms. It's safe around people and pets, but avoid breathing it or getting it in your eyes or on your skin. You should also avoid combining it with an oil spray. If you've previously sprayed oil on a plant, wait at least 4 weeks before applying sulfur. Don't apply sulfur when temperatures exceed 85 degrees F. And be careful if you are applying it to melons, cucumbers, squash, and raspberries, as it may burn the foliage.

Sulfur works best when applied to healthy tissue at the first sign of infection. Once a fungus penetrates a leaf, sulfur won't help.

Sulfur: Tried and True

No wonder sulfur has been used for centuries to prevent plant disease: These before-and-after photographs show the difference it can make.

The gardener treated this scab-infested apple tree with sulfur and also cleaned up all diseased debris underneath, amended the soil, and mulched the tree, producing a healthy and bountiful harvest one year later.

BIOLOGICAL PESTICIDES

It seems logical: Why not use a pest's own diseases against it? And that's just what biological pesticides do. The best part is that they target specific pests. These pesticides generally won't harm people, pets, wildlife, or even nontargeted pests.

Bacteria. Undoubtedly the best known of these agents is *Bacillus thuringiensis* (also called *Bt*). This bacterium destroys the stomach cells of insects that consume it. Several strains of *Bt* are used to control specific kinds of pests. *Bacillus thuringiensis kurstaki,* for example, kills cabbageworms, gypsy moth caterpillars, tomato hornworms, corn earworms, webworms, tent caterpillars, armyworms, loopers, and inchworms. *Bacillus thuringiensis* San Diego targets larvae of the Colorado potato beetle and adults of the elm leaf beetle. *Bacillus thuringiensis israeliensis* wipes out larvae of mosquitoes and blackflies.

Timing Is Everything

Bt works best on newly hatched caterpillars. When you discover the tiny yellow eggs of the cabbage white butterfly (left) on leaves, either scrape them off or spray the plant with **Bt** as soon as the caterpillars begin to emerge (right).

Protecting Petunias

Use *Bacillus thuringiensis (Bt)* to control geranium budworms that devour petunia blossoms (top). The first symptom may be an absence of new blooms (lower left). After being sprayed with *Bt*, the petunia bed returns to good health (lower right). Tip: For best results, spray at the first sign of infestation.

You usually can find the form of *Bt* that kills caterpillars in garden centers under several brand names (Dipel is one). But for special strains you'll likely have to depend on mail-order companies that offer natural pesticides. You'll find these listed in Chapter 8, "Suppliers and Expert Resources." Keep in mind that *Bt* degrades quickly in sunlight, so you should spray it in the early evening. It also works better on young caterpillars than mature ones. Unfortunately, it kills butterfly caterpillars too, so avoid spraying it where they are feeding.

B. t. israeliensis *briquettes kill mosquito larvae in ponds.*

Bt isn't the only biological insecticide worth noting. The *Bacillus popilliae*-Dutky strain, widely known as Milky Spore, kills the grubs of Japanese beetles and June beetles as they feed on grass roots in the soil. When the grubs die and their bodies disintegrate, the spores are released to infect other grubs. Because adult beetles fly long distances, Milky Spore works best when applied to lawns communitywide, rather than just to a lawn here or there. You can buy Milky Spore at most garden centers in areas where Japanese beetles are common.

Protozoa. If grasshoppers devour your garden each summer, you may also be interested in a predacious protozoan called *Nosema locustae*. This microbe targets and kills only grasshoppers and crickets. Infected grasshoppers and crickets spread the disease by laying infected eggs or eating their sick brethren. *Nosema* has a short shelf life and must be refrigerated between uses. You'll have to order this one from a mail-order company.

Chitin. You can combat nematodes, those microscopic wormlike creatures that ferociously attack trees, shrubs, flowers, vegetables, and lawn grasses, particularly in the Southeast, with chitin, a substance that forms the exoskeletons of insects and crustaceans. When you add chitin to the soil, microorganisms produce toxins and digestive enzymes that kill nematodes. Chitin is marketed under the product name of Clandosan and is available by mail order.

Avermectins. Fire ants are an absolute plague in the South. One successful strategy employed against them in recent years involves the use of toxins called avermectins produced by the soil bacterium *Streptomyces avermitilis*. Worker ants feed bait containing avermectins to the queen, killing her and eventually destroying the colony. Similar baits are used against roaches. Although avermectins can be extremely toxic, the version sold in garden centers, abamectin, is quite safe for mammals. However, it's highly toxic to fish, birds, and bees.

Bucket Brigade

Avermectins and other fire ant baits slowly kill the mound. For immediate results, drench the mound with Dursban or Orthene in the morning, when the queen is near the surface.

of commercial pesticides contain it, including rose sprays, bug sprays, and flea and tick sprays.

Synthetic pyrethrins, called pyrethroids, merit greater caution. They work longer than pyrethrins, but they're also more toxic. You'll find them in bug sprays, whitefly and mealybug sprays, roach baits, and hornet and wasp sprays. Look for the common names resmethrin, sumithrin, tetramethrin, permethrin, deltamethrin, tralomethrin, or allethrin on the label.

Rotenone. Made from the roots of several tropical legumes, rotenone comes as a liquid, a wettable powder, or a dust. It kills a host of bad bugs, including cabbageworm, Mexican bean beetle, Colorado potato beetle, Japanese beetle, flea beetle, squash vine borer, and red spider mite. Like pyrethrum, it breaks down quickly. However, it's more toxic to people than malathion or carbaryl (see page 73) and is extremely poisonous to fish.

Neem oil. A product of the neem tree (see page 70), neem oil contains a chemical called azadirachtin that kills soft-bodied insects such as aphids, whiteflies, mealybugs, and mites. Reports suggest it may also prevent such diseases as mildew. Neem oil injures bees, so don't spray it onto blossoms.

PLANT-BASED PESTICIDES

Plant-based pesticides seem like a good alternative to gardeners worried about the effects of synthetics. They control a wide variety of pests and don't persist in the environment. But just because they come from plants doesn't mean you can be careless with them. Swallowing some of them will kill you faster than a synthetic pesticide would.

Pyrethrum. Pyrethrum products, made from a flower in the chrysanthemum family, are the best-known plant-based insecticides. Pyrethrum was the first chemical extracted from the flower. A more potent version, pyrethrin, came along later.

Used properly, pyrethrin poses little danger to people and pets. And it biodegrades quickly. It kills by direct contact and is most effective on soft-bodied pests. Thousands

GROWTH REGULATORS

These hormone-based chemicals disrupt the normal development and reproduction of pests. A good example is methoprene (Vigren). It eradicates fleas in homes and yards by preventing juvenile fleas from becoming egg-laying adults.

Bees and Pyrethrum

Pesticides containing only pyrethrum dissipate in a few hours. If bees are drinking nectar from plants you want to treat, apply these pesticides in the late afternoon, after the bees have stopped feeding for the day. By the time they return the next day, the pesticide will be gone. Avoid using pesticides containing pyrethrins or pyrethroids where bees are present.

OLD MEETS NEW IN PEST CONTROL— THE NEEM TREE

The neem tree *(Azadirachta indica)* has added to the quality of human life for hundreds of years. But only recently have products derived from it started finding their way into the arsenal that western gardeners use to combat garden pests and diseases.

With a wide canopy, height up to 60 feet, and a trunk girth up to 6 feet, the neem tree shelters all below from the hot sun in its tropical and subtropical places of origin. It's found in Southeast Asia, Africa, and similar tropical areas, but in India use of the neem tree has been documented for hundreds of years. The people of India used its twigs as toothbrushes, helping to fight bacterial infections and periodontal disease. They crushed its leaves and rubbed them on wounds to improve healing. Leaves and twigs stored among food grains reduced pest populations in granaries. In India—and in other countries where the neem tree grows—farmers found they could crush and steep the leaves, mix them with water, and apply the liquid as a pesticide to protect crops.

However, the rest of the world did not notice the potential of the neem tree until the 1920s. At that time, a severe locust infestation swept through a portion of India where many neem trees grew. Foliage was stripped from every living plant in the area—except the neem tree.

Since then, much has been learned about this tree, and products derived from it are helping to fight garden pests and diseases. While it is classed as a pesticide and care must be taken to follow its use directions exactly as stated by law, many gardeners are finding it has fewer harmful side effects than other products.

Neem tree

Neem contains a number of active components. The main one, named azadirachtin, works as a pesticide in two ways. First, sprayed on leaves, it repels many insects from landing. Second, it upsets regulatory mechanisms in insects that eat leaves sprayed with it. The insects stop eating, they don't metamorphose to their next stage, and they don't reproduce. In most cases, this means death within just a few days. A wide variety of insects is affected, including aphids, beetles, mealybugs, spider mites, root knot nematodes, caterpillars, locusts, whiteflies, and termites. Like similar insecticides that kill through ingestion of leaf material, neem does not harm the adult form of some beneficial insects—such as ladybugs, lacewings, and predatory beetles—because they eat pollen and nectar, not leaves.

Other components, perhaps the same ones documented as healing bacterial infections, are probably forms of sulfur. And some gardeners have reported that neem products also help stop the spread of mildew and rust (problems that are often controlled by sulfur sprays).

In choosing any pesticide, you need to look at a variety of factors to decide which of the products available is most appropriate for your situation. Those factors include both its effectiveness and its potential harm to you and the environment. Thus far, neem oil products seem to be as effective as products that have greater potential harm as a result of their toxicity levels, the time before they break down in the soil, and off-site movement after application, such as runoff into nearby lakes, streams, or ponds. Just as the past decade saw a number of pesticides based on pyrethrum (which is made from the flowers of the pyrethrum daisy), you'll most likely soon be seeing more products on garden center shelves that are derived from the neem tree.

SOME FINAL THOUGHTS

Whenever you apply pesticides, target your application to a specific pest. Don't blanket the area with "cover sprays," thinking that it's better to kill all insects in the area just in case some may be harmful to your plants. You'll also kill beneficial insects that naturally keep these marauders at bay, so your next pest infestation will be even worse.

Don't be fooled by marketers who try to get you to buy the same chemical over and over by packaging it under different product names, such as Ant Killer, Termite Killer, Lawn and Insect Killer, and Rose and Flower Insect Killer. Look on the label for the chemical's common name. If, for example, all of these products contain chlorpyrifos you may need to buy just one, not four.

Be careful when using a systemic pesticide. A systemic is a pesticide that's absorbed by roots or leaves and incorporated into a plant's living tissue. It can't be washed off with water. Pests die when they eat the plant and ingest the chemical. It is obvious but worth saying that you never should use systemics on vegetables and fruits you plan to eat.

PLANT ALLERGIES—NOTHING TO SNEEZE AT

Although plants benefit people in countless ways, at least 20 percent of us have plant allergies. Certain substances produced by plants can overstimulate your immune system—an allergic reaction resulting in a stuffy nose, itchy eyes, rashes, or even shock.

Allergenic plants contact your body in three basic ways. The first way is when you eat them. Many folks report allergic reactions to tomatoes, onions, garlic, peanuts, and various fruits. Food allergies are easy to overcome, once you know the source. Just avoid eating that particular food.

The second way is when you touch these plants. The leaves and stems of certain weedy plants, such as poison ivy *(Toxicodendron radicans)* and its cousins poison oak *(T. diversilobum)* and poison sumac *(T. vernix)*, as well as Brazilian pepper tree *(Schinus terebinthifolius)* and mango *(Mangifera indica)*, contain oils that may produce a severe rash if they contact skin. Others, such as stinging nettle *(Urtica dioica)*, have tiny, stinging hairs on their leaves and stems. When touched, these hairs produce an immediate burning sensation. Other types of plants, including century plant *(Agave americana)*, plumeria, and many euphorbias, contain a gummy, white sap that can irritate skin. The best way to avoid these reactions is to avoid the offending plants.

Unfortunately, the two most common causes of plant allergies are nearly impossible to avoid because they're in the air—mold spores and pollen. Mold spores are reproductive structures that grow on moist soil. Areas that receive a lot of rain, such as the Southeast, have lots of molds. Pollen grains are tiny pieces of protein produced by the male parts of flowers to fertilize the female parts. Pollen exists just about everywhere. Inhaling mold spores and pollen is the third way to contact allergens.

While little good can be said about mold spores, not all pollen is bad. The pollen produced by plants with showy or fragrant flowers is typically benign. It's too heavy to travel on a breeze; instead, birds and insects, attracted to the flowers, transfer it from plant to plant. However, pollen produced by nonshowy, scentless flowers is entirely different. Because birds and insects ignore these flowers, the only way for their lightweight pollen to reach other plants is by floating on the wind.

The list of usual suspects includes several pollen-producing weeds, such as ragweeds, curly dock, plantains, pigweeds, and lamb's quarter. Some familiar garden plants

Poison ivy

that are notorious distributors of allergenic pollen include Ozark white cedar *(Juniperus ashei)*, eastern cottonwood *(Populus deltoides)*, box elder *(Acer negundo)*, sycamore *(Platanus occidentalis)*, Siberian elm *(Ulmus pumila)*, and privet *(Ligustrum)*. If you have serious allergies, you should think twice before planting any of these serious offenders.

Unfortunately, simply blacklisting "bad" plants won't completely alleviate the problem, for several reasons. First, most common shade trees, including oaks, maples, pines, elms, ashes, hickories, and pecan, produce allergenic pollen, and you can't cut down every tree in your neighborhood. Second, among the worst allergy producers are lawn grasses, particularly those that send up a lot of seed heads, such as common Bermuda, Kentucky bluegrass, and Bahia. You can choose your own grass, but certainly not your neighbor's. And finally, pollen grains are long-distance travelers. Pollen from ragweeds *(Ambrosia)*, the primary cause of hayfever, has been collected at sea hundreds of miles from shore.

So what's an allergy-suffering gardener to do? Blacktop the yard? Hide inside a sterile chamber supplied with filtered oxygen? Hardly. Despite the presence of allergenic plants, you can enjoy your garden by following these simple guidelines:

• Remove common rash-causing plants, such as poison ivy and oak, from your garden. You'll find more information about these weeds in Chapter 7.

• Cut down or remove weeds that produce lots of airborne pollen, including ragweeds, curly dock, plantains, pigweeds, and lamb's quarter. Each of these weeds is pictured and described in Chapter 7.

• Don't dig in the soil just after a rain, when mold spores are numerous. Dig when the soil surface is dry.

• If you can get someone else to cut your grass, do it. Stay indoors while the lawn is being mowed. Don't walk across a freshly cut lawn. If you must cut the lawn yourself, wear a filter mask. Mow it regularly to keep it from blooming and forming seed heads.

• Always change your clothes and bathe after working outside in the garden.

• Stay indoors in early morning and late afternoon, when pollen counts are the highest.

• Run an air conditioner equipped with an electrostatic filter to remove pollen grains from indoor air.

Say your prayers if you're planning to hand-weed this dandelion patch, because you'll be on your knees for a long time. Applying a selective herbicide for broad-leafed weeds is the most practical way to get the problem under control.

PESTICIDES FOR THE HOME GARDEN

The following charts describe insecticides, miticides, fungicides, herbicides, and other pesticides commonly found in garden centers, hardware stores, and home centers in the South. Keep in mind that not all products are registered for use in every state. Moreover, the Environmental Protection Agency periodically reviews each pesticide and may revoke its registration at any time. Check with the local Cooperative Extension Office for registration status and recommended use.

SOME PESTICIDE TERMS DEFINED

Active ingredient. The actual chemical agent that controls the pest or pests listed on the label. It usually comprises a very small percentage of the material in the container and may be listed by its chemical and common names.

Broad-spectrum pesticide. Kills a wide range of pests, as opposed to one that targets a single or limited number of species.

Contact pesticide. Kills when it is touched or ingested by the pest.

Inert ingredient. This is a carrier material into which the active ingredient is mixed in order to permit an even application at the proper strength. Inert ingredients make up the majority of the pesticide but do not by themselves affect targeted pests.

Nonselective herbicide. Kills almost all plants to which it is applied, as opposed to a selective herbicide that eliminates only certain types.

Postemergence herbicide. Kills weeds that have already sprouted and are beyond the seedling stage. Some kill broad-leafed weeds, some destroy grassy weeds, and some kill both.

Pre-emergence herbicide. Inhibits the germination of weed seeds or the growth of young seedlings. It must be applied prior to germination to be effective.

Systemic pesticide. A chemical that's absorbed by plants and incorporated into their tissues.

Translocated. A herbicide that's absorbed by leaves and stems and transported to the roots, killing the entire plant.

Weed-and-feed. A herbicide that's typically blended with a lawn fertilizer in order to feed the grass and kill lawn weeds at the same time.

Repeat Offenders

Some persistent weeds such as sow thistles grow long taproots, making them hard to pull. Any piece of root left in the ground grows a new plant. Applying a translocated herbicide, such as glyphosate (Roundup), kills the weed, roots and all.

SYNTHETIC PESTICIDES

CHEMICAL NAME	PRODUCT NAME	SIGNAL WORD	DESCRIPTION/FORM	TOXICITY/NOTES
INSECTICIDES, MITICIDES, AND MOLLUSCICIDES				
ACEPHATE	Orthene	Warning	Broad-spectrum, systemic control used against aphids, leaf miners, beetles, thrips, bagworms, caterpillars, fire ants, and many other pests. Liquid, granules, or powder	Toxic to bees and birds. Do not use on edible crops
CARBARYL	Sevin	Caution	Broad-spectrum, contact insecticide that controls caterpillars, beetles, fleas, ticks, spittlebugs, and other pests. Will not control spider mites. Liquid, wettable powder, or dust	Highly toxic to bees and fish. May cause fruit drop if sprayed on apple trees
CHLORPYRIFOS	Dursban	Caution	Broad-spectrum, contact insecticide for control of fire ants, fleas, ticks, caterpillars, borers, leaf miners, and many lawn insects. Degrades quickly in sunlight. Liquid, wettable powder, or granules	Toxic to fish, birds, and wildlife
DIAZINON	Diazinon, others	Caution	Broad-spectrum, contact insecticide that controls ants, aphids, beetles, caterpillars, fleas, ticks, white grubs, and other pests. Often used on lawn pests. Will not control spider mites. Liquid or granules	Highly toxic to bees, birds, and fish
DIMETHOATE	Cygon	Warning	Broad-spectrum, systemic pesticide used against sucking pests, such as aphids, spider mites, leaf miners, scales, spittlebugs, and lace bugs. Liquid	Highly toxic to bees, birds, and fish. Do not apply to edible crops
DISULFOTON	Di-Syston	Warning	Broad-spectrum, systemic pesticide often used in rose care products to control aphids, spider mites, leafhoppers, whiteflies, and other pests. Granules	Toxic to fish and wildlife. Do not use around edible crops. May be fatal if swallowed
ENDOSULFAN	Thiodan	Danger	Broad-spectrum, contact pesticide effective against thrips, borers, mites, whiteflies, caterpillars, beetles, and other pests. Liquid or wettable powder	Highly toxic to fish and wildlife. May be fatal if swallowed. Use is restricted in some areas
HEXAKIS	Vendex	Caution	Contact miticide with long residual action. Controls many types of mites, yet does not harm predatory mites that consume harmful species. Liquid or wettable powder	Safe for honeybees. Not sold by itself; instead, is found in broad-spectrum products, such as Isotox. Has replaced dicofol (Kelthane) as the miticide of choice
HYDRAMETHYLNON	Amdro	Caution	A slow-acting stomach poison contained in baits used against fire ants. By not killing ants immediately, it gives worker ants time to feed it to other workers and the queen, eventually killing the mound. Also used in baits to control roaches. Granules, baits	Toxic to fish
IMIDACLOPRID	Merit, GrubEx	Caution	An insecticide targeted at various white grubs that eat grass roots and damage turf. Also controls mole crickets. Labeled for use on some ornamentals. Granules	Less toxic to birds than almost all other lawn insecticides but is highly toxic to fish and other aquatic animals
LINDANE	Lindane, others	Danger	Powerful insecticide used to control borers, leaf miners, pine bark beetles, and twig girdlers. Liquid	Toxic to wildlife. May be fatal if swallowed. May cause irreversible eye damage, so wear goggles. Use is restricted in some areas
MALATHION	Malathion, others	Warning	Broad-spectrum, contact insecticide for use on both edible and ornamental plants. Controls aphids, mealybugs, caterpillars, lace bugs, thrips, and other pests. Liquid or wettable powder	Toxic to bees and fish
METALDEHYDE	Bug-Geta, others	Caution	Molluscicide, often pelletized, that kills slugs and snails	Highly toxic to fish, birds, pets, and other wildlife. May be used in vegetable gardens

SYNTHETIC PESTICIDES (CONTINUED)

CHEMICAL NAME	PRODUCT NAME	SIGNAL WORD	DESCRIPTION/FORM	TOXICITY/NOTES
INSECTICIDES, MITICIDES, AND MOLLUSCICIDES (CONTINUED)				
PHOSMET	Imidan	Warning	A contact insecticide primarily used by growers of apples, peaches, plums, and other stone fruits to contol plum curculios and codling moths. Wettable powder	Toxic to honeybees, so do not apply until petal fall
PYRETHRINS	Numerous	Caution	This is usually available in the synthetic form, pyrethroids, which are stronger and longer lasting than the plant-based chemical. Typically found in sprays, foggers, and baits used to control ants, wasps, hornets, fleas, house-flies, and whiteflies. Examples: resmethrin, permethrin, tetramethrin, sumithrin, deltamethrin, tralomethrin	May be toxic to fish. Do not spray on edible crops
FUNGICIDES				
CALCIUM POLYSULFIDE	Lime sulfur, dormant spray, others	Danger	Used to kill overwintering fungi and insects on fruit trees, roses, and other ornamentals. Usually applied when plants are dormant but may be used with caution during growing season on certain plants. Liquid	Caustic to skin. May cause serious eye injury, so wear goggles
CAPTAN	Captan, others	Danger	Broad-spectrum fungicide now mainly used on fruit crops to control brown rot, black rot, scab, and leaf spots. Wettable powder	Toxic to bees and fish. May cause irreversible eye damage, so wear goggles
CHLOROTHALONIL	Daconil, others	Warning	Broad-spectrum fungicide to control powdery mildew, black spot, botrytis (gray mold), leaf spots, scab, blights, and a variety of lawn diseases. Liquid or wettable powder	Toxic to fish. Irritates eyes and skin. Some people are allergic to the chemical
MANCOZEB	Fore, Manzate, Dithane	Caution	Broad-spectrum fungicide that controls mildew, rust, blight, and leaf spots on vegetables and ornamentals. Chemical combination that includes maneb (see below). Liquid or wettable powder	Moderately toxic to fish
MANEB	Maneb, others	Caution	Broad-spectrum fungicide to control blights, leaf spots, rusts, mildews, and many other diseases of vegetables and ornamentals. Wettable powder	Highly toxic to fish
MYCLOBUTANIL	Immunox	Caution	Broad-spectrum, systemic fungicide used to control mildew, black spot, rust, and other diseases on roses and ornamentals. Liquid	Labeled for use on some fruits
THIOPHANATE-METHYL	Thiomyl, Domain, Cleary's 3336	Caution	Broad-spectrum, systemic fungicide used to control black spot, tip blight, leaf spots, powdery mildew, lawn diseases, and many others. Wettable powder	Do not apply to edible crops
TRIADIMEFON	Bayleton	Warning	Broad-spectrum, systemic fungicide for prevention or eradication of powdery mildew, rust, azalea petal blight, and lawn diseases. Wettable powder	Toxic to fish. Do not apply to edible crops
TRIFORINE	Funginex	Danger	Broad-spectrum, systemic fungicide to control black spot, powdery mildew, rust, and other diseases on roses and ornamentals. Liquid	Keep animals out of treated areas. May cause irreversible eye damage, so wear goggles
HERBICIDES				
2,4-D	Numerous	Caution	Widely used, translocated, postemergence herbicide that controls many broad-leafed weeds. Often mixed with other herbicides in general weed killers. Liquid, granules	Toxic to fish
ATRAZINE	Atrazine, Purge, Bonus S, others	Caution	Pre-emergence and postemergence herbicide that controls grassy and broad-leafed lawn weeds. Leaches readily from soil; may contaminate groundwater. Liquid, granules	Toxic to fish, birds, and wildlife. Do not use near ornamental plantings, streams, or ponds
BENEFIN	Balan	Caution	Pre-emergence herbicide used to control weedy grasses, such as annual bluegrass and crabgrass, in lawns. Granules	Toxic to fish

SYNTHETIC PESTICIDES (CONTINUED)

CHEMICAL NAME	PRODUCT NAME	SIGNAL WORD	DESCRIPTION/FORM	TOXICITY/NOTES
HERBICIDES (CONTINUED)				
CALCIUM ACID METHANEARSONATE	Crabgrass Killer, others	Caution	Postemergence herbicide used to kill crabgrass, nutsedges, and Dallis grass in lawns. Liquid	Keep children and animals out of treated area until 2 days after applying. Repeated use may lead to toxic buildup of arsenic in soil
DICAMBA	Dicamba, others	Caution	Translocated herbicide used against a wide variety of broad-leafed weeds in lawns. Often included with other herbicides in lawn weed killers. Liquid, granules	Leaches readily from soil. Do not use near ornamental plantings
DIQUAT DIBROMIDE	Numerous	Caution	Nonselective, contact herbicide that quickly kills top growth of many garden weeds. Not translocated, so perennial weeds may grow back. Liquid	Toxic to fish, birds, wildlife
DITHIOPYR	Dimension	Caution	Pre-emergence herbicide that controls both grassy and broad-leafed lawn weeds, including crabgrass, annual bluegrass, chickweed, and henbit. Granules	Highly toxic to fish and other aquatic animals. Do not apply more than once a year. Apply only to healthy, established lawns
ETHEPHON	Florel, Etherel, others	Caution	Growth regulator used on fruits and vegetables to hasten ripening, promote flowering, or remove unwanted fruit. Can be used to remove mistletoe from trees. Liquid	Slightly toxic to fish
FLUAZIFOP-P-BUTYL	Fusilade, Grass-B-Gon	Caution	Translocated, postemergence herbicide that controls grassy weeds. Liquid	Leaches readily through soil. Do not apply near streams, ponds, wells
GLUFOSINATE-AMMONIUM	Finale	Caution	Nonselective, postemergence herbicide that controls a variety of broad-leafed and grassy weeds. Not absorbed by roots. Liquid	Breaks down quickly in soil
GLYPHOSATE	Roundup	Caution	Nonselective, translocated, postemergence herbicide that controls a wide variety of actively growing plants, including grasses, perennials, vines, and shrubs. Not absorbed by roots. Liquid	Keep children and pets out of treated area until spray has dried. Do not use on aquatic weeds
IMAZAQUIN	Image, others	Caution	Postemergence herbicide for hard-to-control lawn weeds, such as nutsedges, dollar weed, and wild onion. Liquid	Toxic to fish
ISOXABEN	Gallery, Portrait	Caution	Pre-emergence herbicide that controls many broad-leafed lawn weeds, including dandelion, clover, chickweed, and plantains. Granules	Can be applied on all warm-season and cool-season grasses. One application provides up to 8 months of control
MCPP	Mecoprop	Warning	Translocated, postemergence herbicide used to control many broad-leafed lawn weeds. Often mixed with other herbicides in lawn weed killers. Liquid	Toxic to fish. May cause irreversible eye damage, so wear goggles
OXYFLUORFEN	Triox	Danger	Soil sterilant that kills all vegetation and prevents regrowth for up to 1 year. Leaches through soil and may kill desirable plants. Liquid	May cause irreversible eye damage, so wear goggles
PENDIMETHALIN	Halts	Caution	Pre-emergence herbicide that prevents the germination of many lawn weeds, including crabgrass. Often added to lawn fertilizer. Granules	Toxic to fish and wildlife
TRICLOPYR	Brush-B-Gon, Brush Killer	Caution	Nonselective, translocated, postemergence herbicide used primarily on hard-to-kill woody plants, such as vines, shrubs, and trees. Liquid	Keep children and pets out of treated area until it's dry
TRIFLURALIN	Treflan, Preen	Caution	Pre-emergence herbicide that controls many grassy and broad-leafed weeds in lawns, ornamental plantings, and vegetable gardens. Trifluralin is sometimes blended with benefin (Team) for more broad-spectrum control. Granules	Toxic to fish

NATURAL PESTICIDES

CHEMICAL NAME	PRODUCT NAME	SIGNAL WORD	DESCRIPTION/FORM	TOXICITY/NOTES
INSECTICIDES, MITICIDES, MOLLUSCICIDES, AND NEMATICIDES				
ABAMECTIN	Affirm, others	Caution	Bacterial toxin incorporated into baits that worker fire ants feed to queen, eventually killing the mound. Also found in roach baits. Granules, baits	Toxic to fish
AZADIRACHTIN	Neem, Bioneem, Neem-Away, others	Caution	Chemical produced by a tropical tree that both repels pests and causes them to stop feeding. Controls aphids, beetles, caterpillars, spider mites, whiteflies, and other pests. Liquid	Toxic to bees
BACILLUS POPILLIAE-DUTKY	Milky Spore, Doom, others	Caution	Bacterium that kills white grubs of Japanese beetles that feed on grass roots and damaged lawns	To be effective, needs to be applied communitywide, not just to individual lawns
BACILLUS THURINGIENSIS (*Bt*)	Dipel, Thuricide, Javelin, others	Caution	Bacterium that exists in several strains, including *B. t. israeliensis*, *B. t. kurstaki*, and *B. t.* San Diego, each of which targets a specific pest, including caterpillars, Colorado potato beetles, and mosquito larvae. Wettable powder or dust	Safe around people, pets, birds, fish. Breaks down quickly in sunlight; apply in evening
BOILING WATER		None	An inexpensive and environmentally friendly way to dispatch fire ants. Use caution transporting boiling liquid any distance	It will cook any plants you accidentally spill it on
BORIC ACID	Numerous	Caution	The basis for some of the safest and most effective roach poisons. Roaches, ants, and silverfish pick it up on their feet, ingest it while cleaning themselves, and spread it to others. Powder	Very safe to use
CHITIN	Clandosan	Caution	This substance forms the exoskeletons of insects and crustaceans. When added to soil, microbes produce toxins and digestive enzymes that kill nematodes	Incorporate into soil 2 weeks before planting. Use 50–100 lbs. per 1,000 sq. ft.
DIATOMACEOUS EARTH	Numerous	Caution	Composed of the fossilized, microscopic shells of tiny, water-dwelling organisms called diatoms. These shells cut the exoskeletons and membranes of such pests as slugs, snails, earwigs, ants, silverfish, and roaches, causing them to dry out and die. Powder or dust	Wear breathing mask to avoid inhaling the dust
HORTICULTURAL OIL	Sun Spray, Volck, Oil-Away, others	Caution	Refined oils from plants or petroleum that smother pests, eggs, and disease spores. Especially effective against soft-bodied, sucking pests, such as aphids, mealybugs, whiteflies, and scales. Depending on type, can be used during growing season or as dormant spray. Liquid	Toxic to fish
INSECTICIDAL SOAP	Safer, others	Caution	Not made from detergent but from potassium salts of fatty acids found in plants and animals. Breaks down the cell membranes of soft-bodied pests, such as aphids, mealy-bugs, and mites. Safe to use inside the house. No residual action. Liquid	Toxic to fish
METHOPRENE	Vigren, Precor	Caution	Growth regulator used against fleas and ticks that stops juveniles from becoming adults and reproducing. Fog, spray	Do not inhale fog. Keep animals and children out of treated room for 2 hours after fogging
NOSEMA LOCUSTAE	Nosema, Grasshopper Attack, others	Caution	A microscopic protozoan that kills grasshoppers and crickets when fed to them in bait. Has short shelf life; must be refrigerated between uses	Nontoxic to people, animals, nontargeted insects
ROTENONE	Rotenone	Caution	Plant-based, contact insecticide used against cabbage-worms, flea beetles, squash vine borer, corn borer, and other vegetable garden pests. Wettable powder, dust, or liquid	Extremely toxic to fish

NATURAL PESTICIDES (CONTINUED)

CHEMICAL NAME	PRODUCT NAME	SIGNAL WORD	DESCRIPTION/FORM	TOXICITY/NOTES
FUNGICIDES AND BACTERICIDES				
AZADIRACHTIN	Neem, Bioneem, Neem-Away, Rose Defense, others	Caution	Primarily used to control garden insects but also appears to inhibit black spot, mildew, rust, and some other diseases on ornamentals. Liquid	Toxic to fish
BAKING SODA (SODIUM BICARBONATE)	Baking soda	None	Mixed at 4 tsp. to 1 gal. water, baking soda may control black spot and powdery mildew on roses	Keep it out of fish ponds
COPPER COMPOUNDS	Bordeaux mixture, Kocide 101, others	Caution	Broad-spectrum fungicides and bactericides used on fruits and ornamentals to prevent fireblight, peach leaf curl, shot-hole diseases, downy mildew, and brown rot. Liquid, wettable powder, or dust	Toxic to fish
FUNGICIDAL SOAP	Soap Shield	Caution	Broad-spectrum fungicide of fixed copper mixed with potassium salts of fatty acids. Controls many plant diseases, including fireblight, rust, black spot, powdery mildew, black rot, botrytis (gray mold), and leaf spots. Liquid	May burn the leaves of roses if applied during cool, wet weather
STREPTOMYCIN	Agri-Strep, Agrimycin	Caution	Antibiotic used to kill the bacteria that cause fireblight on apples, crabapples, pears, and other plants. Wettable powder	Degrades quickly in sunlight, so apply in evening
SULFUR	Garden sulfur, Safer Garden Fungicide, others	Caution	Traditional chemical used to control powdery mildew, black spot, brown rot, and apple scab. Liquid, wettable powder, or dust	Avoid getting it in eyes
HERBICIDES				
BOILING WATER		None	An inexpensive and environmentally friendly way to kill weeds growing through cracks in the pavement	It will cook any plants you accidentally spill it on
FERROUS SULFATE	Moss Control, others	Caution	Often used to acidify soil for azaleas, camellias, and other acid-loving plants. Also kills moss in lawns. Apply 1–2 lbs. per 1,000 sq. ft. Do not apply to cement, concrete, stucco, or stone. Granules	Toxic to fish
HERBICIDAL SOAP	Safer Superfast, Scythe, Safer Moss & Algae Killer, others	Caution	Contact, biodegradable herbicides that quickly kill top growth of young, actively growing weeds. May also control mosses, lichens, and algae. Safer Superfast and Moss & Algae Killer are made from potassium salts of fatty acids. Scythe contains pelargonic acid. Neither is translocated. Liquid	Toxic to fish. Perennial weeds need repeated treatments
VINEGAR	Vinegar	None	The acetic acid contained in vinegar can quickly kill herbaceous lawn and garden weeds. Especially effective against weeds growing in cracks in sidewalks, driveways, and patios. Use 5 or 10 percent strength	Nonselective, keep it off desirable plants

BENEFICIAL CREATURES— YOUR GARDEN'S BEST FRIENDS

Believe it or not, pesticides, whether synthetic or natural, aren't your garden's first line of defense. That role belongs to predators that constantly stalk and kill pests that would otherwise savage your plants. Some predators, such as spiders, wasps, praying mantises, toads, lizards, and birds, are highly visible in the garden. The best way to invite them there is by providing shelter, water, and food and not blanketing the whole yard with pesticides.

To repel sudden pest invasions, you may need to reinforce these familiar troops of predators with special pest-fighting forces, known as beneficials. Some folks are lucky enough to be able to buy them from a local organic gardening store. Others have to order them through the mail (see Chapter 8, "Suppliers and Expert Resources"). Once you release these beneficials, they'll quickly move against the bad guys. However, you may have to redeploy them from time to time.

Ladybugs. Also known as ladybird beetles, ladybugs are among those rare insects that people actually like. Famous for consuming scores of aphids at a sitting, both adults and larvae also eat whiteflies, scales, and the eggs of Colorado potato beetles. Trouble is, adult ladybugs fly, so there's no guarantee they will stay in your garden.

Lacewings. Adult lacewings are pussycats— they feed only on nectar and pollen. It's their vicious larvae that garden pests fear. Looking something like miniature alligators, with their pincerlike mouthparts that suck juices from pests' bodies and eggs, lacewing larvae kill aphids, mealybugs, scales, whiteflies, and spider mites, to name a few.

Purchased lacewings are usually shipped as eggs in rice hulls, which you distribute throughout the garden. The

Meet the New Help

Lacewings arrive as eggs shipped in rice hulls, which you spread throughout the garden. After the eggs hatch, the larvae consume a host of harmful insects.

eggs soon hatch and the larvae begin eating. They develop into adults in 1 to 3 weeks, lay eggs, and continue their life cycle. They're especially effective in greenhouses.

Beneficial nematodes. Beneficial nematodes test your trust. Under a microscope they look exactly the same as destructive nematodes. The only difference is what they eat. Destructive nematodes eat plant roots. Beneficial nematodes eat cutworms, cabbage root maggots, white grubs, flea beetle larvae, sod webworms, iris borers, and other pests. Sorry to say, they don't eat destructive nematodes.

Mail-order suppliers and garden centers sell beneficial nematodes in a juvenile, dormant state. You can distribute them in several ways. One is to mix them with a soil amendment, such as vermiculite, and work them either into the top few inches of soil or, if you're adding a new plant to your garden, right

Beneficial Nematodes: Your Partners in Lawn Care
It's easy to apply beneficial nematodes with a watering can (right).
This lawn (above) is treated with applications of nematodes during the
active growing season as part of its routine maintenance program.

at the root level. You can also add them to water and apply them with a watering can or hose sprayer—an especially valuable technique when introducing them to a lawn that's infested with grubs.

Nematodes are sensitive to sunlight and heat, so apply them in late afternoon. Water the area first and keep the treated area moist for several weeks following application. The nematodes will remain active as long as they have something to eat.

Predator mites. Predator mites need trusting, too. They look just like evil mites, but they don't feed on plants. They eat other mites. Some types also eat thrips.

Parasitoid wasps. These aren't like the paper wasps, yellow jackets, and mud daubers you see every day. For one thing, they're tiny—you can hardly spot them. For another, they don't sting. What they do is lay eggs on the larvae and

eggs of many garden pests. The wasp eggs quickly hatch and their larvae consume the victims.

One parasitoid wasp, *Encarsia formosa,* is especially effective against whiteflies in greenhouses. *Trichogramma* wasps destroy the eggs of moths and butterflies, controlling cabbageworms, tomato hornworms, corn earworms, codling moth, cutworms, armyworms, cabbage loopers, and more. *Braconid* wasps lay eggs on the bodies of caterpillars. These eggs form whitish or yellowish cocoons; the larvae inside feed on the fluids of the caterpillar, eventually killing it. One type of braconid wasp targets the tobacco hornworm. Another takes aim at gypsy moth caterpillars.

Adult wasps feed on nectar and pollen, so it's important to have flowering plants in your garden to keep them reproducing. As with other beneficials, avoid widespread spraying after you release them.

Solving
PLANT PROBLEMS

*T*he world isn't perfect, at least the last time we checked. That goes for your garden, too. Sooner or later, some bug, disease, weed, or critter will mess with your own little piece of Eden. But don't panic. Most pest problems have an easy and quick solution. The key is identifying the cause and then applying the appropriate remedy before the problem spreads.

This chapter will help you decide on a course of action. On the following pages you'll find some 250 color illustrations that depict common problems found in Southern gardens. Of course, there isn't room here or even in an entire book to illustrate every problem for every plant you could possibly grow. So we've selected about 140 of the South's most popular plants. Each plant entry includes one or more illustrations of damage caused by insects, diseases, environmental conditions, or poor cultural (gardening) practices, and provides practical solutions.

For more information about the problems highlighted in bold type in this chapter's plant listings, turn to the encyclopedia chapters beginning on page 142. In addition to the color photographs in these chapters, you'll find descriptions of the pest's life cycle, the damage it causes, how to prevent it, and how to get rid of it.

But before we review plant pests in this chapter, let's discuss by plant type some of the issues and problems that confront Southern gardeners.

LAWNS

A beautiful, lush lawn starts with a grass that is well adapted to your area. In general, gardeners in the Upper and Middle South should choose a cool-season grass (Kentucky bluegrass, perennial ryegrass, or tall fescue), while those elsewhere should plant a warm-season grass (Bahia, Bermuda, buffalo grass, carpet grass, centipede grass, St. Augustine, or zoysia). For more details about these grasses, see page 41. Check with your Cooperative Extension Office to learn about grasses recommended for your area.

Water requirements vary for grasses but average about 1 inch per week. Don't water every day for 15 minutes. Instead, water once or twice a week for several hours. The object is to wet the soil deeply to promote deeply rooted grass. Also, never water in late afternoon or night if you can avoid it. Grass that stays wet all night is prone to disease.

Don't cut your grass too short. Lawns mowed to the proper height are thicker, healthier, and have fewer weeds than lawns cut too short. (See "Lawn Scalping," page 234.) Fertilize regularly, using a slow-release fertilizer labeled for your type of grass.

Even if you do everything right, a lot of things can go wrong with your lawn. Trouble is, most problems look pretty much the same—a brown or yellow spot that gets bigger and bigger.

Your task is to figure out what's causing that spot in the lawn—fungus, insect, or the dog. The last cause is easy to uncover. Just watch your dog for a while. But deciding between a fungus and an insect is tougher, especially if you don't know what to look for.

Here's the first thing to do. Cut the bottom out of a coffee can or plastic milk jug. Place the can or jug over an edge where green and yellow grass meet. Fill it with soapy water and wait

> *I tell folks, if there's something wrong with your garden, take ten big steps back and take off your glasses. And if you can't see it, it ain't a problem.*
>
> –Felder Rushing,
> Jackson, Mississippi

Anticipating problems and quickly treating them are the keys to success, whether you're growing (clockwise from upper left) an 'Old Blush' rose and bluebonnets in Texas; tomatoes in Mississippi; perennials and ornamental grasses in Maryland; or flowers, trees, and shrubs in Georgia.

Setting the Stage

A thick, green lawn does more than carpet bare ground. It also ties together the various elements of a garden and brings out flower colors. This St. Augustine lawn in Jacksonville, Florida, shows the benefits of proper watering, mowing, and fertilizing. Attentive care minimizes disease and insect problems.

for a few minutes. If chinch bugs, sod webworms, or some other critters are present in numbers, they'll float to the top.

Nothing floating? Then the problem could be a fungus. To find out, go out to your lawn one morning at dawn when there has been a heavy dew. Look closely at the margin of the dead or dying spot. If a fungus is present, you'll often see a cottony mass of fungal threads right there.

As described in Chapter 5, "Bugs and Other Critters," and Chapter 6, "Plant Diseases and Ailments," the proper insecticide or fungicide can control most lawn problems caused by insects and diseases. Chapter 6 also describes specific lawn problems and ailments under the following headings:

- Brown Patch, page 216
- Dollar Spot on Lawns, page 224
- Fairy Ring, page 227
- Lawn Scalping, page 234
- Lawn Striping, page 234
- Lawns with Dead Patches, page 235
- Melting Out of Lawn Grasses, page 237
- St. Augustine Decline, page 245
- Shade on Lawns, page 247
- Spring Dead Spot, page 251
- Take-All Patch, page 253
- Thatch, page 254

HOUSE PLANTS

House plants have two basic needs. The first is adequate light. No matter how bright a windowsill, it is still considerably dimmer than outdoor light. So make sure you know the light requirements of a house plant before purchasing it and bringing it home. If you don't have a sunny window, stick with house plants that thrive in dimmer light, such as peace lily *(Spathiphyllum)* and snake plant *(Sansevieria trifasciata)*.

The second requirement is the proper amount of water. You may be surprised to learn that more house plants die from too much water than too little. Always make sure that plant containers have a drainage hole, so that excess water can drain away.

The vast majority of other house plant problems can be traced to four little pests—aphids, scales (mealybugs are a type of soft scale), whiteflies, and spider mites. Signs of their presence include puckered leaves, speckled or yellowing leaves, sticky honeydew or black mold on leaves and stems, and tiny webs between leaves and stems.

How did these pests get there? Most came with the plant when you brought it home from the garden center, in the form of tiny eggs and juvenile insects. Once within the safe confines of your home, unchecked by natural predators or harsh weather, pests multiplied amazingly fast.

Vresia bromeliad

The best way to keep insects and mites from infesting your house plants is to carefully inspect the plants before you buy. Reject any with obvious pests or symptoms of infestation. Once you get the plants home, thoroughly spray the stems and leaves (both upper and lower surfaces) with either insecticidal soap or horticultural oil according to label directions. Do this outside before you bring them indoors. You'll find detailed information about aphids, mealybugs, scales, mites, and whiteflies beginning on page 142.

Of course, not all house plant problems are caused by bugs. Probably the most common question about house plants is why the leaves drop from weeping fig *(Ficus benjamina)*. Quite simply, this plant is extremely temperamental. It drops leaves whenever there's an abrupt change in the surrounding light, air temperature, or humidity, usually caused by moving it. If you can't tolerate this annoying habit, choose another house plant.

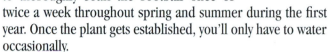

Sweet gum

TREES AND SHRUBS

No plants, sorry to say, are permanent. But trees and shrubs are typically the longest-lived members of the garden. Guaranteeing a long and happy life means getting them off to a good start.

To do this, first make sure the spot you've picked out for them meets their basic needs in terms of sun or shade, water, soil pH, heat and cold tolerance, and sufficient room to grow.

Sourwood

Next, plant them correctly. Dig a hole slightly deeper than the rootball but about three times as wide. Plant the tree or shrub a little high in the hole, so that the top ½ to 1 inch of the rootball is above the soil's surface. Planting high is necessary because the heavy clay soil that pervades much of the South drains poorly. And soil that stays wet causes root rot. Backfill the hole with loose soil around the rootball, water thoroughly, and then cover the rootball with 2 to 3 inches of mulch.

Horticulturists disagree about the benefit of amending existing soil with peat moss, compost, pine bark, or other materials when you plant trees or shrubs. But we think this makes sense: Don't bother amending the soil for trees. Their growth depends on sending out roots far beyond the confines of the original hole. However, if you're planting shrubs with relatively shallow, confined root systems, such as azaleas, boxwoods, and blueberries, amend the soil, especially if the existing soil is poor. You also should amend the soil if you plan to plant acid-loving shrubs in neutral or alkaline soil. (See "Soil pH—the Acid Test," page 23.)

Regular watering is critical to the success of newly planted trees and shrubs. Don't depend on lawn sprinklers—they may wet only the top inch or two of soil. Instead, use the hose to thoroughly soak the rootball once or twice a week throughout spring and summer during the first year. Once the plant gets established, you'll only have to water occasionally.

When selecting a tree or shrub, always keep in mind its growth rate and size at maturity. Sure, that Burford holly looks great under your living room window now, but what are you going to do in 5 years when it is 15 feet tall and no one can see out? Trees and shrubs you must constantly cut back to keep inbounds are more than nuisances—they're also pest prone because they must be constantly hacked back. Choose your plants wisely and save yourself some work.

ANNUALS, PERENNIALS, AND BULBS

Trees and shrubs form the backbone of the garden; annuals, perennials, and bulbs flesh it out with bright color. You have scores of exquisite plants from which to choose. But make sure they fit your garden's conditions *before* you plant them.

With few exceptions, annuals, perennials, and bulbs prefer well-drained soil. If the soil in your garden drains poorly, amend it with large amounts of organic matter, coarse sand, gravel, or expanded slate. Or consider building raised beds.

Removing flowers before they form seed (deadheading) encourages annuals and perennials to bloom longer. Deadheading repeat-blooming summer bulbs, such as cannas and dahlias, keeps the flowers coming. Deadheading spring bulbs, such as daffodils, doesn't extend the bloom, but rather directs

In the world of perennials, Russian sage is a rising czar.

Crinums Never Die

You'll never find tougher, more resilient bulbs than crinum lilies. Often found in older gardens, these fragrant flowers live for decades with absolutely no care.

the plant's energy into making a bigger bulb (for more flowers the following year). Never remove spring bulb foliage until it starts to yellow and wither. If you do, you'll reduce or eliminate next year's bloom.

Some spring bulbs, particularly tulips, need several weeks of temperatures below 45 degrees F in order to bloom well. If your area has short, mild winters, chill tulip bulbs in the vegetable bin of your refrigerator for 8 to 10 weeks prior to planting them in late fall or early winter.

Many perennials and bulbs benefit from periodic dividing. This rejuvenates them and prevents them from becoming too crowded. In general, divide the plants while they're not actively growing. For most, this means autumn or late winter. However, you can divide daylilies and bearded irises in summer. The best time to divide spring bulbs is just as their foliage is dying down in late spring.

Voles, chipmunks, squirrels, and other rodents rank among the most serious pests of perennials and bulbs. Chipmunks and squirrels dig up and eat crocus, tulip, and other bulbs. Voles—small, mouselike creatures that burrow near the soil surface—chew through the roots and stems of perennials, particularly hostas. You can foil these pesky critters by planting bulbs and perennials inside cages fashioned from half-inch wire mesh. Or add coarse particles of expanded slate or sharp gravel into the garden bed before planting.

FRUITS, NUTS, AND BERRIES

Your first consideration when choosing fruit, nut, or berry plants is where in the South you live. Your climate determines what kinds you can grow. For example, citrus is limited to central and south Florida and extreme southern Texas, while cherries do best in the Upper South.

At the core of climatic suitability is the number of annual chill hours your garden receives—the number of hours each winter that the temperature lingers at 45 degrees F or lower. Without adequate chill, many fruit, nut, and berry plants fail to bloom. Your Cooperative Extension Office can tell you how many chill hours your area typically gets, as well as the chill requirements of recommended plant selections. On average, the Upper South gets more than 2,600 chill hours; the Middle South, 1,800 to 2,600 hours; the Lower South, 800 to 1,800 hours; the Coastal South, 300 to 800 hours; and the Tropical South, about 50 to 300 hours.

Pollination is another key to good fruit, berry, and nut production. Although some of these plants are self-pollinating, most require cross-pollination between two or more genetically different selections to produce good crops. Ask your Cooperative Extension Office or local nursery to recommend compatible selections for your area. And if you don't like spraying fungicides, ask about disease-resistant selections, too. You'll also find additional information on these and other topics in the *Southern Living Garden Book*.

THE BIG CHILL

Here are the ranges of chill hours needed for various fruits, nuts, and berries. The lower the number of chill hours, the better the selection performs in warm-winter areas, such as the Lower, Coastal, and Tropical South.

Plant	Chill Hours Needed
Apple	350 to 1,200
Blackberry	200 to 700
Blueberry, highbush	800 to 1,200
Blueberry, rabbiteye	350 to 700
Cherry	800 to 1,200
Fig	100
Grape	100 to 500
Nectarine	250 to 1,200
Peach	150 to 1,200
Pear, Asian	150 to 750
Pear, European	600 to 1,500
Pecan	600 to 900
Persimmon	100 to 200
Plum, European	700 to 1,100
Plum, Japanese	400 to 1,000
Raspberry	800 to 1,700

ALL IN THE FAMILY

Being familiar with the vegetable groups also makes it easier to rotate crops effectively. For example, tomatoes are highly susceptible to wilt diseases and do best when rotated each year, but they should not be replaced by another family member, such as peppers, since the entire *Solanaceae* group can be infected by the same fungus.

Cole crops, or brassicas *(Brassicaceae)*	Cucurbits *(Cucurbitaceae)*	Leafy greens	Onion group	Tomato family *(Solanaceae)*
broccoli	cucumber	chard	garlic	eggplant
brussels sprouts	gourd	endive	leek	pepper
cabbage	muskmelon	lettuce	onion	potato
cauliflower	pumpkin	spinach		tomato
kale	squash	**Legumes**	**Root crops**	
kohlrabi	watermelon	bean	beet	
rutabaga		pea	carrot	
			parsnip	
			radish	
			turnip	

VEGETABLES AND HERBS

Let's get right to the point: Vegetables and herbs need sun. The more sun they get, the better they produce.

Vegetables and herbs also need well-drained soil. If you don't have it, work lots of organic matter, coarse sand, gravel, or expanded slate into the soil. Or build raised beds. In general, vegetables prefer rich, moist soil and regular feedings of fertilizer. Herbs do better in lean, gritty, slightly dry soil.

When planting vegetables, keep in mind the season. Certain vegetables, such as broccoli, lettuce, English peas, and radishes, need cool weather to grow. Others, including beans, corn, eggplant, melons, okra, peppers, and squash, need an extended period of warm weather.

Don't plant the same vegetables or those in the same family (see above) in the same place year after year. Diseases and insects will build up in the soil and devastate your crop. Instead, practice crop rotation. (For more information, see "Gardening—A Moving Experience," page 30.) And always look for disease-resistant selections (see "Disease Resistance by the Letter," page 21).

People aren't the only ones who love fresh vegetables; so do insects and critters. If you'd rather not apply synthetic insecticides to your edibles, use floating row covers and natural insecticides, such as insecticidal soap, *Bacillus thuringiensis (Bt)*, and rotenone. The best way to exclude animal critters is with a fence anchored into the ground. A well-anchored 3-foot-tall fence suffices for rabbits; for deer, however, you'll need one at least 8 feet tall.

The Long and Short of It

Sweet corn (above) needs long, hot summers to develop properly, while lettuce (left) prefers the shorter and cooler days provided by spring, fall, and (in the Coastal and Tropical South) winter weather.

AGERATUM
AGERATUM HOUSTONIANUM
ANNUALS
✓ ZONES: ALL

Ageratum, or floss flower, is a popular annual with small, fluffy, blue, pink, or white blooms atop a mounding green plant. Ageratum needs moist, well-drained soil. Remove old flowers to encourage rebloom.

PROBLEM: Whiteflies *(illustrated above)*. Tiny, white, triangular insects cluster on the undersides of leaves. If disturbed, they fly in a cloud around the infested plant. Plant symptoms include curling or general yellowing of leaves, as well as a black mold that grows on the honeydew excreted by the pests.

Solution: Whiteflies are notoriously difficult to control. Apply horticultural oil, resmethrin, acephate (Orthene), or malathion. If repeated applications don't work, affected plants may have to be replaced.

PROBLEM: Botrytis (gray mold). Brown spots appear on leaves, stems, and blossoms. A woolly gray fungus forms on infected tissues.

Solution: High humidity, poorly drained soil, and cool temperatures favor the disease. Space plants adequately for good air circulation. Promptly remove and destroy dead or spent flowers and dead or dying leaves. Avoid overhead watering. Spray plant with chlorothalonil (Daconil) according to label directions.

OTHER COMMON PROBLEMS: Spider **mite** infestation due to hot weather; the hotter it gets, the quicker mites reproduce. Symptoms include a silver speckling of upper leaf surfaces. Thoroughly spray leaf surfaces with insecticidal soap.

AMARYLLIS
HIPPEASTRUM
BULBS
✓ ZONES: LS, CS, TS; OR INDOORS

Traditional holiday flowers in the South, most selections of amaryllis are usually grown indoors. However, in the Lower, Coastal, and Tropical South most are hardy outdoors and bloom in spring. Trumpet-shaped blooms stand tall on sturdy 2-ft. stems. Strap-like leaves appear after the blooms and last all summer.

PROBLEM: Leaf scorch *(illustrated above)*. Small red spots appear on leaves. These develop into brownish red streaks.

Leaves bend at the point of infection. Spots may spread to flower stalks and flowers. Flowers of severely infected plants dry up before opening.

Solution: Leaf scorch of amaryllis is caused by the fungus *Stagonospora curtisii*. High humidity and overwatering encourage it. Promptly remove and destroy infected tissue. Spray plant every 7 to 10 days with a fungicide containing captan. Begin when leaves first appear in spring and continue until the plant blooms.

OTHER COMMON PROBLEMS: Insufficient light and warm temperatures cause stems of amaryllis bulbs grown indoors to grow so tall that plants tip over.

APPLE
DECIDUOUS FRUIT TREES
✓ ZONES: VARY BY SELECTION

An apple may not be as perfumy as a peach or as exotic as a mango, but it is certainly a top-choice fruit for juice, cooking, and eating fresh. Dwarf trees bear normal-size fruit and take up far less space than standard trees.

PROBLEM: Apple scab *(illustrated above)*. Dull olive green, velvety, fungal growth develops on upper leaf surfaces in spring. Leaves yellow and fall prematurely. Trees may become bare by midseason. Infected fruits display circular rough spots on the surface.

Solution: Cool wet weather favors the disease. Rake and remove fallen leaves and fruit. Beginning at bud break, spray with captan or chlorothalonil (Daconil) at 7- to 10-day intervals until mid-June. Plant scab-resistant selections, such as 'Arkansas Black', 'Grimes Golden', 'Jonathan', and 'Stayman'.

PROBLEM: Cedar-apple rust. Bright yellow or yellow-orange spots form on leaves. Clusters of cup-shaped lesions with fringed edges appear on undersides of infected leaves. Fruit is small and deformed.

Solution: This disease needs two hosts to reproduce: apples and eastern red cedars (*Juniperus virginiana*). Planting selections resistant to cedar-apple rust, such as 'Grimes Golden', 'Granny Smith', 'Freedom', 'Liberty', and 'Priscilla', is the best strategy against this disease. To control rust on other selections, apply a fungicide containing captan, mancozeb, or triadimefon (Bayleton) after flower petals fall and flower buds are first seen.

PROBLEM: Fireblight. Young twigs and branches die back from tips and appear black, burned, or rust colored. Dead leaves and fruit generally remain on the branch. The problem occurs during bloom.

Solution: This bacterial infection is spread by splashing rain. Prune out branches 12 in. below affected areas. After each cut, disinfect pruning tools by dipping them into alcohol or a bleach solution (1 part bleach to 9 parts water). Do not apply high-nitrogen fertilizers. Spray the tree with streptomycin (Agri-Strep) in the evening, just before, during, and just after bloom. Plant fireblight-resistant selections, such as 'Freedom', 'Liberty', and 'Priscilla'.

PROBLEM: Black rot. An apple develops a black, rotten area, usually on the blossom end. As fruit matures, the fungus-caused rot enlarges in concentric bands of black and brown. Dried, shriveled fruit (mummies) remain on

the tree. Leaves show brown spots with concentric rings. Sunken cankers form on branches.

Solution: Destroy diseased fruit, leaves, and branches. Spray with captan. Spray again in spring when new leaves emerge. Repeat at 2-week intervals to 6 weeks before harvest.

PROBLEM: Codling moths. Caterpillars bore into the apple and feed on the seeds. Around the time the apples ripen, the pests tunnel back to the surface of the fruit.

Solution: Jokes about biting into an apple and finding the other half of the worm refer to codling moth caterpillars. A gray-brown moth, barely ³/₈ in. long, lays eggs in developing fruit in early April. As soon as bloom begins, hang sticky traps containing pheromone bait in trees. You can buy them in garden centers and by mail order. For severe infestations, spray trees with *Bacillus thuringiensis kurstaki* (Dipel, Thuricide, Javelin), phosmet (Imidan), malathion, or carbaryl (Sevin).

PROBLEMS AND SOLUTIONS
....
FOR MORE INFORMATION ON PROBLEMS IN BOLD TYPE,
SEE LISTINGS, PAGES 142–307.

OTHER COMMON PROBLEMS: **Aphids, leaf rollers,** eastern **tent caterpillars,** and **scales;** early **fruit drop** due to heavy fruit set or spraying with carbaryl; **powdery mildew;** plum **curculio**

ARBORVITAE
THUJA
EVERGREEN SHRUBS OR TREES
✔ ZONES: US, MS

A flat-needled evergreen that comes in various forms and colors, arborvitae tolerates wet or sandy soils. It is typically used in corner plantings, as a tall screen, and as an accent.

PROBLEM: Bagworms *(illustrated above).* Tiny "pinecones" hang from branches. Caterpillars inside the cones defoliate the plant, turning it partly or entirely brown.

Solution: These pinecones are actually bags made from arborvitae needles and filled with voracious caterpillars. Thoroughly spray needles and stems with *Bacillus thuringiensis kurstaki* (Dipel, Thuricide, Javelin) or with acephate (Orthene), carbaryl (Sevin), or malathion. A second application may be required.

OTHER COMMON PROBLEMS: Brown tips on leaves caused by **leaf miners;** yellowing and speckling of foliage due to spider **mites**

ASH
FRAXINUS
DECIDUOUS TREES
✔ ZONES: US, MS, LS, CS

Ashes grow fairly fast, make good shade trees, are adapted to many different climates, and tolerate a variety of soils. The two most common ashes are green ash *(Fraxinus pennsylvanica),* with foliage that changes to yellow in the fall, and white ash *(F. americana),* with reddish purple fall foliage. Unfortunately, ashes fall victim to a number of diseases and insects.

PROBLEM: Anthracnose *(illustrated above).* Leaves look scorched or burned along the veins.

Solution: Severe infection by this fungus may cause defoliation. Repeated defoliation can weaken the tree, leaving it susceptible to insects, other diseases, and environmental stress. Rake and destroy fallen leaves and twigs. Thin out the tree canopy to improve air circulation and reduce fungal infection. Mulch and adequately water during periods of drought to keep trees vigorous. If the disease returns the following year, spray foliage with lime sulfur, a fixed-copper fungicidal soap (Soap

Shield), chlorothalonil (Daconil), thiophanate-methyl (Thiomyl), or mancozeb. Spray in spring when buds begin to swell, and follow with two to three more sprayings at 10- to 14-day intervals. Follow label directions carefully.

PROBLEM: Canker. Leaves are light green and appear stunted. Cracked, sunken areas appear on the branches, causing them to die back.

Solution: A fungus causes the cankers. Prune out (cut a few inches below the canker) and destroy infected twigs and branches. Water and fertilize regularly to keep trees healthy.

OTHER COMMON PROBLEMS: **Leaf scorch** caused by hot, dry weather; **banded ash borers (see Borers, lilac); aphids;** and **scales**

ASPARAGUS
PERENNIAL

ZONES: US, MS, LS

There is nothing tastier than fresh asparagus from the garden. However, getting an asparagus bed going takes a good bit of work, though well-maintained beds can remain productive for 30 years or more. Absence of winter cold limits asparagus production in the Coastal and Tropical South.

PROBLEM: **Spotted asparagus beetles (see Asparagus beetles)** *(illustrated above)*. Orange, black-spotted beetles eat the tender new shoots of the asparagus as they emerge. Later, they attack and eat the fluffy plumes atop the plant.

Solution: Wash beetles off spears and plants with a jet of water. For infestations, spray plants with rotenone or malathion, taking care to keep pesticides off emerging spears.

OTHER COMMON PROBLEMS: Foliage turns yellow, then brown, then dies due to a **rust** disease (selections 'Mary Washington' and 'Martha Washington' are rust resistant); small spears, caused by lack of fertilizer, poor drainage, or harvesting plants before they are 3 years old.

AZALEA
RHODODENDRON

EVERGREEN OR DECIDUOUS
FLOWERING SHRUBS

ZONES: VARY BY TYPE AND SPECIES

Azaleas are the South's most popular flowering shrubs. Dozens of plant species and hundreds of selections exist. Plants are evergreen, semievergreen, or deciduous and range from 1–15 ft. tall.

PROBLEM: **Chlorosis (see Iron deficiency)** *(illustrated bottom left)*. Shrubs appear very light green or yellow rather than normal deep green. Leaf veins are green but tissue between the veins is yellowish green or yellow.

Solution: Chlorosis in azaleas is caused by lack of iron, which is common in high-pH soils. Feed yearly with an acid-forming azalea fertilizer. If leaves remain yellow, add iron sulfate or aluminum sulfate to the soil, never lime. Test the soil (your county Cooperative Extension Office can do this). Soil pH should be 6 or lower.

PROBLEM: **Lace bugs.** Leaves are speckled with tiny yellow dots. Eventually, the leaves develop a rough, sandpapery look. Dark brown spots of excrement appear on the undersides of leaves. Damage is most severe in summer on plants growing in bright sun.

Solution: Inspect plants for lace bugs beginning in March. Apply insecticidal soap in early May before the first adults lay eggs. Thoroughly coat leaf undersides. If insect numbers begin to build in June, apply acephate (Orthene) or dimethoate (Cygon). Follow label directions carefully.

PROBLEM: **Azalea petal blight.** Tiny, pale fungal spots enlarge rapidly, forming irregular blotches on infected flowers. Flowers quickly turn brown, limp, and mushy. A white mold may cover blooms in humid weather. Diseased blooms dry up and hang on plants for weeks.

Solution: Remove diseased flowers. Rake and destroy fallen flowers. Spray plants with captan, chlorothalonil (Daconil), or triadimefon (Bayleton) just as buds begin to open.

PROBLEM: **Azalea leaf gall.** New leaves become distorted and pale green, appearing thickened and fleshy. As galls mature on leaves, they turn white, then brown and dry, falling by midsummer.

Solution: Fungus spores are released when the galls are white. Older leaves resist infection. Cool moist spring weather favors infection. It is most serious in shady areas where air circulation is poor. Leaf gall affects dense Kurume Hybrids more than Southern Indica Hybrids, but its damage is mostly cosmetic and seldom fatal. Handpick or prune affected leaves from plant before galls turn white. Fungicides have no effect once galls appear. For plants affected by the disease in the past, spraying with triadimefon (Bayleton) before and as leaf buds open and expand in early spring can reduce infection, but timing is critical. Fortunately, sprays are seldom necessary.

PROBLEMS AND SOLUTIONS

FOR MORE INFORMATION ON PROBLEMS IN BOLD TYPE,
SEE LISTINGS, PAGES 142–307.

PROBLEM: Cold, winter injury. Leaves wilt, turn brown, and die, especially near the top of the plant. The bark on individual branches may split, killing the branch back to the main trunk.

Solution: This type of damage often occurs following very cold winters when the soil freezes and the plant is in an exposed location. It may also occur when a series of mild winter days suddenly ends with a severe cold snap. Scratch the bark of affected branches with your fingernail. If the cambium just beneath the bark is green, the branch is still alive and may recover. Prune off all branches where the cambium is brown or the bark has split. Feed the plant with acid-forming azalea fertilizer in spring. Make sure azaleas receive sufficient water in fall and winter, as plants stressed by dry soil are more susceptible to cold injury.

PROBLEM: Wax scales (see Scales). White gobs of a wax-like substance, slightly sticky to the touch, festoon branches.

Solution: The "wax" disguises a female wax scale, plus hundreds of tiny pink eggs. When the eggs hatch in late spring, juvenile scales wander along a stem until they find a spot to settle and begin sucking plant sap. They quickly cover their bodies with the protective wax. Scales secrete a clear, sticky honeydew, which coats leaves and causes sooty mold to grow on them. If you see only a few scales, simply pick them off (wear gloves). Then spray horticultural oil over the entire plant. If you see many scales throughout the plant, spray with horticultural oil every 2 weeks from April to June.

BEAN

ANNUAL BUSH OR VINE

ZONES: ALL

G reat pole and bush beans are easy to grow in any garden, if you know the secrets to success: Buy seed from reliable sources, provide good soil and plenty of sun, plant successive crops 2 weeks apart, and don't plant too early in spring—beans won't tolerate cold, wet soil.

PROBLEM: Mexican bean beetles *(illustrated bottom left).* Leaves are completely eaten, except for the veins. If you examine the leaves, you see small, copper-colored beetles with black spots, accompanied by yellow or orange soft-bodied larvae with spines on their backs. You may also see clusters of yellow eggs on the undersides of leaves.

Solution: Pick adult beetles, larvae, and egg masses from plants. For infestations, spray with rotenone or carbaryl (Sevin).

PROBLEM: Rust. Whitish, minute pimples appear on the undersides of leaves, later becoming distinct, reddish brown spots. Leaves turn yellow, dry, and then drop.

Solution: Rust fungus primarily occurs during cool, wet weather. Water in the morning and do not wet foliage. Avoid overhead sprinkling. Rotate crops every 2 to 3 years. Pull up and destroy plants at the end of the season. Periodic applications of chlorothalonil (Daconil) help protect foliage from rust. Repeat sprayings every 5 to 7 days, if needed.

PROBLEM: Virus. Leaves are puckered and mottled with light and dark green areas. The plants become stunted and produce few beans.

Solution: This problem is due to mosaic virus. Plant a resistant selection, such as 'Topcrop', 'Jade', 'Provider', 'Venture', 'Remus', 'Derby', 'Jumbo', or 'Slender Wax'. Control aphids, which spread the virus, with malathion or diazinon. Avoid spraying if beneficial insects like ladybugs are present in large numbers.

OTHER COMMON PROBLEMS: Seedlings may not emerge or may fall over due to **damping off,** a soilborne fungal disease that occurs in cool, poorly drained soil; semicircle cuts in leaf margins caused by **leaf roller** caterpillars; leaves appear speckled due to spider **mites; powdery mildew**

BEE BALM

MONARDA DIDYMA

PERENNIAL

ZONES: US, MS, LS

W ith brilliant flowers of scarlet, mahogany, pink, or white, bee balm is a choice native plant for butterfly or hummingbird gardens or traditional perennial borders. It needs moist, fertile soil and full sun (part shade in the Lower South).

PROBLEM: Powdery mildew *(illustrated above).* A white powdery fungus covers the plant. Leaves yellow and drop.

Solution: Consider planting mildew-resistant selections, such as 'Colrain Red', 'Jacob Cline', 'Marshall's Delight', 'Raspberry Wine', and 'Violet Queen'. At the first sign of powdery mildew on susceptible plants, spray thoroughly with horticultural oil or a fungicide containing triadimefon (Bayleton) or triforine (Funginex). In the fall, rake and destroy fallen leaves and other plant debris.

BEET

BIENNIAL GROWN AS ANNUAL

ZONES: ALL

Red beet, with its high-protein content and rich color, is one of the most valued garden vegetables. Beets are best planted as early in the season as you can work in your garden. You can also sow them in late summer for a fall crop. Sow successive crops at 3- to 4-week intervals to extend the harvest.

PROBLEM: Flea beetles *(illustrated above)*. Small holes or pits in foliage that leave behind numerous "shot holes."

Solution: This is a sure sign of flea beetles. These small, hard-shelled insects have enlarged hind legs and jump like fleas when disturbed. Their legless larvae are gray white. Flea beetles prefer hot, dry conditions. Serious infestations may kill seedlings and young plants. Spray with insecticidal soap or apply rotenone powder or carbaryl (Sevin). Crop rotation also helps to prevent problems and reduces pest populations, since flea beetles increase in numbers where beets are grown year after year.

PROBLEM: Leaf miners. Tiny, white, irregular lines are on the leaves. These "mined out" areas appear translucent.

Solution: Leaf miner larvae feed on tissue between the upper and lower leaf surfaces. If just a few leaves are affected, remove and destroy them. For severe infestations, spray foliage with malathion or diazinon. Repeat twice more at weekly intervals. Be sure to thoroughly spray the undersides of the leaves.

PROBLEM: Leaf spot. Brown or gray fungal spots with purple borders appear on leaves. Dead tissue may drop out, leaving ragged holes.

Solution: Though unattractive, leaf spot does not significantly reduce the quality of the beet root, but it does ruin the leaves for use as edible greens. No chemical controls exist. Pick off and destroy spotted leaves. Since splashing water spreads the disease, avoid watering with overhead sprinklers.

BEGONIA, WAX

BEGONIA

ANNUALS OR TENDER PERENNIALS

ZONES: ALL (AS ANNUALS)

Wax begonias are among the longest-blooming annuals available. They prefer moist, well-drained, fertile soil and take sun or shade, though diseases may be more prevalent in shade. Begonias with green foliage tolerate sun better than selections with bronze foliage.

PROBLEM: Botrytis (gray mold) *(illustrated above)*. Leaves, stems, and flowers turn brown and rot. A woolly gray fungus forms on decayed tissues.

Solution: High humidity and cool temperatures favor the botrytis fungus. Promptly remove and destroy dead or infected leaves and flowers. Leave enough space between the plants to promote good air circulation. Avoid wetting foliage when watering. If overhead watering is necessary, water early in the day, so foliage quickly dries.

PROBLEM: Powdery mildew. A white powdery fungus coats the leaves. Leaves may then become distorted and curled and may develop brown dying patches.

Solution: Spray plants with horticultural oil or a fungicide containing triforine (Funginex) or triadimefon (Bayleton). In fall, clean up and destroy plant debris.

OTHER COMMON PROBLEMS: Light brown, corky growths, caused by overwatering in periods of high sunlight and high humidity, develop on the undersides of leaves and along the stems; **thrips** cause rusty brown spots to form along the main leaf veins and make the undersides of leaves become silvery and deformed.

BIRCH

BETULA

DECIDUOUS TREES

ZONES: VARY BY SPECIES

Birch trees are fine ornamentals, but not all species perform well in the heat of the South. The native river birch *(Betula nigra)* thrives almost everywhere, but many of the white-barked birches that people plant, especially European white birch *(B. pendula)*, are plagued by a host of problems.

PROBLEM: Borers, bronze birch *(illustrated above)*. Several D-shaped holes appear in the trunk. The tree gradually dies from the top down.

Solution: Borer larvae, the offspring of a small olive brown to black beetle, chew tunnels beneath the bark, destroying tissues that transport the tree's water and nutrients. A few leaves wilt at the top of the tree, then a few twigs and small branches die. Plant resistant species, including river birch, Japanese white birch *(Betula platyphylla japonica),* and monarch birch *(B. maximowicziana).* Do not prune trees in spring. To control borers in susceptible trees, spray tree trunks with lindane, chlorpyrifos (Dursban), or endosulfan (Thiodan) according to label directions. Apply three sprayings at 2-week intervals, beginning in June. Remove and destroy severely infested trees.

PROBLEM: Leaf spot. The leaves have brownish or black spots on the upper surfaces and may drop prematurely.

Solution: Any one of several different types of fungi may cause leaf spot on birches. The problem is typically cosmetic and not life threatening to the tree. To control leaf spot, gather and destroy fallen leaves. Spray healthy foliage with a fixed-copper fungicidal soap (Soap Shield) in late spring.

BLACKBERRY
DECIDUOUS SHRUBS OR VINE
ZONES: US, MS, LS, CS

Blackberries are widely adapted and among the easiest fruits to grow. However, selections differ in winter-chill requirements and susceptibility to diseases. Choosing the right selection for your garden is the key. Ask your Cooperative Extension Office for recommendations.

PROBLEM: **Orange rust (see Rusts)** *(illustrated above).* Newly formed shoots are weak and spindly, and their leaves are stunted or misshapen and pale green to yellowish. Within a few weeks, bright orange fungal blisters cover the lower surfaces of infected leaves.

Solution: Buy only certified disease-free plants. Remove and destroy infected plants (including roots) in spring before blisters break open and discharge spores. Remove all wild brambles, which host the disease, from around the garden site. Clean up and destroy plant debris. Maintain good air circulation for plants by pruning out and destroying old fruited canes immediately after harvest, thinning out healthy canes, and keeping the surrounding area free of weeds.

PROBLEM: **Crown gall.** Warty, rough, tumorlike galls appear on canes. Plants appear stunted. Galls also may form just below the soil line. Young plants may be girdled and killed.

Solution: The bacterium that causes crown gall lives in the soil and enters the plant through wounds in the roots or near the crown. Take care not to nick or injure canes, especially those near the soil line. Do not place plants in soil where this disease has occurred in the past. Remove and destroy infected plants. When pruning, disinfect tools after each cut in alcohol or a solution of 1 part bleach to 9 parts water.

PROBLEM: **Anthracnose.** In the spring, small, purplish, slightly raised or sunken fungal spots appear on shoots. Later, they enlarge and become ash gray in the center with slightly raised purple margins. Small spots with light gray centers and purple margins appear on leaves. The center of each spot later falls out, leaving a hole. Sometimes leaves drop.

Solution: Improve air circulation around plants to allow faster drying of foliage and canes. Avoid using high-nitrogen fertilizers. After harvest, destroy infected canes. Each winter, remove and destroy all canes that fruited the previous summer. Remove wild brambles growing in the area. If disease persists, spray plants with lime sulfur or captan once in April, in May, and in June.

PROBLEM: **Cane borer (see Borers, rose).** Tips of new canes wilt and die due to borers feeding inside the canes.

Solution: Prune canes 2 in. below the wilted area and destroy cuttings. Chemical controls are usually not effective.

OTHER COMMON PROBLEMS: **Japanese beetles, aphids,** and spider **mites**

BLUEBERRY
DECIDUOUS SHRUBS
ZONES: VARY BY PLANT TYPE

Blueberries produce an abundance of fruit if given the same moist, acidic, fertile soil favored by azaleas and rhododendrons. Rabbiteye blueberries need cross-pollination to bear fruit, while highbush blueberries are self-pollinating. Ask your Cooperative Extension Office to recommend selections for your area.

PROBLEM: **Botrytis blight (see Botrytis gray mold)** *(illustrated above).* Flowers and stems turn brown. A gray mold grows on infected tissue. Leaves nearest blooms rot.

Solution: Remove and destroy infected flowers, stems, and leaves. Avoid wetting foliage when watering since splashing water spreads the disease. Space plants adequately to permit air to circulate freely. Spray plants with captan every 10 to 14 days during periods of wet weather. Avoid using high-nitrogen fertilizers, which produce succulent new growth susceptible to disease.

PROBLEM: Root rot. The top of the blueberry bush wilts and eventually dies. Leaves on the affected branches curl inward. Upon close inspection, the small feeder roots appear black and soft. Outer bark of the roots peels away easily. Severely infected plants may die from fungal infection.

Solution: Root rot is the inevitable consequence of planting in heavy, poorly drained soil. No chemical control is available. Plant blueberries in loose, fertile, well-drained soil that contains lots of organic matter. Be careful not to plant too deeply. Let the top ½ in. of the rootball protrude above the soil surface, then mulch thoroughly.

BOUGAINVILLEA

BOUGAINVILLEA

EVERGREEN SHRUBBY VINES

ZONES: CS, TS

Bougainvillea enjoys enormous popularity throughout the Coastal and Tropical South, and rightfully so. Few plants can weather heat and drought better. And its clusters of blooms, in shades of red, pink, salmon, purple, yellow, and white, are spectacular. In winter, plants go dormant and shed their leaves, except in the Tropical South.

PROBLEM: No blooms (see Flowers, lack of) *(illustrated above)*. Despite the best care and healthy-looking foliage, there are no blooms on the plant.

Solution: Give the plant full sun. Bougainvillea blooms better when root-bound, so plant it in a pot or confined bed. Feed every 3 to 4 weeks in spring or summer with water-soluble 20-20-20 fertilizer. Let the soil go slightly dry between thorough waterings. Reduce watering by November. Water only every 3 to 4 weeks. Don't worry if the plant wilts or drops foliage. Resume regular watering and feeding in spring. Plants normally bloom in spring and fall.

PROBLEMS AND SOLUTIONS
....
FOR MORE INFORMATION ON PROBLEMS IN BOLD TYPE,
SEE LISTINGS, PAGES 142–307.

BOX ELDER

ACER NEGUNDO

DECIDUOUS TREE

ZONES: US, MS, LS, CS

Box elder is an undesirable tree that reseeds freely, breaks up in storms, and attracts insects. On the positive side, however, box elder grows in adverse situations where many other trees won't. The selection 'Baron' is reportedly seedless; 'Sensation' offers good red fall color.

PROBLEM: Box elder bugs *(illustrated above)*. Hordes of brownish black beetles with red stripes on their wings feed on the seeds, twigs, and foliage during the summer, accompanied by their young. When cold weather arrives, these bugs invade the house.

Solution: Remove female box elder trees (the ones with seeds). They attract box elder bugs. Seal cracks and openings around doors and windows to keep bugs from entering the house. If bugs do get in the house, use a household insecticide containing a pyrethrin to kill them. For infestations, consult an exterminator.

BOXWOOD

BUXUS

EVERGREEN SHRUB

ZONES: VARY BY SPECIES

Although pruned too often into the shape of a meatball, boxwood is a true garden aristocrat and mainstay of corner plantings and formal design. It grows well in full sun or light shade. Boxwood requires moist, well-drained soil.

PROBLEM: Leaf miners *(illustrated above)*. Yellow-orange to orange blisters or "mines" (tunnels or trails) appear on the leaves in fall or spring. Affected plants are less vigorous and look unhealthy.

Solution: The mines are the result of tiny, maggotlike leaf miner larvae feeding on soft tissue inside the leaf. Leaf miner larvae turn into tiny flies in late spring. The adults then lay eggs on nearby boxwood foliage. This is the best time to spray the foliage with a contact insecticide, such as diazinon, or a systemic insecticide, such as acephate (Orthene) or dimethoate (Cygon). Also, consider planting Japanese boxwood *(Buxus microphylla japonica)* or possibly edging boxwood *(B. sempervirens* 'Suffruticosa'), two types that are less susceptible to leaf miners than the common (American) boxwood species, *B. sempervirens.*

PROBLEM: Psyllids. Leaves are puckered and cup over each other like cabbage leaves. Gobs of white, waxy threads and honeydew appear on leaves. A sooty mold then grows on the leaves.

Solution: Boxwood psyllids overwinter on the plant as eggs. Both adult and juvenile aphids feed by sucking sap. Adult psyllids are light green, aphidlike insects, about $\frac{1}{5}$ in. long. They lay eggs on the tips of boxwood branches in summer. Juvenile psyllids emerge in spring and begin feeding on leaves. To control them, spray boxwood in spring and early summer with a systemic insecticide such as acephate (Orthene) or dimethoate (Cygon). Follow label directions carefully.

PROBLEM: Root rot. Young leaves wilt and turn brown. The tissue just under the bark near the soil line is dark and discolored. Large branches die. Young feeder roots look brown and rotten.

Solution: Heavy, poorly drained soil favors development of this fungal disease. Remove and destroy diseased plants. Plant new boxwoods in loose, fertile, well-drained soil. Plant boxwoods slightly high, so that the top $\frac{1}{2}$ in. of the rootball protrudes above the soil surface, then cover with mulch.

PROBLEM: Cold, winter injury. Leaves that are cold-damaged appear orange or rusty red. This often occurs when warm winter days are followed by severe cold. Twigs may die back.

Solution: Prune damaged branches from the plants. Shelter plants from cold winter winds. Mulch plants in late fall to help soil retain moisture and keep it from freezing.

PROBLEM: Volutella blight. In early spring before new growth begins, leaves on the tips of branches turn pale green, tan, then, finally, yellow. Peeling the bark from the base of infected branches reveals dark, discolored wood. Diseased branches die. Light pink pustules form on the undersides of leaves.

Solution: Volutella blight attacks boxwoods that are stressed by poor growing conditions. It overwinters in dead leaves and other plant debris that accumulates in the crotches of boxwood branches. Prune out and destroy infected branches. Dispose of plant debris. Spray the plant with a fixed-copper fungicidal soap (Soap Shield) or lime sulfur just before growth begins in spring, then three times more at 10-day intervals.

PROBLEM: Nematodes. The shrubs may wilt on hot afternoons, then recover at night. Leaves turn yellow or bronze in color, and leaf size may be reduced. Roots develop small, swollen galls or decayed areas. Plants become stunted and slowly decline, often one branch at a time.

Solution: Common and edging boxwoods are particularly sensitive to the microscopic worms called nematodes, which feed on roots. No chemical control exists for severely infected plants. Remove and destroy them. Incorporate chitin (Clandosan) or Nematrol into the soil before planting new boxwoods to inhibit nematodes. Plant Japanese boxwood, which isn't as vulnerable to nematodes. Or substitute a shrub with similar form, such as dwarf yaupon (*Ilex vomitoria* 'Nana').

BROCCOLI AND CABBAGE

BIENNIALS GROWN AS ANNUALS
ZONES: ALL

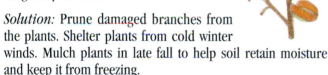

Broccoli thrives in the cooler months in the South. You can eat the undeveloped flower heads raw or cooked. Once the main head is picked, smaller side shoots emerge from the main stalk. Head cabbage (*Brassica oleracea capitata*) produces an edible head of tightly layered leaves. Other cole crops include brussels sprouts, cauliflower, Chinese cabbage (bok choy, napa), collards, kale, kohlrabi, mustard greens, and turnip greens.

PROBLEM: Cabbageworms *(illustrated above).* Irregular holes appear in leaves. Green worms feed on the foliage, leaving behind numerous brown or green pellets on the leaves.

Solution: Cabbage, broccoli, brussels sprouts, and other cole crops often fall victim to cabbage butterfly larvae. If just a few worms are present, pick them off. But when multitudes threaten a crop, spray plants with *Bacillus thuringiensis kurstaki* (Dipel, Thuricide, Javelin), pyrethrin, or malathion. Rotenone powder also offers good control. Floating row covers keep butterflies from laying eggs on plants.

PROBLEM: Club root. Plants yellow and wilt during the hot part of the day. Some plants and plant heads are smaller than previous crops. When you pull the plants, the roots are swollen and misshapen.

Solution: No chemical controls exist for this soilborne fungal disease. Pull and destroy infected plants. Practice crop rotation. Lime the soil, if necessary, to raise the pH to at least 7.2; alkaline soil inhibits the fungus.

PROBLEM: Flea beetles. Leaves have very small, rounded or irregular holes that look like shot holes.

Solution: Flea beetles are small, hard-shelled insects that jump like fleas when disturbed. Both adults and their grublike larvae feed on the leaves. Crop rotation can help, since beetle numbers increase where broccoli and cabbage are grown year after year. Apply rotenone or carbaryl (Sevin) for control.

BUTTERFLY WEED
ASCLEPIAS TUBEROSA
PERENNIAL
ZONES: ALL

This extremely hardy, long-lived wildflower is native to North America. Beautiful bright orange or yellow blooms appear in compact clusters atop branching stems. Flowers produce lots of nectar that attracts butterflies.

PROBLEM: Caterpillar damage *(illustrated above)*. Caterpillars with white, black, and yellow stripes are on the plant devouring the foliage.

Solution: These are the larvae of monarch butterflies. More monarch caterpillars means more monarch butterflies in your garden. They're seldom present in sufficient numbers to do much harm. Chemical control is not warranted. A good solution is to pick them off your butterfly weed and transfer them to other plants they like to eat, such as milkweed and Joe-Pye weed.

CALADIUM
CALADIUM BICOLOR
TUBEROUS-ROOTED PERENNIAL
ZONE: TS

Caladiums are tropical plants with leaves in shades of red and pink or white that have prominent midribs and veins as well as contrasting backgrounds and borders. The variation in color and pattern adds a lush, exotic feel to the garden or landscape. Most caladiums grow best in shade or partial shade, but some tolerate considerable sun, including 'Aaron', 'Fire Chief', 'Lance Whorton', 'Pink Cloud', 'Red Flash', and 'Red Frill'.

PROBLEM: Sunburn *(illustrated above)*. Edges of older leaves turn yellow, then brown. The middle part of the leaves look burned. Burned spots may drop out, leaving the foliage tattered and full of holes.

Solution: Caladiums (especially white-leafed selections) prefer shady areas, particularly during the afternoon. Keep soil moist, but avoid sprinkling leaves. Leaf damage similar to sunburn can be caused by spraying leaves with liquid fertilizer or with cold water during hot, sunny days.

PROBLEM: Tuber rot. Caladium tubers rot in the ground or sometimes in storage.

Solution: Caladiums that rot in the ground have probably been planted too early in spring. Wait to plant until the soil temperature reaches 70°F. Those that decline in storage usually fall victim to a fungus-caused chalky rot. To prevent it, dust tubers with sulfur prior to storing for the winter.

CAMELLIA
CAMELLIA
EVERGREEN FLOWERING SHRUBS OR SMALL TREES
ZONES: US (PROTECTED), MS, LS, CS

When you thrill to the sight of a beautiful camellia in bloom, you know you're in the South. Hundreds of selections exist with flowers of red, pink, or white. Common camellia (*Camellia japonica*) blooms in the winter and the spring. Sasanqua camellia (*C. sasanqua*) blooms in fall and early winter.

PROBLEM: Tea scales (see Scales) *(illustrated above)*. Tiny, white, waxy or cottony, oval specks appear on the undersides of camellia leaves. Closer examination reveals brown specks as well. A sooty mold grows on honeydew that covers leaves. Leaves turn yellow and drop. Twigs may die.

Solution: The brown specks are female scales; male scales are snowy white. Spray the plant thoroughly with horticultural oil, being sure to wet the undersides of the leaves. Repeat every 2 weeks from April through June each year. Spraying according to label directions with a systemic insecticide, such as acephate (Orthene) or dimethoate (Cygon), also provides good control.

PROBLEM: Camellia flower and petal blight. Irregularly shaped, small, brown spots appear on expanding petals. Spots enlarge rapidly until the entire flower is dead and brown. Veins on petals are pronounced, giving the flower a "netted" appearance in the early stages of the disease. Blighted flowers drop.

Solution: The fungus that causes this blight may persist in the soil around the plant for years. Promptly remove and destroy infected flowers. Rake and remove fallen blossoms and other plant debris underneath bushes. Spray plant according to label directions with mancozeb, thiophanate-methyl (Thiomyl), or triadimefon (Bayleton) when blooms first show color. Repeat twice at 14-day intervals. Also spray the ground beneath the plant.

PROBLEM: Sooty mold. There is a sticky substance and black soot that covers the leaves primarily coating the upper surfaces.

Solution: Sooty mold doesn't harm the plant directly, but if it is extensive the mold can block sunlight from reaching leaves, reducing plant vigor. Look for tea scale, mealybugs, or leafhoppers on stems and foliage. These insects suck plant sap and secrete a sticky honeydew on which sooty mold grows. Control insects by blasting them off the plant with a jet of water or by spraying with an insecticide such as acephate (Orthene) or malathion. Without insect honeydew, sooty mold gradually disappears.

PROBLEM: Virus. Irregular yellow or white spots (mottling) or ring spots appear on infected leaves. This is often seen on older, winter-injured leaves. Affected leaves may drop, but plants rarely die.

Solution: There are no controls for viruses, except removing affected plants. Pruning and destroying branches that show symptoms does not control the virus on the rest of the plant.

PROBLEM: Leaf gall. Leaves become distorted, pale green, thickened, and fleshy. As galled leaves mature, they turn white, then brown and dry, falling by midsummer. The galls only affect new growth; older leaves seem to resist the growths. Infection usually takes place in cool, moist spring weather when plants are crowded and growing in shade.

Solution: The problem is mostly cosmetic and seldom fatal. Pick and destroy galled leaves before they turn white. Spraying fungicides after the disease is present has no effect. Applying triadimefon (Bayleton) before and as leaf buds open and expand in early spring can reduce infection, but timing is critical. Fortunately, sprays are seldom necessary.

OTHER COMMON PROBLEMS: **Chlorosis (iron deficiency** indicated by yellow leaves with green veins) caused by planting in soil with a pH higher than 7; root rot due to poor drainage, planting in heavy soil, or planting too deeply; flower-bud drop due to dry soil or cold weather

CANNA
CANNA
TUBEROUS-ROOTED PERENNIALS
ZONES: LS, CS, TS

Old Southern favorites, cannas are subtropical perennials with lovely, large flowers in ivory, yellow, rose, salmon, crimson, or red. Canna foliage is as ornamental as its flowers. Leaves may be pure green, greenish blue, ruby, coppery bronze, or striped.

PROBLEM: Leaf-eating caterpillars. Small holes appear in a line across a leaf *(illustrated above)*.

Solution: This is the handiwork of the yellow woolly-bear caterpillar. Another troublesome caterpillar is the canna leaf roller, which rolls up leaves and hides inside to feed. Infested leaves appear ragged and full of holes. Pick off the woolly bears and destroy them, or spray with *Bacillus thuringiensis kurstaki* (Dipel, Thuricide, Javelin), carbaryl (Sevin), or diazinon. Because canna leaf rollers overwinter in rolled-up leaves, the best way to control them is to cut off and destroy all canna leaves and stems in the late fall.

PROBLEMS AND SOLUTIONS

FOR MORE INFORMATION ON PROBLEMS IN BOLD TYPE, SEE LISTINGS, PAGES 142–307.

PROBLEM: Bud rot. Newly opened leaves develop large, dark brown or blackened spots. Flower buds turn black and die before they open.

Solution: There are no chemical controls for *Xanthomonas cannae*, the bacterium that causes bud rot. Purchase and plant only disease-free plants. Allow sufficient space between plants for good air circulation. Pull and destroy diseased plants.

PROBLEM: Stress and uneven moisture. Parallel tears appear in leaves. The problem resembles insect damage, but on closer inspection, there are no insects present.

Solution: Drought-induced stress followed by an abundance of water causes this problem on cannas. To prevent this damage, water cannas regularly during dry spells. Mulch the soil around them to help even out and retain moisture.

OTHER COMMON PROBLEMS: **Corn earworms** chew leaves and flower buds.

CARPET BUGLEWEED
AJUGA REPTANS
PERENNIAL
ZONES: US, MS, LS

A great ground cover for shaded areas, carpet bugleweed is a favorite of gardeners. Foliage ranges from deep green to purple, variegated, or even gray. Multiple flowers on single spikes, 4–5 in. tall, are usually blue but range in colors from white to dark purple.

PROBLEM: Crown rot *(illustrated above)*. Lower leaves turn yellow. Plants go limp, then leaves turn black and die. Roots rot; plants pull up easily. A white fungus fans out from the base of plants across the soil surface. Large patches of bugleweed may die in the first warm, humid days of spring. Thousands of tiny, white to brick red fungal pellets are visible in the rotted crowns.

Solution: Poor-draining soil is the root of the problem. Once crown rot occurs, little can be done other than preventing a recurrence. Avoid excessive watering. Prior to planting, amend clay soil to improve drainage. Add clean kitty litter (calcine clay) to the soil mix. Calcine clay absorbs limited amounts of water but also allows excess water to drain away.

CARROT
BIENNIAL GROWN AS ANNUAL
ZONES: ALL

Carrots prefer lots of sun and cool to moderately warm temperatures. They have the highest vitamin A content of all vegetables.

PROBLEM: **Distorted roots** *(illustrated above)*. Carrots are forked and distorted instead of nice and straight.

Solution: Carrots thrive in deep, loose, well-drained soil. Avoid planting them in heavy, rocky soils. Short or medium-length selections such as 'Red Cored Chantenay' ('Chantenay Red Core'), 'Danvers Half Long', 'Lady Finger', and 'Thumbelina' are good choices for heavier soils. However, misshapen carrots are still edible.

PROBLEM: Wireworms. Thin, hard worms, 1½–2 in. long, burrow inside carrots.

Solution: Wood ashes provide a good natural control against wireworms, the larvae of click beetles. Sprinkle the ashes over the area to be planted or apply an insecticide containing diazinon to the soil prior to planting.

Rotate crops every year for best results. Never plant carrots in a site where they have grown the previous 2 years.

PROBLEM: Carrot weevils. Small, white grubs, the larvae of weevils, bore large tunnels into the carrots.

Solution: Unfortunately, there is no chemical control available to homeowners. Good garden sanitation is the best alternative. Adult weevils overwinter in fall grass and weeds, so keep these plants mowed. Remove plant debris from the garden each fall. Do not leave carrots in the ground through winter. Early harvest and storage help minimize damage. Rotate crops. Use a floating row cover immediately after planting to prevent adult weevils from laying eggs near plants.

OTHER COMMON PROBLEMS: Carrot roots develop woody cores if left in the ground too long; carrot tops exposed to sunlight turn green and bitter; too much water makes carrots crack.

CATALPA
CATALPA
DECIDUOUS TREES
ZONES: US, MS, LS, CS

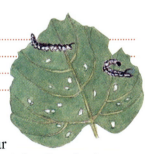

Large, tropical-looking leaves and showy, white flowers in late spring make catalpas popular trees in the South. They grow 50–70 ft. tall and tolerate a wide range of soils.

PROBLEM: **Catalpa sphinx caterpillars** *(illustrated above)*. Large white-and-black caterpillars feed on the catalpa leaves, consuming mass quantities.

Solution: Heavy caterpillar infestations may defoliate trees. Defoliation over several consecutive years can stress and kill trees. For infestations, spray young worms with *Bacillus thuringiensis kurstaki* (Dipel, Thuricide, Javelin) or acephate (Orthene).

CHERRY, FLOWERING
PRUNUS
DECIDUOUS FLOWERING TREES
ZONES: ALL

The white blooms of a Yoshino cherry (*Prunus yedoensis*) float like a cloud above the tree's thick trunk. A few days after Yoshinos bloom, the pink blooms of Kwanzan cherry (*P. serrulata* 'Kwanzan') festoon branches of trees lining numerous avenues in the South. Flowering cherries have been cultivated for centuries in the Orient, where festivals celebrating their blossoms occur each spring. In Macon, Georgia, the annual Cherry Blossom Festival draws thousands of visitors.

SOLVING PLANT PROBLEMS

PROBLEM: Borers (see Borers, peach tree) *(illustrated opposite page, bottom right).* An amber-colored gum mixed with fine sawdust appears on the bark. The bark may look swollen, rough, and crusty.

Solution: Clearwing moths lay their eggs on a limb crotch close to the ground or in a trunk wound. Eggs hatch and larvae bore underneath the bark, where they tunnel and feed. Avoid injuring tree bark. A simple nick in the trunk from a lawn mower is an entry point for borers. If you see signs of borers on the trunk, spray it and major branches with lindane, endosulfan (Thiodan), or chlorpyrifos (Dursban) in late August, again in April, then again in early July.

CHERRY LAUREL
PRUNUS LAUROCERASUS
EVERGREEN SHRUBS
ZONES: US, MS, LS

Cherry laurels deserve wider use in the South. They tolerate sun or shade, as well as aggressive pruning. Their glossy, deep green foliage makes them an excellent choice in foundation plantings, massed plantings, and low screens. Look for compact selections, such as 'Otto Luyken', 'Schipkaensis', and 'Zabeliana'.

PROBLEM: Shot hole *(illustrated above).* Small purple- or rust-colored spots with a yellowish halo appear on leaves in early to midsummer. As spots mature, the centers drop out, resulting in a shot-hole appearance. Severely infected plants may be nearly defoliated. Dark sunken cankers form on the twigs, causing them to die back.

Solution: No chemical control is available. Rake and destroy infected leaves. Prune and destroy cankered twigs. Because the disease spreads from leaf to leaf in splashing water, do not water with overhead sprinklers.

OTHER COMMON PROBLEMS: Root rot due to poor drainage

CHRYSANTHEMUM
CHRYSANTHEMUM
PERENNIALS
ZONES: VARY BY SPECIES

Chrysanthemums bear an abundance of flowers in fall, in a multitude of colors. They prefer fertile, well-drained soil and full sun. For maximum flower production, do not pinch back after July 4. The plants are heavy feeders, so fertilize during the growing season. They don't like root competition from other plants.

PROBLEMS AND SOLUTIONS
FOR MORE INFORMATION ON PROBLEMS IN BOLD TYPE,
SEE LISTINGS, PAGES 142–307.

PROBLEM: Mosaic virus (see Viruses) *(illustrated bottom left).* Buds and flowers are distorted. Leaves are mottled yellow and green and some leaves have yellowish rings. Plants may be stunted and flowers small.

Solution: There is no chemical control for this virus. Pull and destroy infected plants. Insects, mainly aphids, transmit mosaic virus to plants. Control these pests by applying insecticidal soap or diazinon or by spraying a systemic insecticide such as acephate (Orthene).

PROBLEM: Dodder. A Medusa-like tangle of orange-yellow "strings" wraps itself around the leaves and stems of plants.

Solution: Dodder is a parasite that germinates in spring near the host plant. After twining its way around the host, dodder's roots wither away and it survives by absorbing nutrients and water from the host. No chemicals will control dodder on an infested plant. Remove the plant and destroy it. Do this before the dodder blooms and sets more seed. The next spring treat soil with a pre-emergence herbicide, such as trifluralin (Treflan, Preen), to keep dodder from germinating.

OTHER COMMON PROBLEMS: Leaves are dull and off-color, branches wilt, and stems are weak due to bacterial blight; a gray fluffy mold grows on flowers and stems, caused by **botrytis (gray mold)**, a fungal disease; **aphids** cause puckered and distorted leaves; foliage yellows due to **aster yellows.**

CITRUS
EVERGREEN TREES AND SHRUBS
ZONES: CS (HARDIER TYPES), TS;
OR INDOORS

Many citrus species and selections tolerate moderate cold, but won't withstand temperatures below 28°F. In most areas, citruses should be planted in protected locations, such as on the south side of a house or in large pots you can take indoors for the winter.

PROBLEM: Scales *(illustrated above).* Small, hard oyster-shaped bumps appear on plant stems and twigs. A black soot covers the upper leaf surfaces and fruit.

Solution: The hard bumps are scales, insects that suck plant sap and secrete honeydew. Sooty mold grows on the honeydew. Both honeydew and mold disappear once the scales depart. To control scales, spray plants with horticultural oil during the growing season. Or spray with a systemic insecticide, such as acephate (Orthene), according to label directions.

PROBLEM: Citrus scab. Small, pale orange, elevated spots appear on the skin of the fruit. The spots often run together and cover large areas with a corky, scabby growth. Brown scablike lesions cover and distort twigs and leaves. Fruit is stunted and drops prematurely.

Solution: Remove and destroy infected leaves, twigs, and fruit. Keep citrus foliage as dry as possible in spring. Do not water with overhead sprinklers. Apply captan to trees prior to infection, spraying them in late winter before new growth comes in and again after the first flowers fall.

PROBLEMS AND SOLUTIONS
FOR MORE INFORMATION ON PROBLEMS IN BOLD TYPE,
SEE LISTINGS, PAGES 142–307.

PROBLEM: Citrus greasy spot. The leaves develop small blistered areas on their undersides. The blisters turn orange to light brown, with yellowing of the upper leaf surfaces. Eventually, infected areas acquire a dark brown to black, greasy appearance. Infected leaves often drop prematurely.

Solution: Spray foliage with horticultural oil in June or July. For severe infection, spray foliage in June and again in August or spray fruit in July and August with a fixed-copper fungicidal soap (Soap Shield). Practice good garden sanitation by raking and destroying fallen leaves.

PROBLEM: Fruit drop. Many newly formed fruits drop.

Solution: More than one factor can cause fruit drop. Provide adequate watering (particularly during hot and windy weather) and fertilizing of trees, taking care not to overfertilize. In some cases, fruit drop is associated with the lower, more shaded areas of tree canopies. Prune trees well to ensure that sunlight reaches the lower branches. Low potassium levels can also contribute to fruit drop.

OTHER COMMON PROBLEMS: **Aphids** and **mites** cause distorted, discolored leaves; holes in citrus skin and rotten flesh due to **fruit flies;** yellowed leaves caused by high-pH, **alkaline soil;** leaves are a stippled yellow and plants look stunted due to **whiteflies.**

CLEMATIS
CLEMATIS
DECIDUOUS OR EVERGREEN VINES
ZONES: VARY BY SPECIES

Clematis is a popular flowering vine that grows best when placed in full sun with roots mulched to keep them cool. Many selections are available, with blooming periods ranging from early spring to first frost.

PROBLEM: Stem rot *(illustrated above)*. Stems suddenly wilt just as flowers begin to open. Affected stems and leaves turn dark. Sometimes only a single stem is affected.

Solution: The fungus causing this disease usually attacks the large-flowered hybrids. Prune affected stems back to healthy tissue. Spray the plant several times during the growing season with a fixed-copper fungicidal soap, such as Soap Shield.

OTHER COMMON PROBLEMS: Black blister beetles chew tiny holes in leaves; plant is lackluster and stunted from borers chewing the roots; **aphids** cause leaves to pucker; **powdery mildew** coats and disfigures leaves and keeps flower buds from opening.

COCKSCOMB
CELOSIA ARGENTEA
ANNUAL
ZONES: ALL

Celosia flowers bloom as either feather-shaped spikes or flattened crests. Colors range from red to yellow or cream. Plants prefer fertile, moist soil with lots of organic matter and full sun.

PROBLEM: Spider mites (see Mites) *(illustrated above)*. A fine webbing covers leaves and stems. The leaves lose color and appear speckled or dusty.

Solution: Spider mites, which reproduce rapidly in hot, dry weather, spin webs on the undersides of leaves and between leaves and stems, and suck plant juices. For minor infestations, wash them from the foliage with a stiff jet of water. For more serious problems, spray plants with insecticidal soap or horticultural oil, being sure to wet all leaf and stem surfaces. You'll probably have to repeat spraying. You can also spray with a product containing the miticide hexakis (Vendex), such as Isotox.

OTHER COMMON PROBLEMS: **Slugs and snails** chew ragged holes in leaves, leaving a trail of slime on the plants and ground; **aphids** discolor and distort leaves.

COLEUS

COLEUS HYBRIDUS

TENDER PERENNIAL, USUALLY GROWN AS ANNUAL

ZONE: TS

Coleus leaves form a coat of many colors on each plant—crimson, pink, yellow, chartreuse, orange, green, and white. Most selections prefer shade, but some take sun. Rich, moist soil is a must.

PROBLEM: Slugs and snails (*illustrated above*). Plant leaves are chewed and covered with slime.

Solution: These symptoms are evidence of slugs and snails that eat foliage under the cover of darkness. You can protect your coleus plants by spreading diatomaceous earth (see page 33) or wood ashes around them. Or use metaldehyde pellets to bait slugs and snails. Apply the bait in the evening after watering the garden. Follow label directions carefully.

OTHER COMMON PROBLEMS: White cottony tufts, which are actually **mealybugs** sucking juices from the plant, appear in leaf and stem joints; leaves are covered with a fine webbing created by spider **mites** and are speckled or dusty looking.

COLUMBINE

AQUILEGIA

PERENNIALS

ZONES: VARY BY SPECIES

These shade-loving perennials reward gardeners in spring and early summer with beautiful blooms and lacy foliage. Wild columbine (*Aquilegia canadensis*) reseeds itself freely.

PROBLEM: Leaf miners (*illustrated above*). Serpentine "trails" appear on leaves. The trails are easy to see because they are light in color.

Solution: In spring, leaf miners lay eggs on the foliage just a few weeks after leaves emerge. Larvae hatch in 3 to 6 days and burrow into the leaves, making trails or mining tunnels between the upper and lower leaf surfaces. Cut all foliage to the ground immediately after plants bloom. Since the larvae pupate and overwinter in the leaves, dispose of leaf debris completely. Columbine leaves will re-emerge in early summer. If the problem persists, spray foliage when it's a few inches tall in spring with a systemic insecticide, such as acephate (Orthene) or dimethoate (Cygon).

OTHER COMMON PROBLEMS: Crown and stem rot due to planting in wet, poorly drained soil; **aphids; powdery mildew**

CORN

ANNUAL

ZONES: ALL

Corn grows best in well-aerated, warm, fertile soil rich in organic matter. Long, warm summers and regular rainfall help to produce good crops.

PROBLEM: Corn earworms (*illustrated above*). Small green worms eat the kernels at the top of the ear.

Solution: These worms, or caterpillars, may be pink, yellow, green, brown, or almost black. They resemble fall armyworms (see "Armyworms," page 148) in size and appearance. Practicing good garden sanitation is critical to keeping earworms out of your garden. Mow down or remove nearby weeds, which attract these caterpillars to the garden. To control caterpillars, spray corn silks while they are still green with a pyrethrin or carbaryl (Sevin) every 2 to 5 days. You also can gently apply fine sand over each individual ear when the silks begin to show. The grit will eventually work its way down into the top portion of the ear, and the worms are unable to chew. Wash sand from the ears prior to eating. Or, apply 1 tsp. of mineral oil to tips of ears when silks appear.

PROBLEM: Stewart's wilt (see Bacterial wilt). Leaves turn gray green to yellow green and wilt. Infected plants may die.

Solution: Stewart's wilt is spread by flea beetles, so incidence of it tends to be highest near weedy areas favored by the beetles. Remove and destroy diseased plants. Keep weeds mowed. Spray plants with insecticidal soap, rotenone, or carbaryl (Sevin) when beetles first appear. Plant wilt-resistant selections, such as 'Ambrosia', 'Merlin', 'Quicksilver', and 'Silver Queen'.

PROBLEM: Corn smut. Gray or black swollen galls appear on the ears.

Solution: The fungus that causes corn smut affects only the ears. It overwinters in soil, manure, and plant debris, and is spread by splashing water. With a knife or pruners, immediately remove and destroy infected parts of the plant to keep the disease from spreading. After each cut, disinfect tools with alcohol or a solution of bleach and water (1 part bleach to 9 parts water). Do not plant corn in the same location the next year (see page 30). Do not fertilize with fresh manure. Plant disease-resistant selections, such as 'Cherokee', 'Comanche', 'Comet', 'Silver Queen', and 'Sweet Sue'.

PROBLEM: Missing kernels. Corn ears are not fully developed and kernels are missing.

Solution: If pollen doesn't reach corn silks, kernels (corn seeds) will not develop. To ensure corn is properly pollinated, plant it in blocks rather than in long single rows.

OTHER COMMON PROBLEMS: Seed germinates poorly due to planting in cold, wet soil; deer, raccoons, and groundhogs raid corn patches; European corn borers burrow into corn stalks and hollow them out.

COSMOS
COSMOS

ANNUALS

⟋ ZONES: ALL

Cosmos is one of the easiest annuals to grow by sowing seed directly onto the soil. It combines finely dissected foliage with showy flowers of magenta, pink, white, purple, orange, yellow, or white. The flowers are excellent for cutting.

PROBLEM: Spider mites (see Mites) *(illustrated above).* The leaves look speckled, then turn yellow and drop. Tiny webs appear between leaves and stems.

Solution: Spider mites typically attack plants that are stressed from drought. Spraying with a jet of water, insecticidal soap, or horticultural oil usually controls the pests. Keep plants adequately watered. A thin layer of mulch will help to maintain even soil moisture and reduce evaporation.

OTHER COMMON PROBLEMS: Distorted, puckered leaves caused by **aphids**; root rot due to planting in heavy, poorly drained soil; **powdery mildew** causes white spots on leaves.

COTONEASTER
COTONEASTER

EVERGREEN, SEMIEVERGREEN, DECIDUOUS SHRUBS

⟋ ZONES: VARY BY SPECIES

Cotoneasters are a popular and varied group of shrubs. Some are low and spreading, while others can grow up to 18 ft. high. Most people use them as ground covers. They need full sun and good drainage.

PROBLEMS AND SOLUTIONS
....
FOR MORE INFORMATION ON PROBLEMS IN BOLD TYPE, SEE LISTINGS, PAGES 142–307.

PROBLEM: Spider mites (see Mites) *(illustrated bottom left).* Cotoneaster leaves turn light green to silver in color. A fine webbing covers the leaves.

Solution: Most cotoneasters are subject to spider mites, particularly if plants are stressed from inadequate watering. Plant cotoneasters in good fertile soil, water thoroughly during dry spells, and keep them mulched. To control spider mites, spray foliage thoroughly with insecticidal soap, horticultural oil, dimethoate (Cygon), or a miticide containing hexakis (Vendex), such as Isotox.

PROBLEM: Lace bugs. Leaves are speckled or a mottled yellow and green. Brown specks also appear on lower leaf surfaces.

Solution: Lace bugs sucking sap on undersides cause the speckling or mottling. For control, spray with insecticidal soap, pyrethrin, carbaryl (Sevin), or malathion.

PROBLEM: Fireblight. In spring, branches suddenly wilt and turn black as if scorched by fire. The bark at the base of blackened branches develops sunken cankers.

Solution: Cotoneasters are susceptible to fireblight, a very destructive bacterial disease. Unchecked, it can kill the plant. Prune out and destroy blackened limbs, cutting them back about 12 in. beyond dead tissue to green wood. Disinfect pruners after each cut by dipping them into alcohol or a solution of bleach (1 part bleach to 9 parts water). To prevent a recurrence, spray cotoneasters with streptomycin (Agri-Strep) or a fixed-copper fungicidal soap (Soap Shield) when flower buds show color in spring. Repeat three times a week.

OTHER COMMON PROBLEMS: Leaves yellow and drop and branches die back due to **scales**; **aphids** cause distorted, puckered leaves.

CRABAPPLE
MALUS

DECIDUOUS TREES

⟋ ZONES: US, MS, LS

Crabapples produce showy flowers, colorful fruits, and occasionally excellent fall foliage. They're also easy to grow, needing only sun and well-drained soil. Unfortunately, many types are subject to pests, making it essential to choose an improved, resistant selection.

PROBLEM: Apple scab *(illustrated opposite page, bottom right).* Leaves display dark olive green or black spots, then turn yellow and fall. Infected fruits develop olive brown scabby or corky patches.

Solution: Apple scab is caused by a fungus. Premature leaf drop may weaken the tree, but it doesn't kill it. The disease can be prevented on susceptible trees by spraying a fungicide such as captan or chlorothalonil (Daconil) as soon as leaves appear. However, the best strategy is to plant resistant selections (see note under "Apple Scab," page 209).

PROBLEM: Cedar-apple rust. Small yellow spots appear on upper leaf surfaces shortly after bloom. Spots gradually enlarge and become a bright yellow orange. The leaves may drop prematurely.

Solution: During warm, rainy days in spring, native cedars infected with the cedar-apple rust fungus develop bright orange, gelatinous galls. The wind carries spores from these galls to crabapples, with infection occurring on susceptible selections. In late summer, small tubelike structures develop on the undersides of crabapple leaves. Spores released from these structures are blown back to the cedars, completing the disease cycle. To prevent rust on crabapples, spray the foliage with a fungicide such as captan or chlorothalonil (Daconil) during leaf-out. Or plant rust-resistant selections, as listed under "Cedar-Apple Rust," page 218.

PROBLEM: Fireblight. In spring, leaves and infected branch tips suddenly wilt, curl, turn brown or black, and look scorched. Cankers form on the trunk and main branches.

Solution: Fireblight is caused by a destructive bacterium that can kill trees. There are no chemical controls available. However, spraying trees with streptomycin (Agri-Strep) or a fixed-copper fungicidal soap (Soap Shield) when flower buds show color helps prevent infection. Spray three times more at weekly intervals. Plant selections resistant to fireblight, such as 'Adams', 'Harvest Gold', 'Indian Summer', 'Molten Lava', 'Narragansett', and 'Prairifire'.

CREPE MYRTLE
LAGERSTROEMIA INDICA
DECIDUOUS SHRUBS OR TREES
ZONES: US, MS, LS, CS

No better plant exists for the South than crepe myrtle. It combines showy, long-lasting summer blooms, outstanding fall color, and handsome bark. Crepe myrtle does best in full sun and well-drained soil.

PROBLEM: Powdery mildew *(illustrated above).* White powdery spots appear on leaves, stems, and flowers. The spots expand to completely cover leaves in only a few weeks. If the fungus spreads to flower buds, the buds may not open.

Solution: Powdery mildew usually strikes during periods of warm, humid weather. Apply horticultural oil, triadimefon (Bayleton), or triforine (Funginex) at the first sign of the disease. Consider planting a mildew-resistant selection, such as 'Acoma', 'Biloxi', 'Hopi', 'Lipan', 'Miami', 'Natchez', 'Sioux', 'Yuma', and 'Zuni'.

PROBLEM: Sooty mold. A black sootlike mold covers the leaves. Rubbing removes the mold. Underneath, the leaves are green and healthy.

Solution: Look for aphids, scales, or leafhoppers higher in the plant. They secrete a sticky substance called honeydew, on which sooty mold grows. Control these insects by blasting them off with water or by spraying with horticultural oil, azadirachtin (Neem), malathion, or acephate (Orthene). Without the insects and their honeydew, sooty mold will gradually wash away.

PROBLEM: Asian ambrosia beetles. Branches wilt and die back. Sawdust protruding from holes in branches looks like tiny toothpicks stuck to the bark.

Solution: These tiny beetles attack both stressed and healthy plants. They lay eggs inside stems and introduce a fungus (ambrosia) with which to feed their young. The fungus clogs the plant's water transport system and produces toxins, both of which result in wilting. You can reduce stress on plants by making sure they are watered correctly, fertilized annually, and kept free of disease. Once several beetles have invaded the plant, insecticides are not effective. Prune and destroy infested limbs. For prevention, thoroughly spray trunks of susceptible plants nearby with diazinon, endosulfan (Thiodan), or chlorpyrifos (Dursban).

SOLVING PLANT PROBLEMS

CUCUMBER
ANNUAL VINE

✎ ZONES: ALL

Cucumbers require full sun, good air circulation, and well-drained soil. Watering is important during fruit set and development. Cucumbers should never be allowed to wilt. If the first flowers don't set fruit, don't worry. These are probably male flowers. Female flowers, which form the fruit, should follow.

PROBLEM: **Cucumber beetles** *(illustrated above)*. Small, beetles with black stripes chew holes in leaves and stems. The plant wilts in hot weather.

Solution: The striped cucumber beetle carries bacterial wilt and cucumber mosaic virus (see **Virus** below), and spreads these diseases when feeding on plants. Beetle grubs also feed on roots and stems near the soil line. Handpick and destroy beetles. Control infestations by spraying or dusting with carbaryl (Sevin) or spraying with a pyrethrin, rotenone, or malathion. Be sure to apply insecticide over the soil surface around the base of the plant to kill grubs.

PROBLEM: **Wilt (see Bacterial wilt).** Leaves first turn dull green. Then, even after thorough watering, the cucumber plants wilt and eventually die. When you cut and squeeze the stem, a sticky, stringy ooze comes out.

Solution: Cucumber beetles spread bacterial wilt. To control them, cover young cucumber plants with floating row covers until the plants begin to bloom. Then apply insecticides as described under **Cucumber beetles,** above.

PROBLEM: **Virus.** New leaves are stunted, curled, and mottled yellow and green. On older leaves, V-shaped dead areas extend from leaf margins to the middle vein. Fruit is mottled, warty, and misshapen.

Solution: Aphids and cucumber beetles spread cucumber mosaic virus (CMV) from weeds, such as pokeweed and milkweeds, to cucumber plants. There is no chemical control. Remove and destroy infected plants. To prevent a recurrence, keep weeds cut. Plant selections resistant to CMV, including 'Fanfare', 'Park's Whopper', 'Spacemaster', and 'Sweet Success'.

PROBLEM: **Bitter fruit.** Cucumbers taste bitter and are misshapen or shrunken.

Solution: Hot weather, dry soil, poor pollination, or cucumber mosaic virus can cause bitter, misshapen fruit. There is little you can do about this problem other than planting a heat-tolerant, self-pollinating selection like 'Little Leaf' and watering regularly to reduce plant stress.

OTHER COMMON PROBLEMS: Speckling of leaves due to spider **mites**; white spots on upper leaf surfaces due to **powdery mildew** (plant resistant selections 'Fancipak' or 'Park's Whopper'); few cucumbers due to poor pollination

DAFFODIL
NARCISSUS

BULBS

✎ ZONES: US, MS, LS, CS

Daffodils are the South's most dependable spring bulb. Selections generally range in height from 6–18 in., are long-lived, and need fertile, well-drained soil.

PROBLEM: **Bud blast** *(illustrated above)*. Flower buds wither and fall, with few obvious symptoms prior to buds dropping.

Solution: Bud blasting may occur at any stage of bud development, but buds usually fall off when about ½–1 in. long. This condition usually follows a spell of hot, dry weather in early spring. There is nothing you can do other than hope for better weather next year. Double-flowering daffodils are more susceptible than single-flowering types.

PROBLEM: **No blooms (see Flowers, lack of).** Despite healthy foliage, daffodils don't bloom.

Solution: Bloom failure usually results from improper gardening practices, such as planting in deep shade, cutting off bulb foliage before it yellows, planting bulbs that are too small to flower (plant only large, healthy bulbs), failing to plant before January, and letting bulbs become too crowded (lift, divide, and reset them).

DAHLIA
DAHLIA

TUBEROUS-ROOTED PERENNIALS
GROWN AS ANNUALS

✎ ZONES: US, MS, LS

Dahlias have long been a standard in Southern gardens. They grow from tubers planted in spring and produce flowers of many shapes, types, and colors. Dahlias need well-drained, fertile soil and plenty of sun and moisture. Poor soil fertility and shade produce tall, spindly plants.

PROBLEM: Tuber rot *(illustrated opposite page, bottom right).* Tubers in storage develop dark brown sunken areas. After they are planted in spring, new stems yellow and wilt.

Solution: The soil-inhabiting fungus that causes tuber rot attacks tubers that are stored in warm, humid conditions. There is no chemical control. Discard all diseased tubers and plants. Avoid wounding tubers when digging them to store over winter. Store them in peat moss in a cool, dry, dark place.

PROBLEM: **Spider mites (see Mites).** Upper leaf surfaces look stippled and silvery. There is a fine webbing on the undersides of leaves.

Solution: Spider mites cause stippling of leaves by sucking plant juices from the undersides of the leaves. To control them, spray with horticultural oil or insecticidal soap. Repeat applications may be needed.

PROBLEM: **Bacterial wilt.** Plant stems droop and wilt. A wet, soft rot occurs on stems near the soil line. When stems are cut, a yellowish substance oozes out.

Solution: No chemical control is available. Pull and destroy infected plants. Clean up and destroy all plant debris. Do not plant dahlias where the disease previously has occurred, because the bacterium persists in the soil.

PROBLEM: **Verticillium wilt.** Plants wilt even after a thorough watering. If you cut open a stem, you'll see brown streaking inside. Plants may be stunted or killed.

Solution: The fungus that causes verticillium wilt destroys tissues that transport water throughout the plant. No chemical control is available. Destroy infected plants. Do not plant dahlias where the disease has occurred in the past.

PROBLEM: **Crown gall.** Large abnormal growths appear at the base of many plants. Flowers are sparse and very small, plants are stunted, and shoots are leggy.

Solution: Crown gall is caused by a bacterium. Pull and destroy infected plants. Do not plant dahlias where this disease has occurred in the past. Spray tubers with streptomycin (Agri-Strep) prior to planting.

PROBLEM: Borers. Small holes appear at the base of the stem near the soil line, and frass (plant sawdust) protrudes from the holes. Plants droop despite watering.

PROBLEMS AND SOLUTIONS

FOR MORE INFORMATION ON PROBLEMS IN BOLD TYPE,
SEE LISTINGS, PAGES 142–307.

Solution: The larvae of European corn borers feed on young leaves and flowers, then they bore into the stem, causing plant parts above the infested area to die. Because adult moths frequent weedy and unkempt areas, mow or remove nearby weeds. Remove and destroy infested plants. Do the same for all dahlia foliage and stems at the end of the growing season. To prevent a recurrence, spray stems with carbaryl (Sevin) or rotenone every 2 weeks throughout the growing season.

OTHER COMMON PROBLEMS: Puckered leaves due to **aphids**; withered blooms due to **thrips**; **powdery mildew** on leaves

DAYLILY

HEMEROCALLIS

PERENNIALS

ZONES: ALL

Daylilies are one of the South's most versatile, trouble-free perennials. Flower colors include reds, oranges, yellows, pinks, lavenders, as well as bicolors. Daylilies need lots of sun and moist, fertile, well-drained soil.

PROBLEM: Leaf spot *(illustrated above).* Small, irregular, dark brown spots appear on leaves. Leaves develop brown or yellow streaks, then wither and die.

Solution: Various fungi cause leaf spotting. Leaf spotting often occurs during warm, humid weather. Remove and destroy infected leaves. Avoid overhead watering. Provide good air circulation so leaves dry quickly. Spray healthy leaves with maneb or a fixed-copper fungicidal soap (Soap Shield).

OTHER COMMON PROBLEMS: **Thrips** cause leaves to look bronzy and become stunted, and flower buds become twisted and remain unopen; spider **mites** cause leaves to become yellow or dusty looking, with a fine webbing on their undersides.

DOGWOOD, FLOWERING

CORNUS FLORIDA

DECIDUOUS SHRUBS OR TREES

ZONES: US, MS, LS, CS

Spring in the South wouldn't be the same without the white and pink blooms of dogwoods. These native trees need moist, fertile, acid soil that is well-drained. Water thoroughly during periods of drought and give them light shade, particularly during the hot part of the day.

PROBLEM: **Spot anthracnose (see Dogwood leaf spots)** *(illustrated above).* Small reddish spots first appear on flower bracts. Reddish brown spots on leaves follow in late spring.

Solution: Rake and destroy fallen leaves each year. The disease will not significantly damage mature healthy trees. Chlorothalonil (Daconil) fungicide applied just as flowers and leaves emerge in spring can reduce infection. Kousa dogwood *(Cornus kousa)* is moderately resistant to spot anthracnose.

PROBLEM: Leaf scorch. Leaves become brown and crisp around the edges.

Solution: Leaf scorch is the result of the roots' inability to supply enough water to the leaves. It usually occurs in hot, dry summer weather on trees planted in full sun and poor soil. Newly transplanted dogwoods are most often the victims of this condition. To avoid leaf scorch, plant dogwoods in fertile soil containing plenty of organic matter. Mulch the tree with about 2–3 in. of pine straw or ground bark. Soak the rootball once or twice a week during hot, dry spells.

PROBLEM: Botrytis blight (see Botrytis gray mold). Blooms become slimy and covered with a gray, moldy fuzz. When an infected bloom rests or falls on a healthy leaf, it causes a brownish spot to develop on the leaf. Infected flowers and leaves drop.

Solution: This disease is not usually a serious threat. It most often occurs during cool, rainy weather. Pick up and destroy fallen leaves and flowers. To prevent a recurrence, spray flowers and foliage with chlorothalonil (Daconil), maneb, or mancozeb.

PROBLEM: Dogwood anthracnose. This disease initially appears as medium to large, purple-bordered leaf spots and scorched tan blotches that enlarge and kill the entire leaf. Infected leaves cling to stems after normal leaf drop in fall. Cankers form on the main trunk at the junction of each dead twig. The tree eventually dies.

Solution: Wet weather and shade encourage dogwood anthracnose *(Discula destructiva)* fungi. Keep trees healthy and stress-free. Remove and destroy infected twigs and branches. Prune only in dry weather. Spray trees with chlorothalonil (Daconil) or mancozeb in early spring.

PROBLEM: Club gall midge (see Gall-forming insects and mites). Swellings or galls appear at the end of smaller twigs and branches. Leaves usually decline and die above the gall but continue to cling to the tree.

Solution: Galls are caused by a tiny fly (flying midge) that lays eggs in developing leaf buds. Larvae cause twig tissue to swell around them. Heavy infestations can stunt a tree but will not kill it. Prune and destroy galled twigs as soon as they appear. Spraying isn't usually necessary.

PROBLEMS AND SOLUTIONS

FOR MORE INFORMATION ON PROBLEMS IN BOLD TYPE, SEE LISTINGS, PAGES 142–307.

PROBLEM: Powdery mildew. White powdery spots appear on leaves, sometimes as a silvery sheen on upper leaf surfaces. Leaves may have yellow mottling. By mid-June, leaves begin to turn brown and die.

Solution: A severely infected tree may lose half its leaves by summer's end. This fungus usually shows up in cool, rainy weather. Apply protective fungicides such as thiophanate-methyl (Thiomyl) or triforine (Funginex) at first signs of the disease in early May. Keep trees well watered in summer to minimize leaf drop, but do not wet the foliage.

OTHER COMMON PROBLEMS: **Borers,** which usually target stressed, unhealthy trees, cause branch dieback and cracks, and flaking bark on the trunk.

EGGPLANT
ANNUAL

ZONES: ALL

Eggplant requires warm temperatures, full sun, and rich, well-drained soil. Water it well, especially when it is flowering. Pick fruits regularly to keep the plant producing.

PROBLEM: Flea beetles *(illustrated above).* Tiny holes appear in the leaves. The leaves look like they have been peppered by a shotgun. Small, shiny black beetles found on the leaves jump like fleas when disturbed.

Solution: Spray or dust the plants with rotenone, or spray them with insecticidal soap or carbaryl (Sevin), carefully following label directions.

OTHER COMMON PROBLEMS: Plants fail to set fruit due to high temperatures; **Colorado potato beetles** and **hornworms** chew the foliage; **whiteflies, aphids,** and spider **mites** suck plant juices from the undersides of leaves.

ELM
ULMUS
DECIDUOUS OR SEMIEVERGREEN TREES

✂ ZONES: VARY BY SPECIES

American elms *(Ulmus americana),* those stately trees of yesteryear, have been out of favor for some time. They are susceptible to a variety of insects and diseases, the worst being elm leaf beetles and Dutch elm disease. However, recent introductions, such as the American Liberty elms, claim resistance to Dutch elm disease. Chinese elm *(U. parvifolia)* is a fine, fast-growing shade tree resistant to Dutch elm disease, though susceptible to beetles.

PROBLEM: Elm leaf beetles *(illustrated above).* Small, yellowish green beetles with black stripes and their wormlike larvae feed on leaves between the veins. The leaves turn brown and drop. Severely infested trees look scorched.

Solution: Repeated or severe attacks may kill the tree or make it susceptible to further pest problems. At the first sign of beetles and grubs, spray with *Bacillus thuringiensis* San Diego strain. For severe infestations, spray with acephate (Orthene) according to label directions.

PROBLEM: Dutch elm disease. The leaves on the branches near the top of the tree suddenly wilt, turn yellow, and drop. The disease eventually spreads throughout the branches and kills the tree.

Solution: The fungus that causes Dutch elm disease is carried by elm bark beetles that bore into the wood. It may also spread from tree to tree through connected root systems. It primarily attacks American elms. Infected trees cannot be saved and should be promptly removed. Healthy trees may be spared from infection by having a licensed arborist inject them every year with a systemic fungicide.

ENGLISH IVY
HEDERA HELIX
EVERGREEN WOODY VINE

✂ ZONES: ALL

English ivy is the most popular ground cover for shady areas. The plant creeps along the ground but may climb to the top of an unfortunate tree if allowed.

PROBLEMS AND SOLUTIONS

FOR MORE INFORMATION ON PROBLEMS IN BOLD TYPE, SEE LISTINGS, PAGES 142–307.

PROBLEM: Bacterial leaf spot *(illustrated bottom left).* Brown or black spots with yellow halos appear on leaves. Viewed from underneath, the spots look greasy. Leaf stems blacken and shrivel.

Solution: Frequent rain and overhead watering favor this disease. Remove and destroy infected leaves and stems. Avoid overhead sprinkling. Spray healthy foliage with a fixed-copper fungicidal soap (Soap Shield).

PROBLEM: Scales. Oval, light brown spots appear on the stems or midribs of leaves. Stems look crusty, with many brownish bumps. Leaves are dusted with a dark soot.

Solution: The "spots" are female brown soft scales that suck plant juice and excrete a sticky honeydew. Sooty mold grows on the honeydew, thereby inhibiting photosynthesis and healthy plant growth. Control scales by spraying immature crawlers with insecticidal soap, horticultural oil, or a systemic insecticide such as acephate (Orthene). Follow label directions carefully.

OTHER COMMON PROBLEMS: **Leaf scorch** from planting in full sun and dry soil; **root rot (Pythium root rot)** caused by planting in heavy, poorly drained or strongly alkaline soil

EUONYMUS
EUONYMUS
EVERGREEN, DECIDUOUS
SHRUBS; EVERGREEN VINES

✂ ZONES: VARY BY SPECIES

There are many forms of euonymus, including shrubs, vines, and ground covers. In general, they are easy to grow and quite adaptable. However, scales are a major problem, particularly for evergreen types.

PROBLEM: Scales *(illustrated above).* White and brown specks encrust stems and leaves. Leaves yellow and drop; branches die back.

Solution: Those specks are male (white) and female (brown) scales. Scales feed by sucking plant juices, and severe infestations can kill plants. To control these pests, spray with horticultural oil or a systemic insecticide, such as acephate (Orthene) or dimethoate (Cygon), according to label directions.

PROBLEM: Powdery mildew. A white powder covers the leaves. Leaves yellow and drop.

Solution: The fungus that causes powdery mildew on euonymus strikes during both wet and dry weather. At the first sign of the fungus, spray the plant with triforine (Funginex) or thiophanate-methyl (Thiomyl).

FERNS

VARIOUS GENERA AND SPECIES

PERENNIALS

✂ ZONES: VARY BY SPECIES; OR INDOORS

Ferns are among the world's oldest living plants. Some popular ferns include maidenhair *(Adiantum)*, rabbit's foot *(Davallia fejeenisis)*, staghorn *(Platycerium)*, and Boston *(Nephrolepis exaltata* 'Bostoniensis'). Although asparagus fern *(Asparagus setaceus)* and Sprenger asparagus *(A. densiflorus* 'Sprengeri') are commonly called ferns, they are not because they produce seeds rather than spores. Many ferns flourish outdoors in areas of low light, such as the north side of houses; beneath trees; in shaded, damp areas; and, with sufficient light, indoors.

PROBLEM: Scales *(illustrated above)*. Hard brown bumps encrust fronds and stems. Fronds turn yellow and drop. A sticky honeydew is on the fronds.

Solution: Heavily infested indoor plants aren't worth saving. Discard them to prevent scales from spreading to other plants. Remove and destroy infested foliage from outdoor ferns. Spray the foliage of both types outdoors with horticultural oil or a systemic insecticide such as acephate (Orthene) or dimethoate (Cygon).

OTHER COMMON PROBLEMS: **Leaf scorch** from lack of water; burned fronds due to planting in hot sun; Boston fern drops leaves when brought indoors, due to low humidity and insufficient light; **mealybugs**

FIG

DECIDUOUS TREES

✂ ZONES: MS, LS, CS, TS (DEPENDING ON SELECTION)

There is no more traditional Southern fruit than the fig. It's good for eating fresh, drying, or making preserves. Fig trees like lots of sun and fertile, well-drained soil.

PROBLEM: Fig rust (see Rusts) *(illustrated bottom left)*. Small yellow-green flecks appear on fig leaves. The spots become yellower and, finally, a yellowish brown. Upper surfaces of the spots are smooth, but the undersides are blistered. Later, a brown dust exudes from the blisters. Leaves and fruit drop prematurely.

Solution: The fungus that causes rust overwinters in plant debris near the base of the tree or as spores on the bark. Spores germinate in spring and are spread to leaves and fruit by splashing water. Clean up and destroy fallen fig leaves and fruits in fall. Spray the tree with lime sulfur or horticultural oil in winter. Then spray with a fixed-copper fungicidal soap (Soap Shield) every 2 weeks in spring and summer.

OTHER COMMON PROBLEMS: Birds peck holes in the fruit, so protect figs with nylon netting.

FIRETHORN

PYRACANTHA

EVERGREEN SHRUBS

✂ ZONES: VARY BY SPECIES

Firethorn provides colorful fall and winter berries and a hardy, bulldog constitution. Its tolerance for heavy pruning makes it an excellent choice for hedges or espaliers. Firethorn prefers full sun and well-drained soil.

PROBLEM: Fireblight *(illustrated above)*. Blossoms and leaves suddenly wilt and turn black as if scorched by fire. Branches shrivel and curl. Severely affected plants may die.

Solution: Prune and destroy blighted branches. Cut back to healthy wood. Disinfect pruners after each cut by dipping them in alcohol or a bleach and water solution (1 part bleach to 9 parts water). To prevent a recurrence, spray plant in full bloom in early evening with streptomycin (Agri-Strep) or a fixed-copper fungicidal soap (Soap Shield). Spray again 1 week later. Or save yourself some spraying by planting a fireblight-resistant selection, such as 'Apache', 'Fiery Cascade', 'Gold Rush', 'Golden Charmer', 'Mohave', 'Navajo', 'Orange Charmer', 'Rutgers', 'Shawnee', or 'Teton'.

PROBLEM: Scab. Small dark blotches appear on leaves. Eventually leaves turn yellow, then brown, and drop. Berries gradually turn corky and black.

Solution: Scab is a common fungal disease that usually strikes in cool, wet springs. Plant hybrids resistant to scab, such as 'Apache', 'Mohave', 'Orange Glow', 'Rutgers', 'Shawnee', 'Teton', and 'Victory'. Spray susceptible plants with chlorothalonil (Daconil), beginning at bloom in spring and then three more times at 10-day intervals. Rake and destroy fallen leaves and berries.

FORSYTHIA
FORSYTHIA
DECIDUOUS SHRUBS
ZONES: US, MS, LS

Forsythias are best known for their early spring display of golden yellow flowers on arching branches. They require little maintenance and are best used as hedges, screens, and specimens. Forsythia prefers full sun and adapts well to most soils.

PROBLEM: Crown gall *(illustrated above)*. Swollen tumor-like growths appear on the crown (stems and lower branches) of the plant. As these galls enlarge, they become woody and hard. Branches die back and plants look stunted and deformed.

Solution: Crown gall is caused by a soil-inhabiting bacterium that stimulates rapid growth of plant cells. Prune out and destroy infected twigs and branches below galled areas. Sterilize pruning shears after each cut with alcohol or a bleach solution (1 part bleach to 9 parts water). Pull and destroy seriously infected plants.

OTHER COMMON PROBLEMS: **Flowers, lack of,** due to planting in shade, pruning at times other than late spring, or severe winter cold that kills flower buds.

FOXGLOVE
DIGITALIS
SHORT-LIVED PERENNIALS OR BIENNIALS
ZONES: US, MS, LS, CS

The tall, elegant spires of foxgloves literally stop traffic in spring. Although individual plants may persist for a year or two, in most areas, it's better to set out new plants each year.

PROBLEM: Spider mites (see Mites) *(illustrated above)*. Leaves, speckled with tiny yellow spots near the midrib, turn light green, then yellow or bronzy as they die. Fine webbing appears between leaves and stems.

PROBLEMS AND SOLUTIONS

FOR MORE INFORMATION ON PROBLEMS IN BOLD TYPE, SEE LISTINGS, PAGES 142–307.

Solution: Spider mites are difficult to control without resorting to the use of a miticide. Small infestations can be controlled by blasting the pests with a jet of water or spraying with insecticidal soap or horticultural oil. Keep plants well watered so they aren't stressed by periods of drought. If infestation is severe, spray plants with a product containing hexakis (Vendex), such as Isotox, or remove them.

FUCHSIA
FUCHSIA HYBRIDA
EVERGREEN OR DECIDUOUS SHRUBS TREATED AS ANNUALS
ZONE: US

Excellent plants for hanging baskets, fuchsias feature pendulous, single or double flowers in many spectacular color combinations. Hummingbirds like the blooms too. Unfortunately, this plant's dislike of hot weather limits its use in the South.

PROBLEM: Whiteflies *(illustrated above)*. Tiny, white, triangular insects collect on the undersides of leaves or flutter around the host plant. Leaves are pale or discolored, and surfaces are covered with a sticky honeydew.

Solution: Whiteflies are a difficult pest to control. Spray with horticultural oil, insecticidal soap, malathion, or a systemic insecticide like acephate (Orthene). Replace affected plants if repeated applications don't solve the problem.

OTHER COMMON PROBLEMS: Hot weather causes flowers to drop; plant produces deformed new growth and eventually stops blooming due to fuchsia gall mites.

GARDENIA
GARDENIA
EVERGREEN SHRUBS
ZONES: MS (PROTECTED), LS, CS

The gardenia, with its creamy white, perfumy flowers, is a much cherished symbol of the Old South. In areas where it isn't winter-hardy, gardenia makes a handsome greenhouse plant.

PROBLEM: Chlorosis (see Iron deficiency) *(illustrated above)*. The leaves turn yellow between the veins.

Solution: Gardenias need fertile, well-drained soil with a pH between 5.0 and 6.5. Higher-pH soils don't supply the iron gardenias require, causing chlorosis. Feed regularly with an acid-forming fertilizer. If your soil is alkaline, consider growing gardenias in containers or a raised bed.

PROBLEM: Bud drop. Buds drop off the plant without opening.

Solution: Insect damage, root injury, poor gardening practices, and unfavorable weather can each cause bud drop. Don't transplant gardenias while they are in bud. Thrips and aphids commonly damage unopened buds and cause them to drop. Spray aphids with a jet of water or insecticidal soap, thrips with rotenone or carbaryl (Sevin). Make sure that gardenias growing indoors receive bright light, sufficient humidity, and temperatures between 55° and 75°F.

PROBLEM: Sooty mold. A black powdery substance covers the tops of the leaves.

Solution: Sooty mold lives on honeydew secreted by sucking insects, such as aphids, scales, mealybugs, and whiteflies. The mold can prevent sunlight from reaching leaves, thereby reducing plant vigor. Eliminate honeydew by controlling the insects with insecticidal soap, horticultural oil, or acephate (Orthene).

PROBLEM: Whiteflies. Tiny, triangular, white insects infest the undersides of the leaves.

Solution: Whiteflies suck plant juices and secrete a honeydew that attracts sooty mold and ants. To control whiteflies, spray with insecticidal soap, horticultural oil, malathion, or a systemic insecticide like acephate (Orthene). Discard affected plants if repeated applications don't solve the problem.

GERANIUM

PELARGONIUM

TENDER PERENNIALS GROWN AS ANNUALS

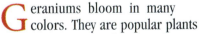

ZONES: CS, TS (PERENNIALS), OR GROW AS ANNUALS

Geraniums bloom in many colors. They are popular plants for growing in annual beds and containers, and grow best in well-drained soil and in full sun to part shade. Keep plants adequately watered during periods of drought to prevent wilting, yellowing, and dropping of leaves. Remove faded flowers to encourage new bloom.

PROBLEM: Rust *(illustrated above)*. Light yellow-orange spots appear on upper leaf surfaces with brown pustules on the undersides of leaves. In severe infestations leaves dry and hang down along the stem.

Solution: Allow enough space between plants for good air circulation. Reduced airflow increases disease problems. Avoid wetting foliage when watering. Pick off and destroy infected leaves. Spray new healthy leaves with chlorothalonil (Daconil) or mancozeb, covering both the upper and the lower leaf surfaces.

PROBLEM: Bacterial leaf spot. Small, slightly sunken spots appear on the undersides of some leaves. Later, leaves wilt, turn brown, then black, and most fall.

Solution: Spray affected plants with fungicidal soap (Soap Shield). Remove and destroy severely infected plants. Prevent disease-favoring conditions by providing air circulation between plants. Maintain proper watering and fertilizing. Water early in the day so plants dry before evening.

PROBLEM: Stem rot (see Pythium root rot). The plant has a dull brown appearance, and the base is mushy and rotten.

Solution: This stem rot is caused by a fungus that thrives in heavy, poorly drained soil. There is no chemical control. Pull and destroy infected plants. Improve soil drainage before planting again.

PROBLEM: Botrytis (gray mold). Flowers are covered with a woolly grayish mold and tend to fade early. Clusters of flowers have a matted appearance.

Solution: Botrytis is one of the most common problems of geraniums. The fungus lives on leaves, stems, and flowers and in plant debris. Good gardening practices eliminate most of the problem. Space plants properly for good air circulation. Remove and destroy fading flowers, dying leaves, and plant debris. Water plants early enough in the day so they dry before evening. For control, spray with chlorothalonil (Daconil), mancozeb, or maneb according to label directions.

GERBERA DAISY

GERBERA JAMESONII

PERENNIAL IN CS AND TS; ANNUAL ELSEWHERE

ZONES: ALL

The exotic gerbera is the queen of all daisies. Its brightly colored flowers range in shades of cream to orange and coral to red, and are excellent for cutting and arranging. Gerberas are also well suited for borders and as bedding plants. Plants overwinter in the Coastal and Tropical South.

PROBLEMS AND SOLUTIONS

FOR MORE INFORMATION ON PROBLEMS IN BOLD TYPE,
SEE LISTINGS, PAGES 142–307.

PROBLEM: Botrytis (gray mold) *(illustrated opposite page, bottom right)*. There is a soft brown rot of the leaves, stems, and flowers. A woolly gray fungus forms on the decayed tissue.

Solution: Gerbera daisies are highly susceptible to botrytis gray mold. High humidity or rainfall and excessive watering favor the fungus. Remove spent flowers immediately. Rake and destroy plant debris. Space plants adequately for good air circulation. Avoid overhead watering. Water early in the day to allow plants to dry before evening. To control the fungus, spray plants with chlorothalonil (Daconil) or mancozeb.

GLADIOLUS

GLADIOLUS
CORMS
ZONES: VARY BY PLANT TYPE

Gladiolus are favorite spring-to-fall flowers in Southern gardens, and choice cutting flowers. Beautiful tubular flowers bloom on sturdy spikes in an array of colors, ranging from white, yellow, and orange to red, purple, and even brown. However, spikes become so full with blooms they often need staking.

PROBLEM: Thrips *(illustrated above)*. Leaves are mottled with brown spots and a silvery white streaking and look stunted. Many flower buds dry and fail to open.

Solution: Thrips are a common problem of gladiolus, usually attacking the flowers during warm, dry, spring weather. Weeds harbor thrips, so keep your garden weed-free. For control, spray with diazinon, chlorpyrifos (Dursban), or carbaryl (Sevin), or use a systemic insecticide like acephate (Orthene) or dimethoate (Cygon). Dust gladiolus corms with carbaryl (Sevin) before storing them over the winter.

PROBLEM: Corm rot (see Fusarium bulb rot). The corms have corky, reddish brown spots. A blue-green mold may grow on the spots.

Solution: Remove and destroy infected corms to keep fusarium bulb rot from spreading. Make sure corms are clean, solid, and healthy before planting them. Periodically inspect corms in storage. Dusting with sulfur or dipping corms into thiophanate-methyl before storing has some benefit.

PROBLEM: Virus. The leaves are puckered, mottled, and malformed. Flowers may be streaked and stunted.

Solution: Aphids often spread yellow bean virus to plants and corms. Control aphids by spraying with insecticidal soap, horticultural oil, diazinon, malathion, or carbaryl (Sevin). Purchase only virus-free plants and corms. Remove nearby weeds since they harbor both insect carriers and the virus. Pull and destroy infected plants and corms.

GRAPE

DECIDUOUS VINES
ZONES: VARY BY SELECTION

Muscadine and bunch are the two types of grapes most commonly grown in the South. Muscadines are thick-skinned and quite tolerant of heat and humidity. Bunch grapes are thin-skinned and more prone to disease. Good selections for the South include muscadines 'Carlos', 'Cowart', 'Noble', 'Scuppernong', and 'Triumph'; and bunch grapes 'Concord', 'Flame', 'Fredonia', and 'Niagara'.

PROBLEM: Black rot of grape *(illustrated above)*. Tiny, reddish brown spots appear on leaves in early summer. The spots enlarge and become brown with black borders. Long black lesions appear on stems and tendrils. A small white spot forms on the fruit, and then rapidly enlarges and rots it.

Solution: The fungus causing black rot attacks all parts of the grape vine and survives on old canes. Select only young disease-free canes to produce this year's crop. Severely prune, then destroy all other canes. Remove and destroy dried grapes, tendrils, and leaves. Eliminate weeds beneath vines. Apply captan early in the season before and immediately after bloom, or spray with a Bordeaux mixture or fixed-copper fungicidal soap (Soap Shield) according to label directions.

PROBLEM: Japanese beetles. Beetles with metallic green bodies and copper-colored wings feed on grape leaves until they are skeletonized, beginning in early June. The beetles eat everything but the leaf veins.

Solution: Handpick beetles if numbers are small. Hold a cup of soapy water beneath the leaves. A light tap of the leaf startles the beetles, causing them to drop into the cup. This is most successful early in the morning, before beetles become active. For severe infestations, spray vines with rotenone, pyrethrin, carbaryl (Sevin), or acephate (Orthene), following label directions. You may need to spray twice a week to control successive beetle hatches. Beetles are usually gone by the time grapes ripen, but leaf damage may reduce fruit quality.

PROBLEM: Anthracnose. Fruit has spots with light gray centers and reddish brown borders. Similarly colored lesions also develop on canes and leaves. The centers drop out of the leaf spots, giving leaves a tattered look. Leaves often become stunted and curl downward.

Solution: This disease is more common on bunch grapes than muscadines. Prune and destroy old canes to help control the spread of disease. Apply liquid lime sulfur in early spring to reduce anthracnose infection.

PROBLEM: Powdery mildew. Green parts of vines are covered with a white powdery substance. Infected fruit splits and either dries up or rots before maturing. A blotchy or netlike pattern of scar tissue appears on already grown fruit.

Solution: Apply wettable sulfur or horticultural oil to leaves starting at petal fall and repeating throughout the growing season. Caution: Sulfur can cause leaf burn on sensitive varieties of grapes, especially when temperatures exceed 85°F.

PROBLEMS AND SOLUTIONS
....
FOR MORE INFORMATION ON PROBLEMS IN BOLD TYPE,
SEE LISTINGS, PAGES 142–307.

PROBLEM: Downy mildew. Yellowish oily lesions appear on upper leaf surfaces. White cottony patches appear on leaf undersides. Infected shoots thicken and curl, turn brown, and die. Young grapes turn gray. In wet weather, a white fungus grows on all infected parts of the vine except older fruit.

Solution: This disease seldom affects muscadines. Apply fungicidal soap (Soap Shield) or spray with captan just before bloom and then every 10 days until 7 days before harvest.

HACKBERRY

CELTIS

DECIDUOUS TREES

ZONES: US, MS, LS

Hackberry is a tough native tree that tolerates alkaline soils, strong winds, and drought. Because it is deep rooted, hackberry is an excellent choice for planting in lawns, parkways, and narrow planting strips.

PROBLEM: Witches'-broom *(illustrated above).* Abnormal growths appear in the crown of the tree. Branches are stunted and grow in matted clumps.

Solution: Witches'-broom is often caused by the presence of a mite and powdery mildew. When practical, prune out and destroy affected areas. Witches'-broom is unsightly and weakens affected branches. Although infected twigs eventually die, trees typically do not suffer any long-term adverse effects. The selection 'Prairie Pride' is resistant to witches'-broom.

PROBLEM: Leaf gall (see Gall-forming insects and mites). The lower surfaces of leaves are covered with small, round or blisterlike growths or galls.

Solution: Hackberry galls form on leaves in response to sap-sucking insects. The problem is mainly cosmetic. No action is required.

HAWTHORN

CRATAEGUS

DECIDUOUS TREES

ZONES: VARY BY SPECIES

Their small size, colorful fall foliage, clusters of pretty blooms, and showy fruit make hawthorns favorite trees for screens, hedges, barriers, and specimen plantings. However, take note that the branches of most hawthorns are covered with long thorns.

PROBLEM: Rust *(illustrated above).* Small yellow spots appear on the upper surfaces of leaves shortly after bloom. Spots gradually enlarge and become bright yellow-orange. Twigs may be deformed.

Solution: During wet, warm weather in spring, the wind carries fungus spores from infected red cedars to susceptible hawthorns. Heavily spotted leaves may drop prematurely. In late summer, small tubelike structures develop on the undersides of hawthorn leaves. Spores are released from these structures and carried by wind back to susceptible cedars or junipers, completing the disease cycle. In spring, spray trees with a fungicide such as chlorothalonil (Daconil) or mancozeb according to label directions.

PROBLEM: Fireblight. The leaves suddenly shrivel, look scorched, and die. Entire limbs die back. Affected bark is dark brown to purplish. Branches develop cankers.

Solution: Fireblight is a common and serious disease of hawthorns. Prune and destroy dead limbs, cutting back 12 in. behind dead tissue to green wood. Sterilize pruners after each cut with alcohol or a bleach solution (1 part bleach to 9 parts water). Avoid using high-nitrogen fertilizer. To prevent occurrences, spray during full bloom with streptomycin (Agri-Strep) or a fixed-copper fungicidal soap (Soap Shield).

HEMLOCK
TSUGA
EVERGREEN TREES

✀ ZONES: VARY BY SPECIES

Hemlocks are among the most graceful of needled trees. When young, limbs are somewhat erect, but droop slightly as the tree matures, cascading from the top of the tree. Hemlocks are often sold as living Christmas trees in December. If you purchase one, keep it indoors no more than 7 days.

PROBLEM: Hemlock woolly adelgids *(illustrated above).* White cottony tufts cling to the tree trunk, twigs, and the base of needles.

Solution: These tufts are woolly adelgids, aphidlike insects that suck sap from the tree. If adelgids are not controlled, they can kill a hemlock in a single year. Suffocate these pests by spraying them with a horticultural oil, taking care to completely cover all tree surfaces. For large trees, you will need to hire a tree-care professional to apply imidacloprid (Merit).

HIBISCUS
HIBISCUS
SHRUBS, PERENNIALS, AND ANNUALS

✀ ZONES: VARY BY SPECIES

Appreciated by Southern gardeners for their large showy flowers and attractive foliage, hibiscus can tolerate a variety of soils and conditions. Some form small trees, and some species tolerate cold winters, while others die back to the ground and serve as perennials. Chinese hibiscus *(Hibiscus rosa-sinensis),* semitropical and the showiest species, is intolerant of freezing weather.

PROBLEM: Aphids *(illustrated above).* Flowers and leaves are wrinkled and distorted. Flower buds may not open. A sticky substance covers the leaves. Leaves yellow and drop.

Solution: Green, yellow, or black aphids are common pests on new growth. They suck plant juices and produce a sticky honeydew. Blasting aphids off the plant with a jet of water generally reduces their numbers. To control heavy infestations, spray with insecticidal soap, horticultural oil, or acephate (Orthene).

PROBLEMS AND SOLUTIONS

FOR MORE INFORMATION ON PROBLEMS IN BOLD TYPE,
SEE LISTINGS, PAGES 142–307.

PROBLEM: Whiteflies. Tiny, white, triangular insects infest the undersides of leaves. The insects fly if disturbed. A sticky honeydew coats the leaves, which become mottled and yellow.

Solution: Whiteflies often attack hibiscus, particularly Chinese hibiscus, and are typically difficult to control. Spray the leaf undersides with horticultural oil, insecticidal soap, malathion, or a systemic insecticide like acephate (Orthene). Replace affected plants if repeated applications don't solve the problem.

PROBLEM: Leaf drop. Chinese hibiscus leaves suddenly turn yellow and fall.

Solution: Letting the soil dry out, even briefly, results in leaf drop. This problem usually occurs during hot summer weather. Give plants plenty of water, particularly those growing in pots. Once watered, most plants quickly recover and replace fallen leaves.

PROBLEM: Japanese beetles. Leaves are chewed and ragged, with only larger leaf veins left intact. Flowers may be entirely eaten.

Solution: This is the work of Japanese beetles, easily identified by their metallic green bodies and copper-colored wings. Handpick beetles if numbers are small. Hold a cup of soapy water beneath the leaves. A light tap of the leaf startles the beetles, causing them to drop into the cup. This is most successful early in the morning, before these pests become active. For severe infestations, spray with carbaryl (Sevin) according to label directions.

HOLLY
ILEX
EVERGREEN OR DECIDUOUS SHRUBS OR TREES

✀ ZONES: VARY BY SPECIES

Whether used in foundation plantings or as hedges, screens, or accents, hollies are valued plants. Some species produce berries without pollination, but most require both a male and a female plant for fruiting to occur.

PROBLEM: Leaf miners *(illustrated above).* Translucent trailing lines or blotches appear on the leaves. Affected leaves may yellow and drop. When you tear open an affected leaf, you may discover a tiny, yellowish white worm that feeds on tissue inside the leaf. American holly *(Ilex opaca)* is the most frequent target of these pests.

Solution: Pick off and destroy affected leaves. For serious infestations, spray foliage in late spring with dimethoate (Cygon) or acephate (Orthene). Spray again in 2 to 3 weeks.

PROBLEM: Wax scales (see Scales). White, brown, or black bumps encrust leaves and stems. A clear, sticky honeydew coats the upper surfaces of leaves. Leaves yellow and drop and branches die back.

Solution: Many types of scales—insects that attach themselves to plants and suck sap—attack hollies. They secrete honeydew, which encourages a sooty black mold to grow. To control scales, spray the plant thoroughly with horticultural oil, dimethoate (Cygon), or acephate (Orthene). You may need to spray again in 2 weeks.

PROBLEMS AND SOLUTIONS

FOR MORE INFORMATION ON PROBLEMS IN BOLD TYPE, SEE LISTINGS, PAGES 142–307.

PROBLEM: Leaf spot. Leaves develop spots with tan to gray centers and brown, black, or dark purple borders. Black pimplelike specks sometimes appear in the centers of the spots. Leaf spots are most numerous during warm, wet weather when leaves stay moist.

Solution: Do not water with overhead sprinklers. Water plants early in the day to allow them to dry off before evening. If practical, pick off and destroy spotted leaves. Spray new healthy leaves in spring with chlorothalonil (Daconil), maneb, or a fungicidal soap (Soap Shield).

HOLLYHOCK

ALCEA ROSEA

BIENNIAL OR SHORT-LIVED PERENNIAL

ZONES: ALL

Hollyhocks are the mainstays and old-fashioned favorites of perennial gardens and borders. Their flowers range in color from snowy white, creamy yellow, and delicate pink to the deepest red and purple.

PROBLEM: Rust *(illustrated above).* Leaves develop orange, yellow, or gray spots. The spots fall out and leave holes. Severely infected leaves wither, and the plant appears sickly.

Solution: Rust is a common problem of hollyhocks. The fungus overwinters on old leaves and stems, so garden sanitation is important. Prune off and destroy infected leaves and stems

as soon as rust appears. Spray healthy foliage and stems with chlorothalonil (Daconil) every 2 weeks throughout the growing season. Cut all flowering stalks to the ground immediately after they finish flowering and destroy them. Do not wet hollyhock foliage while watering.

PROBLEM: Japanese beetles. Leaves are ragged and eaten, with only the larger leaf veins remaining. Flowers are devoured. Beetles with metallic green bodies and copper-colored wings cover the flowers and stems.

Solution: Handpick Japanese beetles if possible, dropping them into a container of soapy water. Spray with a pesticide containing rotenone, pyrethrin, azadirachtin (Neem), carbaryl (Sevin), or acephate (Orthene).

HONEY LOCUST

GLEDITSIA TRIACANTHOS

DECIDUOUS TREE

ZONES: US, MS, LS

Honey locust is a fast-growing, medium to large tree that varies in height from 35–70 ft. Its soft-looking canopy of fernlike leaves casts filtered shade, making it a popular lawn tree. It tolerates acid or alkaline soil, drought, salt, and wind.

PROBLEM: Mimosa webworms *(illustrated above).* Clusters of leaves are webbed together. Leaves turn brown and die, giving the tree a scorched appearance. Small gray or brown caterpillars inside the webs feed on leaves.

Solution: Webworm moths lay eggs on the undersides of honey locust leaves in spring and early summer. Caterpillars then build silken nests and feed on the leaves. Before webbing becomes extensive, spray the foliage with *Bacillus thuringiensis kurstaki* (Dipel, Thuricide, Javelin). To control severe infestations, spray with carbaryl (Sevin), diazinon, or malathion.

HORSECHESTNUT

AESCULUS

DECIDUOUS TREES OR LARGE SHRUBS

ZONES: VARY BY SPECIES

Horsechestnuts, or buckeyes, can be spectacular in spring, with blooms in shades of ivory, yellow, pink, or red. Plants range in height from 12–90 ft.

PROBLEM: Leaf scorch *(illustrated above).* In hot, dry weather, leaves turn brown around the edges and between the veins. The youngest leaves are most affected.

Solution: Leaf scorch is the result of lack of moisture. It can also occur when the weather abruptly changes from a period of cloudy days to sunny, windy weather. Compacted soil, crowded roots, and heat from nearby pavement can also cause leaf scorch. To prevent leaf scorch, water plants thoroughly during periods of drought. Mulch around small trees or shrubs to conserve moisture. If the problem persists, move the plant to a different spot with better soil or replace it with a more drought-tolerant plant.

HOSTA

HOSTA
PERENNIALS

ZONES: US, MS, LS

The beauty of hostas, like coleus plants, is in the shape, coloring, and variegation of their foliage, as well as in their shade-loving nature. Give them rich, moist, well-drained soil. Hostas are excellent companions for ferns.

PROBLEM: Slugs and snails *(illustrated above).* Irregularly shaped holes with smooth edges appear in the leaves. Silvery trails of slime may also be present on plants and on nearby soil. Damage occurs at night.

Solution: Trap slugs and snails by laying a small board on top of a few stones near your hostas to provide an enticing hiding place for the pests during the day. At noon, lift the board and swipe them into a pail of soapy water. Snail and slug baits containing metaldehyde are also effective controls. Be sure to follow label directions carefully.

PROBLEM: Voles. One day the hosta plants look fine. The next morning, they're lying flat and wilted on the ground, severed at the base.

Solution: Voles are small, mouselike rodents that make runways under mulch and beneath the protective foliage of ground covers and fallen leaves. Hostas seem to be their favorite meal. Avoid planting hostas near ground covers that might shelter voles. Do not mulch around them. Incorporate expanded slate (VoleBloc) or sharp gravel into the soil before planting. You can also control voles by placing a mousetrap baited with peanut butter next to your plant. Cover the trap with an upended 1-gal. plastic pot to keep children and pets away. Place a twig under the edge of the pot so the vole can have access to its delicious but final meal.

PROBLEM: Southern blight (see Southern stem rot). The center of the plant collapses and rots. Leaves often look sunscorched and pull easily from the crown. A thick, fanlike white fungus covers the lower leaf stems. Hard yellowish specks appear in the fungal growth.

Solution: Once a plant is infected with Southern blight, it can't be cured. Pull and destroy infected plants. Dig out and dispose of surrounding soil. Place at least 6 in. of new sterile soil atop the old planting bed to bury the fungus and prevent infection of any additional plants.

PROBLEM: Foliar nematodes (see Nematodes). Infested leaves have tannish, water-soaked areas between the veins that look like tan stripes running parallel to the veins. These leaves dry out, shred, and fall from the plant.

Solution: Foliar nematodes, which are microscopic worms, infest the leaves of many herbaceous plants. Strip infested leaves from the plant and destroy them. Avoid overhead watering, as prolonged periods of leaf wetness aid in spreading nematodes across the leaf and from plant to plant. There is no chemical control.

HYACINTH

HYACINTHUS
BULBS

ZONES: US, MS, LS, CS

Hyacinths are fragrant spring-blooming bulbs grown as perennials in the Upper and Middle South and as annuals in the Lower and Coastal South. Bell- or star-shaped flowers range in colors from pure white to the deepest red and purple.

PROBLEM: Short stems *(illustrated above).* The flower stems are very short. Flowers open at near-ground level.

Solution: Short stems usually result from a lack of sufficient winter chilling. Hyacinths require at least 6 to 8 weeks of temperatures below 50°F in order to develop strong stems and large blooms. If you live where winters are short and mild, refrigerate your hyacinth bulbs for 6 weeks before planting them in late fall.

PROBLEM: Bacterial soft rot. The bulbs turn wet and mushy and emit a foul odor. A sticky substance oozes from cracks in stored bulbs.

Solution: This bacterium enters bulbs through wounds. There is no chemical control. Buy healthy, solid bulbs. Avoid wounding bulbs during planting or storing. Pull and destroy infected plants; do not add to compost pile.

PROBLEMS AND SOLUTIONS
....
FOR MORE INFORMATION ON PROBLEMS IN BOLD TYPE,
SEE LISTINGS, PAGES 142–307.

HYDRANGEA, FRENCH
HYDRANGEA MACROPHYLLA
DECIDUOUS SHRUB
ZONES: ALL

Renowned for their huge pom-pom flowers of blue, pink, red, or white, French hydrangeas grow best in a spot that gets morning sunshine and afternoon shade. Drooping leaves are a reminder that the soil is too dry. This shrub is a living litmus test—blue flowers indicate acid soil; pink and red flowers tell you that the soil is probably alkaline.

PROBLEM: **No blooms (see Flowers, lack of)** *(illustrated above).* The shrub appears perfectly healthy but fails to bloom.

Solution: French hydrangeas fail to bloom for several reasons. The most common is not enough sun. Try moving the plant to a sunnier spot. The second is a sudden cold snap in late winter or early spring that freezes the flower buds. There is little you can do to prevent this. The third is that the plant was pruned in fall or winter, thereby removing the flower buds. The safest time to prune is in summer, removing spent flowers and shortening branches that have already bloomed.

IMPATIENS
IMPATIENS
PERENNIALS AND ANNUALS
ZONES: ALL

Near-perfect bedding plants, impatiens are popular for their prolific, nonstop bloom and easy care. Both single and double forms come in colors of white, red, orange, salmon, pink, lavender, magenta, and purple. Impatiens are perennials in the Coastal and Tropical South, where they will survive for years with only an occasional trim. They thrive in filtered or partial shade but tolerate sunny conditions if given plenty of water.

PROBLEM: **Spider mites (see Mites)** *(illustrated above).* Leaves lose their green color and look speckled or dusty. A fine webbing covers the leaves. Plants lose vigor. Leaves dry up and drop.

Solution: Spider mites attack impatiens during hot, dry weather. Hosing off the foliage daily and keeping plants adequately watered usually limits their numbers. To control major infestations, spray plants with insecticidal soap, horticultural oil, or a pesticide containing hexakis (Vendex), such as Isotox. Repeated applications may be required.

PROBLEMS AND SOLUTIONS
FOR MORE INFORMATION ON PROBLEMS IN BOLD TYPE, SEE LISTINGS, PAGES 142–307.

PROBLEM: **Nitrogen deficiency.** The foliage turns a dull green. Leaves are small, and the plant lacks vigor.

Solution: Dull green, spindly leaves tell you that the plant is hungry for nitrogen. Feed it with a balanced (20-20-20) water-soluble fertilizer. Impatiens growing in sandy soils need frequent feeding, about once every 2 weeks. When the foliage improves in appearance, switch over to a bloom-booster fertilizer, such as a 15-40-15.

PROBLEM: Necrotic ring spot virus. Brown, black, or purple spots containing concentric rings appear on leaves. Stems become blackened. Leaves drop prematurely, and the plants are stunted.

Solution: There is no chemical control for this virus. However, controlling the thrips that transmit the virus reduces its incidence. Spray foliage with insecticidal soap, horticultural oil, diazinon, or acephate (Orthene). Pull and destroy infected plants.

OTHER COMMON PROBLEMS: **Aphids** cause puckered and deformed leaves.

INDIAN HAWTHORN
RAPHIOLEPIS INDICA
EVERGREEN SHRUB
ZONES: LS (PROTECTED), CS

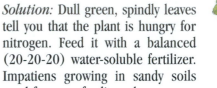

Where soil or climate makes growing azaleas impossible, Indian hawthorn is often an excellent substitute. This slow-growing, rounded evergreen combines glossy, dark green leaves with showy pink, red, or white flowers that appear from late fall to late spring. Indian hawthorn tolerates heat, drought, wind, sandy soil, and salt spray, making it a good candidate for coastal gardens.

PROBLEM: Leaf spot *(illustrated above).* Small red spots appear on new leaves in spring. As the spots enlarge, they turn brown or gray with purple margins. The spots may merge into irregular blotches. Heavily infected leaves drop, weakening the plant.

Solution: This leaf spot is caused by a fungus, *Entomosporium,* that also afflicts photinia (see page 129). It usually occurs in cool, rainy weather and attacks only immature leaves. To control it, pick off and destroy infected leaves. Rake up and destroy fallen leaves. Plant resistant selections such as 'Indian Princess', 'Olivia', and 'Snow White', rather than susceptible ones like 'Pinkie', 'Enchantress', 'Harbinger of

Spring', and 'Heather'. In spring, spray new foliage with chlorothalonil (Daconil) every 14 days until it matures.

PROBLEM: Fireblight. In spring, leaves, flowers, and twigs suddenly shrivel, turn blackish brown, and look scorched. Branches develop sunken cankers and may die.

Solution: Prune and destroy dead limbs, cutting back 12 in. behind diseased tissue to green wood. Sterilize pruners after each cut with alcohol or a bleach solution (1 part bleach to 9 parts water). To reduce occurrences, spray during full bloom with streptomycin (Agri-Strep) or fixed-copper fungicidal soap (Soap Shield). Repeat three times at weekly intervals.

IRIS

IRIS
BULBS AND RHIZOMES
ZONES: VARY BY SPECIES OR TYPE

Irises are among the easiest of perennials to grow. Some prefer well-drained soil, while others thrive with their roots underwater. Spectacular flowers appear in almost every color and combination of colors imaginable.

PROBLEM: Borers *(illustrated above)*; **Bacterial soft rot.** Leaf edges look ragged. Leaves turn yellow and develop dark streaks. Rhizomes become soft, rotten, or hollow. Leaves break off easily and the plant dies.

Solution: Iris borers are the larvae of night-flying moths that tunnel into leaves and rhizomes. Hollowed out rhizomes may become infected with a smelly bacterial rot. To prevent borer attack, pull off and destroy old, brown leaves each fall and winter. In spring, spray foliage when it reaches 5 in. tall with lindane, dimethoate (Cygon), or chlorpyrifos (Dursban).

PROBLEM: Leaf spot. Leaves develop small, oblong, tan spots with reddish borders. The spots rapidly enlarge, and the entire leaf dies.

Solution: Leaf spot is most severe in mild, damp weather where air circulation is poor. Pull and destroy diseased foliage. Rake and destroy plant debris. Protect young, healthy growth by spraying with Bordeaux mixture, mancozeb, or chlorothalonil (Daconil) at 7- to 10-day intervals throughout spring.

PROBLEMS AND SOLUTIONS

FOR MORE INFORMATION ON PROBLEMS IN BOLD TYPE,
SEE LISTINGS, PAGES 142–307.

JAPANESE ANDROMEDA

PIERIS JAPONICA
EVERGREEN SHRUB
ZONES: US, MS, LS

Japanese andromeda is a large, rounded shrub best suited to partial shade. It requires acid soil, and blooms heavily in early spring with pendulous white or pink flowers. New growth is bronzy pink to red. Japanese andromeda is a good companion for rhododendrons and azaleas.

PROBLEM: Lace bugs *(illustrated above)*. The upper surfaces of the leaves show a silvery or yellow speckling, while shiny black spots dot the undersides.

Solution: Lace bugs suck sap from the undersides of leaves. The black spots are excrement. These insects favor plants growing in sunny, dry areas, so plant Japanese andromeda in moist, well-drained soil and light shade. To control lace bugs, spray the undersides of leaves with insecticidal soap, horticultural oil, or malathion. You'll probably need to spray several times. For severe infestations, spray with acephate (Orthene) during late spring.

JAPANESE AUCUBA

AUCUBA JAPONICA
EVERGREEN SHRUB
ZONES: ALL

Japanese aucuba is a handsome, broad-leafed evergreen that performs especially well in light shade. Some types feature glossy deep green leaves while others flaunt emerald foliage speckled or splashed with yellow, gold, or creamy white. Japanese aucuba grows 6–10 ft. tall and wide, though plants sometimes reach 15 ft. It accepts regular pruning. Cuttings root easily in water.

PROBLEM: Sunburn *(illustrated above)*. Dark brown or black patches appear on leaves on the outside of the plant. Leaves become brittle.

Solution: Although Japanese aucuba tolerates morning sun, hot, afternoon sun burns the leaves. Dry soil worsens the problem. Prune off dead leaves then move the shrub to a shadier spot. Remember to keep this plant well watered in hot, dry weather.

PROBLEM: Scales. White, yellow, gray or brown bumps encrust leaves and stems. Leaves turn yellow, then brown, and drop. Stems die back.

Solution: Japanese aucuba plays host to several scale insects. All of them suck plant juices, weakening the plant. Spray the plant with horticultural oil, coating all leaf and stem surfaces. Or apply a systemic insecticide, such as acephate (Orthene), following label directions carefully.

PROBLEM: Anthracnose. Black, greasy-looking spots develop on the leaves, usually along leaf edges or veins. As spots enlarge, they acquire a bull's-eye appearance. Black cankers develop along a stem, girdling and killing it. Leaves on infected stems wilt and turn black.

Solution: Remove and destroy affected stems and leaves. Avoid overhead sprinkling. Provide adequate air circulation around the plant. Rake and remove fallen leaves. As new growth emerges and expands in the spring, spray with chlorothalonil (Daconil), following label directions.

JAPANESE CRYPTOMERIA

CRYPTOMERIA JAPONICA

EVERGREEN TREE

ZONES: US, MS, LS

Japanese cryptomeria is an elegant, fast-growing conifer with attractive red-brown bark. Growing 20–60 ft. tall with a conical shape, it's an excellent choice for tall screens.

PROBLEM: Needle blight *(illustrated above)*. Needles near the bases of branches turn bronze or tan, then eventually grayish. The infection gradually spreads outward toward the branch tips, which remain green. The inside of the tree becomes bare.

Solution: The fungus that causes this disease, *Cercospora,* usually strikes during warm, wet weather. Fortunately, needle blight is seldom fatal. To control it, avoid wetting foliage as much as possible. If practical, prune out and destroy infected branches. Spray the tree once in May, June, and July with triforine (Funginex), chlorothalonil (Daconil), or mancozeb, making sure to cover the interior foliage. Don't confuse this disease with a similar malady, juniper twig blight, which kills branch tips first and moves inward.

PROBLEM: Winter yellowing. The needles turn yellow, bronze, or brownish red in winter and then turn green in spring.

Solution: The discoloration is a physiological response to winter cold and varies from plant to plant. Some selections resist discoloration, including 'Ben Franklin', 'Wintergreen', and 'Yoshino'.

PROBLEM: Cold, winter injury. During very cold weather, needles on the outside of the tree turn brown. A fungus may

grow on these needles, turning them grayish or black. The affected needles do not green up in spring.

Solution: Don't worry about this fungus. It only infects needles damaged by cold or other causes. Prune and destroy damaged foliage and hope for a milder winter next year.

JAPANESE PACHYSANDRA

PACHYSANDRA TERMINALIS

PERENNIAL GROUND COVER

ZONES: US, MS, LS

Japanese pachysandra is an excellent ground cover, easy to grow and seldom bothered by insect pests. It produces a thick carpet of evergreen, waxy leaves 2–4 in. long and can be grown successfully in heavy shade, provided the soil is fertile, moist, acidic, and well drained.

PROBLEM: Leaf and stem blight. The leaves develop large, chocolate-colored blotches and then wither. The stems shrivel and the blotches spread.

Solution: Caused by the fungus *Volutella,* leaf and stem blight is a certain sign that Japanese pachysandra is under stress from drought, poor soil drainage, or insects. Falling autumn leaves that cover the planting compound the problem by creating an overly moist environment that favors fungal development. To control leaf and stem blight, rake fallen leaves off the plants. Remove and destroy any infected plants. Spray healthy plants when new growth starts in spring with chlorothalonil (Daconil) or captan. Spray twice more at weekly intervals. Eliminate problem insects, such as scales, by spraying plants according to label directions with horticultural oil or acephate (Orthene). If problems persist, replace Japanese pachysandra with another ground cover.

PROBLEM: Leaf scorch. The top surfaces of the leaves turn tan or light brown and look burned. Most damage occurs to plants growing in full sun.

Solution: Japanese pachysandra prefers partial to deep shade. Move the plants to a shadier spot or choose a more sun-tolerant ground cover.

JAPANESE PITTOSPORUM

PITTOSPORUM TOBIRA

EVERGREEN SHRUB

ZONES: LS (PROTECTED), CS, TS

Japanese pittosporum is a popular choice for hedges, screens, or windbreaks. It grows in full sun or partial shade and is very tolerant of coastal conditions.

PROBLEMS AND SOLUTIONS

FOR MORE INFORMATION ON PROBLEMS IN BOLD TYPE, SEE LISTINGS, PAGES 142–307.

SOLVING PLANT PROBLEMS

PROBLEM: Scales *(illustrated opposite page, bottom right).* Bumps appear on the undersides of leaves and along the stems. The bumps may be hard and brown or white and cottony. Leaves may yellow and drop. Twigs may die back.

Solution: The bumps are scales, insects that attach themselves to stems and leaves and suck plant sap. Heavily infested plants should be discarded. For light infestations, physically scrape off the scales or spray with horticultural oil, dimethoate (Cygon), or acephate (Orthene).

OTHER COMMON PROBLEMS: **Aphids** may pucker and distort leaves; **Texas root rot** may kill plants growing in heavy, strongly alkaline soils.

JAPANESE YEW
TAXUS CUSPIDATA
EVERGREEN SHRUB OR TREE
ZONES: US, MS

Japanese yews make superb hedges, screens, foundation plants and even ground covers. These needle-leafed evergreens tolerate sun or shade and heavy pruning. But well-drained soil is a must.

PROBLEM: Root rot *(illustrated above).* Branches turn yellow, then brown, and eventually die. The soil around the plant is heavy, moist, and poorly drained.

Solution: Yews do not like having wet feet. Improve soil drainage by amending it with coarse sand, ground bark, sphagnum peat moss, or expanded slate (PermaTill). Plant the shrub slightly high in the hole, so the top ½ in. of the rootball protrudes above the soil surface, then cover the top of the rootball with mulch. Do not plant yews near downspouts or dripping faucets.

OTHER COMMON PROBLEMS: Needles turn yellow and have small notches in them, caused by **weevils**; white cottony **mealybugs** cover stems and needles.

JASMINE
JASMINUM
EVERGREEN, SEMIEVERGREEN, OR DECIDUOUS VINES OR SHRUBS
ZONES: VARY BY SPECIES

Gardeners favor jasmines for their sweetly fragrant blooms, although some species have no fragrance at all. Jasmines prefer fertile, well-drained soil and need an occasional trim to maintain their form.

PROBLEM: Scales *(illustrated above).* Crusty bumps infest stems and the undersides of leaves.

PROBLEMS AND SOLUTIONS
FOR MORE INFORMATION ON PROBLEMS IN BOLD TYPE, SEE LISTINGS, PAGES 142–307.

Solution: The bumps are scales, insects that attach themselves to stems and leaves and suck sap from plants. They often secrete a sticky honeydew on which sooty mold grows. To control scales, spray plants with horticultural oil or with a systemic insecticide, such as dimethoate (Cygon), or acephate (Orthene). Heavily infested plants should be discarded.

PROBLEM: Whiteflies. Tiny, white, triangular insects infest the undersides of the leaves. Leaves yellow and drop. If you jostle the plant, the insects quickly fly.

Solution: Whiteflies are difficult to control. Spray with insecticidal soap, horticultural oil, malathion, resmethrin, or a systemic insecticide like acephate (Orthene). Replace affected plants if repeated applications don't solve the problem.

JUNIPER
JUNIPERUS
EVERGREEN SHRUBS AND TREES
ZONES: VARY BY SPECIES

Junipers are a varied plant group that includes ground covers, shrubs, and trees. Tough and resilient, they require little more than plenty of sun and well-drained soil.

PROBLEM: Spider mites (see Mites) *(illustrated above).* Tiny yellow spots appear on the surface of needles, and the plant has a sickly, yellow appearance. Needles may turn bronze or brown. Tiny webs may cover the needles.

Solution: Inspect plants weekly during hot, dry periods, which favor mite infestations. Control light infestations by spraying junipers with a jet of water from the hose. For heavier infestations involving significant damage to needles, spray plants thoroughly with insecticidal soap, horticultural oil, or a pesticide containing hexakis (Vendex), such as Isotox. Two to three applications at weekly intervals will more than likely be needed.

PROBLEM: Juniper twig blight. Young branch tips turn brown and die. Dead branches gradually turn gray. Tiny black dots appear on dead needles and stems. Young plants may be killed. Mature growth resists infection.

Solution: Prune out and destroy infected branches when plants are dry. Avoid wetting plants late in the day or during

117

evening hours. When new growth begins in spring, spray plants with thiophanate-methyl (Thiomyl) or mancozeb at 2-week intervals.

PROBLEM: Bagworms. Entire branches are defoliated. Plants appear brown and dying almost overnight. Small, grayish brown bags resembling pinecones hang from the branches.

Solution: Those "pinecones" are bags filled with hungry caterpillars known as bagworms. Bagworms are most noticeable in late summer when the bags hang like Christmas ornaments from dead branch tips. Because needled plants do not quickly grow new leaves, a severe attack can spell disaster. Pick off and destroy all bags you can reach. Spray plants in early summer with *Bacillus thuringiensis kurstaki* (Dipel, Thuricide, Javelin) when bags are less than ½ in. long. For older bagworms, spray with a pyrethrin, malathion, diazinon, carbaryl (Sevin), or acephate (Orthene).

PROBLEMS AND SOLUTIONS
....
FOR MORE INFORMATION ON PROBLEMS IN BOLD TYPE,
SEE LISTINGS, PAGES 142–307.

PROBLEM: Cedar-apple rust. Galls, first green, then turning dark brown and hard, develop on branches in the fall. In early spring, the galls develop orange-red, jellylike tentacles.

Solution: This disease usually does not harm junipers but causes significant damage when it spreads to apples and crabapples. Spiky tentacles on galls release fungus spores. Prune out and destroy galls in junipers. Control rust on crabapples and apples using fungicides such as chlorothalonil (Daconil), myclobutanil (Immunox), or triadimefon (Bayleton) when leaves expand in the spring.

LANTANA

LANTANA

EVERGREEN SHRUBS

✔ ZONES: MS (HARDIER FORMS), LS, CS, TS

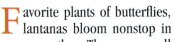

Favorite plants of butterflies, lantanas bloom nonstop in warm weather. They grow well in almost any well-drained soil and tolerate heat, drought, and neglect. For unbounded bloom, plant them in full sun and go easy on the water and fertilizer.

PROBLEM: Whiteflies *(illustrated above).* Tiny, white, triangular insects infest the undersides of the leaves. Leaves become mottled and yellow. When you brush against the plants, the insects quickly fly.

Solution: Whiteflies are common pests of lantana and are difficult to control. Spray the undersides of the leaves with insecticidal soap, horticultural oil, malathion, or a systemic insecticide, such as acephate (Orthene). Replace affected plants if repeated applications don't solve the problem.

LETTUCE

ANNUAL

✔ ZONES: ALL

Lettuce is a cool-season vegetable you can grow in fall, winter, or spring, depending on your climate zone. For a long-lasting harvest, plant successive crops at 2-week intervals and grow selections that mature at different rates.

PROBLEM: Bolting *(illustrated above).* Lettuce begins to flower and leaves taste bitter.

Solution: Some types of lettuce, like 'Bibb', quickly flower and form seed heads (bolt) in hot weather. Lettuce that bolts quickly develops a bitter taste. The best way to avoid this is to plant bolt-resistant types, such as 'Buttercrunch', 'Salad Bowl', 'Red Sails', and romaine selections. They tolerate heat and remain sweet and tender longer.

PROBLEM: Aster yellows. Lettuce appears stunted and may not form a head. Heart leaves turn yellow or white and don't develop properly.

Solution: Microorganisms spread by leafhoppers cause aster yellows. Pull and destroy infected plants. Control leafhoppers by spraying plants with a pyrethrin or carbaryl (Sevin).

LEYLAND CYPRESS

CUPRESSOCYPARIS LEYLANDII

EVERGREEN TREE

✔ ZONES: US, MS, LS, CS

Leyland cypress has become the South's number one choice for tall screens. Once established, it can easily grow 3–4 ft. a year. Just remember, though, that it eventually grows 60–70 ft. tall if unpruned.

PROBLEM: Seridium canker *(illustrated above).* Older interior foliage yellows, then browns. Twigs and branches die. Sunken reddish, dark brown, or purplish cankers form on the bark and ooze sap. Infection usually affects the lower branches first, then travels up the tree.

Solution: There is no chemical control for this disease. Avoid wounding the bark. Any type of wound provides an entry point for the seridium fungus. Prune out diseased branches, cutting 6 in. below the site of infection. Space plants adequately so that air can freely circulate among them.

PROBLEM: Needle or tip blight. During warm, wet weather the needles closest to the inside of the tree turn tan or gray, then die, leaving the inside of the plant bare while the outside remains green. Or needles on the tips of branches turn brown and die, and tiny black dots appear on dead needles and stems.

Solution: These problems usually affect plants growing too close together. The dense foliage restricts air circulation, so foliage doesn't dry quickly. This makes things easy for either of two pathogens—*Cercospora,* which also causes needle blight on Japanese cryptomeria and related species; and *Phomopsis,* which also causes twig blight of juniper. To control these problems, space Leylands 8–10 ft. apart. Avoid wetting the foliage. For recommendations on chemical controls, refer to the entries "needle blight" under "Japanese cryptomeria" and "Juniper twig blight" under "Juniper" in this chapter.

LILAC
SYRINGA
DECIDUOUS SHRUBS
ZONES: VARY BY SPECIES

Lilacs resurrect childhood memories for many gardeners raised in the Upper South. But growing them successfully in the warmer climate zones of the South depends on choosing the right selections.

PROBLEM: Powdery mildew *(illustrated above).* White to grayish powdery spots develop on leaves and on new sprouts in early summer. This powder may completely cover leaves as the season progresses, but seldom causes long-term damage or reduces flowering.

Solution: Prune after blooming to open up the center of the plant and promote good air circulation. Spray the foliage with triforine (Funginex), triadimefon (Bayleton), or horticultural oil at the first signs of disease. Repeat spraying as necessary every 7 to 14 days.

PROBLEMS AND SOLUTIONS

FOR MORE INFORMATION ON PROBLEMS IN BOLD TYPE, SEE LISTINGS, PAGES 142–307.

PROBLEM: No blooms (see Flowers, lack of). Healthy-looking lilacs don't produce any flowers.

Solution: Most lilacs need a long period of winter cold to produce blooms the following spring. In mild-winter areas, plant heat-tolerant types such as 'Miss Kim', 'Blue Boy', 'Lavender Lady', and cut-leaf lilac *(Syringa laciniata).* Planting lilacs in shade also limits bloom. Lilacs prefer full sun.

LILY
LILIUM
BULBS
ZONES: ALL

If you give lilies what they want—sufficient winter chill (in mild-winter areas, refrigerate the bulbs for 6 to 8 weeks), consistent moisture, full sun, and perfect drainage—they'll reward you with magnificent flowers in a variety of sizes, shapes, colors, and fragrances.

PROBLEM: Root rot (see Bacterial soft rot) *(illustrated above).* Lilies grow for a year or two, then die. The foliage turns yellow, and the bulbs seem mushy and emit a foul odor. Some bulbs ooze a sticky substance.

Solution: A harmful bacterium enters bulbs through wounds. There is no chemical control. Buy healthy, solid bulbs. Avoid bruising or wounding bulbs during planting or storing. Pull and destroy infected plants. Do not compost them.

LOQUAT
ERIOBOTRYA
EVERGREEN TREES OR LARGE SHRUBS
ZONES: VARY BY SPECIES

Loquats are rather dense trees. Their attractive broad, leathery dark green leaves are often used in floral arrangements. The most popular species, *Eriobotrya japonica,* blooms in fall and bears edible fruit in winter or spring.

PROBLEM: Fireblight *(illustrated above).* The leaves look scorched and entire limbs die back.

Solution: Although fireblight often attacks flower clusters and may kill a limb or two, it seldom kills the tree. To prevent occurrences, spray during full bloom with streptomycin (Agri-Strep) or fixed-copper fungicidal soap (Soap Shield). Prune and destroy dead limbs, cutting back 12 in. behind dead tissue to green wood. Sterilize pruners after each cut with alcohol or a bleach solution (1 part bleach to 9 parts water). Do not give plants high-nitrogen fertilizers.

MADAGASCAR PERIWINKLE

CATHARANTHUS ROSEUS

ANNUAL SOMETIMES GROWN
AS PERENNIAL

ZONES: ALL

Lavender, purple, pink, red, or white flowers cover this popular bedding plant from spring until fall. Madagascar periwinkle tolerates heat, drought, and humidity, but requires excellent drainage.

PROBLEM: **Root rot (see Pythium root rot)** *(illustrated above)*. Stems and leaves turn yellow, then brown, and eventually die. The soil around the plant is heavy, moist, and poorly drained.

Solution: Planting in heavy clay soil disposes the plant to attack by the fungus *Phytophthora*. Improve drainage by amending the soil with lots of coarse sand, ground bark, sphagnum peat moss, or expanded slate (PermaTill). Do not replant in the same bed where diseased plants have died.

MAGNOLIA

MAGNOLIA

DECIDUOUS OR EVERGREEN TREES
AND SHRUBS

ZONES: VARY BY SPECIES

Deciduous magnolias display spectacular flowers in late winter and early spring before the leaves appear. Fragrant flowers range from white to pink to rosy purple. Southern magnolias sport glossy, leathery evergreen leaves. Their fragrant white flowers appear in late spring or summer depending on the location.

PROBLEM: Algal spot *(illustrated above)*. Velvety pink or pale green spots cover the leaves of Southern magnolias. Twigs may be stunted or die back.

Solution: Cephaleuros virescens, the organism that causes algal spot, favors trees growing in areas with high rainfall. To control it, pick off and destroy spotted leaves. Rake up and destroy fallen leaves. Spray foliage with a copper fungicide, such as Bordeaux mixture or Soap Shield. Algal spot also attacks camellias.

PROBLEM: Scales. Numerous bumps appear on the undersides of leaves and along the stems. The bumps may be hard and brown or white and cottony. Leaves yellow and drop. Twigs may die back.

PROBLEMS AND SOLUTIONS

FOR MORE INFORMATION ON PROBLEMS IN BOLD TYPE,
SEE LISTINGS, PAGES 142–307.

Solution: The bumps are scales, insects that attach themselves to stems and leaves and suck plant sap. Heavily infested plants should be discarded. Overwintering scales can be controlled with dormant oil applied in late winter. For light infestations, physically scrape off the scales or spray with horticultural oil. To kill adult scales, spray with a systemic insecticide such as dimethoate (Cygon) or acephate (Orthene).

MAPLE

ACER

DECIDUOUS TREES OR SHRUBS

ZONES: VARY BY SPECIES

Maples vary greatly in size, shape, adaptability, and fall color. However, they all prefer well-drained soil and adequate moisture during spring and summer. Most maples have shallow, competitive roots.

PROBLEM: Anthracnose *(illustrated above)*. Following warm, wet weather, brown spots advance along leaf veins. The spots often run together, killing the leaves and causing them to drop prematurely.

Solution: Rake and destroy fallen leaves and twigs, and prune dead branches to reduce overwintering fungi. Pruning also improves air circulation and helps to eliminate the wet conditions that favor the fungus. Chemical sprays are rarely justified except when anthracnose causes repeated defoliation. Fungicides labeled for control of anthracnose on maples include chlorothalonil (Daconil), thiophanate-methyl (Thiomyl), mancozeb, lime sulfur, and Bordeaux mixture and other copper fungicides. Spray in spring just after new leaves unfurl. Repeat spraying twice at 2-week intervals. Be sure to follow label directions carefully.

PROBLEM: Verticillium wilt. Leaves on a branch, usually near the top of the tree, suddenly yellow, turn brown, and die. The tree gradually dies, branch by branch. When you peel back the bark of a diseased branch, you discover a dark or olive green stain on the wood underneath.

Solution: The soilborne fungus causing this wilt enters through the roots. There is no chemical control. Prune and destroy dead branches. Fertilize infected trees with a high-nitrogen fertilizer to help them outgrow the infection. If the tree dies, do not replace it with another maple. Plant a wilt-resistant tree, such as an oak, birch, or sweet gum.

PROBLEM: Leaf galls (see Gall-forming insects and mites). A number of small round or blisterlike growths pockmark the leaves.

Solution: Mites stimulate the formation of these unusual growths, or galls. The galls are small, but large numbers of them can cause leaves to curl up. However, the problem is seldom serious enough to warrant chemical control.

PROBLEM: Leaf scorch. During hot, dry weather, the leaves turn brown along the edges and between the veins.

Solution: Scorch usually occurs during hot, windy weather when trees can't take up enough water to replace moisture lost to transpiration (moisture escaping through plant membranes and pores). Trees growing in dry, compacted soil or near pavement are most susceptible. To prevent scorch, water maples deeply in dry weather and mulch the ground beneath them.

PROBLEM: Scales. White cottony insects encrust twigs and branches. A sticky honeydew or sooty mold coats the leaves.

Solution: Cottony cushion scale is a common pest of maples, especially on trees stressed by lack of water or infertile soil. Water deeply during periods of summer drought. Spray branches and leaves with insecticidal soap, horticultural oil, or acephate (Orthene).

PROBLEM: Webworms, fall. Large webs envelop the ends of branches in summer and fall. Caterpillars protected inside these webs strip the branches of leaves.

Solution: If you can reach them, prune and destroy web-covered branches while the webs are still small. If you can't, spray the affected branches with *Bacillus thuringiensis kurstaki* (Dipel, Thuricide, Javelin), carbaryl (Sevin), diazinon, malathion, or acephate (Orthene).

MARIGOLD

TAGETES

ANNUALS AND PERENNIALS

ZONES: VARY BY SPECIES

Among our most popular bedding plants, marigolds bloom from spring until frost, in shades of yellow, orange, gold, and bronze. Few flowers are as easy to start from seed.

PROBLEM: Spider mites (see Mites) *(illustrated above)*. A fine webbing covers the leaves and stems. Leaves lose their deep green color and appear speckled or dusty.

Solution: Keep a close watch on marigolds. At the first sign of mites, spray plants with insecticidal soap or horticultural oil, being sure to wet the undersides of the leaves. For severe infestations, spray with a pesticide containing hexakis (Vendex), such as Isotox. Keep plants well watered. If the problem fails to improve, remove and dispose of the infested plants.

PROBLEM: Slugs and snails. Irregularly shaped holes with smooth edges appear in the leaves. Silvery trails of slime are on the plants and nearby soil. Damage occurs at night.

Solution: Trap slugs and snails by laying a small board on top of a few stones near the plants to provide an enticing hiding place during the day. At noon, lift the board and swipe the offenders into a pail of soapy water. Snail and slug baits containing metaldehyde are also effective in controlling these pests. Be sure to follow label directions carefully.

PROBLEM: Root and stem rot. The leaves wilt and die, and the lower stems turn dark brown and shrivel. When you pull the plant, its roots are rotted.

Solution: Planting marigolds, particularly the African type, in cool, soggy soil disposes them to attack by the *Phytophthora* fungus. Remove and destroy infected plants. Improve soil drainage. Do not overwater. Drench the soil with captan prior to planting marigolds again.

MELONS

ANNUALS

ZONES: ALL

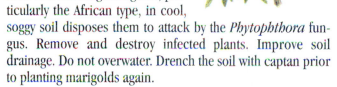

Juicy and delicious, cantaloupes, watermelons, honeydews, and other melons enjoy the South's long growing season. But unlike other melons, watermelon doesn't continue to sweeten after harvest. It must be picked ripe.

PROBLEM: Anthracnose *(illustrated above)*. Small, yellowish, rounded or angular spots appear on leaves. On watermelon plants, the spots turn black; on other melons, the leaf spots turn brown and then drop out, leaving holes. Circular, sunken, dark brown spots develop on the fruit. The fruit shrivels and dies.

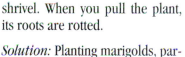

PROBLEMS AND SOLUTIONS

FOR MORE INFORMATION ON PROBLEMS IN BOLD TYPE,
SEE LISTINGS, PAGES 142–307.

Solution: The fungus causing this disease, *Colletotrichum lagenarium,* overwinters in seed and in plant debris. Good garden sanitation is the best way to prevent it. Always use new high-quality seed. Pull up and destroy all vines at the end of the growing season. At the first sign of anthracnose, spray plants in early spring as leaf buds swell. Then apply captan as needed during the growing season.

PROBLEM: Downy mildew. Melon plants are stunted and their leaves curl. Tiny patches of grayish mold grow on the undersides of the leaves. Leaf veins turn yellow, then brown. Leaves die, beginning with the older ones. Fruit quality is poor.

Solution: The fungus that causes this disease spreads by splashing water, so avoid wetting melon foliage. Remove infected leaves from the plant. Spray healthy foliage with chlorothalonil (Daconil). Pull up and destroy melon vines at the end of the growing season.

PROBLEM: Blossom-end rot. A sunken, brown or black rotten spot appears on the blossom end of the fruit. A black mold shows in the rotting area.

Solution: Blossom-end rot in melons usually results from uneven soil moisture, which prevents the plants from absorbing adequate calcium from the soil. To prevent this problem, plant in good, well-drained soil or in raised beds. Water deeply during dry periods and mulch around plants to maintain even soil moisture. Remove affected fruit. If the rot is not at the blossom end, the fruit may have belly rot, a condition caused when melons sit on damp soil. Protect the fruit by mulching under it or allowing it to rest on a shallow can. Blossom-end rot frequently affects plants in sandy or dry soil.

PROBLEM: Angular leaf spot. Greasy, green angular spots appear on the leaves. The spots turn brown and drop out, leaving ragged holes. A fluid may ooze from the spots and then dry into a white residue. Small white spots may appear on the fruit.

Solution: Angular leaf spot is caused by a bacterium that overwinters on seed and in garden debris. It is also spread by splashing water or by working around the vines when they are wet. To control it, start with fresh high-quality seed. Rake and destroy fallen leaves in the fall. Rotate crops (see "Gardening—A Moving Experience," page 30) by planting melons in a different area every 2 to 3 years. Apply a copper fungicide at the first sign of the disease.

PROBLEMS AND SOLUTIONS

FOR MORE INFORMATION ON PROBLEMS IN BOLD TYPE,
SEE LISTINGS, PAGES 142–307.

MIMOSA
ALBIZIA JULIBRISSIN
DECIDUOUS TREE
☀ ZONES: US, MS, LS, CS

The pink "powder puffs" of mimosa flowers appear in early June throughout the South. Fernlike leaves give the tree a lacy, graceful appearance.

PROBLEM: Mimosa webworms *(illustrated above).* Silken webs wrap clusters of leaves together. The caterpillars inside these webs eat the leaves.

Solution: If possible, prune out and destroy webbing and damaged leaves. Thoroughly spray the tree trunk with horticultural oil in early March to suffocate pupating larvae. Rake and destroy leaf debris. Replace mulch under the tree each fall. Spray the tree with *Bacillus thuringiensis kurstaki* (Dipel, Thuricide, Javelin). For serious infestations, spray with carbaryl (Sevin), diazinon, or malathion.

PROBLEM: Wilt. Leaves yellow and droop in early to midsummer. Many drop. Tree branches die over a period of several months.

Solution: There is no control for this soilborne disease that enters through the tree roots. Discovered in the 1930s, it has now spread throughout the South. Remove infected trees. Do not plant new mimosas in the same spot.

MOUNTAIN ASH
SORBUS
DECIDUOUS TREES OR SHRUBS
☀ ZONES: VARY BY SPECIES

Mountain ash bears flat-topped clusters of small white flowers in early summer. Clumps of berries turn orange or red in late summer, often remaining on the tree through most of the winter. Mountain ash tolerates some salt spray.

PROBLEM: Banded ash borers (see Borers, lilac) *(illustrated above).* Numerous holes, accompanied by sawdust, appear in the trunk. Infested branches swell and crack. The tree wilts in hot weather and may die.

Solution: These borers are serious pests of ash, mountain ash, osmanthus, and lilac. Wasplike moths with long, yellow-and-black banded legs lay eggs on the bark. White wormlike larvae with amber-colored heads tunnel beneath the bark where they are protected from insecticides. Spray the tree trunk and branches with lindane or chlorpyrifos (Dursban) in June and again in early September.

PROBLEM: Fireblight. Blossoms and leaves suddenly wilt, turn dark brown or black, and look scorched. Sunken cankers may form on the branches and trunk.

Solution: Although fireblight often ruins flower clusters and may kill a limb or two, it seldom kills the entire tree. To prevent occurrences, spray during full bloom with streptomycin (Agri-Strep) or fixed-copper fungicidal soap (Soap Shield). Prune and destroy dead limbs, cutting back 12 in. behind dead tissue to green wood. Sterilize pruners after each cut with alcohol or a solution of 1 part bleach to 9 parts water. Avoid using high-nitrogen fertilizers.

MOUNTAIN LAUREL

KALMIA LATIFOLIA

EVERGREEN SHRUB

☀ ZONES: US, MS, LS, CS

Mountain laurel is a splendid evergreen shrub that produces beautiful pink, white, or red flowers in late spring. It prefers an acid, moist, well-drained soil and light to moderate shade.

PROBLEM: Leaf spot *(illustrated above).* Tan or brown spots with purplish margins appear on the leaves. The leaves yellow and drop.

Solution: The fungus that causes this leaf spot favors wet foliage, so avoid overhead sprinkling. If possible, pick off and destroy diseased leaves. Spray healthy leaves with chlorothalonil (Daconil) in spring. Spray twice more at 2-week intervals.

OAK

QUERCUS

DECIDUOUS OR EVERGREEN TREES

☀ ZONES: VARY BY SPECIES

From the live oaks along the coast to the huge white oaks of the Appalachian forest, these trees are the kings of the Southern woods. Oaks provide lumber, firewood, and food for wildlife, in addition to welcome shade and sturdy limbs for backyard swings.

PROBLEM: Gypsy moths *(illustrated above).* Large, hairy caterpillars with red and blue spots feed hungrily on leaves. The entire tree may be defoliated.

Solution: Wrap tree trunks with sticky barriers to trap caterpillars. While the caterpillars are small, spray with *Bacillus thuringiensis kurstaki* (Dipel, Thuricide, Javelin). For larger caterpillars and heavy infestations, spray the entire tree with carbaryl (Sevin), phosmet (Imidan), or acephate (Orthene). You may need a tree service to help you.

PROBLEM: Mistletoe. Large tufts of gray-green plants appear in the tree branches. The green masses and white berries are noticeable in winter.

Solution: Mistletoe, a parasitic plant, doesn't kill oaks but can seriously weaken them by robbing them of nutrients and moisture. If the oak is small, prune limbs about 1 ft. below the parasite. To control mistletoe in large oaks, have a professional tree company prune out the parasites or spray the branches with ethephon (Florel, Etherel) when the tree is dormant.

PROBLEM: Oak wilt. Leaves wilt and turn bronze, dull green, yellow, or brown, and then die and drop. The tree may be defoliated. The bark on the trunk may crack, revealing a mat of fungus underneath.

Solution: There is no cure. Remove and destroy infected trees immediately. Do not save the wood for firewood. Do not plant another oak in the same spot. Prune trees only in midwinter or midsummer. Dig a 3-ft.-deep trench between nearby oaks to prevent the disease from spreading by root grafts. Ask a professional tree service about injecting healthy oaks with a systemic fungicide to prevent infection.

PROBLEM: Leaf galls (see Gall-forming insects and mites). Unusual growths form on leaves and stems. Some look like warts, blisters, or felt-covered golf balls.

Solution: Various insects lay eggs on oak leaves and twigs. Their larvae secrete a growth hormone that causes tissue to swell around them. Very little physical damage is done to the tree by galls. If possible, handpick and destroy galls. No other control is necessary.

PROBLEMS AND SOLUTIONS
··
FOR MORE INFORMATION ON PROBLEMS IN BOLD TYPE,
SEE LISTINGS, PAGES 142–307.

PROBLEM: Root damage (see Physical injury). Mature oaks decline and die 1 to 2 years after you move into your newly constructed house.

Solution: Large oaks are sensitive to having their roots cut for water lines, soil piled against their trunks, or their surface roots crushed by heavy vehicles driving over them. To protect a large tree from construction damage, erect a temporary fence around the trunk at the tree's drip line.

OLEANDER, COMMON

NERIUM OLEANDER
EVERGREEN SHRUB

ZONES: LS, CS, TS

Gardeners favor this evergreen shrub for its showy flowers and ease of care. Many selections are available in colors ranging from purest white to cherry red.

PROBLEM: Oleander caterpillars *(illustrated above)*. Several bright orange caterpillars with tufts of black hair feed on the leaves.

Solution: Oleander caterpillars begin as eggs laid by purplish moths that have greenish black wings with white dots. The caterpillars generally feed on leaves in March, July, and December. From November to July, inspect plants weekly for tan eggs on the undersides of leaves. Apply *Bacillus thuringiensis kurstaki* (Dipel, Thuricide, Javelin) as soon as eggs are found, or spray with a systemic pesticide, such as acephate (Orthene) or dimethoate (Cygon).

PROBLEM: Bacterial galls. Warty galls form on the ends of young shoots, distorting the leaves.

Solution: Prune the shoots 4–6 in. below affected areas. Destroy clippings. Disinfect tools in alcohol or a bleach solution after each cut.

ONION

BIENNIAL GROWN AS ANNUAL

ZONES: ALL

Both the bulbs and the leaves of onion plants are edible. The green immature leaves can be used fresh like any type of bunching onion.

PROBLEM: Onion maggots *(illustrated above)*. Small holes appear in onion bulbs. The bulbs may turn mushy. Upon cutting one open, you discover small white maggots inside.

Solution: Onion maggots, the larvae of a small gray fly, are common where onions have been grown in the same location for several years. Practice crop rotation (see page 30). Place floating row covers over onion beds in spring to prevent the flies from laying their eggs. Water beneficial nematodes into the soil. Drench the soil with chlorpyrifos (Dursban) or diazinon prior to planting. Remove and destroy infested plants.

ORCHID TREE

BAUHINIA
EVERGREEN, SEMIEVERGREEN, OR DECIDUOUS TREES OR SHRUBS

ZONE: TS

These flamboyant shrubs and trees feature distinctive, two-lobed leaves and large colorful flowers. They grow in just about any well-drained soil.

PROBLEM: Snow scales (see Scales) *(illustrated above)*. Tiny white specks encrust the leaves and branches. A sticky honeydew, accompanied by a sooty mold, coats the leaves.

Solution: Snow scales suck plant juices and secrete honeydew as a byproduct of their feeding. Sooty mold grows on the honeydew-covered leaves. Heavy infestations can severely damage the tree or even kill it. Spray with horticultural oil as soon as pests appear.

PROBLEMS AND SOLUTIONS

FOR MORE INFORMATION ON PROBLEMS IN BOLD TYPE, SEE LISTINGS, PAGES 142–307.

PROBLEM: Chlorosis (see Iron deficiency). Leaves turn yellow between the veins. If the condition continues, the plant becomes stunted and may slowly die.

Solution: Orchid trees need acid soils with a pH between 5.5 and 6.5. Soils with a higher pH create an iron deficiency in the plant. To correct the problem, amend the soil with garden sulfur and sphagnum peat moss and fertilize the plant with chelated iron.

PALMS

MANY GENERA AND SPECIES

ZONES: VARY BY SPECIES

Palms comprise more than 3,000 kinds that range from ground-hugging shrubs to towering trees. Many folks consider palms to be tropical plants, but several are surprisingly hardy and tolerate brief periods of freezing temperatures.

PROBLEM: Lethal yellows (see note under Aster yellows) *(illustrated opposite page, bottom right)*. Palm fronds yellow and die, beginning at the lower fronds and progressing up the plant. Dead fronds cling to the tree. Flower stalks blacken and do not set fruit. Eventually the tree dies.

Solution: This devastating disease affects many palms, including fishtail palm *(Caryota)*, coconut palm *(Cocos nucifera)*, Chinese fan palm *(Livistona chinensis)*, and Canary Island date palm *(Phoenix canariensis)*. There is no sure-fire chemical control for lethal yellows. Tree companies can inject antibiotics into palms, but this is a temporary and costly solution. It is best to remove diseased palms. Plant disease-resistant kinds of palms such as royal *(Roystonea)*, cabbage *(Sabal palmetto)*, thread *(Washingtonia robusta)*, and queen *(Syagrus romanzoffianum)* palms.

PROBLEM: Frizzle top. Palm fronds become increasingly yellow, then brown. Fronds appear frizzled and then wither and scorch completely. Affected palms usually die if not treated.

Solution: This is a common problem of palms growing in soil deficient in manganese or potassium. A manganese deficiency affects new fronds at the top of the tree first; a potassium deficiency first affects the lower fronds. To cure frizzle top, apply a special palm fertilizer, containing both manganese and potassium, to the soil. Keep soil pH below 7.

PARSLEY
BIENNIAL HERB GROWN
AS ANNUAL
ZONES: ALL

Y ou probably use parsley for cooking and garnishing foods. But the curly-leafed kinds also make excellent deep green edging plants that complement colorful flowers.

PROBLEM: Black swallowtail caterpillars *(illustrated above)*. Yellow and black caterpillars swarm the parsley plants and eat the leaves down to the stems.

Solution: These caterpillars hatch into beautiful butterflies, but just a few can completely defoliate a plant in a matter of days. If they eat too many leaves, manually remove all but one or two. Plant enough parsley so that you'll have what you need and butterflies can flourish.

PROBLEMS AND SOLUTIONS

FOR MORE INFORMATION ON PROBLEMS IN BOLD TYPE,
SEE LISTINGS, PAGES 142–307.

PEA
ANNUAL
ZONES: ALL

P eas are grown for their flowers or seedpods. Pea blossoms are popular and last for more than a week in arrangements.

PROBLEM: Powdery mildew *(illustrated above)*. The leaves, pods, and stems are covered with a white powdery substance. Plants are stunted and eventually die.

Solution: Powdery mildew is common on peas when temperatures are between 68° and 75°F. The soil should be kept moist but not saturated, for maximum growth. Avoid heavy applications of fertilizer, and rotate peas with other plants every growing season. Fixed copper sprays and wettable sulfur offer good control. Be sure to follow label directions. Do not use sulfur on hot days.

PEACH
DECIDUOUS FRUIT TREES
ZONES: VARY BY SELECTION

T he intense burst of flavor enjoyed when biting into a ripe peach convinces many gardeners to plant this traditional Southern fruit. But be warned: Harvesting good peaches from your own tree requires scrupulous care. Be sure you understand the demands of growing peaches before you plant that tree.

PROBLEM: Borers *(illustrated above)*. An amber-colored gum appears near holes on the bark. The bark looks rough, swollen, and crusty. The tree slowly declines.

Solution: Clearwing moths lay eggs at a limb crotch close to the ground or in a trunk wound. Their hatched larvae bore underneath the bark, where they tunnel and feed. Avoid injury to the lower tree trunk. One wound from a lawnmower or string trimmer provides easy access for borer larvae. Spread a layer of mulch around the trunk at least 3 ft. in diameter to prevent weeds where these pests overwinter. If you can, kill single wormlike larva by sticking a wire up the hole. Or spray the trunk and branches with lindane, endosulfan (Thiodan), or chlorpyrifos (Dursban) in April, early July, and late August. Remove and destroy severely infested trees.

PROBLEM: Peach leaf curl. Leaves are puckered and curled as they unfold in spring. Bulging areas on leaves turn to yellow, and then red. A white fungus forms on these leaves, which fall prematurely. Fruit yield is poor.

Solution: Cool, wet weather during leaf emergence favors the fungus that causes this disease. Remove and destroy infected leaves. Do not compost them. Spray the tree just before leaf out in spring with lime sulfur, dormant oil, chlorothalonil (Daconil), or fixed-copper fungicidal soap (Soap Shield). Spray again in fall just after leaf drop.

PROBLEM: Gummosis. Sunken cankers oozing amber sap form on the trunk and branches. Limbs may die back.

Solution: Gummosis is a disease caused by fungi or bacteria that enter the tree through wounds in the bark. Remove affected branches and dead wood while the tree is dormant. Disinfect tools after each cut by dipping them in alcohol or a solution of 1 part bleach to 9 parts water. Stressed trees are more susceptible to gummosis, so keep them healthy with proper watering and fertilizing. Spraying the tree with a copper fungicide in fall offers some control of this disease.

PROBLEM: Peach scab. Small, circular, greenish to black spots develop on the skin of fruits. The fruits may crack and rot. Small brown spots or holes form in the leaves. Twigs die.

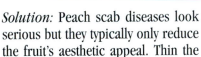

Solution: Peach scab diseases look serious but they typically only reduce the fruit's aesthetic appeal. Thin the tree's canopy to permit penetration of sunlight and air, which helps leaves and fruits dry quickly. Avoid overhead watering. Prune out and destroy infected twigs in late winter. Spray the tree with wettable sulfur, captan, or chlorothalonil (Daconil) just after flower petals drop in spring. Repeat at 10-day intervals until 3 weeks before harvest.

PROBLEM: Brown rot. A brown, firm rot slowly covers the entire fruit. A gray mat of fungal spores blankets the rotted tissue in wet weather. The infected fruit either drops prematurely or dries and remains on the tree.

Solution: Brown rot is the most serious disease of peaches. The responsible fungus also infects the blossoms, stems, and the adjoining twig, causing a canker that kills the twig above it. To prevent brown rot, spray the tree with captan or chlorothalonil (Daconil) every 10 days. Prune infected, blighted twigs. Remove and destroy all dried, infected fruit both on the tree and on the ground.

PROBLEMS AND SOLUTIONS

FOR MORE INFORMATION ON PROBLEMS IN BOLD TYPE, SEE LISTINGS, PAGES 142–307.

PROBLEM: White peach scales (see Scales). Small white specks encrust the branches and trunk. The tree dies back.

Solution: This insect sucks sap from the tree and may eventually kill it. It also attacks cherry and plum trees. To control it, spray branches with horticultural oil. Repeat as necessary.

PEAR

DECIDUOUS FRUIT TREES

ZONES: VARY BY SELECTION

Better keep a napkin handy when you bite into a ripe pear, because the juice will run down your chin. Most pears require cross-pollination between two different selections to produce fruit, although some, like 'Pineapple' and 'Warren', are self-pollinating.

PROBLEM: Fireblight *(illustrated above)*. Young twigs and branches die back from the tips. The leaves appear burned, and the branch tip may curl, resembling a shepherd's crook. Dead leaves and fruit remain on the branches. Cankers may form on branches.

Solution: Infection occurs in early spring during flowering and is favored by wet conditions. Prune and destroy dead limbs, cutting back 12 in. behind diseased tissue to green wood. Sterilize pruners after each cut with alcohol or a bleach solution (1 part bleach to 9 parts water). To reduce occurrences, spray during full bloom with streptomycin (Agri-Strep) or fixed-copper fungicidal soap (Soap Shield). Repeat three times at weekly intervals. Plant fireblight-resistant selections (see note under "Fireblight," page 227).

PECAN

CARYA ILLINOENSIS

DECIDUOUS TREE

ZONES: US, MS (HARDY SELECTIONS); LS, CS

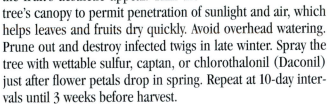

Beloved by Southerners for their tasty nuts, pecan trees are also picturesque and excellent shade trees. But don't plant them near houses in hurricane-prone areas, as they're prone to toppling in high winds.

PROBLEM: Pecan weevils (see Weevils) *(illustrated above)*. Nuts develop small holes and drop prematurely. When you crack them open, you find small, creamy white grubs eating the kernels.

Solution: Weevils are long-snouted beetles. In Florida, adult weevils emerge from the soil in July. Farther north they emerge in late August to September. Weevils feeding on nuts before the shells harden disturbs development of the nuts and causes them to drop. Adults then lay eggs in the nuts. To control weevils, rake up and destroy leaves, fallen nuts, and limbs. Monitor the number of pecan weevils with a Tedders pyramidal trap, which attracts and collects the pests. (Contact your local Cooperative Extension Office for more information.) At the first sign of adult weevils, spray the tree with carbaryl (Sevin). Follow label directions carefully. Spray twice more at 10-day intervals.

PROBLEM: Zinc deficiency. Strange spiraled clusters of leaves form on the ends of branches. Branches die back and the nuts do not fill out.

Solution: Many soils in the South lack sufficient zinc for growing pecans. To correct this deficiency, evenly sprinkle 2–4 oz. of zinc oxide in a 3-ft.-diameter circle around the tree yearly for 2 years. Each year after that, spread 1 lb. of zinc oxide in an 8-ft.-diameter circle beneath the tree. Or spread a special pecan fertilizer containing zinc around the tree according to label directions.

PROBLEM: **Pecan scab.** Small, dark brown patches appear on nuts. Affected nuts turn black and drop prematurely. Olive brown or black spots appear on leaves, which also fall.

Solution: Plant scab-resistant pecan selections such as 'Curtis', 'Houma', 'Kiowa', 'Mohawk', and 'Owens'. Avoid planting susceptible selections such as 'Schley'. Commercial tree-spraying firms can apply preventative fungicides, but this will not control scab on already infected pecans.

PEONY

PAEONIA

PERENNIALS AND DECIDUOUS SHRUBS

ZONES: VARY BY TYPE

With their huge flowers ranging from white to deepest magenta and various shades of pink, peonies are the pride of many a perennial border. Peonies require full sun, fertile soil, good drainage, and some winter chill. Gardeners prize them for their cut flowers, which can last up to 2 weeks in arrangements.

PROBLEM: **Botrytis (gray mold)** *(illustrated bottom left).* Young flower buds blacken and die. Partially opened flowers turn soft, brown, and fuzzy. New shoots wilt, blacken, and die. A fuzzy gray or brown fungus grows on dead tissue.

Solution: Botrytis gray mold occurs during cool, wet springs. Good garden sanitation can prevent it: Remove dead or spent flowers and dead or dying leaves promptly, disposing of all plant debris. Allow enough space between plants for good air circulation. Avoid wetting flowers and foliage. Water early in the day so that leaves and flowers dry thoroughly before evening. Cut and remove old growth in fall. Do not plant peonies in basins that collect water. Don't heap soil around the base of plants. Spraying plants with mancozeb offers good control.

PROBLEM: Phytophthora blight. New growth wilts, turns black, and dies. Older stems turn brown and shrivel. Roots rot and the plant pulls up easily.

Solution: Cool, wet conditions in spring favor the development of phytophthora blight on peonies. The fungus, *Phytophthora,* which is common in most soils, initially attacks either the roots or the developing shoots at the soil level, causing a blackening and decay of stem tissue. These black and often sunken areas are usually several inches long. Flowers, buds, and leaves may turn a dark brown or black color. The disease is most serious in soils that are poorly drained and is spread by splashing rain or contaminated tools, soil, or plant materials. To prevent phytophthora blight, plant peonies in well-drained soil, and thin crowded plantings. If disease symptoms appear, destroy infected plant parts. Peony plants with rotted roots need to be removed together with the adjacent soil. Fungicides may help to control the disease in situations where the roots are not rotted. Spray the foliage, bases of shoots, and nearby soil with mancozeb at 7- to 10-day intervals during rainy periods.

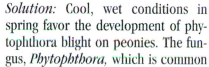

PROBLEMS AND SOLUTIONS
....
FOR MORE INFORMATION ON PROBLEMS IN BOLD TYPE,
SEE LISTINGS, PAGES 142–307.

PROBLEM: **No blooms (see Flowers, lack of).** Despite healthy-looking foliage, the plants are not blooming.

Solution: Because peonies prefer sun, lack of sun is the most common cause of no blooms. Other causes include overly dry soil, overcrowded plantings, a late spring freeze that kills flower buds, and lack of fertilization. Another reason for lack of flowers is planting too deep. Individual eyes (the reddish buds on the roots) should be no more than 1 in. below the soil line. Also, immature plants won't bloom right away, so water and fertilize them properly and be patient.

PEPPER

TENDER PERENNIALS GROWN
AS ANNUALS

ZONES: ALL

Peppers belong to the nightshade family of *Solanaceae,* which also includes potato, tomato, and eggplant. Edible peppers come in a rainbow of colors—orange, purple, red, green, and yellow. Ornamental peppers make excellent bedding plants.

PROBLEM: Blossom-end rot *(illustrated above).* A brown, sunken area near the blossom end of the fruit darkens and enlarges in a widening circle. The area then shrinks, dries, and becomes leathery.

Solution: Blossom-end rot often occurs when plants and fruit are growing rapidly and are then subjected to drought. Alternating between excessively dry and excessively wet conditions generally worsens the problem. Plants set out too early in spring or those planted closely together are more susceptible. To prevent the problem, maintain uniform soil moisture and mulch around plants. Do not cultivate soil next to the plants, as this may damage feeder roots and cause blossom-end rot on developing fruit. Avoid using high-nitrogen fertilizers.

PROBLEM: Sunscald. Many of the peppers appear sunburned. There are spots on the skin that are wrinkled, white, and papery. Black mold grows on the affected areas.

Solution: Fruit exposed to direct, hot sun may be scalded. This usually happens when so many fruits form that the plant falls over. Staking plants prior to fruit set prevents sunscald by allowing the leaves to shade the fruit. Peppers may also get sunscald when a fungus causes the plant to drop most of its leaves. Spraying plants with captan, maneb, mancozeb, or copper fungicides controls most leaf diseases.

PROBLEM: Anthracnose. Black or dark brown spots containing concentric rings form on the fruit.

Solution: The fungus that causes this malady usually appears in warm, wet springs, and spreads by splashing water. To control it, avoid overhead watering. Promptly remove and destroy diseased fruit. Clean up and destroy pepper plants at the end of the growing season. Rotate crops. Only use certified disease-free seed, as the fungus overwinters on seed from infected plants. Spray pepper plants with a fungicide, such as captan or mancozeb at the first sign of the disease.

PROBLEM: Blossom drop. The blossoms of the pepper plant drop off instead of setting fruit.

Solution: Blooms often drop due to adverse weather conditions, such as drought or temperatures below 55°F or higher than 90°F. The condition typically improves once the weather does. Spraying the flowers with a blossom-set product or a solution of 1 tsp. of Epsom salts dissolved in a quart of water may improve fruit set.

PERIWINKLE

VINCA

PERENNIALS

ZONES: VARY BY SPECIES

Periwinkles are excellent evergreen ground covers for shade. They spread quickly and feature showy spring flowers in colors of blue, purple, or white.

PROBLEM: Root and stem rot *(illustrated above).* Leaves and stems wilt and die. Roots rot and plants pull up easily.

Solution: Root and stem rot usually results from planting in wet, poorly drained soil. The soilborne fungus that causes it enters through the roots. Once the disease appears, it is difficult to control. Pull up and destroy infected plants. Improve soil drainage. Avoid overhead watering, and allow the soil to dry between waterings.

PROBLEMS AND SOLUTIONS

FOR MORE INFORMATION ON PROBLEMS IN BOLD TYPE,
SEE LISTINGS, PAGES 142–307.

PROBLEM: Dieback. Brown spots with black specks in the middle appear on leaves and stems. Plants turn yellow or orange. Clumps pull out easily and are blackened at the base. The entire planting may die.

Solution: High temperatures and wet soil combined with low soil fertility predispose vinca to dieback fungus. Remove and destroy diseased plants. Improve soil fertility and drainage. Avoid overhead watering. Spray plants with maneb according to label directions.

PETUNIA

PETUNIA HYBRIDA

TENDER PERENNIAL GROWN
AS ANNUAL

ZONES: ALL

Popular as bedding plants, petunias are also great for containers and window boxes. They come in a dazzling assortment of just about every color you can think of. Easy to grow, petunias need occasional fertilizing. Cutting them back can keep them blooming.

PROBLEM: Slugs and snails *(illustrated opposite page, bottom right).* The leaves and flowers are chewed, but no pests are present.

Solution: Slugs and snails invade your garden at night. Trap them by laying a small board atop a few stones near the plants to provide an inviting daytime hiding place for the pests. At midday, lift the board and scrape the pests into a pail of soapy water. Snail and slug baits containing metaldehyde also control these pests. Be sure to follow label directions carefully.

PHLOX
PHLOX
PERENNIALS AND ANNUALS

✀ ZONES: VARY BY SPECIES

Phlox are wonderful, colorful additions to any garden. The tall types work best in the background of perennial borders, while shorter types make good ground covers or rock garden and edging plants. Remove old flower stalks to extend period of bloom.

PROBLEM: Powdery mildew *(illustrated above).* White powdery patches or spots form on the leaves. The leaves become distorted, turn yellow, curl, and fall.

Solution: At the first sign of powdery mildew, spray thoroughly with a fungicide containing triforine (Funginex) or thiophanate-methyl (Thiomyl). In the fall, rake and destroy fallen leaves and other plant debris. Perennial phlox *(Phlox paniculata)* is especially susceptible to powdery mildew. Consider planting mildew-resistant selections (see note under "Powdery mildew," page 242).

PHOTINIA, FRASER (REDTIP)
PHOTINIA FRASERI
EVERGREEN SHRUB
OR SMALL TREE

✀ ZONES: US (PROTECTED),
MS, LS, CS

The popularity of Fraser photinia just goes to show that nothing succeeds like being obvious. A chance seedling discovered around 1940 at Fraser Nursery in Birmingham, Alabama, Fraser photinia (or redtip, as it is also known) displayed new leaves of bright red rather than the usual green. People flocked to buy it. Today, more homes probably have Fraser photinias than VCRs or indoor plumbing.

PROBLEMS AND SOLUTIONS

FOR MORE INFORMATION ON PROBLEMS IN BOLD TYPE,
SEE LISTINGS, PAGES 142–307.

PROBLEM: Leaf spot *(illustrated bottom left).* Small spots appear on young leaves. As the spots age, the centers turn grayish with a dark purple border. Severely infected leaves drop prematurely.

Solution: The fungus that causes this leaf spot only attacks new, red growth. Mature green leaves are immune. Splashing water and wind spread the disease from leaf to leaf. To prevent it, remove and destroy infected leaves. Do not wet leaves when watering. Avoid summer pruning, which results in a flush of susceptible new leaves. Spray the plant with chlorothalonil (Daconil) every 10 to 14 days from bud break in spring until all new foliage has matured.

PINE
PINUS
EVERGREEN TREES

✀ ZONES: VARY BY SPECIES

Pines are an integral part of the South's landscape. Many species exist, providing food and shelter for wildlife, lumber for homes, ground bark for mulch, and shade for gardens. The whisper of wind through pine needles at night has lulled many a child to sleep.

PROBLEM: Bark borers (see Bark beetles) *(illustrated above).* Pines lose their green color from the top down as needles turn yellow, red, and then brown. Sap bleeds from holes in the bark. Eventually, the tree dies.

Solution: Several species of bark beetles bore through bark and lay eggs underneath. Larvae make serpentine tunnels beneath the bark, eventually severing all of the tubes that transport moisture and nutrients to the top of the tree. Those small holes in the trunk of the tree are exit holes made by mature beetles. Because beetles are attracted to the scent of freshly cut pine trees, schedule pruning in winter. Give trees plenty of water in summer to help them drown invaders with sap. Promptly remove dead or dying pines, as they attract more beetles. Spray the trunks of healthy trees according to label directions with lindane, endosulfan (Thiodan), or carbaryl (Sevin) to control beetles.

PROBLEM: Pine sawflies. Needles on branch tips seem to disappear overnight. Gobs of caterpillarlike larvae with red or black heads can be found on needles.

Solution: These pests are the progeny of nonstinging wasps. The female wasp inserts her eggs into needles and twigs. Spray foliage with acephate (Orthene) or phosmet (Imidan) when sawfly larvae appear.

PROBLEM: Pine tip moths. Needles near branch tips turn yellow or reddish orange. New shoots or "candles" may be hollowed out and turn brown. Dry white resin appears near the base of the needles. Branches look deformed, and die back.

Solution: The damage is caused by moth larvae that tunnel into the branch tip. Treat minor infestations by pruning out and destroying affected branch tips. For major infestations, spray pines with chlorpyrifos (Dursban), carbaryl (Sevin), phosmet (Imidan), or acephate (Orthene) in April, June, and early August.

PROBLEM: Spittlebugs. Gobs of white froth appear on needles near the ends of branches. The needles may yellow and drop.

Solution: Spittlebugs suck sap from pine twigs, and they excrete a sticky liquid. The insects whip the liquid into a white froth, which hides them from predators. The damage is usually only cosmetic. If practical, blast the spittlebug from the branch with a strong jet of water. Severe infestations require spraying the tree with insecticide, but a professional tree service can do this best.

PROBLEM: Diplodia tip blight. The new growth on Austrian, Scotch, or Virginia pine turns yellow, then brown, and dies. Lower branches die first; then the disease steadily advances upward. Dead needles remain attached. Resin oozes from cankers on branches. Eventually the tree dies.

Solution: Don't plant susceptible pines, especially Austrian pine, in areas where tip blight is widespread. Keep pines vigorous with proper watering and fertilizing. Prune infected branch tips back to sound wood during dry weather and destroy diseased wood. Apply protective fungicides, such as thiophanate-methyl (Thiomyl) or chlorothalonil (Daconil), to the tree before bud break. Spray again a week later and then once more in another 2 weeks. Rake up and destroy cones and dead branches beneath the tree.

PROBLEM: Fusiform rust. Swollen stems and spindle-shaped galls appear on the branches and trunk of loblolly and slash pines. In spring, a yellow powder exudes from the swollen area. Large cankers form on older trees. Young trees with infected trunks usually die.

Solution: This rust requires a red oak as an alternate host, and is most common in the Southeast. Prune out and destroy infected branches. Remove and destroy young trees with trunk cankers. Spray healthy trees with triadimefon (Bayleton) in spring just after new growth appears. Spray again 2 weeks later. If fusiform rust is a problem in your area, don't plant loblolly or slash pines.

PINK
DIANTHUS

PERENNIALS, BIENNIALS, AND ANNUALS

ZONES: US, MS, LS

Pinks burst with cheery flowers throughout spring and summer in colors of white, pink, magenta, and red. Flowers often have a spicy, clovelike fragrance. Hardy and easy to grow, pinks prefer a neutral or slightly alkaline soil.

PROBLEM: Alternaria leaf spot *(illustrated above)*. Small yellow spots appear on the leaves. The spots grow and brown, eventually killing large portions of the leaf.

Solution: Stressed plants are most susceptible. Symptoms first appear on leaves nearest the center of the plant. Pick off infected leaves; clean up and destroy fallen leaves. Avoid overhead watering. Maintain good growing conditions by giving plants uniform moisture, plenty of sun, and fertile, well-drained soil. Spray with fixed-copper fungicidal soap (Soap Shield), captan, or chlorothalonil (Daconil) according to label directions.

PROBLEM: Rust. Chocolate brown pustules appear on stems, flower buds, and leaf surfaces. Infected leaves curl and may drop. Plant growth is stunted.

Solution: Cool, wet weather favors development of this fungal disease. Pick off and destroy infected leaves. Avoid wetting foliage. Spray healthy foliage with triforine (Funginex) every 10 days until daytime temperatures are above 90°F.

OTHER COMMON PROBLEMS: **Fusarium wilt, rhizoctonia root and stem rot, virus**

PLUM
DECIDUOUS FRUIT TREES

ZONES: VARY BY SELECTION

Plums are a favorite summer treat for eating fresh right from the tree or for cooking or canning. Plums need well-drained soil. In general, Japanese types perform better in the South than European types.

PROBLEM: Curculios (*illustrated above*). Holes appear in the green fruit. The fruit is deformed and drops prematurely.

Solution: Adult curculios (a type of weevil) lay eggs inside the plums where the hatched larvae feed, leaving brown, rotted interiors. To control curculios, spray trees with rotenone, pyrethrin, malathion, or carbaryl (Sevin). The best time to spray is immediately after petal drop. Do not use malathion within 7 days of harvest.

PROBLEM: Black knot. Dark brown to black, hard swellings form on twigs and branches. In spring, these knots are covered with a dark olive green, feltlike fungus that dries to a black crust as the summer progresses. The growths eventually girdle and kill branches.

Solution: Prune and destroy knots in fall and winter, cutting 3 in. below growths. If knots appear on the trunk, remove them and the surrounding 1 in. of healthy-looking bark. Spray with lime sulfur in winter and with captan in spring just before the buds open.

POTATO
TUBEROUS-ROOTED PERENNIAL
TREATED AS ANNUAL

ZONES: ALL

The potato, like peppers, tomato, and eggplant, belongs to the nightshade family (*Solanaceae*). Potatoes are the fourth largest world crop, surpassed only by wheat, rice, and corn. In the South, plant heat-tolerant selections, such as 'Anoka', 'Caribe', 'Red Pontiac', and 'Yukon Gold'.

PROBLEM: Colorado potato beetles (*illustrated above*). Black-and-yellow striped beetles and larvae voraciously devour the foliage. Entire plants may be defoliated.

Solution: If numbers are small, handpick beetles and grubs and drop them in a bucket of soapy water. Pick off and destroy leaves that have bright yellow egg clusters attached to the undersides. Dust plants with *Bacillus thuringiensis* (*Bt*) San Diego to control grubs in the early stages. To control an infestation, spray or dust plants with pyrethrin, rotenone, azadirachtin (Neem), diazinon, or carbaryl (Sevin). Alternate chemicals to keep beetles from becoming resistant.

PROBLEM: Potato scab. Roughened, corky scabs form on the potato skin.

Solution: The bacterium that causes potato scab enters through pores in stems, through wounds in the potato skin, and through the skin of young, expanding tubers. Keep the soil pH between 5.0 and 5.5 to suppress scab. (You can apply sulfur to the soil to lower the pH and make it more acidic.) Rotate crops, planting potatoes in the same spot only once each 3 years. Plant scab-resistant selections, such as 'Anoka', 'Bison', 'Burbank Russet', 'Cherokee', and 'Sierra'.

PROBLEM: Bacterial soft rot. Potatoes become soft, watery, and slightly granular, and emit a foul odor.

Solution: Bacterial soft rot is common where seed potatoes have been bruised or wounded or when soil temperatures are high. There is no chemical control. Plant only certified disease-free seed potatoes. Thoroughly clean all equipment used for cutting seed tubers in a solution of 1 part bleach to 9 parts water. During the growing period do not apply excessive amounts of nitrogen fertilizer. Harvest tubers only after vines are completely dead. Avoid wounding tubers. Never wash them prior to storage.

PRIVET
LIGUSTRUM

DECIDUOUS, SEMIEVERGREEN, OR
EVERGREEN SHRUBS OR SMALL TREES

ZONES: VARY BY SPECIES

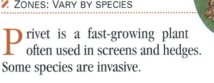

Privet is a fast-growing plant often used in screens and hedges. Some species are invasive.

PROBLEM: Scales (*illustrated above*). White, yellowish, gray, reddish, or brown bumps encrust stems and undersides of leaves. Leaves yellow, brown, and then drop. Stems die back.

PROBLEMS AND SOLUTIONS

FOR MORE INFORMATION ON PROBLEMS IN BOLD TYPE,
SEE LISTINGS, PAGES 142–307.

Solution: These bumps are scales—sap-sucking insects that weaken the plant. Spray with horticultural oil, making sure to coat all leaf and stem surfaces. Or apply a systemic insecticide, such as acephate (Orthene).

PROBLEMS AND SOLUTIONS
....
FOR MORE INFORMATION ON PROBLEMS IN BOLD TYPE,
SEE LISTINGS, PAGES 142–307.

PROBLEM: Leaf spot. Irregularly shaped tan spots surrounded by a dark brown border appear on leaf margins and at the tip. The spots become sunken with age.

Solution: Caused by a fungus, leaf spot is unattractive but not life-threatening to the plant. Selectively prune (thin) dense hedges to improve air circulation through the plants. Avoid overhead sprinkling. Water plants early in the day to allow them to dry completely before evening. If practical, pick off and destroy spotted leaves. On plants previously affected, spray new healthy leaves in spring with a Bordeaux mixture, chlorothalonil (Daconil), or maneb.

QUINCE, FLOWERING

CHAENOMELES

DECIDUOUS SHRUBS

ZONES: US, MS, LS, CS

With its lovely orange, carmine, pink, or white blooms, flowering quince is a handsome landscaping shrub often used in hedges and shrub borders.

PROBLEM: Rust (see also Cedar-apple rust) *(illustrated above).* Yellow or orange spots appear on leaves which turn yellow and fall prematurely. Shrubs may completely defoliate by late summer.

Solution: During wet, warm weather in spring, the wind carries fungus spores from infected red cedars to quinces. In late summer, small tubelike structures develop on the undersides of quince leaves. Spores released from these structures blow back to susceptible cedars, completing the disease cycle. To prevent rust, spray quince trees according to label directions with chlorothalonil (Daconil), fixed-copper fungicidal soap (Soap Shield), mancozeb, or myclobutanil (Immunox) in spring when flower buds show color. Repeat twice more at 10-day intervals.

PROBLEM: Fireblight. Leaves look burned, and entire limbs die back. Sunken cankers form on branches.

Solution: Prune and destroy dead limbs, cutting back 12 in. behind dead tissue to green wood. Sterilize pruners after each cut with alcohol or a bleach solution (1 part bleach to 9 parts

water). Avoid high-nitrogen fertilizers. Spray during full bloom with streptomycin (Agri-Strep) or fixed-copper fungicidal soap (Soap Shield).

RASPBERRY

DECIDUOUS SHRUBS WITH BIENNIAL STEMS

ZONES: VARY BY SELECTION

Raspberry canes are biennial—they grow for a year, produce fruit the second year, then die. New canes then sprout to replace them. Most raspberries perform better in the Upper and Middle South, although some selections do well in the Lower and Coastal South.

PROBLEM: Anthracnose *(illustrated above).* Spots with grayish centers and reddish brown borders appear on canes and leaves.

Solution: Remove and destroy diseased stems and leaves. Avoid overhead sprinkling. Provide adequate air circulation around plants. Rake and remove fallen leaves. As new growth emerges and expands in spring, spray with lime sulfur or captan according to label directions. After harvest, remove and destroy canes that fruited.

PROBLEM: Cane blight. Canes suddenly wilt, crack, and die. Stems develop brownish purple patches from top to bottom as the disease progresses. Black raspberries are the most commonly affected.

Solution: There is no chemical control for cane blight, which invades through wounds on canes and weakens their ability to fruit properly. It can attack black raspberry at points where canes have been snapped off or pruned to force lateral growth. Remove and destroy infected canes. Prune black raspberry canes (to force lateral growth) near the ground, in dry weather, so that cuts heal properly.

REDBUD, EASTERN

CERCIS CANADENSIS

DECIDUOUS SHRUB OR TREE

ZONES: US, MS, LS, CS

Gardeners treasure redbud—a true harbinger of spring—for its showy, purple, pink, or white flowers that appear before the plant leafs out.

PROBLEM: Canker *(illustrated opposite page, bottom right)*. This widespread disease attacks wounded or stressed trees. It causes sunken cankers on the trunk and branches. If a canker encircles a branch or trunk, it kills it.

Solution: Prune branches at least 12 in. below infection. Sterilize pruners after each cut by dipping them in alcohol or a solution of 1 part bleach to 9 parts water. Avoid wounding healthy branches or the trunk. Keep trees healthy through proper watering and fertilizing.

RHODODENDRON

RHODODENDRON

EVERGREEN OR DECIDUOUS SHRUBS

ZONES: US, MS, LS

The genus *Rhododendron* includes both big-leafed rhododendrons and azaleas. Both groups require moist, well-drained, acid soil. Shield them from hot afternoon sun.

PROBLEM: **Rhododendron dieback** *(illustrated above)*. Olive-colored blotches appear on the leaves, and buds turn brown. Leaves roll up and droop. Cankers form on twigs, and twigs die back.

Solution: There is no control for this fungal disease once branches wilt. Prune out and destroy infected branches and twigs. Where cankers are present, cut 2 in. below them to healthy tissue. Examine the center of the branch you leave on the plant. If it is brown or discolored, cut back farther to healthy-looking tissue. Disinfect pruners with alcohol or a bleach solution (1 part bleach to 9 parts water) after each cut. Make sure plants are in loose, fast-draining soil that contains plenty of organic matter. Plant so that the rootball is ½ in. above the soil line. Where dieback is a continual problem and during warm, wet weather that favors the disease, spray new leaves as they emerge with chlorothalonil (Daconil) or mancozeb.

PROBLEM: Root rot (poor drainage). The plant turns yellow. Edges of leaves may dry out. The soil around the plant is heavy and moist.

Solution: Rhododendrons have fine, fibrous root systems. In heavy, wet soil, they suffocate and die. Improve soil drainage by amending it with lots of coarse sand, ground bark, sphagnum peat moss, or expanded slate (PermaTill). Plant each shrub so that the top ½ in. of the rootball protrudes above the soil surface, then cover it with mulch.

PROBLEM: **Borers.** The leaves at the end of a branch wilt and yellow. Small holes and fine sawdust appear on branches and in the crotches of limbs.

Solution: Female clearwing moths lay their eggs in bark cracks and limb crotches in May. The hatched larvae tunnel into the branches, where they feed on the plant and cause the damage you see. Keep plants adequately watered and fertilized. Plant them in well-drained, acid soil that contains lots of organic material. Avoid wounding plants, and minimize pruning. In late spring, spray trunks and branches with lindane or chlorpyrifos (Dursban), carefully following label directions. Spray three times more at 7- to 10-day intervals.

PROBLEM: **Black vine weevils (see Weevils).** Numerous notches appear in the leaf edges. Leaves look ragged.

Solution: Adult weevils spend the day in the soil beneath the shrub. At dusk they emerge and begin feeding on the leaves. This explains why you may see lots of leaf damage during the day without spotting the culprit. Also, weevil grubs feed on plant roots. Spray plants in the evening with rotenone, pyrethrin, or a systemic insecticide such as acephate (Orthene). Treat the soil beneath the plants with diazinon or imidacloprid (Merit, GrubEx) to kill grubs.

ROSE

ROSA

DECIDUOUS OR EVERGREEN SHRUBS

ZONES: ALL

Roses are the world's most popular flowers despite having a reputation of being difficult to grow and maintain. However, many varieties and selections require little care (see "Trouble-Free Roses," page 48) and resist diseases that commonly plague more susceptible roses.

PROBLEM: **Black spot** *(illustrated above)*. Black spots with yellowish halos appear on the leaves. Affected leaves turn yellow and drop.

PROBLEMS AND SOLUTIONS
....
FOR MORE INFORMATION ON PROBLEMS IN BOLD TYPE,
SEE LISTINGS, PAGES 142–307.

Solution: Black spot, the number one rose disease, begins in the fall. Remove and destroy all diseased and fallen leaves. Make sure plants have good air circulation. Spray dormant plants with lime sulfur. Replace mulch every spring. Spray susceptible roses with triforine (Funginex), myclobutanil (Immunox), azadirachtin (Neem), or chlorothalonil (Daconil) weekly from bud break to the first hard frost. Avoid wetting foliage when watering. Plant disease-resistant selections, such as 'Bonica', 'Carefree Beauty', 'Dr. W. van Fleet', 'Flower Carpet', and 'Mrs. B. R. Cant'.

PROBLEM: Powdery mildew. A white powdery coating covers the buds, leaves, and stems. Young leaves are distorted and curled and eventually yellow, then drop. Powder-coated flower buds do not open.

Solution: Avoid wetting foliage when watering. Spray plant thoroughly with a fungicide, such as triforine (Funginex) or azadirachtin (Neem). In the fall, rake up and destroy fallen leaves and other plant debris. Consider planting disease-resistant selections (see page 48).

PROBLEM: Rust. Brownish-orange spots form on the undersides of leaves. Small yellow or brown spots appear on the upper leaf surfaces.

Solution: Plant roses where they have plenty of sun and good air circulation. Avoid wetting foliage when watering. Remove and destroy affected leaves and canes. Rake up and destroy diseased leaves in fall. Apply lime sulfur to dormant plants. Spray new healthy leaves with chlorothalonil (Daconil) or mancozeb, covering both upper and lower leaf surfaces. Consider planting rust-resistant selections, such as 'Cecile Brunner', 'Europeana', 'Fragrant Cloud', 'Garden Party', 'Iceberg', 'Miss All-American Beauty', 'Sexy Rexy', 'Souvenir de la Malmaison', or 'Tropicana'.

PROBLEM: Japanese beetles. Metallic green beetles with copper-colored wings devour the leaves, except the main veins, and flowers.

Solution: Japanese beetles are voracious feeders. Handpick them if numbers are small. Hold a cup of soapy water beneath the leaves. A light tap of the leaf startles the beetles, causing them to drop into the cup. This is most successful early in the morning before beetles become active. For severe infestations, spray plants with rotenone, pyrethrin, azadirachtin (Neem), or carbaryl (Sevin) according to label directions.

PROBLEM: Aphids. Tiny, pear-shaped insects cluster on new leaves, stems, and buds. Leaves and buds are distorted. Also, quite a few ants are around and on the plant.

Solution: Aphids are common pests on new growth. They suck juices from the plant and produce a sticky honeydew that attracts ants. Blasting aphids off the plant with a jet of water generally reduces their numbers. To control heavy infestations, spray with insecticidal soap, horticultural oil, or acephate (Orthene). Do this early in the day so foliage dries by evening.

PROBLEM: Virus. Yellow or brown streaks, rings, or blotches appear on the leaves. The plant may be stunted.

Solution: Rose viruses usually enter the plant during budding or grafting at the nursery. There is no chemical control for infected plants. Buy only certified disease-free plants that show no symptoms. Infected plants may live and bloom for years. Remove and destroy severely stunted plants.

ROSEMARY

ROSMARINUS OFFICINALIS

EVERGREEN SHRUB OR HERB

⚡ ZONES: MS (PROTECTED), LS, CS

Rosemary is a woody shrub grown for its aromatic needle-like foliage. Its small flowers may be white or blue, depending on the selection. Give it full sun and well-drained, fairly dry soil.

PROBLEM: Spittlebugs *(illustrated above).* Gobs of foamy froth appear on stems.

Solution: Spittlebug nymphs produce the froth to hide themselves from predators while they suck plant sap. Blast the pests off the plants with a jet of water or spray them with insecticidal soap.

PROBLEMS AND SOLUTIONS

FOR MORE INFORMATION ON PROBLEMS IN BOLD TYPE, SEE LISTINGS, PAGES 142–307.

SAGE

SALVIA

ANNUALS, BIENNIALS, PERENNIALS, SHRUBS

ZONES: VARY BY SPECIES

Sages have a lot to offer—aromatic foliage; showy, colorful flowers; and a wide range of sizes and textures.

PROBLEM: Slugs and snails (*illustrated above*). Irregularly shaped holes with smooth edges appear in the leaves. Silvery trails of slime may also be present on plants and on nearby soil. Damage occurs at night.

Solution: Trap slugs and snails by laying a small board on top of a few stones near the plants to provide a hiding place for these pests during the day. At midday, lift the board and scrape the pests into a pail of soapy water. Snail and slug baits containing metaldehyde also control these pests. Be sure to follow label directions carefully.

SAGO PALM

CYCAS REVOLUTA

CYCAD

ZONES: CS (PROTECTED), TS

Although the sago palm closely resembles a palm, it's actually a cycad—an ancient cone-bearing relative of conifers. Sago palms make handsome foundation or container plants.

PROBLEM: Scales (*illustrated above*). The leaves become mottled yellow. White or brown bumps encrust the leaves. A sticky honeydew may be present.

Solution: Scales attach themselves to stems and leaves and suck sap from plants. They often secrete a sticky honeydew, on which sooty mold grows. To control them, spray according to label directions with horticultural oil or a systemic insecticide, such as dimethoate (Cygon) or acephate (Orthene). Discard heavily infested plants.

PROBLEM: Frizzle top. Old and new foliage turn yellow. New growth emerges looking frizzled.

Solution: A manganese deficiency in the soil causes frizzle top. Apply manganese sulfate or a palm fertilizer containing manganese to the soil according to label directions. Water thoroughly after treatment.

SASSAFRAS

SASSAFRAS ALBIDUM

DECIDUOUS TREE

ZONES: US, MS, LS, CS

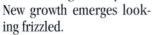

A native from Maine to north Florida and west to Texas, the sassafras turns spectacular colors of red, orange, and yellow in the fall. Don't transplant from the wild. Plant only nursery-grown trees.

PROBLEM: Japanese beetles (*illustrated above*). Metallic green beetles with copper-colored wings feed on leaves, leaving only the main leaf veins.

Solution: If beetle numbers are small, handpick the pests. Hold a cup of soapy water beneath the leaves. A light tap of the leaf startles the beetles, causing them to drop into the cup. This is most successful early in the morning, before beetles become active. For severe infestations, spray with carbaryl (Sevin) according to label directions.

SNAPDRAGON

ANTIRRHINUM MAJUS

PERENNIAL TREATED AS ANNUAL

ZONES: ALL

Snapdragons are favorite perennials for containers, rock gardens, and flower beds, depending on plant size and form. They vary in height from 6 in.–3 ft., and in colors ranging from delicate white to velvety red.

PROBLEM: Root and stem rot (*illustrated above*). In early summer the snapdragon plants wilt suddenly and die within a few days.

Solution: A number of soilborne fungi may attack snapdragons. No chemical controls exist. Dig and destroy affected plants. Do not add them to the compost pile. Improve drainage and soil fertility by incorporating lots of organic matter into heavy soil, which favors fungus growth.

PROBLEM: Rust. Powdery brownish orange bumps appear on the undersides of leaves. The plants seem stunted and may die.

Solution: Rust on snapdragons is often the result of poor air circulation. Space plants farther apart. Avoid wetting foliage when watering. Pick off and destroy infected leaves.

Spray new healthy leaves with chlorothalonil (Daconil), mancozeb, thiophanate-methyl (Thiomyl), or myclobutanil (Immunox), covering both upper and lower leaf surfaces. Consider planting rust-resistant types, such as Deluxe, Double Sweetheart, and Royal Carpet.

SPINACH

ANNUAL

ZONES: ALL

Spinach is a favorite cool-season vegetable grown for its flavorful iron-rich leaves. It can survive severe frosts, but often goes to seed in hot weather.

PROBLEM: Bolting *(illustrated above)*. Plants begin to flower. The leaves taste bitter when cooked.

Solution: Spinach requires cool weather to grow properly. In hot weather, plants may produce flowers and seed, a process called bolting. Selections that resist bolting include 'Avon', 'Bloomsdale Long Standing', 'Hector', 'Melody Hybrid', and 'Tyee Hybrid'.

PROBLEMS AND SOLUTIONS
···
FOR MORE INFORMATION ON PROBLEMS IN BOLD TYPE,
SEE LISTINGS, PAGES 142–307.

PROBLEM: **Leaf miners.** Irregular white lines or trails appear on the upper surfaces of the leaves.

Solution: If you tear open an affected leaf, you may discover a tiny worm that feeds on the tissue inside. The worm is a larva of a small fly. Pick off and destroy infested leaves. Use floating row covers to shield plants from flies. Leaf miners pupate in the soil near plants, so practice crop rotation (see page 30). Remove nearby weeds, which harbor leaf miners.

SPRUCE

PICEA

EVERGREEN TREES OR SHRUBS

ZONES: US, MS

Beautiful and majestic conifers, spruces provide the evergreen backbone for many gardens. However, their dislike of long, hot summer weather limits their use in much of the South.

PROBLEM: **Spruce gall adelgids** *(illustrated above)*. Ugly, brown, pineapple-shaped galls appear on branches.

Solution: Aphidlike insects that suck plant juices cause these galls, which may be green or purple and ½–3 in. wide.

Adelgids' survival depends on spruces and Douglas firs growing in close proximity to each other. Prune out and destroy galls as soon as you notice the problem. For serious infestations, spray new growth in spring with carbaryl (Sevin) or endosulfan (Thiodan) according to label directions. Do not plant spruces near Douglas firs.

PROBLEM: **Bagworms.** Small brown, spindle-shaped bags made of needles woven together with silken threads appear on branches. Entire branches quickly turn brown as needles seem to disappear.

Solution: Voracious caterpillars inside these bags rapidly consume foliage and can quickly defoliate a tree or shrub. When possible, immediately remove and destroy the bags. To control young caterpillars (in bags ½ in. or smaller), spray foliage with *Bacillus thuringiensis kurstaki* (Dipel, Thuricide, Javelin). For older bagworms, spray with pyrethrin, malathion, acephate (Orthene), or carbaryl (Sevin) according to label directions.

SQUASH

ANNUAL

ZONES: ALL

Summer and winter squashes are easy-to-grow garden favorites. Summer squashes, such as yellow crookneck and zucchini, are delicious for eating fresh or for stir-frying, while winter squashes, such as turban, acorn, and butternut, are excellent for cooking, baking, and storing.

PROBLEM: **Squash vine borers** *(illustrated above)*. The vines suddenly wilt and die despite adequate watering. Holes appear in the stems.

Solution: The culprit is a clearwing moth that lays eggs at the base of the vine. Hatched larvae bore into the stem, interrupting water and nutrient flow to the plant. Protect plants from egg-laying moths by using floating row covers over vines until plants begin to flower. Rotate plantings (see page 30) to a different location each year. When vines begin to run, dust or spray plant bases with rotenone, pyrethrin, malathion, or carbaryl (Sevin) every 7 to 10 days throughout the growing season. However, pesticides don't work once borers enter the plant. You can sometimes kill them by filling a garden syringe with beneficial nematodes and injecting these predators into squash stems. Or mix up a small amount of *Bacillus thuringiensis kurstaki* (Dipel, Thuricide, Javelin) in a container, draw the solution into the syringe, and carefully inject 3 cc into squash stems. Repeat this process every 7 days during the growing season.

PROBLEM: Powdery mildew. White to grayish powdery spots develop on leaves, stems, and flowers. Affected leaves dry out.

Solution: Plant mildew-resistant selections such as 'Park's Crookneck PMR Hybrid'. Make sure plants have good light and air circulation. Avoid overhead watering. Keep leaves dry. At the first sign of powdery mildew, spray plants with chlorothalonil (Daconil), fixed-copper fungicidal soap (Soap Shield), wettable sulfur, or horticultural oil. Repeat applications to protect new leaves as they emerge.

OTHER COMMON PROBLEMS: **Squash bugs, leafhoppers,** spider **mites,** and **bacterial wilt**

STRAWBERRY
PERENNIAL
ZONES: ALL

Nothing is better than a bowl of fresh strawberries in the morning. However, growing these sweet berries can exact a price because many diseases attack them in the South. Getting a good harvest depends on choosing a selection that's well adapted to your area.

PROBLEM: Botrytis (gray mold) *(illustrated above).* A woolly tan or gray mold grows on berries. Berries rot.

Solution: The botrytis fungus lives on leaves, stems, flowers, and in plant debris. Good gardening practices eliminate most of the problem. Space plants properly for maximum air circulation. Remove and destroy fading flowers, dying leaves, and plant debris. Water plants early enough in the day so they dry before evening. For control, spray with captan according to label directions.

PROBLEM: Strawberry leaf spot. Small purple spots appear on upper leaf surfaces. As leaves mature, the centers of the spots become grayish, then nearly white. Berries fail to ripen. Strawberry caps or the entire plant may die.

Solution: This is a common fungus-caused problem. Make sure plants have plenty of sun and good air circulation. Plant resistant selections such as 'Allstar', 'Cardinal', 'Chandler', 'Surecrop', and 'Tennessee Beauty'. Spray susceptible selections with captan. Avoid wetting foliage. Gather and destroy strawberry foliage after the growing season.

PROBLEMS AND SOLUTIONS
FOR MORE INFORMATION ON PROBLEMS IN BOLD TYPE,
SEE LISTINGS, PAGES 142–307.

PROBLEM: Black root rot. The plants wilt. Leaves are smaller than normal, turn yellow or red, and then die. Plants pull up easily. Roots are black, dead, and rotted.

Solution: Planting strawberries in heavy, poorly drained soil makes them susceptible to a number of soilborne fungi. No chemical control exists. Pull and destroy infected plants. Improve soil structure by incorporating lots of organic matter and coarse sand, but don't plant strawberries in the same spot for at least 2 years.

OTHER COMMON PROBLEMS: **Slugs and snails,** spider **mites, spittlebugs, virus**

SUNFLOWER
HELIANTHUS
ANNUALS AND PERENNIALS
ZONES: VARY BY SPECIES

Sunflowers continue to amaze young and older gardeners alike, with their bright and colorful single or double flowers ranging from white and primrose to golden yellow and sienna. Most make excellent cut flowers, and many produce tasty seeds. Plants range in size from 18 in.–10 ft. and bloom in late summer and fall.

PROBLEM: Powdery mildew *(illustrated above).* A white powdery film coats the leaves and stems. Leaves yellow and drop. Plants become stunted.

Solution: The powdery mildew common on sunflowers thrives in both wet and dry weather. Rotate plantings each year. Give plants sufficient sunlight, and space plantings for good air circulation. Make sure plants have adequate moisture, but do not keep soil wet. Avoid heavy applications of fertilizer. In the fall, rake and destroy fallen leaves and other plant debris. For control, spray healthy foliage as needed with wettable sulfur (don't spray sulfur in hot weather), fixed-copper fungicidal soap (Soap Shield), horticultural oil, or triforine (Funginex).

PROBLEM: Rust. Small, dark brown, powdery pimples appear on the undersides of leaves. A yellow ring surrounds each bump. Many leaves turn brown and die.

Solution: The rust fungus overwinters on old leaves and stems. Prune and destroy infected leaves and stems as soon as rust appears. Cut all flowering stalks to the ground immediately after they finish flowering and destroy them. Avoid overhead watering. Space plantings to allow maximum air circulation. Spray healthy foliage and stems with chlorothalonil (Daconil) or wettable sulfur every 2 weeks throughout the growing season.

OTHER COMMON PROBLEMS: **Verticillium wilt, white mold**

SWEET POTATO

PERENNIAL GROWN AS ANNUAL

ZONES: US, MS, LS

Sweet potatoes aren't true potatoes, but the tuberous roots of a vine that is closely related to the morning glory *(Ipomoea)*. You can harvest them anytime from 100 to 140 days from planting, depending on the selection. They're fat-free and rich in vitamin A.

PROBLEM: Black rot *(illustrated above)*. Sunken brown or black irregular spots form on the skin. Tiny black specks appear in the centers of the spots. The flesh tastes bitter.

Solution: Black rot can be serious because affected tubers will not store well. There is no chemical control. Remove and destroy all infected plants and their roots. Plant only certified disease-free slips. Do not plant sweet potatoes in the same place for more than 2 years in a row. Do not plant where organic matter in the soil is not well decomposed.

PROBLEM: Scurf. Dark brown or black patches discolor the skin but not the flesh inside.

Solution: Scurf is a common ailment of sweet potatoes planted in heavy, poorly drained soil. Although it does not affect edibility or taste, infection causes the tubers to shrink in storage. Plant only certified disease-free slips. Do not plant sweet potatoes in the same location for more than 2 years in a row. Avoid planting in heavy soil or where organic matter in the soil is not well decomposed.

OTHER COMMON PROBLEMS: **Flea beetles, nematodes**

SYCAMORE

PLATANUS OCCIDENTALIS

DECIDUOUS TREE

ZONES: US, MS, LS, CS

The sycamore, or American plane tree, is a large, fast-growing native tree of the South. Trees in the wild develop massive trunks and may exceed 100 ft. tall. The outer bark flakes off in winter to reveal handsome greenish white bark beneath.

PROBLEM: **Anthracnose** *(illustrated above)*. Leaves first turn brown along the veins. Then they turn completely brown, die, and drop. Black cankers develop along branches. Badly infected trees may die.

Solution: Anthracnose is the most serious disease of sycamores. Wet, cool spring weather favors the fungus that

causes it. Prune off and destroy infected branches and twigs. Rake and destroy fallen leaves. For control, spray the tree at bud break in spring with thiophanate-methyl (Thiomyl), chlorothalonil (Daconil), or a fixed-copper fungicide, such as Soap Shield. Apply the fungicide monthly as long as weather conditions that favor the disease continue. You'll probably need to hire a tree company to do this. London plane tree *(P. acerifolia),* a similar species, is less susceptible.

OTHER COMMON PROBLEMS: **Leaf scorch, powdery mildew, aphids, lace bugs**

TOMATO

PERENNIAL GROWN AS ANNUAL

ZONES: ALL

Tomatoes are one of the easiest, most gratifying garden vegetables to grow. The flavor of store-bought tomatoes pales compared to the sweet, rich taste of home-grown, vine-ripened tomatoes.

PROBLEM: **Fusarium wilt** *(illustrated above)*. Despite repeated watering, the leaves on the bottom of the tomato plant wilt and turn brown. Eventually, the plant dies.

Solution: To identify the problem as fusarium wilt, cut the dead plant stem on an angle near the base and determine the inside color. If it shows streaks of brown, fusarium wilt is the culprit. Warm soil and air temperatures favor the disease. There is no chemical control. Rotate crops each season (see page 30). Plant disease-resistant selections (see page 230). Resistant selections are identified on plant labels or in mail-order catalogs by a capital F following the selection name. Clean up and destroy tomato plants at the end of the season. Do not incorporate them into the compost pile.

PROBLEMS AND SOLUTIONS

FOR MORE INFORMATION ON PROBLEMS IN BOLD TYPE, SEE LISTINGS, PAGES 142–307.

PROBLEM: **Verticillium wilt.** Older leaves near the bottom of the plant wilt, turn yellow, dry, and fall. The disease gradually proceeds upward. Leaves toward the tips of branches usually remain green. The plant doesn't die, but the fruit is small and tasteless.

Solution: Verticillium wilt, like fusarium wilt, is caused by a soilborne fungus. But it occurs primarily in cooler weather. There is no chemical control. Plant tomatoes that are resistant to the disease (they have a V on the plant label or in the catalog listing). Control weeds in the area. Avoid excessive watering. Rotate crops or solarize the soil (see pages 30 and 31).

PROBLEM: Early blight. Tomato seedlings develop dark areas on the stem, then die. Tomatoes on mature plants have ridged black spots that appear sunken at the stem end. Plant leaves develop small spots surrounded by a yellow halo, giving them the appearance of a bull's-eye.

Solution: Early blight is a fungal disease. The dark spots on tomatoes near stem ends cause early fruit rot. Spots on leaves may join together, causing the leaf to turn yellow, dry up, and fall. Defoliation weakens the plant and exposes the fruit to sunburn. Plant resistant selections (see page 226). Remove and destroy plant debris after harvest. Rotate crops. Destroy affected plants. Do not compost. Warm temperatures, abundant rainfall, and high humidity favor the disease. Spray healthy foliage weekly during the growing season with a fixed-copper fungicidal soap (Soap Shield), maneb, chlorothalonil (Daconil), or mancozeb.

PROBLEM: Nematodes. The tomato plants are yellow and don't respond to fertilizing. Regardless of proper watering, they wilt in hot weather.

Solution: Root knot nematodes cause root nodules that block the flow of water and nutrients to plants. Where nematodes are a problem, plant resistant selections (see page 179). Look for the letter N on the plant label. Crop rotation (see page 30) and solarizing the soil (see page 31) will also help. Incorporating Nematrol, a nematicide made from sesame plants, or chitin (Clandosan) into the soil may also provide control.

PROBLEM: Blossom-end rot. A sunken, brown or black spot forms on the end of the tomato opposite the stem.

Solution: Blossom-end rot is the result of uneven soil moisture. It often appears when excessive moisture follows drought. Stressed roots can't absorb sufficient calcium for strong cell walls in the fruit. To guard against wide fluctuations in soil moisture, plant in loose, well-drained soil that contains lots of organic matter. Mulch with pine straw, ground bark, or newspapers. Give tomatoes about 1½ in. of water per week. If soil pH is below 6, add lime. Fertilize with a low-nitrogen fertilizer such as a 5-10-5.

PROBLEMS AND SOLUTIONS

FOR MORE INFORMATION ON PROBLEMS IN BOLD TYPE, SEE LISTINGS, PAGES 142–307.

PROBLEM: Growth cracks (see note under Catfacing). As the tomatoes mature, cracks form in concentric rings around the fruit. Some cracks run down the sides of the fruit.

Solution: Growth cracks usually result when heavy rainfall causes the pulp and seeds inside the tomato to grow faster than the skin, creating expansion lines much like stretch marks. Mulch plants to help reduce extremes in soil moisture. Plant tomatoes resistant to cracking (see page 218).

PROBLEM: Catfacing. Tomatoes are deformed, puckered, and lumpy.

Solution: Catfacing is often a problem when blossoms set fruit during cool weather. Beefsteak-type tomatoes are most susceptible. Plant selections resistant to catfacing (see page 218). Set plants in the ground after the weather warms.

PROBLEM: Tomato leaf roll. The older and lower leaves of some tomato plants roll up and become stiff and leathery but remain green.

Solution: Good news! This is not a disease, but a physiological problem that most often affects staked tomatoes growing in wet soil following a period of heavy rain. The problem does not require control. Plants usually recover after the soil drains. Fruiting isn't affected.

PROBLEM: Septoria leaf spot. Spots with dark borders appear on the lower leaves, smaller than those described in early blight (above, left). Black specks appear in the centers of these spots. The spots eventually turn tan or gray. Leaves turn yellow and fall. Severely infected plants may lose nearly all their leaves.

Solution: Relatively warm temperatures, abundant rainfall, and high humidity favor the development of septoria leaf spot. Remove and destroy plant debris after harvest. Rotate crops annually. For control, spray plants with a Bordeaux mixture, mancozeb, or chlorothalonil (Daconil), every 7 to 10 days during wet weather. Cherry tomato 'Sweet Million' resists septoria.

OTHER COMMON PROBLEMS: **Hornworms, whiteflies, virus**

TULIP

TULIPA

BULBS

ZONES: US, MS;
LS, CS (AS ANNUALS)

Tulips come in nearly every color, and range in size from only a few inches tall to well over 2 ft. Except for certain species, most should be grown as annuals in the South.

PROBLEM: Short stems; Few blooms (see Flowers, lack of) *(illustrated above).* Tulips produce only short, stubby stems and few blooms.

Solution: Short stems and few blooms most often result from insufficient winter chill. If you live where winters are short and mild, keep bulbs in the vegetable bin of your refrigerator for about 10 weeks before planting in late fall. Inadequate watering and fertilizing can also produce shorts stems. Provide plenty of both during and after bloom. Always start with top-size, healthy bulbs.

OTHER COMMON PROBLEMS: **Fusarium bulb rot, virus**

TULIP POPLAR

LIRIODENDRON TULIPIFERA

DECIDUOUS TREE

ZONES: US, MS, LS, CS

Tulip poplar, also called tulip tree and yellow poplar, is the South's tallest-growing hardwood, often exceeding 120 ft. in the wild. Several specimens planted by George Washington still grow at Mount Vernon.

PROBLEM: Leaf drop *(illustrated above).* Following hot, dry weather in mid- to late summer, older leaves yellow and drop.

Solution: Stress from environmental conditions, such as summer drought, is a typical cause of leaf drop. Adequate watering should alleviate the problem. Leaf drop can also result from insect attack, though this is not as common.

PROBLEM: Sooty mold. A sticky substance and a black mold coat the leaves.

Solution: Sooty mold grows on honeydew caused by insects, such as aphids, scales, or leafhoppers, feeding on foliage. Use a hose to wash off mold. Spray foliage with horticultural oil, azadirachtin (Neem), malathion, or acephate (Orthene) to control insects. Once you eliminate the insects, the sooty mold disappears.

PROBLEM: Scales. Large turtle-shaped bumps encrust twigs, branches, and leaves. Leaves yellow and drop. Sticky honeydew and a black mold form on leaves, stems, and bark.

Solution: Tulip tree scales, one of the largest types of scales, measure a diameter of ½ in. They vary in color from grayish green to brown to pinkish orange mottled with black. Several generations can exist in one year. Heavy, continuous attack can weaken a tree, making it vulnerable to stress and other pests. Spray during the growing season with horticultural oil, malathion, insecticidal soap, or a systemic insecticide such as dimethoate (Cygon) or acephate (Orthene). Or spray branches and twigs with dormant oil in winter. Controlling the insects eliminates the sooty mold problem.

PROBLEMS AND SOLUTIONS

FOR MORE INFORMATION ON PROBLEMS IN BOLD TYPE,
SEE LISTINGS, PAGES 142–307.

PROBLEM: Yellow poplar weevils. Small black beetles with long snouts chew holes the size and shape of rice grains in leaves. The leaves develop brown blotches, giving the foliage a scorched look.

Solution: Yellow poplar weevils are a widespread pest, from the Northeast to Florida and west to the Mississippi. Weevil larvae mine the leaves (chew trails between leaf surfaces). Adult weevils feed on buds and leaves. Spring and early summer are the best times to control these pests. Spray the tree with carbaryl (Sevin) or chlorpyrifos (Dursban).

OTHER COMMON PROBLEMS: **Aphids, gall-forming insects**

VERBENA

VERBENA

PERENNIALS, SOME GROWN AS ANNUALS

ZONES: VARY BY SPECIES

Verbenas provide bright, summer-long color. Some species are creeping or spreading, while others are more upright, growing 8–15 in. tall. Cut back faded flowers to maximize bloom.

PROBLEM: Spider mites (see Mites) *(illustrated above).* Leaves become speckled with tiny yellow spots near the midrib. They turn light green, then yellow or bronzy as they die. A fine webbing appears between leaves and stems.

Solution: Spider mites are the culprits, and are usually most active in hot, dry weather. For minor infestations, blast them with a jet of water or spray with insecticidal soap or horticultural oil. Be sure to wet the undersides of the leaves. Keep plants well watered so they aren't stressed by periods of drought, conditions favored by spider mites. If infestation is severe, spray plants with a product containing hexakis (Vendex), such as Isotox.

PROBLEM: **Whiteflies.** Tiny, triangular, white insects infest the undersides of the leaves. Leaves may be mottled and yellow.

Solution: Whiteflies weaken plants by sucking plant juices. They also secrete a honeydew that attracts ants and sooty mold. Spray with insecticidal soap, horticultural oil, malathion, resmethrin, or a systemic insecticide like acephate (Orthene). Pull plants if repeated sprayings don't solve the problem.

OTHER COMMON PROBLEMS: **Aphids, leaf miners**

WEEPING FIG
FICUS BENJAMINA
EVERGREEN TREE
ZONES: TS OR INDOORS

With its leathery, dark green, ovate leaves, weeping fig is a prized tree in the Tropical South and a favorite indoor plant elsewhere.

PROBLEM: **Leaf drop** *(illustrated above)*. An apparently healthy plant suddenly drops many of its leaves.

Solution: Weeping fig is extremely temperamental. Abrupt changes in temperature, humidity, soil moisture, or light (usually the result of moving the plant) cause sudden leaf drop. After a while, the plant should adjust to the new conditions. Make sure the soil is evenly moist and drains well.

OTHER COMMON PROBLEMS: **Scales, mealybugs**

WISTERIA, JAPANESE
WISTERIA FLORIBUNDA
DECIDUOUS VINE
ZONES: US, MS, LS, CS

In springtime, it's easy to spot the fragrant, pendulous purple or white blooms of wisteria just about everywhere you look. Though some species can escape gardens and become pests that rival kudzu, wisteria is still a favorite vine for arbors and trellises.

PROBLEM: **No blooms (see Flowers, lack of)** *(illustrated above)*. The plant appears healthy but doesn't bloom.

Solution: Seedling wisterias may take 10 years to bloom, so plant only named grafted or budded selections. Plant in full sun. Do not fertilize. Tip prune runners in summer. In winter, shorten side shoots growing from the main canes back to three buds and remove spindly growth. If all else fails, root prune in early May by plunging a sharp spade into the ground in a circle around and about 16 in. out from the trunk. Another reason for lack of blooms is extreme cold weather that kills flower buds.

ZINNIA
ZINNIA
ANNUALS
ZONES: ALL

Zinnias are a Southern standby. Their many bright colors, sizes, and shapes make them popular bedding and cut flowers. Zinnias flourish in a variety of soils but require good drainage.

PROBLEM: **Slugs and snails** *(illustrated above)*. The leaves are chewed. Silvery trails appear on the ground around the plants.

Solution: Slugs and snails love zinnias, especially young seedlings. Trap slugs and snails by laying a small board atop a few stones close to the plants to provide an enticing hiding place for them during the day. At midday, lift the board and scrape the pests into a pail of soapy water. Snail and slug baits containing metaldehyde are effective controls. Or sprinkle diatomaceous earth around plants. Follow label directions carefully.

PROBLEM: **Alternaria leaf blight (see note under Early blight).** Reddish brown spots appear on leaves, stems, and flowers. The centers of the spots turn grayish white. Infected tissue turns brown and dies.

Solution: There is no control for this disease. Pick off and destroy infected leaves and flowers. Pull and destroy severely infected plants. Avoid overhead watering. Spray healthy plants with a fungicide, such as chlorothalonil (Daconil), carefully following label directions.

PROBLEM: **Powdery mildew.** A white, powdery film covers leaves and stems. Affected plants are stunted.

Solution: Powdery mildew commonly affects zinnias when temperatures are between 68° and 75°F. Avoid heavy applications of fertilizer. Remove and destroy infected leaves. Avoid crowding plants, making sure to space them well for good air circulation. Do not wet foliage when watering. Do not plant zinnias in the same spot every year. Spray healthy plants with horticultural oil or a fungicide, such as chlorothalonil (Daconil), triforine (Funginex), or thiophanate-methyl (Thiomyl), according to label directions.

OTHER COMMON PROBLEMS: **Botrytis (gray mold),** leaf spot

BUGS AND
Other Critters

A healthy, productive garden supports diversity and balance in both plant and animal life. This chapter tells you how to control common bug (insects, arachnids, mites, and mollusks) and animal pests and also describes beneficial creatures that are good to have around.

There's nothing wrong with having bugs and critters in your garden. Indeed, if nothing lived in it but plants, that would be the time to really start worrying. Plants, bugs, and animals exist together in an ecosystem governed by natural checks and balances. It's only when the system gets out of whack that pests cause problems.

As we mentioned earlier, gardeners pressed for time often feel tempted to shower the yard with pesticide to prevent problems that haven't yet appeared. But such chemical overkill makes problems worse. Indiscriminate spraying kills beneficial insects that prey on harmful ones. It also results in resistant pests that no chemical can control.

Our advice: Put up with a little damage. And do your best to keep plants healthy. Weak plants attract pests; strong ones fend them off. If a particular insect, mite, or animal pest threatens serious damage, use the following pages to identify the pest, then take appropriate action, which may involve chemical, cultural, or physical control.

THE SECRET LIVES OF INSECTS

Insects, six-legged invertebrates with bodies in three segments, make up the vast majority of pests shown and described in this chapter. Each description lists ways of preventing insect damage, as well as controlling infestations. To do either effectively, you need to understand the life cycle of the offending bug. In most cases, you can control the pest by interfering in just a single stage of its life.

Insects grow through a remarkable process called metamorphosis. Almost all begin life as an egg. The egg hatches into a juvenile insect called a larva, which grows by splitting and casting off its rigid external skeleton. Metamorphosis occurs in two forms. In *incomplete metamorphosis*, the larvae, called nymphs, look like miniature versions of their parents. Cicadas are a good example. But in *complete metamorphosis*, the young insect begins as a wormlike creature that doesn't resemble an adult at all. Examples include butterfly caterpillars, beetle grubs, and fruit fly maggots. The young insect then goes through a pupal stage, during which it transforms itself into the adult form.

Insect development ranges from the astonishingly fast to the amazingly slow. A fruit fly, for instance, passes through its entire life cycle in just a few days. But cicadas develop and feed underground for more than a decade.

> *A handful of patience is worth a bucketful of brains.*
> —Dutch proverb

If the same insect bugs your garden every year, knowing its life cycle can help you deal with it. Just about all insects suffer weak points in their development when they're particularly vulnerable to control. For example, mature armored scales are impervious to most pesticides. But catch them in their juvenile crawler stage and any number of natural or chemical pesticides will do them in.

Of course, control doesn't have to involve pesticides. Maybe you need to change the timing of your planting (you'll have fewer problems with Colorado potato beetles if you plant a fall crop of potatoes rather than a spring one). Or maybe you just need to plant something else. Why fuss over a plant that needs spraying twice a week when another plant that's just as good needs no care?

Swallowtail butterfly caterpillars (upper left and lower right) seldom cause enough damage to warrant control. The same can't be said for aphids (lower left). Squirrels (upper right) entertain us with their antics, but also rob gardens of fruits, nuts, bulbs, and vegetables.

Life Passages

Insects go through stages, or metamorphosis, during their lives. Squash bugs hatch from eggs (inset, left), then molt through nymph (juvenile) stages until they attain wings and adult size (above). Moths also hatch from eggs (above, right) but have a more complex and complete metamorphosis. The larval, or caterpillar, stage (right) is when they do the most damage in the garden by eating the leaves of plants. Then they enclose themselves in a pupa (below, right) from which they emerge as adult moths.

A Matter of Form

The larvae of garden pests, such as moths and butterflies, beetles, and flies, have distinctive forms, each with its own name. Moths and butterflies produce larvae in the form of caterpillars (left, above inset), while beetle juveniles are known as grubs (inset, left). The maggot (right), which is legless (and sometimes looks headless), is the larva of a fly. Typically, the larvae of insect pests cause more damage to garden plants than adults.

GUERRILLAS IN OUR MIDST

Some of our most troublesome and aggressive insect pests are accidental imports from other lands. Natural predators that evolved along with them kept them in check in their native habitats. However, once loosed upon our land and lacking predators, they spread faster than rumors at a boarding school.

Exotic pests don't always walk across our borders or fly across the waters to reach our shores. Many stow away in the holds of cargo ships. That's how the red imported fire ant *(Solenopsis invicta)* cruised into the South. It came by boat from South America to Mobile, Alabama, sometime in the 1930s. From there it quickly hitched rides in the rootballs of nursery plants being trucked to other states. In the fire ant's homeland, its natural predators kill so many of its foraging workers that it isn't a serious pest there, but here, without their control, the pest has firmly entrenched itself throughout most of our region, and is headed north.

Gardeners in the Upper and Middle South have cursed the Japanese beetle *(Popillia japonica)* for decades. This voracious bug devours the foliage and flowers of just about every kind of plant you can think of. It, too, was a stowaway, entering the U.S. by way of New Jersey in 1916. From there it quickly spread north, west, and (alas) south. Japanese beetles have been recently sighted in the northern half of the Lower South. Entomologists predict they will eventually reach the Gulf Coast.

Some insect invasions took place fairly recently. The Formosan termite *(Coptotermes formosanus)* first infiltrated the South near Charleston, South Carolina, toward the end of World War II. Undetected until 1969, it quietly established colonies along coastal areas from South Carolina to Texas. Ground-zero for its attack has been the grand wooden buildings of historic New Orleans, many of which have already been seriously damaged by the pest.

Unfortunately for the South, 1985 was a very good year for the Asian tiger mosquito *(Aedes albopictus)*. It arrived in Houston aboard old water-filled tires, found the South to its liking, and flew in to explore its new home. In little more than ten years, it has conquered almost all of the South and set its sights on the North. In fact, Asian tiger mosquitoes have been found as far north as Minnesota. What's the big deal? Mosquitoes infest just about every place that isn't arid. Well, for one thing, the Asian tiger mosquito transmits diseases, such as dengue fever, eastern equine encephalitis, and canine heartworm. For another, unlike most other mosquitoes that goof off during the day, this one hungrily pursues its victims day and night.

What can we do to forestall such invasions? Not much really. Globalization has many more than just economic implications. It means that previously isolated regions of the world are now within easy reach by sea and air. As careful as customs inspectors are, they can't catch every pest trying to sneak in. Our best strategy may be to import some of the natural enemies of these pests from their homelands. The worry is, once a natural predator gets rid of a pest, will the predator become an even bigger pest?

THE REST OF THE PESTS

You can't blame all plant damage on insects. Other small creatures that people often mistakenly lump together with insects take part in the plant carnage too. Mites, for example, are arachnids. Possessing eight legs and only two body segments, they're related to spiders, scorpions, chiggers, and ticks. Snails and slugs are mollusks, belonging to the same family as oysters and clams. Sowbugs and pillbugs are crustaceans, cousins of lobsters and shrimp. And nematodes are microscopic worms.

Why are these distinctions important? Because the methods you use to control one group of insects won't necessarily work on other groups. Whether you employ a physical, natural, or chemical strategy, you need to tailor your defense to the specific type of pest. This goes for pesky animals, too.

You'll find natural and synthetic controls listed for most of the pests in this chapter. For more information about these products, turn to Chapter 3, "A Pound of Cure."

Something Wicked This Way Comes

When it comes to aphids, this ladybug larva is one mean baby. A beneficial predator of insect pests, it has a voracious appetite for aphids and consumes many more of these insects than adult ladybugs do.

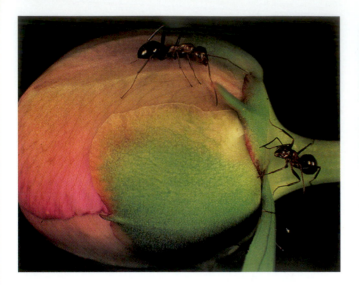

ANTS

GARDEN PESTS, BENEFICIALS; HOUSEHOLD PESTS

ZONES: ALL

There's no getting away from ants. The dozens of species inhabiting the South range from black to red, from specklike to nearly an inch long. Some shepherd flocks of aphids for their honeydew; others tend fungus farms. But most ants are dedicated predators of insects, spiders, mites, and even small animals. They're also fond of anything sweet, like fruit and candy, and occasionally nibble plants. And some ants invade houses.

The black carpenter ant *(Camponotus pennsylvanicus)* is among the most common types. Nearly an inch long, it nests in rotting wood, usually in trees but sometimes in houses. Unlike termites, carpenter ants don't eat wood; they merely remove it. Texas leaf-cutter ants *(Atta texana)* build huge, crater-shaped mounds. They cut leaves from hackberry, hickory, oak, and sweet gum, then drag them into their nest to cultivate a fungus that they eat. The Argentine ant *(Iridomyrmex humilis)*, an invader from South America, is brown and about ⅛ in. long. It aggressively drives out other ants, eats insects and seeds, and sometimes invades houses looking for sweets. The red imported fire ant *(Solenopsis invicta)* is the South's most notorious species (see "Putting Out the Fire," at right).

Target: Insects, mites, spiders, ticks, chiggers, small animals, and anything sweet or greasy

Damage: Ants usually do little damage to plants, although they may nibble seedlings or swarm over fruit lying on the ground, and some place aphids on plants. Many types build unsightly mounds in lawns. Carpenter ants may hollow out trees, making the trees prone to wind damage, and occasionally damage houses. Fire ants sometimes girdle the trunks of young citrus and pecan trees in dry weather or chew holes in apples on the tree; they also inflict painful stings if disturbed. Texas leaf-cutter ants may defoliate small trees.

Life cycle: Winged males and females (queens) appear about once a year. After mating, males die and females lose their wings. Each female creates a nest and lays large numbers of eggs that become worker ants. Some fire ant mounds have more than one queen. Populations swell during summer and fall. Colonies overwinter in soil, garden debris, trees, and houses.

Prevention: Don't leave sweets, food scraps, pet food, or fruit lying about. Destroy isolated mounds in your lawn before ants spread. Apply a sticky barrier, such as Tanglefoot, to the trunks of fruit trees.

Control: To control leaf-cutter ants, spray small trees with carbaryl (Sevin), malathion, or diazinon according to label directions. If carpenter ants have invaded your home, consult an exterminator. To kill Argentine ants and other home invaders, mix boric acid (available in drugstores) with apple jelly. Place small amounts around the home in places frequented by ants but inaccessible to children and pets. Boric acid is an environmentally friendly stomach poison that ants will carry back to their colony and eat. For serious infestations, call an exterminator. To destroy ant mounds in lawns, drench with boiling water. Or drench mounds with an insecticide containing chlorpyrifos (Dursban), diazinon, or acephate (Orthene). You can also apply these chemicals in granular form.

PUTTING OUT THE FIRE. *Since cruising to Mobile by boat from South America in the 1930s, the imported fire ant has become one of the South's most troublesome pests. Reddish brown and about ⅛ in. long, it outcompetes native ants, attacks ground-nesting birds and other wildlife, and inflicts a painful sting. It also builds large, obtrusive mounds.*

Fire ants are much easier to control in home lawns and gardens than on farms and ranches. Slow-acting poisons, such as hydramethylnon (Amdro) and abamectin (Affirm), kill entire mounds over a period of weeks. For quicker results, drench mounds with boiling water. Or drench with an insecticide containing chlorpyrifos, diazinon, or acephate. (You can also apply these chemicals in granular form.) Do this in early morning, when the queen is higher up in the mound. A promising biological control now being tried in Florida and Texas is a parasite called a phorid fly (Pseudacteon sp.). This tiny fly lays an egg on the ant's head. After the larva hatches, the ant's head falls off. Phorid flies terrorize fire ants so much that the ants stop foraging and hide underground. Without food, the colony starves or is pushed out by other ant species.

Fire ant with aphids

APHIDS

GARDEN AND HOUSE PLANT PESTS

❦ ZONES: ALL

Aphids (or plant lice) are those familiar, slow-moving, soft-bodied insects that cluster on the new growth of roses, perennials, and other plants and suck their juices. More than 1,300 species inhabit North America. Pear shaped and usually wingless, they measure 1/16–1/4 in. long and may be green, pink, yellow, tan, gray, white, or black. Woolly aphids, found on trees and shrubs, are noted for the white wool-like tufts that grow on their backs. Large numbers give the appearance of a cottony, waxy coating on the branches. Woolly apple aphids *(Eriosoma lanigerum)* are shown in the photo above, right.

Target: Aphids feed on an extremely wide range of plants. The green peach aphid *(Myzus persicae)* favors peach and other fruit trees, vegetables, flowers, bougainvillea, citrus, clematis, and English ivy. The black citrus aphid *(Toxoptera aurantii)* attacks citrus, camellia, ixora, and pittosporum. The cotton aphid *(Aphis gossypii)* targets hibiscus and mallows. The rose aphid *(Macrosiphum rosae)* attacks roses. Woolly aphids attack apple, elm, cotoneaster, hawthorn, maple, and pyracantha.

Damage: Both adults and juveniles (nymphs) damage plants by piercing the leaves, stems, and flowers and sucking sap and other fluids, weakening plants and leaving them discolored and stunted. Roses and other flowers bloom poorly. Foliage may look puckered or distorted. Some aphids transmit viruses.

Aphids cannot digest all the sugars they ingest with plant fluids. They excrete the excess in the form of a sticky honeydew, which supports the growth of an unsightly fungus called sooty mold (see page 250). Ants often farm aphids to feed on their honeydew, tending them as if they were sheep and actually placing them on target plants. Honeydew dripping from trees can soil cars, garden furniture, and paving, a particular problem with tulip poplars *(Liriodendron tulipifera)* infested with the tuliptree aphid *(Illinoia liriodendri)*.

Life cycle: Aphids have a complex reproductive cycle. Depending on the point in the cycle, females may lay eggs or bear live young. They may give birth without mating or after being fertilized by a male. Some generations are born with wings to help them migrate to other plants. Others are born wingless and remain on the original plant. Populations explode in warm weather. Reproduction is continuous in the Coastal and Tropical South. Elsewhere, eggs overwinter on target plants.

Prevention: Encourage or introduce natural enemies of aphids, including assassin bugs, lacewings, ladybugs, parasitoid wasps, soldier beetles, and syrphid flies. Destroy ant mounds in flower and vegetable beds. Spray woody plants with dormant oil in winter to destroy overwintering eggs. During the growing season, spray foliage periodically with a strong jet of water to remove aphids before they become established.

Control: Kill aphids on edible plants by dusting the foliage with diatomaceous earth or spraying with insecticidal soap. You can make your own "insecticidal soap" by mixing 5 or 6 drops of liquid detergent in a quart of water. For other plants, spray with azadirachtin (Neem) according to label directions.

ROSE? WHAT ROSE? *One way to control aphids on rosebushes is to underplant them with garlic. The pungent leaves seem to confuse or repel the pests.*

Severe infestations are difficult to control because aphids often hunker down in folds of leaves, flower buds, and new growth. Try spraying with horticultural oil or an insecticide containing a pyrethrin, diazinon, malathion, or acephate (Orthene) according to label directions. To avoid killing beneficial insects, spray only infested plants.

ARMYWORMS

VEGETABLE AND LAWN PESTS

ZONES: ALL

Armyworms are large caterpillars named for their unsettling habit of marching in troops, devouring all vegetation in their path. Most armyworms, including the true armyworm *(Pseudaletia unipuncta)* and yellow-striped armyworm *(Spodoptera ornithogalli),* pictured above, conduct maneuvers at night. However, the fall armyworm *(S. frugiperda)* eats anytime, though it prefers early morning and late evening.

Armyworms are 1–2 in. long. The true armyworm is yellowish or brownish green with a brown head and three dark stripes. The yellow-striped armyworm is nearly black with two bright yellow stripes. The fall armyworm may be green, tan, or nearly black with a prominent white marking, like an upside-down Y, on its face.

Target: Armyworms attack beans, beets, cabbage, corn, cucumber, lettuce, spinach, and tomato. The fall armyworm also favors turf grasses and can destroy a small lawn in a single night.

Damage: The foliage of vegetables may be chewed or skeletonized; tomatoes and beans, gouged or pitted. Lawns may look ragged, and heavy infestations may leave large brown patches.

Life cycle: Adult moths lay eggs in early to midsummer. From 2 to 20 days later, depending on species, larvae emerge and immediately begin feeding. After 2 to 4 weeks, they drop and pupate underground in earthen cells. Adult moths emerge 2 to 4 weeks later. Several generations may occur each year.

Prevention: Get rid of surrounding weeds and grasses that harbor eggs. If practical, dig a steep-sided, 6-in.-deep trench around your vegetable garden. Armyworms will march in, but they can't march out.

Control: Encourage natural enemies, such as assassin bugs, tachinid flies, tiger beetles, and spined soldier bugs. Introduce trichogramma wasps, which parasitize armyworms. Use *Bacillus thuringiensis kurstaki* (Dipel, Thuricide, Javelin) against armyworms less than an inch long. To control larger caterpillars, spray the foliage of vegetables with azadirachtin (Neem) or carbaryl (Sevin). Or on ornamentals only, spray acephate (Orthene). Use carbaryl, diazinon, or chlorpyrifos (Dursban) to kill fall armyworms in lawns.

ASIAN AMBROSIA BEETLES

TREE PESTS

ZONES: ALL

A tiny, foreign invader now threatens peach, plum, pear, pecan, and many other trees in the South—the Asian ambrosia beetle *(Xylosandrus crassiusculus).* Less than ¼ in. long and cylindrical in shape, it is dark brown, reddish brown, or black and may have pitted wing covers. It entered this country in 1974 near Charleston, South Carolina. Since then, it has spread into North Carolina, Georgia, Florida, Alabama, Mississippi, Louisiana, and Texas.

It's much easier to detect the beetle's presence than the insect itself. A telltale clue is a white, toothpicklike spike of boring dust that protrudes about 1½ in. from the trunk. Female beetles produce these spikes as they excavate galleries or corridors inside the tree for laying eggs.

Target: Peach, plum, pear, pecan, persimmon, magnolia, sweet gum, Chinese elm, crepe myrtle, and many other kinds of hardwood trees. Young trees with trunks 1–4 in. in diameter are at highest risk.

Damage: These aggressive beetles attack both healthy and stressed trees. Attacks on healthy plants usually occur near ground level or at wound sites. As many as 50 beetles may infest a single tree. Beetles excavate a maze of tunnels and cultivate ambrosia fungus *(Fusarium solani)* on the tunnel walls to feed their developing young. Infested trees may wilt and die.

Life cycle: While adult beetles are present most of the year, they require high humidity to reproduce. Major activity occurs in March. Females bore into stems, twigs, branches, or trunks of young trees. They deposit eggs within tunnels and introduce the fungus. Females remain with their young until they mature and exit the tree. Hatching females mate before leaving the tree to infest a new host.

Prevention: Keep trees vigorous with adequate watering and fertilization. Avoid wounding them. Spray trunks with chlorpyrifos (Dursban) or endosulfan (Thiodan) late in the day, so the chemical can dry overnight and avoid breakdown due to sunlight and heat. You can also spray with diazinon. Follow label directions carefully.

Control: Once beetles are in the tree, no chemical will help. Remove and burn the infested tree.

ASPARAGUS BEETLES

ASPARAGUS PESTS

✏ ZONES: US, MS, LS

Most folks relish tender asparagus spears. Unfortunately, so do asparagus beetles. These pests are about ¼ in. long. The spotted asparagus beetle *(Crioceris duodecimpunctata)*, shown above, is orange with black spots. The common asparagus beetle *(C. asparagi)* is blue-black or brown with yellow markings and a red head.

Target: The asparagus beetle and its larvae attack only asparagus, though other plants, such as ferns, may be hosts.

Damage: Asparagus beetles chew tender new spears of asparagus. The chewed part of the spear grows more slowly and twists, so that spears emerge crooked from the ground. Spears may also look distorted, chewed, or scarred, with most damage during the harvest period in early spring. Later in the season, adults and larvae chew on stems and the ferny leaves of asparagus plants.

Life cycle: Adults overwinter in plant debris, flying in to feed just as asparagus shoots sprout from spring soil. Adult females lay dark eggs that protrude horizontally from spear tips. Within a week, orange or olive green grubs hatch, feeding on asparagus stalks and leaves. After a few weeks, they burrow into the ground to form yellow pupae. There are two or three generations per year.

Prevention: Clean up garden debris in asparagus beds in the fall to eliminate overwintering adult beetles. Use floating row covers over asparagus beds in the spring to keep eggs off the spears.

Control: In a small garden, the easiest method of managing these pests is to handpick adult beetles and larvae. Natural enemies include birds, ladybug larvae, and spined soldier bugs, which eat the beetle's larvae and eggs. Adult beetles may be easily washed off edible spears of asparagus plants with a jet of water. You can also wash off beetles found later in the season on the foliage, or you can kill them by spraying with an insecticide containing rotenone or malathion. Don't spray insecticide onto emerging spears, as the insecticide may distort them. Spraying shortly after harvest will reduce large populations of asparagus beetles and their larvae. Be sure to follow label directions.

ASSASSIN BUGS

BENEFICIALS

✏ ZONES: ALL

Every garden needs its share of assassins—assassin bugs, that is. This group of more than 160 species in North America are named for their habit of sneaking up on insect victims and then stabbing and sucking them dry. Assassin bugs are about ½ – ¾ in. long with narrow, long heads, curved beaks, long antennae, and distinct "necks." They are usually brown, black, or gray, but many sport brilliant red markings. Among the largest and most easily recognized assassins is the wheel bug *(Arilus cristatus)*. The adult is about 1¼ in. long, gray, with a spiked crest just behind its head that resembles the spokes of a wheel.

Assassin bug nymph

Target: Aphids, armyworms, the larvae and eggs of asparagus beetles, fall webworm, gypsy moth caterpillars, leafhoppers (pictured at top), mites, sawfly larvae, and tomato hornworms

Damage: Assassin bugs are not particularly discriminating and will attack other beneficial insects as well as pests. In addition, some assassins, such as the wheel bug, can inflict a painful bite if humans handle them.

Life cycle: Adult females lay rows of barrel-shaped eggs on the leaves of garden plants. The eggs hatch into juveniles, called nymphs, which are smaller, wingless, and darker than adults and may be brilliantly colored (wheel bug nymphs are blood red with black markings). The nymphs gradually grow wings as they reach full size. There are one or more generations per year.

Prevention: Assassin bugs pose no danger to plants. However, anyone attempting to handle them is well advised to wear gloves. Bites may cause burning, itchy welts in sensitive individuals.

Control: No control is needed. To keep from killing these beneficial bugs accidentally, avoid blanket spraying of insecticides. Precisely target sprayings to infested plants only.

AZALEA CATERPILLARS

AZALEA PESTS

ZONES: ALL

Azalea caterpillars *(Datana major)* love company. Both big and small ones feed in groups. Young caterpillars are ¼ in. long, reddish to brownish black, with white and yellow stripes. Mature caterpillars are black, 2 in. long, with multiple rows of yellow dots down and across the body. Heads and legs are mahogany red. If disturbed while feeding, the caterpillars stop moving and raise their front and back ends in unison, hanging onto foliage with middle pairs of legs. The adult insect is a light brown, night-flying moth with a 2-in. wingspan and threadlike antennae.

Mature azalea caterpillar

Target: Azaleas, particularly Southern Indica Hybrids

Damage: Young caterpillars skeletonize the leaves, leaving only a netting of veins. Older larvae consume entire leaves and may completely defoliate small plants overnight. The most damage usually occurs in late August and September. Because feeding occurs late in the season, it rarely kills azaleas. However, it may slow their growth.

Life cycle: Adult moths emerge in late spring, laying eggs on leaf undersides. After hatching, larvae feed on leaf undersides for several days. In late summer, having completed their growth, the caterpillars drop to the ground. They overwinter as pupae in the soil under host plants. Only one generation exists per year.

Prevention: Examine the undersides of the leaves every 2 weeks in summer. For small infestations, pick off and destroy the affected leaves or prune away affected branch. Wear gloves when you do this, as the caterpillars emit a secretion that can stain your hands.

Control: For serious infestations, spray with a biological insecticide containing *Bacillus thuringiensis kurstaki* (Dipel, Thuricide, Javelin) in early evening. Or spray according to label directions with a broad-spectrum, contact insecticide, such as malathion, carbaryl (Sevin), diazinon, rotenone, or acephate (Orthene).

BAGWORMS

TREE AND SHRUB PESTS

ZONES: ALL

The amazing thing about a bagworm is that it does its dirty work right under people's noses and almost always gets away with it. That's because the guilty caterpillar *(Thyridopteryx ephemeraeformis)* hides inside a bag that many folks confuse with a pinecone—even if the tree it's hanging on isn't a pine! The spindle-shaped bag, up to 2 in. long, consists of bark and leaves woven together with silk.

Target: Primarily needle-leafed evergreens, including arborvitae *(Thuja),* juniper, spruce, and false cypress *(Chamaecyparis),* but also deciduous trees, such as honey locust and bald cypress

Damage: The caterpillar rapidly consumes needles and leaves, defoliating entire plants before your very eyes. Deciduous plants may recover, but evergreens frequently die.

Life cycle: Eggs (500 to 1,000) overwinter in each bag. In May or June, hatched, blackish larvae crawl out, spiraling downward on a silken strand. Each larva creates its own body bag. When ready to pupate, it permanently attaches its bag to a host. Male moths, furry, blackish, with clear wings, emerge in August. Females never resemble moths. They have yellowish, soft, almost hairless bodies, and no wings, legs, antennae, eyes, or functional mouthparts. Females stay in the bag, where they mate, lay eggs, and die. Males die shortly thereafter.

THE BASHFUL BAGWORM. *A bagworm caterpillar eats by sticking its head and front legs out of the top of its silken bag home. When threatened, it quickly retreats into the bag and pulls the entry closed with a silk drawstring.*

Prevention: Remove and destroy bags as soon as they appear.

Control: If only a few bags are present, handpick and destroy them. To control the young caterpillars (bags of ½ in. or less), spray foliage in early evening with *Bacillus thuringiensis kurstaki* (Dipel, Thuricide, Javelin). For older bagworms, spray foliage according to label directions with malathion, diazinon, carbaryl (Sevin), a pyrethrin, or acephate (Orthene).

BARK BEETLES

TREE PESTS

✔ ZONES: ALL

Bark beetles prove that even the smallest insect can bring down the biggest plant. These dark, shiny, hard-shelled bugs are about ¼ in. long (some are even smaller) and live on and in between the bark plates of large trees. It isn't just their chewing that kills the host trees. In many cases, the telling factor is the disease these beetles transmit.

Types include the European elm bark beetle *(Scoly-tus multistratus),* which carries Dutch elm disease, and a trio of pests that attack pines—the black turpentine beetle *(Dendroctonus terebrans),* the Ips or pine engraver beetle *(Ips pini),* and the Southern pine beetle *(Dendroctonus frontalis),* shown above, right. The latter pest transmits a blue-stain fungus that damages the sapwood, shown above, left, blocking the passage of water and nutrients. Damage from the Southern pine beetle has reached epidemic proportions in the pine forests of Alabama and other Southeastern states.

Pine bark beetle

Target: Pines (especially loblolly, slash, and shortleaf), spruce, arborvitae, cedar, and elm. Homing in on a scent given off by stressed trees, beetles will fly long distances to attack trees suffering from drought, disease, or other problems.

Damage: Larvae chew tunnels in the green layer under the bark, called the cambium, disrupting the flow of nutrients and water through the tree. Branches and trunks may be girdled and die. Conifers may ooze pitch mixed with frass (sawdust left by feeding larvae) through holes in the bark. On cedars, small twigs die first and hang down.

Infested pines lose their green color from the top down, with needles turning yellow, red, and then finally brown. Pines under attack usually bleed large amounts of pitch or sap from the entrance holes. However, severely weakened trees may exhibit only brownish sawdust at the holes. More than one species of pine beetle may attack a stressed tree simultaneously. The fungus they carry hastens the tree's demise, which usually occurs in a single year. Trees die singly or in groups. Garden specimens are just as susceptible as forest trees.

Life cycle: Adult male beetles locate stressed trees, then often emit a pheromone to invite females to dinner. Females lay eggs within the bark or into the ends of branches. Larvae tunnel through the cambium to feed, creating elaborate galleries. They pupate under the bark, then chew their way out, emerging as adults to fly to other trees. Usually one to three generations occur per year, but the Southern pine beetle may produce as many as nine generations.

Prevention: Promptly remove and burn dead, dying, or lightning-damaged pines, because these act like a magnet to attract egg-laying beetles. Plant pines that bark beetles don't favor. Keep pine trees healthy and vigorous through proper watering and fertilizing. Protect them from damage to the bark. Prune pines in winter, since beetles are attracted to the scent of freshly cut pine trees. Do not compact the soil beneath them by parking vehicles or heavy equipment within the dripline of the tree. Do not store cut branches or firewood near trees. Spray pine trunks according to label directions with lindane, chlorpyrifos (Dursban), endosulfan (Thiodan), or carbaryl (Sevin). Spray elm trunks in May and June with acephate (Orthene).

Control: There is no chemical control once beetle larvae have entered the tree. Thorough watering and fertilizing may help some trees to recover by oozing enough pitch to kill grubs. But heavily infested pines and elms should be immediately destroyed, before the infestation spreads.

GOING DUTCH? *Many older Southerners recall entire avenues lined with massive American elms* (Ulmus americana), *their wide-spreading branches forming majestic canopies over the roads. Then tragedy struck in the late 1920s. A virulent disease called Dutch elm disease (named after the country in which it was first studied) entered North America on burled elm logs sent from Europe. It killed elms by the millions and spread to nearly every U.S. state. Today, isolated large American elms survive, often protected by yearly injections of systemic fungicide. Our best hope for elm-lined streets in the future are hybrids that appear to resist the causal fungus,* Ophiostoma ulmi. *They include the American Liberty series, 'Delaware #2', 'New Harmony', 'Valley Forge', and 'Washington'.*

BEES

BENEFICIALS

☀ ZONES: ALL

As the primary pollinators of many flowers, vegetables, and backyard fruit trees, bees are vital to the garden. European in origin, the honeybee *(Apis mellifera),* shown above, left, was introduced to North America during the 1600s as a pollinator for apple orchards. This bee is about an inch long and has gold-and-black markings and two pairs of clear wings. The native bumblebee *(Bombus sp.),* shown above, right, is a large, black, fuzzy bee with a yellow or reddish stripe on its middle. It is the primary pollinator of tomato, eggplant, and pepper plants.

Target: Honeybees and bumblebees feed on pollen and nectar from the flowers of garden plants and flowering trees.

Damage: If disturbed, bees will sting. People who are allergic to bee stings may experience swelling, dizziness, or difficulty in breathing; in some cases, without quick medical attention, they may die. Sometimes bees are a nuisance when they build their nests in buildings or too near the garden.

Life cycle: Honeybees live in colonies around a dominant female, called a queen, who lays many thousands of eggs in her lifetime. These eggs hatch into sterile female worker bees. Some workers become males, or drones, which mate with the queen, then die. Other eggs bear new queens. When a honeybee hive becomes too crowded, thousands of the bees leave in a swarm, usually in late winter or early fall. During the summer, honeybees gather nectar and pollen and transform them into honey and wax in the hive. In the shorter, chillier days of winter, they retire to their hives to feed off stored honey. Bumblebees nest in the soil or sometimes in a compost pile. A bumblebee colony may be as small as a dozen bees with a single queen that overwinters by hibernating underground. Bumblebees don't create usable honey or wax, but are important crop pollinators. All bees die after stinging, because the stinger and venom sac are ripped out when the bee flies away.

Prevention: When left to their foraging, bees will not sting. If you are concerned about allergic individuals, you can have hives removed by a professional beekeeper or pest control professional.

Control: To encourage bees to frequent your garden, plant nectar flowers and provide a water source. Bees may be killed if the flowers they feed on have been sprayed with pesticides; carbaryl (Sevin) is especially toxic to bees. To protect them, use only insecticides that degrade quickly, such as a pyrethrin or rotenone. Apply them late in the evening, when bees are in their hives. If you are accidentally stung by a bee, apply wet mud to the wound to draw out the stinger—or scrape the stinger off your skin with a fingernail—then apply first aid. Persons who are allergic to bee stings should keep antihistamine first aid kits handy and seek medical attention immediately when stung. Swarms or hives should be removed only by a professional beekeeper or pest control professional.

KILLER BEES. *The Africanized honeybee, also called the "killer bee," looks just like an ordinary honeybee but is smaller. It is, however, particularly aggressive; if disturbed, swarms will pursue and attack humans and other mammals. The sheer volume of stings can be fatal. Introduced from Africa to South America, this bee has traveled northward through Mexico and appeared in Texas and New Mexico. The Africanized honeybee is expected to extend its range, particularly as viruses and mites reduce naturalized European honeybee populations. Africanized bees are extremely dangerous: they can be disturbed by the noise of a lawn mower several hundred yards away and can pursue humans for as much as half a mile, zeroing in on head and face. If these insects move into your area, use extreme caution around any hives; swatting or killing a foraging bee releases an odor trigger that draws nearby bees to attack. If attacked, pull a shirt over your head to protect your face and eyes, and run away as fast as possible, seeking cover indoors or in a car.*

BIG-EYED BUGS

BENEFICIALS

✿ ZONES: ALL

If you're a bug, you'd better keep out of sight when a big-eyed bug is around. This hungry insect predator, about ⅛ in. long, looks like a chinch bug, but its huge, bulging eyes distinguish it. Big-eyed bugs *(Geocoris sp.)* are typically black with silver wings, but may be pale tan or whitish. If you look at a big-eyed bug with a magnifying glass, you may notice minute black spots on the head and thorax. Their bodies are stout and slightly flattened. Juvenile big-eyed bugs, called nymphs, are small, gray, wingless versions of the adults.

Target: Big-eyed bugs eat insect eggs and soft-bodied pests, such as aphids, leafhoppers, mealybugs, spider mites, thrips, whiteflies, and various caterpillars, including small cabbage loopers, corn earworms, tobacco budworms, and armyworms. They also eat chinch bugs—as many as 50 each in a single night.

Damage: No damage, unless you're a chinch bug or spider mite.

Life cycle: Big-eyed bugs reside on and around a wide variety of plants. Females deposit eggs on stems and leaf undersides near prey insects. A distinct red spot marks each whitish egg. The nymphs emerge in 2 weeks and mature in about 4 weeks. Each nymph can devour up to 1,600 spider mites before it matures. An adult may eat 80 spider mites a day. When disturbed, both nymphs and adults drop to the ground. When prey is scarce, they survive on nectar and honeydew. Several generations occur each year. Adults hibernate in garden debris.

Prevention and control: No measures needed. Instead, encourage their presence by providing ample shelter in the form of low-growing plants. Nectar-producing flowers will supply supplementary food. Target insecticide spray carefully, so you don't kill big-eyed bugs, too.

BORERS, BRONZE BIRCH

BIRCH PESTS

✿ ZONES: US, MS, LS

You can always tell your new neighbors aren't from the South when they start planting white birch trees. Most birch species don't survive here for long, for two reasons—the hot climate and the bronze birch borer.

The adult bronze birch borer *(Agrilus anxius)* is a small, olive brown to black beetle, about ½ in. long, with a blunt head, slender body, and pointed tail. The larva is a flat-headed, wormlike borer, cream colored, and about ¾ –1 in. long. Two brownish spines extend from the tail.

Target: Birches, especially European white birch *(Betula pendula)* and paper birch *(B. papyrifera)*. Older, stressed trees are particularly vulnerable.

Damage: The larvae chew extensive tunnels through the inner bark of the tree. Ridges on the outer bark atop these tunnels resemble bulging or varicose veins. Continued feeding cuts off the flow of sap, causing limbs to die. Limb dieback starts at the top of the tree and proceeds downward. Eventually, the tree dies.

Life cycle: Female beetles lay eggs in the cracks of bark near the tops of birches from June through August. The eggs hatch and the larvae quickly chew their way into the bark. If the tree is healthy, sap may fill the tunnels and drown the borers. But weakened trees have no such defense. The larvae overwinter in the tree and pupate in spring. Adults then chew their way out of the tree, leaving telltale, D-shaped exit holes on the branches or trunk.

Prevention: Plant only borer-resistant species of birches, such as river birch *(B. nigra),* Japanese white birch *(B. platyphylla japonica),* and monarch birch *(B. maximowicziana).* Plant birches in moist, well-drained, fertile soil that contains plenty of organic matter. Water freely during droughts. Don't prune in spring, as birches bleed profusely then, and the loss of sap may put them under stress. Spray the trunks of susceptible birches with lindane, dimethoate (Cygon), chlorpyrifos (Dursban), or endosulfan (Thiodan) according to label directions.

Control: Remove and destroy severely infested trees.

BORERS, DOGWOOD

ZONES: ALL

If your new dogwood tree is dying, the dogwood borer or pecan borer *(Synanthedon scitula)* could be the reason. The swift-flying adult moth, ½ in. long, is active during the day. It has a wasp-shaped, bluish body with yellow stripes and yellow legs. Wings are clear and rimmed in black. Mature borer larvae, ½ in. long, are whitish with pale brown heads. Young larvae are light brown.

Adult borer

Target: Dogwood, pecan, elm, hickory, willow, and other trees

Damage: Leaves turn prematurely red in midsummer. Trunk areas injured by larval feeding appear lumpy. Eventually tree bark sloughs off swollen areas, and a coarse, brown "sawdust" called frass may be visible under damaged bark. As the infestation progresses, abnormal branch and twig growth may occur, and foliage begins to die back at upper tree areas. Newly transplanted trees are especially susceptible and may die. Mature trees usually survive initial infestation, but will die if attacked in successive years.

Life cycle: Larvae overwinter under tree bark, pupating in spring. Adults emerge in May and June, remaining active until September. Females lay eggs in injured areas of the bark. Hatched larvae crawl over branches and enter through tree wounds, scars, or crevices in the tree crotch. Larvae feed within the inner bark until winter, making meandering tunnels. There is one generation per year.

Prevention: Healthy trees are less susceptible. Fertilize and water adequately. Do not prune dogwoods during summer when moths are laying eggs. Avoid wounding or injuring trees with mowers or string trimmers, as the resinous smell released from the wound attracts borers. Consider planting Kousa dogwood *(Cornus kousa)*.

Control: Spray trunk and damaged areas with an insecticide containing chlorpyrifos (Dursban) or lindane, beginning in mid-May. Repeat according to label directions. You can sometimes kill borer larvae under the bark by inserting a wire up the entry hole.

BORERS, IRIS

ZONES: US, MS, LS, CS

The pernicious iris borer *(Macronoctua onusta)* is the bane of iris fanciers throughout the South. The plump, pinkish white larva of a sneaky night-flying moth hollows out rhizomes and opens the door to a smelly, nasty disease called bacterial rot (see page 212).

Target: Irises, particularly bearded (German) and Japanese types

Damage: Pinhole scars appear on young leaves. Leaf edges may look ragged. Young larvae bore into the leaves, feeding as they proceed toward the rhizome. Yellowing foliage develops dark, streaked, or watery areas. As mature larvae feed on rhizomes, their tunnels appear as multiple holes. Or they may completely hollow it out. Borers excrete slimy waste matter, called frass, which is a breeding ground for soft-rot bacteria, giving iris a slimy look at ground level. Leaves break off easily; rhizomes become soft, watery, and smelly.

Life cycle: Adult moths can lay up to 1,000 eggs in the fall onto brown, dried iris leaves. The eggs hatch in April. Larvae feed on young, rapidly growing leaves. By June, the larvae move down to the rhizome. In August, they turn into brownish black, shiny pupae, resting 2 in. deep in the soil for about 2 weeks. New adult moths emerge in September. There is one generation per year.

> **BORING BUT NOT BORED.** *Maybe it's just an illusion, but it seems the old-fashioned, unimproved bearded irises fall victim to borers less than the award-winning hybrids. By today's standards, the old solid yellow, blue, and white irises may be a bit dull. But at least they stay alive.*

Prevention: Good sanitation is key. Each fall and winter, remove and destroy old, brown iris leaves. Don't purchase infested plants. Inspect leaves by letting the sun shine through. If borers are present, they may be visible. When dividing rhizomes, place them in the sun for a few days to let cut surfaces heal over before replanting. Discard all damaged leaves.

Control: Spray foliage at 5 in. tall, according to label directions with chlorpyrifos (Dursban), dimethoate (Cygon), endosulfan (Thiodan), or lindane.

BORERS, LILAC

SHRUB AND TREE PESTS

⚡ ZONES: US, MS, LS, CS

Two borers attack lilacs in the South. They look alike, do similar damage, and sometimes have overlapping territories. The true lilac borer *(Podosesia syringae),* shown above, attacks lilacs and privet mainly east of the Mississippi River. The banded ash borer *(P. aureocinta),* formerly found west of the Mississippi River but now in overlapping territory with the lilac borer, also attacks lilacs but prefers ash *(Fraxinus),* mountain ash *(Sorbus),* and osmanthus. Both borers are offspring of clearwing moths that look and act like paper wasps.

Target: Lilac, privet, ash, mountain ash, osmanthus

Damage: Borers tunnel into the main stems, causing the plant to wilt in hot weather. Numerous holes appear in the bark. Sawdust-like frass accumulates at entry points. Infested stems swell and crack and may break away from the plant. Repeated infestations may kill the plant.

Life cycle: Adult moths of the lilac borer emerge in May. After mating, females lay eggs at the base of lilac or privet trunks. Larvae hatch in 10 to 14 days and immediately bore into the host. They continue growing and feeding until spring, then pupate. Banded ash borer moths emerge from July to September to mate. The larvae enter the host in fall, feed until the following summer, and then pupate. Both borers have one generation per year.

Prevention: Borer moths frequently lay eggs near wounds. So avoid pruning target plants when borers are active. Be careful not to injure the bark with lawn mowers or string trimmers.

Control: Prune off and destroy heavily infested stems and branches in fall and winter. For lilac borer, spray trunks and main branches with chlorpyrifos (Dursban) in mid-May. Repeat about a month later. For banded ash borer, spray trunks with lindane, chlorpyrifos (Dursban), or endosulfan (Thiodan) in early June and again in early September.

BORERS, PEACH TREE

FRUIT TREE PESTS

⚡ ZONES: US, MS, LS, CS

If your peach tree is dying or you see sap oozing from the trunk, peach tree borers could be the reason. Two different borers, cousins of the dogwood borer (see opposite page), attack peach and other fruit trees in the South. The greater peach tree borer *(Synanthedon exitiosa),* shown above, is a white caterpillar with a brown head, ¾–1 in. long. The lesser peach tree borer *(S. pictipes)* looks quite similar but is ½–¾ in. long. Both are larvae of blue-black clearwing moths.

Target: Both pests attack fruiting and ornamental peach, apricot, cherry, nectarine, and plum trees.

Damage: Both borers chew tunnels under the bark, interfering with the tree's ability to transport water and nutrients. The greater peach tree borer does most of its damage to the main trunk, operating from 1–2 ft. above ground to 2–3 in. below ground. The lesser borer targets the upper trunk and major limbs.

Life cycle: Female moths of the greater borer emerge in summer and early fall. They lay eggs in the cracks of bark. Larvae hatch and burrow into the bark to feed, overwintering inside. They leave the tree in late spring to pupate in the soil. The lesser borer follows much the same pattern but pupates inside the tree, covering the exit hole with a silken web. Both borers have one generation per year.

Prevention: Avoid damaging the bark as nicks provide easy entry for borers. Closely inspect trunks and main branches for holes that ooze sap. Remove and destroy severely infested trees as these attract more borers.

Control: If your tree has just a single borer, try sticking a wire up the hole to kill it. Otherwise, spray the trunk and major branches of fruit trees with endosulfan (Thiodan), lindane, or chlorpyrifos (Dursban) according to label directions. Spray in late August, again in April, and again in early July.

BORERS, RHODODENDRON

SHRUB PESTS

✎ ZONES: US, MS, LS

Rhododendrons aren't the easiest shrubs to grow in the South. The rhododendron borer *(Synanthedon rhododendri)* is one reason why. The adult is a day-flying moth that looks a lot like a wasp. Its abdomen is black and blue with three horizontal yellow stripes. Its black head has green-and-white markings and long antennae.

Target: Rhododendrons and occasionally mountain laurel and deciduous azaleas, particularly if these shrubs are planted near infested rhododendrons

Damage: The larva, a yellowish white caterpillar about ½ in. long, tunnels into the wood of trunks and branches. Wilting leaves turn pale green, then olive, and finally yellowish. Branches grow slowly and break off. Many show scars from previous infestations. Holes also occur in V-shaped crotches of limbs. Severely infested plants die.

Life cycle: Moths emerge in late May and feed on plant nectar. Females place eggs in bark crevices, old pruning scars, V-shaped crotches, and old larval tunnels. The eggs quickly hatch. Larvae immediately chew entry holes into the shrub's inner bark. Larval feeding creates long tunnels. Sawdust accumulates on the bark and on the ground around the plant. Larvae begin hibernating in late fall, then resume feeding. Feeding resumes in March. Larvae chew cells into the outer bark, form cocoons, and pupate. As they mature, they wriggle out of the cocoons, cut exit holes in the bark, partially emerge, then change into moths.

Prevention: Borers prefer plants stressed by inadequate care and poor growing conditions. Keep plants well watered and fertilized. Plant them in well-drained, well-aerated, acid soil containing plenty of organic matter. Avoid wounding them with lawn mowers and string trimmers. Keep pruning to a minimum.

Control: Inspect rhododendrons frequently. Prune out and destroy infested branches in fall, winter, and very early spring, before egg-laying moths emerge. In late spring, after they emerge, spray the trunks and branches according to label directions with lindane or chlorpyrifos (Dursban). Spray three more times at intervals of 7 to 10 days.

BORERS, ROSE

ROSE PESTS

✎ ZONES: ALL

If you find holes in canes, boring insects may be attacking your roses. Many types of borers plague roses, particularly the larvae of the rose-stem sawfly *(Hartigia trimaculata)*, the rose-stem girdler *(Agrilus aurichalceus)*, and carpenter bees *(Xylocopa sp.)*, shown above. The adult rose-stem sawfly is a small wasplike insect with transparent wings. Its larvae grow to ¾ in. long and are yellowish white with brown heads. The adult rose-stem girdler is a ¼-in.-long, metallic green beetle. Its larvae are whitish. The adult carpenter bee is ³⁄₁₆ in. long and metallic green or metallic blue-black. Its larvae are curled and yellowish.

Target: Roses and other plants, depending on the borer

Damage: Rose borers tunnel around and into canes and under bark. Their feeding destroys pathways for nutrients and water. Wilting foliage often indicates the presence of borers, as does dieback or stunting of the cane. A slight swelling may appear on the cane where the borer is feeding. If you cut into the swelling, you'll see the borer.

Life cycle: The life cycle of rose borers varies. The rose-stem sawfly appears in June and punctures current-season canes to lay its eggs. The feeding larvae initially girdle infested canes, then bore within, traveling downward. There is usually only one borer per cane. The rose-stem girdler adult lays its eggs under the bark. Emerging grubs eat spiral tunnels around the canes. The canes then swell and split as the plant grows. Small carpenter bees burrow into the center of pruned stems and deposit eggs. Slitting the stem lengthwise usually reveals a half-dozen or so grubs. Most borers produce only one generation per year.

Prevention: Keep roses healthy with adequate water and fertilizer. Use candle wax, glue, or caulk to seal the cut ends of pruned canes.

Control: Chemical controls aren't needed nor are they effective. Prune infested canes back to healthy wood.

BORERS, SHOT-HOLE

FRUIT TREE PESTS

ZONES: US, MS, LS, CS

The shot-hole borer *(Scolytus rugulosus)*, a common pest of fruit trees, can be identified by a pattern on tree branches of small, pencil-point holes, shown above. Sap may be running out of the holes, which have been made by a black beetle so minute it is often hard to see. To determine if the damage has been caused by the shot-hole borer, peel back the bark to look for galleries of holes running 1–2 in. lengthwise down the cambial layer. This is where the beetle has laid its eggs. The larval stage, which causes the damage, is a tiny worm the size of a pinhead.

Target: The shot-hole borer most often attacks cherry, peach, and plum trees, particularly trees that are infrequently watered, already diseased, poorly pruned, or otherwise stressed.

Damage: Shot-hole borers interrupt the flow of nutrients. In severe cases, branches may be girdled and die back.

Life cycle: Adult female beetles dig holes within the bark and lay their eggs on the cambium. The hatching larvae feed and pupate under the bark. There may be one or two generations per year; the last generation overwinters inside as larvae and emerges as adult beetles the next spring.

Prevention: Keep fruit trees well watered and fertilized; routinely prune off dead or dying branches; correct any other disease or insect problems on the tree. Do not leave pruned limbs or cut firewood near fruit trees, as the beetles may lay their eggs there instead.

Control: Healthy fruit trees can withstand shot-hole borers by exuding resinous sap, which drowns and kills the borer larvae. The sap oozing through trunk holes indicates that this cure is taking place. Water and fertilize affected trees and prune off dead or infected branches. In early spring, spray the bark with an insecticide containing lindane or chlorpyrifos (Dursban), carefully following directions on the label.

BOX ELDER BUGS

MAPLE AND HOUSEHOLD PESTS

ZONES: US, MS, LS, CS

Many gardeners never know the name of that tree outside of their window, until strange bugs invade the house in winter. Then a frantic call goes out to the Cooperative Extension Office, and they find out. The adult box elder bug *(Leptocoris trivittatus)* is dark brown to black and ½ in. long. Distinctive red-orange stripes decorate its wings. Juvenile bugs are bright red with black legs and wing patches.

Target: Female box elders *(Acer negundo)* and occasionally seed-bearing silver maples *(A. saccharinum)*

Damage: Both young and adults feed on tender twigs, leaves, flowers, and seeds of box elder and silver maples. They use long, slender, piercing mouthparts to suck sap. Other than deforming some leaves, this really doesn't harm the tree. Most complaints come when box elder bugs enter homes in fall to avoid winter cold. They don't do much harm, but emit a sickening odor if you smash them. This is called "revenge."

Life cycle: In April and May, females lay clusters of red-orange eggs in bark crevices of box elders, as well as on stones, leaves, and other nearby trees. The eggs hatch in about 2 weeks. Normally solitary, females mass in huge numbers in October on the sun-facing side of trees, fences, and houses. They fly in swarms toward warm, dry sites, often entering buildings through small cracks around windows and doors. They hibernate over winter, but may awaken during winter warm spells. Usually, only one generation occurs per year, but two are possible in the Coastal South.

Prevention: Find out which of your trees is a female box elder (females have seeds) and get rid of it. Don't plant silver maples. Seal around windows and doors to close entry points.

Control: Outdoors, spray swarms with a pyrethrin, malathion, or diazinon. Follow label directions carefully. Indoors, vacuum up bugs or use a household insecticide containing a pyrethrin. For large infestations indoors, consult a pest control company.

BUDWORMS, TOBACCO

FLOWER, VEGETABLE, AND CROP PESTS

✔ ZONES: MS, LS, CS, TS

Tobacco budworm *(Heliothis virescens)* feeds mostly on tobacco in the South but eventually turns to flowers. The adult budworm, a close relative of the corn earworm (see page 162), is a light green moth. The larva is a striped caterpillar up to ¾ in. long. Depending on the food it's eating, the caterpillar varies in color from brown to green to red.

Originally a subtropical pest, tobacco budworm doesn't overwinter in areas where the ground freezes or winter temperatures dip below 20°F, but its pupae may overwinter in the soil of potted plants taken inside for winter. They may also survive in protected spots near building foundations.

Target: Tobacco, ageratum, geranium *(Pelargonium)*, impatiens, marigold, nicotiana, penstemon, and petunias. Ivy geraniums are resistant.

Damage: Young larvae tunnel into flower buds and feed from the inside. Older caterpillars chew holes in the flowers and leaves. Buds of geranium, penstemon, and petunia may appear dried up and not open, or the blossoms may open tattered and full of holes.

Life cycle: Moths lay eggs singly on host plants. After they hatch, caterpillars feed a few weeks before pupating. Some pupate during the summer within the dried-up buds. Others pupate over the winter in earthern cells several inches below the soil surface. The moths die in freezing weather. There may be more than one generation per year.

Prevention: People living near tobacco farms will naturally have more budworm problems. However, you can reduce your future budworm population by pulling up and destroying infested plants at the end of the season to get rid of eggs and pupae. Tilling soil in late fall may also reduce the numbers of surviving pupae.

Control: Tobacco budworms are notorious for building up resistance to pesticides. Get around this problem by alternating sprayings of *Bacillus thuringiensis kurstaki* (Dipel, Thuricide, Javelin) with carbaryl (Sevin), acephate (Orthene), or a pyrethrin.

CABBAGEWORMS

VEGETABLE AND FLOWER PESTS

✔ ZONES: ALL

Several caterpillars are called cabbageworms. The European or imported cabbageworm *(Pieris rapae)*, shown above, is the larva of a white butterfly often seen hovering around cabbage-family plants. The velvety light green larva grows to 1½ in. long. The native cabbage looper *(Trichoplusia ni)* is about the same size. It has a humpbacked gait like that of an inchworm. This is the larva of a nocturnal gray moth. Also common are the smaller, ¼-in.-long green caterpillars of the diamondback moth *(Plutella xylostella)*, which wriggle rapidly when disturbed. The striped, yellowish gray caterpillar of the cabbage webworm *(Hellula rogatalis)* bores into stems, buds, and stalks in fall. The cabbage maggot *(Delia brassicae)*, the larval form of a fly, is ¼ in. long and white; it lives underground, feeding on plant roots.

Target: Cabbageworms attack cole crops, including broccoli, brussels sprouts, cabbage, cauliflower, and radicchio. Cabbage loopers also feed on the foliage of beet, carnation, lettuce, nasturtium, and spinach. The cabbage maggot attacks the roots of cole crops.

Damage: Caterpillars chew holes in leaves, ruining edible foliage and florets. Plants attacked by cabbage maggots are yellowed and stunted and wilt during the hot part of the day, even when watered.

Life cycle: Adults lay eggs on or near host. Caterpillars hatch in a few days and begin to feed immediately. Larvae of imported cabbageworms, cabbage loopers, and diamondback moths pupate in a cocoon on the plant. Cabbage maggots pupate underground.

Prevention: Shelter plants from egg-laying adults with floating row covers, especially in early spring. Crop rotation can limit cabbage maggots in soil. Between crops, clear and till beds to remove lingering adult moths, eggs, or pupae. Fall crops have fewer pests.

Control: Handpick caterpillars and cocoons. Natural predators include trichogramma wasps, yellow jackets, and lacewings. As soon as you notice white butterflies, spray with *Bacillus thuringiensis kurstaki* (Dipel, Thuricide, Javelin). Or, use rotenone, a pyrethrin, azadirachtin (Neem), or carbaryl (Sevin); follow directions carefully. Beneficial nematodes help control cabbage maggots.

CANKERWORMS

TREE PESTS

ZONES: ALL

These pests are also known as "inchworms" because their bodies hump up as they crawl. The names of the two kinds, spring cankerworm *(Paleacrita vernata)* and fall cankerworm *(Alsophila pometaria)*, are misleading—both do their damage in spring and early summer. These caterpillars may be green or brown with yellow side stripes. Fall cankerworms, shown above, have three pairs of legs at the front and rear of their bodies; spring cankerworms, two.

Target: Oaks, maples, hickories, ash, linden, beech, and occasionally apple

Damage: Young cankerworms chew buds and young leaves. As they grow, they skeletonize leaves. Defoliation may occur. Cankerworms also annoy people by spinning down from trees on silken strands and dropping in numbers onto people, cars, and picnic tables.

Life cycle: Spring cankerworms emerge as adult moths in February or March. Females lay eggs on tree branches just as leaves begin to unfurl. Larvae feed until late June, when they drop to the ground. They burrow into the soil 1–4 in. to pupate over winter. Fall cankerworm moths emerge in fall from pupal cases in the ground. They lay eggs on the trees in November and December, which hatch the following spring.

Prevention: Cankerworms are the lemmings of the insect world. Their numbers rise and fall precipitously from year to year, due to the presence or absence of natural enemies. Wrap trunks of susceptible trees with a 4–6-in.-wide band of horticultural sticky tape. Place the band 4–6 ft. high on the trunks, but beneath the first branches. This traps wingless female moths crawling up the trunk. Or make your own sticky tape by coating duct tape with a sticky substance called Tanglefoot, which is available in many organic gardening catalogs.

Control: Thoroughly spray the trunk during winter with horticultural oil to kill overwintering eggs. To kill young larvae, spray foliage in spring with *Bacillus thuringiensis kurstaki* (Dipel, Thuricide, Javelin), applying it in early evening. To kill large caterpillars, spray trees according to label directions with malathion, phosmet (Imidan), diazinon, rotenone, or acephate (Orthene).

CATALPA SPHINX CATERPILLARS

CATALPA PESTS

ZONES: ALL

The familiar catalpa sphinx caterpillar or catalpa worm is the larva of the seldom-seen, yellowish brown catalpa sphinx moth *(Ceratomia catalpae)*, which flies mostly at night. This large caterpillar (1–3 in. long) sports a distinctive black "horn" on the rear. It comes in two different color forms. One form bears a broad, black band down the entire length of its back. Its sides are white or pale yellow. The other has a black head, lacks the black band, and has greenish yellow sides with black dots and vertical black lines.

Target: Catalpa trees

Damage: Catalpa worms eat only catalpa leaves. Newly hatched caterpillars feed as a group and skeletonize single leaves. Mature larvae go their separate ways and consume entire leaves, except for the midribs and large veins. Entire trees may be defoliated. Catalpas quickly sprout new leaves, but successive generations of these pests may defoliate trees again, seriously weakening them.

Life cycle: Catalpa worms overwinter as pupae in the soil. Adult moths emerge in spring. Females lay up to 1,000 whitish eggs on the undersides of leaves. Larvae hatch within a week. Fully grown caterpillars drop to the ground to pupate. The life cycle is about 6 weeks. Two generations per year may occur in the Upper South; four in the Lower South. Generations may overlap, and caterpillars of different stages may infest a single tree at the same time.

GONE FISHIN'. *Catalpa worms make great fish bait. Many Southerners plant catalpas just for the worms. So if your friend's not home and the catalpa is bare, you'll probably find your buddy at the lake.*

Prevention: A type of stingless braconid wasp, *Apanteles glomeratus,* parasitizes and kills the caterpillars. The only other means of prevention is not to plant catalpas.

Control: Pesticides aren't usually needed. For serious infestations, however, spray the tree according to label directions with *Bacillus thuringiensis kurstaki* (Dipel, Thuricide, Javelin) or acephate (Orthene) when caterpillars are still small.

BUGS AND OTHER CRITTERS

CHINCH BUGS

LAWN PESTS

ZONES: ALL

Southern chinch bugs, *Blissus insularis,* suck the sap from grass blades and are a major pest. Adults have folded, flat, white wings with a distinctive triangular black marking. Their black bodies measure only ⅙ in. long. Newly emerging wingless nymphs are yellow, later turning red with a light-colored band across the back.

Target: Lawns, particularly St. Augustine grass

Damage: Small yellow or brown patches of dying grass appear in scattered areas, with each patch increasing in size until the entire lawn is affected. Damage is worse in hot, dry weather, and areas in full sun are more severely affected.

Life cycle: Chinch bug adults overwinter in protected places in and around lawns. Adults emerge in spring, feed, and mate. Pinhead-size nymphs hatch from eggs in about 2 weeks, mature in about a month, and live about 2 months. There are four to seven generations per year.

Prevention: Choose selections of St. Augustine grass, such as 'FX-10', 'Floralawn', and 'Floratam', that resist chinch bug damage. Also consider planting other grasses.

Control: Early diagnosis and treatment are key to controlling chinch bug damage. To check for these pests, press one end of a can (open at both ends) about 3 in. into the soil around an affected area. Fill the can with water and wait about 5 minutes. If chinch bugs are present, they will float to the surface. With severe infestations, part the grass and watch for movement of these insects away from the light. Controlling chinch bug infestations requires treatment of the entire lawn. Use a spray or granular insecticide containing chlorpyrifos (Dursban), applying it in early evening. Because several generations of chinch bugs can be present, repeated control applications may be necessary. However, insecticides also destroy beneficial big-eyed bugs (see page 153), predators of chinch bugs. These beneficials resemble chinch bugs, but have much wider eyes. Do not overfertilize, as this increases pest populations. Water lawns well to suppress pest numbers and promote the beneficial fungus *Beauveria bassiana,* which infects chinch bugs.

CICADAS, PERIODICAL

TREE PESTS

ZONES: ALL

Summer in the South wouldn't be the same without the deafening hum of cicadas, those large, bug-eyed insects people mistakenly call locusts. The reddish orange eyes, legs, and wing veins are distinguishing features of this 1-in.-long, dark, stout, wedge-shaped insect with long, wide wings. Many species appear every year. But the ones that cause folks to stand up and take notice are the periodical cicadas—residents of a sort of insect Brigadoon. Some populations emerge simultaneously every 13 years. Others take 17 years.

17-year cicada

Target: Hardwood trees, including oaks, dogwoods, hickories, peaches, gums

Damage: Larvae (nymphs) suck sap from tree roots. Adults occasionally suck sap from twigs. Such damage is usually minor. The real blow comes when adult females cut slits near the ends of branches, into which they deposit eggs. Branch tips die and remain on the tree for some time before falling. A heavily infested tree will look disfigured for years. Young trees may be seriously injured.

Life cycle: A female lays 400 to 600 eggs in tree bark. Antlike nymphs hatch in 6 weeks and drop to the ground, where they burrow and live on sap from roots. Each population remains underground for 13 or 17 years. Then, on one evening from April through June, all the nymphs—up to 40,000—emerge at once. Only male cicadas hum. It's their mating call. The noise, mating, and egg laying continue for about a month. Then the adults die en masse. Piles of corpses do raise a stink.

Prevention: Contact your Cooperative Extension Office to see if periodical cicadas inhabit your area and when the next invasion is due. Avoid planting new trees for 2 years prior to a predicted onslaught. Cover young trees with netting.

Control: Invasions of periodical cicadas cannot be controlled. You can spray small trees with carbaryl (Sevin) when adults first appear, but chemical control for large trees isn't possible.

CODLING MOTHS

FRUIT AND NUT PESTS

✂ ZONES: US, MS, LS, CS

This is usually the culprit found in rotting fruit either on the tree or on the ground. The codling moth caterpillar *(Laspeyresia pomonella)* is under 1 in. long, with a pink or whitish body and a dark brown head. The adult moth, gray-brown with copper brown bands, has a wingspan of less than an inch.

Target: The codling moth is a major pest of apples, pears, plums, and walnuts.

Damage: Apple skins may be blemished with holes and dark spots, and the fruit tunneled and ruined with blackish fecal waste. Apples, pears, and walnuts may drop prematurely, with the caterpillar still inside.

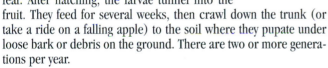

Adult codling moth emerging from pupal skin

Life cycle: Shortly after bloom time in midspring, the adult moth lays single eggs on a small developing fruit or a nearby leaf. After hatching, the larvae tunnel into the fruit. They feed for several weeks, then crawl down the trunk (or take a ride on a falling apple) to the soil where they pupate under loose bark or debris on the ground. There are two or more generations per year.

Prevention: Sanitation is key. Rake away fallen leaves and dropped fruit under the tree throughout the year to destroy pupae.

Control: A combination of controls is the most effective strategy. In early spring, use sticky traps with pheromone bait. The traps will tell you when the moths are in the egg-laying mood. Then you can introduce biological controls, such as parasitoid wasps, to kill caterpillars as they hatch. Wrap the trunks with sticky barriers to trap larvae as they crawl down. Rake away dropped fruit and leaves. For severe infestations, spray trees with *Bacillus thuringiensis kurstaki* (Dipel, Thuricide, Javelin), malathion, phosmet (Imidan), or carbaryl (Sevin). The sprays will be effective only if the larvae are caught before they enter the fruit.

COLORADO POTATO BEETLES

VEGETABLE PESTS

✂ ZONES: ALL

The adult Colorado potato beetle *(Leptinotarsa deremlineata)* can quickly make duds of your spuds. The adult beetle, shown above with grubs and eggs, is ⅓ in. long with showy, black-and-yellow-striped wing covers and an orange-and-black-spotted "vest" behind its head. This distinguishes it from other beetles that target potato plants. The larva of the potato beetle is a humpbacked grub that is red with a row of black spots on each side.

Target: The foliage of potato, tomato, eggplant, and related tomato-family (Solanaceae) plants such as tomatillo and ground cherry

Damage: Both adult beetles and grubs feed voraciously on leaves and stems, leaving behind spots of black excrement. Large infestations completely defoliate potato plants.

Life cycle: Adult beetles emerge from the soil in early spring to feed on young plants and lay eggs on the undersides of leaves. A single female may lay hundreds of eggs at a time. After a week, the eggs hatch and the larvae begin feeding for a few weeks, then burrow into the ground to pupate. Pupae may overwinter. There are one to three generations per year.

Prevention: In spring, floating row covers or a thick straw mulch can help prevent the adult beetles from reaching the plants and laying eggs. Strongly scented companion plants such as marigold, catnip, and tansy planted around potato and tomato seedlings may also keep the flying adults from identifying their target by smell. Remove plant debris and weeds from potato beds each fall.

Control: Adult beetles, egg clusters, and grubs can be handpicked and destroyed by dropping them in soapy water. A dusting of *Bacillus thuringiensis (Bt)* San Diego strain (also known as M-1 or *B. t. tenebrionis*) controls the grubs in the early stages. Natural predators of the larger grubs and beetles include birds, spined soldier bugs, and parasitic nematodes. To kill adult beetles and grubs, spray or dust plants with a pyrethrin, rotenone, azadirachtin (Neem), diazinon, or carbaryl (Sevin). Be sure to follow label directions.

CORN EARWORMS

VEGETABLE AND FLOWER PESTS

ZONES: ALL

This is the pest you worry about when you bite into an ear of corn and find only half a worm. The larva changes from a tiny white caterpillar with a black head to one that is over an inch long, green or pink or dark brown, with zigzag stripes along its length. The adult form of corn earworm (*Heliothis zea*) is a night-flying moth that migrates long distances.

Target: Besides corn, this caterpillar attacks the fruits of tomato, pepper, even bean and pea plants. It also feeds on garden flowers such as canna, geranium, nicotiana, penstemon, petunia, and sunflower.

Corn earworm adult

Damage: Earworm eggs and caterpillars are found in the silks or tips of ripening corn. Salvage the ear by cutting off the spoiled tip. On flowers, buds and leaves will be chewed and plants may not bloom at all, or blossoms may open tattered.

Life cycle: The adult female moth lays domed, ridged white eggs singly on silks or leaf undersides. Caterpillars hatch and feed for several weeks, then crawl down to pupate in the soil. There can be up to seven generations per year, on various host plants.

Prevention: An old method that still works is to place fine sand or 20 drops (about a teaspoon) of mineral oil on the tip of each ear when silks appear, to deter the egg-laying moth. Pinch the top of each ear with a rubber band to keep caterpillars out. Or grow tight-husked selections such as 'Country Gentleman'.

Control: Spray with a pyrethrum or carbaryl (Sevin), according to label directions; target-spray directly onto the silks every 2 to 5 days, as long as the silks are still green. Introduce or encourage beneficial insects, such as lacewings and trichogramma wasps. (Any eggs found on plants that are black, not white, have already been parasitized by the trichogramma wasp.) Dust petunias with *Bacillus thuringiensis kurstaki* (Dipel, Thuricide, Javelin). Tilling the soil between crops helps kill overwintering pupae.

CUCUMBER BEETLES

VEGETABLE AND FLOWER PESTS

ZONES: ALL

There are two types of cucumber beetles to watch for in the South. Striped cucumber beetles (*Diabrotica acalymna vittata*), shown above, are the most common. Adults are greenish yellow with three black stripes down the back. Spotted cucumber beetles (*Diabrotica sp.*) are yellowish green with a dozen black spots on the back. Both types are about ¼ in. long. Their larvae are slender and white, about ¼ – ½ in. long, with brown heads and brown patches on their first and last segments.

Target: Striped cucumber beetles attack cucumber, cantaloupe, muskmelon, and squash. Spotted cucumber beetles attack these plants and also corn, dahlias, roses, and other ornamentals.

Damage: Adult beetles chew holes in leaves, buds, and flowers and rip ragged lesions in stems. But they do the most damage by spreading diseases, such as bacterial wilt and mosaic virus, to vegetable crops. The larvae of spotted cucumber beetles also chew roots of corn (which is why these pests are also known as corn rootworms), killing seedlings in a few days or wilting and stunting plants later in the season.

Life cycle: Adults appear in late spring. Females lay eggs in the soil around host plants. Larvae burrow into the soil and chew plant roots, then pupate in a few weeks. One to four or more generations occur per year. The beetles overwinter as adults, hiding and hibernating under fallen leaves and garden debris.

Prevention: Use floating row covers to keep adult beetles off of your plants. But be sure to remove the covers when flowers appear to allow insects to pollinate the plants. Keep corn plants well watered so they'll quickly replace munched roots. Collect and destroy garden debris in fall to reduce the number of overwintering beetles. To control beetles on roses, use rose food containing the systemic insecticide disulfoton (Di-Syston). Do not use disulfoton on edibles.

Control: If you have just a few beetles, pick them off the plants. Birds and tachinid flies provide natural controls. For infestations, spray plants according to label directions with rotenone, a pyrethrin, malathion, or carbaryl (Sevin).

CURCULIOS, PLUM

FLOWER AND NUT PESTS

ZONES: US, MS, LS, CS

Plum curculios *(Conotrachelus nenupthars)* know how to get out of trouble. When disturbed, they roll up in a ball and play dead. These small weevils with long, curved snouts are about ¼ in. long. Their grayish brown color makes them difficult to see on the branches of backyard orchard trees. But they cause noticeable damage to plum and apple fruit in the form of a distinctive crescent- or mushroom-shaped scar. The larvae, seen only in spring, are grayish white legless grubs, ⅓ in. long.

Target: Plum curculios feed on fruit and nut trees, especially plum and stone fruit trees, and on blueberry plants.

Damage: Adults chew holes in flower buds, blossoms, and green fruit. The larvae tunnel through fruits and nuts, leaving rotting brown interiors. Fruits and nuts are deformed and drop prematurely.

Life cycle: Adult curculios overwinter in fallen leaves and garden debris. In spring females make a crescent-shaped incision in developing fruit and lay their eggs inside. After hatching, the larvae feed for two to three weeks within the fruit. When the fruit drops, the larvae crawl out to pupate in the soil. Adults emerge from the soil from midsummer to late fall. There may be one or two generations per year.

Prevention: Clear fallen leaves and dropped fruits from under fruit trees on a regular basis, to reduce hiding places for adult curculios and to keep larvae from reaching the soil to pupate.

Control: Place a cloth underneath the tree and shake the branches, and curculios will fall in little balls onto the cloth where they can be gathered up and destroyed. You can also kill adult curculios by spraying tree branches with a pyrethrin, rotenone, malathion, phosmet (Imidan), or carbaryl (Sevin), applied according to label directions. Spraying is most effective if done right after petal drop, the time when adult curculios are actively crawling on branches and beginning to lay eggs. Once the eggs and larvae are in the fruit, no amount of spraying will deter them.

CUTWORMS

VEGETABLE, FLOWER, AND LAWN PESTS

ZONES: ALL

Cutworms are the hairless caterpillar larvae of various night-flying moths. They come in several colors and may be up to 2 in. long. Cutworms feed only at night but you'll often find them on the soil during the daytime, curled up into a C shape. They are particularly common in new gardens created from areas that had previously been lawn or a long-standing weedy patch.

Target: Cutworms eat almost any type of grass, vegetable, or flowering plant.

Damage: Cutworms attack seedlings or recently transplanted garden vegetables or flowers, severing stems and leaving what's left of the young plants lying on the ground. In lawns, they wreak havoc during spring and summer, causing small patches of sod to turn brown and die. Grass blades around the margins of the affected areas show jagged holes along their edges. The entire lawn looks ragged.

NIGHT MOVES. *Cutworms work under cover of darkness. To check for them, inspect seedlings or the lawn at night with a flashlight.*

Life cycle: Adult moths lay tiny white eggs in garden debris and soil. The caterpillars feed at night, retiring for the day to the cover of soil or a leaf. After feeding for several weeks, they burrow into the soil to pupate, then emerge as adult moths. There may be several generations per year.

Prevention: Before sowing seeds or transplanting seedlings, clear and till garden beds thoroughly to destroy any eggs, caterpillars, or pupae. To protect transplants, encircle each one with a stiff paper collar (a paper cup with the bottom cut out works well), pushed 1–2 in. into the ground and extending 1–2 in. above the soil level.

Control: Introduce natural predators, such as beneficial soil nematodes, parasitoid wasps, ground beetles, soldier beetles, rough stinkbugs (see page 190), and tachinid flies. Spread diatomaceous earth around seedlings to deter caterpillars. Treat lawns with diazinon or chlorpyrifos (Dursban). Apply according to label directions.

DAMSEL BUGS

BENEFICIALS

✔ ZONES: ALL

Damsel bugs aren't shy and demure when it comes to dealing with other insects. Slender and tan, gray, black, or brown, they resemble the assassin bug (see page 149), another beneficial predator. Adult bugs are about ½ in. long. They have four wings, which when folded make an X-like mark across their backs. Some plant-destructive bugs also have X-like marks on their backs, but you can identify damsel bugs by their long, narrow heads.

Juvenile damsel bugs, or nymphs, resemble the adults, but are smaller and darker and have no wings. Both the adults and the nymphs are distinguished by long, jointed legs and angled antennae. They move quickly to hunt slower-moving prey and may fly away if disturbed.

To attract damsel bugs to your garden, add ornamental grasses, ground covers, or a wildflower meadow to your garden. Limit your use of pesticides.

Target: Damsel bugs eat aphids as well as the caterpillars or nymphs of armyworms, asparagus beetles, corn earworm, imported cabbageworm, leafhoppers, and sawflies. They also eat the eggs of moths and the Colorado potato beetle.

Damage: Damsel bugs do not damage plants.

Life cycle: Adults lay eggs on many plants, including grasses and weeds. The eggs hatch into nymphs that crawl around to hunt. They gradually attain wings after they molt. Depending on the climate and species, there may be several generations per year.

Prevention and control: No measures are needed.

DAMSELS IN DISTRESS. *Damsel bugs have their own enemies, often falling victim to fungi and beneficial tachinid flies and parasitoid wasps. (Any soldier bugs in shining armor out there?)*

DRAGONFLIES

BENEFICIALS

✔ ZONES: ALL

Imagine you're a mosquito with a dragonfly in hot pursuit. It must feel like meeting Godzilla and smelling like a plate of fish. Approximately 450 species of dragonflies inhabit North America, ranging in length from ¾ – 5 in. They resemble their close relatives, the damselflies, but there's an easy way to tell them apart — dragonflies rest with their wings spread, while damselflies hold their wings together parallel to their bodies. Also, a dragonfly's body is rather stout, while a damselfly's is thin and delicate.

Dragonflies come in many colors — iridescent blue or green, yellow, black, brown, and rust-red. Four long, powerful wings move independently, enabling the insects to fly forward, backward, or hover. Huge, compound eyes help them spot prey. Juvenile dragonflies, called naiads, live in water and look nothing like their parents. But they're ferocious predators, too.

ONE BIG, BAD BUG. *Some dragonflies in Central America belonging to the genus* Coerulatus *boast wingspans of up to 8 in. But that's nothing compared with prehistoric dragonflies. Some of these scary arthropods paraded wingspans of 30 in. or more. A single one could make off with an entire bologna sandwich!*

Target: Adult dragonflies consume mosquitoes, midges, gnats, and other flying insects. Naiads eat mosquito larvae and other aquatic insects, worms, tadpoles, and even small fish.

Life cycle: Dragonflies spend most of their time near ponds, marshes, and streams. After mating in flight, the female deposits eggs in a plant or simply drops them into the water or mud. Naiads hatch and spend 1 to 3 years in the water, eating, growing, and molting up to 15 times. They emerge in spring, molt one final time, and become adults. Adults usually fly from June through October.

Prevention and control: No prevention is needed, unless your last name is Mosquito. Dragonflies are highly beneficial to the garden and should be encouraged to proliferate. The primary requirement for having them around is fairly still, non-chlorinated water.

EARWIGS, EUROPEAN

VEGETABLE AND FLOWER PESTS

ZONES: ALL

Contrary to the old wives' tale and the modern horror film, earwigs do not crawl into people's ears and bore into their brains. Introduced from Europe in the early 1900s, the European earwig *(Forticula nuricularia)* is now found throughout North America. Although they have wings, these insects rarely fly, preferring to run for cover with a quick, scurrying crawl when they are disturbed. Measuring ¾ in. long, they're easily identified by the pointy pincers on the tail end of their abdomens.

Target: Earwigs lodge in all garden plants, crawling out to feed at night on decaying plant remains. During the day they often congregate in dark, damp places in the garden, such as under rocks.

Damage: Earwigs are often blamed for damage in the garden that is usually the fault of another pest. Young earwigs do like to nibble tender plant tips, so they can be destructive in the springtime. Mostly they are happy to be part of your garden's cleanup crew, helping to transform garden debris into useful humus. But large infestations may be a nuisance, and the insects can inflict a painful pinch.

Life cycle: Earwigs are active from spring through late fall; they hibernate through the winter. Adult females lay clusters of 20 to 60 eggs in the soil in the autumn or early spring, tending the nest until the eggs hatch. There is usually one generation per year.

Prevention: Keep the garden clean of debris and remove earwig hiding places.

Control: Make earwig traps by placing damp, loosely rolled-up newspapers on the ground near plants. The insects will crawl into the rolls, which you can then discard. Or fill a low-sided can, such as a cat-food can, with ½ in. of vegetable oil and place on the ground. Special earwig traps with poison bait are available at garden centers; place them near areas where earwigs are likely to be—in woodpiles, under wooden stairways or decks, near old wooden fences and arbors. For severe infestations, spray soil around plants with diazinon in the late afternoon or evening, according to label directions.

ELM LEAF BEETLES

TREE PESTS

ZONES: ALL

Found throughout the South, this beetle *(Xanthogaleruca luteda)* feeds on elm leaves both as a grub and as an adult. Adults are oval, about ¼ in. long, with pale yellow wing covers with a lengthwise black stripe. The ½-in.-long grub is yellow with black stripes. Both hide on the undersides of elm leaves.

Target: The elm leaf beetle concentrates on trees in the elm family, *Ulmaceae.* European elms are often hardest hit; American elms, Chinese elms, and zelkova are less frequently attacked.

Damage: Adult beetles riddle foliage with holes; grubs skeletonize entire leaves. In the worst cases they defoliate branches or whole trees. Large grub populations chew so much foliage that the weakened tree becomes susceptible to the elm bark beetle, which often carries Dutch elm disease.

Elm leaf beetle larvae

Life cycle: Female beetles lay yellowish, teardrop-shaped eggs in spring on undersides of leaves. Larvae feed for several weeks, then drop to pupate in leaf mold. Bright yellow pupae are often found near the tree trunk. From one to five generations exist per year, more in the Coastal and Tropical South.

Prevention: Avoid planting European elms. Keep existing trees healthy and well watered. Prune off dead or dying branches, which may provide a resting place for adult beetles.

Control: *Bacillus thuringiensis* (*Bt*) San Diego strain kills both beetles and grubs but will not harm beneficial predators. Apply *Bt* to the undersides of leaves every few days after you first notice larvae. Heavy infestations may require banding or spraying with acephate (Orthene), phosmet (Imidan), or carbaryl (Sevin). For large trees a tree professional can inject the tree through the bark with a systemic insecticide. Wrap sections of tree trunk with a sticky barrier to trap beetles and larvae that crawl on the bark. Native predators include several tiny parasitoid wasps and a black tachinid fly that lays its eggs in beetle larvae.

FLEA BEETLES

VEGETABLE AND FLOWER PESTS

ZONES: ALL

Flea beetles *(Altica sp.)* are shiny oval blue-black, brown, or bronzy green beetles about ⅒ in. long. Some species have white or yellow markings. All jump like fleas when disturbed. The legless larvae are tiny and gray white. Flea beetles prefer hot, dry conditions.

Target: Adults relish many garden vegetables, including broccoli, cabbage, chard, corn, eggplant, pepper, potato, radish, sweet potato, tomato, and turnip; they also like black-eyed Susan, marigold, and nasturtium.

Damage: Adult flea beetles chew leaves, leaving pits or small holes in foliage. While older plants withstand some damage, seedlings may dry out and die. Flea beetles also spread plant diseases, such as early blight (see page 226) and bacterial wilt (see page 212); tomatoes are often a victim.

Tobacco flea beetle adult

Life cycle: Adults overwinter in weeds such as horse nettle and pokeweed and garden debris. In late spring they lay tiny white eggs under the soil around host plants. Larvae feed and pupate underground. There are one to four generations per year.

Prevention: Clean the garden to remove havens for overwintering adults. Rotate crops to reduce pest populations. To protect seedlings in spring, use floating row covers. Keep garden beds well irrigated in summer. Plant vegetables close together, so leaf cover keeps the ground moist and less attractive to egg-laying adults.

Control: Lightly misting the leaves of vegetables and ground covers under siege may make the foliage less attractive to flea beetles. You can kill adult beetles by spraying with an insecticidal soap or with an insecticide containing rotenone or carbaryl (Sevin), applied according to label directions. Tilling between crops will cut down the number of eggs, larvae, and pupae in soil.

FRUIT FLIES

FRUIT PESTS

ZONES: ALL

An apple a day won't keep fruit flies away. The larvae of these small flies eat their way through all kinds of fruit, leaving a soft, wormy, disgusting mess. Species common to the South include the Mexican fruit fly *(Anastrepha ludens);* Caribbean fruit fly *(A. suspensa),* shown above; vinegar fly *(Drosophila melanogaster);* and apple maggot fly *(Rhagoletis pomonella).*

Target: Ripening, ripe, and rotting fruit of all kinds. The Mexican fruit fly is a serious pest in the citrus groves of the Rio Grande Valley of Texas. The Caribbean fruit fly attacks citrus, mangoes, and other orchard fruits in Florida. The apple maggot targets apples, cherries, plums, and pears. The vinegar fly frequents rotting produce and sweet liquids and often finds its way into your kitchen.

Damage: Infested fruits look soft and wormy. Apple skins may be pitted or dimpled. Citrus fruits have holes in their skins and rotten flesh and fall from the tree prematurely.

Life cycle: Adult flies lay eggs under the skins of developing fruits. The larvae, which are tiny maggots, burrow into the fruit to feed. At maturity, they eat their way out and drop to the ground to pupate. There may be one to several generations per year. The vinegar fly multiplies rapidly indoors, placing eggs near the surface of fermenting foods or other moist organic materials. Breeding may occur throughout the year. It can even take place in drains, garbage disposals, trash cans, and recycling bins.

Prevention: Promptly pick up and destroy fallen fruit. Refrigerate ripe fruit. Never bring fruit from foreign countries into the U.S. as it may harbor exotic fruit fly species that could devastate domestic orchards.

Control: To control apple maggots, hang sticky pheromone traps (available at some garden centers or by mail order) from the branches. Spray fruit trees according to label directions every 10 days throughout the fruiting season with malathion, phosmet (Imidan), or carbaryl (Sevin). Wait 7 days after spraying before picking fruit. Do not spray carbaryl on young apples, however, as it may cause them to drop. Once maggots enter fruits, chemicals are not effective.

GALL-FORMING INSECTS AND MITES

TREE AND SHRUB PESTS

ZONES: ALL

Several hundred different species of wasps, aphids, adelgids, midges, mites, moths, and sawflies create galls—weird, distorted, sometimes colorful growths on leaves, twigs, and flowers. Galls may look like pustules, corky nodules, fuzzy balls, spiky lumps, or, in the case of oak apple gall (pictured above) like small ripening apples. Although galls appear on many different trees and shrubs, most of them native, oaks are by far the favorite hosts.

Gall wasp laying eggs

Target: Oaks, beech, cottonwood, dogwood, elm, grape, hackberry, honey locust, linden, maple, poplar, red bay, spruce, willow, witch hazel, and yaupon

Damage: Damage is purely cosmetic in the vast majority of cases. However, severe infestations can weaken a plant.

Life cycle: Adult gall-makers either feed or lay one or more eggs in the soft tissue of a leaf or the thin bark of a twig. When the egg hatches, a larva begins to feed on the plant. Secretions from the larva irritate the plant, which protects itself by sealing off the intruder inside bumpy, raised scar tissue. Gall shapes, which are specific to the insect involved, may look like a bubble, blister, or ball. Depending on the species, gall-makers live from weeks to years within the gall, which gradually increases in size. The larvae eventually emerge to pupate. There may be several generations per year.

Prevention: This isn't practical in most cases. However, if you're considering planting a honey locust, the selection 'Shademaster' is known to resist gall-forming insects.

Control: Controlling galls in big trees isn't practical or necessary as the damage is mostly cosmetic. For smaller trees and shrubs, prune off the affected twigs and leaves and destroy them.

GRASSHOPPERS AND FIELD CRICKETS

VEGETABLE AND FLOWER PESTS

ZONES: ALL

Those "locust plagues" you may have read about in the Bible were really giant swarms of grasshoppers, shown above. More than 600 native species exist. The insects may be brown, black, green, or yellow. Adults are winged, 1–2 in. long, with large hind legs. Juvenile grasshoppers, called nymphs, are smaller and wingless. Brown field crickets *(Gryllus sp.)* are smaller than grasshoppers and chirp at night during mild weather.

Target: Grasshoppers usually annoy farmers more than home gardeners. During hot, dry weather, they decimate vegetable and grain crops. Crickets feed on foliage, seeds, flowers, and other insects.

Damage: Grasshoppers and crickets seldom pose serious problems. But in large numbers, they can strip plants to the ground. They usually appear in late summer and fall.

Life cycle: Grasshoppers and crickets commonly overwinter as eggs in the soil or on weeds. Nymphs hatch out in midspring, molting their skins five or six times as they grow. As they reach sexual maturity, they grow wings and reproductive organs. They mate in the fall, lay eggs, and die with the first hard frost. There is one generation per year.

SO WHO NEEDS THE WEATHER CHANNEL? *Male crickets chirp to attract females. And the hotter the weather, the faster they chirp. You can calculate air temperature by counting the number of chirps in 15 seconds, then adding 40. Thus, 30 chirps in 15 seconds means the temperature is 70°F.*

Prevention: Keep the yard clear of weeds, which can harbor these pests. Cover vegetable gardens with floating row covers.

Control: A biological control, *Nosema locustae*, kills grasshoppers and crickets. It works best when applied to an entire neighborhood, rather than a single yard. To stop a marauding swarm, spray with diazinon, carbaryl (Sevin), malathion, or azadirachtin (Neem), according to label directions. Chemical control isn't necessary for minor infestations of grasshoppers and crickets.

GROUND BEETLES

BENEFICIALS

⚡ ZONES: ALL

There are many species of predatory ground beetles, ranging from pea-size to over an inch long. Shiny black, often with an iridescent sheen to their wing covers, they have knobby heads with small antennae and large, conspicuous jaws. Although they can fly, they prefer to crawl and can run quickly on their medium-size legs. They live in burrows in the soil, emerging to hunt and feed at night. Often found crawling around potting sheds and compost piles, they will scurry off at a speedy run, when discovered, to hide. The larvae live underground and are rarely noticed; they also hunt insect prey.

An insect-eating ground beetle

Target: Small ground beetles hunt and eat other insects, caterpillars, soil maggots, and soil grubs. Some larger species, such as the one shown above, eat snail and slug eggs along with small snails and slugs; these ground beetles come equipped with long, narrow jaws, which they use to reach into snail shells to bite and pull out the snail that is hiding inside.

Damage: Despite the fearsome appearance of the larger ground beetles, they do not bite humans or damage plants.

Life cycle: Ground beetles live quiet lives underground and in the shadows of garden structures, patios, and decks. The eggs are laid and hatched beneath the soil; the larvae tunnel around in search of soft-bodied prey, such as root maggots and cutworms. After pupating in soil or in the rotten wood of decaying logs, they emerge as adult beetles to meet and mate. Depending on the species, there are from one to several generations per year.

Prevention and control: No measures are needed.

GROUND PEARLS (PEARL SCALE)

LAWN PESTS

⚡ ZONES: MS, LS, CS, TS

Ground pearls *(Margarodes sp.)* are scale insects that infest the roots of lawn grasses in the South. One of many pests that cause dead patches in lawns, they can be identified by pulling up and inspecting the roots of still-living grass at the edge of a damaged area. Ground pearls resemble pearly cysts or nodules on grass roots. Don't confuse them with the larger white nodules found on the roots of clover in the lawn, created by nitrogen-fixing bacteria that benefit the soil.

Target: Ground pearls attack warm-season grasses, especially Bermuda, Bahia, centipede, St. Augustine, and zoysia grasses.

Damage: Because ground pearls siphon off water and nutrients from grass roots, the lawn may appear dull and off-color. Large, circular patches of grass turn brown and die. The worst damage occurs when the lawn is already stressed by drought, improper mowing, or lack of fertilizer.

Life cycle: Female ground pearls lay eggs in the soil in spring. The eggs hatch into tiny crawlers, which attach themselves to grass roots and begin feeding. Roots respond by forming cysts that engulf the insects, but the damage continues. Immature scales overwinter within the cysts, then emerge in spring as mature breeding females that crawl through the soil to new feeding sites. The life cycle takes 1 to 2 years.

Prevention: Buy only certified, pest-free sod. Check the roots for cysts or nodules.

Control: No pesticides have shown to be effective. If you discover ground pearls in your lawn, remove and dispose of the affected sod. Help your lawn recover by watering regularly, fertilizing properly, mowing at the correct height (see pages 41 and 234), and aerating every spring.

GYPSY MOTHS

TREE PESTS

ZONES: US, MS

A voracious pest that has defoliated millions of acres in the eastern United States, the gypsy moth *(Lymantria dispor)* has steadily moved south since it was accidentally released in 1869 in Massachusetts. It is quite a traveler, often laying egg masses on cars and trucks. The hatched caterpillars can float through the air on silken strands. The adult female moth is white with brown markings and has a wingspan of about 1¾ in. The dark tan male moths are smaller. The caterpillars are distinctive: up to 2 in. long, hairy, and dark, with red and blue spots on their backs. Do not confuse them with tent caterpillars (see page 191).

Target: Many trees, but especially oaks

Damage: Gypsy moths can kill trees. Caterpillars cluster, chewing large holes in leaves; a heavy infestation can completely strip a tree or shrub. Conifers may die as a result of a single defoliation; deciduous species can withstand 2 to 3 years of defoliation before dying.

Life cycle: Eggs overwinter in 1-in.-long, suedelike pouches on tree trunks. In spring, the larvae crawl up the bark to the leaves, feeding until midsummer, then crawl back down to form mahogany-colored pupae in the cracks of bark. Adults emerge in late July or August. After mating, females crawl up trees or other rough-surfaced objects to lay eggs. There is one generation per year.

Prevention: Gypsy moths are well entrenched in the Upper and Middle South, and they're heading farther south. Be careful not to introduce the pest: When traveling from affected areas, check vehicles and camping gear for egg pouches; when moving, examine hoses, lawn mowers, and garden furniture.

Control: Wrap tree trunks with sticky barriers to prevent adult females from climbing up to lay eggs, and to trap larvae traveling down. Encourage or introduce natural predators—assassin bugs, spined soldier bugs, parasitoid wasps, tachinid flies. Spray with *Bacillus thuringiensis kurstaki* (Dipel, Thuricide, Javelin) to kill the larvae when they are still small. Kill larger caterpillars with insecticide sprays containing azadirachtin (Neem), carbaryl (Sevin), phosmet (Imidan), or acephate (Orthene), following the label directions.

HEMLOCK WOOLLY ADELGIDS

HEMLOCK PESTS

ZONES: US, MS

Might the South witness the eradication of another beautiful native tree, as happened to the American chestnut in the early 20th century? The jury is still out, but the hemlock faces mortal danger, thanks to a small, aphidlike pest called the hemlock woolly adelgid. Native to Asia, this dark-colored insect *(Adelges tsugae)* entered the Pacific Northwest in the 1920s. By the 1950s, it had advanced into Maryland, West Virginia, and Virginia. Dead hemlocks stood silently in its wake. Now as its legions march steadily southward, it's knocking on the door of the great hemlock forests of the Smoky Mountains, the Blue Ridge Mountains, and the Appalachians. Foresters tremble at the prospect.

Target: Eastern and Carolina hemlocks

Damage: Named for the white woolly egg sacs it attaches to the needles of infested trees, the woolly adelgid greedily sucks sap from the twigs. It also injects a toxic saliva while feeding that helps to kill existing needles while inhibiting the tree's ability to grow new ones. Within months of the initial attack, needles turn grayish green, then drop. The tree may defoliate and die within 1 year.

Life cycle: Females may reproduce without mating, laying up to 300 eggs in a single egg sac, from February through June. The hatching juvenile adelgids are called crawlers. Some become wingless females that remain on the host tree and lay more eggs. These eggs hatch from June through mid-July. The hatchlings go dormant in the heat of summer, then resume growing in October. A new cycle starts the following February. Other crawlers become winged adults that fly to and infest additional hemlocks.

Prevention: Scientists have discovered a small, predacious beetle that keeps the adelgid under wraps in Japan. They're trying it out here, but the results aren't in. No other methods have proven effective.

Control: Spray hemlocks thoroughly with horticultural oil once from June through August. Spray once again from October to April. Cover the trees completely. To save large trees, hire a professional tree service to apply imidacloprid (Merit).

HORNWORMS, TOBACCO AND TOMATO

VEGETABLE, FLOWER, AND CROP PESTS

ZONES: ALL

These giant green caterpillars are the larvae of huge sphinx moths. The tobacco hornworm *(Manduca sexta)*, shown above, has seven white, diagonal stripes on each side. The horn on its rear is curved and red. The tomato hornworm *(M. quinquemaculata)* bears eight white, V-shaped markings on its side. Its horn at the rear is straight and black. Rapacious feeders, hornworms are hard to spot because they are green like the plants and cling to the undersides of leaves and stems.

Target: Members of the Solanaceae family, such as angel's trumpet, eggplant, nicotiana, pepper, petunia, potato, tobacco, and tomato

Damage: Hornworms greedily munch the leaves and stems of target plants, often stripping them bare. Once they devour all the leaves of a tomato plant, they'll eat the ripening tomatoes as well. Buds, leaves, and blooms of plants may be shredded.

Life cycle: Hornworms overwinter in the soil as pupae. Moths emerge in late spring through summer. Females hover over plants at night, laying one pale green egg on the underside of each leaf. Larvae hatch in about 4 days, feed for 3 to 4 weeks, and then burrow into the soil to pupate. There are one to four generations per year.

Prevention: Rotate vegetable crops to prevent a buildup of pupae in soil. To kill pupae, till soil well before planting. Floating row covers can protect crops when moths are most active, typically June and July.

Control: If numbers are small, handpick caterpillars. Natural enemies include birds, lacewing larvae, and parasitoid wasps. Spraying plants in early evening with *Bacillus thuringiensis kurstaki* (Dipel, Thuricide, Javelin) will kill small (1–2 in. long) caterpillars. Spray larger caterpillars according to label directions with a pyrethrin, rotenone, or carbaryl (Sevin).

GET OFF MY BACK! *If you see a hornworm with small white cocoons stuck to its back, it has been parasitized by the trichogramma wasp. Place the caterpillar in a jar and watch as the tiny (and people-friendly) wasps slowly finish it off. Then release the wasps so they can find more hornworms.*

JAPANESE BEETLES

TREE, SHRUB, VEGETABLE, FLOWER, AND FRUIT PESTS

ZONES: US, MS, LS

Native to Japan, the Japanese beetle *(Popillia japonica)* is a major pest in the Upper and Middle South and is gradually spreading farther south. The body of the ½-in.-long, oblong adult beetle has a distinctive metallic green sheen. The wing covers are copper colored. The larvae, which dwell in soil, are white, C-shaped grubs that can measure up to 1 in. long. Adults feed on flowers and foliage during the day; they can fly as far as 5 miles at a clip.

Target: This beetle feeds on an amazing variety of fruiting and ornamental flowering plants, including fruit trees, grapevines, rosebushes, annuals, perennials, and bulbs. The grubs chew the roots of grasses and garden plants.

Damage: The voracious adult Japanese beetle dines singly or in crowds, chewing leaves until they are skeletonized and eating away at flowers until they are mere shreds. Defoliation of entire shrubs is not uncommon. The grubs are serious pests of lawns, creating brown dead patches that spread during the season.

Life cycle: Adult beetles fly, feed, and mate from June to August. Through the summer, female beetles burrow into the soil to lay eggs. The eggs hatch and the larvae feed on roots. When the soil warms up in spring, the grubs move upward to feed on roots once again. The larvae pupate in May or June, emerging from the soil as adults shortly after. There is a new generation every year.

Prevention: Use care to avoid bringing infested plants or soil into unaffected areas. New sod should be treated to kill grubs.

Control: Handpick beetles off plants when you see them, drowning them in soapy water. Spraying the foliage of roses with the botanical insecticide azadirachtin (Neem) appears to deter beetles from feeding on rosebushes. Larvae in lawns may be killed by introducing parasitic nematodes or treating the soil with chlorpyrifos (Dursban), diazinon, or imidacloprid (Merit, GrubEx). Kill adult beetles by spraying with a pesticide containing rotenone, a pyrethrin, azadirachtin (Neem), carbaryl (Sevin), phosmet (Imidan), or acephate (Orthene), applied according to label directions.

BUGS AND OTHER CRITTERS

LACE BUGS

SHRUB AND TREE PESTS

ZONES: ALL

Lace bugs (*Corythuca sp.*) work undercover, sucking sap from the undersides of leaves. Most are whitish or pale brown, ⅛ in. long, with a boxy shape and transparent, lacy wings. Wingless nymphs, which may have spines, are darker than adults. Adults rarely fly; instead, they move with slow, sideways movements.

Target: Lace bugs target many ornamental trees and shrubs, especially ash, azalea, cotoneaster, Japanese andromeda (*Pieris japonica*), poplar, rhododendron, and sycamore. Different species attack specific host plants only.

Damage: As these pests suck nutrients from leaves, the dry, dying areas of foliage lose chlorophyll and appear speckled, splotched, or stippled with bleached-looking spots. Excrement left by feeding insects on the undersides of leaves looks like hard, black spots. Trees usually show damage in summer, dropping their leaves prematurely. Flowering shrubs lose vigor and may bloom poorly.

Life cycle: Adult lace bugs lay egg clusters within leaf veins. Nymphs hatch in late spring, maturing through molts. Some species lay eggs on the undersides of evergreen leaves and hide them underneath excrement spots that remain over winter. Other species overwinter as adults, hiding under loose plates of tree bark. There are several generations per year.

Prevention: Plant azaleas and Japanese andromeda in moist soil and light shade, as lace bugs favor plants growing in sunny, dry sites. Spray plants (infested the previous year) with horticultural oil in late spring. Be sure to coat the undersides of the leaves.

Control: Pluck off and destroy any heavily infested leaves. Lace bugs may be washed off with a jet of soapy water or killed by spraying with insecticidal soap or horticultural oil, or with contact insecticides containing a pyrethrum product, malathion, diazinon, or carbaryl (Sevin) according to label directions. It is important to spray the undersides of leaves, where these pests congregate. Severe infestations on broad-leafed evergreens, such as azaleas, may be stopped by using a systemic insecticide such as dimethoate (Cygon) or acephate (Orthene) during late spring when the nymphs are feeding.

LACEWINGS

BENEFICIALS

ZONES: ALL

Lacewings fit their name. They are flying insects with lacy, netted wings that extend in a graceful oval beyond their slim bodies. Green lacewings (*Chrysopa sp.*) measure about 1 in. long, including their long antennae, with pale green wings, distinct legs, and copper-colored eyes. The brown lacewing (*Hemerobius sp.*), shown above, is half the size. The immature form of the brown and the green lacewing is shaped like an alligator, ½ in. long, with visible legs and pincers, and is often called an aphid lion. Larvae can be spotted or striped and may be green or brown.

Target: Lacewing larvae eat mites, aphids, leafhoppers, hornworms, thrips, mealybugs, whiteflies, and psyllids. Winged adults do not eat insects; they feed only on nectar, pollen, and honeydew from garden flowers.

Brown lacewing larva (inset, top) and green lacewing larva (bottom)

Damage: Lacewings and their larvae cause no damage to plants.

Life cycle: Lacewings lay their oval, white eggs singly, balanced on a threadlike stalk attached to a trunk or stem. Larvae crawl to hunt aphids and other small, soft-bodied insects. They feed for a week or two, then spin a spherical pupa and attach it with silk to a tree trunk or to the underside of a leaf. Adults emerge in about 5 days. They die when the weather gets cold.

Prevention: No preventive measures are needed.

Control: You can bring lacewings into your garden by purchasing eggs that are ready to hatch. Three or more releases, spaced a week apart, may be needed to effectively reduce aphids and whiteflies. To attract lacewings to your garden, plant nectar sources such as butterfly bush, coneflower, lantana, butterfly weed, buckwheat, and yarrow.

ARSENIC AND OLD LACEWINGS. *Don't use pesticides if you're introducing lacewings into your garden or you'll poison these good guys, too.*

LADYBUGS

BENEFICIALS

✎ ZONES: ALL

The colorfully spotted ladybug, or ladybird beetle, is a welcome guest in gardens. Most types are about ¼ in. long. Their rounded, shiny wing covers may be orange or red with black spots, or solid orange, brown, yellow, or black with no spots at all. The immature or larval form looks like a small, six-legged alligator about ¼ in. long, with a roughened or corrugated hide and markings of orange and black spots or stripes.

Target: Adult ladybugs and ladybug larvae hunt and feed on aphids, mites, and other soft-bodied insects. They are often introduced into gardens for this purpose, although recent research suggests they are less effective than lacewings for insect pest control.

Damage: Ladybugs cause no plant damage. In the South, one species has a tendency to swarm by the thousands and invade houses. Although they are harmless, this can be a nuisance.

Life cycle: Female beetles lay clusters of elongated orange eggs on a variety of host plants. These hatch into the larvae that immediately begin to hunt and feed on aphids and other prey. After pupating on host plants, ladybugs fly to mate and seek food sources. There may be from one to several generations per year.

Prevention: No prevention measures are needed. Tightly fitting window and door screens may be the most effective barriers against ladybugs that invade homes.

Control: Mail-order suppliers and garden centers sell ladybugs, usually as bags of adult beetles or larvae. Released ladybugs may fly off rather than settle down to the business of eating aphids. One way to retain them is to wet down garden foliage with water or a diluted sugar-water solution before releasing them, since captured ladybugs are often thirsty. Releasing ladybugs at ground level in the cooler temperatures of late evening also helps. To increase populations of ladybugs, avoid or limit spraying of insecticides. Most pesticide formulations, from insecticidal soaps to chemical preparations, will kill ladybugs and their larvae.

LEAF-CUTTING BEES

LEAF AND STEM PESTS; BENEFICIALS

✎ ZONES: ALL

You can identify leaf-cutting bees *(Megachilidae sp.)* by the damage they leave behind: precise circles or ovals in foliage, their edges as clean as if they had been cut with a small pair of scissors. The bees themselves are small and hairy, and either black, green, purple, or blue. Their wings have a metallic sheen.

Target: Leaf-cutting bees seem to prefer the foliage of roses, although any tree or shrub that has a shiny, firm leaf may be cut.

Damage: Affected foliage is cut from the edges in scalloped, circular, or oval patterns that are about ¼ in. in diameter. Bees may also cut circles out of rose petals. The edges of the cuts become dry and turn brown. While they are unsightly, the cuts do not affect the health of rosebushes or other plants, but the damage may ruin the foliage of roses earmarked for cutting or exhibition. These bees are docile and rarely sting humans.

Leaf-cutting bee

Life cycle: Leaf-cutting bees live in small colonies, gathering pollen and nectar during the warm months and hibernating during the winter season. Female worker bees cut foliage with their mouthparts and then use the material to construct their nests, which are built on the ground under cover of weeds or garden debris, under house shingles, or in woodpiles.

Prevention: In home gardens, leaf-cutting bees should be tolerated, since they are important pollinators for many plants. You can eliminate potential nesting sites around rosebushes by clearing away weeds and leaf debris. To protect roses intended for exhibition or as cut flowers, cover plants with floating row covers when you first notice leaf-cutting bee damage.

Control: No controls are recommended for this native insect and useful pollinator.

LEAFHOPPERS

VEGETABLE, FRUIT, SHRUB, AND TREE PESTS

ZONES: ALL

There are some 2,500 species of these small, wedge-shaped insects. Many leafhoppers are handsomely colored and patterned, while others are camouflaged green to blend in with foliage. When disturbed, they run sideways; as the name implies, they also leap from plant to plant, although adults can fly. Adults are ¼ in. or smaller. The wingless nymphs are smaller still. The grape leafhopper (*Erythroneura lawsoniana*) is shown above.

Target: Some leafhopper species savor just one kind of plant, while others enjoy a broad menu. Noticeably affected plants include apple, aster, bean, beet, carrot, eggplant, grape, and potato. The rose leafhopper (*Edwardsiana rosae*) attacks rosebushes and apple trees.

Damage: Both adults and nymphs suck plant juices, making leaves look bleached or mottled with whitish spots. Sometimes leaves turn brown and curl at edges, a condition called hopperburn that is often found on potato plants. Black excrement specks may ruin grapes and apples, though they can be scrubbed or peeled from apple skins. Severe infestations cause stunting and leaf drop in flowers and vegetables. Certain species like the beet leafhopper transmit plant diseases such as curly top virus (see page 256).

Life cycle: Adult leafhoppers lay yellowish, curved eggs in the stems or leaf veins of plants. Nymphs reach full size within one month. There may be one to six generations per year; the rose leafhopper has two per year. Leafhoppers overwinter as eggs in cold-winter climates; in warm-winter climates, some species overwinter as adults.

Prevention: Clear weeds and brush to remove cover for overwintering adults and eggs. Use floating row covers to protect potato, carrot, and other susceptible crops.

Control: Lure leafhoppers to yellow sticky traps, or wash them off with a jet of water or insecticidal soap. Natural predators include birds, green lacewings, and parasitoid wasps. Apply a dormant oil spray in winter to kill overwintering eggs of the rose leafhopper. For crop infestations, apply a pyrethrum product, azadirachtin (Neem), rotenone, malathion, or carbaryl (Sevin), following label directions, especially to undersides of leaves.

LEAF MINERS

VEGETABLE, FLOWER, AND SHRUB PESTS

ZONES: ALL

The name "leaf miners" is a catchall term for certain moth, beetle, and fly larvae that tunnel between the upper and lower surfaces of leaves, leaving behind a near-transparent trail in a characteristic pattern. On vegetables, the most common leaf miners are the larvae of tiny black flies with yellow markings.

Target: Various species of leaf miners attack boxwood, columbine, holly, and other perennials, as well as annual flowers and vegetables.

Damage: Leaf miners do the most damage on leafy edible crops such as chard, lettuce, and spinach, which may be ruined. On ornamental plants such as holly, the foliage may be unsightly. However, the damage is slight unless there is a severe infestation, in which case the loss of chlorophyll can result in a weakened plant.

Leaf miner larvae

Life cycle: Adults lay eggs under the leaf surface, usually on the underside of the foliage. Larvae hatch and feed on the soft tissue between the leaf ribs. After feeding, leaf miners drop off the leaf to pupate underground or under cover of plant debris. There can be several generations per year, depending on the species.

Prevention: To protect edible leafy crops, use floating row covers to prevent adult insects from laying eggs on the foliage. To prevent larvae from pupating near plant roots, lay a plastic mulch under leafy crops and keep your vegetable beds well weeded during the growing season. Rotating crops and tilling the soil between crops helps destroy pupae. Parasitoid wasps, natural enemies of leaf miners, lay their eggs on larvae or near leaf miner egg sites.

Control: Pick off and destroy infected leaves. Light infestations require no attention. For serious infestations on ornamentals, spray with a systemic insecticide, such as acephate (Orthene) or dimethoate (Cygon), according to label directions.

LEAF ROLLERS

TREE AND SHRUB PESTS

✿ ZONES: ALL

The name "leaf roller" applies to many different caterpillars that roll foliage around themselves as they feed, creating shelter from predators such as birds. The caterpillars spin sticky webbing as they roll, attracting dust and dirt, which also helps conceal them. Adult moths are ½–2 in. long and wide; larvae are ½–1 in. long.

The fruit-tree leaf roller *(Archips argyrospila),* found throughout the South, is a thin, light green caterpillar with a black spot on its head. When disturbed, it wriggles vigorously and tries to escape by dropping to the ground on a thread of silk. The adult form is a brown moth.

Target: Some leaf rollers target specific plants, while others enjoy a varied diet. The fruit-tree leaf roller feeds on apple trees as well as on buckeye, maple, oak, poplar, and willow.

Damage: Leaf rollers rarely do enough damage to hurt shrubs and flowers, but the fruit-tree leaf roller is an exception. It feeds on new growth, leaving foliage ragged or stunted. The tree or plants beneath are covered with silken threads. In severe infestations, defoliation may occur, weakening the plant, though it may produce a second crop of spring leaves. Some leaf rollers eat and scar fruits.

Life cycle: Adults lay masses of eggs on host plants. Larvae, or caterpillars, begin to feed, sometimes moving from leaf to leaf as they grow. Fruit-tree leaf rollers pupate within rolled leaves or attached to bark with a brownish silk cocoon, emerging as adults 2 weeks later. Leaf rollers have one to three generations per year and overwinter as eggs or pupae.

Prevention: Natural enemies of leaf roller caterpillars include birds and parasitoid trichogramma wasps, which can be encouraged or introduced to the garden. Where the fruit-tree leaf roller is a problem, apply dormant-oil spray during the winter, thoroughly covering the branches with oil to smother and kill any egg masses.

Control: Pick off and destroy infested leaves. Spray or dust the foliage in the evening with *Bacillus thuringiensis kurstaki* (Dipel, Thuricide, Javelin) or phosmet (Imidan) according to label directions.

LEAF SKELETONIZERS

TREE PESTS

✿ ZONES: ALL

Skeletonizers aren't ghouls but insects that feed on the green tissue between the upper and lower surfaces of leaves. The result is a leaf that is ghostly and pale between the veins. Leaf skeletonizers are the larval form of several insects that are called casemakers, named for their cigar-shaped cocoon with longitudinal ribs. Species common in the South include the oak skeletonizer *(Bucculatrix ainsliella),* the birch skeletonizer *(B. canadensisella),* and the apple skeletonizer *(B. pomifoliella).*

Target: The oak skeletonizer feeds on oak and chestnut leaves. The birch skeletonizer attacks only birches. The apple skeletonizer targets fruit trees belonging to the apple family, including apple, cherry, crabapple, hawthorn, and serviceberry.

Damage: Skeletonizers feed on the tissue between the upper and lower surfaces of leaves, emptying it of chlorophyll. As they grow, they also chew the undersides of leaves, eventually forming translucent windows between the veins. Damage is mostly cosmetic. Rarely do skeletonizers affect enough leaves to influence the health of the tree.

Life cycle: Flying adults lay eggs on leaves. The larvae chew through the leaf surface and then feed on the green tissue inside. Once they've grown to full size, about ¼ in., the caterpillars exit and attach cigar-shaped, white silk cocoons to the leaves and then pupate. There may be one or two generations per year.

Prevention: To reduce the numbers of skeletonizers, remove and destroy leaves that show the characteristic "windows."

Control: Control isn't necessary in most cases as the damage is superficial. For severe infestations, rake and destroy infested and fallen leaves in fall. Then spray the foliage of shade trees with acephate (Orthene) the following spring as soon as damage appears. Spray fruit trees with malathion or carbaryl (Sevin). Follow label directions carefully.

LOOPERS

TREE, SHRUB, AND VEGETABLE PESTS

🖊 ZONES: ALL

This large and varied group of caterpillars gets its name from the way they hunch up as they crawl, forming the shape of a loop. Other common names include inchworms, measuring worms, spanworms, and geometers. (Cankerworms are also called inchworms. For more information about them, see page 159.)

A number of different loopers damage plants. They include the cypress looper (*Anacamptodes pergracilis*), shown above, eastern pine looper (*Lambdina pellucidaria*), hemlock looper (*L. fiscellaria*), barberry looper (*Coryphista meadii*), and holly looper (*Thysanopyga intractata*). Each species has its own pattern and color combination, such as black and gold, green and white, or green and gold. Loopers often drop from plants on a silken thread if disturbed. More than one type of looper may feed on a single plant.

Target: Bald cypress, barberry, hemlock, holly, and pine; the cabbage looper feeds on broccoli, cabbage, and other cole crops. For information about this species, see "Cabbageworms," page 158.

Damage: Needles and leaves turn a straw color or brown. Outer twigs may be defoliated by midsummer. The leaves of American holly (*Ilex opaca*) initially display notched margins; the plant may then be partially or completely defoliated. Shade trees suffer skeletonized leaves, then defoliation. Repeated infestations weaken plants, making them susceptible to subsequent attack by borers and bark beetles.

Life cycle: Looper populations boom one year, then bust the next, probably because of environmental factors and natural predators. Some loopers overwinter as pupae at the foot of host trees while others overwinter as eggs on needles, twigs, and bark. Moths or caterpillars usually emerge in early to midspring, but moths can appear as late as November.

Prevention: Keep trees and shrubs healthy by proper watering, fertilizing, and pruning. Rake and destroy debris each fall.

Control: While caterpillars are still, spray in early evening with *Bacillus thuringiensis kurstaki* (Dipel, Thuricide, Javelin). For large caterpillars, spray with acephate (Orthene), carbaryl (Sevin), or phosmet (Imidan). Follow label directions.

MEALYBUGS

FLOWER, SHRUB, AND HOUSE PLANT PESTS

🖊 ZONES: ALL

Common on house plants, these tiny sap-feeding scale relatives also plague plants outdoors. Their bristly gray coats make them look like powdery or cottony fluff when they mass in colonies on leaves and stems. Their waxy coating shields them from most pesticide sprays. Citrus mealybugs (*Planococcus citri*) are shown above.

Target: Mealybugs feed on the soft green tissue of house plants. They also favor cacti, succulents, citrus, and many other ornamental plants.

Damage: Mealybugs weaken plant tissues by sucking plant juices. Leaves may be stunted, distorted, discolored, spotted, or yellowed. When mealybugs feed, they excrete a sugary honeydew that attracts ants. It also encourages a sooty mold fungus that appears as black sticky goo on leaves and stems.

Life cycle: Mealybugs quickly become large colonies, since each adult female lays up to 600 eggs at a time. The eggs are usually laid beneath leaves in a white cottony sac. Nymphs hatch in about 10 days and crawl to feeding sites, usually in the crotches between leaf petioles and stems. There may be several generations per year. Mealybugs overwinter as eggs or adults; they proliferate quickly indoors.

Prevention: Controlling ants around succulents is a good strategy, since ants often cultivate mealybugs in exchange for honeydew.

Control: Natural predators to encourage or introduce include green lacewings and ladybugs, particularly a ladybug species known as the mealybug destroyer. On a cool or overcast day, spray branches and leaves of citrus trees with a light horticultural oil. For severe infestations, apply an insecticide containing a pyrethrum product, azadirachtin (Neem), malathion, diazinon, or, for ornamentals only, acephate (Orthene), following label directions.

SHE MAKES A MEAL OF MEALYBUGS. *The mealybug destroyer (Cryptolaemus montrouzieri) is a black-and-orange ladybug. These beneficial insects need warm temperatures and high humidity, so their usefulness is limited to greenhouses and warm months in the garden.*

MEXICAN BEAN BEETLES

VEGETABLE PESTS

ZONES: ALL

Mexican bean beetles *(Epilacthina varivestis)* cause serious damage to bean crops throughout the South. Closely related to ladybugs, they resemble these helpful insects in size and shape, but the bronze or coppery sheen of their wing covers gives them away. Adult bean beetles have rows of black spots on their backs. The immature or larval form is ⅓ in. long and yellowish, with rows of spines on the back.

Target: Mexican bean beetles attack most varieties of bean plants.

Damage: Adults and their larvae feed on the undersides of leaves, chewing away leaf tissue and leaving skeletonized stems behind. Bean pods may also be chewed. Heavily infested plants may die. The worst damage occurs in July and August.

Life cycle: Bean beetles overwinter as adults in garden debris or in wooded areas. In spring, females emerge to feed lightly and lay eggs in a yellowish cluster on the undersides of bean leaves. After hatching, the larvae feed for 2 to 5 weeks, then pupate on the leaves. Adults are plain yellow when they first emerge from pupa. Their spots appear later, after voracious feeding in late summer.

Prevention: Beetles prefer wax beans, snap beans, and lima beans (in that order). So if they're a serious pest in your area, choose your beans wisely. Use row covers in spring to shield bean plants from egg-laying adults. Check the undersides of the leaves on young bean plants for yellow egg masses. In the fall, clean up garden debris and brush in nearby wooded areas to remove havens for adult beetles.

Control: Place a cloth beneath bean plants and shake the plants; the beetles will drop off onto the cloth and can be gathered up and destroyed. Handpick and destroy adult beetles, larvae, and egg masses. Natural predators to encourage or introduce include toads, birds, tachinid flies, spined soldier bugs, and parasitoid wasps. If bean crops are severely or repeatedly infested, spray plants with an insecticide containing rotenone, a pyrethrum product, malathion, or carbaryl (Sevin) according to label directions, and be sure to spray the undersides of leaves, where the insects congregate.

MILLIPEDES AND CENTIPEDES

VEGETABLE, FRUIT, AND HOUSEHOLD PESTS; BENEFICIALS

ZONES: ALL

Centipedes, shown above, at left, look like 1-in. worms with many feet. They are brown and somewhat flattened, with one pair of legs per segment. They run fast and hunt at night, paralyzing smaller insect prey with venomous claws. Millipedes, shown above, at right, have hard-shelled, cylindrical and segmented bodies, with two pairs of short legs per segment. They measure 2 in. long and may be black, pink, or gray brown. Most coil up when disturbed. They prefer a damp environment.

A LEG UP. *Despite their name, millipedes do not have 1,000 legs, but may have as many as 400. North American centipedes typically have about 30 legs. Some tropical centipedes have several hundred legs and reach 12 in. long.*

Target: Centipedes are beneficial soil dwellers that gobble up insects, baby snails, and slugs. Millipedes benefit gardens by feeding on decaying plant material, helping to create humus. They may eat fallen fruit.

Damage: Centipedes do not eat plants but occasionally bite humans (feels like a bee sting). Millipede feeding may damage fallen fruit; some species can irritate the skin when touched. Both can be a nuisance when they invade homes or gardens in large numbers.

Life cycle: Adult centipedes and millipedes overwinter underground. In the spring, they lay clusters of translucent eggs in or on the soil. These eggs hatch into nymphs that are smaller versions of the adults. There is one generation per year.

Prevention: Protect fruits that ripen on the ground, such as strawberries, by mulching the soil around plants with dry straw or diatomaceous earth. To prevent centipedes from entering your home, eliminate damp areas around house foundations.

Control: Swat indoor invaders or spray with a household insecticide containing a pyrethrin. To control millipedes in garden beds, sprinkle diatomaceous earth or ashes between rows. These materials irritate the millipede's many feet but make an effective barrier only if replaced when wet. For infestations, treat the soil with diazinon or chlorpyrifos (Dursban). Apply according to label directions.

MITES

TREE, SHRUB, FLOWER, FRUIT, VEGETABLE, AND HOUSE PLANT PESTS

 ZONES: ALL

Mites are tiny but cause big problems. They are not insects. Rather, as their eight legs indicate, they are arachnids and closely related to spiders. Mites are red, black, green, tan, or yellow and about the size of a pinpoint. They are nearly invisible, except when clustered together. Most people don't know these diminutive pests are around until they cause serious damage, which coincides with stretches of hot dry weather and poorly watered plants.

If you suspect mites on a plant, hold a piece of white paper under the plant and gently tap the stem or leaf. Mites will drop onto the paper, looking like slowly crawling specks of pepper. The spider mite *(Tetranychus sp.),* shown above, is probably the most familiar to home gardeners. It strings tiny webs between the leaves and stems of a plant.

Tomato russet mites, magnified

Target: While some mites, such as the citrus red mite *(Panonychus citri)*, the spruce mite *(Oliogonychus milleri)*, and the boxwood mite *(Eurytetranychus buxi)*, attack specific plants, spider mites and other types have more cosmopolitan tastes, feasting on a wide range of annuals, perennials, vegetables, trees, shrubs, and house plants.

Damage: Mites suck juices from leaves, stems, and flower buds. Heavily infested plants weaken and die. Affected foliage or flowers may appear speckled, spotted, yellowed, bronzed, scorched, or distorted. Foliage, buds, and stems eventually dry out and turn brown. On tomatoes, petunias, potatoes, and other members of the potato family (Solanaceae), greasy yellow to bronze-colored leaves are a sure sign of the tomato russet mite *(Aculops lycopersici)*.

Life cycle: Mites go through several stages as they grow from an egg to an adult. Some types produce a new generation every 3 to 7 days in warm dry weather. However, spruce mites are active mainly in the cooler days of spring and fall. Outdoors, mites may overwinter in plant litter as eggs or adults.

Prevention: Dry air encourages mites, so water plants regularly and wash off their foliage. Check any plants you purchase from a garden center for webbing (examine the joints of stems) or other signs of infestation. Before planting, spray stems and leaves (both upper and lower surfaces) with insecticidal soap or horticultural oil. Avoid repeatedly spraying the garden with carbaryl (Sevin), as it tends to worsen mite problems. Rake and destroy plant debris at the end of the growing season.

Inspect susceptible plants for mites throughout the growing season, especially during dry weather. Succeeding generations of mites tend to spread from the undersides of leaves to stems, flower buds, and upper surfaces of leaves. At this point the damage is easy to spot. However, once damage is obvious, control may be difficult.

Control: For light infestations, use a stiff spray of water to wash off mites. You can also introduce ladybug larvae, lacewings, and predatory mites into the garden. These critters eat destructive mites. On vegetable plants, such as tomato, dusting the undersides of the foliage with garden sulfur will kill many mites. You can also spray with insecticidal soap, a light horticultural (summer) oil, or dimethoate (Cygon). Heavily infested vegetable, ornamental, and foliage plants are best thrown out. Spray citrus and deciduous trees and shrubs with dormant oil in late winter to smother overwintering mites and eggs. Thoroughly cover branches and stems. Light summer oils can be used on citrus and broadleaf evergreens during the growing season, as long as the temperature isn't above 90°F. Some oils discolor the foliage of conifers, so if these needle-leafed evergreens have mites, check the product label before spraying.

For heavy infestations, use a miticide, such as hexakis (Vendex), often added into general-purpose pesticides, such as Isotox. Don't use insecticides, such as carbaryl (Sevin) and malathion. Mites aren't insects, so these products won't kill them. In fact, by wiping out the mites' competitors, you could worsen the problem.

IT SOFTENS HANDS, TOO!

You'll find one of the cheaper, easier-to-use, environmentally friendly mite controls right in your own kitchen—liquid detergent. Mix 5 to 6 drops in a quart of water, fill a spray bottle, and spray the solution onto leaves and stems in the morning or evening. It kills mites almost immediately.

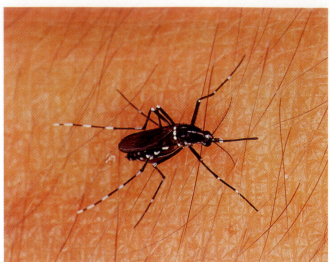

MOLE CRICKETS

LAWN PESTS

ZONES: LS, CS, TS

Few insects can destroy a lush lawn faster than mole crickets. There are three kinds, all invaders from South America, that now infest the South. The short-winged mole cricket *(Scapteriscus abbreviatus)* lives only in Florida, is flightless, and does not "sing." The Southern mole cricket *(S. borellii),* shown above, and tawny mole cricket *(S. vicinus)* have invaded the entire Southeast, as well as Louisiana and Texas. They fly and sing. The Southern mole cricket plays dead when caught, while the tawny mole cricket does not. All three are about 1½ in. long.

Target: Warm-season lawns, particularly those with heavy thatch

Damage: Mole crickets use huge claws on their forelegs to dig through the lawn and soil surface, uprooting large patches of grass. The Southern mole cricket is a predator, feeding mostly on insects it finds. The tawny mole cricket and the short-winged mole cricket feed on roots, stems, and leaves of lawn grasses and vegetable seedlings.

Life cycle: The life cycle varies somewhat according to the species. Generally, females lay eggs in underground chambers, 4–12 in. below the surface, in April through June. Eggs hatch in about 3 weeks; the parental crickets die shortly thereafter. The juvenile crickets, called nymphs, cannibalize each other at first, then begin feeding on plant roots. They molt six or seven times throughout the summer as they feed and grow. They overwinter as nymphs or adults. There is one generation per year.

Prevention: Because heavy thatch encourages mole crickets, avoid heavy watering and fertilizing. Dethatch your lawn as needed. Test for mole crickets by pouring soapy water on a patch of lawn. This will force them to the surface.

Control: A beneficial nematode, *Steinernema scapterisci,* is a good, long-term control of Southern and tawny mole crickets when applied to the lawn in March–April or in September–October. You'll likely have to order these beneficials by mail. Imidacloprid (Merit, GrubEx) provides the best chemical control for all mole crickets. Apply it in May or June. Or you can apply diazinon granules.

MOSQUITOES

HUMAN AND ANIMAL PESTS

ZONES: ALL

More than 100 species of mosquitoes inhabit North America. Not only do they pester us with their bites, but they also sicken people and animals with the diseases they transmit.

Mosquitoes that plague the South fall into three main groups. Anopheles mosquitoes, shown on opposite page, breed in permanent marshes. They're not a problem in most cities and suburbs. Culex mosquitoes are. They breed in standing water, such as swimming pools, birdbaths, ponds, gutters, and water barrels. Aedes mosquitoes make up the third group. They generally breed in salt marshes and flooded areas. However, an imported species of this group, the Asian tiger mosquito *(Aedes albopictus),* shown above, breeds in water collected in hollow trees, discarded tires, tin cans, buckets, and flower pots. Named for its black-and-white-striped legs, it's thought to have entered this country in 1985 aboard a batch of used tires.

Only female mosquitoes bite. They consume blood and also use it to produce eggs. Most feed at night, although the voracious female Asian tiger mosquito bellies up to the bar 24 hours a day. Male mosquitoes feed on nectar and plant juices.

Target: Humans and animals

Damage: When mosquitoes bite, they inject a tiny amount of saliva, which causes an allergic reaction in most people. Usually, the damage is limited to an itchy, red bump. However, some mosquitoes spread disease. Anopheles mosquitoes can transmit malaria—a few cases are reported almost every year in the Southeast. In rare instances, Culex mosquitoes give humans eastern equine encephalitis, which causes a potentially deadly inflammation of the brain. Asian tiger mosquitoes have been known to transmit eastern equine encephalitis, dengue fever, and dog heartworm.

Life cycle: After mating, females place eggs on or at the edge of standing water. Depending on species and location, overwintering eggs hatch or adults emerge from hibernation in spring. Whitish larva called wrigglers often gather just below the water surface. When they swim, it's usually tail first, in a wriggling manner. They eventually become C-shaped pupae called tumblers, which swim in

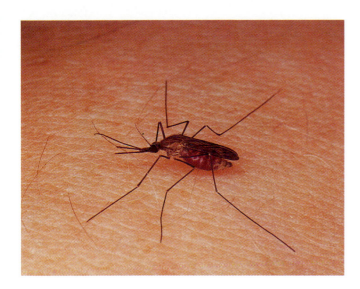

an active, tumbling fashion. Mosquitoes leave the water as adults. Most species hide during the day in dark, sheltered places, such as dense shrubbery. Depending on the species, there may be from one to ten generations per year.

Prevention: Keep mosquitoes from breeding by preventing water from stagnating in barrels, flower pots, old tires, and gutters. Change the water in birdbaths daily. Stock ponds with fish. Trim hedges and thin heavy brush to remove hiding places and improve air circulation. Keep the air moving. Most mosquitoes are weak fliers. A strong fan on the deck or porch will blow them away.

To keep mosquitoes from zeroing in on you, try these things. First, take a shower—this removes lactic acid and other compounds that attract mosquitoes from the skin. Second, wear white—like little Draculas, mosquitoes prefer the colors of the night. Third, use repellents. Products containing deet, such as Off! and Cutter, are quite effective. However, extra-strength sprays can be toxic to small children. For them, use less concentrated products, such as Off! Skintastic for Kids and Cutter Insect Repellent Just for Kids. Fourth, burn citronella candles. The volatile oils released into the air confuse mosquitoes and keep them from finding you.

EVERY NIGHT IS LADIES' NIGHT. *Just like the notorious Count, mosquitoes prefer biting women. The estrogen-like compounds that women secrete through their skin drive the busy little bloodsuckers wild. That's why hubby can happily relax in his lawn chair each night, while his wife's red blood cell count drops like a concrete beignet.*

Control: Forget electric bug zappers. Mosquitoes find you by smell, not sight. The carbon dioxide (CO_2) you exhale as you breathe leads them right to you. Directing insect foggers into brush provides temporary control. Doughnut-shaped briquettes called Vectobac, which contain *Bacillus thuringiensis israeliensis* (also see page 68), dropped into birdbaths, ponds, and other bodies of standing water can kill mosquito larvae for up to 30 days and do not harm fish.

NEMATODES

VEGETABLE, LAWN, FLOWER, TREE, AND SHRUB PESTS; BENEFICIALS

ZONES: ALL

Nematodes are microscopic worms less than 1/16 in. long. Root nematodes live in the soil and feed on plant roots. Foliar nematodes live in stems and leaves. Nematodes may be found wherever there is moist, rich soil. They move from garden to garden on transplants, garden tools, water, ants, and shifted earth. The South's most troublesome species is the Southern root knot nematode (*Meliodogyne incognita*). However, some nematodes are beneficial because they attack harmful insect pests.

Target: Southern root knot nematodes attack tomato roots, shown above, and other vegetable crops. Other types attack trees, shrubs, flowers, and lawn grasses. They are a serious problem in Florida and the Coastal and Tropical South.

Damage: Nematode damage causes leaves to yellow and become wilted or stunted. Roots look stunted and show lumpy nodules that shelter nematodes and help them siphon off nutrients and water.

Life cycle: Generations are continuous, though nematodes are most active in warm soil. They overwinter as eggs or as adults.

Prevention: Rotate vegetable and flower plantings. Vegetable selections that resist nematodes include 'Atkinson', 'Beefmaster', 'Celebrity', and 'Nematex' tomatoes; 'Wando' pea; 'Bountiful' and 'Tender Pod' beans; and 'Apache', 'Hopi', and 'Nemagold' sweet potatoes.

Control: Pull and destroy infected plants, including roots. Natural enemies include a soil fungus that can be encouraged by digging in organic matter such as leaf mold. But soil solarization and crop rotation are more effective. For severe cases, consult a pest control professional about soil fumigation. Applying Nematrol or incorporating chitin (Clandosan) into the soil may also control pests.

THE WORM TURNS. *Certain beneficial nematodes, available for purchase, attack some 400 varieties of borers, caterpillars, and insect root pests by parasitizing their grubs or releasing bacteria that kill the larvae. Follow label directions carefully when applying to target areas.*

OLEANDER CATERPILLARS

OLEANDER PESTS

ZONES: CS, TS

When your oleander practically disappears before your very eyes, this pest may be the culprit. The oleander caterpillar *(Syntomeida epilais jucundissima)* is bright orange with tufts of long, black hair rising from black bumps. At full size, it reaches 1½ in. long. Adult moths are active during the day. They are small, with a purplish body and greenish black wings. Small white dots are scattered over the moth's body, wings, legs, and antennae. The abdominal tip is red-orange. It is sometimes called the polka-dot moth or polka-dot wasp moth.

Adult moth

Target: Oleander

Damage: New oleander shoots turn light brown, then are skeletonized. Later in the season, entire leaves disappear and defoliation occurs. Loss of foliage does not kill the plant, but does stress and weaken it, increasing its susceptibility to other pests, such as scale.

Life cycle: In early March, females lay pale yellow egg clusters on undersides of leaves. Groups of emerging caterpillars feed on the leaves for about 8 days, then become solitary for about 19 days, feeding on entire leaves. They pupate in groups on tree trunks, emerging as moths to start another generation. There are three overlapping generations per year.

Prevention: No measures are needed. There are several natural enemies of these caterpillars, including stinkbugs, tachinid flies, and various caterpillar-attacking diseases. Diseased caterpillars are often dark in color and quite soft. Leaving them on the plant allows the pathogen to spread through the caterpillar population.

Control: Prune and destroy infested foliage. Handpick larger caterpillars and drop in a pail of soapy water. Oleander plant sap is poisonous, so wear gloves and wash hands with soap afterwards. Control small caterpillars with *Bacillus thuringiensis kurstaki* (Dipel, Thuricide, Javelin). Chemical insecticides are not recommended, but for infestations, spray with acephate (Orthene) or dimethoate (Cygon).

PILLBUGS AND SOWBUGS

FRUIT AND FLOWER PESTS; BENEFICIALS

ZONES: ALL

Many gardeners find it difficult to distinguish between these dark gray, crawling crustaceans with segmented backs and wavy antennae, commonly known as "roly-polies." Here's how to tell them apart: sowbugs *(Porcellio sp.)*, shown above, right, have two tail-like appendages on their rears; only pillbugs *(Armadillium vulgare)*, shown above, left, will roll up into a round, tight ball when disturbed. While adapted to dry land, both are related to crabs and crayfish; neither is classified as an insect. They rest in dark, moist places during the day and venture out at night to feed on decaying plant matter. Plentiful in moist, organic soils, sowbugs and pillbugs can be a nuisance to gardeners who have no reason to fear them.

Target: Pillbugs and sowbugs are often wrongly blamed for chewing holes in strawberries and flowers, since daylight finds them curled up in a hole that was already chewed by snails, slugs, or nocturnal insects. They prefer to munch on decaying vegetation, which is why they are often found near damaged fruits or foliage.

Damage: Colonies of pillbugs and sowbugs perform a useful function in the garden by breaking down plant debris into humus. But when their numbers are high, they may nibble on the tender tips of foliage or fruit at ground level.

Life cycle: Like kangaroos, females carry their young in a pouch on their bodies. The immature pillbugs and sowbugs are smaller, paler versions of their elders. There are from one to three generations per year.

Prevention: Pillbugs and sowbugs need moist hiding places. Remove leaf piles, grass clippings, boards, rock piles, and other debris from the garden. Improve drainage in low, wet spots. Keep fruits and vegetables from resting on the ground.

Control: Small numbers of sowbugs and pillbugs don't do serious damage and require no control. Insecticides containing carbaryl (Sevin), chlorpyrifos (Dursban), diazinon, or a pyrethrin are effective against major infestations.

PINE SAWFLIES

TREE AND SHRUB PESTS

ZONES: ALL

Those gobs of caterpillars voraciously consuming your pines and other conifers aren't caterpillars at all but larvae of small non-stinging wasps called sawflies. These pests are most active in spring and summer. Types common in the South include the redheaded pine sawfly *(Neodiprion lecontei),* shown above, a yellowish green or whitish worm with six rows of black spots on its back and sides and a distinctive red head; the black-headed pine sawfly *(N. excitans),* which has an olive green body with black stripes and a black head; and the European pine sawfly *(N. sertifer),* which has a grayish green body, light and dark gray stripes, and a black head.

Target: Pine sawflies favor two- and three-needle pines, which include loblolly, mugho, red, Scotch, shortleaf, and slash pines. The redheaded pine sawfly also attacks deodar cedar, larch, Norway spruce, and white pine.

Damage: Sawflies feed en masse. Severely infested trees may be completely defoliated. If defoliation happens late in the growing season and conifers are not able to produce another flush of growth before winter, the weakened trees may not survive.

Life cycle: Adult sawflies emerge in spring. Females use a special sawlike blade at the tip of their abdomens to cut slits in the needles, into which they deposit eggs. Light yellow spots appear on damaged needles. The newly hatched larvae feed in hordes, usually from the top of the tree down. Depending on the species, they may feed on new growth, last year's growth, or both. After defoliating a tree, they may crawl several yards over the ground to locate a new tree. Sawflies spend the winter in a pre-pupal stage inside a cocoon hidden in plant debris under trees. They pupate in spring and become adults shortly thereafter. However, some remain as pupae for 2 to 3 years.

Prevention: Keep a watchful eye on susceptible pines. Sawflies can appear seemingly overnight.

Control: If possible, prune and destroy infested branches. To control serious infestations, spray foliage with carbaryl (Sevin), malathion, diazinon, phosmet (Imidan), or acephate (Orthene). Follow label directions. Spraying large trees requires professional help.

PINE TIP MOTHS

TREE AND SHRUB PESTS

ZONES: ALL

It's hard to keep pines in tip-top shape when all of their branch tips are brown. This is the damage caused by various pine tip moths that inhabit the South. These small moths, which are orange to reddish brown with silvery gray markings, produce tiny caterpillars that bore into branch tips. Dry weather and poor soil exacerbate the damage.

Target: Nantucket pine tip moth *(Rhyacionia frustrana)* attacks all two- and three-needle pines except longleaf and slash. Loblolly pine is its favorite target. European pine shoot moth *(R. buoliana)* favors Austrian, Japanese black, mugho, red, and Scotch pine. Pitch pine tip moth *(R. rigidiana)* prefers loblolly, red, Scotch, slash, and Virginia pines. In Florida, the subtropical pine tip moth *(R. subtropica)* attacks spruce and Virginia pines.

Damage: New branch shoots, called "candles," may be hollowed out and turn brown. Needles near branch tips turn yellow and small deposits of pitch form around new bud clusters. Resin-coated silk webbing shows around needles. Shoots die back and heavily infested trees appear reddish brown. Repeated infestations may deform and kill young pines.

Life cycle: Moths emerge in early spring. The female lays eggs singly onto pine needles, buds, or shoots. Larvae hatch in about 10 days and bore into the base of needles or buds, then into pine shoots. Larvae or pupae may overwinter in damaged shoots or in the ground. Some species produce one generation per year. Nantucket pine tip moth may have four.

Prevention: Don't plant susceptible pines if pine tip moths are present in your area. Clean up and destroy plant debris under pines to reduce the numbers of overwintering larvae and pupae.

Control: When practical, cut off and destroy infested branch tips. Spray pines with an insecticide containing carbaryl (Sevin), chlorpyrifos (Dursban), phosmet (Imidan), or acephate (Orthene) in April, June, and early August. Be sure to follow label directions carefully.

PRAYING MANTISES

BENEFICIALS

✎ ZONES: ALL

Say your prayers if you're a bug in the clutches of a praying mantis. One of the most fearsome predators of the insect world, the praying mantis eats any creature (head-first and alive) it can catch, including most insects and even mice, small lizards, and frogs.

Several features distinguish the mantis. Its triangular head, containing sharp mouthparts, can swivel 180°. Large, compound eyes see incredibly well. When the mantis seizes its prey with its spiny front legs—which fold into the predator's trademark "praying" position—the strike comes in less than fifty thousandths of a second.

Three species are common to the South. The Chinese praying mantis *(Tenodera aridifolia sinensis)* is light brown and 3–5 in. long. The European mantis *(Mantis religiosa)*, above, is bright green and 2–3 in. long. The Carolina praying mantis *(Stagmomantis carolina)* is brown or gray and less than 2 in. long. Male mantises fly; females are often wingless.

Mantis egg case

Target: Anything alive they can catch and overpower, even their own young and other adult mantises. However, they also eat lots of harmful bugs as well.

Damage: None to plants, but significant to bugs

Life cycle: After mating, the female attaches a rounded or tube-shaped, papier-mâché-like egg case (see inset photo) to a twig or stem. Eggs hatch in spring and nymphs (juveniles) emerge, consuming every insect in sight, including each other. Nymphs molt six to seven times as they mature. One generation occurs per year.

Prevention and control: Encourage mantises to populate your garden. Many mail-order suppliers sell mantis egg cases.

HONEYMOON JITTERS. *It's a sad, macabre fact of mantis reproduction. After a male mates with the much larger female, she often repays his efforts by biting off his head and eating him.*

PSYLLIDS

TREE AND SHRUB PESTS

✎ ZONES: ALL

Psyllids are small, winged insects that resemble aphids. No more than ⅕ in. long, they hold their clear wings in a rooflike triangle over their heads. Adults are typically green or brown, while the juveniles (nymphs) often have a white cottony coating. Both adults and nymphs feed by sucking sap.

Target: Psyllids usually attack specific plants, as indicated by some of the following names: boxwood psyllid *(Cacopsylla buxi)*, hackberry gall-maker *(Pachypsylla sp.)*, pear psyllid *(Cacopsylla pyricola)*, and yaupon psyllid *(Gyropsylla ilicis)*.

Damage: Most psyllids cause primarily cosmetic damage, although the pear psyllid can reduce yields. Feeding by boxwood psyllids causes new foliage to become cupped and puckered. Hackberry psyllids cause blister- or nipple-shaped galls to form on leaves, while pear psyllids excrete copious amounts of honeydew, which promotes the growth of sooty mold (see page 250) on leaves. Yaupon psyllids cause leaves to curl up into brownish red galls.

Life cycle: Boxwood psyllids overwinter on the plant as eggs; nymphs hatch as boxwood buds begin to open in spring; adults appear in May or June. Overwintering adult hackberry psyllids emerge from cracks and crevices in May; females deposit eggs on the undersides of new hackberry leaves; nymphs develop inside the galls and become adults in the fall. Female yaupon psyllids lay eggs on just-opened foliage in early spring; nymphs live inside the galls that form until they mature about 10 months later. Adult pear psyllids overwinter in bark crevices or leaf debris; females lay eggs in spring; and the microscopic nymphs become adults in a month. Unlike other psyllids, which produce one generation per year, the pear psyllid may have three to five.

Prevention: Apply horticultural oil to dormant plants to kill overwintering adults.

Control: Spray boxwoods and yaupons in spring and early summer with a systemic insecticide containing acephate (Orthene) or dimethoate (Cygon). Follow label directions carefully. Spray pear trees with horticultural oil in late winter and with carbaryl (Sevin) or malathion in late spring. Controlling hackberry psyllids is impractical.

RED HUMP CATERPILLARS

TREE PESTS

ZONES: ALL

The festive-looking red hump caterpillar *(Schizura concina)* is chunky, 1 in. long, and yellow with black and white stripes and spiny black warts all over its back; when older, it has a large lacquer red bump located two segments from the head end. The adult form is a brownish gray moth.

Target: Native to most of North America, the red hump caterpillar has a variety of deciduous host trees, from sweet gum and birch to walnut and willow. It is an occasional pest on fruit trees, significant only when found on young trees.

Damage: Red hump caterpillars feed in large groups. Slow-moving, they may attack only a single branch of a tree, but they can succeed in defoliating that branch completely. Infested branches are usually at the top of a tree; the first evidence of damage may be a pile of droppings on the ground below. Young fruit or nut trees are most harmed by defoliation. Larger landscape trees can easily recover the next year.

Life cycle: Adult moths first appear in late spring, and females lay shiny round eggs in clusters of 25 to 100 on the undersides of leaves. After hatching, the caterpillars feed on leaves, taking several weeks to reach full size. Then they drop to the ground and pupate in a hard, reddish brown shell on or just under the soil. There can be one to three generations per year.

Prevention: From May to July, periodically inspect leaves on new or recently planted trees for egg masses or caterpillars.

Control: If possible, handpick leaves that hold egg masses or cut off infested branches. For severe infestations, spray the tree with carbaryl (Sevin), phosmet (Imidan), or *Bacillus thuringiensis kurstaki* (Dipel, Thuricide, Javelin).

SADDLEBACK CATERPILLARS

TREE AND SHRUB PESTS

ZONES: ALL

A saddleback caterpillar *(Sibine stimulea)* may not float like a butterfly, but it does sting like a bee . The "hairs" on its body are hollow spines that protect it from attack by birds and other predators. Once the spines penetrate the skin, they pump venom into the wound, causing an intense burning sensation, redness, swelling, dermatitis, and sometimes nausea. The full-grown caterpillar is about 1 in. long and 3/8 in. wide. The name "saddleback" comes from the purplish-brown, saddle-shaped oval atop the caterpillar's green back.

Target: Plum, cherry, oak, chestnut, basswood, hibiscus, and palm

Damage: The saddleback caterpillar eats the foliage of a variety of trees and shrubs. However, it is rarely present in sufficient numbers to do any damage of consequence.

Life cycle: Female moths lay eggs on the plant. Larvae feed on leaves in late summer, hibernate in winter, and pupate in spring.

Prevention: Don't touch a saddleback caterpillar. If you get stung, don't rub the spot. Examine it first to see if any spines are sticking to the skin. If so, apply cellophane tape to the skin and then pull it off to remove the spines. Wash the area and apply an ice pack. Steroid creams may help reduce swelling.

Control: Saddlebacks work singly and usually in such small numbers that no chemical control is needed.

EEEOW!!! IT'S AN IO! *The saddleback isn't the only caterpillar that stings. Touching the Io (pronounced "EE-OH") caterpillar (Automeris io) smarts, too. The bottlebrush clusters of poisonous spines that line its body feel like a bee sting. It is 2–3 in. long and pale green, with white and red stripes on its side. The puss caterpillar (Megalopyge operularis) packs a punch that's even worse. It looks like a brown, fuzzy hairball about 1 in. long, and hangs out in hardwood trees. Its sting is the most painful of all the South's stinging caterpillars.*

SCALES

TREE, SHRUB, AND HOUSE PLANT PESTS

ZONES: ALL

Scale insects look more like a disease than a pest, because they appear as a crusty, fuzzy, or bubbly growth on leaves, stems, branches, and tree bark. Look closer and you will notice they are individual rounded bumps, each one hard, waxy, or fuzzy. This insecticide-resistant coating protects a tiny, wormlike creature within. Varying in size, shape, and color, scales cling, immobile, like barnacles on their host plants. Remotely related to aphids and mealybugs, scales are just as ubiquitous. Most scales are classified as either "soft" or "armored." The so-called soft scales have leathery or waxy coatings, while armored scales have stiff, lacquered coatings. Soft scales produce honeydew as a byproduct of their feeding, and this may be seen as a sticky substance on leaves and stems. Common scales are oyster shell scale (*Lepidosaphes ulmi*), an armored scale shown above, right; white cottony cushion scale; brown soft scale (*Coccus hesperidium*), shown above, left; euonymus scale (*Unaspis euonymi*); white peach scale (*Pseudaulacaspis pentagona*); tea scale (*Fiorinia theae*); oleander scale (*Aspidiotus nerii*); and snow scale (various pests).

Target: Some scales attack the foliage of many evergreen plants, including azalea, citrus, camellia, English ivy, euonymus, ferns, Japanese aucuba, Japanese pittosporum, oleander, pine, privet, and palms; others live on the bark, branches, and leaves of deciduous trees, such as black gum, magnolia, maple, orchid tree, tulip poplar, and willow. Scales also frequently attack house plants.

Damage: Immobile for most of their life, scale insects suck plant juices from underneath their protective coatings. On conifers, needles and shoots covered by scale turn a sickly yellow or brown. On other evergreens, leaves turn yellow or grow weakly. Infested twigs and bark may be covered with black sooty mold fungus. Heavy infestations may seriously weaken or kill a plant.

Life cycle: Scales lay eggs under their protective shells. The tiny offspring, called crawlers, travel short distances on the host plant to settle in. Once they attach their mouthparts—which provide both a sucking tool and an anchor—and start feeding, they begin to create their protective covering. They remain in one place and move again only to mate. The males of some species, such as cottony cushion scale, leave their shells to spin cocoons. After pupating, they emerge winged and fly to mate with wingless females. Armored scales usually have several generations per year, so a small infestation may quickly become a large, unsightly mess. Soft scales have only one generation per year.

Prevention: Avoid introducing scales into your garden when you come home from the garden center with plants. Spray the new plants with horticultural oil according to label directions before putting them in your garden or bringing them indoors. Don't try to save severely infested plants. Throw them in the trash instead.

Scale with sooty mold

Control: If only a few plants are infested, remove scales by hand using a nail file or your fingernail. On trees, you can rub them off with a plastic scouring pad from the kitchen. Scales have many natural enemies, including lacewing larvae and beetles that attack them in the crawler stage; some beneficial wasps pierce the hard shells and lay eggs within to parasitize the scales. If you see scales that appear to have a hole at the top, these are likely to be empty shells that have been successfully parasitized. See Chapter 8, "Suppliers and Expert Resources," page 316, for sources of beneficial wasps.

Spraying with a light horticultural oil during the growing season will control many scales on fruit trees, house plants, and ornamentals. The oil will smother the insects as they hatch and begin to crawl. Repeated spraying may be needed.

Spraying contact insecticides rarely removes or even inconveniences the pests. However, if you are lucky enough to spot scales in their crawler stage, you can kill them by spraying with insecticidal soap, carbaryl (Sevin), malathion, or diazinon. Always apply insecticides according to directions on the product label. To kill adult scales encrusting leaves and stems, spray with a systemic insecticide such as dimethoate (Cygon) or acephate (Orthene). But don't use systemics on fruit trees. Another very good option is spraying the affected plant with dormant oil while it is dormant. This smothers overwintering scales.

SLUGS AND SNAILS

FLOWER AND VEGETABLE PESTS

ZONES: ALL

These slimy critters are mollusks, not insects, and are closely related to shellfish such as clams and oysters. Snails have shells; slugs do not. Both travel by extending the length of their bodies along a patch of slippery, silvery slime.

Target: Slugs and snails eat any and all garden plants. They seem to especially relish basil, delphinium, hosta, marigold, petunia, salvia, zinnia, and leafy garden vegetables. Only herbs with stiff, highly scented foliage, such as lavender, rosemary, and sage, appear to be unpalatable.

Damage: Snails and slugs use toothlike jaws to rasp large, ragged holes in leaves and flowers. Seedlings and new transplants may be eaten entirely, with just a slime trail left behind to tell the tale. These pests feed at night and on overcast or rainy days, hiding under cover when the sun shines. They are most active during warm, rainy springs.

Life cycle: Every slug and snail has both male and female sex organs, so after mating, any individual can lay clusters of up to 80 small gelatinous eggs in soft soil. After hatching, snails and slugs may take from a few months to a few years to reach their full adult size. Once grown, they lay eggs up to six times per year. Native snails adapted to cold-winter areas hibernate in topsoil. During hot seasons or droughts, snails can seal themselves up with a membrane and stay dormant for up to 4 years.

Prevention: The first step to managing snails and slugs is to eliminate any daytime hiding places near your vegetable and flower beds. Boards, stones, bricks, unused flowerpots, and ground covers in shady places are favorite haunts. To protect newly planted seedlings, surround the beds with copper stripping 3–4 in. high. Snails and slugs will not cross copper; something in their slime reacts with this metal to give them a small electric shock. Do not lay the copper flat on the soil; keep it vertical, like a little fence. It can be stapled to raised beds, wrapped around citrus tree trunks or flowerpots, or curled into a collar to protect individual plants. Wood ashes, crushed eggshells, and diatomaceous earth irritate the bodies of slugs and snails and thus also make good barriers. Dur-

ing rainy springs, hunting, handpicking, and laying bait traps for snails and slugs early in the season may prevent a population explosion later on.

Control: Handpick snails (you can also hunt them at night, with a flashlight) and destroy them by crushing them in a paper bag and tossing their remains into the compost pile. Follow slime trails to find their hiding places—snails often hang upside down from the undersides of flower boxes or attach themselves to the wood of decks or stairs. Trap slugs and snails by laying a small board on top of a few stones near plants to provide an enticing hiding place during the day. At noon, lift the board and swipe the offenders into a pail of soapy water.

Encourage in your garden natural enemies of snails and slugs: predaceous ground beetles, birds, toads, and salamanders. Chickens, geese, and ducks are also efficient snail hunters.

Dishes baited with beer will lure slugs to their deaths. Commercial snail baits containing metaldehyde are most effective against slugs and snails; they also control millipedes and sowbugs. Granular snail baits will be more effective if you wet the ground first; read product labels carefully before applying. However, heavy rain or water on the pellets usually dissolves them before snails can get them. Set out poison baits in the late evening and try to clear them in the morning, since many formulations can be poisonous to birds and pets. Metaldehyde poison in the form of a caulky paste lasts longer through rainy weather and makes a good barrier when snaked along the edge of paving or garden paths. Poison baits are highly toxic to fish, so don't use them near ponds or streams.

Sprinkling salt on snails and slugs does kill them, but salt is bad for the soil and can be harmful to plants.

WHY WASTE GOOD BEER?

Lots of people know about filling shallow containers with beer and leaving them in the garden for slugs and snails. The intemperate mollusks drink until they pass out and drown. While this may be kinder than coating the pests with salt (which we don't recommend), it's also a waste of good beer. You can achieve the same result by mixing a teaspoon of brewer's yeast into a cup of water.

SOLDIER BEETLES

BENEFICIALS

ZONES: ALL

When it comes to aphids, caterpillars, and other soft-bodied insects, the predatory soldier beetle takes no prisoners. Common throughout the South, these hunters are sometimes called leatherwings. They are long and slender, about ½ in. long, and vary in color from yellow to red with brown or black wings. Some species resemble lightning bugs but do not produce light.

All soldier beetles are helpful in the garden as insect predators. When disturbed, the adults often curl their heads under their bodies and drop to the ground. Their larvae, which live underground, are rarely seen. The only complaint people have about soldier beetles is that, like ladybugs, they sometimes invade houses during the winter to escape the cold. However, they cause no harm there.

To attract soldier beetles to your garden, provide a water source and plant nectar-producing flowers. You can buy soldier beetles in packages to be released in spring or summer. After you release them, refrain from or limit pesticide use to help soldier beetles become established in your garden.

Target: Adult soldier beetles attack and feed on aphids and other soft-bodied insects. They also feed on pollen and nectar from flowers, such as goldenrod. The tiny larvae prey upon small soil-dwelling insects.

Damage: Soldier beetles and their larvae do not damage plants.

Life cycle: Soldier beetles lay their eggs in clusters on the soil. Once hatched, the slender, wormlike larvae burrow into the soil to feed on underground prey and then pupate. These insects may overwinter in damp soil or garden debris as eggs, larvae, or pupae. Depending on the species, there may be several generations per year.

Prevention and control: No measures are needed.

SPINED SOLDIER BUGS

BENEFICIALS

ZONES: ALL

Each time a spined soldier bug (*Podiscus maculiventris*) deals with a caterpillar, it does so with a vengeance. This dark gray or brown beneficial stinkbug has a triangle etched on its back. Adults are about ¾ in. long; juveniles, or nymphs, are small, dark, and flat. Both adults and nymphs brandish long, daggerlike mouthparts, which they use to stab and suck the juices of the insects they feed on. They eat both eggs and larvae. The spined soldier bug shown above is attacking a cabbage webworm (*Hellula rogatalis*).

You can purchase spined soldier bugs as beneficials in either adult or nymphal form. After you release them in your garden, either refrain from or limit pesticide use until they become well established.

Target: Spined soldier bugs attack an incredible array of harmful insects, including asparagus beetle, cabbage looper, cabbage webworm, codling moth, Colorado potato beetle, corn earworm, eastern tent caterpillar, elm leaf beetle, fall armyworm, fall webworm, gypsy moth caterpillar, imported cabbageworm, Mexican bean beetle, spotted cucumber beetle, spring cankerworm, tobacco budworm, two-lined spittlebug, as well as other stinkbugs.

Damage: Adult spined soldier bugs do not damage plants. Young nymphs may suck plant juices, but after their first molt they become full-time predators.

Life cycle: Each female spined soldier bug lays up to 40 clusters of about 30 bronze-colored eggs on garden plants. Eggs hatch into nymphs that develop into adults in a few weeks. The growing season may see several succeeding generations, their numbers waxing and waning according to the numbers of available prey. Because adults can fly, they often leave an area once they exhaust the food supply.

Prevention and control: No measures are needed.

SPITTLEBUGS

TREE, SHRUB, FLOWER, FRUIT, AND LAWN PESTS

Z ZONES: ALL

The signs of spittlebugs are unmistakable—gobs of foamy froth oozing over stems and leaves. The froth hides and protects the feeding nymphs of spittlebugs, of which there are many different species. These small, triangular insects may be green or brown—although you probably won't be able to see them through the foam. The adult insects, which are oval and brownish or gray, produce no foam and are quite mobile. They hop or fly from plant to plant.

Target: Spittlebugs attack a wide range of annuals, perennials, and herbs. Rosemary and strawberries are favorite targets. Pecan spittlebug (*Clastoptera achatina*) attacks pecan trees. Pine spittlebug (*Aphrophora cribatta*) is a serious pest of pines. Two-lined spittlebug (*Prosapia bicincta*) afflicts warm-season grasses, particularly centipede and Bermuda. It also feeds on holly.

Spittlebug

Damage: Spittlebugs do only minor damage to most plants unless they're present in large numbers. However, pecan spittlebugs can kill terminal shoots of pecans and reduce yields. Two-spotted spittlebugs can yellow and brown the lawn.

Life cycle: In spring, spittlebug nymphs hatch from overwintering eggs and begin feeding by sucking plant juices. They mature in a week or two; then their spittling days are over. Adult females lay eggs on host plants. Depending on the species, there may be one to three generations per year.

Prevention: Regular dethatching will prevent a buildup of spittlebugs in the lawn.

Control: Spined soldier bugs (see opposite page) are a natural control. Or you can apply a lawn insecticide containing diazinon or chlorpyrifos (Dursban) to the lawn. Follow label directions carefully. Contact a professional tree service to control spittlebug infestations in trees. Pesticides aren't usually necessary elsewhere. You can blast the foam off foliage with a jet of water.

SPRINGTAILS

LAWN PESTS; BENEFICIALS

Z ZONES: ALL

Less a pest than a nuisance, springtails live in soil and lawns. These grayish or blue-black insects are less than ¼ in. long and have a tiny forklike appendage on their rear. This is not a fang or a stinger; instead it enables them to jump into the air when threatened. Attracted to damp places, they often jump or fall into swimming pools and garden fountains. Springtails are usually found in damp soils, in potted plants, and on the soil beneath lawns.

Target: As beneficial insects, springtails gobble up microorganisms beneath the soil and help turn decaying plant matter into useful humus.

Damage: Most springtails feed on decaying plant matter, but a species that affects lawns will chew on the root hairs of grasses, especially if the grass is very soggy. Recently laid sod lawns may not thrive if this insect is prevalent, as the grass may be unable to resist fungus infections, such as rust, that also attack damp turf. When the sod is lifted up, clusters of springtails may jump up from the damp soil.

Life cycle: Successive generations appear throughout the year.

Prevention: Since these tiny pests love a damp environment, letting garden soil dry out between waterings generally keeps them underground. When setting new sod lawns, be sure the soil underneath is well graded and fast draining.

Control: Small populations of springtails should be tolerated, as springtails help build good soil. The presence of springtails in potted plants usually means the pots are being overwatered. Reducing watering will also keep down populations in lawns. Where lawns are severely infested, drench the turf and soil below with diazinon. Always apply pesticides according to label directions.

SPRUCE BUDWORMS

TREE PESTS

❚ ZONES: US, MS

Spruce budworms *(Choristoneura fumiferana)* are caterpillars that attack conifers, especially spruce and fir. These pests are 1¼ in. long and reddish brown with raised spots. The adult is a gray moth with brown markings and a wingspan of ½ in. The moth and its larval form are common in much of the Upper and Middle South, but are rarely seen in the Southwest.

Target: Fir, hemlock, larch, and spruce

Damage: In spring and summer, budworm larvae chew the tender tips of new growth, covering the needles as they feed with a silky webbing that binds them together and creates a hiding place from birds. Webbing appears on affected needles by midsummer. Large sections of a tree may turn brown and die.

Life cycle: Budworm epidemics are cyclical, with severe outbreaks every 10 years or so. Females lay clusters of pale green eggs near branch tips in late summer. After the eggs hatch, the larvae are quite small; they retire to crevices in bark to spin a silk case where they hibernate over the winter. As the weather warms in spring, the larvae begin feeding heavily, burrowing into needles and buds. After about a month, they pupate on the tree and then emerge as adult moths. There is one generation per year.

Prevention: No preventive measures are needed in most years. Monitor firs and spruces in early summer for the presence of webbing on new growth. If you see an outbreak in your area, treat buds on susceptible evergreens with *Bacillus thuringiensis kurstaki* (Dipel, Thuricide, Javelin). Repeated applications may be required.

Control: Hose off webbing and pry apart wrapped needle bunches, then kill the exposed larvae by dusting or spraying with *Bacillus thuringiensis kurstaki* (Dipel, Thuricide, Javelin), or treat the branches with an insecticide containing acephate (Orthene) or carbaryl (Sevin), applied according to label directions.

SPRUCE GALL ADELGIDS

TREE PESTS

❚ ZONES: US, MS

An attack of spruce gall adelgids is about the worst Christmas present a Chrismas tree grower can suffer. These insects cause ugly, brown, pineapple-shaped galls to form on the ends of the branches. The Cooley spruce gall adelgid *(Adelges cooleyi)* is the most common species in the South.

Target: Norway and Colorado blue spruce are principal targets. Douglas fir *(Pseudotsuga menziesii)* is an alternate host.

Damage: On the leaf tips of infected spruce trees, needles become slightly enlarged and turn reddish brown, shown above. After the needles fall from infested stems, the stems become rubbery, flattened or pineapple-shaped galls. The galls may be green or purple and ½ – 3 in. wide. The galls are caused by chemicals secreted by the nymph as it sucks plant juices from needle tips; the tree reacts by forming an enclosure around the offending insect. The galls turn brown and may persist for many years. On Douglas fir, needles may be discolored or may drop.

Life cycle: This pest has a complicated lifestyle, alternating between two different hosts, spruce and Douglas fir trees. Winged adelgid adults lay eggs on either tree. Nymphs that hatch on spruces in the spring begin sucking plant juices, which then create the gall. By midsummer, the nymphs within the galls molt and exit as winged adults, which migrate to Douglas fir. They settle into cones or needle tufts, produce white cottony stuff to make a nest, then give birth to a new generation of nymphs. These nymphs feed on Douglas fir until some develop wings, which they use to migrate back to spruces.

Prevention: Do not plant Douglas fir and spruce trees close together, as this provides the ideal habitat for this pest.

Control: Prune infested foliage while the galls are still green, and destroy it. Wash the cottony deposits off Douglas firs with a jet of soapy water. Natural predators to be encouraged or introduced into the garden include ladybugs and lacewings. For serious infestations, spray new growth in spring with carbaryl (Sevin) or endosulfan (Thiodan) according to label directions.

SQUASH BUGS

VEGETABLE PESTS

ZONES: ALL

Squash bugs (*Anasa tristis*) belong to a group that includes stinkbugs. The almond-shaped adults are dark brown or black and about ½ in. long. From under the wings, a squash bug's orange-toned body protrudes a bit, looking like edging. The nymphs are smaller and yellowish green with red heads. Both adults and nymphs hide on the undersides of leaves; they can run quickly on their long legs. When they are caught and crushed, their bodies emit a foul odor.

Target: Squash bugs attack plants in the cucurbit family, feeding on cucumber, gourd, melon, pumpkin, and squash.

Damage: Both nymphs and adult squash bugs suck plant juices. At first, leaves may show spots that turn yellow and then brown; then the stems of affected plants wilt and blacken. Infested plants are weakened, and younger plants may die. The outsides of squash may show signs of feeding by adult bugs.

Life cycle: After overwintering in garden debris, adult squash bugs fly to lay clusters of shiny, reddish brown eggs on the leaves and stems of cucurbits. Nymphs group together to feed, eventually growing into the darker adults. There is one generation per year.

Prevention: Check the undersides of transplanted or newly sprouted squash plants for egg masses; pick off affected leaves and destroy them. Tidy vegetable beds each fall to get rid of weeds and plant debris where adult squash bugs could overwinter. Plant resistant selections, including 'Butternut', 'Early Summer Crookneck', 'Improved Green Hubbard', 'Royal Acorn', and 'Table Queen'. Crop rotation can be helpful too (see page 31).

Control: You can kill nymphs and adults by spraying the undersides of leaves with insecticidal soap. Spined soldier bugs (see page 186) provide natural control. For severe infestations, spray the undersides of leaves with rotenone, applied according to label directions.

SQUASH VINE BORERS

VEGETABLE PESTS

ZONES: ALL

A common pest throughout the South, the squash vine borer (*Melittia satyriniformis*) is the larval form of a large moth that is orange and black with clear wings. The caterpillars can be found within the stems of squash vines; if you slit a stem lengthwise with a knife, you may find a fat white worm about 1 in. long.

Target: The squash vine borer attacks squash and pumpkins. Occasionally it targets cucumber and melon vines. Butternut squash usually resists this pest.

Damage: The borer tunnels through squash vine stems, disrupting the flow of water and nutrients. Vines suddenly wilt and collapse, even though the plants may be well watered. Bubbly, greenish yellow frass, or insect excrement, appears near holes in the stems. Wilted plants usually die.

Life cycle: The adult female moth appears on squash plants in late spring and lays its eggs on the vines in June and July. The larvae bore into plant stems and feed for 4 to 6 weeks. Then they crawl out of the stems and into the ground to pupate over the winter. There is one generation per year.

Prevention: To protect squash plants from flying adults, cover crops with floating row covers. Remove the covers when flowers appear, to allow access by pollinating insects. Crop rotation and early planting are helpful, too. Borers overwinter in garden soil and debris, so if they ruin your squash one year, plant squash in a different area the next. Or skip a year of planting.

Control: Once vines begin to run, dust or spray the base of the plant with rotenone, a pyrethrum product, malathion, or carbaryl (Sevin) every 7 to 10 days. However, insecticides are useless once the borer has penetrated a vine stem. If only parts of a vine are affected, try to save the remaining crop by cutting away the wilting portions. If you notice frass around a hole, slit the vine near the hole to locate and destroy the borer. Or try to kill the borers by injecting beneficial nematodes or 3 cc of *Bacillus thuringiensis kurstaki* (Dipel, Thuricide, Javelin) into stems with a syringe. After harvest, pull up old vines, destroy crop debris, and till the soil to kill resting pupae.

STINKBUGS

VEGETABLE, FRUIT, AND NUT PESTS; BENEFICIALS

ZONES: ALL

Stinkbugs are the skunks of the insect world. When disturbed, they produce a stench foul enough to convince predators (and people) to leave them alone. Not all stinkbugs are pests. Some, like the spined soldier bug (see page 186) and the predaceous stinkbug *(Euthyrhynchus floridanus)*, eat harmful insect pests and even other stinkbugs. You can tell the good guys from the bad guys this way: The former have spines at the corners of their shield-shaped bodies; the latter generally don't. Also, the good guys sport short, sharp beaks for piercing prey and the bad guys don't.

Three of the most common stinkbugs in the South are the green stinkbug *(Acrosternum hilare)*, shown above, the brown stinkbug *(Euschistus servus)*, and the Southern green stinkbug *(Nezara viridula)*. They're most numerous where tall grass, weeds, and garden debris provide shelter for them during winter.

Target: Vegetables, fruits, and nuts, including beans, broccoli, cabbage, corn, okra, peaches, pecans, strawberries, and tomatoes

Damage: Affected leaves and fruits are usually spotted, blemished, or distorted. Strawberries, peaches, and tomatoes may also show "catfacing"—a deformity in which the fruits look gnarled, creased, or twisted. Pecans develop bitter, discolored spots; the kernels may turn brown and shrivel; and the nuts drop prematurely.

Life cycle: Adults overwinter in weeds or leafy debris, then in spring lay barrel-shaped eggs in tens on a leaf or stem. Nymphs feed for a few weeks, then become winged adults without a pupal stage. There may be three or four generations per year.

Prevention: Remove and destroy garden debris each year in late fall. Keep weeds cut. Mow grass regularly beneath pecan trees. Use floating row covers in home vegetable gardens to keep out stinkbugs.

Control: The tachinid fly *Trichopda pennipes* parasitizes adult Southern green stinkbugs, while a tiny, parasitoid wasp, *Trissolcus basalis,* parasitizes the eggs of that stinkbug as well as others. These two predators and the spined soldier beetle usually do a good job of controlling stinkbug populations. However, for major infestations, spray with carbaryl (Sevin) according to label directions.

SYRPHID FLIES

BENEFICIALS

ZONES: ALL

Syrphid flies, a large group of about 900 species in North America, occur in all parts of the South. Like hummingbirds, they possess the ability to hover in flight, so many people know them as "hover flies." Although these flies vary in color and size, most are brown or black with yellow bands on the abdomen and resemble wasps and bees. But they don't bite or sting. Look for them in the garden among your flowers. Adults feed only on pollen or nectar. But their sluglike or maggotlike larvae, which may be greenish, brown, or translucent with no visible head or legs, greedily devour aphids and other troublesome pests.

Syrphid fly larva eating aphids

To attract syrphid flies to your garden, provide a source of water for adult flies and plant nectar-producing flowers. Winged adult males often establish territories around certain plants when they're in bloom, welcoming females but chasing off males and other nectar-gathering insects. Planting flowers, flowering herbs, and vegetables together provides an attractive environment for syrphid flies; limiting the use of insecticides in your garden keeps them around.

Target: Larvae of syrphid flies hunt and feed on soft-bodied insects, such as aphids, mealybugs, and scales in the crawler stage. They use tiny fangs to impale and carry off prey, then drain them of fluids, leaving only the skin behind.

Damage: Unless you're an aphid or mealybug, you have nothing to fear.

Life cycle: Adult flies lay their eggs near colonies of aphids and other prey. Larvae hatch and feed on their victims. There may be several generations per year.

Prevention and control: No measures are needed.

TACHINID FLIES

BENEFICIALS

ZONES: ALL

The tachinid fly looks like something you ought to swat and has a face only a mother could love. But these gray and bristly insects prove that not all flies are a nuisance. Approximately 1,300 species exist in North America. Many resemble the common housefly but are a little larger, about ¼–½ in. long. Other tachinids look like bees or wasps.

Adult flies feed only on flower nectar, but their larvae parasitize many kinds of pest insects.

To attract tachinid flies to your garden, provide a water source and plant flowers that produce nectar. Plant flowers, herbs, and vegetables together. Limit the use of insecticides, spraying only if a major pest insect invasion ensues.

Target: Tachinid flies parasitize cutworms, grasshoppers, stinkbugs, and the larvae of some beetles. Individual species attack specific pests. For example, *Lespesia aletiae* parasitizes fall armyworms, cabbage loopers, imported cabbageworms, and oleander caterpillars. Another species, *Ormia depleta,* also known as red-eye fly, wreaks havoc on Southern and tawny mole crickets. It locates these crickets by their song and deposits its larvae on or near the cricket. Red-eye flies have been released in Florida as a biological control for mole crickets.

Damage: Tachinid flies cause no damage to plants.

Life cycle: Most tachinid flies lay eggs directly on the body of the host insect. After an egg hatches, the larva burrows into the body of the host and feeds inside. When fully developed, the larva chews its way out, drops to the ground, and pupates in the soil. Other tachinids lay their eggs on foliage. The eggs hatch inside the host insect after it foolishly eats the foliage. Still others, like the red-eye fly, deposit live larvae on the host.

Prevention and control: No measures are needed.

TENT CATERPILLARS, EASTERN

SHADE AND FRUIT TREE PESTS

ZONES: ALL

Silken nests in the crotches of tree branches in spring are the handiwork of eastern tent caterpillars *(Malacosoma americanum)*. You can easily identify these black, 2-in.-long critters by the white stripe down their back and row of blue spots along their sides.

Target: Tent caterpillars attack many trees and shrubs. Their favorite targets include black cherry *(Prunus serotina),* apple, and crabapple trees.

Damage: Caterpillars build gauzy nests in the crotches and forks of tree branches. They leave these nests during the day to feed on foliage. Entire branches and large portions of severely infested trees may be defoliated.

Eastern tent caterpillar web

Life cycle: Adult female moths crawl up tree bark to lay collarlike egg masses that may encircle branches and twigs. The first crop of caterpillars hatches in early spring, spins webbing for nests, and feeds until early summer. The full-grown caterpillars then drop to the ground or lower themselves on silken threads to pupate in leaf litter. These pests overwinter as egg masses on twigs. There may be one to several generations per year.

Prevention: Check tree bark in the winter and remove egg masses if you see them. Also check wooden garden structures. Introduce or encourage natural caterpillar predators, such as ground beetles, spined soldier bugs, tachinid flies, and parasitoid wasps.

Control: Spray or dust the nest in early evening with the microbial control *Bacillus thuringiensis kurstaki* (Dipel, Thuricide, Javelin), which will kill the caterpillars. Caterpillars and their webs can also be removed by hand, but wear gloves since many people are allergic to these pests. For severe infestations, spray trees with diazinon, phosmet (Imidan), carbaryl (Sevin), or malathion, applied according to label directions.

TERMITES

HOUSEHOLD AND TREE PESTS

ZONES: ALL

These industrious pests eat wood and operate in colonies of more than 50,000. Subterranean termites cause 95 percent of the estimated annual $2 billion of structural damage in the U.S. About ¼ in. long, they belong to several castes. Workers are creamy white and sterile. Soldiers have huge heads and strong jaws. Reproductive swarmers have long, narrow wings, blackish bodies, and big eyes. Each colony contains at least one queen.

Target: Wood, cardboard, paper, and anything composed of cellulose

Damage: Termites hollow out major structural supports, such as joists and beams. Extensive damage usually takes 3 to 8 years. Termites also infest the heartwood of trees.

Life cycle: On a warm spring day, winged swarmers leave the colony to start new ones. Underground colonies thrive in moist soil. They travel to food sites through extensive, tubelike tunnels. If the wood isn't touching soil, they may build mud tubes to it, to avoid contact with outside air, which would dry out and kill them. The colony may grow for 3 to 4 years before it swarms.

Prevention: Inspect wooden structures yearly. Don't let untreated wood touch soil. Look for mud tubes that cross concrete foundations. Termites love moisture, so make sure downspouts, faucets, lawn sprinklers, and condensation pipes don't place water near the foundation. Don't place woodpiles or bark mulch against the house. Use chemical termite baits around the foundation. Follow label directions.

Control: Contact a licensed exterminator.

TERMITE ALERT! *Since entering the U.S in the 1940s, the voracious Formosan termite* (Coptotermes formosanus) *has spread through the Southeast. It secretes an acidic substance that helps it tunnel through rubber, lead, asphalt, plastic, and plaster. It doesn't need ground contact to enter houses. New Orleans has been hard-hit, with annual cost of structural damage and treatment exceeding $200 million. The insect has also hollowed out many of the city's beloved live oaks.*

THRIPS

FLOWER, SHRUB, VEGETABLE, FRUIT, AND BULB PESTS

ZONES: ALL

Thrips are so tiny (about $\frac{1}{20}$ in. long) that most folks never see them. But there's no overlooking the damage they cause. Brown, yellow, or black with bodies shaped like a grain of rice, they tear the tissues of leaves and flowers as they suck the juices. The damage looks similar to that caused by mites (see page 177), without the characteristic webbing. Adults have two pairs of narrow, feathery wings. The smaller and wingless juveniles, called nymphs, may be light green or pale yellow.

Target: Thrips attack vegetables, annuals, perennials, bulbs, fruits, and shrubs. Favorite targets include azaleas, cacti, citrus, dahlias, dracaenas, ferns, gladiolus, greenhouse plants, palms, rhododendrons, roses, and succulents. Flower thrips (*Frankliniella tritici*), the most abundant species, cluster on buds, flowers, and new growth of many plants. Greenhouse thrips (*Heliothrips sp.*), shown on opposite page), infest seedlings and house plants in greenhouses. Gladiolus thrips (*Taeniothrips simplex*) ruin gladiolus blooms all over the South.

Damage: Adult thrips and their nymphs chew and suck plants vigorously, scraping away the chlorophyll on leaves where they feed. The surface of damaged leaves looks silvery or bronzy. Leaves may be speckled, streaked, spotted, or stunted. Flowers may fail to open normally, appearing twisted, discolored, or dried up. Although thrips often hide within flowers or on the undersides of leaves, telltale specks of black excrement reveal their presence. Infestations usually peak during periods of hot, dry weather.

Life cycle: Like aphids, some kinds of thrips can reproduce asexually, so a small infestation quickly becomes a big one. After hatching, the nymphs go through two larval stages, a pre-pupal and pupal stage, and then change into winged adults. The entire life cycle takes only 2 to 3 weeks. Reproduction is continuous in the Coastal and Tropical South. Elsewhere, thrips overwinter as eggs laid within plant tissues by adults.

Prevention: Thrips prefer dry plants, so keep plants properly watered. Periodically rinse off the leaves of target plants to discourage thrips.

Control: One way to control thrips in flower and vegetable gardens is to use yellow sticky cards (see page 33). These act like flypaper to thrips attracted to the color. You can make your own sticky traps by painting a piece of cardboard yellow, then coating it with oil or petroleum jelly.

Beneficial insects, such as parasitoid wasps, soldier beetles, and especially the green lacewing (see page 171), whose larvae hunt and kill the nymphs, are useful too. Dusting the undersides of infested foliage with garden sulfur or diatomaceous earth will also kill nymphs. To kill adults on most plants, spray with insecticidal soap, horticultural oil, a pyrethrin, rotenone, malathion, diazinon, or carbaryl (Sevin) according to label directions. Do not use systemic insecticides on edible crops.

To control thrips ruining the blooms of roses or gladiolus, pick off and destroy infested blooms. Spray new buds and blooms with acephate (Orthene) or dimethoate (Cygon). If it's necessary to store gladiolus corms indoors over winter in your area, first dust them with carbaryl and then store them at 40–45°F.

Thrips that infest ornamental trees and shrubs often are hard to kill because these insects hide within new leaf and flower buds. Spiders are useful predators against thrips on shrubs because they will crawl into buds to reach their prey. Parasitoid wasps and lacewings provide additional control. But when foliage starts to look like that of the azalea, shown on the opposite page, it's time to bring out the big guns. Spray the plant with a systemic insecticide, such as acephate (Orthene) or dimethoate (Cygon), according to label directions.

TIGER BEETLES

BENEFICIALS

ZONES: ALL

With the name "tiger beetles" (*Cicindela sp.*), these beneficials sound like hunters, and they are. Fortunately, they hunt and eat other insects. Adults are from $3/8 – 7/8$ in. long and feature long, threadlike antennae and prominent, large eyes. They may be metallic black, blue, bronze, green, orange, or purple. Powerful grinding mouthparts are sickle shaped, very sharp, and lined with teeth. Tiger beetles run and fly rapidly. In both adult and larval forms, they're ferocious insect eaters.

Tiger beetles prefer open, sunny habitats—beaches, pathways, roads, and mud-flats. Adults stalk their prey and capture it with sheer speed. The name "tiger" reflects their ability to pounce on prey. Once they grab it, they bang it against the ground until it's dead, then eat it.

MY GIRL. *Male tiger beetles don't know how to share. After mating, they engage in a curious practice called "mate guarding." The male grasps the female, crawls onto her back, and rides around for a prolonged period to discourage other suitors.*

Target: Ants, aphids, smaller beetles, caterpillars, flies, worms, and spiders

Damage: No damage to plants; plenty of damage to bugs

Life cycle: Female beetles deposit eggs in the ground in summer. The emerging grublike larvae are whitish, S-shaped, and spiny. They sport large, hard heads and long, curving jaws. The larvae live in vertical underground burrows about 12 in. deep. When small insects wander by or fall into the burrows, the tiger beetle larvae seize them, drag them into the bottom of the burrows, and eat them. Larvae overwinter underground, then pupate in chambers dug into the sides of the burrows. Adults emerge in summer. Depending on species, the life cycle takes 1 to 3 years.

Prevention and control: No measures are needed. In fact, these beetles need to be protected, as many are endangered in the wild due to loss of habitat and widespread use of pesticides.

TWIG GIRDLERS

TREE PESTS

ZONES: ALL

Not all falling branches are the fault of the wind. The culprit may be the twig girdler *(Onicideres cingulata)*, a stout, gray-brown, hard-shelled beetle about ¾ in. long. Distinguishing marks include a light stripe across the wings and antennae, as long as its body. The larvae are cylindrical, light brown to brownish gray, about 1 in. long, with small heads.

Target: Oak, pecan, hickory, dogwood, and other shade, nut, and fruit trees

Damage: Twigs up to 3 ft. long drop to the ground beneath the tree. The broken end of the twig seems to have been ground smooth all the way around, although the center may appear cracked. Dead twigs hang from the tree until dislodged by the wind. Although affected trees appear ragged, the injury isn't life threatening. However, severe infestations may deform young trees.

Life cycle: Adult beetles emerge from mid-August through early October. Females chew V-shaped grooves into twigs near the ends of branches and deposit three to eight eggs into each groove. Then they chew a continuous notch around the twig, girdling it. The notch restricts the flow of sap into the twig, killing it, but provides the necessary conditions for the larvae to develop. The twig breaks and falls to the ground, where the larvae overwinter in the twig. They resume feeding in spring, boring farther down into the twig. They pupate in the twig cavity and emerge as adults in late summer. There is one generation per year.

Prevention and control: Gather and burn all girdled twigs that fall to the ground. Do this in fall, winter, or early spring. If practical, prune off any infested twigs remaining on the tree and burn them too.

WASPS AND HORNETS

PESTS; BENEFICIALS

ZONES: ALL

Wasps and hornets have a bad reputation but serve useful purposes. They pollinate crops, although not as efficiently as honeybees, and kill garden pests, such as caterpillars. Unfortunately, many wasps and hornets inflict painful stings if disturbed, and unlike bees, they can sting repeatedly.

Wasps and hornets are not mutually exclusive groups. In fact, all hornets are wasps. The term *hornets* generally refers to larger wasps that build large nests and sting aggressively.

Probably the most familiar wasp is the pesky eastern yellow jacket *(Vespula maculifrons)*, shown above. About ⅝ in. long with yellow and black stripes, it builds nests under rocks or in the ground. Because yellow jackets love sweets and meat, they often hover around garbage cans and picnic tables, making people miserable. They also sting with little provocation.

That bread loaf–shaped nest you see hanging in the tree is the home of the bald-faced hornet *(V. maculata)*. About an inch long with black-and-white markings, it aggressively hunts caterpillars and other insects. It doesn't sting unless provoked, but jostling its nest courts disaster.

Paper wasps *(Polistes sp.)*, opposite page, build nests consisting of small combs of cells attached by a single stalk to a roof or overhang. About ¾ in. long with reddish brown and yellow markings, they hunt insects. They don't sting unless disturbed.

Two huge wasps you definitely want to avoid are the cicada killer *(Sphecius speciosus)* and the European giant hornet *(Vespa crabro)*. The cicada killer resembles a yellow jacket but is much larger, about 1½ in. long. The females sting and paralyze cicadas and then drag them into underground burrows to feed their young. Though possessing very powerful stings, cicada killers aren't aggressive toward people.

The same can't be said for the European giant hornet. The largest wasp in North America at 1⅝ in. long, it has a stout, reddish brown body and orange stripes. It chews the bark off of lilacs, birches, boxwoods, and other plants to use in building nests. When defending these plants, it attacks without provocation and delivers a sting that will knock you down.

Target: Plants (for nectar), insects, and people (for revenge)

Damage: Though the European giant hornet damages plants by girdling stems, most wasps benefit the garden. The trick for gardeners is keeping out of their way.

Life cycle: Adult, mated females generally overwinter in protected places. In spring, they build nests and lay eggs. Offspring become workers that maintain the nest and find food. By summer's end, males and females fly away, mate, and start new colonies.

Prevention: Don't leave trash, empty drink cans, fruit, meat, or garbage uncovered outdoors. In summer, use screens on windows and doors and don't walk barefoot. Do not disturb nests unless absolutely necessary.

Control: Use a jet-spray wasp and hornet killer to destroy nests of yellow jackets and paper wasps. Do this after dark and follow label directions exactly. Spray trunks of lilacs, birches, and other susceptible plants with carbaryl (Sevin) in July and August to foil the European giant hornet. Leave cicada killers and bald-faced hornets alone. However, if you need to eradicate them, consult a professional exterminator.

TINY TITANS. *Some of the most helpful flying insects in the garden are parasitoid wasps, usually so small that five or six could fit on the head of a pin. Many species inhabit gardens naturally. To attract them, plant nectar flowers and provide a water source. Encarsia and Trichogramma wasps are commonly available to home gardeners in packages; they may be released into the garden to help control whiteflies, scales, beetles, and a variety of harmful larvae. Since these tiny wasps can fly, they effectively attack fruit tree pests, such as codling moth larvae, that may be unreachable in tall trees. They are quite specialized—certain species attack only certain pests—so they can be effective as a targeted control for harmful fruit tree insects. These tiny wasps live only briefly, so weekly releases are recommended.*

WEBWORMS, FALL

TREE PESTS

 ZONES: ALL

Despite its name, fall webworm *(Hyphantria cunea)* operates in summer as well as fall. Novice gardeners often confuse it with the eastern tent caterpillar *(Malacosoma americanum)* (see page 191), which spins silken webs in trees in spring. But the two are easy to distinguish. The latter constructs nests in the crotches of branches close to the trunk. The fall webworm builds its nests out on the ends of branches.

Two races of fall webworm exist. Adult moths of the Southern race appear about mid-March. They have white wings with dark wing spots, and their larvae have black heads. Moths of the Northern race appear about a month later. They're pure white, and their larvae have red heads. Territories of the two may overlap.

Target: Pecan, walnut, persimmon, sourwood, maple, mulberry, crabapple, ash, honey locust, and many other species of deciduous trees

Damage: The larvae or caterpillars eat the foliage within the nest and enlarge the nest as they grow. Damage to the tree is seldom serious, but severe infestations can defoliate and stress a tree.

Life cycle: Adult moths lay eggs on the undersides of tree leaves in spring and early summer. The eggs hatch in about 10 days and young caterpillars quickly build silken nests to hide themselves as they feed. If disturbed, the caterpillars react in unison with jerky movements. Larvae go through many stages of development. After they mature, they form cocoons and change into moths. There may be one to four generations per year, depending on the length of the growing season.

Prevention: Inspect susceptible trees for nests. If possible, prune out the infested branch and burn it.

Control: Break up newly formed nests with a jet of water, then spray them with *Bacillus thuringiensis kurstaki* (Dipel, Thuricide, Javelin) in early evening. For severe infestations, spray nests and foliage with carbaryl (Sevin), diazinon, acephate (Orthene), or malathion according to label directions.

WEBWORMS, SOD

LAWN PESTS

✏ ZONES: ALL

Ever stir up flocks of small gray or tan moths as you walk across the lawn in early evening? If so, sod webworms are probably munching your grass. Several sod webworm species *(Cramus sp.)* inhabit the South. Adults are streamlined moths about ¾ in. long, with a distinctive beaklike projection on the head. Larvae feed at the crowns of grass plants during summer and fall.

Target: Lawn grasses, particularly Bermuda, St. Augustine, centipede, zoysia, and Kentucky bluegrass; and young corn plants

Damage: The larvae feed on grass blades at night. During the day, the green, brown, or pinkish white worms remain curled in a C-shape at the soil surface. The damage usually goes unnoticed for weeks. Eventually, though, home owners discover irregular patches of closely cropped turf that turn yellow or brown. Individual grass blades may be chewed along the sides or skeletonized. Lawns recover quickly from mild infestations. But severe infestations, accompanied by drought, may turn the lawn brown.

Life cycle: Larvae overwinter among the roots of grasses and weeds or just under the soil surface. They begin feeding in spring on grass blades and roots they pull into silken nests at ground level. In late spring, they construct cocoons, pupate, and emerge as moths a week or two later. Adults live only a few days. Females fly at dusk and drop eggs helter-skelter over the grass. These eggs hatch in a week or so. There may be one to three generations per year.

Prevention: Keep lawns vigorous through proper watering, fertilizing, aerating, and mowing. Many beneficial insects control sod webworms, so avoid killing the good guys with widespread use of pesticides. Treat the lawn with beneficial nematodes.

Control: Prior to treatment, mow the grass, then water for several hours. Then in early evening, spray the lawn with *Bacillus thuringiensis kurstaki* (Dipel, Thuricide, Javelin) or apply a granular lawn insecticide containing chlorpyrifos (Dursban) or diazinon. Follow label directions carefully.

WEEVILS

LAWN, SHRUB, TREE, FRUIT, AND NUT PESTS

✏ ZONES: ALL

Several long-snouted beetles, or weevils, can cause serious harm to plants. Pecan weevils *(Curculio caryae)* can destroy 80 percent of a pecan crop. The adult black vine weevil *(Otiorhynchus sulcatus),* shown above, and its larvae attack ornamental shrubs and trees. Billbugs *(Sphenophorus sp.)* can wipe out entire lawns. They range in size from ¹⁄₁₀–¾ in. long.

Target: Pecan, hickory, rhododendron, azalea, hemlock, yew, and warm-season grasses

Pecan weevil larva

Damage: Pecan weevils feed on developing pecan and hickory nuts, causing them to drop. Adults lay eggs in the nuts. Their creamy white grubs then feed on kernels. Black vine weevils primarily attack evergreens, such as rhododendrons, azaleas, and yews. Adults chew leaves, while grubs feed on roots. Grubs may also girdle the plant, killing the top. Billbugs chew rows of holes in grass blades. Their white grubs eat both blades and roots.

Life cycle: Most weevils overwinter as pupae in the soil. Adults emerge in spring and lay eggs near or on target plants. Larvae feed in spring and summer and pupate in fall. There is one generation per year. Pecan weevils emerge in July in Florida and late August and September farther north, with one generation every 2 years.

Prevention: In July, check for pecan weevils by wrapping sticky tape around tree trunk or deploying weevil traps. Begin spraying about 7 days after you catch the first weevils. Avoid heavy mulching, and water only when necessary. Check for billbugs by drenching a section of lawn with soapy water, which brings them to the surface.

Control: For pecan weevils, spray trees with carbaryl (Sevin) when shells begin to harden. Spray twice more at 10-day intervals. For black vine weevils, spray in the evening with acephate (Orthene), azadirachtin (Neem), a pyrethrum product, or rotenone. To control grubs of black vine weevils and billbugs, add beneficial nematodes to the soil or treat with imidacloprid (Merit, GrubEx) or diazinon.

WHITEFLIES

FLOWER, VEGETABLE, SHRUB, AND HOUSE PLANT PESTS

ZONES: ALL

Like aphids, whiteflies appear in hordes, sucking sap from the leaves of vegetables and flowering plants. The immature form is a nearly transparent, wingless nymph; when feeding it excretes honeydew, a sticky sweet substance that attracts ants. Adults look like tiny white moths. They typically feed together and fly up in a cloud when disturbed. Whiteflies flourish year-round in the Coastal and Tropical South but mainly during summer elsewhere. Warm still air is the perfect environment for whiteflies, making greenhouses a favorite haunt. A mixture of nymphs and adults is shown above.

Target: A variety of plants including shrubs, annuals, perennials, vegetables, house plants, and fruits

Damage: By sucking plant juices, whiteflies weaken plants and stunt their growth. Affected foliage may be stippled yellow, then may curl and turn brown. Honeydew attracts sooty mold fungus. Some whiteflies transmit viruses from plant to plant.

Life cycle: Adults lay eggs on the undersides of leaves. Nymphs hatch out within a day or two, then begin to feed. As they molt, they become nearly immobile transforming into pupae. Winged adults emerge shortly thereafter. There are many overlapping generations each year.

Prevention: Use your hand to brush leaves of bedding and vegetable plants at the garden center before you bring them home. If whiteflies fly off, leave the plants there. Thoroughly spray all plants brought home from a greenhouse or garden center with insecticidal soap or horticultural oil to kill whitefly nymphs and eggs.

Control: Natural enemies include lacewing larvae and parasitoid wasps. For small infestations, use yellow sticky traps, handpick infested leaves, or hose down leaves with soapy water. Kill whiteflies and nymphs by spraying with insecticidal soap, horticultural oil, or with resmethrin, azadirachtin (Neem), or malathion. Be sure to spray the undersides of leaves. For infestations on ornamentals, spray with acephate (Orthene) or dimethoate (Cygon), according to label directions. Alternate insecticides as whiteflies often become resistant to repeated use of a product.

WHITE GRUBS

LAWN PESTS

ZONES: ALL

It would be nice if beetles confined themselves to destroying plants above ground, but they don't know the meaning of moderation. The larvae of several types, including Japanese beetles, June bugs, and rose chafers, damage lawns by chewing roots. Generally, the larvae are white with brown heads and three pairs of legs. They usually lie immobile in the soil, curled up in the shape of the letter C. The larvae are grouped together under the catchall name of "white grubs."

Target: Lawn grasses

Damage: White grubs eat the roots of grasses. Unable to absorb water or nutrients, grass plants turn brown and die. Following severe infestations, patches of chewed turf can be rolled up like carpet. Armadillos, raccoons, and skunks, rooting around for grubs to eat, may do this job for you. Mole activity may also increase, because grubs are a principal food of moles.

Life cycle: Adult beetles lay eggs on grass blades in the summer. The larvae hatch and burrow underground to feed. They usually remain within 3 in. of the surface and sometimes emerge at night to chew grass blades. Most species burrow deeper into the soil as winter approaches, hibernating through the colder months. In spring, the grubs feed vigorously once more, before pupating. Adults emerge in late spring or early summer. There is one generation per year.

Prevention: Buy only certified, grub-free sod.

Control: Add beneficial nematodes to the lawn. These microscopic worms parasitize white grubs. Adding the biological control called Milky Spore (*Bacillus popilliae*-Dutky) to the lawn will kill Japanese beetle grubs. The botanical insecticide azadirachtin (Neem) seems to disrupt the reproductive cycle of Japanese beetles when sprayed on the lawn in summer. You can also control white grubs in general by treating the lawn in spring with a granular insecticide containing imidacloprid (Merit, GrubEx), diazinon, or chlorpyrifos (Dursban). These products work better if you first dethatch the lawn.

SPIDERS

and Other Arachnids

While they give most gardeners the willies, spiders and most other arachnids are considered beneficial because they hunt and eat insects. But some arachnids are dangerous to humans and worth knowing about—if only to give them a wide berth whenever you see them.

Most homes, gardens, and woodlots harbor many species of spiders. Not classified as insects, but rather as arachnids, they are more closely related to lobsters and crabs. Arachnids have eight legs, which they use to move quickly when chasing prey. Home and garden spiders may be active or passive hunters. Some species chase their quarry and inject them with a paralyzing venom. Other kinds spin broad webs to trap their victims as they fly by or tumble in. Jumping spiders, lynx spiders, and wolf spiders are skilled hunters that ambush and overpower their victims. Outdoors, hunting spiders rest in leaf debris and establish hunting areas under shrubs and hedgerows and around rows of vegetable crops and bedding annuals. Each spider can be counted on to consume several insects a day.

HAZARDOUS TO HUMANS

Of the few spiders that pose real danger to humans, the most poisonous are the black widow spider (*Latrodectus mactans*) and the brown recluse (*Loxosceles reclusa*), which is also called the violin spider. Fortunately, these spiders are well marked and easy to identify. The black widow spider is shiny black, about ½ in. long, with a distinctive red hourglass shape on its rounded abdomen. The brown recluse is a dull brown spider of about the same size, with a mark shaped like a violin, in darker brown, on its back.

If poisonous spiders are attacked or disturbed, they will bite humans. Their venom can cause a serious allergic reaction. The bite of the black widow spider can be toxic and perhaps even fatal, if medical attention is not sought promptly. The bites of the brown recluse spider do not heal; instead they ulcerate the skin and cause permanent scars. The venom of all these spiders can damage internal organs in humans and animals. If a person or pet is bitten by any spider or other arachnid, apply ice to the wound to slow the spread of the venom, and seek medical attention immediately.

To prevent being bitten by a spider, leave webs alone, if possible, and use care when working in garden areas where these poisonous species congregate. Rockeries, crawl spaces under gazebos and garden structures, dark corners of potting sheds, and stacked woodpiles and compost piles are usual nesting places of black widow and brown recluse spiders. Wear gloves when clearing out these areas, to avoid spider bites. Black widow spiders seem to be fond of nesting in the metal ground boxes that shield drip irrigation valves or outdoor lighting wires; use caution and gloves when opening lids of these boxes to inspect valves or wires.

Merchants of Menace

Two poisonous spiders you definitely want to avoid are the black widow (top, its egg case in inset) and the brown recluse (bottom), also called the violin spider. Black widow bites can be fatal; brown recluse bites cause permanent scars.

In southwestern Texas, gardeners should look out for scorpions and tarantulas. Shaking out garden boots or rustling a corner of the potting shed may surprise a small scorpion, which will sting if it can't scurry away to cover. If you find large numbers or nests of these dangerous pests, call a professional exterminator.

Species of desert scorpions range in length from 1 in. to several inches—about the size of a fist. The larger desert arachnids tend to be nocturnal hunters, but they may also be found in the daytime, sunning on rocks or resting in the shade.

Life cycles of arachnids can be a fascinating study—at a distance, of course. Scorpions and spiders fight with their own kind; some species, such as the black widow, devour their competitors and even their mates. They reproduce by laying eggs, which hatch into small crawlers that molt into larger sizes. Some web-spinning spiders are so small when they hatch that they can be carried along by wind on a single silken thread, to relocate far from their original nest. This process, called ballooning, is common to most species; spiders traveling in the air have been found as high as several thousand feet up in the atmosphere, and by this method of transport they may be carried hundreds of miles, even across oceans.

Arachnids usually produce one generation per year. Many species are highly visible in the fall, when they leave the reduced cover of fading vegetation to find winter shelter indoors. Other species die with the approach of cold weather, the next generation safely overwintering as eggs, protected by silken pouches tied to leafy debris or to high positions on garden structures.

Many types of large and small spiders sport fangs that paralyze or poison prey. Emboldened by the venom they carry, spiders and scorpions will attack much larger creatures and fiercely fight until they or their victims succumb. Unlike bees, which die after they sting, spiders and scorpions can repeatedly bite or stab their victims, injecting more venom each time.

To control spiders in the home, you can squash them or spray individual spiders with household insecticides. You can kill individual scorpions by crushing them with a shovel or spade if they pose a threat.

TICKS AND CHIGGERS

Other members of the arachnid group that trouble gardeners are centipedes (see page 176), mites (see page 177), ticks, and chiggers.

Ticks are parasites that feed on the blood of animals, including human beings. Commonly found in wooded areas, ticks drop down from leafy perches to hitch a ride on mice, deer, humans, or other mammals, attaching themselves under the fur and sucking blood through jawlike mouthparts. Fully engorged with blood, a tick may expand its abdomen by six to ten times, and at this point it may be noticeable in a pet's coat.

Tick

Some wild ticks carry diseases, including Lyme disease and Rocky Mountain spotted fever. Fever, muscle aches, and welts or wounds shaped like bull's-eyes signal the initial stages of diseases that ticks transmit. When in areas where deer are prevalent, wear long pants tucked into the tops of your socks, and check equipment, clothing, and skin afterwards for ticks. Spray clothing and skin with insect repellent.

To remove a tick from a human or an animal, coat the pest with heavy cooking oil. The tick will react to this treatment by pulling out of its host. At this point, you can remove the tick with tweezers. Do not attempt to burn or pull out a tick from the skin; the mouthparts can break off and remain embedded, causing both an ulcerated wound and further exposure to diseases.

Chigger

Chiggers are tiny parasites that attack people and animals by burrowing under the skin and sucking blood. Their larvae bite into a hair follicle and leave behind swollen, itchy, red welts. They usually attack people around the ankles or behind the knees, but also affect the skin in armpits, in elbow creases, around the crotch area, or under a belt or collar.

Chiggers are also commonly known as harvest mites, jiggers, and red bugs. Several species are common to the South, including *Trombicula alfreddusgesi, T. batatas,* and *T. splendens.* Adults are about $\frac{1}{20}$ in. long and usually bright red with hairy bodies. Their microscopic orange-yellow to dark red larvae are barely $\frac{1}{150}$ in. across. The larvae are most active during spring and summer. Adults feed only on vegetable matter and insect eggs.

Chigger larvae are sensitive to carbon dioxide. When humans and animals exhale as they pass by, the larvae leap onto them. Wear long pants, socks, and high boots when walking through weeds and brush. Spray clothing and exposed skin with an insect repellent containing deet, according to label directions.

Just Hanging Out

Argiope spiders (below) are common sights in summer and fall. They often hang in the middle of orb-shaped webs they build in flower borders or below porch lights. Although these large arachnids look fearsome, they pose no danger to people.

GOOD CRITTERS,

Bad Critters

The economic boom that turned the Sunbelt into the fastest-growing region in the country has come at a price—the loss of woods, farms, and wilderness to widespread suburban development. The rampant destruction of wildlife habitat means that the birds, rodents, reptiles, deer, and other animals that formerly lived in the wild now live side by side with us. And when they get hungry, our homes and gardens are often the first place they come looking for a meal.

MISSED AGAIN! *Ever wonder why your apple, crabapple, maple, or birch tree looks peppered with buckshot holes? No, it's not because Cousin Harley missed again while pursuing his favorite cultural activity—blowing away rural traffic signs. Instead, the culprit is a feathered vandal called the yellow-bellied sapsucker. This woodpecker drills parallel rows of holes into trunks (shown above), then laps up the oozing sap. Fortunately, the damage is seldom serious, unless insects or diseases enter through the holes. About the only way to foil this culprit is by wrapping the trunks with burlap. Maybe if you wrapped Cousin Harley, you could save the traffic signs too.*

Many animal pests prefer to feed after dusk or in early morning, so you may not see them close up. But they cause distinctive types of damage that help you pinpoint the culprit. Birds, for example, often peck holes in ripe fruits and vegetables just before harvest. Rabbits munch seedlings and young plants near the ground. Voles cut off plants near ground level and leave the tops lying wilted on the ground.

Folks usually enjoy seeing wildlife in their gardens. But when animal guests outstay their welcome, you may need to use traps, barriers, or repellents to protect your plants.

BIRDS AND BATS

Birds do many good things. They entertain us with song, thrill us with beauty, and relieve us of thousands of insects. But they also gobble grass seed, strip fruit trees and berry bushes, pillage fish ponds, and pull up seedlings.

A protective barrier supplies the best defense against birds. Cover newly seeded lawns with straw. Enclose berry bushes and small fruit trees in plastic netting. Hide vegetable seedlings beneath floating row covers. You can also scare birds away by employing reflective mylar tape or suspended pie tins. Inflatable plastic snakes and owls frighten birds too, but you need to move them around every day or so. Birds may have bird brains, but they're not that dumb!

Winging It

Most folks welcome birds, like the house finch (top), to their gardens, luring them with feeders and birdbaths. But some birds, like the common starling (middle), become nuisances when they descend in large numbers. The only winged mammals, night-flying bats, such as the little brown bat pictured at left, frighten some people. However, many types do us a favor by consuming any number of insects.

People with fish ponds who live near large bodies of water should keep an eye out for marauding blue herons and other fish-eating birds. Submerged rock ledges give fish good places to hide.

Bats, though often feared, should be welcome in the garden. Many types will eat millions of mosquitoes and other night-flying insects. Occasionally, however, a colony takes up residence in someone's attic. These should be removed only by professionals, as many endangered Southern bat species are protected by law. Contact your zoo, wildlife rescue service, or local office of the U.S. Fish and Wildlife Service for advice.

SQUIRRELS AND CHIPMUNKS

No doubt about it—squirrels and chipmunks are cute and entertaining. But in a garden, they can be quite destructive. Squirrels loot bird feeders, fruit trees, and tomato plants; uproot transplants; and invade attics. Chipmunks dig underground burrows, and devour tulip and lily bulbs and crocus corms.

Various barriers and repellents help to control squirrels. Use special baffles, mounting poles, and squirrel-proof bird feeders to protect bird seed. Cover fruit trees with netting. Apply pepper spray or a repellent such as Ropel to ornamental plants or wooden objects to keep squirrels from chewing them. Seal openings into the attic with hardware cloth or wire mesh. Use a squirrel trap to capture the offending rodent and release it in the wild.

To foil chipmunks, line the bottom and sides of a planting bed for bulbs with fine wire mesh. Set the bulbs in the bottom and cover them with another layer of wire mesh attached to the sides. Then fill in with soil. The flowers and leaves will pass through the mesh, but chipmunks can't get in.

Chipmunk

MOLES AND GOPHERS

Moles and gophers are underground assassins, tunneling unseen through the soil in search of food. Moles eat grubs and insects, not plants. But they damage gardens and lawns by leaving a spongy network of tunnels and ridges in their wake. Gophers are far worse. They voraciously consume roots, tubers, and bulbs, push up large mounds of soil, and often tunnel hundreds of feet in a single night.

Pocket gopher

Mole and gopher traps provide the best control. Applying lawn insecticide to kill underground insects and grubs may send moles elsewhere to find a meal. If you're particularly energetic or know someone who is, you can also try lining planting beds or lawns with wire mesh, burying it at least 2 ft. deep.

VOLES, MICE, RATS, AND SNAKES

Voles do most of the dirty work for which moles get blamed. These small, mouselike rodents scurry along or just under the soil surface, hidden from predators by leaf litter. They chew roots and bulbs, undermine plants, and sever perennials at ground level. Voles favor soft, organic soil and are particularly troublesome near the woods.

Vole

Friend or Foe?

Squirrels (top) may look darling, but they pillage bird feeders, rob fruit trees, and dig up transplants. Moles (inset) dig tunnels (above) beneath lawns and gardens looking for grubs. Snakes are generally feared, but unnecessarily, as most are nonpoisonous. Small snakes, like the eastern garter snake (right), hunt insects and earthworms, while larger snakes rid the garden of rodents.

Rogue's Gallery

Common garden pests include (top to bottom) rats that hide in brush and wood piles, invade houses, and spread disease; hungry deer that devour every plant in sight; wayward skunks that root through gardens looking for worms and grubs; and raccoons that often raid garbage cans and fish ponds.

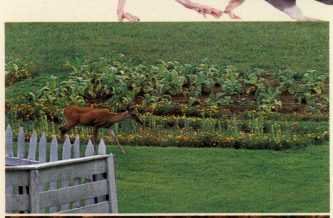

To deter voles, try wrapping the roots of shrubs and perennials (especially hostas) with fine wire mesh before planting. Or line the entire planting bed with wire mesh, burying it 6 in. into the ground. Another trick is to add a couple of shovelfuls of sharp gravel around the roots of a plant at planting time. Incorporating expanded slate aggregate (VoleBloc) into the soil before planting also discourages voles. Be sure to pull away mulch from around the base of plants, as voles use mulch for protective cover.

Mice mainly damage plants by chewing bark during the winter. You can stop this by pulling mulch away from the base of the tree or shrub. Then wrap wire mesh or plastic tree guards around the trunks.

Rats pose a health threat and sometimes invade houses. The best way to discourage rats (and mice) is to eliminate their favorite nesting sites. Cut tall grass and brush. Remove debris, especially near wooded areas. Also, eliminate garbage and other food sources. The fewer rodents there are, the fewer snakes will come around, because many snakes eat rodents.

DEER

Deer will never make the endangered species list. Because people have killed off most of their natural predators, many times more deer inhabit the South today than 200 years ago. And now that we've wiped out much of their habitat, they're making our gardens their lunchtime deli.

Hungry deer eat almost everything, from daylilies and rhododendrons to tree bark and corn. (For a list of plants deer don't *normally* eat, see page 428 of the *Southern Living Garden Book*.) And they're difficult to discourage, since an adult deer can easily and gracefully leap over a 7-ft. wall or fence.

White-tailed deer

But there are solutions. If you have the inclination and the money, you can surround your garden with an electrified fence that supplies a mild electric shock. Here's the trick: Coat the wire with peanut butter (but turn off the current while you're doing it). Deer love peanut butter, so when they lick the wire and get a mild zap, they quickly learn to avoid the fence.

Other solutions include spraying vulnerable plants with deer repellents, such as Hinder, Deer Away, Ropel, Deer-Off, and even wolf or lion urine (word to the wise—don't try collecting this yourself). Of course, you must reapply most repellents following heavy rains. Too much trouble? Consider erecting an 8-ft.-tall deer fence constructed of wire mesh.

MISCELLANEOUS BAD GUYS

If you have a vegetable garden, sooner or later a rabbit or groundhog (woodchuck) will visit. Frustrating rabbits is easy. They can't climb, so surround your garden with a chicken wire fence, 2–3 ft. high, that's anchored 6 in. in the ground. Foiling groundhogs is not as easy. They can climb, so a wire fence isn't much of a hindrance. Our advice—get an animal trap or a large, hungry dog.

Eastern cottontail

Raccoons and skunks are the worst kinds of pests because they're smart and persistent. Raccoons most often show up to raid garbage cans, so keep your cans inside your garage or tool shed. To evict a problem raccoon from your garden, use an animal trap. Skunks come looking for grubs in the soil, as well as unattended pet food. If they become frequent guests, treat your soil with chlorpyrifos (Dursban) to kill the grubs. Keep pet food indoors. Do not attempt to trap a skunk. You might just catch one. Then who will draw the odious task of letting the angry animal go?

Armadillos, a common sight lying belly-up along Southern interstates, have become frequent garden pests in recent years. They use powerful claws to tear up lawns in search of grubs and other food. One answer is treating the lawn with chlorpyrifos (Dursban) to remove the food source. Or you can trap the offending beast. If all else fails, consider building an interstate highway through your yard.

Pet dogs and cats can cause as much damage to gardens as wild animals. Fences will keep out neighborhood dogs. Keeping your own canine inside a fenced dog run is the easiest way to help your pet and plants peacefully coexist. Cats annoy gardeners by using planting beds for litter boxes. You can discourage this by applying animal repellent to the bed or covering it with clipped rose branches, pinecones, or sweet gum balls.

Digging It

Known to Southerners as "possum on the half-shell," the weird-looking armadillo digs through lawns for grubs to eat. You can either spray your lawn with an insecticide to kill the grubs or trap the armadillo and take it away.

HOMEGROWN TIPS

Each month *Southern Living* magazine prints a garden tip of the month on its "Letters to Our Garden Editors" page. Many of the tips sent in by readers deal with the problem of controlling pesky critters. Here's a sampling of tips received over the years. Keep in mind that these are ideas readers say work for them. *Southern Living* does not test them.

Voles. *Mrs. Basil L. Irwin of Lake Wylie, South Carolina,* baits a mousetrap with a mixture of peanut butter and birdseed. Place the trap next to the vole hole and cover it with a clay flower pot. *Helen M. Poindexter of East Bend, North Carolina,* recommends placing human hair on the ground around your plants.

Deer. *Gladys Watson of Hill Top Lakes, Texas,* scatters mothballs throughout her flower beds and around her specimen shrubs two or three times a year. As long as the odor of the moth balls is detectable, the deer don't bother her plants. (Keep children and pets away from mothballs.)

Armadillos. *Margaret Gould of Lake Providence, Louisiana,* suggests sprinkling ground red pepper around plants and throughout the yard where armadillos dig.

Moles. *Kerry Crockett of Manassas, Virginia,* took used kitty litter out to the garden, opened up the visible mole tunnels, and put a scoop of used litter in each one. The moles packed up and moved out.

Squirrels. *Louise Parham of Augusta, Georgia,* recommends sprinkling black pepper on flower borders where squirrels dig. *Barbara Doster*

of Gadsden, Alabama, keeps squirrels from robbing fruit trees by spreading human hair around the base of the trees. *Regina Askew of El Dorado, Arkansas,* sprinkles red pepper over her bulb beds to keep squirrels from digging.

Snakes. *Mrs. S. E. Welch of Lexington, Kentucky,* rid her garden of snakes by sprinkling mothballs throughout the flower beds and along fencerows. (Keep children and pets away from mothballs.)

Cats. To keep her cat from digging in a planter, *June Buffone of Charlotte, North Carolina,* covers the top of the planter with chicken wire, then cuts small holes in the wire for the plants. *Grace Holmes of San Antonio, Texas,* grinds up a handful of jalapeño peppers in a blender filled with water, then pours the solution around her potted plants.

Dogs. *Susan S. Grohoski of Fort Riley, Kansas,* had trouble keeping her dog from digging in the flower bed. So she stapled chicken wire over the bed, covered it with a thin layer of soil, and then sowed flower seeds. *Pamela Tsai of Raleigh, North Carolina,* has a German shepherd that likes to nap in her perennial border. She stopped this by spreading pinecones in all the bare spots between plants. *Ann Harrison of Austin, Texas,* protects seedlings and young transplants from her dog by temporarily covering them with tomato cages.

Birds. *Sharon Brian of Winnfield, Louisiana,* stuffs green nylon net under the foliage and over the top of the soil of hanging baskets to keep birds from building nests. The barrier does not interfere with watering.

PLANT DISEASES
and Ailments

*T*he *health of a plant depends not only on genetics, but also on environmental conditions and the care it receives. This chapter tells you how to prevent and to cure common diseases and ailments.*

Plants get sick, just like people. Coaxing them back to health depends on accurately diagnosing the cause. Sometimes changing weather results in plant ailments. Gardeners, too, can sicken plants by subjecting them to improper gardening or cultural practices, such as overwatering, improper pruning, or compacting the soil. However, in most cases, the culprit is a disease.

PLANT DISEASES, IN A NUTSHELL

Plant diseases have many causes. The usual suspects fall into one of three main categories—fungi, bacteria, or viruses.

Fungi. Fungi are predominantly multicelled organisms that lack chlorophyll, the green pigment that allows plants to turn sunlight into food—a process called photosynthesis. Because fungi can't photosynthesize, they feed on organic matter.

In most cases, their actions are beneficial. Fungi break down dead plant and animal materials, recycling their nutrients into the environment. But when they act on living plants, gardeners take exception.

Fungi normally multiply by means of microscopic spores, the fungal equivalent of seeds, which they produce in mind-boggling quantities. Wind, rain, watering, tools, machinery, insects, and gardeners themselves may disseminate the spores. Most spores don't find their target at first. They rest indefinitely on the ground, rocks, pavement, or tools, sometimes surviving very adverse conditions. When they finally land on a moist leaf, stem, or flower of a host plant, they germinate and produce hyphae, threadlike structures that make up the mycelium, the body of the fungus. The mycelium feeds on plant tissues and produces a variety of symptoms, including rotting fruit, spotted leaves, mildews and molds, and stunted and wilted plants. Fortunately, fungicides and proper gardening practices usually provide adequate control.

Bacteria. Bacteria are single-celled organisms. Like fungi, they can't manufacture their own food, so they feed on organic matter. But unlike fungi, bacteria must remain inside a host plant or plant debris in order to survive. In moisture and warmth, they multiply extremely rapidly by division. A dry climate, therefore, may inhibit their growth, until watering supplies just the right amount of moisture they need. Anything they contact—insects, people, animals, tools, splashing rain—spreads them. Bacteria can enter a host plant through a wound or natural opening and then begin to feed and multiply.

Bacteria can cause symptoms such as galls, rot, leaf spots, cankers, and oozes. The best control is removing the source of bacteria—plant debris or infected plant part. Applying an antibiotic, such as agricultural streptomycin (Agri-Strep), eradicates certain bacteria.

You find all the things in a garden that you find in life— birth, death, triumph, failure, enlightenment, joy, and despair.

—Lee May, Atlanta

Viruses. Smaller than bacteria, viruses lack the ability to reproduce on their own. Instead, they multiply by entering host cells and hijacking the host's genetic material in order to clone themselves. This process can seriously disrupt the host. The resulting disease produces abnormal growth, leaf spots, unusual leaf coloration, damaged fruit, or stunted plants.

Sap-sucking insects, including aphids, leafhoppers, and thrips, often spread viruses. Eliminating them and discarding infected plants work best to control spread of infection. Once a virus enters a plant, chemical control is impossible.

Regularly inspecting plants in your garden will alert you to the first signs of trouble, so you can take appropriate steps. The chlorotic rose (upper right) shows the effects of overly alkaline soil. Leaf spots on apple leaves (lower left) result from apple scab, a common fungus.

PREVENTING PLANT DISEASE

The recipe for spreading any plant disease depends on three key ingredients: the pathogen (disease-causing organism), a susceptible plant, and a favorable environment. You can short-circuit this troublesome trio with the following strategies.

Ban the pathogen. Use only certified, disease-free seed. Examine nursery plants before buying and reject any with problems. Keep tools clean and disinfect them after use (as described in "Getting It Under Control," below).

Plant resistant selections. A plant's genetic makeup determines its susceptibility to diseases. Improved selections often resist common ailments, making disease controls unnecessary. You'll find lists of disease-resistant plants throughout this chapter and in Chapter 2, "An Ounce of Prevention."

Create an unfavorable environment. Avoid planting the same plants in the same spot every year. Leave enough space between plants to allow good air circulation. Don't overwater and don't water from overhead late in the day—diseases love foliage that stays wet all night. Don't overfertilize, especially with nitrogen. Finally, make sure your soil drains well. Wet soil encourages root rot, mold, and damping off.

GETTING IT UNDER CONTROL

No matter how conscientious you are, sooner or later disease will rear its ugly head in your garden. When it does, use the following methods to keep problems from escalating.

Prune and destroy diseased plant part. But be practical. Don't cut off an entire branch if a single spraying will solve the problem. If a diseased plant requires major surgery, you probably should just replace it.

MAKING A HEALTHY CUT

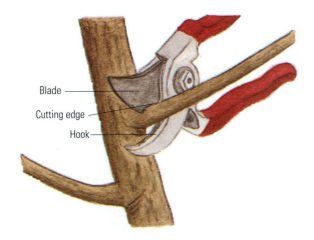

Blade

Cutting edge

Hook

To correctly prune off a diseased plant part, hold pruning shears with the blade closest to the stem or plant part that will remain. To cut back to a bud, make an angled cut with the higher end of the cut above the bud and the lower end opposite it. Note that the shears are also slanted to produce a slightly angled cut.

When removing diseased parts, use pruning shears for branches up to ¾ inch in diameter, loppers for branches from ¾ inch to 2 inches, and a pruning saw for larger branches. Cut well below the diseased part of the plant, removing growth back to a bud or a crotch (see illustration below).

Restrict spread of disease. Don't work in the garden when the plants and soil are wet. Plant pathogens transfer easily this way. And weed your garden regularly. Many weeds harbor diseases and disease-spreading insects. Removing weeds also improves air circulation, which discourages disease.

Disinfect pruning tools used on infected plants after each cut. Dip them into rubbing alcohol or a solution consisting of 1 part bleach to 9 parts water. This way, you won't unwittingly spread the disease.

Finally, promptly dispose of disease-ridden plant debris. Don't add into compost.

When to use chemicals. Treat chemicals as a last resort. Use only chemicals specifically labeled for the disease identified. Follow directions carefully. If you have questions, contact your local Cooperative Extension Office.

You'll find fungicides listed under "Control" for many of the diseases in this chapter. For more information about these products, turn to Chapter 3, "A Pound of Cure."

CULTURAL PROBLEMS

The fact that your town doesn't have its own symphony orchestra may seem like a cultural problem to you, but this is not how we use the term in this book. Rather, we define a cultural problem as a plant ailment caused by poor growing conditions or improper gardening practices.

A cultural problem often masquerades as a disease, but no pathogen is at fault. Blossom-end rot of tomatoes is a good example. How can you look at the black, sunken, rotting end of a ripe tomato and not blame an evil fungus? But the truth is, blossom-end rot results when the plant can't absorb enough calcium from the soil due to fluctuating moisture levels. So spraying it with a pesticide won't do any good. The only way to fix the problem is to even out the levels of soil moisture.

However, diseases can attack a plant weakened by a cultural problem. For example, plant a boxwood or Japanese yew in poorly drained soil and you're just begging for an assault by pythium or phytophthora root rot. Top your innocent shade tree and you can rest assured that eventually you'll be dealing with heart rot of that tree. Watering in late afternoon or at night is another common mistake. Foliage that stays wet at night becomes an easy mark for fungal diseases.

You can avoid most cultural problems by using good gardening practices (see Chapter 2, "An Ounce of Prevention"). Also, don't hesitate to compare notes with other gardeners in your neighborhood. If they've seen the problem before, they may know how to handle it.

AIR POLLUTION DAMAGE

CULTURAL

ZONES: ALL

Sulfur dioxide, peroxyacetyl nitrate (PAN), ozone, ethylene, and nitrogen dioxide are the air pollutants most troubling to plants. These chemicals are breakdown products of gases released into the air by trucks, cars, and industry. Air pollution problems grow worse during the warm weather of mid- to late summer. Plants in urban areas suffer most from air pollution, but dirty air has followed businesses and heavy traffic to the suburbs, making those areas less healthy for plants as well. Even in the mountains, trees may be damaged by pollution and therefore more vulnerable to pest attack. Air pollution affects plants through leaf pores, which absorb pollutants that disrupt cell membranes. Ozone damage is shown above.

Symptoms: The tissue between leaf veins turns grayish green to pale brown or light tan. Leaves may curl, then drop. Upper leaf surfaces may develop white to tan flecks. On some plants, both the upper and the lower leaf surfaces are affected. The needles of pines and other conifers may be blotched. The tips of new needles may abruptly turn reddish brown or gray, and needles may drop. Fruit may fall prematurely from fruit trees. PAN causes a silvering or bronzing of lower leaf surfaces.

THESE TREES BREATHE EASY. *The following trees tolerate polluted air: Chinese elm, Chinese pistache, crepe myrtle, eastern red cedar, ginkgo, goldenrain tree, green ash, hackberry, honey locust, Japanese zelkova, littleleaf linden, live oak, Norway maple, sweet gum, sycamore, and yaupon*

Prevention: If you live where the air is heavily polluted, select pollution-tolerant plants (see note above for pollution-tolerant trees).

Control: Before attributing plant damage to air pollution, check for other factors that may cause leaf, blossom, or bark damage—for instance, insects, nutrient deficiencies, lack of water, soil problems, and diseases. Fertilize and water injured plants to encourage their recovery.

ALKALINE SOILS

ENVIRONMENTAL

ZONES: ALL

Depending on the types of plants you grow, alkaline soil can be a blessing or a curse. Alkalinity, indicated by a pH above 7, is caused by abundant calcium, sodium, and other substances in the soil. It may also result from lime that leaches from cement or brick walkways or patios. Soil is usually alkaline in areas that receive less than 20 in. of rain per year or where large deposits of limestone lie beneath the soil. Soil pH often determines what nutrients are available for plant use. Above a pH of 7, some nutrients, such as manganese, iron, copper, and zinc, become less available to the plant. This in turn affects the ability of plant roots to absorb water and other nutrients. Most plants grow well in slightly acid soils with a pH between 6.0 and 6.8.

Symptoms: Plants growing in soil that is too alkaline for their needs may develop chlorosis—yellow areas between the veins on their newest leaves (also see page 232). In severe cases, all the leaves become chlorotic. Because yellow leaves can't manufacture food, the plant slowly weakens and dies.

Prevention: Test soil pH, either with a kit from a garden center or through your Cooperative Extension Office. Test across the entire planting area, rather than at just one spot, as pH may vary from one place in your garden to another. Select plants, such as Texas red oak, eastern red cedar, and yaupon, that grow well in alkaline soils (see page 51). For other plants, correct the soil pH, or use raised beds or containers with purchased soil or soil-less mixes. Add organic material before planting.

Control: Add sulfur to the soil. A soil test done by the Cooperative Extension Office will tell you how much sulfur your soil needs. Use a fertilizer that encourages an acid soil reaction, such as one designed for azaleas, camellias, rhododendrons, or hydrangeas. Use an acid-forming mulch, such as pine straw or shredded bark. Work chopped leaves, compost, grass clippings, and plenty of sphagnum peat moss into the soil.

PLANT DISEASES AND AILMENTS

ANTHRACNOSE

FUNGUS

⚡ ZONES: ALL

Anthracnose appears early in the growing season. It affects many different plants, but seldom kills them. On trees, infected leaves can look burned, much like those produced by leaf scorch (see page 236) in hot, dry weather. However, leaf scorch browns leaf edges, while anthracnose generally browns leaves along the veins.

Target: Many herbaceous and woody plants, including English ivy, hydrangea, Japanese aucuba, pansy, cane berries (such as blackberry and raspberry), grape, lettuce, melon, pepper, strawberry, and tomato; trees including ash, dogwood, elm, maple, oak, Southern magnolia, and sycamore

Symptoms: Symptoms depend on the affected plant. In general, the anthracnose fungi cause sunken spots of gray or tan to dark brown on leaves, stems, fruit, or twigs. The spots may enlarge to cover the leaf. Leaves may wither and drop.

On tomatoes and peppers, small, circular water-soaked spots increase as fruit approaches maturity. As the spots darken and deepen, they often have concentric markings. In warm weather, the spots soon penetrate and spoil the fruit.

Prevention: Wetness encourages these fungi. Grow vining plants on trellises or poles to keep them dry. Use mulch to decrease splashing of rain or sprinkler water. Avoid overhead watering, or do it in the morning to give plants a chance to dry. Give plants sufficient space for good air circulation.

Control: Remove and destroy affected fruit, twigs, and branches. Rake fallen leaves. Chemical control depends on the type of plant affected. For vegetables, spray with chlorothalonil (Daconil), maneb, or mancozeb as soon as disease appears. For fruit, spray plants with calcium polysulfide (lime sulfur) in early spring as leaf buds swell. Then apply captan as needed during the growing season. For ornamentals, spray with chlorothalonil (Daconil) in early spring. Be sure to follow label directions carefully.

DOOM FOR THE DOGWOODS. *Dogwood anthracnose has killed thousands of dogwoods in the Southeast. Many Southerners fear that their beloved flowering dogwood (Cornus florida) will ultimately go the way of the disease-ravaged American chestnut (Castanea dentata) and American elm (Ulmus americana).*

Dogwood anthracnose is caused by a fungus, Discula destructiva, which overwinters on dead twigs and leaves. It then spreads by rain and splashing water. The disease first appears as large, irregular, tan to brown blotches near leaf tips and petal edges. On leaves, the blotch usually spreads down to the midvein, giving the diseased area a wedge shape. Leaves may also display brown spots with dark brown to purple margins. Infected leaves usually drop before autumn. Infected twigs develop cankers that grow until they girdle and kill the twigs.

Unlike other leaf spots, this ruthless fungus also invades the main trunk, causing extensive cankers. Dieback symptoms first appear on lower branches, then often spread to the entire tree. Dogwood borers (see page 154) may attack as the tree weakens. Infected trees often succumb 3 to 5 years after the onset of symptoms.

Now for the good news. Dogwood anthracnose favors cool, moist weather. So far, it's mainly a problem in upland forests in the Upper and Middle South. It prefers forest and understory trees to lawn trees and single specimens, probably because the foliage of trees growing in the open dries faster. Also, closely grouped trees spread the disease more quickly.

One way to protect your dogwoods from anthracnose is to spray them according to label directions with chlorothalonil (Daconil) or mancozeb. Spray first in spring at bud break, then at weekly intervals until the leaves mature. Rake up and burn all fallen dogwood leaves in autumn. Prune out and destroy cankered twigs. Avoid overhead watering of trees. You might also consider planting stellar dogwood (Cornus rutgersensis), a spectacular hybrid of flowering dogwood, and kousa dogwood (C. kousa). These species resist the disease.

APPLE SCAB

FUNGUS

 ZONES: ALL

Apple scab, the most widespread apple disease in the world, is severe in most of the South. It is especially damaging to apples and crabapples in the Upper and Middle South. *Venturia inaequalis*, the fungus that causes it, thrives in cool, moist weather. It overwinters on dead apple leaves on the ground. Spores carried by spring winds quickly infect developing young twigs, foliage, flowers, and fruit. In only 6 hours of wetness at 70°F, the fungus can infect fruit around the bloom. Visible infections occur 1 to 2 weeks later. Immature leaves and fruit are most susceptible.

Target: Apple and crabapple trees

Symptoms: Initially, dark olive green or blackish irregular patches, scabby and sometimes blistered, develop on upper leaf surfaces. Velvety spots may enlarge to cover the entire leaf undersurface. Leaves become twisted, puckered, and yellow. Infected leaves may fall early; severely affected trees may lose all leaves. Olive brown scabby patches appear on fruit skin, then develop a white rim around a dark, velvety center. The rim later disappears, and the centers become raised, corky, and tan. Severe attacks result in small, distorted, and possibly cracked fruit that drops early.

Prevention: Plant selections with multiple-disease resistance (see below). Prune trees to increase air circulation and reduce the amount of wettable foliage. Rake up and discard fallen leaves and fruit.

Control: Apply triforine (Funginex), chlorothalonil (Daconil), captan, garden sulfur, or calcium polysulfide (lime sulfur) early, according to label directions, from bud break until leaves are fully expanded in early spring. Once scab appears, it cannot be cured.

ON STRIKE AGAINST SCAB. *These selections resist apple scab: Apple—'Arkansas Black', 'Freedom', 'Golden Delicious', 'Grimes Golden', 'Jonathan', 'Liberty', 'Mollie's Delicious', 'Paulared', 'Priscilla', 'Roxbury Russet', 'Stayman'; Crabapple (Malus)—'Adams', 'Callaway', 'Donald Wyman', 'Indian Summer', M. zumi calocarpa, 'Prairifire', 'Snowdrift', 'Strawberry Parfait', 'Sugar Tyme', 'Weeping Candied Apple'*

ASTER YELLOWS

PHYTOPLASMA

 ZONES: ALL

Aster yellows is a severe plant problem. Its symptoms are most noticeable in warm weather and seldom seen at temperatures below 50°F. Aster yellows is caused by microorganisms called phytoplasmas. Phytoplasmas may overwinter on weeds and they multiply in leafhoppers, which transmit the disease to plants while feeding.

Target: Annuals, perennials, bulbs, and vegetables

Symptoms: On flowers—such as asters, chrysanthemums, and petunias—foliage yellows and leaf veins become pale. New leaves are distorted. Older leaf edges may turn brown. Flowers are nonexistent, or small and deformed, often turning greenish yellow. Bulb tops are killed, and plant growth is usually stunted. Gladiolus have many thin, weak leaves that turn yellowish green. Flower spikes are twisted and deformed. Flowers often remain green.

On vegetables, symptoms vary. Outer leaves of carrots become reddish or purple. New leaves are yellow and stunted. Many tiny leaves grow from the root top. Carrot roots are distorted (also see page 223) and small. Dense tufts of hairlike rootlets may grow from the main root. Carrots taste bitter. Celery stems curl and twist. Lettuce is stunted and may not form a head. The heart leaves, which may be pale yellow to white, fail to develop normally.

PALM KILLERS. *When phytoplasmas attack palms, the result can be lethal yellows, a disease that has devastated coconut palms in south Florida. There is no cure. Avoid planting susceptible palms, such as coconut palm, fishtail palm, date palm, and Canary Island date palm.*

Prevention: Lay floating row covers over plants to protect them from leafhoppers. Promptly remove and discard any infected plants.

Control: Uproot and destroy infected plants. Remove any weeds, particularly dandelions, plantains, and thistles, that may be carrying the disease or harboring leafhoppers. To control leafhoppers, spray with a pyrethrin, azadirachtin (Neem), rotenone, malathion, or carbaryl (Sevin) according to label directions.

AZALEA LEAF GALL

FUNGUS

ZONES: ALL

Azalea leaf galls are swollen, cauliflower-like growths caused by the fungus *Exobasidium vaccinii.* Infection occurs in the spring from spores that are splashed onto leaves by rain or carried on the wind. Warm wet weather, deep shade, and poor air circulation favor development of this disease. Evergreen azaleas with dense foliage, such as Kurume hybrids, fall victim more often than lankier types, such as Southern Indica hybrids. In most cases, the problem is merely cosmetic and not a cause for alarm. However, severe infestations can cause azaleas to lose so many leaves that their growth and flower production diminishes significantly.

Target: Evergreen azaleas and occasionally rhododendron

Symptoms: All or parts of young leaves become swollen, fleshy, and severely distorted. They may have a balloon shape and appear velvety and whitish or pale green due to fungus spores on the leaf surface. Later, the infected leaf portions, or galls, become brown and woody. Sometimes a fleshy rosette of leaves appears at the tip of a branch. Whole flowers, petals, or seedpods may become thick, hard, waxy galls. In moist weather, the surface of affected flower parts becomes covered with a white to pink powdery fungus.

Prevention: Improve air circulation around azaleas. Avoid watering them with overhead sprinklers, especially at night. Quickly pick off and destroy any galls you see. Plant open, upright azalea types, rather than dense, mounding forms. Do not purchase plants with galls.

Control: Handpicking of galls usually provides adequate control. For severe infestations, spray plants thoroughly with a fixed-copper fungicidal soap, such as Soap Shield, or triadimefon (Bayleton). Be sure to spray new, young foliage prior to infection, as fungicides will not remove the galls from leaves already infected. Spray again the following spring just as new leaves appear.

OF ALL THE GALL. *Azaleas aren't the only ornamental plants defaced by unsightly growths on their leaves.* Exobasidium camelliae, *a relative of azalea leaf gall fungus, causes similar galls on camellia leaves (see page 95).*

AZALEA PETAL BLIGHT

FUNGUS

ZONES: ALL

Petal blight, caused by the fungus *Ovulinia azaleae,* results in extensive damage to azaleas in the South. Infection is greater when heavy fog, dew, or rain combines with high humidity during the flowering period. Fungus spores overwinter on blighted flower petals, remaining on the plant and within plant debris and top layers of mulch. These spores can survive for 2 years or longer. In spring, the spores become airborne and are carried to early-blooming azaleas, creating spots on petals within 12 hours. Wind, splashing rain, and pollinating insects then disperse spores on blighted petals to later-blooming azaleas. Sometimes nearly all the azalea blooms in a particular area seem to collapse simultaneously. All azaleas are susceptible to this disease. However, Kurume hybrids tend to have fewer problems.

Target: Azalea and rhododendron

Symptoms: Small, irregularly shaped spots on infected flower petals may be visible before flowers fully open. Spots on colored flowers are white, while those on white flowers are brown. Flowers look freckled, and those on lower branches are usually affected first. Petals become slimy within 24 hours of initial infection and resemble brown mush within 3 days. They often stick to nearby leaves. Infected blossoms usually remain on the plant, but some may drop. Nearly all flowers on a plant become infected when conditions are optimum for the disease. Petal blight does not affect leaves.

Prevention: Avoid overhead watering. Space plants well and prune to provide good air circulation, which also helps to keep foliage and flowers dry and the disease at bay.

Control: Spray with a fungicide containing captan, chlorothalonil (Daconil), or triadimefon (Bayleton), just as flower buds begin to show color. A second application may be necessary if the disease has been severe in the past. Spray a few flowers first as a test, because some fungicides ruin flowers. (Daconil may discolor the blooms of certain selections.) Remove and destroy any infected flowers. Rake up and discard fallen flower debris, as well as the top inch of soil or mulch from around plants. Replace soil or mulch with clean material.

BACTERIAL CANKER

BACTERIA

ZONES: ALL

The bacterium that causes bacterial canker, *Pseudomonas syringae,* generally causes no problems for healthy plants. However, with weather and growing conditions that favor the bacterium, it invades plants through wounds, leaf scars, and buds, killing the tissues. The wounds can be caused by frost damage, physical injury, or early pruning. Trees that are stressed are more susceptible.

Target: Peach, nectarine, cherry, and other stone fruit trees, as well as flowering cherry trees

Symptoms: Irregularly shaped, brown, water-soaked cankers appear in early spring on the bark of tree trunks or branches. The cankers may expand to encircle entire branches. As the tree leafs out, a brown, sour-smelling substance may emerge from the canker margins. Leaves may not appear in spring or may wilt on affected branches as weather warms. New tree shoots often appear at the rootstock. When the disease is severe, trees may die.

Prevention: Avoid planting stone fruit trees in sandy or shallow soils that may have nematodes (see page 179). Nematode feeding weakens trees, making them more vulnerable to disease. If the tree is to go into a spot with shallow soil over hardpan, break through the hardpan before planting. Flowering cherry trees may be more prone to the disease if exposed to strong morning sun, particularly during winter. In the Middle and Lower South, plant flowering cherry trees in areas protected from morning sun and temperature extremes. Keep trees adequately watered and fertilized. Use a protective covering if the temperature drops to freezing during bloom or early fruit growth.

Control: Bacterial canker is difficult to control; prevention is the key. In summer, prune out infected twigs and branches, cutting a few inches below the infected site. Sterilize shears after each cut with rubbing alcohol, shellac thinner, or a solution of 1 part bleach to 9 parts water (caution—bleach tends to rust tools quickly). Although copper sprays are not always effective, you can try using them to manage bacterial canker. Spray in fall at the initial leaf drop.

BACTERIAL LEAF SPOT

BACTERIA

ZONES: ALL

Bacterial leaf spot and stem rot, caused by *Pseudomonas* and *Xanthomonas* bacteria, is a common flower and vegetable disease. *Pseudomonas syringae* causes a devastating leaf spot and blight disease of lilacs. Damage caused by the *Xanthomonas* bacteria is shown above. Leaf spot bacteria, which can live in plant debris for 3 to 6 months, are spread by garden equipment and splashing water. Mild, wet spring weather favors progression of bacterial leaf spot, as does rapid plant growth.

Target: Geranium, zinnia, begonia, pepper, tomato, beans, brussels sprouts, celery, cucumber, and other flowers and vegetables; also English ivy, cherry laurel, and lilac

Symptoms: Symptoms vary, depending on the pathogens at work and the affected plant. On brussels sprouts, tiny black to purplish spots with yellow halos appear on outer leaves. These spots eventually grow together to form light brown, papery areas. On celery leaves, a water-soaked spot appears, then becomes bright yellow. The center of the spot gradually turns brown, with a yellow halo. On English ivy, brown and black spots with red margins appear on leaves. Leaf stems turn black and shrivel. On geranium cuttings, a black rot may develop at the cutting base. Leaves may have slightly sunken, ¼-in. dark spots. Leaves may remain on the plant or may drop. Blue-black rotting occurs on many or all stem parts. The stems may partially recover and produce new leaves at the terminals. If an infected stem is cut open, a thick yellow liquid filled with millions of bacteria may ooze from the cut surface.

Prevention: Inspect plants regularly to detect the disease early. Avoid sprinkler or overhead irrigation. Do not handle transplants when they are wet. If possible, plant only in dry weather.

Control: Remove small plants that are infected. Prune infected branches and stems from larger plants. Do not replant the area with susceptible crops the following year. Disinfect cutting tools after use. Spray affected plants with copper or fixed-copper fungicidal soap (Soap Shield) or in combination with mancozeb as soon as disease appears. Repeat every 7 to 10 days during rainy weather.

BACTERIAL SOFT ROT

BACTERIA

✗ ZONES: ALL

Any diseased, weak, or overripe fruit or vegetable is susceptible to bacterial soft rot, which also can infect some healthy plants. The bacteria *(Erwinia)* overwinter in infected plant debris and soil, entering plants through wounds. Enzymes produced by the bacteria break down plant cells. At high temperatures, damage rapidly progresses—the disease is severe at 80–85°F in moist conditions.

Target: Fruits, especially melons; vegetables, particularly broccoli, carrot, celery, lettuce, onion, and potato; cacti; flower bulbs and rhizomes, especially iris, hyacinth, and lily

Symptoms: Small, water-soaked areas appear on foliage, stems, some underground vegetables, bulbs, and rhizomes, and then rapidly enlarge. Plant tissue rots, becoming soft and mushy. The affected parts have a foul smell, appear sunken, and may collapse. Bacteria and cell debris may ooze through growth cracks; the sticky ooze dries and may turn brown, gray, or tan. Foliage on infected plants may yellow, wilt, and die, and the plant may eventually die. On potatoes, a slimy, foul-smelling decay appears in tubers and can cause complete rot within 10 days.

Prevention: Plant only healthy plants, in well-drained soil, leaving ample space between them to promote good air circulation. Avoid overwatering and overhead watering, and do not use stagnant water sources. Control pest insects. Avoid injuring bulbs, tubers, and rhizomes when digging or dividing them.

Control: On cactus, cut out the diseased area with a knife, removing about ½ in. of healthy tissue around the rot. This disfigures the plant but may stop the rot from spreading, and save the plant. Remove and discard all bulbs and plants showing signs of decay. There is no cure for many of the bacterial soft rots.

BACTERIAL WILT

BACTERIA

✗ ZONES: ALL

The bacterium *Erwinia tracheiphila* causes this disease of plants in the cucumber (Cucurbit) family. (A related bacterium, *Erwinia stewartii,* causes Stewart's wilt in corn; see page 99.) It overwinters in the bodies of the striped and the 12-spotted cucumber beetles and is transmitted to the plant by beetle feeding. As beetles chew on affected leaves, which they seem to prefer, their mouth parts become contaminated with bacteria that they then carry to unaffected plants. An entire plant can be infected within 2 weeks. However, infection occurs only if there is a film of water on leaf tissue.

Target: Cucumber, cantaloupe, pumpkin, squash, white gourd; however, watermelon is not affected

Symptoms: Dull green flabby patches appear on leaves, followed by sudden wilting and shriveling of foliage. Stems shrivel and dry but do not turn brown. If you cut a wilted stem near the plant's base, bacteria ooze out in white sticky masses. If you touch this ooze with a knife or other utensil and withdraw it slowly, the white ooze strings out in a fine thread. Affected plants may die. Partially resistant plants may be dwarfed, with excessive blooming and branching, wilting during the day but partially recovering at night. Fruit wilts and shrivels.

> **NAME THAT DISEASE.** *Bacterial diseases are often categorized by their symptoms. For example, bacteria that penetrate a plant's water-conducting system are known as* wilts. *Bacteria that stimulate growths at a plant's base are called* crown galls. *Bacteria that kill plant tissue are called* blights.

Prevention: Control beetles early in the season. Avoid overhead watering. Do not overwater or crowd plants. Cover plants with floating row covers to deter cucumber beetles. Clean up and destroy plant debris, where beetles tend to overwinter. Rotate plants with less susceptible crops (see page 30).

Control: There are no chemical or other cures for the disease once it takes hold. Promptly remove and discard affected plants.

BITTER FRUIT OF CUCUMBER

CULTURAL/ENVIRONMENTAL/VIRUS

✎ ZONES: ALL

Too little fertilizer, poor soil, very hot weather, drought, and wide fluctuations in temperature can cause cucumbers to taste bitter. In most cases, the bitter taste is limited to the cucumber skin and the flesh just beneath it, as well as to the stem end. Cucumber mosaic virus (see page 256), spread by aphids and cucumber beetles, may also cause bitter fruit.

Target: Cucumber

Symptoms: When caused by poor cultural practices or unfavorable weather, bitter cucumbers look misshapen. The end of the fruit opposite the stem becomes shrunken, as if someone had let the air out.

Misshapen fruit

Prevention: Cucumbers are about 95 percent water, so once they start growing, they must have a steady supply of moisture in the soil. During dry weather, be sure to soak soil thoroughly. Mulching around plants will help conserve moisture and keep roots cool during hot, dry weather. Consider planting naturally sweeter selections, such as 'Sweet Slice', 'Sweet Success', 'The Duke', 'Aria', and 'Jazzer'. As a general rule, newer selections are less likely to become bitter than older types. Controlling aphids and cucumber beetles helps to prevent cucumber mosaic infection, as does controlling perennial weeds. Plant selections resistant to cucumber mosaic virus (see page 21, "Disease Resistance by the Letter").

Control: There's no changing a bitter cucumber into a sweet, tasty one. However, remove the stem end, then peel off the skin and a thin layer of flesh just beneath it to see if that solves the problem. The rest of the cucumber may taste fine. Later pickings from the same row may not have the problem. If cucumber mosaic virus is the culprit, destroy infected plants as soon as you see the damage. This virus cannot be cured.

BLACK KNOT OF PLUM

FUNGUS

✎ ZONES: US, MS, LS, CS

Black knot of plum, caused by the fungus *Apiosporina morbosa*, occurs primarily on twigs and branches, but occasionally on trunks and scaffold limbs. The fungus overwinters on the tree and releases spores during spring rains. Infection stimulates excessive production of cells in tissue surrounding affected area, thereby producing knots. The knots progressively cut off water and nutrient supply. The disease can cause stunting, the dying off of affected tree parts, or occasionally death of the tree. It is more common in the Upper and Middle South and often attacks neglected trees.

Target: Cultivated and wild plum trees; prune, apricot, peach, cherry, and flowering plum and cherry *(Prunus)* trees

Symptoms: Warty swellings or knots appear on new tree shoots in autumn. Initially, knots are pulpy soft and covered with a velvety, olive green fungus. Eventually, they elongate, becoming black, rough, hard, and brittle. Knots range from ½–12 in. long, and to 2 in. wide, sometimes encircling a branch. A secondary fungus *(Trichothecium roseum)* usually invades older knots.

Prevention: Never purchase trees with visible knots or abnormal swellings. When planting plum or prune trees, avoid placing them next to or downwind from areas with a significant black knot problem. Plant resistant selections, such as 'President' (highly resistant); 'AU-Producer', 'AU Roadside', 'AU Rosa', 'Bradshaw', 'Crimson', 'Formosa', 'Homeside', 'Milton', 'Ozark Premier', 'Santa Rosa', and 'Shiro' (all moderately resistant). Avoid susceptible plums, such as 'Damson' and 'Stanley'.

Control: Spraying is only partially effective. Thorough control requires removing wild plum and cherry seedlings and pruning and destroying affected tree parts in neighboring areas as well. Pruning out and destroying knots in fall and winter also help to control the disease. On branches, prune 3 in. below knots. On tree trunks, remove knots and about 1 in. of surrounding healthy-looking bark. Check trees yearly. To kill the fungus, spray the tree with calcium polysulfide (lime sulfur) in winter. Spray again with captan in spring just before the buds open.

BLACK ROT OF GRAPE

FUNGUS

⚡ ZONES: ALL

Black rot of grape, caused by the fungus *Guignardia bidwelii,* can destroy an entire crop within a few days. It is particularly destructive during hot humid weather. The fungus overwinters in canes and tendrils, fallen leaves, and mummies (black, shriveled, hard grapes). In spring, thousands of infectious spores are released and spread by wind or splashing rain. Maximum spread occurs in rains lasting from 1 to 3 hours. Infection can take place wherever water remains on grape vine surfaces for more than 8 hours. Disease incubation ranges from 1 to 3 weeks.

Target: Bunch and muscadine grapes

Symptoms: Initial infection appears in early June. Tiny, angular or circular, reddish brown to tannish brown leaf spots form on upper leaf surfaces. Minute black dots that are actually thousands of spores appear just inside the margins of the spots. Sunken, dark lesions may also appear on shoots, stems, and tendrils. Large leaf areas may be affected, but defoliation seldom occurs. On the fruit, black rot appears as rapidly enlarging tan-colored spots on the surface of half-grown grapes. Affected areas rot and shrivel. Within 7 to 10 days of infection, the entire grape becomes mummified but usually remains attached to the cluster. Minute black fungal fruiting bodies also form on the mummies.

Prevention: Prune and retie grape vines annually. Plant grapes in sunny open areas with good air circulation. Eliminate weeds beneath vines to help plants dry faster during wet weather. Remove and destroy all plant debris, mummies, and diseased tendrils at the end of the season. Or plant resistant selections, such as 'Southern Home' and 'Florida Fry'.

Control: Early in the season before and immediately after bloom, spray with a fungicide containing captan. Or use Bordeaux mixture or fixed-copper fungicidal soap (Soap Shield) according to label directions. Spray vines every 10 to 14 days throughout the growing season, if necessary. Be sure to cover the fruit completely.

BLACK SPOT

FUNGUS

⚡ ZONES: ALL

Black spot, the bane of all rose lovers, is caused by *Diplocarpon rosae,* a fungus that overwinters on rose canes and fallen leaves. It thrives in warm, moist environments. Spores spread to other plant parts through splashing rain or overhead watering.

Target: Rose

Symptoms: The disease initially appears on young leaves as black circles with irregular margins. These spots, which are fungus colonies, grow to about ½ in. wide and may be surrounded by a yellow halo. Leaves may turn yellowish and drop. In severe cases, roses lose most or all of their leaves. A new crop of leaves may appear, only to be lost again. Repeated defoliation weakens plants. Flowers are small and fewer in number.

Prevention: Plant resistant selections, such as 'Bonica', 'Carefree Beauty', 'Carefree Wonder', 'Dr. W. Van Fleet', 'Flower Carpet', Lady Banks's rose, and 'Mrs. B. R. Cant'. Avoid planting susceptible roses next to one another to prevent the fungus from transferring by splashing rain or watering. Give roses lots of sun and good air circulation. Water during hours of full sun so the leaves can dry before nightfall; avoid overhead watering. In fall, rake up and destroy infected leaves. Spray plants with calcium polysulfide (lime sulfur) while they're dormant in winter. Spread fresh bark or straw mulch under plants every spring.

Control: If a favored plant continually develops black spot in one location, try moving it to a sunnier place with better air circulation. At the first appearance of black spot, spray leaves thoroughly with fungicidal soap (Soap Shield), azadirachtin (Neem), or wettable or liquid sulfur. On susceptible grandiflora, floribunda, and hybrid tea roses, and in the Middle, Lower, and Coastal South, spray with triforine (Funginex), myclobutanil (Immunox), or chlorothalonil (Daconil) at weekly intervals from bud break in spring to first hard frost in fall. However, in drier climates, such as West Texas and western Oklahoma, this kind of intensive spraying is not necessary.

BLOSSOM DROP
CULTURAL/ENVIRONMENTAL
✂ ZONES: ALL

Temperature variations during pollination in spring may cause the blossoms of vegetables, trees, flowers, or fruit-producing plants to drop. For example, the optimal temperature range for peppers and eggplant is 58–85°F; pollination will not occur if night temperatures fall below 58°F, and blossoms may fall if the temperature rises above 85°F. Hot winds exacerbate the problem. Rain that deters bees also may cause pollination problems.

Tomato flowers are usually self-pollinating, but if temperatures fall below 55°F more than four nights in a row, blossoms may drop unfertilized. Freezing weather may cause fruit tree blossoms to drop. Flowers may also drop at day temperatures above 90°F or 75°F at night.

THREE HOT TOMATOES. *If your tomatoes stop bearing during the summer swelter, try planting 'Heatwave', 'Solar Set', or 'Sunmaster' next year. These heat-tolerant selections set fruit even when the mercury rises well above 90°F.*

Symptoms: Blossoms fall. Little or no fruit appears on the plant. Fruit that does appear may have a rough skin or may be misshapen.

Prevention: Choose plants that cope best with your garden conditions. Avoid planting eggplant, tomatoes, and peppers too early in spring. If nights are cold, plant in the warmest area of your garden. Use a protective covering to warm the air around plants. Where summer temperatures are very high or where hot, dry winds are common, avoid planting midsummer beans. Fertilize according to directions on the label; do not overfertilize. Give adequate water.

Control: There is no control for this problem once it occurs. However, if air temperature stays warm and stable, plants that lose blossoms early in the season may still provide a full fruit crop and may do well. Watering when temperatures are warm will cool plants and help reduce blossom loss. Decrease fertilization, following instructions on the label for the specific plant. Gentle plant shaking may help tomato pollination: tap the flowers lightly on a warm, sunny day between 10 A.M. and 2 P.M. Discard misshapen and rough-skinned fruit that may slow down later production.

BLOSSOM-END ROT
CULTURAL/ENVIRONMENTAL
✂ ZONES: ALL

Blossom-end rot has multiple causes, all stemming from a plant's inability to utilize calcium in the soil. Soil calcium is available to the plant only when soil is evenly moist, so the most common causes of this disorder are drought and extreme variation in soil moisture—going consistently from soaked to very dry and back again. Other causes of blossom-end rot include strongly acid soil, root damage from excessive or improper cultivation, heavy soil resulting in an inadequate plant root system, temperature swings, and high salt content in the soil.

This disorder in tomatoes, peppers, squash, and watermelon often appears on immature fruit but can also appear on ripe fruit. It can dramatically reduce both quality and quantity of tomatoes. Blossom-end rot frequently affects plants in sandy or dry soil.

Symptoms: A soggy-looking sunken area develops on the blossom end (opposite the stem end) of affected fruits, often at earliest fruit set. This damaged area becomes dark brown or black and leathery. It may be flat or concave. As the rot develops, the damaged area enlarges and eventually may cover half the fruit. A black mold caused by fungi may appear on the rotting area, which adds to the damage.

Prevention: A timely combination of water and adequate levels of calcium (lime and gypsum are good sources) prevents blossom-end rot. Plant vegetables in well-drained, good garden soil or raised beds. Place 2–3 in. of mulch around your plants, especially tomatoes, to conserve and balance soil moisture. Avoid damaging roots when cultivating; don't dig more than 1 in. deep within a 1-ft. radius of the plant. Supply plants with adequate water, about 1½ in. per week during fruiting. Infrequent deep waterings are better than frequent light waterings. However, do not let plants dry out completely; soil should be moist. Avoid using high-nitrogen fertilizers.

Control: Correct any soil drainage problems in your garden. Add lime to strongly acid soils to maintain a soil pH of 6.0–6.5. Mix gypsum into soil around plant. If improving garden practices does not halt blossom-end rot, have your soil tested for a mineral imbalance. If the water or soil in your area contains too much salt, water more thoroughly to help leach salts through the soil.

BOTRYTIS (GRAY MOLD)

FUNGUS

ZONES: ALL

The fungus that causes botrytis gray mold, *Botrytis cinerea*, invades weak and damaged plant tissue. Flowers are very susceptible during bloom, while berries are attacked at all stages of development. Gray mold spores survive in plant debris and are spread through the air during the whole growing season. Spores may also spread by splashing water or contact with infected plant parts. Cool temperatures, high humidity, and standing water on plants favor the disease, as do close plant spacing and overhead watering. Gray mold is more severe if crops are not rotated.

Target: Flowers, vegetables, and fruits, including peony, blueberry, grape, strawberry, bean, ageratum, begonia, dogwood, Gerbera daisy, geranium, and zinnia

Symptoms: Water-soaked lesions appear on leaves, stems, blossoms, or fruit. In advanced stages of the disease, lesions may be covered with gray spore masses like those shown above. On peonies, young flower buds turn black and wither; older buds turn soft and brown; and stems wilt and die.

GOLDEN MOLDY. *Botrytis may be an enemy to home gardeners, but it's a hero to many wine-grape growers who actually inoculate their grapes with the fungus. Botrytis causes grapes to shrivel, increasing their sugar concentration. When botrytis strikes, how sweet it is!*

Prevention: Create good air circulation by spacing plants properly. If possible, orient crop plants in the same direction as the prevailing winds. Mulch with pine needles, straw, or plastic to keep fruit off the ground. Harvest small fruits every few days when ripe. Remove faded flowers from annuals and perennials.

Control: Remove and discard all dead or infected plant parts. To control gray mold on peonies, spray with mancozeb. For grapes, strawberries, and other fruits, use captan. For annuals and perennials, apply chlorothalonil (Daconil). Apply all fungicides according to label directions.

BROWN PATCH

FUNGUS

ZONES: ALL

Brown patch (*Rhizoctonia solani*) is one of the most prevalent lawn diseases. Initially, infected patches tend to be just a few inches in diameter, but they can expand to several feet wide. Both shoots and roots are killed. Weeds may invade the patch center where the lawn has died. Patch fungi may overwinter in plant debris. Symptoms usually appear after a day or more of overcast, rainy weather. Extended dry periods suppress the disease.

Target: All lawn grasses, particularly St. Augustine, centipede grass, and zoysia

Symptoms: This disease appears as brown, irregularly shaped or circular areas in a lawn. The margin of each affected area may be surrounded by a darker grass ring. This is where the fungus is advancing most actively. Crowns and roots are generally intact. After a few weeks, the centers of affected areas may recover somewhat, giving them a doughnut appearance. In the Coastal South, this disease may appear on St. Augustine lawns in winter; in the Middle and Upper South, it shows up on tall fescue lawns during hot wet weather.

Prevention: Avoid excess amounts of fertilizer, as lush growth makes the grass more susceptible. Provide good drainage. Water only in the morning. Raise mower height in the summer, since close mowing makes the grass vulnerable. Rake off mowed grass and excess thatch. If growing tall fescue or Kentucky bluegrass, plant a mixture of three or more improved selections.

Control: Apply a fungicide containing chlorothalonil (Daconil), mancozeb, thiophanate-methyl (Thiomyl, Domain), or triadimefon (Bayleton). Apply all treatments according to label directions. Water well before and after treatment, so fungicides penetrate to the depth of the grass roots.

BROWN ROT OF STONE FRUIT

FUNGUS

✂ ZONES: ALL

Brown rot is a most common and destructive disease of peaches and other stone fruits. *Monilinea fruticola,* the fungus that causes brown rot, overwinters in rotted fruit that remains on the ground, in dried rotted fruit remaining on the tree, and in infected twigs. In spring, wind and rain carry spores to healthy fruit-tree buds. Flowers can be infected from the time buds open until petals fall. Most fruit rot develops the month before harvest. Brown rot is most severe in mild moist weather.

Target: All stone fruit trees, including cherry, peach, and plum

Symptoms: Brown rot begins as a browning and wilting of blossoms and leaves. Dead blossoms may remain on trees for a long time. After killing flowers, the fungus grows into nearby twigs, producing brown, sunken cankers oozing with a gummy substance. During moist weather, small, rotting brown circles appear on mature fruit and spread rapidly to cover it. Light brown or gray powdery fungus spores, sometimes in concentric rings, soon cover the rotted skins. Fruit eventually shrinks, darkens, and dries out. It sometimes drops, but often remains on the tree—such fruits are known as mummies.

Prevention: Maintain good garden-cleanup practices. Control insects. Avoid wetting blossoms.

Control: Inspect trees before growth begins in spring. Prune out and dispose of fruit mummies, damaged twigs, and any branches with gummy cankers. Thin trees to encourage good air circulation. Spray healthy blossoms and fruit with captan, wettable sulfur, or chlorothalonil (Daconil) to prevent infection. Repeat every 10 days until 3 weeks before harvest. Follow label directions carefully.

CAMELLIA FLOWER AND PETAL BLIGHT

FUNGUS

✂ ZONES: ALL

Infection by the fungus *Ciborinia camelliae* begins any time after camellia flowers begin showing color. This fungus attacks only flower parts, not leaves, stems, or roots. Hard brown or black fungus bodies (sclerotia) develop in the base of old infected flowers. These fungus bodies later produce mushroomlike growths, which in turn produce spores that cause new petal infections. The fungus, which can survive at least 5 years in the soil, is spread by wind to new flowers. Germination occurs when there is condensed moisture on the foliage. In an attempt to prevent the spread of this serious and widespread fungus, some states may quarantine shipments or gifts of camellias or require that they be certified free of this disease.

Target: Camellia

Symptoms: Small tan or brown spots appear on petals, then enlarge, and eventually may cover entire petals—after a few days, the entire flower may be brown. Darkened veins give a netted appearance to the brown coloration. Dark brown to black fungus bodies, an inch or more in diameter, are visible in the flower base after the flowers fall to the ground.

Prevention: To avoid introducing camellia blight into the garden from contaminated soil, buy bare-root plants—those without attached soil. On plants in containers, pick off and destroy all flower buds before planting. On existing plants, always rake up old leaves, flowers, and other plant debris throughout the garden, but especially under camellias. Avoid overhead watering, or water only at times when plant leaves will dry quickly.

Control: Remove and discard diseased camellia flowers, buds, and flower and leaf debris. Carefully remove any existing mulch, replacing it with a fresh mulch at least 4 in. thick. Spray with a fungicide containing thiophanate-methyl (Thiomyl, Domain), triadimefon (Bayleton), or mancozeb. Always apply fungicides according to directions on the product label.

PLANT DISEASES AND AILMENTS

CATFACING ON TOMATO

CULTURAL/ENVIRONMENTAL

ZONES: ALL

Catfacing results from abnormal development of the tomato flower as it first develops into a fruit. One of the most common factors contributing to catfacing is cool weather, particularly if it drops below 55°F. However, weather above 85°F, periodic drought, feeding by stinkbugs (see page 190), or accidental contact with herbicides can also cause catfacing. Sometimes only the early fruit is affected. Catfacing does not spread from one plant to another or from tomato to tomato. Large beefsteak-type tomatoes are most prone to this disorder.

Symptoms: Rough, dry brown blotches or lines with little zipper-like crossbars appear on the fruit, usually near the blossom end (bottom). Fruit is severely malformed, most often by deep surface folds and puckering. Fruit ripens unevenly and is of poor quality.

Prevention: Little can be done if unfavorable climatic conditions occur. Most tomatoes thrive in day temperatures of 65–80°F. Don't plant tomatoes outdoors unless both day and night temperatures are above 55°F. Keep soil evenly moist, watering deeply during dry weather. If possible, water in early morning so leaves dry thoroughly before dark. Avoid exposing plants to herbicide drift when spraying weeds in the area. Plant tomato types other than beefsteak. 'Homestead 24F' resists catfacing; so does 'Monte Carlo'. 'Hayslip' is somewhat resistant.

Control: There is no cure for catfacing once it occurs.

TOMATO CRACKS. *Don't confuse catfacing with blossom-end rot (see page 215) or tomato cracking, which includes cracks radiating out from the stem and running down the sides of the fruit, and concentric rings around the fruit. Wide variation in soil moisture as fruit enlarges causes cracking. Infectious organisms often enter the cracks. Plant tomatoes resistant to cracking, such as 'Bragger', 'Early Girl', 'Jet Star', 'Marglobe Supreme', and 'Roma'. Mulch around plants to even out soil moisture. Avoid heavy applications of nitrogen fertilizers.*

CEDAR-APPLE RUST

FUNGUS

ZONES: ALL

The *Gymnosporangium* fungi that cause rust diseases require specific alternate hosts each year. Cedar-apple rust often attacks apple trees one year and red cedar and junipers the next.

Target: Apple, crabapple, hawthorn, red cedar, mountain ash, quince, and upright junipers

Symptoms: In spring or early summer, a small, greenish brown swelling may appear on a host cedar tree or on juniper needles and stems. By fall, the swelling enlarges into a hard, brown gall about 1½–2 in. across. These galls, covered with small, circular depressions, do not damage the tree. However, during wet warm weather the following spring, the galls absorb water, swell up, and display orange jellylike (telial) horns up to 1 in.

Gall with telial horns

long. The spores produced by these horns may infect apple trees up to 4 miles away. From mid- to late spring, tiny yellow spots appear on fruit and upper leaf surfaces of infected apple and hawthorn trees. These spots slowly enlarge and turn orange, spotted with minute black dots. In summer, spores appear within brown, cuplike, fringed growths on lower leaves. Wind blows spores back to cedars and junipers, restarting infection.

Prevention: Don't plant susceptible plants within several hundred yards of red cedar. Plant rust-resistant selections such as 'Freedom', 'Liberty', 'Priscilla', 'Pristine', and 'Stayman' apples; and 'Callaway', 'Donald Wyman', 'Indian Summer', 'Prairifire', 'Strawberry Parfait', and 'Sugar Tyme' crabapples *(Malus)*.

Control: Spray flowering trees and shrubs with fixed-copper fungicidal soap (Soap Shield) in spring when the flower buds show color. On rust-susceptible crabapple and apple trees, spray with captan, chlorothalonil (Daconil), mancozeb, myclobutanil (Immunox), or triadimefon (Bayleton) during leaf out. Repeat spraying twice more at 10-day intervals. Follow label directions.

CITRUS GREASY SPOT

FUNGUS

ZONES: CS, TS

Greasy spot, caused by the fungus *Mycosphaerella citri*, is a major problem for all citrus fruits. Typically, the peak period of infection is May through early September. Rain, watering, or heavy dew triggers the release and spread of spores, which remain on fallen leaves throughout the year. Combined high humidity and high temperature, especially at night, favor the disease.

Target: All citrus and kumquat selections, and orange jessamine

Symptoms: On foliage, initial symptoms appear as tiny blisters on lower leaf surfaces. The blisters turn from orange to brown, and then to black. As the infection progresses, leaf surfaces appear splattered by a black greasy substance. Leaves drop prematurely in autumn, with leaf fall continuing to spring. Leaf loss reduces fruit production the following season. Pinpoint black specks may appear between oil glands of fruit. On grapefruit, specks may join together to produce a symptom called greasy spot rind blotch. Fruit color near the specks may retain a green color longer than normal.

Prevention: Remove and destroy fallen leaves. Reduce insect populations, such as aphids and scales, by spraying with horticultural oil. Lemons, grapefruit, and tangelos are most susceptible to this disease. 'Valencia' oranges, 'Temple' and 'Murcott' tangors, and tangerines are less susceptible. Leaf drop during February indicates the need for controls to prevent future infection.

Control: For control of greasy spot on foliage, apply a fixed-copper or horticultural oil spray in June or July. Copper fungicides provide a higher degree of consistent control than oils. However, spraying with oil usually controls mild infections. Oil sprays applied even after infection occurs may prevent or delay appearance of symptoms. For severe foliar infection, spray with a fixed-copper fungicide in June and again in August. It is essential to thoroughly spray leaf undersides. To control greasy spot on fruit, spray with fixed-copper in July or August.

CITRUS SCAB

FUNGUS

ZONES: CS, TS

Spores of the fungus *Elsinoe fawcetti* cause citrus scab on fruit, leaves, and twigs of susceptible citrus types. This disease is rare on round oranges but can be severe on lemons, sour oranges, 'Temple' and 'Murcott' tangors, 'Minneola' tangelos, Satsuma mandarin oranges, and sometimes grapefruit. Rain, watering, and wind distribute spores released from overwintering lesions found on fruit and leaves in early spring. While temperature has little affect on infection, rain and heavy dew promote spore germination. Tender new growth is more readily infected.

Target: Citrus

Symptoms: Small, pale orange, somewhat circular, elevated spots appear on young leaves. The spots gradually become wartlike growths on one side of the leaf, often with a conical depression on the underside. The crests of these growths usually become covered with a pale-colored, scabby, corky tissue, which may also turn dark if colonized by other fungi. The corky areas often run together and cover large areas of the leaves. Badly infected leaves may be quite crinkled, distorted, and stunted. The disease also manifests itself as small corky outgrowths on twig surfaces. On young fruits it appears as scabby, cream-colored or pale yellow spots; on older fruits, as olive-gray spots. These spots may grow together in large irregular patches. Scabs on grapefruit may flake off as the fruit matures, with the affected areas remaining green and tending to flatten out. Fruits severely attacked when young will often become misshapen, with predominant warty projections or conical growths extending from the surface.

Prevention: Do not overwater. Keep foliage as dry as possible during the spring growth period. Remove and destroy dead twigs and branches and infected fruit. Spray trees with captan prior to infection. Spray in late winter just before new growth begins and again just after flowers fall.

Control: Once citrus scab appears on trees, it cannot be treated. However, infected fruit is edible if peeled.

CLUB ROOT
FUNGUS

/ ZONES: ALL

Club root fungus *(Plasmodiophora brassicae)* causes abnormal cell growth and division within the root. Affected roots may become oddly club shaped. Because these damaged roots cannot supply water or nutrients to the plant, young plants will not grow well. In later stages of the disease, rotting of the roots spreads millions of fungus spores into surrounding soil, and from there they spread by watering or garden tools to other plants.

Target: Cabbage, broccoli, and cauliflower, as well as most other cruciferous crops

Symptoms: Initial symptoms of leaf wilting and leaf yellowing usually occur on a hot, sunny day. The plant recovers from wilting at night, only to droop again as the next day warms up. If you pull out the plant, you will see swollen, thickened roots in a gnarled mass. Younger plants attacked by club root fungus may die. Mature plants can survive, but the crop produced is not worth harvesting.

Prevention: Purchase certified disease-free seedlings and plant in disease-free soil. If club root has been a problem in the past, don't plant members of the cabbage family in the same soil for at least 7 years. Club root prefers moist, acid soil. Improving drainage and adding lime to raise the pH to 7.2 should prevent it.

Control: An infected plant cannot be cured. Dig up and discard the whole plant, including the roots. Clean tools after using them in infected soil.

JOIN THE CLUB. *Other things cause weird-looking growths on roots besides club root. Among the most common of these are Southern root knot nematodes. These microscopic wormlike creatures live in the soil and feed on roots. Affected roots develop lumpy nodules, and the plant becomes stunted and wilts in bright sunshine. Root knot nematodes attack many flowering plants and vegetables, particularly tomatoes. For more information, see Nematodes, page 179.*

COLD, WINTER INJURY
CULTURAL/ENVIRONMENTAL

/ ZONES: ALL

Even warm-weather areas can be subject to sudden cold spells. Tender plants, warm-season lawn grasses like centipede grass, seedlings, and plants raised indoors and brought out too early in spring are most susceptible to freezing injuries. So, too, are normally hardy trees and shrubs that "wake up" too early during mild spells in winter, only to be devastated by a late, hard freeze. Sudden cold can result in discolored leaves and stems that may die. Tree branches heavily coated with snow or ice may fall. Alternating freezes and thaws can cause more problems than the frost itself. Frozen plant sap expands upon thawing, bursting the cell walls of plants. Repeated freezing temperatures alternating with thaws bring waterlogged soil and subsequent root damage.

Symptoms: Leaves wilt and appear water-soaked. Shortly afterward, leaves and stems turn black. Tree bark may develop longitudinal cracks, often on the south and southeast sides, or bark can split completely around the trunk. These cracks are caused by expansion and contraction of the wood during sudden cold-spell temperature changes.

Prevention: Choose plants adapted to your climate. Or in the fall bring indoors the tender plants that won't survive your winter; you can also place them in a greenhouse or on a protected porch. Wait until hedges, trees, and shrubs are completely dormant in fall before pruning. Pruning in late summer often results in a new flush of growth that is killed. Keep plants well watered—drought-stressed plants suffer more cold damage. Mulch around plants in early winter to insulate roots. Shield broadleaf evergreens from winter sun and wind, which can damage foliage. Remove snow and ice loads from plants promptly. Don't put out tender plants in spring until after the last frost.

Control: Once winter damage has occurred, it cannot be remedied. Shelter plants to prevent further damage. Maintain good gardening practices to restore plant health.

PLANT DISEASES AND AILMENTS

CORN SMUT

FUNGUS

ZONES: ALL

Corn smut (*Ustilago maydis*) is most likely to occur in these situations: when soil is high in nitrogen; when plants have been injured by hail, blowing sand, insects, or careless use of garden tools; when summer temperatures are 80–90°F; or when there is moderate rainfall as ears mature. The spores, which spread from plant to plant by watering, wind, and manure, can affect just a few ears or an entire crop. Where they germinate, they form galls that look like puffballs, tumors, or boils. Overwintering in soil, garden refuse, and manure, the spores can live up to 7 years, waiting for a host and suitable weather conditions.

PASS THE SMUT, PLEASE. *To most Southerners, corn smut looks absolutely gross. But some people in Mexico consider the corn smut growths a delicacy and actually eat them. Plant pathologists agree that eating corn smut won't hurt you, but don't hold your breath waiting to get a recipe printed in* Southern Living!

Target: Corn

Symptoms: Damage appears on any aboveground part of the corn, after the corn ears and tassels have formed. The kernels and cobs are replaced by pale greenish white and later black-covered galls, particularly on sweet corn. Smut-infected plants are small, their corn ears quite disfigured. While some galls are pea size, others may grow to 6 in. wide.

Prevention: Some corn selections, such as 'Silver Queen', are resistant. Ask your local Cooperative Extension Office about selections most successful in your area. Keep plants adequately watered; even resistant types can show smut symptoms if summers have been very hot and dry. Eliminate galls before they open and release spores to infect more corn plants. Discard galls; do not place in a compost pile. Clean up corn debris after harvest, and discard debris if smut has appeared in the last several years. Do not use any manure fertilizers on corn, as they may transmit the fungus. Don't plant corn in the same area each year.

Control: There is no chemical control.

CREPE MURDER

CULTURAL

ZONES: ALL

It's the high crime of horticulture—the senseless, annual chopping back of beautiful crepe myrtles. Drive through any Southern neighborhood in early spring and, before long, you'll encounter a spiritually fulfilled suburbanite, pruning saw in hand and a pile of crepe myrtle branches on the ground.

Why do well-intentioned gardeners keep repeating this crime? Some people think they need to prune off old seed heads to have blooms the following year. This is absolutely false. Others hack back these plants to keep them from getting too big. These folks need to remember that crepe myrtles are small trees, not foundation shrubs. If the plants seem to need pruning every other week to keep them from covering the windows or walk, they're planted in the wrong place. Finally, crepe murder is a copycat crime. A lot of people engage in it because they see their neighbors doing it.

Symptoms: People shorten crepe myrtles by 6 ft. or more, turning beautiful trunks into thick, ugly stubs. Repeated pruning to the same point creates gnarled, knobby "knuckles" on the ends of the trunks. A thicket of long, weak, whiplike branches then sprouts from each knuckle. These whips are too weak to support the flowers and hang straight down like cooked spaghetti.

Prevention and control: Find out the mature height of a selection *before* planting it. If your crepe myrtle grows too big for its spot, move it to where it has more room. Or replace it with a dwarf or semidwarf selection. Prune only to maintain natural form. Select four or five well-spaced main trunks; remove any others at ground level. Train these trunks to grow upward and outward from the base of the plant. As they grow taller, gradually remove all side branches up to a height of 4–5 ft. This exposes the smooth, handsome bark. Early each spring, remove weak, spindly growth and all branches that are growing in toward the center of the plant. Prune large branches back to a crotch. Never leave thick stubs.

CROWN GALL

BACTERIA

ZONES: ALL

Crown gall may seriously harm plants, as well as deform them. It can invade your garden from diseased nursery stock and be spread by contaminated pruning tools. The bacterium that causes it, *Agrobacterium,* enters plants through open wounds and stimulates abnormal cell growth, which forms the galls, often during summer months. Galls usually appear at the crown but also may form lower in the roots and are occasionally seen on aboveground parts. The galls interrupt the flow of both water and nutrients through the plant. Sometimes the galls crack, creating an opening through which secondary organisms may enter and damage the plant. Crown gall bacteria can infest soil for several years.

Target: Roses, ground covers, annuals, perennials, shrubs, vines, berries, and fruit, nut, and ornamental trees, particularly flowering pear, cherry, apple, and crabapple

Symptoms: Galls—hard, rough, whitish, irregularly shaped, tumorlike growths—appear near the soil line and on stems and roots. The galls range from the size of a pea to that of a baseball. Larger galls may split open. On young trees, the galls may initially be soft, spongy, or wartlike, but they become brown and woody with age. Plants with many galls may weaken and grow slowly; leaves may turn yellow.

Prevention: Inspect nursery stock before buying, and reject any plant with gall symptoms, including suspicious bumps. If crown gall has occurred in your garden in the past, do not place susceptible, healthy new plants in that area. Be careful not to wound plants when planting them or cultivating around them. Control insects, especially those that may damage plants around the soil line.

Control: Remove and destroy infected plants. When pruning, use only disinfected tools (disinfect with denatured or rubbing alcohol, or with a solution of 1 part bleach and 9 parts water). Solarizing soil (see page 31) for 5 weeks helps to kill bacteria.

DAMPING OFF

FUNGUS

ZONES: ALL

Damping-off disease is caused by various fungi, including *Botrytis, Fusarium sp., Phytophthora, Pythium,* and *Rhizoctonia solani.* Varying amounts and types of these fungi normally reside in the soil. They attack young plants when encouraged by cold soil, damp soil with a high nitrogen level, crowding, shade, high humidity, or cloudy days. The disease frequently kills young seedlings just as they emerge from the soil. Older seedlings resist attack.

Target: Vegetable, flower, and grass seedlings

Symptoms: Seedlings may not emerge, or if they do, they may grow to about 1 in. high and then suddenly wilt and fall over. You may not see them go, but there will be gaps in planting areas where they have disappeared. Seedlings may have discolored or water-soaked lesions at the soil line where fungi have rotted the stems. A white, cottony fungal mass may cover the soil.

Prevention: Use new flats or pots, or thoroughly wash and disinfect old containers before using. Use only pasteurized potting soil, never soil from the garden. Be sure that the seed packet is stamped for use in the current year, as fresh seed is less likely to incur damping-off disease. Try seeds treated with a fungicide. Be careful to plant seeds at the correct depth, and do not overwater them. Scatter a thin layer of sand or perlite on the soil surface to keep seedlings dry at the soil line. Thin seedlings so they are not crowded together and give them ample light. Add fertilizer only after seedlings have formed their first true leaves. Delay planting seeds in the garden until soil warms up; seedlings will be stronger and grow faster.

Control: As soon as you see signs of damping off, stop watering and allow the soil to dry slightly around the plants. However, do not let soil around seedlings dry completely or the seedlings will die. If seedlings are in cold frames or flats, give them as much air and light as possible—the better the growing conditions, the less likely damping off will continue.

DIPLODIA TIP BLIGHT

FUNGUS

⚡ ZONES: US, MS, LS, CS

A fungus, *Sphaeropsis sapinea* (formerly *Diplodia pinea*), causes a devastating disease of many pines. Austrian pines (*Pinus nigra*) growing in the Upper South have been particularly hard hit. The fungus overwinters on infected needles, twigs, and cones, both on the tree and on the ground. Brownish black spores ooze from dead tissue during wet weather from early spring through fall. Insects, birds, wind, tools, and splashing rain spread the spores to other branches and trees. Diplodia tip blight affects young buds, cones, shoots, and needles. Mature tissues resist it.

Target: (In order of susceptibility) Austrian, Scotch, red, mugho, and Virginia pines

Symptoms: New, young shoots become stunted, turn brown, and die. Dead needles remain attached to the tree. New growth on lower branches usually dies first. The disease gradually proceeds up the tree. Resin oozes from enlarging cankers at the base of infected shoots and branches. If not controlled, diplodia tip blight eventually kills the tree.

Prevention: Don't plant susceptible pines in any areas where the disease prevails. Gardeners in the Upper South should not plant Austrian pines. Stressed trees are more likely to contract the disease, so keep pines growing vigorously by watering thoroughly during droughts and fertilizing each year in early spring.

Control: Spray the tree just before bud break in the spring with a fungicide, such as chlorothalonil (Daconil), thiophanate-methyl (Thiomyl, Domain), mancozeb, or fixed-copper fungicidal soap (Soap Shield). Follow label directions carefully. Spray again a week later, then once more 2 weeks later. Depending on the size of the tree, a tree service may have to do this for you. Prune off diseased branches during dry summer weather. Disinfect pruning tools after each cut, using a solution of 1 part bleach and 9 parts water. Rake up and destroy dead branches and cones underneath the tree.

DISTORTED ROOTS IN CARROT

CULTURAL/ENVIRONMENTAL/PEST/DISEASE

⚡ ZONES: ALL

Carrots grow best in sandy or loamy soil free of rocks. Their roots have problems penetrating and expanding in clay or rocky soil. Transplanted carrots develop crooked roots more often than seed-sown carrots, but crowded seedlings also fail to develop properly. Carrots given excess nitrogen produce poor-tasting, rough carrots with branched roots. Nematodes, microscopic worms, may feed on plant roots, producing stunted, knobby carrots. Rot fungi, prevalent in wet, heavy soils, can cause carrot forking, and prolonged hot weather can stunt growth. If hot weather is followed by rain, carrot roots may rapidly expand and develop cracks. Any extreme fluctuations in soil moisture between wet and dry causes root cracking.

IMMIGRANT ROOTS. *The first carrots, it is believed, came from Afghanistan and were colored purple. Yellow carrots followed, then Dutch breeders developed the orange carrot. Early settlers, who brought seeds from home, introduced "carrots" in America. Today's carrot is an excellent source of Vitamin A, containing almost 8,000 International Units per average-size root.*

Target: Carrot

Symptoms: Roots of carrots are forked, twisted, or misshapen; numerous side roots develop.

Prevention: Plant carrot seeds in sandy loam soil that is rock free. In heavier soil, grow short, stocky types, such as 'Chantenay Red Core' and 'Danvers 126'; short, round kinds, such as 'Parmex', 'Planet', and 'Thumbelina'; or heirlooms, such as 'Danvers Half Long' or 'Oxheart'. Good miniature selections include 'Babette', 'Lady Finger', 'Minicor', and 'Short 'n Sweet'. Plant seeds 3 per in. and ¼ in. deep in rows 12 in. apart. Thin to 3 in. apart when seedlings are 1 in. tall. To grow longer carrots, dig up 9 in. of soil, remove any rocks, and replace soil with a mixture of compost, coarse sand, and purchased or existing soil. Or plant in a raised bed of humus-rich soil. Fertilize carrots with a balanced vegetable fertilizer.

Control: Misshapen carrots can't be changed, but they're edible.

DOGWOOD LEAF SPOTS

FUNGUS

ZONES: ALL

Many different fungi cause leaf spot diseases on flowering dogwood (*Cornus florida*), one of the South's most beloved trees. The most common is spot anthracnose, produced by the fungus *Elsinoe cornii*. It most often seems to affect white dogwoods grown in full sun. Two other common leaf spot problems are cercospora leaf spot (*Cercospora cornicola*) and septoria leaf spot (*Septoria cornicola* and *S. floridae*).

Leaf spot fungi overwinter on infected twigs, branches, and plant debris. During wet spring weather, infectious spores spread to new growth with splashing rain and water. Infection occurs only if the foliage or flowers are moist. Although these diseases don't kill dogwoods, repeated infection and subsequent defoliation reduce their vigor, making them more susceptible to environmental stresses.

Target: Flowering dogwood; septoria leaf spot also attacks redtwig dogwood (*C. stolonifera*)

Symptoms: Spot anthracnose produces pinhead, reddish-brown spots with yellow to tan centers, first on flower bracts and later on leaves. In severe cases, the spots connect into large, darkened patches. Leaves and bracts become distorted and smaller than normal. Infected flower buds may not open or may produce stunted, malformed, spotted flowers. Cercospora leaf spot appears as irregular, tan or brown spots of varying sizes without definite borders. Septoria leaf spot produces angular lesions between the leaf veins. The spots have grayish centers with dark purple margins.

Prevention: Do not water with overhead sprinklers. Provide good air circulation to allow foliage to dry quickly. Plant pink- or red-flowering dogwoods instead of white ones. Rake up and burn dogwood leaves in fall. Spray trees with chlorothalonil (Daconil) or mancozeb according to label directions when trees are blooming. Repeat 4 weeks later and again in September after flower buds form.

Control: Once infection occurs, no controls are effective during the growing season. Begin a prevention spray program (see above) in the fall to break the disease cycle.

DOLLAR SPOT ON LAWNS

FUNGUS

ZONES: ALL

Warm wet weather in May and June and fall weather with cool nights encourage this disease, which is caused by the fungus *Sclerotinia homeocarpa*. Most prevalent in lawns lacking nitrogen and in underfertilized, compacted, poorly drained soils, the disease—also called small brown patch—spreads by shoes or garden equipment. Lawns usually recover on their own over a period of several months if watering, aeration, and fertilization are improved.

Target: Many lawn grasses, especially Bermuda; creeping fescue; Kentucky bluegrass; tall fescue; zoysia; and, on occasion, centipede grass

Symptoms: Small, round, brown spots appear in the lawn, later becoming straw colored. Initially measuring 1–2½ in. wide, they sometimes merge to form bigger, irregularly shaped patches that cover large areas and possibly the entire lawn. Leaf blades have tan blotches with reddish brown margins. Dieback from leaf tips often occurs. A white cobwebby fungus growth, which you can see in early morning before the dew dries, may cover dying leaf blades.

Prevention: Plant resistant selections such as 'Pennlawn' creeping fescue or 'Jamestown' Chewings fescue; or 'Columbia', 'Majestic', 'Parade', 'Vantage', or 'Victa' bluegrass. Fertilize regularly with a balanced lawn fertilizer. Water deeply and infrequently to encourage a deep, strong root system. Water only in the morning, so the lawn has a full chance to dry during the day.

Control: If dollar spot develops, do not walk on affected parts of the lawn. Keep deep watering to a minimum—only water in the morning, once or twice a week. Improve soil aeration and apply a fertilizer containing nitrogen if there is a nitrogen deficiency. Rake thatch and discard. For severe infestations that do not clear up after a few months, spray with chlorothalonil (Daconil), thiophanate-methyl (Thiomyl, Domain), or triadimefon (Bayleton) according to label directions.

DOWNY MILDEW

FUNGUS

ZONES: ALL

Downy mildew is caused by fungi of the genera *Bremia*, *Peronospora*, and *Plasmopara*. These fungi must survive on living tissue, so they rarely kill infected cells or their host plants. But affected plants may be stunted and may fruit poorly. Downy mildew fungi overwinter on infected plant debris, weeds, and existing plant parts. High humidity, cool temperatures, fog, drizzle, and heavy dew encourage development and spread of the disease.

Target: Alyssum, bachelor's button, beet, cane berries, cabbage family, grape, lettuce, melon, onion, pansy, pea, rose, and others

Symptoms: Each downy mildew fungus is host specific. Alyssum leaves become slightly deformed, ranging from puckered to curled. A whitish to grayish mold grows in puckered areas on the leaf undersides. On cane berries, small, conspicuous patches appear on the upper leaf surface. These patches change from yellow to deep wine red. Stems show red streaking. Fruits dry and shrivel, a condition called dryberry disease. Berries may split, appearing to be two berries on one pedicel (the stalk that supports the fruiting organ). Leaves, shoots, and tendrils of grapevines become brown and brittle. Grapes may be covered with a white cottony growth or may shrivel and discolor. On lettuce, older leaves are attacked first. Upper leaf surfaces have light green or yellowish areas; undersides are patched with a downy substance. The upper leaf surfaces of pansies turn yellow. A light gray-brown, feltlike growth, shown above, appears on undersides of leaves. Rose leaves show purplish red to dark brown irregular spots. Leaflets are yellow but may contain a "green island." Leaves may drop if infection is severe.

Prevention: Plant disease-free seeds and healthy, disease-resistant plants. Do not take cuttings from roses with symptoms of the disease. Water in the morning and remove debris from around plants.

Control: Remove and discard infected plants and plant parts. For grapes, plant muscadines (which resist the disease) rather than bunch grapes, or spray with Bordeaux mixture or fixed-copper fungicidal soap (Soap Shield) according to label directions. For vegetables, spray with maneb or chlorothalonil (Daconil).

DUTCH ELM DISEASE

FUNGUS

ZONES: ALL

The fungus causing Dutch elm disease, *Ophiostoma ulmi*, is carried and spread by elm bark beetles. Initially the beetles feed in upper sections of a tree. The fungus multiplies and spreads through the tree, producing a toxin that interferes with the tree's water-conducting system. Symptoms begin in late spring.

Target: American and European elm trees

Symptoms: There are two forms of Dutch elm disease: an acute form and a slower, chronic form. In the acute form, water-deprived leaves suddenly wilt, sometimes so rapidly that leaves dry, curl, and fall while still green. Trees with the acute disease may die within a few weeks. In the chronic form, symptoms are gradual. Infected trees leaf out late in the season. Starting near the tree top, one or more branches may be covered with yellowing leaves, and their bark may have small holes. Many leaves drop off. Infected twigs and branches may be ringed with brown dots just under the bark—these are the clogged water-conducting tubes. Infected trees linger but eventually die. Get positive identification of Dutch elm disease by checking with a cooperative extension agent.

NO DUTCH TREAT. *This disease is not of Dutch origin; it was first identified in Holland, about 1918. In 1930, the disease reached the U.S. in elm burl logs imported for furniture veneer. It spread quickly and has threatened the existence of the native American elm.*

Prevention: Plant resistant elms, such as Chinese and American Liberty elms. Having a licensed arborist annually inject an elm with a fungicide may extend its life.

Control: Early detection is the key. Inspect susceptible elms each spring and late summer, promptly removing and destroying any infected trees. Elm bark beetles feed only on healthy wood, but they breed in dead or dying wood. Do not save logs for firewood or wood chips for mulch; strip off bark on tree stumps below ground level and destroy it. If one of a group of trees becomes infected, consult a professional arborist. You may need to remove all of them.

EARLY BLIGHT (ALTERNARIA BLIGHT)

FUNGUS

ZONES: ALL

Heavy dews, frequent rains, and warm air temperatures usually accompany severe outbreaks of early blight (also known as alternaria blight and alternaria leaf spot). The fungus, *Alternaria solani*, affects both old and new plants; it is most severe toward the close of the growing season. Poorly fertilized tomato and potato plants are particularly susceptible, as are heavily loaded tomato vines. The disease is more frequent when plants are watered from overhead. Spores survive in plant debris for at least a year.

Target: Tomato, potato, and eggplant; pinks, zinnia

Symptoms: Small, dark brown to black spots, oval or irregularly shaped, appear on leaves. Leaf tissues around the spots may turn yellow, and the entire leaf may yellow. Ridged concentric rings in the lesion center form a bull's-eye. The lowest, oldest plant leaves are infected first; they droop, dry out, and die. Tuber lesions are brown to black sunken spots, less than ½ in. wide. Mature tomato fruit develops dark, leathery, sunken spots near the stem that may have concentric ridges like those on infected leaves.

Prevention: Use certified disease-free seed potatoes. Rotate crops that do not get early blight with potatoes and tomatoes. Plant resistant tomatoes, such as 'Early Cascade', 'Miracle Sweet', 'Mortgage Lifter', 'Quick Pick', 'Sunmaster', and 'Walter Villemaire'. Avoid overhead watering. Fertilize according to soil test analysis. Thin plants so light and air reach all parts. Handle fruit carefully because injuries attract the fungus. Destroy plant debris. Eliminate weeds.

Control: Throw out infected tubers; do not compost. Spray weekly with chlorothalonil (Daconil), maneb, mancozeb, or fixed-copper fungicidal soap (Soap Shield) according to label directions.

ZAPPING ZINNIA LEAF SPOT. *A form of early blight, Alternaria zinniae causes reddish brown leaf spots on zinnias. In severe cases, leaves, stems, and flowers brown and die. To control, pick off and destroy infected leaves, stems, and flowers. Do not water overhead. Spray with chlorothalonil (Daconil), according to label directions.*

EDEMA

VARIOUS CAUSES

ZONES: ALL

Edema is a physiological disorder that is often mistaken for a pathogen-caused problem. Although scientists are not certain of all the causes of edema, we do know that it can result from injury—from insect feeding (particularly by thrips and aphids), from windblown soil particles, and from chemical applications. The problem usually occurs with a combination of environmental conditions, such as high soil moisture, low light levels, and high relative humidity. However, edema is also seen in very dry areas.

Target: Indoor and outdoor plants, including annuals, vegetables, and perennials; outdoors, begonia, camellia, geranium, and ivy are most often damaged. Other plants include eucalyptus, hibiscus, privet, and yew.

Symptoms: Edema most frequently occurs during late winter and early spring. Watery blisters or small galls—from just a few to many—appear on leaves, primarily on lower leaf surfaces. Blisters may harden and turn brown, yellow, or rust colored. Affected leaves may yellow and drop. On camellias, leaf undersides may develop brown, corky, roughened swellings. On foliage plants, these lesions, which may be concentrated near leaf margins, may be lighter in color than surrounding leaf areas. On tomatoes, edema shows up as very small, clear, watery, and sometimes numerous blisters. As the blisters dry, they turn opaque and usually reddish brown. On cabbage and cauliflower, the disorder usually begins on lower leaf surfaces. Initially a few watery blisters appear, then they turn dark brown, yellow, or rust. The symptom may be mistaken for a rust or bacterial infection.

Prevention: Plant several vegetable selections, instead of just one or two, as plants differ in susceptibility. Provide good drainage; water plants early in the day so soil can drain and does not remain saturated at night. Be sure plants have adequate light. Fertilize regularly with a fertilizer recommended for the plant type. Control insects. Harvest crops before the heavy fall rains that saturate the soil.

Control: Control insect populations, such as aphids and thrips. Do not overwater plants.

FAIRY RING
FUNGUS

ZONES: ALL

From late spring to early fall, fairy ring mushrooms can disfigure a lawn. The disease is especially a problem in acid soils and in areas where there is buried wood. As the mushroom fungus multiplies, its white underground growth, or mycelium, becomes so dense and tough that water cannot penetrate the lawn. Starved and thirsty as weather warms up, grass around the mushrooms initially begins to die. However, the dying mycelium provides nutrition to the grass above it, which turns green again. Fairy rings may be small or several hundred feet wide. They expand about 1–2 ft. per year.

Target: All lawn grasses

Symptoms: Fairy ring damage appears in a target pattern: a brown area surrounded by a wide circle of dark grass. Small, tan mushrooms appear within or just outside the grass circle. Sometimes there is an inner circle of dark green grass as well. The grass in these circles may be greener than any other grass in your lawn.

Prevention: Rake or pick all mushrooms as soon as they appear in a lawn, before the mushroom caps open up and release spores. On new home sites, remove old tree roots and stumps, as well as wood left over from construction, before installing a new lawn.

Control: No grasses are resistant. Apply lawn fertilizer containing nitrogen to revitalize fairy ring center. Use a core aerator twice during the growing season to break up the mycelium and bring water to lawn roots. Water and mow more often. There is no chemical control.

FIREBLIGHT
BACTERIA

ZONES: ALL

Fireblight *(Erwinia amylovora)* is a very destructive disease, particularly when the weather is mild and wet during bloom season. Bacteria multiply quickly within the host plant: a single bacterium can cause massive damage, eventually killing a previously healthy tree.

Target: Apple, pear, firethorn *(Pyracantha)*, cotoneaster, hawthorn, Indian hawthorn, flowering crabapple and pear, as well as loquat, mountain ash, quince, and redtip *(Photinia)*

Symptoms: In early spring, infected blossoms and leaves suddenly shrivel, turn blackish brown, and die. Young twigs wilt from tips back, appearing black and twisted as if burned. Damaged bark is an abnormal dark brown to purplish color and appears sunken. Branches develop cankers, which in warm moist spring weather ooze a thick liquid. Within the liquid are fireblight bacteria that are spread to other plants by insects, birds, squirrels, and splashing rain. Fruit may have black spots or may turn entirely black.

FIRE FIGHTERS. *These plants resist fireblight:* apple—'Empire', 'Enterprise', 'Freedom', 'Grimes Golden', 'Liberty'; flowering (callery) pear—'Bradford', 'Capital', 'Chanticleer'; fruiting pear — 'Ayers', 'Baldwin', 'Delicious', 'Duchess', 'Kieffer', 'Moonglow', 'Orient', 'Tyson', 'Warren'; firethorn (pyracantha)—'Apache', 'Fiery Cascade', 'Mohave', 'Teton'

Prevention: Select fireblight-resistant plants (see list at right). Control insects, such as leafhoppers, ants, aphids, and bark beetles, that spread fireblight. If you have fruit trees, don't plant susceptible ornamental trees nearby. Don't overfertilize; lush new growth is particularly susceptible.

Control: In spring and summer, prune infected twigs and branches at least 12 in. below diseased area. Repeat pruning in fall. Destroy cuttings. Disinfect pruning tools in alcohol or a bleach solution of 1 part bleach to 9 parts water. Spray susceptible trees with copper sulfate, fixed-copper fungicidal soap (Soap Shield), or streptomycin (Agri-Strep) when flower buds show color. Repeat three times weekly.

FLOWERS, LACK OF
CULTURAL/ENVIRONMENTAL

✎ ZONES: ALL

The number one cause of few or no flowers is lack of sun. To produce flowers, plants need appropriate light. Plants that require full sunlight will not bloom well, or at all, in shade. Plant bloom is also keyed to seasonal sunlight and air temperatures. Sometimes unusually cool and cloudy weather delays or prevents bloom.

Flowering can be affected by the plant's normal cycle. All plants need to reach a minimum age or size before they will flower. For example, seedling-grown Southern magnolia and wisteria often take 10 years or so to begin flowering. Biennial plants (those with a 2-year life span) seldom bloom their first year; expect blooms the second year under good garden conditions. Some plants, such as cleome, marigold, and petunia, slow down flower production when older faded blossoms are left on the plant—these blooms form seeds, diverting plant energy from flowering.

Another cause of poor flowering or nonflowering can be over- or underfertilizing. All plants need nitrogen to grow and flower properly, but excess amounts bring lush leaf growth at the expense of flowers. Severe winter cold can also kill flower buds. Finally, some plants, such as peony or spider lily, resent disturbance and may skip a year of flowering after transplanting.

Symptoms: Apparently healthy plants with leaves that look normal fail to produce flowers or produce flowers that are quite small.

Prevention: Research the planting time, blooming time, light requirements, and optimal garden conditions for your plants. When planting seeds, follow the information on the seed packet. Purchase only large, healthy bulbs or corms; while undersized bulbs and corms may eventually reach blooming size, they may not be able to withstand adverse weather conditions.

Control: Thin out overcrowded plantings. Remove old flower heads. Give plants the proper amount of sun. Plant named selections that have been grafted or budded rather than unnamed seedlings. Avoid overfertilizing with nitrogen.

FRIZZLE TOP
CULTURAL/ENVIRONMENTAL

✎ ZONES: CS, TS (MAINLY FLORIDA)

People aren't the only ones who need proper nutrition. Palms do too, and when they don't get it, problems result. One of the most obvious is a curious condition called frizzle top, in which the newest fronds look withered, scorched, and, well, *frizzled.* The condition usually occurs in alkaline soils that don't supply enough manganese to the plant. However, it can also result from a potassium deficiency.

Target: Palms, including queen palm (*Syagrus romanzoffianum*), royal palm (*Roystonea*), pygmy date palm (*Phoenix roebelenii*), and sago palm (*Cycas*)

Symptoms: A manganese deficiency affects the new fronds at the top of the plant. They appear smaller and weaker than older fronds and turn light yellow with streaks of dead tissue. As the condition worsens, the new fronds appear frizzled. Eventually, only dying frond stubs emerge. Death of the main palm bud quickly follows, causing the tree to die.

A potassium deficiency initially affects oldest fronds, then progresses to new fronds. Yellow or orange spots appear on the fronds with dead tissue along the leaf margins. On date palms, the frond tip is discolored, rather than the margins. Eventually, entire fronds appear frizzled. The frond midrib usually remains green, but can turn orange. With severe potassium deficiency, the canopy is much smaller and the trunk narrower than usual. New fronds are small, yellow, and frizzled. Without proper treatment, the palm dies.

Prevention: Palms require a continuous supply of balanced nutrients. Apply a slow-release fertilizer specifically formulated for palms according to label directions. Sprinkle the fertilizer under the canopy, but do not allow it to touch the trunk, as this may injure young roots. Add sulfur to the soil to lower the pH below 7.

Control: Correct a manganese deficiency by applying manganese sulfate or a special palm fertilizer containing manganese to the soil according to label directions. Frizzled fronds will remain that way, but new ones will be normal. Applying a special palm fertilizer should also correct potassium deficiency.

FRUIT DROP

CULTURAL/ENVIRONMENTAL

✎ ZONES: ALL

Some fruit drops every year in a natural thinning process that adjusts the tree's load to its nutrient capacity. Normal fruit drop occurs in pome fruit trees—those bearing fruit with a core with small seeds, such as apple and pear—and in citrus. These fruit trees generally produce a heavy, mature fruit crop one year, then undergo a substantial fruit drop the following year, resulting in a normal light crop. Fruits containing the weakest or fewest seeds usually fall first. Fruit drop may be preceded by blossom drop (see page 215).

Abnormal fruit drop results from a number of factors. Large quantities of fruit may drop when the tree is stressed by overwatering, underwatering, high heat, extreme cold, or rapid changes in air temperature and moisture. Unusual spring frosts can freeze and kill developing young fruit. Too much nitrogen fertilizer can cause fruit drop. So can lack of pollinating insects, or spraying apple trees in spring with carbaryl (Sevin).

PICK IT UP. *Don't leave fallen fruit lying on the ground even if it's too small to make a decent snack. Not only does the rotting fruit attract yellow jackets, fruit flies, animals, and other pests, it may also harbor insects and diseases that will spread right back to your trees. So pick it up. Bury it. Or put it out with the trash. Don't compost it.*

Symptoms: Large amounts of young, newly formed fruit drop from a tree that does not appear to have insect or disease problems. Fruit drop continues until the fruit is a diameter of ½–1 in.

Prevention and control: Plant trees that do not need an insect pollinator; if they require a tree pollinator, be sure you have the correct one. Give trees adequate water, and supply extra water if the weather has been particularly warm or windy. Use a general fruit tree fertilizer containing nitrogen, but avoid overfertilization. Do not spray apple trees with carbaryl (Sevin). Protect fruit trees from frost by planting them on a slope or choosing later-flowering selections.

FRUITING PROBLEMS

CULTURAL

✎ ZONES: ALL

Certain fruit trees—such as nectarine, apple, pear, peach, and Japanese plum—tend to produce a lot of small, often poorly flavored fruit if trees are not thinned or pruned adequately. When fruit-bearing wood is not pruned during the dormant season, the tree may set many more fruits than it can nutritionally support to full size, so most fruit fails to develop. A normal variability in color, quality, and size can occur on large trees, where the amount of sunlight reaching fruit on foliage-shaded inner branches is different from that reaching fruit on outer branches. Smaller fruit can also result from poor pollination.

Symptoms: A tree that displays no sign of pests or disease produces many small fruits.

Prevention: Buy self-fertile fruit trees, which will produce a crop without a pollinating selection nearby. During the dormant season, prune the tree properly. During the fruiting season, thin to balance the distribution of fruit. This helps prevent overloaded branches from breaking. It also diminishes the alternation of heavy and light crops from year to year, a problem with some pome fruit trees (those having a core with small seeds, such as apple and pear).

Control: On mature trees, thin immature fruits, about 4 to 8 weeks after bloom, when they are the size of a nickel. Remove unhealthy, malformed, or damaged fruits first, then reduce the number that remain, leaving only the largest fruits. Apples should have a single fruit every 6 in. along branches. For early peaches, leave 6–8 in. of space between fruits. For late peaches, thin after the June fruit fall, leaving 5 in. of space between fruits. Thin Japanese plums to one fruit every 4–6 in. Thin pears at midsummer, leaving one fruit per cluster, unless crop is light—then leave two fruits per cluster. You do not need to thin cherry, persimmon, or orange trees unless overloading is so severe it threatens to break branches. If you are planting a fruit tree that needs cross-pollination or one that is not reliably self-fertile—many sweet cherries, apples, and pears fall into this category—be sure to select the correct pollinator. Ask at a local nursery or Cooperative Extension Office for advice.

FUSARIUM BULB ROT

FUNGUS

ZONES: ALL

This destructive fungus, *Fusarium oxysporum,* attacks both growing plants and bulbs in storage. The disease usually enters a planting or storage site through infected bulbs, corms, soil, or tools, and infects stored bulbs through wounds or abrasions. Plants in the ground are infected through their roots and then decay in the ground. The disease particularly attacks trumpet daffodils, daffodils forced for indoor use in winter, and Madonna lilies. Bulb rot is prevalent in warm climates where temperatures rarely drop below freezing; it is worst when soil temperatures reach 60–70°F. It persists in the soil indefinitely.

Target: Cyclamen, daffodil, dahlia, freesia, gladiolus, iris, lily, narcissus, onion, tulip, and other bulbs and corms

Symptoms: Leaves turn yellow, and the plant is stunted and dies prematurely. When dug up, affected bulbs may have few or no roots and often fall to pieces. Flower bulbs in storage develop a chocolate, bluish gray, or purple-brown spongy decay easily visible if you pull away the outer fleshy bulb scales. White fungal strands sometimes grow on the bulbs. Corms affected by this fungus show small, reddish brown lesions, more often on the lower half of the corm. These lesions enlarge in storage, and the entire corm may become a hard, dry, brownish black mummy.

Prevention: Purchase clean, healthy bulbs; reject any that are shriveled, show rot, or are soft when pressed. Do not plant healthy bulbs in an area where diseased plants have grown; rotate planting beds from year to year. When digging up bulbs for storage or transfer, be careful not to bruise them, and dry them rapidly.

Control: There is no chemical control for fusarium bulb rot. Discard all diseased plants, bulbs, and bulb remnants, as well as the soil surrounding any infected bulb for 6 in. in each direction. Bulbs lifted from affected planting areas can be dipped in the fungicide thiophanate-methyl (Thiomyl, Domain).

FUSARIUM WILT

FUNGUS

ZONES: ALL

The *Fusarium oxysporum* fungi overwinter in soil, some species surviving indefinitely. They can be transmitted by seed, contaminated soil and other growing media, garden equipment, watering, plant roots, or other vegetative parts. Soil temperatures above 80°F and air temperatures above 70°F favor wilt diseases.

Target: Annuals, perennials, and vegetables, such as basil, cyclamen, dahlia, marigold, melon, spinach, squash, and tomato

Symptoms: Initially plants wilt in warm weather, partially recovering in the evening. Wilting intensifies as the season goes on. Leaves may turn yellow, and on cantaloupe and tomato, leaves appear scorched; lower leaves are most affected at first, as shown above. Lightly infected plants may be stunted and produce fewer leaves; severely infected plants may die—either gradually, or suddenly with heat stress. Cutting across the stem of an infected plant shows dark or discolored fungus-clogged tissue. A mildewy growth may appear on cantaloupe stems near the crown of the plant. Dying watermelon stems show a pinkish white cottony growth near ground level. Infected asparagus stalks are yellow and stunted.

Prevention: Rotate crops each season. Plant resistant selections (see below). Obtain transplants grown from treated seed. In catalogs, look for selection names with an F, noting fusarium resistance. Plant seeds in sterile soil or potting mix, in new pots or in used pots that have been thoroughly disinfected. You can also use the sun's rays to solarize (sanitize) the planting site (see page 31). Fertilize and water adequately to promote vigorous plants.

Control: Inspect plants weekly. Immediately remove infected plants. Do not use diseased plants as mulch or in compost.

AGAINST THEIR WILT. *The following vegetable selections resist fusarium wilt:* tomato—'Atkinson', 'Beefmaster', 'Big Beef', 'Celebrity', 'Early Girl', 'Floramerica', 'Jet Star', 'Roma VF', 'Sweet Million'; cantaloupe—'Athena', 'Classic', 'Durango', 'Easy Rider', 'Gold Star'; spinach—'Jade'; watermelon—'Mini-Jubilee', 'Paladin', 'Tiger Baby'

HARDPAN

CULTURAL/ENVIRONMENTAL

✎ ZONES: ALL

Hardpan is a soil layer, often hidden under topsoil, that allows very little water to pass through. In Texas and the Southwest, it is usually caused by a caliche (calcium carbonate) layer where soils have not weathered and the soil particles are cemented together by minerals. In other areas, the soil particles in the hardpan layer are cemented together by iron and aluminum compounds. At times this very compacted soil seems to hold water like a bucket, as shown above. Hardpan, usually within a foot of the soil surface and as much as 3 ft. deep, is immediately evident when you try to dig through it. Because plant roots cannot penetrate the hardpan, they are restricted to the shallow soil layer above it. This limits their ability to obtain nutrients and to obtain a firm ground hold. The shallow soil above the hardpan can retain only small amounts of water, so plants wilt rapidly in hot, dry weather.

Symptoms: Trees and shrubs grow slowly and may fail to thrive. Trees, particularly large ones, may fall over when heavy rains combine with wind. Fruit trees have a limited harvest.

Prevention: Avoid repeated rototilling of garden soil. Determine if hardpan is present in your target planting area by digging down 2–3 ft. deep. Avoid planting large trees and shrubs in hardpan areas. Instead, use raised beds for vegetables and flowers and aboveground containers for smaller trees and shrubs. In areas with high water tables or poorly drained soil, install a drainage system, such as a French drain, dry stream bed, or dry well.

Control: Water affected plants frequently, but do not overwater. Profuse watering can drown the plants, by overfilling soil pores and eliminating oxygen from the hardpan-confined root zone. The longer the air supply is cut off, the more damage occurs. Repeated instances may result in permanent plant damage. While it is not always easy, you can penetrate hardpan. Use a crowbar, jackhammer, or power posthole digger (these can be rented) to punch holes in the hardpan. Fill the drainage holes with good soil.

HEART ROT

FUNGUS

✎ ZONES: ALL

Heart rot is usually an old-age disease, one of nature's ways of recycling old trees. The disease is caused by various fungi that normally rot dead wood, such as fallen trees. However, when wounds—caused by insects, physical injury, and weather damage—provide an entrance, heart rot fungi may also invade the heartwood of living trees. Healthy trees may stop the infection by producing cells that wall off the invading fungi, but older trees that have many wounds may have little resistance to decay-causing organisms. Decay spreads throughout the heartwood, weakening affected branches, which break and fall during storms. The fungus spores are spread by the wind.

Target: Ornamental, shade, and fruit trees

Symptoms: Yellowish to brown mushroomlike or woody growths may appear on the tree bark exterior; invisible beneath them is internal decay, shown above inside a stump. When the growths are hard, they are called conks. They may remain on affected trees for many years. During storms, branches fall from the tree. The wood in the area of the break looks discolored and may be spongy. A dark ooze may trickle from cavities in the trunk following a heavy rain.

Prevention: Promote the health and longevity of your trees with good gardening practices, including adequate fertilization. Water appropriately, making certain water gets down to the tree roots. Avoid wounding trees.

Control: Once conks appear on tree trunks, it is too late to do anything about heart rot; no chemical control is possible. Where practical, after a decayed branch has cracked and fallen, cut off the remaining stub, flush with the trunk or a larger branch. If the disease appears on large, specimen, or prized trees, consult a professional arborist to determine the extent of the decay. If the decay is severe, the entire tree may have to be removed for safety reasons. It's always a good idea to have a professional arborist examine large older trees that are located adjacent to residences or to anything else that might be damaged by falling trees or limbs.

HERBICIDE DAMAGE

CULTURAL

⚡ ZONES: ALL

Gardeners often use herbicides to kill or inhibit weeds. Herbicides include plant growth regulators, defoliants, soil sterilants, and desiccants. If accidentally sprayed onto or carried by wind to desirable plants, such products may severely injure or kill those plants. Mulching or amending soil with clippings from an herbicide-treated lawn or with manure treated with an herbicide can also damage plants. Some herbicides, such as atrazine (Purge, Bonus S), may leach through the soil following heavy rains and injure sensitive trees, shrubs, and flowers.

Herbicide damage is sometimes mistaken for a virus infection. If herbicide-sensitive plants such as tomato, potato, grape, pepper, or redbud show stem spiraling (twisted stems) or leaf distortion, the cause is probably an herbicide. A virus usually affects one specific plant group but doesn't damage other plants in the area.

Symptoms: Leaves are cupped, leathery, or thickened, and have an uncharacteristic fan shape. They may develop a mosaic pattern of light and dark green areas or turn yellow or brown around the edges. Leaf stems twist or spiral. Fruit and vegetable production diminishes. Trees may completely defoliate. Although they usually survive, growth may slow. Soil sterilants, which kill all plants, can be absorbed by the roots of nearby trees. Sensitive trees may die in a short time without showing symptoms of herbicide damage.

Prevention: Always apply herbicides during still, cool mornings. Avoid using them near a vegetable garden. Compost grass clippings or manure for at least 2 months to ensure they are free of herbicide residue. Whenever you use a pre-emergence herbicide (weed preventer), follow label directions about length of time required before planting in the treated area. Don't use strong herbicides, such as soil sterilants, in the vicinity of trees.

Control: If you accidentally spray herbicide on a plant, wash it off immediately with a garden hose. Once a plant absorbs the herbicide, there is nothing you can do to prevent damage. Keep affected plants as healthy as possible with adequate water and fertilizer.

IRON DEFICIENCY AND CHLOROSIS

CULTURAL

⚡ ZONES: ALL

Iron aids in production of the green plant pigment chlorophyll, as well as in plant enzyme functions. If the soil is too alkaline, with a pH over 7, iron may not be available to the plant. Overly alkaline soils can result from lime leached from concrete or subterranean limestone. Soggy, poorly aerated soils also inhibit iron release. In iron-deficient soil, the early leaves of a plant get whatever is available. Once the iron is absorbed by these plant tissues, it cannot be reused by new leaves, which then suffer the most severe damage.

Chlorotic leaves on gardenia

Symptoms: Leaves lose green color, starting at the outer edge and progressing inward—a condition called chlorosis (also see page 88, Azalea; and page 238, Nitrogen Deficiency). Leaf veins usually remain green. The newest leaves are most affected. In plants with severe iron deficiency, these leaves are very small and may turn completely white or bright yellow, while older leaves remain green. On fruit trees, yield may be small and fruit flavor poor.

Prevention: Test soil pH before planting in any area. Many garden centers have kits for soil testing; or you can consult your cooperative extension agent. If necessary, correct the soil pH to the recommended levels before putting in plants. Adding organic matter, such as sphagnum peat moss, before planting will also help. Check your garden's drainage and improve it as needed. Use mulches to increase soil water retention. Probably the easiest answer is to select plants that like alkaline soil and don't need extra iron.

Control: Apply a fertilizer containing chelated iron according to directions on the label. Recheck soil pH after all treatment. If the pH is 7 or higher, add sulfur according to the recommendations of your soil test. When incorporating any additives, remember that feeder roots are close to the soil surface. Work carefully, preferably at shallow levels, to avoid further plant stress.

JUNIPER TWIG BLIGHT

FUNGUS

⚡ ZONES: ALL

Also known as phomopsis twig blight, juniper twig blight is caused by *Phomopsis juniperovora*. This fungus enters the plant through wounds or healthy tissue. Older, mature foliage resists infection, but new growth is susceptible, especially in wet, humid weather. Excessive pruning or shearing in summer stimulates new, succulent foliage that is prone to infection. Plants grown in too much shade are also highly vulnerable. Overhead watering, insects, tools, and splashing rain spread the spores. The disease overwinters on dead needles.

Target: Junipers, especially creeping junipers *(Juniperus horizontalis)*; arborvitae *(Thuja)*; false cypress *(Chamaecyparis)*; Japanese cryptomeria *(Cryptomeria japonica)*

Symptoms: In the spring, needles, twigs, and smaller branches turn dull red or brown, then ash gray. Tiny black dots, which are the fruiting bodies of the fungus, may appear on needles and stems after the needles have dried and turned gray. Small gray lesions often girdle branch tips, generally on the final 4–6 in. of branches, and kill the foliage beyond the diseased tissue. Repeated blighting in early summer can result in abnormal bunches of shoots that resemble a broom. Young trees or shrubs may be stunted, with discolored foliage, and plants under 5 years old are often killed.

BLIGHT OR DROUGHT?

Juniper twig blight damage sometimes resembles drought damage. However, the change from healthy tissue to damaged tissue is gradual with damage from drought, whereas plants infected with this blight show a sharp change.

Prevention: Plant in sites with good air circulation and sunlight. Avoid wounding the twigs. Keep plants as dry as possible consistent with good growth; avoid watering during evening hours. Do not overfertilize.

Control: Prune out and destroy affected twigs and branches. Spray plants with thiophanate-methyl (Thiomyl, Domain) or mancozeb at 2-week intervals in spring, when growth begins.

LATE BLIGHT

FUNGUS

⚡ ZONES: ALL

Late blight results from infection by *Phytophthora infestans,* the Latin name for "potato destroyer." This is the fungus responsible for the Irish potato famine of the mid-19th century. Infected tomato and potato plant parts harbor the fungus, which overwinters in compost piles or garden debris, including infected potato tubers. Spores, dispersed by the wind, germinate when they encounter condensed moisture on susceptible plants.

Target: Tomato and potato

Symptoms: Small, dark, water-soaked spots appear on leaves and stems. Under cool, moist conditions, they rapidly enlarge, forming purplish black lesions, shown above. In humid areas, a white or gray mold may appear on the leaf undersides. On green tomatoes, gray-green, sunken spots form. They expand, join, and darken, causing the fruit to be malformed. Potato tuber skin discolors from brown to purple. Later, a brownish dry rot with an unpleasant odor sets in. In cool, wet weather, late blight may advance rapidly, ruining an entire field of potatoes or tomatoes in a few days.

Prevention: Use certified disease-free potato seed. Keep tomato and potato growing areas as separate as possible. On potatoes, regularly apply fungicides containing mancozeb every 7 days, starting when shoots are 6 in. high; continue treating vines as long as they are green. Potatoes planted in early spring and harvested before fall wet weather are more likely to escape severe infection. Avoid watering overhead. Remove and destroy tomato and potato plant debris at the end of the season. Space and stake tomato plants to provide good air circulation.

Control: Remove and destroy infected leaves of tomato or potato as soon as they show spots. Do not dig potatoes infected with late blight until at least 14 days after vines have been killed by frost or herbicide; do not harvest potatoes when soil is wet. Do not hold potato seed over from one year to the next or put rotten potatoes on the compost pile. In early spring, spray tomatoes with Bordeaux mixture, fixed-copper fungicidal soap (Soap Shield), chlorothalonil (Daconil), or mancozeb. Be sure to follow label directions.

LAWN SCALPING

CULTURAL

✄ ZONES: ALL

Scalping is the odious practice of cutting grass much too low, often close to the soil surface. The weakened lawn immediately turns brown and opportunistic weeds invade. Overgrown grass may present similar symptoms even if mowed at the appropriate height: mower cutting exposes the lower grass segments to sudden bright sun, and they burn. Scalping may also result from a buildup of thatch (see page 254), which gives the lawn a spongy texture that causes the mower to bounce, scalping the lawn in spots. Mowing just after a rain worsens this problem.

Symptoms: Yellow patches appear shortly after mowing. Several days later, the patches may turn tan or brown and die.

Prevention: Adjust mower blades to the appropriate height for the specific lawn type. Keep mower blades sharpened. Mow often enough so that mowing does not remove more than ⅓ of the grass-blade height. If the grass is quite tall, adjust the mower height to ½ the grass height and lower it gradually over the next few mowings. Remove excess thatch using dethatching equipment available at garden centers. The best time to dethatch warm-season grasses is early spring. Dethatch cool-season grasses in early fall.

Control: Don't scalp! Cut grass at the proper height.

THE RIGHT HEIGHT. *Here are the recommended mowing heights for various lawn grasses: Bahia grass, 3–4"; Bermuda, common, ½–1½"; Bermuda, hybrid, ½–1½"; buffalo grass, 1–6"; carpet grass, 1–2"; centipede grass, 1–2"; Kentucky bluegrass, 2–3"; perennial ryegrass, 1½–2½"; St. Augustine grass, 2–4"; tall fescue, 2–3"; zoysia, 1–2".*

LAWN STRIPING

CULTURAL

✄ ZONES: ALL

You can always spot the new neighbors on the block by their stripes—the ones that show up for all to see about a week after they fertilize the lawn.

Dark green stripes meander across the lawn with pale green stripes between. It looks a bit like a green version of Old Glory. Of course, your neighbor meant well—it's just that once fertilizer leaves the spreader and hits the grass, it becomes nearly invisible. And unless you have the memory of an elephant, you forget where you've fertilized. But don't worry. The lawn stripes will remind you where you left off about 7 days later.

Symptoms: Dark green stripes appear on the lawn about 6 to 7 days after fertilizing. The grass between the stripes remains pale or yellowish green.

Prevention and control: The people most likely to stripe their grass are those who use drop spreaders. That's because these spreaders drop the fertilizer in a narrow band beneath the spreader. So unless you overlap the bands, some areas of the grass will get fertilizer while others won't.

One way to make striping less likely is to use a broadcast spreader. It distributes fertilizer in wide bands across the lawn, so you won't miss many places. But broadcast spreaders can make it hard to apply weed-and-feed products, as they may sling "weed" granules onto the leaves of desirable plants and injure them.

Fortunately, there's an easy solution to this problem, no matter which kind of fertilizer spreader you choose. Fill the hopper of the spreader with half of the fertilizer required for your lawn, then distribute it by going back and forth, lengthwise, across the lawn. After you've covered the whole lawn that way, fill the hopper with the remaining fertilizer, then distribute it by going back and forth, widthwise. This way, the fertilizer will be distributed evenly.

LAWNS WITH DEAD PATCHES

CULTURAL

✂ ZONES: ALL

Chemicals such as gasoline, fertilizers, pesticides, and hydrated lime may burn grass if accidentally spilled or applied improperly. Dog urine contains salts that burn lawns. Damage takes up to 5 days to become visible. Lawns suffer the most damage during hot, dry weather.

Symptoms: Dead or dying grass patches, round or irregular, appear in lawn. If caused by dog urine or fertilizer, each spot may be encircled by a ring of dark green grass. The damage depends on the intensity or strength of the damage-causing agent, the amount spilled, and the lawn condition at the time damage occurs.

Prevention: Store chemicals in their original containers with their original instructions. Apply fertilizers, pesticides, and hydrated lime according to directions on the product label. Never combine chemicals unless the manufacturer specifically recommends doing so. Water immediately and thoroughly after fertilizer application, so the product does not rest on the plant surface for an extended time and so the fertilizer gets down into the grass root zone. Fill spreaders and sprayers on an unplanted surface, such as a driveway, rather than on the lawn. Water the grass regularly to minimize the odor that attracts dogs.

Control: If the damaging material is water soluble, water the area thoroughly, as much as six times longer than you ordinarily would. If the damaging material is not water soluble—such as gasoline or weed oil—inundate the area with a mixture of water and dishwasher soap, which will cut through the gasoline and oil. Then water heavily. Some substances, such as pre-emergence herbicides, cannot be eliminated from the soil after an accidental spill. You must replace the top layer of soil in the affected area and overlap slightly into unaffected parts of the lawn. Try to keep dogs off grass. Since dogs tend to return to the same elimination areas, try a commercial chemical repellent to disguise prior scents. As with other lawn chemicals, apply according to directions on the label.

LEAF DROP

CULTURAL/ENVIRONMENTAL

✂ ZONES: ALL

Leaf drop has many causes: too much water, too little water, root damage caused by diseases or insects, or insufficient sunlight. However, leaf drop can be normal. Deciduous trees drop their leaves in fall, although a stressed tree may drop leaves in midsummer. The foliage of evergreen plants has a life span of 1 to 4 years; leaf drop may occur every year or every second or third year. Hollies tend to lose their leaves in late winter, while pine trees and other conifers drop needles at various seasons, depending on the species. Normal leaf drop also occurs when new growth shades older, interior growth.

Symptoms: All or part of the plant may wilt. Lower, older needles or leaves turn yellow, brown, or reddish, then drop. Or many leaves of all ages and sizes suddenly may turn orange or red and drop. Leaf dropping may progress until only the stems are left. The problem may develop over a few days, several weeks, or longer. Insect or disease damage may be visible. Leaves on apparently healthy trees fall off.

DROPPING BY. *Leaf drop often results from fungal attack. Anthracnose, a disease of trees such as ash and sycamore, causes major leaf drop in late spring (see page 208). Apple scab (page 209), black spot (page 214), and peach leaf curl (page 239) also cause leaf drop.*

Prevention: Provide appropriate amounts of water, fertilizer, and light.

Control: If the soil of container plants is soggy and leaves have fallen or turned mostly yellow, repot the plant using new potting soil. Make sure in-ground plants have good drainage and well-aerated soil. Fertilize according to plant needs. Look for insect or disease symptoms, and treat as appropriate.

LEAF SCORCH

CULTURAL/ENVIRONMENTAL

ZONES: ALL

Leaves release moisture from their surfaces through a process called transpiration. If the amount of water getting to the leaves is less than the amount the plant releases or transpires, the leaves dehydrate and may die. Anything that disrupts the balance between water input and water output can cause leaf scorch. Conditions that decrease water uptake include fewer roots due to recent transplanting, diseases such as root rot, salt burn on young plants, and frozen soil. Drying winds, the combination of drought and high temperatures, and too much sun increase water loss. When water balance is disrupted, the greatest loss usually occurs at leaf margins and at leaf tips. Flowering dogwoods are especially sensitive to leaf scorch.

Symptoms: Browning leaf margins are the primary symptom. Entire leaves may wilt. Damage usually occurs first on newer leaves. On trees, the damage is most severe on youngest branches, with many leaves dropping during late summer. Trees do not usually die from leaf scorch.

Prevention: Select plants adapted to your climate. Place shade-loving plants in shade. Keep plants adequately watered, wetting the entire root system; during very hot, dry weather, reduce transpiration by gently sprinkling the foliage several times a day. Apply a mulch around plants to conserve moisture. This is especially important for shallow-rooted plants, such as dogwood and Japanese maple. Leach salts from soil with very heavy watering. Protect plants from strong winds. If freezing temperatures are expected, keep soil moist.

Control: Leaves damaged by leaf scorch do not recover. Proper watering reduces further damage, as do adding mulch and providing shade. Inspect affected plants for disease or physical injury (see page 241), and treat appropriately.

LIGHTNING INJURY

ENVIRONMENTAL

ZONES: ALL

Tall trees are among lightning's favorite targets. Although there may be no outward signs of electrical shock, trees may die suddenly from burned roots or internal damage. Or trees may show external damage immediately. Tall trees growing in open areas or along riverbanks are most vulnerable. In some instances, deep-rooted species and decaying trees may be more prone to lightning injury than shallow-rooted species or healthy trees.

Symptoms: Trees may burst into flame during an electrical storm. Tops of trees or branches may explode, leaving a jagged stub. A piece of bark may be burned or stripped from the entire length of the tree. Part or all of the tree suddenly may turn brown and die.

With palms, the fronds may suddenly droop around the trunk, beginning with the lower fronds. They may remain green initially, but change rapidly to yellow and then to brown. About 2 weeks after the lightning damage, most will have drooped or fallen off. The central bud area wilts and bends over. A reddish fluid may be seen along the trunk. No pests are visible on the dying fronds.

Prevention: Water your trees well, especially during droughts, to reduce damage by increasing the overall health of the trees. Do not plant trees that will attain considerable height, such as tulip poplars. Select trees that are not as susceptible to lightning injury, such as birch, beech, and horsechestnut. Consult a professional arborist about lightning protection for valuable old trees in thunderstorm areas.

GROUND ZERO. *While it's a bad idea to stand beneath any tree in a thunderstorm, it's most unwise to do so beneath an oak, maple, pine, tulip poplar, or ash. Lightning tends to strike these trees first.*

Control: Some trees may recover from lightning strike. To help a tree in this process, remove all loose and injured tree bark. Water well, and fertilize adequately for the tree variety. Remove dead trees so they do not become a safety hazard.

MELTING OUT OF LAWN GRASSES

FUNGUS

ZONES: ALL

Melting out is a common disease of Kentucky bluegrass and tall fescue caused by the fungus *Drechslera poae*. A similar fungus (formerly grouped with *Drechslera* but under the heading *Helminthosporium*) causes melting out of Bermuda grass. The disease spreads by windblown spores and on infected grass pieces carried by shoes, mowers, and tires. It overwinters in thatch. Cloudy weather, high humidity, high nitrogen levels, low mowing, and temperatures between 65° and 75°F favor its development. It first appears as a leaf spot, which usually isn't serious, but the fungus may then attack the crowns of grass plants, which is serious.

Target: Kentucky bluegrass, tall fescue, perennial ryegrass, Bermuda grass

Symptoms: Circular to elliptical, brown or purple spots that have straw-colored centers appear on grass blades and stems. Leaves turn yellow, then tan, and eventually drop. Shaded lawn areas are affected first. Crowns and roots eventually develop a dark brown rot. The lawn may appear yellow if nitrogen levels are low or blackish brown if nitrogen is abundant. The end result is a browning and thinning of the lawn that is most apparent in hot weather.

Prevention: If growing Kentucky bluegrass, use disease-resistant selections, such as 'Adelphi', 'Bonnieblue', 'Glade', 'Majestic', 'Merion', 'Parade', and 'Touchdown'. A blend of at least three different selections is best. Remove excess thatch in spring. Improve drainage through annual aeration. Mow grass at its highest recommended height (see pages 41 and 234). Water in early morning, not late afternoon or night. Do not apply high-nitrogen fertilizers in spring. Use balanced, slow-release fertilizers instead. Apply a fungicide containing chlorothalonil (Daconil), mancozeb, captan, or maneb according to label directions.

Control: Providing proper growing conditions usually controls melting out. If the problem persists, apply chlorothalonil (Daconil) according to label directions.

MUSHROOM ROOT ROT

FUNGUS

ZONES: ALL

This disease is caused by an *Armillaria* fungus, a native parasite often found in tree roots on newly cleared land. It can live many years in old tree roots and stumps. The fungus breaks down root tissue and eventually girdles plants. Infected plants may die rapidly or may linger for years. Infection is most severe in heavy, poorly drained soil.

Target: About 700 species of woody and herbaceous plants, including blackberry and red raspberry, grape, strawberry, rose, stone fruit and nut trees, and oak and willow trees

Symptoms: On infected plants, the initial symptoms are a decline and dieback in which the leaves turn yellow, wilt, and die. On blackberries, leaf damage may occur on only one side of the plant or in just one or two canes; few berries are produced. During fall and wet winter weather, clumps of honey-colored mushrooms, each 2–5 in. across, may appear on the crowns of infected plants or on nearby soil if roots are near the surface. White fans of feltlike fungus grow on an infected plant's crown and roots between the bark and the wood at ground level and just below it.

NAME GAME. *Mushroom root rot goes by several aliases, including armillaria root rot, oak root fungus, shoestring fungus, and honey mushroom.*

Prevention: Avoid placing susceptible plants in locations where mushroom root fungus is known to have occurred or where *Armillaria* fungi are likely to be present, such as on old orchard sites. When you clear trees, shrubs, or brush from a new planting site, remove and destroy all roots larger than 1 in. in diameter. Plant resistant species, such as catalpa, cedar, fig, sweet gum, madrone, magnolia, maple, pecan, pear, apple, and Chinese pistache. Provide good drainage.

Control: No chemical control is available. When plants are severely affected by mushroom root fungus, remove them and replant with a resistant species. If the tree is a prized one that you would prefer not to replace, consult a professional arborist when you first notice symptoms.

NITROGEN DEFICIENCY

CULTURAL/ENVIRONMENTAL

ZONES: ALL

Plants need nitrogen at all times. But they require particularly large quantities when plant growth is rapid, from early spring through early summer. Without sufficient nitrogen, plants transfer nitrogen from older leaves to new leaves, thereby damaging the old leaves. Most soils require additional nitrogen to support healthy plant growth. Commercial fertilizers provide nitrate nitrogen, which is readily available to plants. It acts quickly and is effective in both cold and warm soils. Organic nitrogen—found in blood meal, cottonseed meal, fish meal, fish emulsion, and manure—must be decomposed by soil microorganisms before it is available to plants. Decomposition speed depends on soil temperature and moisture.

DON'T OVERDO IT. *Overfertilizing with nitrogen results in lush, leafy growth at the expense of flowers and fruit. It also encourages insects and diseases.*

Symptoms: Plant growth is slow and plants are spindly. Older, lower leaves, which are affected first, may turn yellow and remain on the plant or may drop. New leaves and blossoms may be smaller than normal. In severe nitrogen deficiency, leaf undersides of some plants may turn bluish purple.

Prevention: Use a fertilizer containing nitrogen, according to label directions. A synthetic nitrate fertilizer is most effective if applied in frequent, light feedings unless formulated as a timed-release product that replaces nitrogen automatically during a specified time period. Amending soil with large amounts of fresh sawdust, ground bark, or peanut hulls can create an artificial nitrogen deficiency in the soil. When adding organic material to soil, be sure it is properly composted and add it a little bit at a time. Mix in additional nitrogen fertilizer because organic material increases microbial activity in soil and reduces the amount of nitrogen available to the plant. Blood and fish meals are the organic materials highest in nitrogen content. Make certain that mulches contain some nitrogen.

Control: Use a commercial fertilizer containing nitrogen according to directions on the label. Water in the fertilizer adequately.

OAK WILT

FUNGUS

ZONES: US, MS, LS, CS (SOUTHWEST)

Oak wilt, caused by the fungus *Ceratocyctis fagacearum*, has killed millions of oaks throughout the Southwest, particularly in the Texas Hill Country. The main infection period occurs in spring. Sap and oak bark beetles carry the fungus from diseased trees to wounded areas of healthy trees. The fungus may also spread from tree to tree through connecting roots of adjacent oak trees. The rapidly multiplying fungus blocks water-conducting vessels of trees.

Target: Oaks, including chinkapin oak (*Quercus muehlenbergii*), live oak (*Q. virginiana*), pin oak (*Q. palustris*), Shumard red oak (*Q. shumardii*), Southern red oak (*Q. falcata*), and water oak (*Q. nigra*); chestnut (*Castanea*) and apple trees (*Malus*)

Symptoms: Leaves turn dull green, bronze, or tan along tips and edges, then toward leaf center. Leaves also may turn yellow or brown along the veins, then droop, curl lengthwise, and wilt. Leaves fall in all stages of discoloration, and even when green. Defoliation may be slight or complete. On oaks, fungal mats may appear between the bark and the wood, with the bark cracking from fungal pressure. The fungus attracts damaging insects. Most diseased oaks die within a year, but some die within a few months. White oaks, bur oaks, and post oaks usually resist the disease.

Prevention: Inspect oaks regularly, removing and destroying any with oak wilt. Do not keep infected wood for firewood. Destroy connecting roots of diseased and healthy trees by digging a 3-ft.-deep trench between them. Prune only in the hottest summer months and the coldest winter months. Fresh pruning wounds at other times may attract beetles contaminated with oak wilt fungus. Treat all fresh pruning cuts with a tree wound dressing or sealer. Sterilize tools with rubbing alcohol after each cut. If pruning must be done in spring or fall, consult a certified arborist. Don't plant a new oak within the root zone of one that has died from oak wilt. Fungicide injections may keep a prized tree from becoming infected, but you'll need a tree service to do this.

Control: There is no known method of saving an oak infected with this fungus.

PEACH LEAF CURL

FUNGUS

⚡ ZONES: ALL

Peach leaf curl is one of the worst diseases affecting peach trees. It usually occurs when spring weather is cool and wet. The spores of the fungus *Taphrina deformans* overwinter on peach tree bark, having been carried there by wind or rain. Spring rain carries the spores to developing buds. At the end of the season, a grayish white powdery fungus forms on leaf surfaces. This blows onto the bark, setting the stage for next year's cycle of peach leaf fungus.

Target: Peach and nectarine trees

Symptoms: New leaves are abnormally thick, and they pucker and curl as they grow. Yellow or reddish blisters appear on the leaves, later turning a powdery white. Entire leaves may turn red, yellow, or pale green, and develop a white covering. In early summer, the leaves shrivel, turn black, then fall. A second crop of leaves may form after the first ones drop from the tree. Infected trees are weak and as a result become vulnerable to other diseases. Fruit may not appear; if it does, it may be misshapen, cracked, and covered with raised, wrinkled lesions of varying shapes. Such deformed fruit drops before it is ripe. Several years of peach leaf curl defoliation weakens the tree severely and causes considerable reduction in the fruit crop. It rarely kills the tree.

Prevention: To prevent recurrence the next year, spray the tree with calcium polysulfide (lime sulfur), dormant oil, chlorothalonil (Daconil), or fixed-copper fungicidal soap (Soap Shield) in the fall just after the leaves drop and in spring just before leaf-out.

Control: There is no cure for infected leaves. Remove and destroy them; do not put them in the compost heap.

PEACH SCAB

FUNGUS

⚡ ZONES: ALL

The fungus that causes peach scab, *Cladosporium carpophilum*, overwinters in lesions on affected twigs. After petals fall in spring, wind and rain carry infectious spores to healthy leaves, twigs, and fruit. Typically, symptoms develop after an incubation period of 1 to 2 months. While infection usually occurs 3 to 4 weeks after petal fall, the fruit remains susceptible through harvest.

Target: Peach, nectarine, and apricot trees

Symptoms: Initial infections appear as tiny, circular, olive green to black spots on surfaces of half-grown fruit. The spots usually cluster near the stem end, but they can occur any place on the fruit surface. Older lesions become greenish brown and velvety. If the spots are especially numerous, they may join together in a crustlike covering over misshapen fruit. Severely infected fruit may crack open to the pit. These cracks become entry points for several fruit-rotting fungi. Sometimes the fruit drops prematurely. Tiny, brownish lesions (cankers) with irregular margins appear on current-season twigs, though twigs are usually not seriously injured. On leaves, pale green to brownish spots that eventually turn yellowish brown to dark brown appear on leaf surfaces. These spots may fall out, leaving "shot holes" in the foliage. With severe infections, premature defoliation may occur.

Prevention: Thin tree canopy through proper and regular pruning to promote better air circulation and to allow foliage and fruit to dry quickly. Pruning also allows better spray penetration if this becomes necessary. Avoid placing trees in low-lying sites where heavy dew collects. Avoid overhead watering. Drip irrigation works best.

Control: Once the disease appears on fruit, it is too late to control during the current season. In the following season, prune and destroy infected twigs before new growth starts. Beginning with petal fall, spray with a fungicide containing wettable sulfur, captan, or chlorothalonil (Daconil). Repeat as directed on the product label.

PECAN SCAB

FUNGUS

 ZONES: ALL

Pecan scab, caused by the fungus *Cladosporium caryigenum*, is the most destructive disease of pecans in the South. The fungus overwinters on infected leaves, twigs, and shucks, both on the ground and on the tree. In spring, wind and rain carry the spores to young, rapidly growing shoots, leaves, and developing nuts. Only growing tissue is susceptible, and the fungus causes infection only if there is adequate moisture. Mature foliage and nuts are immune to scab. The disease is most prevalent in areas with frequent rainfall and high humidity.

Target: Pecan trees

Symptoms: Small dark brown to black circular patches appear on nuts. As the patches enlarge, they become slightly sunken. Severely infected nuts fail to develop properly, or they turn black. They may drop prematurely or remain attached to the shoots for an indefinite period. Enlarging, round or irregular, olive-brown to black spots appear on leaves, often near leaf veins. Infected leaves fall in late summer. This premature leaf drop deprives the trees of nutrients needed for nut development the following season.

Prevention: Plant scab-resistant selections, such as 'Barton', 'Caddo', 'Cheyenne', 'Curtis', 'Davis', 'Elliott', 'Houma', 'Kiowa', 'Mohawk', and 'Owens'. Remove and destroy old shucks, leaves, and other plant debris from around base of tree at season's end. Inspect for debris around the tree once more before it begins to leaf out in spring. Prune low-hanging branches to let in more sunlight and improve air circulation. This allows leaves and nuts to dry quickly after heavy dews or rains, making them less prone to scab. Healthy, vigorously growing trees are much less susceptible, so give them sufficient fertilizer and water. If you have scab-prone pecans such as 'Schley' and 'Success' and wish to use a preventative fungicide, this requires several applications and specialized equipment to cover large trees. Contact a commercial tree-spraying firm. Never spray after shucks begin to split open.

Control: There is no control once pecan scab has affected the current nut crop.

PHOTINIA LEAF SPOT

FUNGUS

ZONES: ALL

Photinia leaf spot is caused by the fungus *Entomosporium maculatum*. Spores survive on infected plants and are released from late winter through most of the growing season. They spread to healthy plants by a combination of splashing water and wind. Light infections cause cosmetic damage; severe infections cause early and heavy leaf drop. Leaf spotting is most severe following wet spring weather. While this disease rarely kills the plant, extensive defoliation slows its growth and increases sensitivity to environmental and cultural stresses.

Target: Photinia, as well as hawthorn, Indian hawthorn, flowering pear, loquat, cleyera, and other plants

Symptoms: Tiny, bright red, circular spots appear on the upper and lower surfaces of young expanding leaves. By the time the spots are a diameter of ½ in., their edges are purple, then later turn ash brown to gray. On heavily diseased leaves, the spots merge, forming irregular blotches. Black specks found in spot centers are fruiting bodies of the fungus. Heavily spotted leaves usually drop.

Prevention: Do not purchase plants with any leaf spot symptoms, and keep new photinias well away from established plants affected by the fungus. Space plants to improve air circulation and evaporation of moisture from foliage. Avoid summer pruning as it tends to promote a flush of highly susceptible new growth.

Control: There is no way to get rid of leaf spots once they appear on leaves. If practical, remove and destroy infected leaves. Regularly rake up and destroy fallen leaves. If photinias had a leaf spot problem in the prior year, spray in spring with a preventative fungicide containing chlorothalonil (Daconil), timed from bud break and applied every 10 to 14 days until all foliage has matured. This will break the disease cycle.

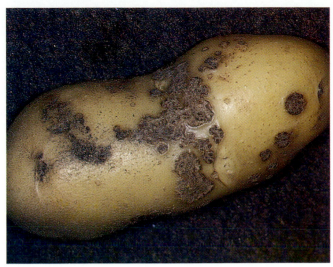

PHYSICAL INJURY

CULTURAL

ZONES: ALL

Most people don't harm plants intentionally—they just don't know they're doing it. Lawn mowers and string trimmers can strip the bark from young trees. Vehicles parked on the lawn crush roots and compact soil. On a construction site, workers can injure and kill trees by cutting roots, piling soil atop the root zone, gouging the trunk, and driving tractors over the roots. Affected plants slowly decline and often fall victim to diseases and insects.

Symptoms: The plant may wilt, and leaves may turn yellow, then brown. Wounds or cankers may appear on any part of the plant. There may be holes, surrounded by sap or sawdust, in a tree trunk or its branches. Overall growth is poor. If damage is severe, the plant may die.

Prevention: Be careful not to wound plants while mowing, trimming, or cultivating around them. Place edging, curbing, or other plant guards around garden beds or large plants to protect them from lawn mowers and string trimmers. Mulch an area 2–3 ft. in diameter around base of trees and shrubs to reduce the risk of mower or trimmer damage. Do not plant delicate plants near walkways or play areas. During construction, set up temporary fencing around trees, shrubs, and other plantings that could be harmed. Discuss with workers the need to take care around plants.

Control: Keep an injured plant adequately watered to speed its recovery. Fertilize if necessary.

DO NOT DISTURB. *The larger the tree, the more sensitive it is to disturbance of its roots. This is particularly true of hardwoods, especially oaks. Running heavy vehicles over the root zone, piling up soil against the trunk, cutting roots to put in water lines, and changing drainage patterns are all good ways to kill a big tree. The tree won't die right away. Instead, it will probably kick off after a year or two, following a drought.*

POTATO SCAB

BACTERIA

ZONES: ALL

Potato scab results from infection by *Streptomyces scabies,* a bacterium. The disease may be introduced initially by infected seed pieces; it is also transmitted by insects, handling, and wounds from tools, as well as through pores in the tuber skins during rapid growth. Most damage occurs when air temperatures are between 75° and 85°F and the soil is dry. A soil pH of 5.7–8.0 encourages potato scab. The bacterium survives in the soil indefinitely, withstanding temperature and moisture extremes. The bacterium also survives on infected tubers remaining in the garden.

Target: Potato

Symptoms: Potato scab infection begins with black specks on tubers. The specks expand rapidly, forming conspicuous, circular, brown corky pits, or scabs that may eventually join to cover most of the tuber. Usually scabs are only superficial, although occasionally pitted scab may occur, with lesions that may be ½ in. deep. Leaves and stems are not affected.

Prevention: Use only certified disease-free seed potatoes. Test and correct the soil to pH 5.0–5.5, using sulfur or acid-forming fertilizers. Water regularly, especially in the first two weeks as plants emerge and tubers form. Do not fertilize with manure from animals that have fed on scabby potatoes, as scab bacteria can pass intact through the digestive tracts of plant-eating animals. Instead, use commercial fertilizer such as a 5-10-5 or cottonseed meal. Foliar feed with fish emulsion as soon as you hill up the plants. If you have had a scab problem before, plant potatoes in the same garden area only once every 3 years.

Control: No chemical control is available for potato scab. Your best bet is to increase soil acidity and plant scab-resistant selections, such as 'Anoka', 'Bison', 'Buffalo', 'Carola', 'Cherokee', 'Russet Burbank', and 'Sierra'.

POWDERY MILDEW

FUNGUS

❚ ZONES: ALL

There are many different powdery mildew fungi. The fungus spores overwinter on fruit trees. In spring, the fungus begins to grow, and spores are released to travel on the wind to young leaves. Powdery mildew thrives where cool nights follow warm days. Insufficient sunlight and poor air circulation favor its development.

Target: Bee balm, begonia, clematis, dahlia, euonymus, hydrangea, lilac, pansy, phlox, rhododendron, rose, sunflower, zinnia; bean, grape, pea, potato, pumpkin, squash, strawberry, tomato; apple, dogwood, peach, crepe myrtle, maple, oak, and sycamore trees

Symptoms: A white or gray powdery fungus appears on foliage and flowers. Round, white spots on upper leaf surfaces expand and merge, covering both sides of leaves. Infected leaves turn yellowish green to brown. New growth may be stunted, curled, and distorted. Infected blossoms may not set fruit; fruit may develop a rough skin or be covered with the powdery fungus. Fruit drops early or is dwarfed.

NO-POX PHLOX. *In the humid South, powdery mildew targets perennial phlox* (Phlox paniculata). *But these selections resist the disease: 'David' (white), 'Eva Cullum' (pink with red eye), 'Franz Schubert' (lilac pink), 'Katherine' (lavender blue), 'Pax' (white), and 'Sandra' (scarlet).*

Prevention: Plant resistant selections; see the *Southern Living Garden Book* under the "Practical Gardening Dictionary" or individual plant listings for suggestions. Give plants sufficient light and air circulation. Water plants from underneath rather than above to keep leaves dry.

Control: Reduce nitrogen fertilizer. Pick off and destroy infected leaves and flowers. Spray ornamentals with horticultural oil, triforine (Funginex), thiophanate-methyl (Thiomyl, Domain), azadirachtin (Neem), or triadimefon (Bayleton). Spray fruits and vegetables with wettable sulfur or horticultural oil. Discard infected flowers of annuals and leftover produce in fall.

PYTHIUM ROOT ROT

FUNGUS

❚ ZONES: ALL

Because the fungus spores may swim short distances through soil water to attack the roots of susceptible plants, *Pythium* and *Phytophthora* are sometimes called water molds. They are most active in warm soils (55–80°F), but can survive in dry, cold soils while they wait for favorable conditions. Lawns and flower beds that are frequently watered often have pythium root rot problems, as do areas with heavy, poorly drained soils.

Target: Lawns; azalea, geranium, Madagascar periwinkle, rhododendron, and other ornamental plants

Symptoms: Symptoms develop over several weeks to several months. Young leaves turn yellow and wilt. Affected plants may be stunted and may flower prematurely, or the entire plant may wilt and die, even though the soil is moist. Plant stems or trunks show a dark discoloration close to ground level. If you peel back the stem covering or bark at the plant's base, you may see a distinct margin between the dark diseased plant tissue and the white healthy tissue.

Prevention: Do not overfertilize plants. Keep the soil moist; do not allow plants to dry out, but do not overwater them. Diminish the water needs of susceptible plants by placing those that are in containers in a more shaded area and by creating shade for ground-growing plants. Improve drainage by incorporating sand, composted bark, or expanded slate (PermaTill) into the soil or using raised beds. If drainage cannot be improved, use plants that are resistant to root rot, such as American arborvitae *(Thuja occidentalis)* and Pfitzer juniper.

Control: No controls exist. Destroy diseased plants.

WHAT ROT. *The symptoms of rhizoctonia root and stem rot (see opposite page) on some plants may look similar to those of pythium root rot. But Rhizoctonia fungi often favor well-drained, fertile soils, whereas Pythium tends to prefer soils that are poorly drained. Like pythium root rot, drought stress causes wilting, but drought stress can be alleviated by watering. Watering may increase the severity of pythium root rot.*

REDBUD CANKER

FUNGUS

ZONES: ALL

Redbud canker most often affects plants that have been injured, attacked by insects, nematodes, or disease organisms, or stressed by drought, frost, sunscald, nutritional deficiencies, or defoliation. Spores of the source fungus, *Botryosphaeria dothidea,* also colonize weakened, dead, or freshly pruned twigs and branches. In spring and summer, spores are spread by wind, rain, and watering, especially high-angle sprinkler systems. Optimum temperature for development of the disease is 80–91°F. The fungus slowly spreads through the tree in all directions, cutting off nutrition and water to affected sites. Although it is the most destructive disease of redbud, it seldom attacks healthy plants.

Target: Redbud and many other plants, including blueberry, camellia, grape, rhododendron, rose; citrus, dogwood, hickory, peach, sweet gum, and willow trees

Symptoms: Multiple, oval to elongated cankers of varying sizes develop on branches and occasionally on the trunk. Leaves wilt, wither, and eventually die. Leaves above the diseased area have abnormal coloration and produce little new growth. On affected branches, buds may fail to open in spring. Killed bark becomes sunken, rough, and dark. Old cankers may be surrounded by a ridge of callus (tissue that forms around a wound). Wood is discolored to at least an inch below the canker. On plants other than redbud, symptoms vary, depending on the plant part attacked and the source of stress.

Prevention: Avoid wounding trees. Prune in dry weather. Fertilize and water thoroughly during dry weather to maintain vigorous growth and prevent stress. Keep sprinkler angle low. Avoid watering with overhead sprinklers.

Control: The most effective way of controlling redbud canker is to regularly remove and destroy all dead and dying plant parts, cutting at least 3 in. below any visible discoloration in the bark. Take care to sterilize pruning tools between cuts. Paint wounds immediately. No effective chemical control is available.

RHIZOCTONIA ROOT AND STEM ROT

FUNGUS

ZONES: ALL

The fungus *Rhizoctonia solani* can be found in most soils, its many pathogenic strains causing a variety of diseases. The fungi that cause rhizoctonia root and stem rot enter the plant through the root system or the main stem at the soil line. The infection moves into other stems and the lower leaves, then progresses up the plant. This fungus thrives in warm, moist, fertile conditions and in aerated, well-drained soils.

Target: Ornamentals such as calendula, carnation, geranium, poinsettia, and sunflower; vegetables such as bean and lettuce

Symptoms: All leaves may turn pale and wilt, sometimes suddenly. Lower leaves and stems may rot. On bean seedlings, elongated, sunken, reddish brown lesions appear on stems and roots. Upper portions of affected plants wilt and die, and the stems may decay. If you remove the plant from the ground, you may find that the roots are very dark and perhaps badly rotted, even if it has been planted in soil with good drainage.

Prevention: Provide moisture as needed, but avoid overwatering. Sow seed when environmental conditions favor rapid germination and growth of seedlings.

Control: If all the leaves are wilted, remove and replace the plant. Less severely affected plants can be saved by reducing watering and by drenching the soil with a fungicide containing thiophanate-methyl (Thiomyl, Domain). If you have a container plant that will grow from cuttings and it has a healthy top, try removing the top and rooting it in sterile potting soil, perlite, or vermiculite. Discard the infected soil, and wash the pots thoroughly, disinfecting them in a solution of 1 part bleach and 9 parts water for about 30 minutes.

TWO ROTTEN LOOKALIKES. *The symptoms of rhizoctonia root and stem rot are similar to those of pythium root rot. However,* Pythium *fungi most often appear in heavy, poorly drained soils.* Rhizoctonia solani *fungus attacks seedlings as well as mature plants. It is also one of the fungus species that causes damping off.*

RHODODENDRON DIEBACK

FUNGUS

ZONES: ALL

Rhododendron dieback is a serious problem in the Southeast. Plants infected with the fungus *Phytophthora cactorum* look as if they have been killed by cold. The fungus spores survive for years in soil and plant debris, spreading to plants through infected soil, splashing water, rain, wind, infected tools, and contact with diseased plants. Infection usually occurs in warm, wet weather. In hot weather, the entire plant may die.

Target: Rhododendron and azalea

Symptoms: Buds turn brown. Olive-colored blotches appear on leaves. These blotches later turn brown and may have a dark red margin. Leaves on one or two branches suddenly roll up and droop. In shady locations, leaves have spots that appear water-soaked. Discolored, sunken cankers often appear on stems, twigs, and branches. Plant parts above the cankers shrivel, wilt, and die back from the tip. Eventually, the entire plant wilts and dies, even though the soil feels moist.

Prevention: Rhododendrons need excellent drainage. The soil should be loose and contain lots of organic matter. Plant them so that the tops of the root balls are ½ in. above the surrounding soil, then cover root balls with mulch. Space plants well for good air circulation. Avoid overhead watering. Do not plant rhododendrons where other rhododendrons have died from the disease. Do not overfertilize. Rake up and destroy dead leaves around plants. Rhododendrons that resist dieback include 'Roseum Elegans', 'Caroline', 'Cynthia', 'Anah Kruschke', 'Anna Rose Whitney', 'English Roseum', 'County of York', 'Rocket', and 'Vulcan'.

Control: Once branches wilt, no chemical will control the disease. Prune diseased twigs and branches 2 in. below the affected part. Disinfect tools between cuts in alcohol or a solution of 1 part bleach and 9 parts water. Destroy prunings. If rhododendron dieback is a continual problem, spray new leaves as they emerge with a fungicide containing chlorothalonil (Daconil) or mancozeb when the conditions favor development of the disease.

RUSTS

FUNGUS

ZONES: ALL

There are at least 4,000 types of rust diseases. Rust is present throughout most of the world. Most strains infect only specific plants. The fungi can overwinter on living leaves, in stems, and in plant debris. The spores become active in moist conditions. They are spread by wind and splashing water. Some may travel as far as 300 miles on the wind, although most are more local. The spores also may spread via the gardener's handling when the plant is wet.

Target: Zoysia grass; apple, crabapple, and pine; hawthorn, Oregon grape, fuchsia, geranium, hollyhock, pinks, quince, rose, snapdragon, sunflower, juniper; asparagus, onion, snap and dry beans, fig, pear, and blackberry

Symptoms: Rust initially appears as powdery pustules or pimples on undersides of lower leaves. The pustules are usually orange yellow to rusty brown but may be purple, red, white, or black. Each pustule contains millions of microscopic spores. As the disease progresses, upper leaf surfaces may be spotted with yellow, then turn completely yellow. Severely infected plants wither and die. Fruit quality is poor and fruit may drop early.

Prevention: Plant rust-resistant selections of apple and crabapple (see Cedar-Apple Rust, page 218), asparagus, bean, blackberry, roses, and lawn grasses. Give plants maximum air circulation. Immediately remove and destroy rust-infected leaves and plant debris. If watering from overhead, be sure plants will dry before dusk.

Control: Among the effective fungicides are those containing chlorothalonil (Daconil), mancozeb, and myclobutanil (Immunox). Contact your Cooperative Extension Office before choosing a fungicide.

RUSTPROOFING, ROMAN STYLE. *The Romans prayed to the sun god Apollo, who was in charge of making plants ripen, to shield their growing fields from dreaded rusts and other diseases. In the late 1800s, a new rust disease attacked the main coffee-growing plantations in Ceylon. Planters started growing tea instead, and the English became a nation of tea drinkers.*

PLANT DISEASES AND AILMENTS

ST. AUGUSTINE DECLINE
VIRUS

✎ ZONES: LS, CS, TS

St. Augustine decline (SAD), also called centipede mosaic, is caused by Panicum mosaic plant virus. The disease is widespread in Texas and also found in Arkansas and Louisiana. While most St. Augustine grasses tolerate moderate shade, in dense shade the virus becomes more severe. It may be transmitted within infected seed or by infected stolons, plugs, or sod.

Target: St. Augustine and occasionally centipede grasses

Symptoms: Yellow mottled leaves become progressively worse until the grass completely yellows. Leaves and stolons die, leaving bare spots in the lawn. Weeds move into affected areas, crowding out the weakened St. Augustine grass.

Prevention: Plant a resistant selection, such as 'Floralawn', 'Floratam', 'Seville', or 'Raleigh'. Avoid 'Bitter Blue' and 'Floratine', which are susceptible to the virus. Keep grass healthy. While St. Augustine tolerates a range of soils, it does not like waterlogged, compacted, or dry soil. It requires moist, somewhat fertile soil, and mild winter temperatures. For proper growth, remove excess thatch, water during droughts, do not overfertilize, and maintain a mowing height of 2–4 in.

Control: Chemical controls are not available. Replace diseased grass with a virus-resistant selection or another grass type. Verify SAD through your local Cooperative Extension Office.

ACID TEST. *Take-all patch (see page 253), which also affects St. Augustine grass as well as Bermuda grass, is easily confused with SAD. The fungus responsible for take-all patch,* Gaeumannomyces graminis, *causes blades to turn yellow and roots to turn brown or black. Mowing diseased grass spreads the infection. Chemical control is difficult. Keep St. Augustine grass vigorous by watering deeply, aerating, removing thatch, providing good drainage, and not overfertilizing. Maintain soil pH below 6.5, because the fungus doesn't thrive in acid soil.*

SALT DAMAGE
CULTURAL/ENVIRONMENTAL

✎ ZONES: ALL

Salt damage to plants is most prevalent along the coast, but it can occur anywhere. Salt accumulation in soil may come from fertilizers (including manure), soil composition, or water. Salt spray from a nearby ocean or other body of water drifts on the wind. Normally, rainfall or watering washes the salt through the soil layers and away from plant roots. However, at least 30 in. of rain each year is necessary to leach salt through the soil. Both salt spray on foliage and salt in the soil cause damage to plants by drawing out moisture. The desiccating or drying effect of salt on plants is worse in the winter when dormant or near-dormant plants are more easily stressed.

Target: Plantings in salt-laden soil and along the coast

Symptoms: Leaves may yellow. Salt deposits on leaf tips or margins cause them to turn a dark brown that looks like a burn. Leaves may drop. Plant growth slows or stops. A dark or white crust may form on the soil.

Prevention: Choose salt-tolerant plants (see note below and page 57). Consider putting in windbreaks if salt spray is a problem. Water adequately and thoroughly. Do not overfertilize with commercial fertilizers. Avoid fertilizing plants with fresh manure, which has a high salt content.

Control: Increase watering by at least 50 percent to leach salt through the soil. Improve the soil drainage by amending it with organic matter. Add gypsum to saline soil to remove harmful sodium.

SALTY SURVIVORS. *The following plants tolerate salt spray: bougainvillea, cabbage palm, cape honeysuckle, century plant, eastern red cedar, Indian hawthorn, Japanese pittosporum, live oak, Natal plum, oleander, prickly pear, sea grape, shore juniper, thorny elaeagnus, yaupon, and yucca. For other salt-air plants, see page 56.*

SEED SPROUTING FAILURE

CULTURAL/ENVIRONMENTAL

 ZONES: ALL

Seeds fail to sprout well for a number of reasons. Heavy watering or rainfall may have washed them away or buried them too deep. Or you may have planted them too deep. Seeds sown far below the surface will suffocate from lack of oxygen.

In addition to oxygen, seedlings need water to sprout. Without it, seed coats do not soften enough to permit the seedling to break through, or if the seedling does emerge, it may be weak and therefore vulnerable to damping-off organisms. Seeds placed in dry soil will not germinate. Too-shallow planting will speed the effects of soil drying. When soil has a crust, water fails to penetrate even when applied in sufficient quantity. Tiny seedlings cannot push their way through crusted soil. Soil temperature is also a factor; each plant has its own preferred sprouting temperature.

In addition to problems in soil, air, and water conditions, several soil-dwelling fungi attack and kill emerging seedlings. Also, birds may nip seedlings as they emerge.

Symptoms: Seedlings fail to germinate or sprout.

Prevention: Loosen soil before planting, using soil amendments as necessary. Purchase seed selections appropriate for your soil and site, and plant them properly and at the correct time of year. Make certain the packet bears a current date; seeds lose viability after a year. Place seeds at the recommended depth and distance apart. Keep soil slightly moist, watering gently with a fine hose spray. The tiny root systems of seedlings have no protection against even short periods of drought; in hot, sunny weather you may have to water more than once a day. Take protective measures against birds: place floating row covers, netting, or rustproof chicken wire over newly seeded areas. Be sure the covering is high enough that birds cannot reach the seedlings through it; anchor the edges. Eliminate weeds, since weed seeds may attract some birds.

Control: You can protect seed from disease during germination by coating them with a fungicide containing captan. Follow directions on the label. You can also use treated seed.

SEPTORIA LEAF SPOT ON TOMATO

FUNGUS

 ZONES: ALL

This very common leaf spot, *Septoria lycopersici,* can occur at any time during the growing season, but it generally becomes more severe after blossom set. The fungus overwinters in infected plant debris and seed, and in weeds such as nightshade, jimsonweed, and horse nettle. It may also be introduced into the garden from infected transplants. Fungus spores are released in spring and initially infect leaves near the soil. Moderately high temperatures, heavy dew, frequent rainfall, and high humidity increase the severity of the disease. Severe infection causes defoliation, which results in fewer tomatoes and sunscald damage on fruit. The fungus survives at least 3 years on infected debris.

Target: Tomato

Symptoms: Small water-soaked spots appear on lower, inner leaves. The circular lesions, which have a $\frac{1}{16}$–$\frac{1}{8}$ in. diameter, turn tan or gray with a dark margin. They may be numerous enough to cover the entire leaf. Fungus spores form within minute black specks (visible with a hand lens) in the lesion's center. As the disease progresses up the plant, infected leaves turn yellow, dry, and then fall. In severe infections, all the leaves may drop except a few at the tips of stems. While lesions sometimes form directly on stems, they do not form on tomatoes.

Prevention: Purchase healthy transplants. Clean up and destroy tomato plant debris. Remove weeds. Do not plant tomatoes in the same location every year. Avoid overhead watering. Do not work around wet plants. Keep plants growing vigorously.

Control: Use a fungicide containing chlorothalonil (Daconil) or mancozeb as soon as symptoms appear. Reapply according to label directions.

SPOTTING TOMATO DISEASES. *Septoria leaf spot is often confused with early blight (see page 226), a fungus that causes tomato leaves and mature fruit to develop dark lesions with "bull's-eyes" in the center. Early blight lesions may also appear on stems.*

SHADE ON LAWNS

CULTURAL/ENVIRONMENTAL

✄ ZONES: ALL

Maintaining a healthy lawn in shade is difficult. Shade blocks out sunlight needed for proper growth and general health. The trees that provide the shade may also absorb many of the nutrients and water needed by the grass.

Symptoms: Grass growing under trees becomes thin and spotty; it may die out altogether. Leaf blades are thin and dark green. Moss and algae may grow on the soil. Diseases that thrive in shade, such as powdery mildew, may appear.

Prevention: When planting shade trees in lawns, keep in mind their size at maturity, and choose trees that cast filtered shade. Keep trees pruned to let light reach plants. Select shade-tolerant grasses (see note at right). Or plant a shade-tolerant ground cover in lieu of lawn (see page 46). Water and fertilize more heavily under trees so there is an ample supply for both trees and the plants underneath. Set mowing height for shaded grass higher than for grass that is in full sun. Rake up fallen leaves regularly so they do not block light to plants under trees.

BLADES FOR THE SHADE. *All lawn grasses grow better in full sun. But carpet grass, centipede grass, red fescue, tall fescue, and zoysia tolerate light shade. The best warm-season grass for moderate shade is St. Augustine, especially the selections 'Bitterblue', 'Palmetto', and 'Seville'.*

Control: If shade is a severe problem and alternative plantings are not feasible, consider using an attractive bark or pine straw mulch instead of lawn grass or other plants.

SHORT STEMS ON BULBS

CULTURAL/ENVIRONMENTAL

✄ ZONES: LS, CS, TS

Our warm Southern climate may be great for crepe myrtle, live oak, and magnolia, but it isn't well suited for tulips and Dutch hyacinths. These mainstays of spring bulb displays thrive on long, cold winters, short, cool springs, and hot, dry summers. In mild-winter areas, especially the Lower, Coastal, and Tropical South, they grow poorly and are short-lived. Even where they survive from year to year, they steadily decline in performance and are best treated as annuals.

Large-flowered tulips and Dutch hyacinths require at least 6 to 8 weeks of cool weather, 40–50°F, to bloom properly. Ten to 12 weeks of winter chilling is even better. Without sufficient chilling, bulbs develop abnormally short stems. If this is coupled with unseasonably warm weather in spring, the bulbs may bloom at ground level. Improper winter storage at temperatures above 60°F, even for a short while, may also contribute to a disappointing spring display.

Symptoms: Flower stems are unusually short. Leaves seem healthy, but flowers appear stunted. Flowers may open while still at ground level. Bulbs left in the ground may fail to bloom the following year.

Prevention: In early October, purchase top-size bulbs from a reputable dealer to ensure they have been stored properly. Store the bulbs inside mesh bags in the vegetable bin of your refrigerator (*not* the freezer) for 10 to 12 weeks before planting. Do not store them with ripening fruit, because the fruit gives off a gas that harms bulbs. After this time, plant them outside in fertile, well-drained soil. Planting them in filtered sun may keep them from blooming too early in mild-winter areas.

Control: Nothing can be done for bulbs with short stems. Dig and discard them and plant new bulbs next fall. Realize that in most areas of the South, tulips and Dutch hyacinths do best when treated as annuals.

SHOT HOLE

BACTERIA

ZONES: ALL

When shot hole attacks your garden, you may wonder whether local goose-hunters have suddenly turned their sights on your plants. This disease, caused by the bacterium *Xanthomonas pruni*, affects trees and shrubs in the cherry family, causing numerous holes in the leaves, as well as cankers in the twigs.

Shot-hole bacteria overwinter in infected twigs. The bacteria ooze onto twig surfaces in spring when it rains or there is a heavy dew. Rainfall or water then splashes them onto healthy leaves and stems, where they multiply. New infections can occur throughout the growing season. Rainy, windy weather and temperatures 70°–85°F favor the disease. Serious infections can defoliate trees and shrubs, making them vulnerable to winter damage, insects, and other diseases.

Target: Cherry laurel, cherry, peach, and plum trees and shrubs

Symptoms: Small, rounded, angular, or irregular spots appear on leaves, usually near the tip and around major leaf veins. Spots may be deep purple, rusty brown, or black. The centers of the spots dry up and fall out, leaving multiple, ragged "shot holes" each about 1/8 in. wide. Leaves turn yellow and drop prematurely. Dark, sunken, or blistering twig cankers occur, causing twigs to die back. Fruit is cracked and malformed and develops dark, sunken spots.

Prevention: Buy healthy, disease-free trees and shrubs from a reputable nursery and inspect them carefully for leaf spots and shot holes. Plant in sunny areas that have well-drained soil and good air circulation. Do not water with overhead sprinklers. Prune only during dry weather.

Control: Rake up and destroy infected leaves. Prune out and destroy cankered twigs. Fertilize plants to encourage healthy growth. Spraying plants with streptomycin (Agri-Strep) during and just after bloom in spring may provide control.

SLIME FLUX

BACTERIA

ZONES: ALL

Slime flux, also called wetwood, is a bacterial disease occurring primarily during the growing season. It may be stimulated by environmental stress, such as very warm weather or drought. The bacterium *Erwinia nimmipressuralis* infects a tree's heartwood, causing fermentation in tissues. Gases produced by fermentation force sap out of wounds, cracks, and other tree openings, a symptom called flux. It is not usually a serious disease.

Target: Ornamental trees, including birch, elm, hickory, maple, oak, poplar, and willow; fruit and nut trees

Symptoms: Sour-smelling sap oozes from the tree trunk. As the slime is exposed to air, it becomes darker and dries on the bark, causing unsightly gray or black streaks, which may enlarge and thicken. Bacteria and yeasts working within the flux cause it to become increasingly foul smelling with age, and insects are attracted to it. Where the flux drips onto a lawn, it can cause dead spots. The amount of flux increases markedly when the tree is growing rapidly. You may see wilting and scorched leaves if the tree is also suffering from water stress.

Prevention: Be careful not to wound trees. Maintain trees in good health, and fertilize and water them adequately.

Control: There is no cure for slime flux. The flux might stop by itself, but it also might continue for years. Slime flux causes interior wood to be discolored and wet. Remove any loose bark you find, to allow the wood to dry out. Since this disease indicates a weakened tree, subject to decay, you should consider the tree hazardous. Diseased limbs and those that hang over houses or driveways should be removed for safety. When pruning infected trees, disinfect tools with alcohol or a solution of 1 part bleach and 9 parts water. Homeowners were once advised to insert drainage pipes into the tree just below the oozing wounds. But this practice can lead to heart rot (see page 231), a far more serious disease.

SLIME MOLD

FUNGUS

ZONES: ALL

Slime molds are caused by any of several types of fungi. Because they are nonparasitic, they are harmless. They use leaf blades as support for their reproductive structures. The spores are spread by the wind. Slime molds are most likely to appear abruptly, following lawn watering. They are more common during cool, humid, or wet weather, particularly in the fall, but they also appear in spring and summer after heavy watering or rains.

Target: All grasses and many other small plants

Symptoms: This fungus initially makes a sudden appearance as a gray, watery white, or yellowish white slimy growth that crawls over plants. You can easily rub it off the plants if you don't mind slimy stuff all over your hand. After a few days, the growth moves up onto any nearby plant parts and changes into pinhead-size balls of purple-brown, black, white, or bluish gray. This phase is easier to spot than the slime phase. A profusion of these globular or spherical balls may cover grass patches ranging from a few inches to several feet wide. The balls, composed of fungus spores, feel powdery when you rub them between your fingers. When these balls break, masses of fine, dark spores are released. An abundance of the powdery spores covering the grass may block the sunlight and turn the grass yellow.

Prevention: Preventing thatch buildup on your lawn may help.

Control: In most instances, these unsightly molds will disappear if left alone. If you wish to remove them, sprinkle with a strong water spray during dry weather, rake them away, mow the lawn, or sweep the area with a broom. Chemical control is not necessary or useful.

SOIL COMPACTION

CULTURAL

ZONES: ALL

You may like it when folks beat a path to your door, but your lawn and other plants don't. Continual foot traffic—even the temporary weight of heavy-duty construction equipment—will compress the top 2–4 in. of soil into a compacted mass. The tightly packed soil particles leave little space for air or water. Roots are deprived of oxygen and can't penetrate the mass to reach areas where oxygen is available. Water penetrates compacted soil slowly, causing puddling and runoff, which in turn result in water-stressed plants. Clay soils are more prone to compaction than other types.

PUTTING THE SQUEEZE ON. *Don't dig or cultivate in your vegetable garden until the soil dries out in spring. If you work the soil while it's muddy, you'll compact it; when it dries, it'll be as hard as bricks. To check dryness of soil, give it the squeeze test. Pick up a handful of soil and squeeze it. Relax your hand and toss the compacted soil around. If the soil holds together in a ball, it's too wet. If it falls apart, it's okay.*

Symptoms: The lawn becomes sparse and overrun by weeds. Trees and shrubs are stunted and may die. Plants may become diseased, mainly from root and crown rots.

Prevention: Create walkways to direct people around planted areas. Protect plants by placing barriers—such as fencing—to keep traffic off garden areas, or install raised beds. If vehicles or heavy equipment must be temporarily driven across the lawn, make certain the soil is as dry as possible.

Control: Aerate compacted soil. On lawns, use a lawn aerator to poke 3-in.-deep holes at least 3 in. apart; air and water will then be able to reach plant roots. If large areas to be planted are badly compacted, use a pick to break up the hard surface, then use a rotary tiller. Add plenty of sand and organic matter—such as peat moss, well-aged manure, or compost—during tilling. Tilling in kiln-fired expanded slate (PermaTill) will also help considerably.

SOOTY MOLD

FUNGUS

ZONES: ALL

Sooty molds are also called black molds. These unsightly molds are caused by several species of fungi. More than one sooty mold fungus may appear on the same plant at the same time, feeding on the honeydew of numerous insects. Fungal growth takes place from spring through early fall. Splashing rain or water may spread the fungus to other plants.

Target: Trees, particularly crepe myrtle; shrubs, vines, annuals, and perennials

Symptoms: Sooty mold usually appears as a dark, brown-black powdery fungus growth covering leaf surfaces and twigs. It can also look like a thin, dark film or black spots. In severe cases, the fungus almost completely covers a leaf's surface. Although the fungus is considered fairly harmless because it does not feed on plants, extremely heavy infestations can block sunlight from reaching the leaves, which may yellow and fall prematurely.

Prevention: Control scale, aphids, mealybugs, whiteflies, and other honeydew-excreting insects, as well as ants.

Control: On small plants, wipe or wash off the molds with a small sponge and water. On large trees, use a hose-end sprayer to wash off mold. Spray plants with malathion, horticultural oil, azadirachtin (Neem), or acephate (Orthene) to control insects that secrete honeydew.

STICKY SITUATION. *Some sap-sucking insects do not fully digest plant sap. The undigested portion is excreted as a sweet, sticky liquid called honeydew. If copious amounts of honeydew form on trees, sidewalks and other surfaces below may become coated with it and the sooty mold that follows. Ants add to the problem by collecting and tending honeydew-excreting insects, such as aphids, scale, and mealybugs. They milk the insects for the honeydew, which they take back to other ants for food. Ants also transfer honeydew-excreting insects from plant to plant.*

SOUTHERN STEM ROT

FUNGUS

ZONES: LS, CS, TS

This disease, also known as Southern blight, is caused by the fungus *Sclerotium rolfsii*. It is most common in warm, moist soils deficient in nitrogen. The fungi overwinter in affected plant parts or in soil, where they can survive for many years. It is most damaging in the Lower and Coastal South during hot, wet summers.

Target: Wide range of hosts that includes Japanese aucuba, carpet bugleweed *(Ajuga),* and most flowering annuals and perennials; vegetables such as carrot, beans, melons, sweet potatoes, tomato, and pepper; and fruits such as apple, crabapple, and peach

Symptoms: Infected plants wilt and leaves yellow. Plant stem at soil line appears soft and sunken, and develops a brown to black discoloration. In moist conditions, a white, fanlike fungal growth occurs on the lower stem near the soil surface, on fruit and leaves in contact with the soil, and on plant debris around the base of the plant. The fungus may spread more than 3 ft. through the soil and from plant to plant within a row.

Prevention: Soil solarization for 4 to 6 weeks (see page 31) effectively suppresses the disease. Rotate crops (see page 30). Rake up and destroy all dead leaves and other plant debris from the soil surface prior to planting. Place a collar of aluminum foil around the bases of tomato plants. Space plants to improve air circulation.

Control: Chemical control is not practical. Remove and destroy all infected plants. Remove the soil surrounding any affected plant to a depth of 3 in. and for 6 in. beyond. Discard plant debris. Do not replant susceptible plants in the same soil for at least 3 years.

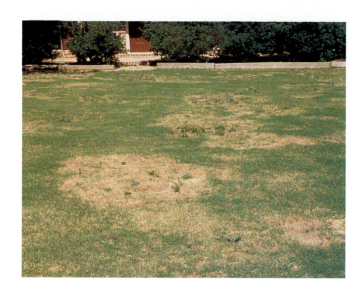

SPRING DEAD SPOT

FUNGUS/CULTURAL

ZONES: US, MS, LS, CS

Sometimes diseases attack on their own. And sometimes they need a little help from us. Spring dead spot of lawns is a good example of the latter. It results when improper cultural practices, coupled with an unusually cold winter, make things easy for several different kinds of soilborne fungi, including *Gaeumannomyces graminis* and *Ophiosphaerella herpotricha*. The infection and subsequent damage begin in fall but are masked by winter dormancy. In spring, when lawns resume normal growth, damage becomes apparent. Ironically, well-maintained, well-fertilized lawns suffer more from this disease than neglected ones.

Target: Bermuda grasses (especially the named hybrids) and occasionally zoysia

Symptoms: Circular or arc-shaped, slightly depressed patches of straw-colored, dead grass appear when the lawn greens up in spring. These patches range from a few inches to a few feet in diameter and occur randomly. As they grow, they may coalesce, until they cover most of the lawn. During early stages of this disease, the centers of the patches may remain alive, creating a "frog's-eye" pattern. Later, the centers die. If you dig up a piece of turf, you'll see dark brown or black, rotted roots, instead of white, healthy roots. The fungi may leave a toxin in the patch that makes regrowth difficult. Diseased patches reappear on the same sites for several years. Opportunistic weeds often invade the dead spots.

Prevention: Do not overfertilize. Do not apply quick-release, high-nitrogen fertilizer after August 1. Apply a slow-release, "winterizer" fertilizer in fall that contains extra potassium, such as 8-8-25. Maintain the soil pH between 5.8 and 6.2. Remove excess thatch.

Control: Apply triadimefon (Bayleton) according to label directions when symptoms appear. Then water the lawn thoroughly.

STRAWBERRY LEAF SPOT

FUNGUS

ZONES: ALL

The fungus that is the causal agent, *Mycosphaerella fragariae*, overwinters on old infected leaves. A long rainy season and temperatures over 50°F favor its development in spring and fall or in moist summers. There are many other leaf spot diseases, some caused by bacteria (see page 211).

Target: Strawberry

Symptoms: Initially leaves are red or purplish, gradually becoming grayish. Tiny fungus spots with a whitish center and red margin scatter widely over the leaf surface, fruit stalks, runners, and berry caps. Fruit is small. Berries attacked before ripening may never fully ripen and are inedible. Strawberry caps or the entire plant may die. Plantlets growing from infected plant runners are weak and may produce a small crop. Black seed disease may cause unripe berries to develop one to ten brownish black, hard, leathery spots. The fruit does not rot, but it discolors under the spot.

SICK STRAWBERRIES. *Many diseases infect strawberries, including armillaria root rot, white mold, verticillium wilt, black root rot, botrytis (gray mold), powdery mildew, red stele, and various viruses. Some diseases may occur simultaneously. For help in identifying the disease, take an infected plant in a sealed plastic bag to a cooperative extension agent.*

Prevention: Plant resistant selections, such as 'Allstar', 'Apollo', 'Cardinal', 'Chandler', 'Earliglow', 'Surecrop', and 'Tennessee Beauty'. Moderately resistant selections are 'Atlas', 'Tribute', and 'Tristar'. Set healthy plants in well-drained soil.

Control: After harvesting June-bearing plants, remove their foliage and mow them about ½ in. above the crown. This reduces fungi overwintering on old leaves. Do not mow everbearing strawberries, but remove foliage. Discard plant debris at the season's close. Spray with a fungicide containing captan. Treatment may have to be repeated at 7- to 10-day intervals, stopping several days before harvest, according to label directions. Avoid overhead watering.

SUNBURN

CULTURAL

ZONES: ALL

Plants that are grown in low light conditions can be sunburned if moved abruptly to a sunnier location. Indoor or porch plants moved directly outdoors in the spring or summer are especially vulnerable. Even cacti and other sun-loving plants can be damaged by sunlight if suddenly relocated from low light to high light. While sun damage often coincides with damage from wind (see page 259) or inadequate watering (see page 258), the three are not interconnected. Sun bleaching and burn, shown above, result when light and heat break down chlorophyll, the green pigment of plants. Too much exposure to sunlight also results in leaf scorch (see page 236) and sunscald (at right). In very sensitive plants, such damage may cause plant death.

Symptoms: Plants develop faded yellowish white, yellow, pale green, or brown leaves on the section of the plant facing the sun. Leaves may become brittle. Growth may be poor. The damage is worse if the plant is allowed to dry out. Plants may wither and die.

Prevention: Grow shade-loving plants in shade. Water them adequately—for plants in containers, this may mean watering as often as twice a day during heat waves. Wrap the trunks of newly transplanted trees—especially those with smooth, thin bark—with tree-wrapping paper or burlap to prevent sunscald. Do not move sun-tolerant plants abruptly from low light areas to sunnier areas; place them in partial shade for several days so they can adjust. When selecting new plants, choose native plants and others that are adapted to local growing conditions.

Control: Move plants suffering from too much sun to a shadier spot. Water well after moving; prune off badly damaged leaves to improve the plant's appearance.

RED-FACED BUT UNBURNED. *Did you ever wonder why the leaves of certain plants, such as sourwood, photinia, and Japanese cleyera, have a red tinge when they unfurl in the spring? Scientists speculate the ruddy pigment protects tender leaves from ultraviolet radiation until they can toughen up.*

SUNSCALD

CULTURAL

ZONES: ALL

Overexposure to sun causes sunscald. The problem commonly occurs when young trees are moved from a protected situation, such as a shaded nursery, to an open garden site. Trees that have been shaded have thin and tender bark. If exposed to sudden intense sunlight, tree bark cells heat up rapidly. Since they are not adapted to very high temperatures, they are easily injured or killed. Sunscald may also occur on cold, clear winter days with sudden, intense sunlight. Recently pruned or transplanted trees are more susceptible to sunscald, as are young trees and species with smooth, thin bark. Sunscald may also occur on shade-loving plants, such as camellias, rhododendrons, dogwoods, and Japanese maple. Dry soil conditions intensify sunscald problems.

Symptoms: Bark turns dark brown, splits open, and dies. The splits form patches or long cracks, usually on the southeast side of the tree. The damaged bark and wood may be invaded by decay organisms, which enter the wood and cause cankers. Young trees may be killed. On shade-loving plants, sunscald causes leaf centers to turn a bronze color. Severely affected areas turn brown and die. Flowers may appear bleached.

Prevention: Transplant in cool, overcast weather. Use burlap or tree-wrapping paper, available at garden centers, to wrap trunks and major branches of recently transplanted trees. You can also whitewash the trunk. Place shade-loving plants in shade. Water immediately after transplanting, and do not let plants get too dry.

Control: Unless there is major damage, trees suffering from sunscald will usually recover, given proper care. Fertilize to encourage new growth. As the transplanted tree takes hold and adapts, its bark will eventually thicken to withstand differing intensities of sun. Water regularly, deep enough to reach tree roots.

TAKE-ALL PATCH

FUNGUS

⚡ ZONES: LS, CS, TS

Some pathogens aren't happy making things miserable for just a single plant. A fungus called *Gaeumannomyces graminis* is a good example. It attacks Bermuda, centipede, and zoysia grasses, and is responsible for spring dead spot (see page 251). And when it sets its sights on St. Augustine grass, it causes a disease called take-all patch.

This fungus overwinters in thatch and infected plant tissue. It may also enter the garden on infected sod. Although it's most active during cool, moist weather, the symptoms don't usually appear until a stretch of hot weather in spring or summer. Conditions that favor the disease include high soil pH, low or unbalanced soil fertility, poor drainage, and excessive thatch.

Target: St. Augustine, Bermuda, centipede, and zoysia grasses

Symptoms: Leaves yellow and eventually die. As roots and stolons become infected, straw-colored, circular or ring-shaped dead patches appear in the lawn. These range from a few inches to 20 ft. in diameter. Dying grass near the edge of a patch may have a purplish tinge. Grass plants pull easily from the ground due to dark brown or black rotted roots. Dead patches may last for years before opportunistic weeds invade.

Prevention: Buy only certified, disease-free sod. Maintain soil pH between 6.0 and 6.5 by adding sulfur if necessary. Remove excess thatch in spring. Improve drainage through annual aeration of lawn. Fertilize with a balanced, slow-release fertilizer formulated for your type of grass. If take-all patch has been a problem in the past, apply a fungicide containing triadimefon (Bayleton) in the fall according to label directions.

Control: This fungus is difficult to control. Applying triadimefon (Bayleton) fungicide according to label directions in fall and spring may help. Water the lawn thoroughly after each application.

TEXAS ROOT ROT (COTTON ROOT ROT)

FUNGUS

⚡ ZONES: MS, LS, CS (SOUTHWEST)

Texas root rot *(Phymatotrichum omnivorum)*, also known as cotton root rot, attacks more than 2,000 plant species. It is most prevalent in areas with mild winters and warm, heavy, alkaline soils with a pH between 7.2 and 8.5. Symptoms usually occur from June through frost, though aboveground symptoms may not be obvious until the fungus has destroyed plant roots. The disease invades by continual slow growth through the soil, growing at 5–30 ft. per season around fruit trees. The fungus may also be carried on roots of transferred plants. It can survive for at least 3 years in soil, and may be found as far as 3 ft. deep.

Target: Fruit, shade, and nut trees; cotton and many other plants

Symptoms: Leaves become slightly yellow or bronze. Upper leaves may wilt within 48 hours after discoloration; lower leaves, within 72 hours. Permanent wilting often occurs on small plants by the third day, with the plant dying shortly thereafter. Trees and shrubs may survive for several years, showing stunted new growth, yellowing, and dieback. Brown, gray, or dirty-yellow woolly fungus strands may cover the root surface. Root bark is brown and decayed. Affected areas may appear as an ever-enlarging circle of dead plants. During moist weather, fungus spore mats 2–12 in. wide may appear on soil surface. The mats initially appear white and cottony, and later tan and powdery.

Fungus spore mat

Prevention: Purchase disease-free plants. Incorporate organic material into the soil and improve drainage. Replace diseased plants with types resistant to root rot. Tolerant plants, although infected, may survive. Contact your local Cooperative Extension Office for a listing of disease-resistant plants for your area. Members of the grass, palm, lily, amaryllis, iris, onion, and orchid families are usually immune.

Control: No chemical control is available. Improve drainage and add organic matter to soil. Dig and destroy affected plants. Increase soil acidity. Use a fertilizer containing nitrogen.

THATCH

CULTURAL

ZONES: ALL

Thatch is a layer of intermingled dead roots, partially decomposed grass stems, and debris that has accumulated below the grass blades and above the soil surface. A thatch layer of ¼ – ½ in. thick is normal. Deeper thatch stops water and fertilizer from reaching the soil and grass roots. It also encourages and harbors harmful diseases and insects, such as spittlebugs; pest and disease management becomes more difficult because pesticides can't penetrate the thatch. Excess thatch also predisposes these grasses to drought and cold injury. Thatch builds up when the lawn is overfertilized or overwatered, or when the soil is too acid or compacted. Some grasses—Bermuda, centipede grass, Kentucky bluegrass, St. Augustine, and zoysia—form more thatch than others. Perennial ryegrass seldom forms heavy thatch. To determine if your lawn has a thatch problem, cut and lift a few 2-in.-deep grass plugs. If the stringy, feltlike material between the grass and soil surface is more than ½ in. thick, you have a problem.

Symptoms: Large patches of grass suddenly go dormant during summer heat and drought. Grass thins out, and weeds appear in the thinning portions. The lawn feels spongy. When you mow, particularly just after a rainfall, the mower bounces, sometimes enough to cause scalped spots in the lawn. Diseases occur.

Prevention: Rake lawns regularly. Practice core aeration (see page 35). Do not overfertilize, particularly warm-season grasses.

Control: Thatch may accumulate over many years and should not be removed all at once. Instead, dethatch annually until you correct the problem—in early spring to early summer for warm-season grasses, in early fall for cool-season grasses. Avoid dethatching while lawn is turning green. A dethatching machine may be available from garden-equipment rental outlets, or a professional garden service can do the job. Read instructions before using a machine, as you could damage the lawn if you use it improperly. Remove thatch debris, then fertilize and water to hasten lawn recovery.

TOMATO LEAF ROLL

CULTURAL/ENVIRONMENTAL

ZONES: ALL

Tomato leaf roll usually occurs during the change from spring to summer weather. In spring, tomato plants grow vigorously, and top growth often exceeds root development. When the first days of warm summer weather occur, the plant responds to this change as though it's a problem, and attempts to reduce transpiration (loss of moisture) by rolling its leaves. This is usually a temporary condition that disappears after about a week. Other conditions can also instigate leaf rolling, including excessive rainfall or overwatering, abrupt weather changes, very hot days, and heavy cultivation. Leaf roll is more frequent on trained and pruned plants and more apparent on some tomato types than others. But it's completely normal for some tomato selections, such as 'Big Boy', 'Floramerica', and 'Beefsteak'. However, if the condition persists, some form of root injury may have occurred. Should leaves curl and change color or fruiting become affected, the problem may be caused by a virus, a fungus, or herbicide damage (see page 232).

Symptoms: Initially, lower, older leaves roll up at the margins. The leaves develop a cupped appearance, with margins sometimes touching or overlapping. The rolling leaf problem proceeds upward on the plant until it affects most of the leaves. Leaves remain green. Plants may lose leaves, especially on staked or pruned plants. The rolling is often accompanied by leaf thickening, giving the leaf a leathery texture. Plant growth does not seem to be greatly affected. Yields are normal.

Prevention: Plant tomatoes in well-drained soil. Maintain uniform soil moisture. Avoid drought conditions or overwatering. In hot weather, use a thick layer of mulch, which can reduce water loss.

Control: Although unattractive, tomato leaf roll is not a serious problem and does not require control.

TOPPING TREES

CULTURAL

ZONES: ALL

You wouldn't expect to thumb through the yellow pages and find physicians advertising "bloodletting" or credit services touting "loan-sharking." Yet look under "Tree" and you'll find more companies offering "topping" than you can shake a severed branch at.

Topping is about the worst thing you can do to a large shade tree. What it means is using a chain saw to cut the tops out of trunks and main branches, leaving large, ugly stubs. Not only does it permanently ruin the appearance of the tree, but it shortens its life and makes it prone to damage from insects, heart rot (see page 231), and storm damage.

Why do people top trees? Mainly because they don't know any better and a fellow with a chain saw in the back of his pickup truck persuades them it's the right thing to do. The reason most often given is keeping large branches from falling on the house. Problem is, topping eventually makes branches more likely to fall. And if the tree rots because of topping, the whole tree could come down.

Symptoms: The main trunk and major branches are cut back severely, leaving thick stubs. These stubs frequently die back and rot. Rot may spread to the heartwood of the tree. A thick broom of long, whiplike branches sprouts near the end of each stub. Their joints are quite weak, so they easily break and fall during storms.

Prevention and control: Never top your shade trees. If someone asks to do it, show him the door. Should your trees need pruning, consult a professional arborist. The good ones belong to the Society of Consulting Arborists or the International Society of Arboriculture. Make sure anyone who does tree work on your property is licensed and insured. Ask how large, unwanted branches can be safely removed without disfiguring the tree or damaging its health.

CAN YOU TOP THIS? *Local power companies periodically top trees to keep branches away from power lines. But keeping the lights on doesn't have to mean mangling your trees. Ask the power company if you can be on hand when it trims your trees. You'll probably reach a compromise on the trimming that will leave both you and them smiling.*

TRANSPLANT SHOCK

CULTURAL

ZONES: ALL

Even with careful handling and good all-around conditions, transplanted plants may lose leaves, flowers, or buds after being moved. Damage to the plant's hairlike water-absorbing rootlets decreases the amount of water taken in by the plant. The plant wilts due to water stress, even though the ground around it is wet. In hot, dry weather, the plant suffers even more.

Symptoms: Transplanted seedlings or mature plants die or fail to thrive. Flower buds drop off before opening, and older flowers also fall. Double-flowered plant species may produce only single flowers. Leaves yellow and droop and may drop. The plant wilts during daylight hours, even though the soil seems adequately watered.

Prevention: Lack of water and damage to roots are the major causes of transplant shock. Plant as quickly as possible after purchasing plants or digging them up. The best time to transplant is when plants are dormant. Transplant on cooler or cloudy days, in the early morning or late afternoon. Dig holes at least twice as wide as the full root system; amend the soil according to local recommendations. Be as gentle as possible when digging up plants or taking them out of their containers. Try not to disturb the soil around the roots. If root disturbance occurs, and plants are older or very large, prune the foliage by one-third to decrease the amount of water needed to survive. Water immediately after transplanting, making certain that roots are fully wetted, and continue to water diligently, not allowing soil to dry. Protect newly installed plants from cold, heat, or drying. In hot weather, shade transplants with white shade cloth or floating ground covers for a week. Lightly wet foliage in late morning to early afternoon to minimize heat and moisture stress. Instead of transplanting annual or vegetable seedlings from cell packs, sow them where they are to grow. Or purchase or grow plants in individual peat pots that go directly into the ground without disturbing the root system.

Control: Plants suffering from transplant shock often recover if their root zones get adequate water, with no dry periods, and if they're temporarily protected from drying winds and too much sun.

VERTICILLIUM WILT

FUNGUS

✔ ZONES: ALL

More than 200 plants are infected by the fungi *Verticillium dahliae* and *V. albo-atrum*. Plants may contract verticillium wilt through infected seed, plant debris on the soil, or direct contact. Fungi multiply in plants during cool, moist seasons but become obvious in warm, dry weather when plants are stressed. Verticillium wilt damages plants by clogging their water-conducting tissues. It is more common on herbaceous plants but does affect young trees early in the bearing season. Overfertilization with nitrogen may favor this disease. Infested soil can harbor the fungi for many years, and in some instances they may be impossible to eradicate. Weeds harbor these fungi.

WIN AGAINST WILT. *Resistant trees include beech, birch, dogwood, oak, sweet gum, sycamore, and conifers. In seed catalogs, look for the letter V, which indicates verticillium-resistant selections. Plant resistant tomato selections like 'Beefmaster', 'Better Boy', 'Celebrity', 'Early Girl', 'Heatwave', 'Lemon Boy', and 'Roma'.*

Target: Tomato, strawberry, and brambles; dahlia; trees including catalpa, redbud, and maple, particularly Norway and silver maples; roses

Symptoms: Tree branches may die. Fruit and flowers may be stunted or may not appear. The plant may survive for weeks to years with the infection. On roses, leaves turn yellow. If only a few canes are affected, they may die back. On many herbaceous plants, the wilting starts with lower leaves and progresses up the stem. Tissue between leaf veins turns yellow, then brown, giving leaves a mottled appearance. Severely infected plants may be stunted.

Prevention: Plant resistant selections (see above). Control weeds. Avoid excessive watering, severe pruning, or other measures that promote heavy leaf growth. In areas where verticillium wilt is present, grow susceptible crops in containers with pasteurized soil. Use nitrogen fertilizer at minimal rates, sufficient only to provide normal growth. Practice crop rotation or solarize soil (see pages 30 and 31).

Control: Prune out dead branches to improve tree appearance.

VIRUSES

DISEASES

✔ ZONES: ALL

Viruses don't just sicken your kids the day before a family vacation. They attack plants too. Some viruses attack one particular plant, while others attack a wide range. Some unfortunate plants fall victim to multiple viruses, and symptoms may overlap. Symptoms may also vary according to the time of year the virus is contracted.

Mosaic virus diseases of chrysanthemum, bean, cucumber, and rose, as well as camellia yellow mottle-leaf virus, may spread by insects, contaminated seed, or infected plants and plant debris. Contaminated clothing, hands, and tools may also spread them. Tobacco mosaic virus (TMV) may enter the garden aboard cigarettes and other tobacco products. Tulip virus is spread by aphids and diseased bulbs. Viruses seldom kill plants directly. However, virus-stressed plants have a hard time fending off insects, other diseases, drought, and temperature extremes. Even when they survive, they suffer poor growth, decreased yields, and malformed parts.

Target: Cucumber, tomato, pepper, bean, camellia, chrysanthemum, gladiolus, rose, tulip, lily, and other plants

Symptoms: Cucumber mosaic virus (CMV) causes stunted, curled, and crinkled leaves that are mottled yellow and green. Fruit develops wartlike bumps with whitish green areas between the bumps. Sometimes the skin is white and smooth, a condition known as "white pickle." Fruit is misshapen and bitter, and yields are diminished.

TMV attacks tomatoes and peppers. In general, tomato leaves become long and stringy. They usually show a subtle light- and dark-green mottling. Young plants are stunted and fruit quality and yield suffer. However, if plants begin fruiting before they're infected with the virus, fruit may develop normally. Infected pepper plants develop mottling, crinkling, or yellow-green spots on younger leaves that later drop. Fruit may appear normal or become yellow and wrinkled.

Two mosaic viruses attack beans, causing leaves to pucker and become mottled yellow and green. The plant becomes stunted, yields are reduced, and seeds inside the pods are small and shriveled.

Rose mosaic virus, shown on the opposite page, causes leaves to develop a yellow zigzag pattern, ringspots, and mottling. New leaves

may be distorted. Sometimes only a few leaves show symptoms, although the entire plant is infected. Flowering may be normal.

Camellia yellow mottle-leaf virus, shown on opposite page, appears as irregular or round, yellow or white specks, spots, and large blotches on leaves. Leaves are smaller than normal. Colored flowers often display white specks or spots. White flowers do not.

Plants suffering from chrysanthemum mosaic virus have mottled leaves that are smaller than normal. Leaf veins turn pale yellow. Flowers are small and may have brown streaks. Plant parts are malformed.

Flowers of virus-infected tulips are irregularly streaked, spotted, or mottled. The leaves may also be streaked or mottled with light green or white. Plants are stunted and flowering is poor.

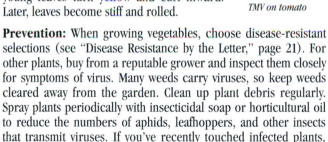

TMV on tomato

Curly top virus is spread by the beet leafhopper. Symptoms vary, but in general, young leaves turn yellow and curl inward. Later, leaves become stiff and rolled.

Prevention: When growing vegetables, choose disease-resistant selections (see "Disease Resistance by the Letter," page 21). For other plants, buy from a reputable grower and inspect them closely for symptoms of virus. Many weeds carry viruses, so keep weeds cleared away from the garden. Clean up plant debris regularly. Spray plants periodically with insecticidal soap or horticultural oil to reduce the numbers of aphids, leafhoppers, and other insects that transmit viruses. If you've recently touched infected plants, wash your hands thoroughly before handling other plants.

Control: No chemical control exists. Immediately remove and destroy infected plants.

SICK CHIC. *Think no nursery would sell you a virus-ridden plant? Think again. One of the South's most popular (and overused) shrubs, a dwarf nandina called 'Nana Purpurea', owes its mottled yellow-green and purple-red puckered leaves to a virus. Sure wish they'd find a cure.*

WATERING, EXCESSIVE

CULTURAL

ZONES: ALL

Overwatering is an easy way to kill plants with kindness. Heavy and poorly drained soils are particularly susceptible to getting waterlogged. Roots growing in waterlogged soil may die because they cannot absorb the oxygen they need to function normally. The longer the air is cut off, the greater the root damage. The dying roots decay and cannot supply the plant with nutrients and water.

Damage caused by overwatering is frequently misdiagnosed as pest damage. However, pest damage rarely causes roots to concentrate near the surface of the soil. Damage could also be caused by a downspout located too near a plant (shown above).

Symptoms: Plants are stunted, slow growing, weak, and they may die. Leaves are greenish yellow; fruit cracks. Roots concentrate just under or just above the soil surface, where soils dry out faster and oxygen is more available. Plants suffer from leaf burn or leaf scorch (see page 236). Edema causes water-soaked spots or pale green blisters form on stems and leaves. Root rot diseases appear.

Prevention: Water to meet plant needs, and be careful not to overwater. Adding large amounts of well-composted organic matter, expanded slate (PermaTill), and coarse sand to heavy soil will help loosen it, allowing more air and water to enter. Where soggy soil cannot be prevented, use bog or other plants that are tolerant of wet soil, create raised beds, or install French drains.

Control: Allow soil, especially clay soil, to dry partially between waterings, so air can get into it. If soil drains poorly, take steps to improve its drainage.

WATERING, INADEQUATE

CULTURAL

ZONES: ALL

Plants suffer more from lack of water than from any other problem. Water is stored in plant cells, which are kept plump from pressure exerted by the water. As water evaporates from the cells—faster in warm weather—it needs to be replaced. If watering or rainfall isn't sufficient, the entire plant's metabolism is disturbed. This can in turn encourage insects and disease and prevent uniform maturation of fruits.

A soggy ground surface does not necessarily mean you've applied sufficient water. The water may have run off, rather than getting down to the roots. In clay and compacted soils, water penetrates very slowly. It quickly penetrates sandy soil, but doesn't remain there long.

Symptoms: With mild water deficiency, plants grow slowly and look stunted. Under long-term stress, plants permanently wilt or stop growing, and may die. Bare spots appear in ground covers. Water-stressed plantings fall victim to weeds, insect pests, and diseases.

Prevention: Add lots of organic matter to the soil to improve its moisture retention. Till heavy soil to reduce compaction. Use mulches to slow evaporation. If the water-retaining layer of soil is shallow (perhaps above a layer of hardpan—see page 231) and cannot be deepened, water more frequently or use shallow-rooted plants, such as annuals. Most vegetables, fruit trees, lawns, and ornamentals need about 1 in. of water per week. Water whenever the top 2 in. of soil feel just barely moist. Keep sprinkler heads in good repair so they do not become clogged and leave some spots dry. Drip irrigation systems are very useful with sandy soils. During hot, dry weather and in low-rainfall areas, such as Central and West Texas and western Oklahoma, thoroughly wet soil every 5 to 7 days.

Control: When you water, water deeply. Badly damaged plants may not survive; however, try letting them recuperate before giving up on them. If water from sprinklers tends to puddle or run off, turn them off for an hour or so and reapply.

WHITE MOLD

FUNGUS

ZONES: ALL

White mold, also called sclerotinia rot and watery soft rot, results from infection by the fungus *Sclerotinia sclerotiorum*. It overwinters as small black structures (sclerotia) attached to decomposing infected plant parts. It may also survive several years in soil. In early spring or fall, the sclerotia produce small, cup-shaped fruiting structures, resembling tiny mushrooms, which release spores into the air. The sclerotia also produce vegetative strands that can infect many plants. Moist, cool conditions favor infection. White and gray mold (*Botrytis cinerea*) can occur simultaneously.

Target: Bean, carrot, lettuce, strawberry, sunflower, tomato, marigold, zinnia, and many other plants

Symptoms: On snap beans, most infections occur near the ground as a result of fallen, infected blossoms. If fungi invade the main stem, most leaves will yellow and wilt. On the types of beans that are often dried, such as pinto beans and red kidney beans, rapid wilting and plant death may occur if fungi invade stems near the soil line. Lesions on dry infected stems and vines are beige to white; stem surfaces may be papery. On carrots, the disease is sometimes called cottony soft rot for the cottony white growth on the surface of soft lesions on the carrot root. On tomatoes, affected stems may turn a tan color. They are also covered with a white cottony fungus growth dotted with hard black fungal sclerotia. In general, water-soaked lesions appear on plant stems, leaves, and pods. You may also see a fluffy white fungus embedded with hard black fungal sclerotia.

Prevention: Choose plant selections that do not produce excessive foliage near ground level. Do not grow any very susceptible hosts, such as lettuce, in the same place every year; rotate them with plants—such as onion—that are not susceptible. Position plants so that air circulates between rows. Do not overwater.

Control: Control isn't possible once the infection is moderate to severe. No fungicide for white mold is currently available for home use. Since sclerotia remain near the soil surface, solarization may reduce their numbers (see page 31).

WIND DAMAGE

CULTURAL/ENVIRONMENTAL

ZONES: ALL

Wind causes leaves to lose moisture more rapidly than a plant's root system can replace it. Wind causes the most damage when it is very hot or very cold. Dry or frozen soil aggravates the problem because the soil does not provide replacement water. Branches damaged by injury, disease, or insects may be brought down by even moderate winds. Wind may also dash sand against plant parts, damaging them. Young or newly transplanted plants with limited root systems are quite susceptible to wind damage. High winds during storms can bring down large trees.

Symptoms: Leaves or entire plants wilt. Leaf scorch from winds may make young and exposed leaves brown and dry, especially around the leaf margins and near the tips. Trees and shrubs constantly exposed to prevailing winds on the beach or prairie become one-sided and windblown. Leaning trees, or those pushed by the wind, can pull loose and fall over with part or all of the roots attached. Trees with heart rot or hollow trunks may break and fall.

Prevention: Plant trees adapted to your climate, particularly those like oaks that have strong rather than brittle wood. Select native plants; they are often well adapted to local conditions. Use hedges, tall evergreens, or fencing as windbreaks. Water and fertilize regularly to maintain plant health. Mulch after plants are dormant to reduce the depth of frost penetration into the soil. Deep-water trees to encourage deep rooting. Remove hollow, rotten, or leaning trees. In areas with high winds, thin out or prune back some branches to reduce the tree's resistance to wind load. Isolated trees are more prone to wind damage than those in groups.

Control: Tip and margin browning caused by wind damage cannot be corrected. Pick off damaged leaves if they are unsightly, and water plants deeply. Plants may recover when the wind diminishes.

WITCHES'-BROOM

VARIOUS CAUSES

ZONES: ALL

The numerous causes of witches'-broom include bacteria, viruses, phytoplasmas, mistletoe, dodder, chemical damage, and insect attack; shown above is witches'-broom caused by the honeysuckle aphid. On potato, the cause is a phytoplasma transmitted by several leafhopper species and by potato seed pieces. On hackberry, the cause is believed to be a powdery mildew combined with a mite. On oleander, the culprit is a fungus. Although witches'-broom is unsightly and weakens the affected branches, it may not seriously damage the entire plant. However, it may be accompanied by a disease or an insect that can cause considerable harm.

Target: Ornamentals, such as rose, elm, oleander, lilac, and rhododendron; vegetables, such as potato; and trees, including cherry and hackberry

Symptoms: On oleander, multiple small shoots sprout just below branch tips, then turn brown and die. On hackberry, broomlike clusters of twigs become noticeable in the tree after the leaves fall. Affected branches break easily in storms. On potatoes, stunted plants have multiple and highly branched stems; leaves, which have yellow margins, roll up. Tubers are plentiful but quite small. In general, shoots on the broom quickly die and turn brown. Branches are weak and easily damaged.

Prevention: Prevention depends on the causative agent, which may be difficult for the home gardener to identify. Consult your Cooperative Extension Office for help in diagnosing the problem.

Control: If practical, prune out infected branches at least 12 in. below the brooming. There is no general chemical control.

Weeds and Other
PESKY PLANTS

For centuries, weeds—the gardener's bane—have turned otherwise peaceful gardens into horticultural war zones. But hope is at hand. In this chapter, you'll find the advice you need to prevent and even dispatch these plant pests.

"A weed," said the late J. C. Raulston of North Carolina State University, "is a plant dealing with an unhappy person." There are plenty of reasons a weed could make the average gardener unhappy. Perhaps the weed robs desirable plants of water, nutrients, and sunlight, as purslane and sow thistles do in the vegetable garden. Or maybe it's poisonous, like deadly nightshade, or causes allergic reactions, such as poison ivy and ragweeds.

My crabgrass is out to get me and my chickweed and I are engaged in a mutual vendetta.

—Allen Lacy,
Home Ground

Some rampant weeds, such as Chinese wisteria, can strangle trees or tear gutters from houses. Others merely detract from the beauty of the landscape—for example, violets invading a lawn or Chinese privet blotting out the woods.

But weeds have their good points, too. Many are edible. Crabgrass, an introduced weed, was planted by settlers who used its seed as a grain. Dandelion, another foreign import, has leaves you can eat and flowers good for making wine. All parts of kudzu are edible—its leaves, flowers, and huge tubers.

When you get right down to it, weeds are simply opportunists. They set up shop whenever less adaptable plants vacate the premises because of clearing, compacted soil, close mowing, or poor drainage. Reproducing by windborne seeds, slithering rhizomes, splitting bulbs, and rooting stems, weeds seem to spread in the blink of an eye.

Knowing the reproductive strategies of weeds suggests ways you can stop them before they gain a foothold. For example, do not disturb the soil unnecessarily. Mulch bare soil immediately or plant a blanketing ground cover. Cut your lawn at its highest recommended height (see pages 35 and 234) to shade the soil surface and keep weed seeds from germinating. And be careful not to inadvertently admit weed seeds into your garden through contaminated topsoil, compost, nursery plants, or hay bales.

To get a leg up on weeds, you have to know what kind you have. This is especially true if you're using herbicides. A chemical that controls grassy weeds may not work on broadleafed weeds. And a product that dispatches annual weeds may show little effect on perennials.

Thus, correct identification of the target weed is essential. The following chapter describes and shows 95 of the South's most common weeds. It gives advice on how to prevent minor problems from becoming major ones, as well as how to control serious infestations. But if you can't find a particular weed in these pages, take a sample to your local cooperative extension service for identification.

WHACKING THOSE WEEDS

In most cases, physical control takes care of a weed problem over time. Hand-weeding or hoeing is the first line of defense, particularly against annual or biennial weeds, such as henbit or lamb's quarter. By persistently removing these plants before they set seed, you can greatly reduce their numbers in your garden. Unfortunately, anytime you dig in your garden,

There is no escaping weeds, such as poison ivy (upper right) and violets (lower left). A dandelion's long taproot (lower right) makes it hard to pull. But tilling the vegetable garden (upper left) turns many weeds under and enriches the soil.

you're also going to bring weed seeds to the surface. Your next task, therefore, is to keep them from sprouting. One way to do this is by thoroughly mulching bare soil. You can also kill many weed seeds by solarizing the soil (see page 31).

Perennial weeds are harder to physically control than annual weeds because they develop persistent root systems, rhizomes, bulbs, and tubers. Pulling them usually leaves some of these reproductive structures in the ground, which allows the original plants to regenerate quickly. Dig these weeds instead, removing as much of the root system as possible. You may have to repeat this several times for it to be effective.

You can also kill perennial weeds by repeatedly mowing or cutting the tops. This works better on tall, single-stemmed weeds, such as milkweeds and blackberry, than on short weeds with tufts of foliage, such as violets and dandelions.

Or you can try smothering perennial weeds. After removing the top growth, lay down a thick mulch of cardboard, newspaper (at least three dozen sheets thick), or black plastic. Overlap these materials so that weeds can't grow through the cracks. Top off this mulch with a layer of pine straw or shredded bark. Leave the mulch in place for at least one full growing season.

PESTICIDES: HANDLE WITH CARE

Care should be taken whenever you use pesticides, particularly near edible crops. Be sure to read the labels on any product you bring into your garden and use it only as its label directs—it's against the law to do otherwise. Pesticide registrations change rapidly, so some products mentioned in this book may be removed from the lists of approved products or their label directions may be changed over time as additional research becomes available. If you have questions concerning current regulations, consult your local nursery or Cooperative Extension Office.

TYPES OF HERBICIDES

Herbicides are classified according to what types of weeds they kill and the particular point in the target plant's life cycle at which you apply them.

Pre-emergence herbicides, such as benefin (Balan), trifluralin (Treflan, Preen), trifluralin and benefin (Team), and pendimethalin (Halts), inhibit the germination of seeds and the growth of seedlings.

Postemergence herbicides kill growing plants. They're divided into two groups: contact herbicides and translocated herbicides. *Contact herbicides,* such as herbicidal soap (Superfast, Scythe), and diquat dibromide kill only the plant parts that you spray; perennial weeds may grow back from the roots. *Translocated herbicides,* including glyphosate (Roundup), fluazifop-P-butyl (Fusilade, Grass-B-Gon), and triclopyr (Brush-B-Gon, Brush Killer), are absorbed by various parts of the plant and carried down to the roots. They're the ones to use on perennial weeds, though they'll kill annuals too.

Use caution when applying any herbicide. Follow label directions to the letter. Using herbicides in a reckless manner could end up killing a lot more than your weeds.

You'll find chemical controls listed for most of the weeds in this chapter. For more information about these herbicides, turn to Chapter 3, "A Pound of Cure."

COMPOST WEEDS— YES OR NO?

You can safely compost annual and perennial weeds, as long as they don't have flowers or seeds. You can also compost the top growth of perennial weeds that haven't flowered. However, toss roots of perennials and any weeds with flowers or seed heads into the trash. Even a very hot compost pile may not kill all the seeds. Using the resulting compost may infest your garden.

TYPES OF SPREADING STEMS

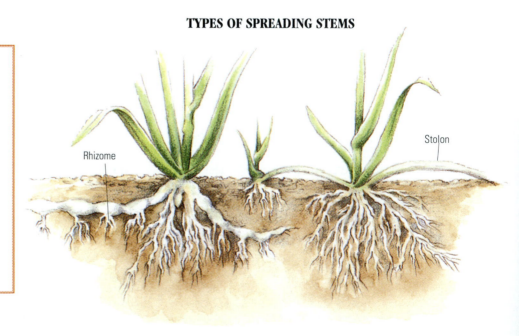

Rhizome

Stolon

ALGAE

SEVERAL FAMILIES AND SPECIES

MICROSCOPIC ORGANISMS

⚡ ZONES: ALL

Algae are tiny organisms lacking roots, stems, or leaves. They grow in ponds and in overly wet, shaded lawns and other damp spots in the garden. In ponds, algae turn the water an unattractive pea green, especially in newly filled ponds and in early spring as the water warms. On land, algae show up as slimy or scummy areas ranging in color from green to black.

Life cycle: These primitive organisms reproduce by cell division, fragmentation, or spores.

Prevention: In ponds, the key to reducing growth of algae is maintaining an ecological balance. Algae thrive where ample sunlight coincides with high levels of dissolved nutrients in the water. Reduce the nutrients by preventing runoff from fertilized areas of the garden. You can also give fish less food; in a balanced pond, fish often survive on insects and plants with little or no additional food. Adding submerged or oxygenating plants—such as anacharis, cabomba, and eelgrass—is also helpful: they compete with algae for dissolved nutrients. Aeration by means of a waterfall, a fountain, or even a trickling hose adds needed oxygen, as do mechanical or biological filters.

Control: To control algae on soil, loosen the soil to reduce compaction, improve drainage, reduce watering, and prune nearby vegetation so more sunlight reaches the ground. Spray with wettable sulfur in early spring and again a month later. To remove algae from walls, benches, and other surfaces, scrub with a mixture of ½ cup bleach to 1 gal. of water. Rinse thoroughly. Or use a herbicidal soap, such as Scythe.

ANNUAL BLUEGRASS

POA ANNUA (POACEAE)

ANNUAL GRASS

⚡ ZONES: ALL

Annual bluegrass germinates and grows during the cool weather of fall, winter, and early spring, forming a bright green tuft of softly textured, 1–2-in. leaves with curved, prowlike tips. Pyramidal clusters of small whitish flowers appear throughout the growing season, giving a white haze to infested lawns. With the arrival of hot, dry weather the clumps die, leaving unsightly brown patches in lawns. Annual bluegrass also grows in vegetable beds, in flower and shrub borders, between paving stones, and in orchards.

Life cycle: Germinates in fall, flowers and sets seeds in late winter and spring, then dies when weather turns hot.

Prevention: Maintain a thick lawn by improving drainage, aerating every spring, mowing at the correct height, watering regularly, and fertilizing appropriately.

Control: If chemical control is necessary, in late summer apply a pre-emergence herbicide containing dithiopyr (Dimension), pendimethalin (Halts), or benefin (Balan). Check the label to be sure the product is safe for your type of grass. Carefully spot-treat clumps of annual bluegrass in lawns or the garden with a product containing glyphosate (Roundup) or fluazifop-P-butyl (Fusilade, Grass-B-Gon). Take care not to get any of these chemicals on desired plants.

BLUEGRASS NOTES. *Kentucky bluegrass (Poa pratensis), one of the most widely planted cool-season lawn grasses, is a perennial relative of annual bluegrass. Its leaves also have the characteristic tip shaped like a boat prow or canoe. Rough-stalked bluegrass (P. trivialis), another perennial relative, is very tolerant of shade and damp soil. This species is sometimes included in seed mixtures for planting in such conditions, although it can become weedy.*

BAMBOOS

PHYLLOSTACHYS, PLEIOBLASTUS, SASA, AND OTHER GENERA
(POACEAE)

GIANT GRASSES

ZONES: ALL

While bamboos can be dramatic and useful plants in the land-scape, some species spread rapidly and invade other plantings or creep unbidden under a fence from a neighboring garden. All bamboos have woody stems (culms) divided into sections or internodes by joints (nodes). Leafy branches grow from buds in the upper nodes. Bamboos spread by underground stems (rhizomes) that give rise to new vertical shoots. The rhizomes of running bamboos (those listed above and others) can grow varying distances from the parent plant before sending up shoots. These bamboos form large groves and can be difficult to manage. Clumping bamboos (*Bambusa* and other genera) are the safest bet for most home gardens, as their rhizomes will extend only a short distance from the main clump.

Life cycle: Perennials that reproduce by rhizomes; the canes usually live for several years.

Control: Cut off all shoots at ground level, and repeat as they sprout again, cutting the new shoots before they reach 2 ft. This eventually starves the roots, but it takes patience and time. You can also dig out the entire clump. Cut back the stems to make it easier to get at the roots. Using a mattock and spade, remove all of the rhizomes. Generally, the rhizomes do not grow deeply in the soil, but they may be widespread. Any left behind will resprout.

To combine physical and chemical controls, cut the stems almost to the ground. Then with an ax, chop vertical gashes in the stumps. Immediately spray or paint glyphosate (Roundup) on the cut stumps. This method requires less of the chemical than spraying the entire plant. You are also less likely to accidentally damage nearby desired plants. Expect to repeat this treatment.

BAMBOO BARRIER. *To contain running bamboo, install a barrier around the root, 1½ ft. into the soil. Poured concrete edging or strips of galvanized metal are effective. You can also plant running bamboo in large containers, such as bottomless oil drums or flue tiles, sunk into the ground.*

BARLEY, WILD

HORDEUM MURINUM LEPORINUM (POACEAE)

ANNUAL GRASS

ZONES: ALL

Also known as hare barley, common foxtail, and farmer's foxtail, this grass flourishes in vegetable and flower gardens, lawns, and orchards and along roadsides. A winter annual, its seeds germinate from November to March; the plant matures in late spring or summer. The seedling's hairy foliage gives it a velvety look, but older leaves are smooth and dull green. As it matures, wild barley forms a branching plant 6–36 in. tall. The stems at the lower nodes (joints) often bend downward, and the plant takes on a prostrate form in mowed lawns. The leaf blades are ⅛–⅓ in. wide and 2½–6 in. long. At the base of each leaf blade, a well-developed auricle (an ear-shaped lobe or appendage) clasps the stem. Foxtail-shaped flowering spikes, 2–3 in. long and often tinged red, may be partially covered by the uppermost leaf sheath. The spikelets (flower groups) are 1½–3 in. long and tipped with stiff bristles. These long, sharp bristles, which can injure animals, are a distinctive feature of wild barley.

Life cycle: Annual that reproduces by seed

Prevention: Pull or hoe wild barley when the plants are young. You need to remove it before it sets seed to avoid future infestations. A mulch kept in place throughout the year will prevent seeds of wild barley already in the soil from germinating. Soil solarizing (see page 31) during the heat of summer will kill seeds.

Control: Nonselective herbicides containing glufosinate-ammonium (Finale) or glyphosate (Roundup) or herbicidal soap (Superfast, Scythe) eliminate young plants. Take care not to get these chemicals on desired plants.

BARNYARD GRASS

ECHINOCHLOA CRUS-GALLI (POACEAE)

ANNUAL GRASS

ZONES: ALL

Barnyard grass, also called Japanese millet, jungle rice, cockspur grass, and watergrass, is a vigorous warm-season annual. In mowed lawns it grows only a few inches tall, but in the garden it can reach 4–5 ft. The seedling plant has a flattened, reddish stem and gray-green leaves. The coarse, upright stems of the mature plant retain the reddish tint at the base. The light green leaf blades are about ½ in. wide and lack the membrane (auricle) and the fringe of hairs (ligule) that many other grasses have at the junction of the leaf blade and the stem. Erect or drooping flower heads, 2½–4 in. long, are usually reddish to dark purple with bristle-like projections (awns). Seed heads, which may also have a purplish cast, are crowded with relatively large seeds.

Leaf bases of barnyard grass

Life cycle: Annual that germinates in spring, sets seed and dies in fall.

Prevention: In vegetable and flower gardens, hoe or hand-pull barnyard grass while the plants are small; as they mature they develop an extensive, fibrous root system that is difficult to remove. And because a single plant of barnyard grass can produce as many as a million seeds, it is essential to remove this weed before it sets seed. A thick mulch prevents germination of the seeds; solarization (see page 31) effectively kills them. In lawns, improve conditions so the grass is thick enough to resist weed infestations.

Apply a pre-emergence herbicide containing benefin (Balan), dithiopyr (Dimension), or pendimethalin (Halts) to prevent germination of barnyard grass in the lawn. Check to be sure the particular herbicide is safe for your type of grass. Use trifluralin (Treflan, Preen) or trifluralin and benefin (Team) around ornamentals.

Control: For postemergent control, use a selective herbicide containing fluazifop-P-butyl, such as Fusilade or Grass-B-Gon. Or spot-treat with herbicidal soap (Superfast, Scythe), diquat dibromide, or glyphosate (Roundup). Avoid spraying desired plants.

BEDSTRAW

GALIUM TINCTORIUM (RUBIACEAE)

BROAD-LEAFED, HERBACEOUS PERENNIAL

ZONES: ALL

At home in swamps, marshes, ditches, and other wet places, bedstraw also resides in moist, poorly drained areas of the lawn and garden. If unmowed, its flimsy stems reach 6–24 in. long, often flopping to the ground. Downward-pointing prickles along its four-sided stems allow it to clamber easily over grass and other plants. Whorls of four to six straplike leaves, each about ½ in. long, occur at each node along the stem.

Life cycle: From early spring to early summer, bedstraw bears clusters of two to three, small, white flowers. Perched on short stalks on the ends of branches, the flowers give rise to smooth, black fruits that look like tiny eggs stuck together. The fruits, containing seed, separate when they mature. Seeds sprout in spring and summer.

Prevention: Keep the lawn thick and vigorous with proper watering and fertilization. Mow the lawn at its tallest recommended height (see "Lawn Scalping," page 234). Aerate to improve drainage and reduce compaction (see "The Air Down There," page 35). Mulch garden beds to keep weed seeds from germinating.

Control: Bedstraw is an easy weed to pull, if you don't have too much of it. Regular hoeing or mowing will prevent it from flowering and reseeding. It will also exhaust the plant's food reserves and prevent it from resprouting. Treat infested lawns with a selective, liquid or granular postemergence herbicide labeled for your type of grass. In garden beds, spot-treat with a herbicide containing glyphosate (Roundup); 2,4-D, MCPP, and dicamba (Weed-B-Gon, Weed-Stop); glufosinate-ammonium (Finale); or with herbicidal soap (Superfast, Scythe). Be sure to follow label directions carefully and avoid spraying desired plants.

BEGGAR-TICKS

BIDENS, VARIOUS SPECIES (COMPOSITAE)

BROAD-LEAFED, HERBACEOUS ANNUALS

ZONES: ALL

How do you distribute seeds far and wide when they're too heavy to blow through the air? That's easy—equip them with barbs, so they hitchhike to new locations on the fur of animals or the clothing of people passing by.

Beggar-ticks grow 1–5 ft. tall. They frequently inhabit roadsides, fields, and pastures. Although they prefer moist to wet soils, they tolerate dry soils as well.

Several species make the South their home. *Bidens bipinnata,* also called Spanish needles, is quite showy in bloom. Large, bright yellow, daisylike blooms adorn finely dissected foliage in late summer and fall. But its major faults as a garden plant are that its seeds stick to you and your pets, and it reseeds with abandon. *Bidens frondosa,* devil's beggar-ticks, is a weed, pure and simple. Its leaves consist of three lance-shaped leaflets with toothed margins. Drab, orange-yellow blooms, sometimes with petals absent, don't exactly inspire poetry. The flowers give way to devilishly constructed, ¼–½-in.-long dark brown to black seeds. Each is armed with two barbed spines that snag just about anything passing by.

Life cycle: Annual, nonwoody weed that reproduces by seed dropped during summer and fall. Seeds germinate from midspring through late summer.

Prevention: To keep from bringing beggar-ticks home, avoid brushing seed-bearing plants while walking through fields. Mulch garden beds to keep seeds from sprouting.

Control: Pull or dig new seedlings in spring. Hoe, cut, or mow them to prevent flowering and seed production. In lawns, spot-treat with a selective, postemergence herbicide labeled for your type of grass. In garden beds, spot-treat with glyphosate (Roundup), glufosinate-ammonium (Finale), diquat dibromide, or herbicidal soap (Superfast, Scythe). Be sure to follow label directions carefully.

BERMUDA GRASS

CYNODON DACTYLON (POACEAE)

PERENNIAL GRASS

ZONES: ALL

Also called devil grass or wire grass, Bermuda grass is a popular lawn grass. However, it can also be a troublesome weed in other kinds of lawns and in beds of flowers, shrubs, and vegetables. Bermuda grass spreads by underground stems (rhizomes), aboveground runners (stolons), and seed. Many possibilities for regeneration make it an aggressive competitor with other plants. Both the rhizomes and the stolons root at the nodes, forming new plants that spread to make a dense mat of wiry stems and short, 1–4-in. bluish green leaves. A fringe of white hairs is visible where the leaf blade joins the stem. The flower head of Bermuda grass is composed of three to seven slender, 1–2-in.-long spikes radiating from a single point at the tip of the stem. (In contrast, the flower spikes of crabgrass can arise from several points on the stem, and they are attached to the main stem by a short stalk.) Seeds form throughout the summer and germinate readily in warm soil. Pollens can cause allergic reactions in some people.

Life cycle: Perennial that reproduces by stolons, rhizomes, and seed

Prevention: If you have a Bermuda grass lawn, prevent its spread into other parts of the garden with a deep barrier or edging. Dig up stray clumps before they form sod, taking care to remove all of the underground stem, as it can generate new shoots. Repeated pulling and digging are generally necessary. To avoid spreading this grass, take care not to transport soil containing roots or rhizomes to other parts of your garden. Mulches in beds will slow growth, but eventually Bermuda grass grows through most of them. Solarization (see page 31), if carried out during the hottest part of summer, over a period of at least 6 weeks, kills the seed of Bermuda grass and rhizomes that are not too deeply buried.

Control: Use a selective herbicide containing fluazifop-P-butyl (Fusilade, Grass-B-Gon), or spot-treat with glyphosate (Roundup) according to label directions. Take care not to get these chemicals on desired plants. Applying atrazine (Purge, Bonus S) to St. Augustine, centipede grass, carpet grass, and zoysia lawns will remove unwanted Bermuda grass.

BINDWEED, FIELD

CONVOLVULUS ARVENSIS (CONVOLVULACEAE)

VINING BROAD-LEAFED PERENNIAL

ZONES: US, MS, LS, CS

Field bindweed is a persistent pest in vegetable and ornamental gardens. This weed's many common names—including wild morning glory, cornbind, creeping Charlie, creeping Jenny, and greenvine—attest to its troublesome nature. The 1–4-ft.-long vining stems of field bindweed crawl over the ground and twine over and around any plants they encounter. The extensive root system can penetrate 10 ft. into the soil, producing many underground stems or rhizomes that give rise to new plants. New plants also grow from seeds. The seedling leaves are large and rounded, with a notch on the end. The first true leaves are spade shaped. As the plant matures, the leaves usually become arrow shaped, although they vary in size and shape depending on soil fertility and moisture. Flowers are white or pink funnels that open in the morning and close in the afternoon.

Life cycle: Perennial that reproduces by rhizomes and seed

Prevention: Field bindweed is difficult to manage. If pulled, the stems break off, and regrowth occurs from the roots and rhizomes. The seeds can sprout even after lying dormant in the soil for 50 years. Therefore, remove young plants as soon as you see them, before they have a chance to form a root system or to bloom and set seed. Repeatedly digging out the roots can eventually control bindweed, but you must be persistent. A herbicide containing trifluralin (Treflan, Preen) may provide pre-emergent control around many ornamentals.

Control: For postemergent control in lawns, use a herbicide containing 2,4-D and dicamba. Follow label directions carefully. Spot-treat bindweed in ornamental plantings with a product containing glyphosate (Roundup). These chemicals are most effective when the weed has a few flowers but has neither reached full bloom nor set seed. Repeated treatments are usually needed to destroy the entire root system. If bindweed is twined around desirable plants, detach it before treating with herbicide.

BLACKBERRY

RUBUS, VARIOUS SPECIES (ROSACEAE)

ARCHED BRAMBLES

ZONES: US, MS, LS, CS

Every summer, Southerners with pails in hand take to the woods during blackberry-picking time. However, in your yard, blackberries can quickly form a dense thicket if not checked, like those above smothering a patch of daisies. The greenish or reddish stems have five angles and are studded with sharp thorns. Mature leaves are compound, with three or five leaflets that have toothed edges. Five-petaled white flowers appear in large terminal clusters in spring, followed by tasty, shiny black fruits in midsummer. The rhizomes (underground stems) spread rapidly, sending up shoots to form new plants. Birds enjoy the berries and scatter the seeds, sowing blackberries in pastures, along roads, and in gardens, where they turn up in lawns, paths, flower beds, shrub borders, and ground covers.

Life cycle: Plants are perennial; canes sprout and grow the first year, flower, fruit, and then die the next year.

Prevention: Pull young plants in spring, before they have time to develop a perennial root system. To kill established clumps, repeatedly prune back the stems as they sprout. This eventually exhausts the roots, and they will die. Mowing or cutting back the stems to ground level in summer and digging out the roots with a shovel and pickax slows down growth more effectively, although some canes will still sprout again from rhizomes left in the soil. More cutting and digging will then be needed. Cover cleared areas with a dense mulch—cardboard, black plastic, or several layers of landscape fabric, topped with bark or chopped tree debris—for at least one season to prevent any remaining rhizomes from sprouting.

Control: Cut stems to the ground and apply glyphosate (Roundup) to the stubs as soon as possible after cutting. Spot-treat any new shoots with glyphosate as they appear. Or you can spray triclopyr (Brush-B-Gon, Brush Killer) or glyphosate on mature leaves. With either herbicide, take care to avoid contact with nearby desirable plants. Do not spray fruiting plants in areas where berries could be picked and eaten.

BRACKEN

PTERIDIUM AQUILINUM PUBESCENS (POLYPODIACEAE)

PERENNIAL FERN

ZONES: ALL

Bracken is a large, coarse fern that often grows in or near open woodlands in sandy, acid soil. Although useful as a tall ground cover or screen in untamed areas of the garden, bracken can become a tough, invasive weed. The fronds are leathery in texture, much divided, and hairy on the underside. The fronds, which grow from 2–7 ft. tall, emerge directly as a single stem, without branching, from creeping, woody rhizomes that spread widely.

Life cycle: Perennial that reproduces by creeping rhizomes and by spores

Prevention: Try to dig out as much of the rhizome (underground stem) as possible. Digging probably will need to be repeated several times as new fronds sprout from missed pieces of rhizome.

FATAL FRONDS. *Do not gather and cook young bracken fronds as you would fiddle-heads; brackens slowly poison unsuspecting humans who ingest them. The fronds also poison horses and sheep, so check for bracken where they are grazing.*

Because bracken prefers to grow in acidic soil, changing the pH of your garden soil to make it more alkaline discourages this weed. Have the soil tested to learn exactly how acid it is and how much lime is needed to approach a neutral pH.

Control: Spray glyphosate (Roundup) to actively growing fronds, or cut off the fronds and apply the herbicide to the cut stems. Take care not to get this chemical on desired plants. Translocated herbicides containing dicamba are also effective; apply carefully to avoid damaging nearby broad-leafed ornamentals.

BROOM SEDGE

ANDROPOGON VIRGINICUS (GRAMINEAE)

PERENNIAL GRASS

ZONES: ALL

Broom sedge grass is a horticultural orphan, usually growing unnoticed and uncared for in old farm fields, on roadsides, and in open, sunny areas. This native meadow grass treads where few other plants dare because it tolerates the poorest of dry, rocky, infertile soils. In many cases, it doesn't fit the definition of a weed because it performs beneficial functions. For example, by quickly colonizing disturbed or cutover land, it reduces erosion by water and wind. Moreover, few things surpass the simple beauty of a solid field of orange-brown broom sedge lit by the late fall sun.

Each tuft of broom sedge features slightly flattened, erect stems that branch near the top. Leaves, 6–12 in. long and ¼ in. wide, start out light green and become a darker green as they mature. The upper surface of the leaf blade may be hairy toward the base.

Broom sedge blooms from midsummer to early fall. Flower heads emerge from the joints of leaves on the upper half of the stem. The green to reddish purple flower heads consist of two to four fingerlike clusters covered with tufts of long, silky, white hairs. With the onset of cooler fall temperatures, the leaves turn a handsome orange brown and remain this color throughout the winter.

Life cycle: Perennial grassy weed (or a handsome pasture grass, depending on your point of view) that reproduces by seed and by short rhizomes

Prevention: Broom sedge thrives on neglect. Given good soil, regular watering and fertilizing, and competition from other plants, it invariably disappears.

Control: Dig or pull plants. Mow plants to prevent flowering and reseeding. Spot-treat problem plants with a herbicide containing glyphosate (Roundup). Be sure to follow label directions carefully.

BUTTERCUP, CREEPING

RANUNCULUS REPENS (RANUNCULACEAE)

BROAD-LEAFED PERENNIAL

✔ ZONES: ALL

Introduced from Europe as an ornamental, this plant, like its showier double-flowered form, *Ranunculus repens* 'Pleniflorus', is now considered a weed in most locations. A vigorous plant with thick, fibrous roots and hairy stems that root at the lower nodes, creeping buttercup can spread several feet in a season. The leaves are hairy and deeply cut, with toothed margins. Bright yellow flowers appear in spring on 1–2-ft.-high stems and are followed by greenish seed heads.

Life cycle: Perennial that reproduces by seed and by rooting at the nodes of creeping stems

Prevention: In lawns, improve drainage to help prevent the establishment of creeping buttercup, which flourishes in perpetually moist soil. If improving drainage is not possible, consider planting a ground cover that is tolerant of damp soils instead of trying to grow grass. In garden beds, mulch to prevent seeds from germinating.

Control: To kill established creeping buttercup in garden beds, remove the top growth and, for one season, cover the roots with plastic or cardboard topped with organic mulch. In lawns, dig up and discard isolated plants. If chemical control is necessary, use a product containing 2,4-D, MCPP, and dicamba (Weed-B-Gon, Weed-Stop). Follow label directions carefully.

BATTLING BUTTERCUPS. *Other weedy buttercups that sometimes appear in Southern gardens include tall buttercup and hairy buttercup. Tall buttercup (R. acris) is a perennial growing as tall as 3 ft., with hairy, deeply lobed, narrow leaves and yellow or cream-colored flowers. Hairy buttercup (R. sardous) is a winter annual or short-lived perennial, usually less than a foot tall, with hairy leaves and bright yellow flowers. Control of these buttercups is the same as for creeping buttercup.*

BUTTONWEED, VIRGINIA

DIODIA VIRGINIANA (RUBIACEAE)

BROAD-LEAFED, HERBACEOUS PERENNIAL

✔ ZONES: ALL

A denizen of ditches, stream banks, marshes, seeps, and other areas with wet soil, Virginia buttonweed also flourishes in lawns and gardens. And like an unwanted guest who appreciates a free meal, this weed often outstays its welcome.

In the wild, Virginia buttonweed may grow 8–24 in. tall. Unfortunately for homeowners, it tolerates close and frequent mowing. Once it is established in the lawn, an extensive system of underground stems (rhizomes) makes it a major pain in the hindquarters to eradicate. Its leaves are leathery, light to dark green (sometimes tinged red), about 1–3 in. long, and joined to the stem by a membrane with several hairs. Branching stems may extend 2 ft. long, rooting at the leaf joints. Virginia buttonweed blooms from early summer to early fall, bearing small, white, starlike flowers both above and below ground. Flowers are followed by rows of leathery seedpods that give the plant its name.

Life cycle: Spreads by seed, rhizomes, and rooting stems. It's most troublesome in warm weather.

Prevention: Keep lawns thick and vigorous with proper watering, mowing, aeration, and fertilization. Like all weeds, this one is an opportunist and quickly invades bare spots. In garden beds, pull or hoe plants, then mulch to prevent seed from germinating.

Control: Established plants are difficult to control in lawns. However, applying a postemergence herbicide containing dicamba, imazaquin (Image), or calcium acid methanearsonate (Crabgrass Killer) has proved effective. But you'll probably have to spray more than once. Make sure the product you use is labeled for your type of grass and follow directions carefully. In gardens, regular cultivation usually provides good control.

CARPETWEED

MOLLUGO VERTICILLATA (AIZOACEAE)

BROAD-LEAFED, HERBACEOUS ANNUAL

✀ ZONES: ALL

True to its name, carpetweed produces a dense mat of stems and leaves that sometimes smother surrounding plants. The stems radiate from a central point and stretch outward in a starburst pattern. This weed commonly inhabits damp, rich soil. But it also flourishes in dry, gravelly, or sandy soil, which is why you often find it growing in paths, walkways, and neglected areas. It seldom poses a serious problem for established lawns, but may temporarily infest newly seeded lawns.

Whorls of three to eight light green, spoon-shaped leaves occur at each stem joint. By the end of summer, the stems may extend 18 in. or more. Clusters of two to five small, white, five-petaled flowers appear on slender stalks from mid- to late summer, followed by egg-shaped seed capsules containing orange-red or orange-brown seeds. The kidney-shaped seeds break away when ripe.

Life cycle: This annual, nonwoody weed germinates in late spring. It flowers and sets seed in summer and fall. Seeds lie dormant through the winter.

Prevention: Keep lawns thick and vigorous with proper watering, fertilization, aeration, and mowing. Mulch garden beds to keep weed seeds from germinating or apply a pre-emergence herbicide containing trifluralin (Treflan, Preen) or trifluralin and benefin (Team). Because carpetweed gets off to a relatively slow start in spring, a well cared–for lawn and garden can crowd it out.

Control: Like bedstraw (see page 265), this weed is an easy one to pull, as long as your yard isn't filled with it. Seedlings grow quickly, so pull or hoe them while they're young. Spot-treat mature plants with a postemergence herbicide containing glyphosate (Roundup), glufosinate-ammonium (Finale), diquat dibromide, or herbicidal soap (Superfast, Scythe). Be sure to follow label directions carefully.

CHICKWEED

STELLARIA MEDIA (CARYOPHYLLACEAE)

BROAD-LEAFED ANNUAL

✀ ZONES: ALL

Chickweed is a low-growing succulent weed found in lawns and gardens. Generally, it grows most vigorously in the cool weather of fall, winter, and spring, then sets seed and dies when hot weather arrives. But it sometimes lives through the summer in cool, shaded gardens. Chickweed has slender stems with many branches and a line of white hairs on one side of each branch. The leaves are smooth and pointed, ¼–1 in. long, bright green on the upper surface and paler on the underside. Starry white flowers appear from midwinter to early spring, borne on slender stalks that rise from the base of the leafstalks.

Mouse-ear chickweed

Life cycle: Annual that reproduces by seed and by creeping stems that root at the nodes

Prevention: Keep lawns healthy and growing thickly through proper fertilization, watering, and mowing. If just a few chickweed plants appear, pulling them is easy, especially while they're young. You can also use a pre-emergent containing pendimethalin (Halts) on lawns or trifluralin (Treflan, Preen) around the ornamentals listed on the label.

Control: For postemergent control on lawns, use a product containing 2,4-D, MCPP, and dicamba (Weed-B-Gon, Weed-Stop). Spot-treat chickweed with herbicidal soap (Superfast, Scythe), glyphosate (Roundup), or glufosinate-ammonium (Finale). Be careful not to get these products on desired plants.

CHICKWEED CHECKUP. *Although mouse-ear chickweed (insert above) looks much like common chickweed, it's a perennial plant of a different genus,* Cerastium. *Its small rounded leaves are hairy and look like mouse ears. Pull or dig this weed out before it sets seed. Chemical controls include postemergence herbicides containing MCPP or dicamba for use in lawns or glyphosate (Roundup) among ornamentals.*

CHICORY

CICHORIUM INTYBUS (ASTERACEAE)

BROAD-LEAFED PERENNIAL

✘ ZONES: US, MS, LS

Chicory, also called blue daisy, coffeeweed, or succory, occurs along roadsides and fencerows, in ornamental and vegetable gardens, and sometimes in lawns, especially in alkaline soil. It tolerates poor, dry soil. Chicory grows from a tough, deep, woody taproot. The basal rosette (leaf whorl at base of the plant) of 3–8-in.-long leaves resembles that of dandelion, but chicory's leaves are rougher and hairy. From the rosette grow 1–3-ft. branched stems, with small, clasping leaves. The leaves, stems, and roots contain a bitter-tasting, milky juice. Chicory flowers, which appear in midsummer, are daisy-like, up to 1½ in. wide, and usually a pretty sky blue but occasionally purple or white. The flowers close in the afternoon.

Life cycle: Reproduces by seed and pieces of the taproot

Prevention: Pull or cut young chicory plants as soon as you see them. Older plants are more difficult to remove. Dig up the plant, removing as much of the taproot as possible. It may sprout again, but after you pull or cut it several times, chicory usually does not regrow. In any case, remove the plants before they set seed. If there are many chicory plants growing in your garden, cut them back to the ground and cover the area with a thick mulch, such as black plastic or cardboard topped with an organic mulch. Leave the mulch in place for a full growing season.

Control: If chemical control is needed, use a product containing dicamba or MCPP, or triclopyr (Brush-B-Gon, Brush Killer). Don't get these products on desired plants.

A BITTER BREW. *As weeds go, chicory is a useful one. Its thick roots have traditionally been dried, roasted, and ground to serve as a pleasantly bitter-tasting coffee substitute. The young leaves, which also taste somewhat bitter, can be added to spring salads or cooked as a vegetable. From the wild form of chicory gardeners have selected and cultivated the plant now known as radicchio. Endive, curly endive, and escarole are closely related vegetables.*

CHINESE PRIVET

LIGUSTRUM SINENSE (OLEACEAE)

WOODY, SEMIEVERGREEN SHRUB

✘ ZONES: MS, LS, CS, TS

Chinese privet is another example of an ornamental plant that became a nightmare. A popular shrub in Europe, it was brought to the South in the late 1800s for use as a hedge and screening plant. Birds quickly discovered its berrylike fruits and scattered the seeds all over creation. Apparently, every single seed germinated too, which is why it's hard to find a woodland or abandoned lot in the entire Southeast that isn't choked by this pest.

Growing 10–15 ft. tall and wide, Chinese privet forms a dense thicket of leaves and shoots. It thrives just about anywhere, in bright sun or dense shade, in cracks in the pavement or along stream banks and bogs. The elliptical leaves are 1–2 in. long and are usually a dull dark green. However, a popular selection, called 'Variegata', sports foliage with a creamy white edging. It's the only form of Chinese privet you can now buy, which is fortunate.

Chinese privet flower

Life cycle: This woody shrub bears clusters of rather sickeningly sweet, small white flowers in late spring and early summer. Masses of small, blue-black, berrylike fruits appear in fall. Birds eat the fruits and pelt the countryside with the seeds, which sprout and grow on nearly every molecule of soil they hit. As if that weren't enough, the shrub also propagates by suckers.

Prevention: If you already have variegated Chinese privet, prune it regularly to keep it from flowering and producing seed.

Control: Pull or dig young seedlings. Repeatedly cut established shrubs to the ground. Spray entire plant with a nonselective, translocated herbicide containing triclopyr (Brush-B-Gon, Brush Killer) or glyphosate (Roundup). You may have to spray more than once. Follow label directions carefully.

CHINESE WISTERIA

WISTERIA SINENSIS (FABACEAE)

DECIDUOUS, TWINING, WOODY VINE

ZONES: US, MS, LS, CS

Chinese wisteria is proof that beauty has its price. Among the most spectacular of all flowering vines, this native of the Orient literally drips with foot-long chains of fragrant, violet blue flowers in spring. But it spreads by both seeds and suckers, can grow 20 ft. in just one season, and will climb an 80-ft.-tall tree without hesitating. In the Lower South, it cascades over hillsides, strangling small trees within the iron grip of its merciless tentacles. Its vining branches also crush arbors and trellises, rip the gutters off houses, and can bend an iron railing as if it were taffy.

Life cycle: Perennial vine that flowers in spring, then sets beanlike seedpods. The seeds ripen in fall and germinate the following spring. The vine also spreads by suckers at the base of the plant.

Prevention: Plant Chinese wisteria only where you can manage and control it. Do not let it climb up trees or escape into the woods or unmanaged areas. Pull up unwanted seedlings. Consider planting less aggressive native species, such as American wisteria *(Wisteria frutescens)* or Kentucky wisteria *(W. macrostachya)*.

COUSINS IN CRIME. Japanese wisteria (W. floribunda) is just as popular and troublesome as its Chinese cousin. Even experienced gardeners have a difficult time telling them apart. But take a closer look: Chinese wisteria twines counterclockwise; Japanese wisteria twines clockwise.

Control: Cut the main stem near ground level, then paint the cut surface with a herbicide containing triclopyr (Brush-B-Gon, Brush Killer). Or spray the vine according to label directions with triclopyr or glyphosate (Roundup). Another good way to terminate Chinese wisteria is to fill a large bucket with a solution of glyphosate mixed to regular strength. Then push as many of the leaves and young, flexible shoots into the bucket as you can and leave them there for a day or so. The leaves and stems will gradually absorb the chemical and carry it down to the roots.

CLOVER, WHITE

TRIFOLIUM REPENS (FABACEAE)

BROAD-LEAFED PERENNIAL

ZONES: ALL

White clover, also known as white Dutch clover, is a common lawn weed. Not everyone dislikes it, though. Some folks actually recommend adding it to lawns because, like other legumes, it captures nitrogen from the air and adds it to the soil.

White clover has branching stems that grow close to the ground, rooting at the joints. Under open conditions it may grow up to 12 in. tall, but it remains much shorter in mowed lawns. The leaves are compound, divided into the three leaflets characteristic of clovers. Each leaflet of white clover is marked by a white crescent. The round flowering head is made up of a cluster of small white flowers, which may turn pink and droop as they age.

Life cycle: Perennial that reproduces by seed and by rooting at the nodes of creeping stems

Prevention: Follow good lawn management practices, including providing sufficient nitrogen fertilizer and water to help the lawn grasses compete with the clover. Mowing the grass at its tallest recommended height (see pages 35 and 234) helps shade out white clover. In vegetable and ornamental beds, cultivate to remove young plants. Pull or dig older plants before they set seed. A mulch not only helps prevent germination of white clover seeds, but also loosens the soil, so that it is easier to pull weeds.

Control: Treat lawns with a product containing 2,4-D, MCPP, and dicamba, such as Weed-B-Gon or Weed-Stop, or imazaquin (Image).

TIP-TOE THROUGH THE CLOVER. White clover in the lawn makes things dicey for those who enjoy traipsing barefoot across the grass. Honeybees tending the clover flowers tend to sting angrily when stepped on. But if you avoid the bees, you'll appreciate their hard work. The delicious, light-colored honey they make from white clover tastes mild and very sweet.

CRABGRASS

DIGITARIA, VARIOUS SPECIES *(POACEAE)*

ANNUAL GRASSES

⚡ ZONES: ALL

Probably the most infamous of annual summer weeds, crabgrass infests lawns, as well as vegetable and ornamental gardens. This weed thrives in hot, damp areas. Seeds germinate in early spring, as soon as the first few inches of the soil remain at 50–55°F for 3 to 7 days. The young plant's first true leaf is flat, pale green, and covered with coarse hairs. Tufts of hair at the junction of the stem and leaf blade distinguish crabgrass from other annual grasses. As crabgrass grows, it branches from the base; joints often root where the stems touch the soil. The inflorescence (flowering part), which appears in mid- to late summer, is made up of 3 to 11 slender branches that arise near the tip of the stem. A single plant may produce more than 8,000 seeds.

Life cycle: Annuals that reproduce by seed and by roots growing from swollen joints in the stems

Prevention: Crabgrass is an opportunist. It quickly invades sparse, struggling lawns that result from compacted, infertile soil and scalping (see page 234). Growing a thick, healthy lawn is the best prevention. Fertilize and water regularly, aerate every spring, and mow at the highest recommended height for your type of grass (see pages 35 and 234). You can also apply a pre-emergence herbicide, such as benefin (Balan), trifluralin (Treflan, Preen), trifluralin and benefin (Team), dithiopyr (Dimension), or pendimethalin (Halts), in late winter or early spring.

Control: For postemergence control in ornamentals, use a product containing fluazifop-P-butyl (Fusilade, Grass-B-Gon) or herbicidal soap (Superfast, Scythe). For postemergence control in lawns, use a product containing calcium acid methanearsonate (Crabgrass Killer) or dithiopyr. Nonselective herbicides containing glufosinate-ammonium (Finale), diquat dibromide, or glyphosate (Roundup) also kill crabgrass. Take care not to spray these products on desired plants.

CUDWEED

GNAPHALIUM, VARIOUS SPECIES *(ASTERACEAE)*

BROAD-LEAFED ANNUALS OR BIENNIALS

⚡ ZONES: ALL

Several species of cudweed crop up as weeds in lawns and garden beds, especially in poor soils lacking organic matter. Some cudweeds are aromatic, with a pungent or sweet scent. The white, woolly stems are useful dried as everlastings.

Cotton batting plant (*Gnaphalium chilense, G. stramineum*), like other cudweeds, looks white, silky, and hairy. If unmowed, it can grow from 6 in. to 2½ ft. tall, with long, narrow leaves and clusters of small, inconspicuous greenish yellow flower heads at the ends of the stems. Purple cudweed (*G. purpureum*) generally grows 4 in. high in lawns, but can reach 24 in. tall if left unmowed. When young, its leaves are covered with a dense coating of white, woolly hairs, but the leaves become greener and smoother as they age. Brownish or purple flower heads appear on the stem or at the base of the leafstalks. A third species, lowland cudweed (*G. palustre*), is a low-growing plant, to 12 in. high, with a dense, spreading growth habit. It has dense tufts of woolly hair along the stems and in the leaf axils (the juncture of leaf and stem). The flower heads are small, borne at the ends of branches and in the leaf axils.

Cudweed seedling

Life cycle: Annuals or biennials that reproduce by seed

Prevention: Spotting these white, woolly plants among lawn grasses and other plants is easy, so it is not difficult to find them and pull them up before they set seed. In vegetable and ornamental beds, a thick mulch will help prevent existing seeds from growing. Improving the soil by adding compost will deter growth of this weed. Fertilize lawns to thicken the grass, making it less hospitable to weeds. Apply a pre-emergence herbicide containing isoxaben (Portrait, Gallery).

Control: Spot-treat cudweed in lawns with a selective postemergence herbicide containing 2,4-D, MCPP, and dicamba (Weed-B-Gon, Weed-Stop), imazaquin (Image), or atrazine (Purge, Bonus S).

DALLIS GRASS

PASPALUM DILATATUM (POACEAE)

PERENNIAL GRASS

ZONES: MS, LS, CS, TS

Dallis grass grows in low, wet areas, but tolerates drought once established. Though found in vegetable and ornamental beds, it is especially troublesome in lawns. Its coarse, flat stalks stick out among finer-textured lawn grasses, and it regrows quickly after mowing. A clumping grass, dallis grass grows from a hard, knotty base. It reproduces by seed, which germinate in spring, and by rhizomes. Its dark green foliage resembles that of other grasses, which makes the seedling plant difficult to identify. However, as the plant matures, a firm, membranous ligule (projection) shows up at the base of the leaf where it joins the stem. Leaf blades have only a few hairs

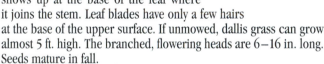

Dallis grass flowering head

at the base of the upper surface. If unmowed, dallis grass can grow almost 5 ft. high. The branched, flowering heads are 6–16 in. long. Seeds mature in fall.

Life cycle: Perennial that reproduces by seed and rhizomes (underground stems)

Prevention: In lawns, pull isolated plants. If dallis grass is a persistent problem in your lawn, you probably should take steps to improve the drainage. In garden beds, cultivate to remove dallis grass seedlings. Dig out larger plants before they set seed. Mulch to prevent seeds already in the soil from germinating. Apply a product containing trifluralin (Treflan, Preen), trifluralin and benefin (Team), or dithiopyr (Dimension) as a pre-emergence herbicide in the kinds of lawns and among the ornamentals listed on the labels.

Control: To treat dallis grass during the growing season, choose a product containing calcium acid methanearsonate (Crabgrass Killer); several treatments may be necessary. You can also spot-treat clumps with a herbicide containing glyphosate (Roundup) or fluazifop-P-butyl (Fusilade, Grass-B- Gon) according to label directions.

DANDELION

TARAXACUM OFFICINALE (ASTERACEAE)

BROAD-LEAFED PERENNIAL

ZONES: ALL

Dandelion arrived in the South during colonial times. It was cultivated for its edible greens and also for its flowers, which were used to make dandelion wine. It quickly escaped the vegetable garden to become one of our most recognizable and persistent lawn weeds. The newly sprouted light green seed leaves of dandelion unite at the base, forming a shallow cup. As the plant matures, a deep taproot forms. The leaves arise from the taproot, forming a rosette; shallow to deep lobes etch the edges of the leaves, which end in sharp points. Both leaves and flower stems exude a milky, bitter-tasting juice when torn. Bright yellow flowers appear from late winter or spring until frost, followed by circular balls of seeds that are dispersed by wind.

Life cycle: Perennial that reproduces by seed and by sprouting root crowns and pieces of taproot

Prevention: To discourage dandelions, thicken the lawn by aerating, proper fertilization, watering, and mowing. Pull dandelions from lawns and gardens when they are young, before they produce a taproot. Once the taproot has formed, you must remove all of it to get rid of dandelions; new plants sprout from even a small piece. In gardens, maintaining a year-round mulch helps prevent dandelion seeds from germinating.

Control: For chemical control in lawns, spray with a selective postemergence herbicide containing 2,4-D, MCPP, and dicamba (Weed-B-Gon, Weed-Stop) in spring or fall.

DICHONDRA

DICHONDRA MICRANTHA; ALSO CALLED D. CAROLINENSIS OR D. REPENS (CONVOLVULACEAE)

BROAD-LEAFED PERENNIAL

ZONES: MS, LS, CS, TS

In many areas of California, dichondra is a favored ground cover and is even grown as a lawn. But here, it's just another good-for-nothing weed. It spreads by slender stems that creep along the ground, rooting freely at nodes and forming a dense mat of foliage. It often invades flower and shrub beds, as well as other ground covers and lawns. Dichondra has smooth, kidney-shaped leaves, ¼–½ in. wide. In sun the leaf stems remain short, but in shade they may grow 6 in. tall. The flowers are small and inconspicuous, growing in the axils (junctures) of leaf and stem.

Life cycle: Perennial that reproduces by rooting surface runners and by seed

Prevention: Keep lawns thick and vigorous to crowd dichondra out. Mulch garden beds to prevent seed from germinating. Apply a pre-emergence herbicide containing atrazine (Purge, Bonus S).

Control: Dichondra is an easy weed to pull. One good yank usually removes a foot or two of it. For serious infestations, use a herbicide containing 2,4-D, MCPP, and dicamba (Weed-B-Gon, Weed-Stop). Be sure to follow label directions carefully.

DICHONDRA ON THE ROCKS. *No, this isn't a crazy, new drink. It's a way of using dichondra that actually looks good. If you have an unmortared stone path or terrace, simply cast dichondra seeds between the stones in spring. Bright green leaves will quickly fill in the gaps and provide a soft, lush look.*

DOCK, CURLY

RUMEX CRISPUS (POLYGONACEAE)

BROAD-LEAFED PERENNIAL

ZONES: ALL

Curly dock is a tenacious weed that grows from a thick, fleshy taproot. It is mainly a lawn pest, but also occurs in vegetable and flower gardens. The weed grows 2–5 ft. tall in the open garden, but remains a low rosette of leaves in frequently mowed lawns. The seeds of curly dock germinate from early spring into summer. As the plant grows, it produces lance-shaped, curly-edged, bluish green leaves, 3 in.–1 ft. long. Erect stems grow from the base; they are slightly ridged and usually reddish. The small, green-tinged flowers form dense clusters at the top of the stems from May until frost. The seeds are spread by wind or water. A single plant can produce as many as 40,000 seeds; once buried, these remain viable for up to 80 years. Pollens can cause allergic reactions in some people.

Life cycle: Perennial that reproduces by seed and by regrowth of pieces of taproot and crown

Prevention: In lawns and gardens, dig out young plants, removing as much of the root as possible. Kill large plants by cutting the top growth every week or two until the roots stop resprouting and die. Be sure to get rid of curly dock before it sets seed. In garden beds, mulch to prevent germination of seeds already in the soil.

Control: For chemical control in lawns, use a postemergence product containing 2,4-D, MCPP, and dicamba (Weed-B-Gon, Weed-Stop). For nonselective control, spot-treat with glyphosate (Roundup), taking care not to get this chemical on desired plants.

DODDER

CUSCUTA, VARIOUS SPECIES (*CUSCUTACEAE* OR *CONVOLVULACEAE*)

ANNUAL PARASITE

ZONES: ALL

Startling when first encountered in the garden or in the wild, dodder is a leafless parasitic plant that lacks chlorophyll. Its yellow to bright orange stems twine over host plants, creating a mass of smothering growth. Dodder, a flowering plant, produces seeds that germinate from late winter through summer. The small seedling has a thread-like stem that swings about slowly and twines upon any support it encounters. If the support is not a suitable host, the seedling dies. If the host is suitable, dodder produces wartlike suckers that penetrate the stem of the host, drawing in nourishment. The lower part of the seedling then withers and dies, and the dodder plant becomes entirely parasitic, weakening or killing the host. Dodder grows rapidly, producing branches that soon attach to neighboring plants. Clusters of cream-colored flowers appear from July to October.

Dodder flowers

Life cycle: Parasitic annual that reproduces by seed

Prevention: Remove all traces of dodder from flowers, vegetables, or shrubs. Then apply a thick mulch to garden beds to keep dodder seeds from germinating.

Control: There is no reliable way to completely remove dodder from infested branches, as even the smallest piece left behind will grow again. Therefore, cut away the entire branch, dodder and all, and burn it or place it in the trash; do not compost dodder. Sometimes the only way to get rid of it is to remove the entire host plant.

DOLLAR WEED (PENNYWORT)

HYDROCOTYLE, VARIOUS SPECIES (*UMBELLIFERAE*)

BROAD-LEAFED, HERBACEOUS PERENNIAL

ZONES: ALL

Named for its rounded leaves that resemble silver dollars or pennies, dollar weed can cost proud lawn owners their sanity. Given moist soil and a little bit of shade, it forms dense mats in a short time. Trailing stems grow from tubers and spreading rhizomes (underground stems). They root along the ground at every leaf joint. With the leaf stalks joined to the bottoms of the leaves, individual leaves resemble umbrellas.

Several species of dollar weed inhabit the South, including coastal plain pennywort *(Hydrocotyle bonariensis)*, water pennywort *(H. umbellata)*, and whorled pennywort *(H. verticillata)*. Depending on the species, flowers may occur in long spikes or rounded clusters, followed by round, greenish fruits. All species tolerate close mowing. Dollar weed is a major lawn pest in the Coastal and Tropical South, especially where lawns are either poorly drained or irrigated with lawn sprinklers daily.

Life cycle: Perennial that reproduces by seed, rhizomes, and tubers

Prevention: Avoid overwatering. Improve poor drainage through proper aeration. Keep lawns thick and vigorous with proper mowing and fertilization. Apply a pre-emergence herbicide containing isoxaben (Portrait, Gallery) on Bahia grass, Bermuda grass, centipede grass, St. Augustine, and zoysia lawns only. In areas where wet soil and too much shade make establishing a lawn difficult, grow an appropriate ground cover instead. In garden beds, spread landscape fabric over the soil around desired plants, then cover it with mulch.

Control: Pull or dig isolated plants. Treat infested lawns with a selective, postemergence herbicide or weed-and-feed labeled for your type of grass. This may include 2,4-D and MCPP, imazaquin (Image), or atrazine (Purge, Bonus S). In garden beds, spot-treat with a herbicide containing glyphosate (Roundup). Follow label directions carefully.

FESCUE, TALL

FESTUCA ARUNDINACEA (POACEAE)

PERENNIAL GRASS

ZONES: ALL

Tall fescue is a clump-forming grass popular in the South as a cool-season lawn. However, it can invade warm-season lawns. Its appearance there is quite objectionable in winter, as its bright green foliage mars the carpetlike quality of the surrounding brown lawn. When mowed, tall fescue grows as a flat, spreading clump, with stiff leaf blades up to ⅓ in. wide that form a 90° angle with the stems. The leaves, which may be flat or rolled, have prominent ridges on the upper side and tiny stiff hairs along the margins.

Life cycle: Perennial grass that reproduces by seed

Prevention: Remove clumps of tall fescue from lawns by cutting under the root crown with a knife or sharp shovel. This grass does not spread by runners, so digging out the clumps usually gets rid of it. If the digging leaves large empty spots, fill them with soil, then sow grass seed or lay sod. In gardens, dig out tall fescue, removing the plants before they set seed, to prevent later problems. A thick mulch will prevent any seeds already in the soil from germinating.

Control: For chemical control, use a product containing fluazifop-P-butyl (Fusilade, Grass-B-Gon)—a selective herbicide that controls grasses—around the broad-leafed ornamentals listed on the label. Or spot-treat with a nonselective herbicide containing glyphosate (Roundup), taking care not to get the chemical on desired plants. Applying a weed-and-feed fertilizer containing atrazine (Purge, Bonus S) to St. Augustine, centipede grass, carpet grass, and zoysia lawns will remove unwanted tall fescue.

FLORIDA BETONY

STACHYS FLORIDANA (LABIATAE)

BROAD-LEAFED, HERBACEOUS PERENNIAL

ZONES: MS, LS, CS, TS

A fast-spreading nuisance in lawns and gardens, Florida betony grows in full sun to partial shade and tolerates a wide range of soils from wet to dry. It's often called "rattlesnake weed," because it produces white, segmented tubers that resemble a rattlesnake's tail. Other distinctive features include square stems and lance-shaped leaves with slightly toothed or serrated edges. At one time this aggravating weed was confined to its native Florida. However, it was accidentally distributed throughout the South in pots containing nursery stock, and now makes its home from Florida to Virginia and Texas.

Life cycle: Florida betony sprouts from seeds or tubers in the fall, then grows and spreads rapidly, eventually reaching 2 ft. tall. It grows through the winter in most of the South, flowers and sets seed in spring, then goes dormant in summer.

Prevention: Keep the lawn thick and vigorous through proper watering, fertilizing, aerating, and mowing. Healthy lawns can outcompete Florida betony for light, water, and nutrients. Apply a pre-emergence herbicide or weed-and-feed containing atrazine (Purge, Bonus S) to carpet grass, centipede grass, St. Augustine, and zoysia lawns only in late October. In garden beds, spread landscape fabric over the soil around desirable plants and cover it with mulch.

Control: Dig isolated weeds, being sure to remove all of the tuber. Treat infested lawns in late February with a selective, postemergence herbicide or weed-and-feed labeled for your type of grass. This may involve 2,4-D, MCPP, and dicamba (Weed-B-Gon, Weed-Stop) or atrazine (Purge, Bonus S). In garden beds, spot-treat Florida betony with a herbicide containing glyphosate (Roundup). You may have to spray more than once. Be sure to follow label directions carefully. Do not let the spray drift onto desired plants.

FLORIDA PELLITORY

PARIETARIA FLORIDANA (URTICACEAE)

BROAD-LEAFED, HERBACEOUS ANNUAL OR PERENNIAL

ZONES: ALL

Although Florida pellitory is a particular nuisance in St. Augustine lawns in Florida, this weed also occurs throughout the Southeast and all the way north to the New England states. It favors moist, shady areas where the grass is sparse. Its oval, three-veined, 1-in.-long leaves are alternately arranged on stems that can sprawl more than a foot long over the grass. A unique feature of the leaf is that the leaf stem can be as long or longer than the blade.

Life cycle: Although Florida pellitory can be perennial, it's a short-lived summer annual in most of the South. Seeds germinate in spring and seedlings grow quickly. Clusters of tiny, green flowers appear at the bases of leaves from spring until fall. The plant sets seed, then usually dies.

Prevention: As with all lawn weeds, the best way to head off an invasion is to maintain a thick, healthy lawn. Fertilize, water, aerate, and mow properly to encourage the grass to quickly fill bare spots. Mowing the grass at its highest recommended setting (see pages 35 and 234) will shade the soil surface and keep Florida pellitory seed from sprouting. Mulch garden beds.

Control: Individual plants are easy to pull. Treat infested lawns with a selective, postemergence herbicide or weed-and-feed labeled for your type of grass. For most lawns, use a combination of 2,4-D, MCPP, and dicamba (Weed-B-Gon, Weed-Stop). Atrazine (Purge, Bonus S) should be used on carpet grass, centipede grass, St. Augustine, and zoysia lawns only. In garden beds around trees and shrubs, spot-treat Florida pellitory with a herbicide containing glyphosate (Roundup), glufosinate-ammonium (Finale), diquat dibromide, or herbicidal soap (Superfast, Scythe). Apply when weeds are actively growing. Be sure to follow label directions carefully.

FLORIDA PUSLEY

RICHARDIA SCABRA (RUBIACEAE)

BROAD-LEAFED, HERBACEOUS ANNUAL

ZONES: MS, LS, CS, TS

Also known as Florida purslane, Florida pusley (say *puhslee*) isn't fussy about where it lays down its roots. It settles comfortably in bare spots in the lawn and garden beds or in the cracks and crevices of driveways and sidewalks. In just a short time, it produces a dense, smothering patch of stems and leaves that may reach 4–12 in. tall and spread to 2 ft. or more. Florida pusley especially flourishes in the sandy soils of the Coastal and Tropical South. Its fuzzy, oblong leaves may be 1–3 in. long. Like most lawn weeds, it tolerates close mowing.

GEE, THANKS A LOT, GUYS. *Richardia, the group of weedy plants that includes Florida pusley, was named for Richard Richardson, an English physician. What an honor. In retrospect, he probably would rather have had a watch.*

Life cycle: Seeds germinate in spring and seedlings grow quickly. White, funnel-shaped clusters of flowers appear on the ends of stems from early summer until frost. Flowers are followed by bumpy, leathery fruits containing seeds that drop from the plant before it dies. The seeds sprout the following spring.

Prevention: A thick, healthy lawn without bare spots won't give Florida pusley the chance to get started. Be sure to water, fertilize, and aerate properly, and mow your lawn at its highest recommended height (see pages 35 and 234). Apply a pre-emergence herbicide containing benefin (Balan) in early spring. Mulch garden beds to keep weed seeds from germinating, or apply a pre-emergence herbicide containing trifluralin (Treflan, Preen) in early spring.

Control: Treat lawns with a selective, postemergence herbicide or weed-and-feed labeled for your type of grass. A combination of 2,4-D, MCPP, and dicamba (Weed-B-Gon, Weed-Stop) will do for most lawns. Atrazine (Purge, Bonus S) gives good control, but should only be used on carpet grass, centipede grass, St. Augustine, and zoysia lawns. In garden beds, pull isolated plants or spot-treat with glyphosate (Roundup), glufosinate-ammonium (Finale), diquat dibromide, or herbicidal soap (Superfast, Scythe).

FOXTAILS, ANNUAL

SETARIA, VARIOUS SPECIES *(POACEAE)*

ANNUAL GRASSES

ZONES: ALL

Foxtails are annual grasses that grow in lawns and vegetable and flower gardens. Seeds of both yellow foxtail *(Setaria pumila,* also called *S. glauca)* and green foxtail *(S. viridis),* shown above, germinate from early spring into summer. The seedlings are difficult to differentiate from other annual grasses. As they mature, plants of yellow foxtail grow 1–3 ft. tall, with upright stems. The leaf blades are smooth, $1/8$–$3/8$ in. wide, with a spiral twist. Distinct long hairs grow at the base of the leaf. The seed heads are dense, bushy spikes, 1–5 in. long, with yellowish to reddish brown bristles and relatively large seeds. Green foxtail grows 6–32 in. tall. Its angled stalks bend downward at the lower joint. The leaf blades lack the hairs at the base that are characteristic of yellow foxtail. Green foxtail also has a smaller seed head, with pale yellow to purplish bristles, and smaller seeds than those of yellow foxtail; both plants flower and set seed from July to September.

Life cycle: Annuals that reproduce by seed

Prevention: Dig or pull foxtail plants before they set seed, removing the entire plant, roots and all. If parts of the crown remain in the ground, they will reroot, and you will need to weed again. Improving the quality of turf through regular fertilizing and adequate watering discourages annual foxtails. In garden beds, a thick mulch prevents foxtail seeds from germinating. Solarize beds (see page 31) before planting to kill seeds. If chemical prevention is needed, in late winter to early spring apply a pre-emergence herbicide containing dithiopyr (Dimension), pendimethalin (Halts), trifluralin (Treflan, Preen), or trifluralin and benefin (Team) to lawns or around ornamentals listed on the label.

Control: For spot control, apply a herbicidal soap, glufosinate-ammonium (Finale), or glyphosate (Roundup), taking care not to get these chemicals on desired plants.

GOLDENROD

SOLIDAGO, VARIOUS SPECIES *(ASTERACEAE)*

BROAD-LEAFED, HERBACEOUS PERENNIALS

ZONES: ALL

Goldenrod has a public relations problem, and it's guilt by association. Many folks still think it causes hayfever, even though the true culprit is ragweed *(Ambrosia),* a plain-looking roadside weed that blooms at the same time. The dogged persistence of this belief keeps gardeners from realizing that goldenrod can be an outstanding ornamental plant.

More than 100 species of goldenrod inhabit North America. They range in height from a few inches to 6 ft. or more. From midsummer through fall, their showy, golden yellow blossoms illuminate roadsides, meadows, ditches, pastures, and fencerows. Some species, such as Canada goldenrod *(Solidago canadensis),* spread aggressively by rhizomes (underground stems) and are best left to the wild. However, others form clumps and are well-behaved, carefree perennials that blend well with asters, salvias, ironweed, as well as other late-season perennials. Desirable goldenrods include seaside goldenrod *(S. sempervirens),* rough-leafed goldenrod *(S. rugosa),* tall goldenrod *(S. altissima),* and sweet goldenrod *(S. odora).*

Life cycle: Plants flower in summer and fall. Fleecy white seed clusters release seeds that ride the wind to new homes and germinate in spring. Some species also spread by rhizomes.

Prevention: Mow nearby weed patches to keep seeds from blowing in. Mulch garden beds to keep seeds from germinating.

Control: Regular mowing usually eliminates goldenrod from lawns. If not, spot-treat it with a selective, postemergence herbicide labeled for your type of grass. In garden beds, hoe, dig, or pull young plants when the soil is moist. Remove older plants before they flower and set seed, digging out as many of the rhizomes as you can. Spot-treat problem plants when they're blooming with a herbicide containing glyphosate (Roundup). Follow label directions carefully.

GOOSEGRASS

ELEUSINE INDICA (POACEAE)

ANNUAL GRASS

✂ ZONES: ALL

Also known as silver crabgrass, wiregrass, and crowsfoot, goosegrass is a tough summer annual, most often found in sparse lawns and in paths where the soil is compacted. Seedlings emerge in spring when the soil has warmed, several weeks later than crabgrass. Seedlings are light green, with a thin, papery appendage (ligule) at the base of the leaf blades. The mature plant can grow to 3 ft. in height, but it stays much lower in mowed lawns. The leaf blades are flat or folded, 1/8 – 1/3 in. wide, with soft, whitish hairs that extend to the sheath. The flattened stems are pale green or silver at the base; the blades are darker green. Unlike crabgrass, goosegrass does not root at the stems but instead grows in tufts. The inflorescence, like that of crabgrass, forms a whorl of fingerlike spikes at the tip of the stem. Sometimes one or two spikes appear just below the tip of the stem. Goosegrass can flower and set seed even when closely mowed.

Life cycle: Annual that reproduces by seed

Prevention: In lawns, improving the growing conditions to favor lawn grasses will discourage goosegrass. Aerating the soil to reduce compaction is especially important. If any part of the lawn is subject to heavy foot traffic and continual compaction, consider replacing the grass with a path. You can also apply a pre-emergence herbicide containing benefin (Balan), pendimethalin (Halts), dithiopyr (Dimension), trifluralin (Treflan, Preen), or trifluralin and benefin (Team) in early spring.

Control: A selective postemergence herbicide containing fluazifop-P-butyl (Fusilade, Grass-B-Gon) or calcium acid methanearsonate (Crabgrass Killer) controls goosegrass; it is most effective if applied when the weed is less than 8 in. tall. Nonselective herbicides containing herbicidal soap (Superfast, Scythe), glufosinate-ammonium (Finale), or glyphosate (Roundup) can be used to spot-treat goosegrass. Take care not to get these chemicals on desired plants.

GROUND IVY

GLECHOMA HEDERACEA (NEPETA HEDERACEA) (LAMIACEAE)

BROAD-LEAFED PERENNIAL

✂ ZONES: ALL

Ground ivy can be an effective ground cover in shady, moist locations, but it can also spread quickly and widely beyond its allotted area. Also known as creeping Charlie, ground ivy often becomes a pest in lawns and gardens. Its 1½-in.-wide leaves, in opposite pairs, are bright green, slightly hairy, and scalloped around the margins. In spring and summer, small, trumpet-shaped blue flowers appear in the leaf axils (where the leaves join the stem). The plant grows only 3 in. tall, but the trailing stems or stolons reach 1½ ft. or more, rooting at the nodes (joints) as they grow. Broken pieces of the stem also root, forming new plants.

Ground ivy in bloom

Life cycle: Perennial that reproduces by seed and by stolons

Prevention: If you want to grow ground ivy as a ground cover, contain its spread with an edging of bricks, steel, concrete, or other barrier. Should it escape and invade the lawn, pull or dig it out as soon as possible; raking helps remove the stems, which have shallow roots. You usually need to weed out ground ivy several times over the course of one or two growing seasons, as bits of stolons left behind will resprout. Fertilize the lawn to help it compete with this weed, and take care not to overwater. In gardens, pull or rake ground ivy, repeating as necessary. Once you remove the top growth, use landscape fabric covered with a mulch to prevent its return.

Control: For chemical control of ground ivy in lawns, use a herbicide containing 2,4-D, MCPP, and dicamba (Weed-B-Gon, Weed-Stop), following label directions. Spot-treat ground ivy in ornamental beds with glyphosate (Roundup), taking care not to get this nonselective herbicide on desired plants.

GROUNDSEL, COMMON

SENECIO VULGARIS (ASTERACEAE)

BROAD-LEAFED ANNUAL

ZONES: US, MS, LS

Common groundsel—also known as grimsel, bird-seed, and (like several other weeds) ragwort—is an annual native to Eurasia. It appears at the edges of lawns, among shrubs and perennials, and in vegetable gardens. Seedlings of common groundsel are tiny rosettes of sharply notched, dull green, red-tinged leaves. The mature plant varies in height from 4–24 in., usually with branching stems that are ridged and succulent; under crowded conditions the plant may form a single stem, rather than branching. The lower leaves are purplish on the underside, 1–4 in. long and ½–1½ in. wide, with jagged margins. Upper leaves are smaller and clasp the stem. Many small, yellow, cylindrical flower heads cluster together, surrounded by black-tipped bracts at the base. The flower heads mature into puffball seed heads, which separate, allowing the wind to disperse the seeds. Seeds are able to germinate as soon as they ripen; thus common groundsel can produce several generations in a single year.

Life cycle: Annual that reproduces by seed

Prevention: To reduce later problems, hoe or pull common groundsel before the plants set seed. Mulch to prevent seeds already in the soil from germinating. Before planting a new ornamental or vegetable bed, solarize the soil to destroy seeds.

Control: For postemergent control, spot-treat with glyphosate (Roundup), glufosinate-ammonium (Finale), diquat dibromide, or herbicidal soap (Superfast, Scythe), taking care not to get these chemicals on desired plants.

HENBIT

LAMIUM AMPLEXICAULE (LAMIACEAE)

BROAD-LEAFED ANNUAL

ZONES: ALL

Henbit, also known as dead nettle, is a winter weed in lawns and gardens, especially in areas with rich soil. Seeds usually germinate in fall. The plants grow slowly over the winter, becoming most obvious in spring, and die as soon as the weather turns hot. Henbit grows 12–16 in. high, with the square stems typical of the mint family. The stems lie close to the ground at the base, where they may root at the nodes (joints), then curve upward. Coarsely toothed leaves are paired, opposite one another; lower leaves have long stalks, while the upper leaves clasp the stem. Small, slender, purplish red flowers appear in clusters in the axils (where the leaves join the stem) of the upper leaves in spring.

Bud of the henbit flower

Life cycle: Annual that reproduces by seed and stolons

Prevention: Henbit is easy to pull by hand. You can greatly reduce the number of plants in your lawn and garden by weeding in late winter and early spring. Keep the lawn healthy and growing vigorously to crowd out henbit seedlings. Mulching garden beds will prevent seeds that are already in the soil from germinating. You can also apply a pre-emergence herbicide containing pendimethalin (Halts) or dithiopyr (Dimension) on lawns or trifluralin (Treflan, Preen) on ornamentals listed on the label.

Control: For postemergent control in lawns, use a product containing 2,4-D, MCPP, and dicamba (Weed-B-Gon, Weed-Stop), or imazaquin (Image). Make sure these products are labeled for your type of grass. In gardens, spot-treat with herbicidal soap (Superfast, Scythe) or a product containing glyphosate (Roundup).

HORSE NETTLE

SOLANUM CAROLINIENSE (SOLANACEAE)

BROAD-LEAFED, HERBACEOUS PERENNIAL

ZONES: ALL

Horse nettle is one weed you don't want to tackle without a good set of gloves. Vicious, yellowish or white prickles arm its leaves and stems, just waiting for a shot at bare flesh. Sharp prickles also guard the midribs of the leaves, as well as the leaf stems.

Horse nettle grows 1–3 ft. high and typically occupies roadsides, pastures, and overgrown lots. But it can also invade garden beds. Leaves are 2–6 in. long and about half as wide. They may have lobed or wavy margins. All parts of the plant are poisonous to both people and animals.

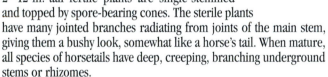

Horse nettle's green berries

Life cycle: This nonwoody perennial blooms from spring to early fall, producing clusters of light purple to white flowers with bright yellow centers that resemble the blooms of potato plants. Flowers give rise to pea-size, yellow berries that wrinkle as they age. Each berry contains numerous seeds. A single plant can produce 5,000 seeds, which germinate in spring and summer. The plant also spreads by creeping rhizomes. Any part of a rhizome left in the ground can produce a new plant.

Prevention: Mow nearby weed patches. In garden beds, lay landscape fabric around desirable plants, and cover fabric with mulch.

Control: Pull or dig plants when they're young. Remove as much of the root system as possible. Regular mowing usually eliminates horse nettle from lawns. If it doesn't, spot-treat it with a selective post-emergence herbicide labeled for your type of grass. A combination of 2,4-D, MCPP, and dicamba (Weed-B-Gon, Weed-Stop) is appropriate for most lawns. In garden beds, spot-treat with glyphosate (Round-up) according to label directions.

HORSETAILS

EQUISETUM, VARIOUS SPECIES (EQUISETACEAE)

PERENNIALS

ZONES: ALL

Rushlike survivors of the Carboniferous Age, several species of horsetails are native to the South. Common horsetails (*Equisetum hymale*), or scouring rush, shown above, produce slender, hollow, bright green stems, up to 4 ft. tall, with distinctive black and ash-colored rings at each joint. Horsetails are nonflowering plants related to ferns: conelike spikes at the end of each stem bear spores. Common horsetails is the species most often planted in gardens, but it may easily escape from its allotted area, becoming a pest in lawns and gardens. Field horsetails (*E. arvense*) has two types of mature plants, fertile and sterile. The 2–12-in.-tall fertile plants are single-stemmed and topped by spore-bearing cones. The sterile plants have many jointed branches radiating from joints of the main stem, giving them a bushy look, somewhat like a horse's tail. When mature, all species of horsetails have deep, creeping, branching underground stems or rhizomes.

Sterile plants of Equisetum arvense

Life cycle: Perennials that reproduce from spores and creeping rhizomes (underground stems)

Prevention: If you decide to plant horsetails, confine them to a container to prevent their escape. If horsetails spread into your lawn or garden, dig out as much of the root system as possible. When new sprouts appear, cut them off and dig up the roots again. Then spread a mulch of landscape fabric or cardboard, topped with organic matter, to discourage further growth.

Control: Chemical control of escaped, established plants is just about impossible. Plant them at your own risk.

HORSEWEED

CONYZA CANADENSIS (ASTERACEAE)

BROAD-LEAFED ANNUAL

ZONES: ALL

Horseweed, also known as mare's tail, is found in gardens, in lawns, and along roadsides, mainly in dry areas. The seeds germinate from fall through spring, producing a low rosette of dull green leaves covered with soft, short hairs. As the plant matures, it sends up a rough stem that grows to 7 ft. tall and that branches near the top, fanning out in a shape that resembles a horse's tail. The leaves are bristly and crowded closely along the stem. Lower leaves are spatulate or spoon-shaped, and the leaves farther up, along the stem, are lance shaped or linear. Many small flower heads form across the top of the plant. Individual flower heads have greenish white "petals" and a yellowish center. Horseweed blooms in summer, producing seeds that will float away on white bristles in late summer and fall.

Life cycle: Annual that reproduces by seed

Prevention: Young horseweeds are easy to pull or hoe. Be sure to remove the plants before they set seed. A mulch around vegetables and ornamentals will prevent seeds already in the soil from germinating. You can also apply a pre-emergence herbicide containing isoxaben (Portrait, Gallery) to keep seeds from sprouting. As seeds of horseweed can easily blow in from wild areas or pastures, it may appear again after you have removed the weed from your garden.

Control: For chemical control, spot-treat horseweeds with glufosinate-ammonium (Finale), diquat dibromide, herbicidal soap (Superfast, Scythe), or glyphosate (Roundup); take care not to get these chemicals on desired plants.

IVIES, ENGLISH AND ALGERIAN

HEDERA HELIX, H. CANARIENSIS (ARALIACEAE)

EVERGREEN WOODY VINES

ZONES: ENGLISH IVY: ALL; ALGERIAN IVY: CS, TS

Ivy is one of the South's most popular ground covers and climbing vines. It's also an aggressive spreader that can quickly invade areas beyond its allotted territory, smothering small plants in its path. Ivy spreads by trailing branches that root at the nodes as it grows along the ground, or by aerial rootlets that cling to walls, fences, or trees. English ivy *(Hedera helix)* has dull, dark green leaves 2–4 in. wide at the base and equally long, with three to five lobes. Algerian ivy *(H. canariensis),* shown above, has shiny, rich green leaves that are 5–8 in. wide and have three to five shallow lobes. The leaves of the variegated form are edged with yellowish white. Both ivies exhibit a mature phase once the vine has grown vertically for several years. The vine then develops stiff branches with unlobed leaves and flowers and produces black berries. Algerian ivy is usually more vigorous than English ivy. Both can be weedy and both can harbor rodents.

English ivy

Life cycle: Evergreen woody vines that spread by roots forming at nodes (joints) on the branches and by seed

Prevention: Confine ivy used as a ground cover within a bed surrounded by edging or paving. Do not let it climb.

Control: To remove ivy growing as a ground cover, mow it close to the ground with a heavy-duty mower. Then dig up as many roots as possible. As ivy is deep rooted, expect regrowth from roots you have missed, and further digging. Then cover the area with a double layer of landscape fabric, black plastic, or cardboard, topped with several inches of pine straw or shredded bark, for at least a full growing season. To control climbing ivy, cut and pull it down in sections. Dig out the roots, repeating until they stop sprouting.

Chemical control of established ivy is quite difficult. Repeated sprayings of glyphosate (Roundup) according to label directions will be necessary.

JAPANESE HONEYSUCKLE

LONICERA JAPONICA (CAPRIFOLIACEAE)

EVERGREEN OR SEMIEVERGREEN, WOODY, PERENNIAL VINE

ZONES: ALL

When you smell the sweet scent of its flowers or taste a drop of its sugary nectar, it's hard to envision Japanese honeysuckle as one of the South's all-time worst weeds. But it's true. Shortly after it arrived in this country from Asia as an ornamental vine in the 1800s, it escaped to the wild. Tolerating sun or shade, dry or moist soil, it quickly conquered peaceful woodlands, turning unspoiled forests into impenetrable thickets. This rapacious vine can climb to 30 ft., smothering shrubs and strangling small trees along the way. Believe it or not, it's still used as an ornamental in West Texas, because the vine isn't so rampant in arid regions. Southern hunters also plant it as winter forage for deer.

Japanese honeysuckle flower

Life cycle: Showy, fragrant flowers appear in spring and summer. They change from white to yellow after they're pollinated. Shiny, black berries containing seeds ripen in fall. Birds eat them and spread the seeds, which germinate in spring. The vine also spreads by suckers at the base of the plant that root at the leaf joints.

Prevention: If possible, eliminate Japanese honeysuckle from nearby woods. Don't plant Japanese honeysuckle. Instead, plant trumpet honeysuckle *(Lonicera sempervirens),* a noninvasive species that bears beautiful red or yellow flowers in spring.

Control: Pull, dig, or hoe seedlings as soon as you notice them. Remove vines before they climb trees. Pull up as much of the root system as possible. To kill established vines, spray with a herbicide containing glyphosate (Roundup). Or cut the vine near ground level and paint the stem's cut surface with triclopyr (Brush-B-Gon, Brush Killer) in late summer. Be sure to follow label directions carefully. Regular mowing often eliminates Japanese honeysuckle from lawns. If it doesn't, spot-treat plants with a selective, postemergence herbicide labeled for your type of grass. A combination of 2,4-D, MCPP, and dicamba (Weed-B-Gon, Weed-Stop) is appropriate for most grasses.

JAPANESE ROSE (MULTIFLORA ROSE)

ROSA MULTIFLORA (ROSACEAE)

DECIDUOUS, WOODY SHRUB

ZONES: US, MS, LS

Where this plant is concerned, the bloom is definitely off the rose. Native to eastern Asia, it was brought to this country to provide hardy rootstocks for grafted roses. It was also touted in ads on the back pages of Sunday tabloids as a "miracle living hedge" that would combine beautiful blooms with a carefree, fast-growing screen. Highway departments also planted it down the medians of interstate highways. Word had it that Japanese rose grew so thick it would stop a runaway tractor-trailer at 70 mph. Unfortunately, the plant escaped to the wild, where it has taken over fields, pastures, roadsides, and unmanaged areas. Growing 8–10 ft. tall and wide, it forms a fountain of long, curving, cascading branches armed with sharp thorns.

Life cycle: Japanese rose blooms in mid- to late spring, bearing clusters of small, white flowers that resemble blackberry blooms and smell like honeysuckle. Bright red, egg-shaped rosehips containing seeds appear in early fall. Birds eat them and spread the seeds, which germinate in spring. The plant also spreads by rooting wherever the canes touch the ground.

Prevention: Do not plant Japanese rose. If you notice suckers with lustrous, bright green foliage growing up from beneath the graft union of your rose bush (marked by a notch on the main stem), cut them off immediately. They may come from a Japanese rose rootstock. If you leave them, they'll eventually crowd out the good rose.

Control: Pull or dig seedlings when they're young. To kill established plants, spray with a herbicide containing glyphosate (Roundup) or triclopyr (Brush-B-Gon, Brush Killer) in summer. You may have to spray more than once. Be sure to follow label directions carefully.

JOHNSONGRASS

SORGHUM HALEPENSE (POACEAE)

PERENNIAL GRASS

ZONES: ALL

Johnsongrass is a tough, spreading perennial grass that can be troublesome in lawns and vegetable and flower beds. This grass reproduces from seed or from its thick, white, fleshy underground stems (rhizomes), which are segmented and break apart easily. With stems growing 2–8 ft. high, johnsongrass has a coarse, leafy appearance. Its leaf blades are ¼–1 in. wide and bright green, with a conspicuous white midvein that breaks when the leaf is folded over. The large, reddish purple flowering top, 6–22 in. long, is made up of branches bearing many shiny spikelets; it droops with age.

Life cycle: Perennial grass that reproduces by seed and by spreading rhizomes

Prevention: Repeated mowing discourages johnsongrass by preventing seed formation and weakening the roots. But digging out whole plants is more effective. Remove as much of the root system as possible. Any roots remaining in the soil will sprout, making repeated digging necessary. Rototilling is not recommended, as the machinery breaks the rhizomes into short segments, spreading the weed rather than eliminating it. To prevent regrowth, cover cleared areas with a double layer of landscape fabric, black plastic, or cardboard, topped with bark or pine straw, for at least one growing season.

You can also apply a pre-emergence herbicide containing trifluralin (Treflan, Preen) around ornamentals listed on the label or pendimethalin (Halts) on lawns.

Control: To control existing plants, spray with fluazifop-P-butyl (Fusilade, Grass-B-Gon) or glyphosate (Roundup) according to label directions.

KNOTWEED, JAPANESE

POLYGONUM CUSPIDATUM (POLYGONACEAE)

DECIDUOUS BROAD-LEAFED PERENNIAL

ZONES: US, MS, LS

Sometimes planted as an ornamental, Japanese knotweed has escaped from cultivation to become a weed of roadsides, pastures, and gardens. This tough, vigorous plant forms large clumps of reddish brown, stout, wiry stems growing 4–9 ft. high each year. The woody stems, which die back in fall, have swollen nodes or joints, giving the plant its common name of bamboo or Mexican bamboo (though it is not related to true bamboo). The large, 2–6-in.-long leaves, nearly heart shaped with a narrow pointed end, are borne on short stalks. Greenish white flowers in large, plumelike clusters appear at the ends of the stems and in the leaf axils (the juncture of leaf and stem) in late summer and fall.

Life cycle: Perennial that reproduces by spreading rhizomes (underground stems)

Prevention: Do not plant it.

Control: Getting rid of Japanese knotweed requires persistence. Cut the stems to the ground, repeating as new shoots appear. As it stores substantial food reserves in an extensive system of rhizomes, Japanese knotweed can continue to send up new shoots for months or even several growing seasons. If possible, let the infested area go dry during the summer to help slow it down.

For chemical control, spot-treat whole plants or paint cut stems with glyphosate (Roundup) or triclopyr (Brush-B-Gon, Brush Killer). This is most effective in late summer when Japanese knotweed has just begun to flower. Follow label directions carefully.

KNOTWEED, PROSTRATE

POLYGONUM ARENASTRUM; ALSO CALLED *P. AVICULARE*
(POLYGONACEAE)

BROAD-LEAFED ANNUAL

ZONES: ALL

Prostrate knotweed grows in lawns and vegetable and flower gardens, especially in areas with compacted soil. It also appears in cracks in sidewalks and driveways. This weed germinates from late winter to midspring, quickly forming a spreading, low-growing plant with wiry stems 1–3 ft. long. The stems are swollen at the joints, with many branches. There is a silvery, papery sheath where the leaves emerge from the joints; leaves are bluish green, narrow, and about ½–1 in. long and ³⁄₈ in. wide. Tiny white or pink flowers appear in clusters in the leaf axils (the juncture of leaf and stem) in summer and fall. Prostrate knotweed somewhat resembles another low-growing weed, spotted spurge, but lacks the purple spots found on the leaves and its milky juice.

Life cycle: Annual that reproduces by seed

Prevention: Aerating, fertilizing, and providing adequate water for lawns helps prevent the establishment of prostrate knotweed. If the soil in parts of your lawn remains compacted because of constant foot traffic, consider replacing the grass with a permanent path. Pull or hoe prostrate knotweed from lawns and gardens; the weeds are not difficult to pull when young, especially if the soil is damp. Mulch to prevent the germination of prostrate knotweed seeds in flower and vegetable gardens. You can also apply a pre-emergence herbicide containing pendimethalin (Halts) in late winter.

Control: To control prostrate knotweed in lawns use a selective herbicide for broad-leafed weeds containing 2,4-D, MCPP, and dicamba (Weed-B-Gon, Weed-Stop). Spot-treat this weed in other areas, such as in sidewalk cracks, with a product containing glyphosate (Roundup), glufosinate-ammonium (Finale), diquat dibromide, or herbicidal soap (Superfast, Scythe), taking care that these nonselective herbicides do not contact desired plants.

KUDZU

PUERARIA LOBATA (FABACEAE)

DECIDUOUS, SEMIWOODY, PERENNIAL VINE

ZONES: MS, LS, CS, TS

When kudzu made its American debut as an ornamental plant at the 1876 U.S. Centennial Exposition in Philadelphia, little did the organizers and visitors suspect that this harmless-looking plant would later become "The Vine That Ate the South."

Many consider kudzu to be the world's fastest-growing plant. It's reputed to grow up to a foot in a single day and more than 100 ft. in a single season. Its leaves consist of three leaflets arranged alternately along the stem. These leaflets have one to three lobes and reach

Kudzu leaves

6–7 in. long and 5 in. wide on mature plants. The vine itself grows from an enormous tuber that buries itself several feet into the ground.

In the early 1900s, kudzu was planted as a forage crop for cattle, as a cover crop to add nitrogen to the soil, and as a ground cover by highway departments to control erosion. It quickly blanketed entire fields and woods and now engulfs trees, utility poles, abandoned houses and schoolbuses, and everything else in its path. (Of course, to be fair, it has also reduced erosion.)

Life cycle: Kudzu blooms in midsummer to early fall, producing reddish purple flowers that smell like grape juice. Flattened, reddish brown seedpods mature in late summer and contain kidney-shaped seeds that germinate the following spring. The vine also spreads by trailing stems that root at the leaf joints when they touch the ground.

Prevention: If possible, eliminate kudzu from adjoining woods and overgrown lots. Don't let it climb trees, arbors, trellises, telephone poles, or anything else you ever want to see again.

Control: Spray the foliage with a herbicide containing glyphosate (Roundup) when vines are actively growing in summer. Or cut the stem near the ground and paint the cut end with triclopyr (Brush-B-Gon, Brush Killer). Be sure to follow label directions carefully. If you live on a farm, graze cattle on kudzu. They love the stuff.

LAMB'S QUARTER

CHENOPODIUM ALBUM (CHENOPODIACEAE)

BROAD-LEAFED ANNUAL

ZONES: ALL

A common weed in gardens and along roadsides, lamb's quarter is also called fat hen, white pigweed, and wild spinach. Its seeds germinate from early spring through fall. The seed leaves are easy to recognize: on top they have a mealy texture and are dull green; on the underside they are bright purple. The white mealy texture or powder is also found on the leaves of mature plants, especially on the undersides. This characteristic helps distinguish this weed from pigweeds (species of *Amaranthus*), which have smoother leaves. The ½ – 4-in.-long leaves of lamb's quarter are triangle shaped; some have smooth edges, others are lobed or wavy edged. Lamb's quarter grows 1 – 6 ft. tall, depending on the fertility of the soil, with a main stem bearing many branches. The flowers, which are greenish, small, and mealy, grow in clusters at the tips of the stems. Pollens can cause allergic reactions in some people.

HUNGRY? REALLY HUNGRY?
Tender leaves of lamb's quarter can be cooked like spinach. The scented leaves of a close relative, epazote, or Mexican tea (Chenopodium ambrosioides), are sometimes used to flavor Mexican dishes, especially beans.

Life cycle: Annual that reproduces by seed

Prevention: Lamb's quarter is fairly easy to pull, especially when young. Remove the plants from the garden before they set seed, as the seeds are very long lived; seeds of this plant found in a 1,700-year-old archaeological site in Denmark survived and germinated. Mulch around vegetables and ornamentals to prevent seeds already in the soil from germinating. Solarization (see page 31) is also effective, as is applying a pre-emergence herbicide, such as pendimethalin (Halts) for lawns and trifluralin (Treflan, Preen) for ornamentals.

Control: Spot-treat established plants with herbicidal soap (Superfast, Scythe), glufosinate-ammonium (Finale), or glyphosate (Roundup), according to label directions. Take care not to get these chemicals on desired plants.

MALLOWS

MALVA PARVIFLORA, M. NEGLECTA (MALVACEAE)

BROAD-LEAFED ANNUALS OR BIENNIALS

ZONES: ALL

Mallows are sometimes called cheeseweed, because the fruit resembles a round of cheese. Mallows infest lawns and vegetable and flower gardens. The seeds germinate from November to April. The plants grow quickly, becoming bushy and branched, and ranging from a few inches to 2½ ft. in height. The rounded leaves grow on 1 – 6-in.-long stalks and are 1 – 5 in. wide. The leaves have five to seven lobes and a distinctive folded or accordionlike appearance. Pinkish white, five-petaled flowers are borne singly or in small clusters in the leaf axil. Fruits turn from green to brown as they mature, separating into sections, each containing a seed.

Mallow flower

Life cycle: Annuals or biennials that reproduce by seed

Prevention: In lawns, fertilize and water to promote dense growth of grasses and to crowd out mallow and other weeds. In gardens, hoe or pull mallow plants when they are young. As they mature, mallows develop a long, tough taproot. To remove older plants, cut the taproot below the crown (the area where the branches originate) with a sharp hoe or shovel. Mulch to prevent germination of seeds already in the soil. Solarize new beds to kill seeds (see page 31). You can also use a pre-emergence herbicide containing isoxaben (Portrait, Gallery) to control mallow in lawns and around ornamentals listed on the product label.

Control: To control mallow growing in lawns, apply 2,4-D, MCPP, and dicamba (Weed-B-Gon, Weed-Stop). Spot-treat young mallow plants with glufosinate-ammonium (Finale) or glyphosate (Roundup), taking care not to get these chemicals on desired plants.

MEDIC, BLACK

MEDICAGO LUPULINA (*FABACEAE*)

BROAD-LEAFED ANNUAL OR SHORT-LIVED PERENNIAL

ZONES: ALL

Black medic—also known as black clover, trefoil, or yellow tre-foil—is a low, trailing plant that grows in lawns and in flower and vegetable gardens, as well as in orchards and meadows. Seeds of black medic germinate in March and April. The four-angled, hairy stems branch from the taproot, trailing 1–2 ft. along the ground. The com-pound leaves have three parts or leaflets; each finely toothed leaflet is about ½ in. wide. The central leaflet has a longer stalk than the other two. Clusters of small, bright yellow flowers appear in May and June, followed by the seedpods in August, or later in frequently mowed lawns. The curved seedpods are kidney shaped and hairy.

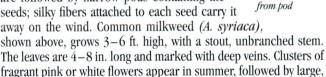

Black medic seed pods

Life cycle: Annual or short-lived perennial that reproduces by seed

Prevention: Hoe or hand-pull young plants before they set seed. Older plants develop a fairly tough taproot; dampen the soil to pull them more easily. A thick mulch will help prevent existing seeds in the soil from germinating. Soil solarization (see page 31) can kill black medic seeds.

Control: For chemical control, apply a postemergence herbicide containing 2,4-D, MCPP, and dicamba (Weed-B-Gon, Weed-Stop) on lawns. Spot-treat black medic with a product containing herbi-cidal soap (Superfast, Scythe), glufosinate-ammonium (Finale), or glyphosate (Roundup). Be careful not to apply these chemicals to desired plants.

MILKWEEDS

ASCLEPIAS, VARIOUS SPECIES (*ASCLEPIADACEAE*)

BROAD-LEAFED PERENNIALS

ZONES: ALL

Milkweeds occasionally invade the yard, but you find them mainly in fields and on roadsides. Their flowers and foliage attract butterflies, especially mon-archs. Milkweed leaves exude a sticky latex when broken. Many milkweed species are poisonous to livestock. Showy milkweed (*Asclepias speciosa*), which is native to much of Texas, is a pale green or gray-green plant growing 2–4 ft. high. The soft, woolly leaves are oval, 4–7 in. long, with prominent veins. The purplish pink flowers are followed by narrow pods containing the seeds; silky fibers attached to each seed carry it away on the wind. Common milkweed (*A. syriaca*), shown above, grows 3–6 ft. high, with a stout, unbranched stem. The leaves are 4–8 in. long and marked with deep veins. Clusters of fragrant pink or white flowers appear in summer, followed by large, hairy seedpods.

Milkweed seeds emerging from pod

Life cycle: Perennials that reproduce by seed and by creeping rootstocks

Prevention: Regular mowing in lawns or open fields will eventually control established colonies of milkweed. In garden beds, hoe or chop the stems of milkweed at or below soil surface, repeating as they grow again. Also hoe or pull any seedlings that appear. Be sure to get rid of milkweed before seeds form, to avoid later problems.

Control: For chemical control, apply glyphosate (Roundup) when milkweed is flowering. Take care not to get this chemical on desired plants.

MISTLETOES

PHORADENDRON, VARIOUS SPECIES *(VISCACEAE)*

PARASITIC EVERGREEN SHRUBS

ZONES: ALL

Mistletoes are parasitic plants that grow on woody plants, taking nutrients and moisture from their hosts. They infect many trees, including ash, birch, black walnut, box elder, cottonwood, honey locust, mesquite, and fruit and nut trees. But their favorite hangouts are oaks, especially water oak *(Quercus nigra).*

Mistletoes have green or gray-green stems and leaves; the leaves are oval shaped and thick and firm in texture. Small, sticky white or pinkish berries are spread by birds or by humans working in infected trees. Mistletoes can grow to 3 ft. high, forming a dense rounded clump attached to the host tree. While they seldom kill their host, they can seriously weaken it.

Mistletoe leaves

Life cycle: Parasitic evergreen shrubs that reproduce by seed

Prevention: Some species of trees are somewhat resistant to mistletoe. The list includes Chinese pistache *(Pistacia chinensis),* crepe myrtle *(Lagerstroemia),* ginkgo, goldenrain tree *(Koelreuteria paniculata),* sweet gum, persimmon, sycamore, and conifers.

Control: Prune out the branch of the infested tree, at least 1 ft. below the place where the mistletoe is attached. If the mistletoe is attached to the trunk or a main branch that is too large to prune, cut the mistletoe flush with the trunk or branch. This will slow the spread and growth of the mistletoe, but it will grow back. To prevent regrowth, wrap the cut area with several layers of landscape fabric or black polyethylene and tie it with flexible tape. This keeps light from reaching the parts of the mistletoe that are still in the tree; however, even under these conditions it may take several years for the mistletoe to die. If the covering becomes detached, be sure to replace it.

For chemical control, use a product containing the plant growth regulator ethephon (Florel, Etherel). When sprayed onto mistletoe in dormant trees, it causes the mistletoe plant to detach and fall from the tree. The mistletoe may grow back, so repeated applications may be necessary.

MORNING GLORIES

IPOMOEA, VARIOUS SPECIES *(CONVOLVULACEAE)*

ANNUAL VINES

ZONES: ALL

Morning glories can be pesky weeds, twining around desired plants, choking or smothering them. Tall morning glory *(Ipomoea purpurea),* native to tropical America, is often grown as an ornamental. Its heart-shaped leaves have no lobes and are 3–4¾ in. long and 1½–3 in. wide at the base; they are covered with short hairs. Its flowers may be white, pink, purple, or blue; stems grow 5–13 ft. long. Another escaped ornamental, Japanese morning glory *(I. nil),* shown above, grows vigorously to 15 ft. or more with twining, angled stems. The 1–3½-in.-long leaves have three lobes; the large flowers are light blue or purple. Red morning glory *(I. coccinea),* native to tropical America and the Southwest, has reddish, ridged stems. The leaves are 1½–2½ in. long, heart shaped on some plants and deeply lobed on others. The narrow, trumpetlike flowers are scarlet red.

Life cycle: Annual vines that reproduce by seed

Prevention: Hoe or pull seedlings as soon as you spot them. If morning glories have grown large enough to twine around other, more desirable plants, carefully untangle them and pull out the roots. To prevent future infestations, remove morning glories before they set seed. A mulch around vegetables, flowers, and other plants will prevent seeds already in the soil from germinating.

You can also use a herbicide containing isoxaben (Portrait, Gallery) as a pre-emergent in garden beds. Apply according to label directions.

Control: To kill established plants, paint the leaves with a solution of glyphosate (Roundup) or triclopyr (Brush-B-Gon, Brush Killer) according to label directions.

MOSSES

MANY FAMILIES AND GENERA

NONFLOWERING, NONVASCULAR, ROOTLESS PLANTS

ZONES: ALL

While gardeners value moss as a soft and beautiful ground cover in wooded gardens, when it grows in lawns or on pathways it is usually considered a weed. Garden moss is a mat made up of thousands of tiny, rootless plants. Generally no taller than 2 in., moss forms a green, velvety cover over the soil, rocks, or paths. It most often invades shady lawns, growing on compacted, poorly drained, acid soil.

DON'T FIGHT MOTHER NATURE. *If ridding your lawn of moss proves next to impossible, take this hint: Consider replacing the grass with a shade-loving ground cover, such as Japanese pachysandra, mondo grass, or English ivy. Or cultivate a moss lawn.*

Life cycle: Nonvascular plants that reproduce from stem pieces and from spores

Prevention: Changing your existing soil conditions is the best way to eliminate moss from lawns. Test the soil to determine its pH; add lime as needed to raise the pH to 6.5 or higher. Aerate the lawn to improve drainage. If water continues to puddle, you may need to install a drainage system. Prune trees or shrubs, if possible, to let in more sunlight. Remove moss from the flat surfaces of brick or concrete paths with a wide spatula or flat shovel.

Control: For chemical treatment of moss in lawns or on structures, use a product containing potassium salts of fatty acids (Safer Moss & Algae Killer) or pelargonic acid (Scythe), applied according to label directions. Or apply ferrous sulfate to lawns only at a rate of 1–2 lbs. per 1,000 sq. ft. These chemicals will not destroy the moss permanently; in time it will grow back unless the conditions that favor it are changed.

MUGWORT

ARTEMISIA VULGARIS (ASTERACEAE)

BROAD-LEAFED PERENNIAL

ZONES: US, MS

Also known as wild chrysanthemum, mugwort inhabits pastures, roadsides, and gardens. Mugwort is invasive, spreading widely and quickly by extensive, running roots. It grows 3–7 ft. high, with erect leafy stems, woody at the base, that rise from the rootstocks. The 2–6-in.-long leaves have three to five deep notches or lobes. Leaves, dark green on the upper side and whitish green and mealy underneath, have a strong odor reminiscent of sage. Long flowering branches appear in summer, bearing clusters of greenish flowers on short stalks.

Life cycle: Perennial herb that reproduces by seed and rootstocks

Prevention: Eliminating mugwort—and other plants with spreading rootstocks—demands patience. Cut off the stems and dig out as many of the roots as possible. In a few weeks new shoots will appear from pieces of root left behind. At this time, cut back these shoots and dig out the roots again. Cover cleared areas with a mulch of landscape fabric or thick cardboard to help suppress any remaining roots. Mulch also prevents seeds of mugwort from germinating.

Control: If chemical control is necessary, first cut back the stems. When the plant regrows to flowering stage, treat it with glyphosate (Roundup). Repeat treatments may be necessary. Take care not to get this chemical on desired plants.

MULLEINS

VERBASCUM, VARIOUS SPECIES *(SCROPHULARIACEAE)*

BROAD-LEAFED BIENNIALS

ZONES: ALL

Mulleins form a large group of plants that includes favorites for the flower border but also weeds of gardens, orchards, and roadsides. Common mullein *(Verbascum thapsus),* shown above, also called Aaron's rod or blanket leaf, is a weed found in dry, infertile soil. The plant produces a large, thick rosette of furry, gray-green leaves the first year. In its second year, it sends up a single, stout, erect stem, 1–6 ft. tall. Leaves alternate along the lower part of the stem; closely spaced flowers are borne on 1–3-ft.-long terminal spikes (stalks) at the top of the plant. The yellow, five-lobed flowers are followed by woolly, egg-shaped capsules holding a multitude of tiny dark brown seeds. A single plant can produce as many as 200,000 seeds. Moth mullein *(V. blattaria)* produces a rosette of smooth, dark green leaves with shallow teeth. In spring of the second year, a slender, dark green, 1½–5-ft.-long flower stalk shoots up. The flowers are about an inch wide, usually yellow, but in some forms they bloom pale pink or white, with showy purple stamens. Wand mullein *(V. virgatum)* has large, lance-shaped, dark green leaves at its base in its first year, followed by a 2–5-ft.-long, gently curving, flowering stalk the second spring. The bright yellow flowers with reddish centers are ¾–1 in. across.

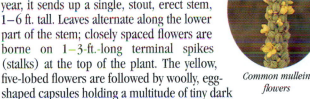

*Common mullein
flowers*

Life cycle: Biennials that reproduce by seed

Prevention: Try to pull, hoe, or dig out mullein plants during the first year, before they have a chance to flower and set seed. Be sure to dig out the taproot, which may resprout if it is not removed completely. Mulch around vegetables and ornamentals to prevent seeds already in the soil from germinating.

Control: For chemical control, spot-treat mullein with glufosinate-ammonium (Finale) or glyphosate (Roundup). These herbicides are most effective on seedlings or young plants. Take care not to get these chemicals on desired plants.

MUSTARDS

BRASSICA, VARIOUS SPECIES *(BRASSICACEAE)*

BROAD-LEAFED ANNUALS

ZONES: ALL

Wild mustards are familiar weeds in the South. Most are winter annuals, sprouting in fall, growing slowly over winter, and bursting into a sea of yellow flowers in spring. One species, called wild mustard *(Brassica kaber),* grows 1–3 ft. tall, with erect stems that have stiff hairs on lower portions. The leaves are 2–8 in. long, 1–4 in. wide; the lower leaves have lobes, and the upper ones are toothed. The four-petaled flowers are followed by 1¼–2-in.-long seedpods. Black mustard *(B. nigra)* is often taller, up to 8 ft. high. Its leaves are 2–10 in. long, 1–6 in. wide, sometimes with stiff hairs, and similar in shape to those of wild mustard. Its seedpods are less than an inch long and are carried close to the stem; the pods of wild mustard are larger and spreading.

WEED OR FEED? *The young leaves, flower buds, and flowers of these mustards are edible; they give a peppery flavor to early spring salads.*

Life cycle: Annuals that reproduce by seed

Prevention: In lawns, increase the vigor of the grass by regular fertilizing and overseeding in fall. Pull or hoe mustards when they are young. The plants are easy to pull from moist soil. To prevent future problems, be sure to remove the plants before they set seed. As these weeds often crop up in fall-planted vegetables, solarize vegetable beds in summer (see page 31) before planting, to kill mustard seeds.

You can also apply a pre-emergence herbicide containing isoxaben (Portrait, Gallery) in fall.

Control: For chemical control of established plants, spray with products containing 2,4-D, MCPP, and dicamba (Weed-B-Gon, Weed-Stop), glufosinate-ammonium (Finale), or glyphosate (Roundup) according to label directions.

NETTLE, STINGING

URTICA DIOICA (URTICACEAE)

BROAD-LEAFED PERENNIAL

ZONES: US, MS, LS, CS

The painful welts caused by the stinging hairs of this weed are familiar to hikers and gardeners. Preferring moist, shaded sites, stinging nettle infests shrub borders, orchards, fields, riverbanks, and roadsides. It grows 2–9 ft. tall, spreading widely by underground stems or rhizomes. The four-angled stems often branch from the base; they have stinging hairs and stiff bristles. Coarsely toothed leaves, 2½–5 in. long, grow in pairs along the stem. Stinging hairs cover the undersides. Spiky clusters of whitish green flowers appear on slender branches at the base of the leafstalks in summer.

Nettle seedlings

Life cycle: Perennial that reproduces by seed and by creeping underground stems or rhizomes

Prevention: You can prevent nettle seeds from spreading in garden beds by applying a product containing trifluralin, such as Treflan or Preen.

Control: Wear gloves and long sleeves when working around this weed. Mow or cut it, repeating when new growth appears. Eventually the roots will stop growing, but this may take several seasons. Digging up the roots and removing as many of the rhizomes as possible will control stinging nettle more quickly. Or, once the top growth is cleared, cover the area with a thick mulch, such as a double layer of landscape fabric or cardboard, topped with bark, for at least one growing season.

If chemical control is necessary, treat stinging nettle with a selective herbicide for broad-leafed weeds, such as Weed-B-Gon or Weed-Stop. Or you can spot-spray with glyphosate (Roundup).

NIGHTSHADES

SOLANUM, VARIOUS SPECIES (SOLANACEAE)

BROAD-LEAFED ANNUALS OR SHORT-LIVED PERENNIALS

ZONES: ALL

Several nightshades—close relatives of tomatoes, potatoes, and eggplant—are weedy pests. Their foliage and berries contain toxic alkaloids poisonous to animals and humans. Black nightshade *(Solanum nigrum),* shown above, also known as deadly nightshade or garden nightshade, is probably the most common species in gardens. A variable plant, it grows from 6 in.–2½ ft. tall, with branching stems that may stand erect or lie on the ground. The leaves are egg shaped, with smooth or wavy margins. White or pale blue flowers resemble tomato flowers. Small berries appear in bunches, dull green when young, maturing to black. Black nightshade is usually an annual, but can live for several years in warm climates. Hairy nightshade *(S. sarrachoides)* is similar to black nightshade, but it has spreading foliage that is hairy and somewhat sticky to the touch. Its flowers have white petals, and the green to yellowish berries are half enclosed by the calyx (leaflike parts at the base of the flower). Hairy nightshade, an annual, grows 2½ ft. high.

Life cycle: Annuals or sometimes short-lived perennials—all reproduce by seed

Prevention: Pull or hoe plants when they are young, making sure to get rid of this pest before the berries and seeds form. Mulch to prevent seeds that are already in the soil from germinating. Solarization (see page 31) is effective in killing seed, as is applying a pre-emergence herbicide containing isoxaben (Portrait, Gallery).

Control: To kill established nightshade, spray with glufosinate-ammonium (Finale) or glyphosate (Roundup). Be sure to follow label directions carefully.

NUTSEDGES, YELLOW AND PURPLE

CYPERUS ESCULENTUS, C. ROTUNDUS (CYPERACEAE)

PERENNIALS

ZONES: ALL

Also called nut grass, nutsedges rank among the South's most troublesome lawn and garden weeds. They favor moist, poorly drained soil. Yellow nutsedge *(Cyperus esculentus)*, shown above, grows 6–30 in. tall, with true leaves that rise from the base of each stem. Leaflike bracts (small, leaflike structures) radiate out below the flower cluster, which consists of spreading yellowish brown spikes. The flowering stem is about as long as the basal leaves. Purple nutsedge *(C. rotundus)* grows 1–2 ft. high; its basal leaves (the lowest leaves on the plant) are generally shorter than the flowering stem. Flowers are purplish brown. (In mowed lawns, flower stalks are usually not produced.) Both nutsedges reproduce by seed but also by underground stems (rhizomes) and "nutlets" (tubers), which allow them to spread rapidly. The edible nutlets of yellow nutsedge taste a bit like almonds, giving rise to one of the plant's alternate names, earth almond. The globe-shaped nutlets are smooth and brown; one nutlet grows at the end of each rhizome. By contrast, the oblong, bitter-tasting nutlets of purple nutsedge grow in a chain along the rhizomes.

Life cycle: Perennials that reproduce by seed, rhizomes, and tubers

Prevention: Remove nutsedges when they are young—with fewer than five leaves or less than 6 in. tall. Older and taller plants are mature enough to produce the nutlets from which they can regrow. When you dig or pull the plant, the nutlets break off, remaining in the soil to sprout and start a new plant. To suppress nutsedges, remove as much of the weed as possible and cover the area with several layers of landscape fabric or with cardboard. Top with bark or pine straw. Leave the cover in place for at least one growing season. You should also be careful to buy only clean topsoil and certified sod to prevent nutsedge from being introduced into your yard.

Control: For postemergence chemical control of young plants, apply a selective herbicide containing imazaquin (Image) or spot-treat with glyphosate (Roundup) according to label directions. These herbicides will not affect any nutlets that have become detached from the treated plant. Take care not to get the chemical on desired plants.

ONION AND GARLIC, WILD

ALLIUM CANADENSE, A. VINEALE (LILIACEAE)

PERENNIALS

ZONES: VARY BY SPECIES

Wild onion and wild garlic are some of the worst and hardest-to-control weeds of Southern lawns. Their dark green clumps of narrow leaves are particularly objectionable when growing in the middle of dormant, warm-season lawns that have turned brown for the winter. Wild garlic *(A. vineale)* grows from a cluster of bulbs covered with a papery sheath, like cultivated garlic. The leaves are hollow and round, pointed at the tip. Wild garlic sends up a solid, 3-ft. flowering stem in spring or summer, topped with a terminal cluster that usually contains small bulbils (a bulblike organ) rather than flowers. The bulbils fall to the ground, sprouting in fall or spring to form new plants. The original bulbs also sprout again. Wild garlic also multiplies by bulblets that split off from the central bulb. Wild onion *(A. canadense)* looks very similar but does not form bulblets.

Wild onion

Life cycle: Perennials that reproduce by bulbs and seed

Prevention: If you have just a few clumps, dig them up before they set seed. Cover cleared areas with a thick mulch, such as cardboard or black plastic, topped with bark or pine straw, for at least a full growing season.

Control: To control widespread infestations, spray with a product containing 2,4-D, MCPP, and dicamba (Weed-B-Gon, Weed-Stop), or apply imazaquin (Image). Be sure to follow label directions carefully.

ORIENTAL BITTERSWEET

CELASTRUS ORBICULATUS (CELASTRACEAE)

WOODY, PERENNIAL, DECIDUOUS VINE

ZONES: US, MS, LS

The story of oriental bittersweet illustrates the law of unintended consequences. Introduced into this country from Asia as an ornamental vine in the late 1800s, it has choked acres of woodlands in the Upper South. It did this with a major assist from birds, which eat the colorful fruits and spread the seeds hither and yon.

Actually, the South is home to two species of bittersweet. Telling them apart is easy. The native species, American bittersweet *(Celastrus scandens)*, produces clusters of fruits on the ends of its branches. Oriental bittersweet fruits all along the length of the vine. American bittersweet is considerably less aggressive and not usually a pest. The same cannot be said of its Asian cousin. Although handsome in garden settings (and prized for colorful fruits used in holiday decorations), when set loose in the wild it becomes a monster. It quickly engulfs nearby trees and shrubs, scrambling to heights of 30–40 ft. Its twining stems often throttle and kill young plants.

Life cycle: Small, greenish white flowers appear in leaf axils (the juncture of leaf and stem) along the stems from late spring to early summer. They're usually hidden by green, rounded leaves that are 2–5 in. long. In the fall, flowers give rise to pea-size, three-lobed seed capsules. As the seeds ripen, the yellow-orange capsules split open to reveal fleshy, bright red seeds. Birds eat the seeds and spread them with their droppings. The vine also propagates by suckers.

Prevention: The best way to keep this vine from becoming a problem is not to plant it. Buy bittersweet branches for holiday decorations from a florist.

Control: Repeatedly cut back stems to the ground. Eventually, the vine will stop sprouting. For chemical control of short vines (10 ft. or less), spray according to label directions with triclopyr (Brush-B-Gon, Brush Killer) or glyphosate (Roundup). To kill vines up in trees, cut through the stem near ground level, then paint triclopyr on the stem's cut surface.

OXALIS

OXALIS, VARIOUS SPECIES *(OXALIDACEAE)*

BROAD-LEAFED PERENNIALS

ZONES: VARY BY SPECIES

Two species of oxalis are persistent perennial lawn weeds in many areas of the South. Yellow oxalis (*Oxalis corniculata,* all zones), also called creeping wood sorrel, produces spreading stems, 2–12 in. long, initially growing from a single taproot. The stems soon root at the joints, eventually invading large areas. The green or purplish compound leaves are made up of three heart-shaped leaflets carried at the tip of 1–2-in. stalks. The small, $\frac{1}{4}$–$\frac{1}{3}$-in.-long yellow flowers have five petals. They are followed by cylindrical seed capsules; when the seeds are ripe the capsules burst open, shooting seeds as far as 10 ft. away. The two different species called pink wood sorrel (*O. crassipes, O. rubra*), both native to South America, were brought to the South as ornamentals but quickly escaped into lawns and gardens. The foliage typically sprouts in late winter. Showy pink flowers appear in spring. Leaves die down in summer. Pink wood sorrel is most common in the Middle and Lower South.

Yellow oxalis or creeping wood sorrel

Life cycle: Perennials that reproduce by rooting at stem joints, by seed, or by small bulbs

Prevention: Pull or dig small plants of yellow oxalis before they form seeds. You can also apply a pre-emergence herbicide containing pendimethalin (Halts) or dithiopyr (Dimension). To manage pink wood sorrel you need to get rid of the bulbs. Dig the whole plant in late winter, sifting through the soil to remove as many of the small bulbs as possible. Solarization (see page 31) will help. Both kinds of oxalis can be suppressed, although not completely exterminated, by covering a cleared area with landscape fabric or cardboard, topped with mulch, for at least a full growing season.

Control: To kill established yellow oxalis, spray with a product containing 2,4-D, MCPP, and dicamba (Weed-B-Gon, Weed-Stop). Repeated applications may be necessary. Spot-treat pink wood sorrel with glyphosate (Roundup). Follow label directions carefully.

PIGWEEDS

AMARANTHUS, VARIOUS SPECIES *(AMARANTHACEAE)*

BROAD-LEAFED ANNUALS

ZONES: ALL

Several species of pigweed populate Southern gardens. One of the most common is redroot pigweed *(Amaranthus retroflexus),* shown above, also called rough pigweed, green amaranth, or careless weed. This coarse, branching, upright plant can grow as tall as 7 ft., but it is more likely to grow to 1–3 ft. The lower stems and the taproot are reddish. Leaves are oval, 1–3 in. long, with wavy margins and distinct veins on the underside; they are borne on stems ½–1½ in. long. Both the stems and leaves are covered with short, rough hairs. Dense flower spikes with inconspicuous flowers grow at the ends of the stems and from the leaf axils (the juncture of leaf and stem). Smooth pigweed *(A. hybridus),* reaching 7–8 ft. tall, has smooth, deep green leaves and stems. Its flowering stem is longer and more slender than that of redroot pigweed. Prostrate pigweed *(A. blitoides)* forms a 6–24-in. mat with smooth, branching stems. Leaves are oval, about ½ in. wide, light green, sometimes reddish underneath. Flower spikes are borne in leaf axils. Tumble pigweed *(A. albus)* is a rounded, bushy, branching plant 6–36 in. tall. The stems are light green; the oblong, 1–2-in.-long leaves are light green on top and can be reddish on the underside. When the plant is mature, the main stem breaks easily, releasing the plant to tumble away in the wind, scattering seed. All pigweeds are prolific seed producers; a single redroot pigweed can produce more than 100,000 seeds. Pollens can cause allergic reactions in some people.

Life cycle: Annuals that reproduce by seed

Prevention: Pull or hoe pigweed seedlings when they are small. Mulch to prevent seeds already in the soil from germinating. Solarization (see page 31) is also effective. A pre-emergence herbicide containing trifluralin (Treflan, Preen) will also kill seeds.

Control: Spot-treat pigweed in lawns with a herbicide containing 2,4-D, MCPP, and dicamba (Weed-B-Gon, Weed-Stop). In gardens, treat with products containing glyphosate (Roundup), diquat dibromide, herbicidal soap (Superfast, Scythe), or glufosinate-ammonium (Finale), taking care not to get these chemicals on desired plants.

PLANTAINS, BROADLEAF AND BUCKHORN

PLANTAGO MAJOR, P. LANCEOLATA (PLANTAGINACEAE)

BROAD-LEAFED PERENNIALS

ZONES: ALL

Two species of plantain abound throughout the South, often in compacted soils that are low in organic matter. Broadleaf or common plantain *(Plantago major),* shown above, can grow up to 16 in. tall, but it usually remains shorter, especially in areas that are mowed or walked on. Forming a rosette, the thick leaves are dark green, 2–7 in. long, and somewhat egg shaped. Their short, V-shaped stem grows from the base of the plant; parallel veins mark the leaves from end to end. The flower stem is leafless, rising 4–16 in. from the base of the plant. It curves upward, topped with a dense spike crowded with many small, greenish white flowers. Buckhorn plantain *(P. lanceolata),* also called narrowleaf plantain, grows up to 18 in. tall, with leaves 3–10 in. long and less than 1½ in. wide. The leaves are covered with soft hairs and have three to five prominent veins that run the length of the leaf blade. The flowering stalks are 6–20 in. tall, ending in dense spikes of small green flowers with prominent white stamens. Pollens can cause allergic reactions in some people.

Life cycle: Perennials that reproduce by seed

Prevention: To reduce infestations of plantains in lawns, keep the lawn thick by consistent fertilization. Aerate the lawn to reduce compaction. Adding plenty of organic matter, such as compost, before planting new lawns or garden beds helps reduce the numbers of this weed. In vegetable and ornamental gardens, dig out plantains before they set seed. As they can regrow from pieces of their fibrous rootstalk left behind in the soil, it is important to remove as much of the root as possible; a dandelion weeder is helpful. Mulch to prevent seeds already in the soil from germinating.

You can also use a pre-emergence herbicide containing isoxaben (Portrait, Gallery) around the ornamentals listed on the label.

Control: For existing plants in lawns, use a selective herbicide containing 2,4-D, MCPP, and dicamba (Weed-B-Gon, Weed-Stop). Spot-treat plantains with glyphosate (Roundup), taking care not to get this chemical on desired plants.

POISON IVY AND POISON OAK

TOXICODENDRON RADICANS, T. DIVERSILOBUM (ANACARDIACEAE)

DECIDUOUS SHRUBS OR VINES

ZONES: ALL

Poison ivy and poison oak are toxic plants. A resin on their leaves, stems, fruits, and roots causes severe contact dermatitis in most people. These plants are spread by birds, which eat the fruits and disperse the seeds. Poison oak and poison ivy can appear in gardens as low shrubs, or they can twine around trees or other shrubs, developing an extensive root system before they are noticed.

Poison ivy *(Toxicodendron radicans),* shown above, usually grows as a trailing or climbing vine. The stems grow from branched, creeping horizontal rootstocks, which can spread several yards from the parent plant, sending up new shoots. The leaves, arranged alternately on the stem, are compound and borne at the end of a stalk. Each leaf is composed of three shiny, oval, pointed leaflets, which are often reddish when young, becoming glossy dark green in summer. The edges may be smooth, toothed, or lobed. Clusters of small greenish flowers appear in summer, followed by round, ridged, cream to yellow fruits that are ¼ in. wide. The foliage turns bright orange to scarlet in fall.

Poison oak *(T. diversilobum),* shown above right, grows as a dense, leafy shrub in open or partially shaded areas; in deeper shade it becomes a vine, climbing with aerial roots. Like poison ivy, it has extensive creeping horizontal rootstocks. Its leaves are also compound, made up of three leaflets, although at first glance the leaflets look like individual leaves. The central or terminal leaflet has a stem, or petiole, but the side leaflets do not have distinct stems. The margins of the leaflets of poison oak are scalloped, toothed, or lobed. The new growth is tinged red, usually becoming shiny green in summer, then turning scarlet in fall. In spring the plant develops clusters of small white flowers, which develop into waxy, white berries.

BEATING THE ITCH. *If you know you'll be walking among poison ivy, oak, or sumac, applying a pre-exposure lotion to your skin will provide temporary protection. You can get this product from mail-order suppliers, drugstores, and hardware stores.*

Life cycle: Deciduous shrubs or vines that reproduce by creeping horizontal rootstocks and by seed

Control: How much poison ivy or poison oak is present and where it is growing will affect your decision on how to manage it. A few small plants in the garden can be grubbed out physically. Wear protective clothing—tightly woven long-sleeved shirt and pants and washable cotton gloves over thick plastic gloves. Carefully cut and remove the top growth, then dig out the roots to a depth of 8 in. Do not compost the stems or roots; wrap them and put in the trash, or bury them deeply in the ground. This can be done in winter when the plants are leafless, but be careful—the stems contain the toxic resin and are still dangerous. Never burn poison ivy or poison oak, as inhaling the smoke can cause severe injury. Wash your clothing separately after contact with poison ivy or poison oak. Also wash your tools carefully, including the handles. Rinse the tools in alcohol, then dry and apply oil to prevent rust.

For chemical control, spray the foliage of actively growing plants with glyphosate (Roundup) or triclopyr (Brush-B-Gon, Brush Killer). Glyphosate is most effective when applied after the berries have formed. If most of the vine is up in a tree, you can kill it by pulling as much of it as you can off of the trunk (wearing gloves, of course), being careful not to break the stem. Fill a bucket with glyphosate or triclopyr solution, and stuff as much of the vine as possible into the bucket. The vine will carry the chemical down to the roots and die. As these herbicides will kill any other plants they contact, take care not to get them on desired plants.

WANTED—GULLIBLE GOATS. *Looking for a novel way to rid your fields of poison ivy? How about hiring a friendly herd of goats? That's right. Goats will gobble this noxious vine right down—along with any piles of tasty tin cans you may have lying around.*

POKEWEED

PHYTOLACCA AMERICANA (PHYTOLACCACEAE)

BROAD-LEAFED HERBACEOUS PERENNIAL

ZONES: ALL

Also known in the South as inkberry, pokeberry, and poke salad, pokeweed proves that hungry adventurers will try to eat almost anything. Despite the fact that all parts of the plant are poisonous, especially the roots and seeds, some desperate but intrepid soul way back when discovered that if you boil the tender, young, spring leaves three times and throw away the water, they make a zesty, safe addition to a dinner salad. Unfortunately, the raw leaves can sicken dogs, cats, and farm animals too, and such critters seldom remember the part about boiling. Pokeweed can also carry mosaic viruses (see page 256), which feeding insects can transmit to lettuce, peppers, and potatoes growing nearby.

This native American weed inhabits roadsides, overgrown lots, fencerows, cemeteries, pastures, and home gardens. Both Native Americans and early European settlers in the South used the inky, red juice in its many-seeded berries for dye.

Life cycle: Seeds germinate in spring and summer. As the seedlings grow, the young leaves are pale green and the undersides of the leaves and leaf stems turn purplish red. Red, succulent stalks may eventually reach 9 ft. tall and carry leaves that are 4–12 in. long. Small, white to greenish flowers appear in midsummer in drooping, grapelike clusters. The juicy berries turn purplish black when ripe. The berries fall to the ground, where they release their seeds.

Prevention: Cut nearby weed patches. Pull young plants before they flower and set seed. Regular cultivation and maintenance of home gardens will eliminate most pokeweed.

Control: Pull, dig, or hoe young plants. Use a mattock to dig out the fleshy roots of established plants. Spot-treat pokeweed plants with a nonselective herbicide containing glyphosate (Roundup). Be sure to follow label directions carefully.

PRICKLY LETTUCE

LACTUCA SERRIOLA (ASTERACEAE)

BROAD-LEAFED ANNUAL OR BIENNIAL

ZONES: ALL

Prickly lettuce usually inhabits fields, overgrown lawns, and roadsides, especially in areas with dry soil. When it first sprouts in winter or spring, seed leaves are about ⅓ in. long and ⅙ in. wide, with a few bristles on top; bristles also appear on the midveins on the underside of the leaf. Leaves exude a milky juice when broken or pulled from the crown. The main stem grows 1–5 ft. tall from a deep taproot. The lower part of the stem is prickly or bristly, but it is nearly smooth toward the top. Light green leaves alternate along the stem; leaf blades clasp the stem. They are somewhat twisted at the base and may point north and south (prickly lettuce is sometimes called compass plant). Lower leaves are 2–10 in. long, usually lobed, and soft hairs scatter the top. The underside of the leaf has a prominent whitish midvein lined with curved prickles. Upper leaves are smaller and generally not lobed. The inflorescence (flowering head) is spreading and branched. Individual flower heads, ⅛–⅓ in. across and yellow, often dry to a bluish color. The seeds, tufted with white hairs, float away on the wind.

Life cycle: Annual or biennial that reproduces by seed

Prevention: Pull or hoe seedlings. Dig or pull larger plants before they set seed. Mulch around vegetables and ornamentals to prevent weed seeds from germinating. Or use a pre-emergence herbicide containing isoxaben (Portrait, Gallery) around ornamentals that are listed on the label.

Control: Spot-treat with glufosinate-ammonium (Finale), herbicidal soap (Superfast, Scythe), or glyphosate (Roundup), taking care not to get these chemicals on desired plants.

LETTUCE LOOKALIKE. *Prickly lettuce is sometimes confused with annual sow thistle* (Sonchus oleraceus). *But the midribs on the undersides of the leaves of prickly lettuce have curved prickles, while the undersides of annual sow thistle leaves are smooth. Although prickly lettuce is not edible, it is related to salad lettuce,* Lactuca sativa.

WEEDS AND OTHER PESKY PLANTS

PRICKLY PEAR

OPUNTIA HUMIFUSA (CACTACEAE)

BROAD-LEAFED, SUCCULENT PERENNIAL

⚡ ZONES: ALL

One of the hardiest and most widespread of North American cacti, prickly pear grows almost any place where there is plenty of sun and well-drained soil. You'll find it on the sand dunes of Atlantic beaches and on the deserts of southwest Texas. Its flat, fleshy pads, 2–6 in. long, serve several functions—they photosynthesize just as leaves do, they store water, and they help the plant reproduce. Stems root along the lower margins wherever they touch the ground to form an ever-widening clump. Pads that break off also root. There are several other species of prickly pear that have become such pests on Texas ranches that ranchers resort to aerial sprays of herbicides.

CHUNK LIGHT OR SOLID WHITE? *Prickly pear fruits are edible and can be used to make jelly. Believe it or not, some grocers sell the fruits under the name "tuna." Some may wonder how long it will take them to start selling the pads as "caviar."*

Prickly pear rarely produces large spines. However, each pad is armed with a polka-dot array of tiny, reddish brown, barbed bristles called glochids. These irritating bristles detach easily and embed themselves in skin and clothing, making them difficult to remove.

Life cycle: Prickly pear blooms mainly in late spring and early summer. Bright yellow blossoms, often with red centers, appear singly on the edges of the pads. Flowers are followed by 2-in.-long, pear-shaped fruits that turn purple to reddish brown when ripe. Animals eat the fruits and spread the seeds. The plant also reproduces by rooting stems and pads.

Prevention: In home gardens, keep prickly pear confined. Pick up and discard fallen pads before they root.

Control: Mow, hoe, or cut prickly pear regularly until new growth no longer emerges. Spot-treat problem plants with a nonselective herbicide containing glyphosate (Roundup). Be sure to follow label directions carefully.

PURSLANE

PORTULACA OLERACEA (PORTULACACEAE)

BROAD-LEAFED ANNUAL

⚡ ZONES: ALL

Purslane, also called pusley or wild portulaca, is a low-growing summer annual found in gardens and orchards, between stepping-stones, and in cracks in pavement. It thrives in moist conditions but withstands considerable drought. Seeds germinate in late spring. The seed leaves are teardrop shaped, succulent, and tinged with red. As the plant matures, it produces many branched stems, 6 in.–3 ft. long, that form a mat. Five-petaled yellow flowers appear in leaf axils (the juncture of leaf and stem), opening in sun and followed by globe-shaped seedpods filled with black seeds. One plant can produce more than 50,000 seeds.

Purslane seedlings

Life cycle: Annual that reproduces by seed and by stem fragments that root in damp soil

Prevention: Purslane is easy to pull or hoe. Pieces of stem can reroot easily, so remove them from the garden. Remove plants that have begun to flower as they can ripen seed even after being pulled. Mulch to prevent seed germination. Purslane seeds can be killed by soil solarization (see page 31) or by applying a pre-emergence herbicide containing trifluralin (Treflan, Preen), trifluralin and benefin (Team), dithiopyr (Dimension), or pendimethalin (Halts).

Control: Treat purslane growing in lawns with a product containing 2,4-D, MCPP, and dicamba (Weed-B-Gon, Weed-Stop). In gardens, spot-treat young plants with herbicidal soap, diquat dibromide, glyphosate (Roundup), or glufosinate-ammonium (Finale), taking care not to get these nonselective herbicides on desired plants.

PURSLANE ANYONE? *Purslane leaves and stems are edible, and have a tart, lemony flavor. They are used in both French and Mexican cuisines in salads, soups, stew, and egg dishes. Some gourmet vegetable seed companies sell strains of purslane that produce extra-large leaves.*

QUACK GRASS

ELYTRIGIA REPENS (POACEAE)

PERENNIAL GRASS

ZONES: US, MS

Quack grass is an aggressive perennial weed that invades lawns and vegetable and flower gardens. It is also called witch grass or devil's grass. Quack grass can grow as tall as 3 ft., but it stays much lower in mowed areas. The leaf blades, ¼–½ in. wide, are flat, thin, pointed at the tip, and green to blue green in color. Small grasping auricles—earlike projections—clasp the stem at the base of each leaf blade. The seed heads, which are dense spikelets resembling wheat, are borne on erect stalks in summer. Quack grass produces an extensive mass of long, slender, yellowish white, branching rhizomes (underground stems) that can spread laterally 3–5 ft. The rhizomes are able to penetrate through hard soil and into roots and tubers of other plants, such as potatoes and bearded iris.

Quack grass leaf bases showing auricles

Life cycle: Perennial that reproduces by seed and by rhizomes

Prevention: Quack grass is difficult to manage. However, before planting, thoroughly dig the area and remove all visible pieces of root to slow down its growth for a few years. Apply a pre-emergence herbicide containing trifluralin (Treflan, Preen). Watch carefully for any new sprouts and remove them immediately. Quack grass can also be suppressed by cutting back the top growth and covering the area with a mulch of black plastic. Leave the cover in place for at least one year. In lawns, frequent close mowing reduces the nutrient reserves in the roots of this weed. If the infestation is severe, it is usually best to kill the lawn and weeds with an appropriate herbicide and replant.

Control: For postemergent chemical control, use fluazifop-P-butyl (Fusilade, Grass-B-Gon). Or spot-treat with glyphosate (Roundup) in spring when quack grass has 6–10 in. of new growth. Take care that this chemical does not get on desired plants.

QUEEN ANNE'S LACE

DAUCUS CAROTA (UMBELLIFERAE)

BROAD-LEAFED, HERBACEOUS BIENNIAL

ZONES: ALL

Queen Anne's lace signals the start of the "lacy" days of summer. When its graceful, white blossoms bob in the breeze along the roadside or in a meadow, it's hard to believe this is a foreign invader, an introduced weed from Asia and Europe. Really just a carrot with showy blooms and inedible roots, this plant is a welcome guest in many gardens. But beware: One seedpod can quickly fill your garden with seedlings.

Life cycle: Seedlings germinate in spring. In the first year, they resemble parsley, producing a tuft of grayish green, ferny leaves. In the second year, hollow stems, 1–3 ft. long, emerge from the tuft. The stems carry a few finely dissected leaves that get progressively smaller near the top. When crushed, they emit a strong, carrotlike odor.

Queen Anne's lace flower

Flowers appear on second-year plants from early summer until fall, bearing flat or concave clusters of lacy, white flowers, sometimes tinged with rose, at the ends of stems. When flowers fade, the edges of the cluster lengthen and curl inward over the center. Over the next few weeks, it dries out and begins to look like a bird's nest. As it breaks down, the seeds are released and the plant dies. A single plant can produce more than 4,000 seeds.

Prevention: Apply a 2–3-in. layer of mulch in garden beds in late fall to keep seeds from germinating. Or apply a pre-emergence herbicide containing isoxaben (Portrait, Gallery). Be sure to follow label directions carefully.

Control: Pull young plants when soil is moist to remove the taproot. Regular mowing will eliminate Queen Anne's lace from lawns. In garden beds, spot-treat with a nonselective herbicide containing glyphosate (Roundup) according to label directions.

RAGWEEDS

AMBROSIA (ASTERACEAE)

BROAD-LEAFED ANNUALS AND PERENNIALS

ZONES: ALL

Ragweeds typically inhabit fields and roadsides. They produce copious amounts of pollen carried by the wind, causing hay fever in late summer. Common ragweed *(Ambrosia artemisiifolia),* shown above, is an annual that grows up to 4 ft. high. Its leaves and upright, branched stems are blue green and covered with fine hairs. The feathery and fern-like leaves are 2–4 in. long. Greenish male flowers grow on terminal spikes (stalks at top of plant), producing pollen. Western ragweed *(A. psilostachya),* found in Texas and Oklahoma, is a perennial with a running root-stock or rhizome. It grows 1–4 ft. tall, with aromatic, grayish green stems and leaves that are covered with short white hairs. The feather-shaped leaves are 1¼–4¾ in. long. Greenish flowers are borne on terminal spikes. Giant ragweed *(A. trifida),* an annual, may grow taller than 10 ft. in moist sites but is shorter in dry areas. Its large leaves are quite different: large, 2½–12 in. long, and shaped like hands, usually with three lobes but sometimes five. Both the leaves and stems are rough. Flower clusters are often more than 6 in. long.

DON'T BLAME GOLDENROD. *Although goldenrod is often blamed for hay fever because its showy flowers appear at the same time as ragweed's, its pollen is too heavy to become airborne. Ragweed is the hayfever-causing culprit.*

Life cycle: Annuals and perennials that reproduce by seed; perennial western ragweed also spreads by running roots.

Prevention: Pull, cut, or mow older plants before they flower and set seed. Be sure to remove the roots of western ragweed as it can grow from pieces left behind in the soil. Mulching prevents ragweed seeds already in the ground from germinating, as does using a pre-emergence herbicide containing isoxaben (Portrait, Gallery).

Control: Treat ragweed plants with a selective herbicide containing MCPP, 2,4-D, and dicamba (Weed-B-Gon, Weed-Stop) or use a nonselective herbicide containing glyphosate (Roundup). Take care not to get this chemical on desired plants.

SANDBURS

CENCHRUS (POACEAE)

ANNUAL GRASSES

ZONES: ALL

Sandburs are annoying weeds: Their sharp, stiff spines can stick to socks, shoes, and the coats of animals. They grow in lawns, gardens, orchards, and fields and along roadsides throughout the South, especially in sandy soils. Southern sandbur *(Cenchrus echinatus)* grows 6–24 in. tall. The stems, often reddish at the base, sometimes bend at the leaf nodes (joints) and root to the ground. The 2–6-in.-long leaves may feel smooth or sandpapery. At maturity, the flower spike, 1–3 in. long, bears 10 to 20 burs, each with light purples spines. Field sandbur *(C. incertus,* also listed as *C. pauciflorus)* looks similar but has slightly smaller burs. Sandburs can produce more than 1,000 seeds per plant. The seeds are spread when the burs hitchhike on clothing or the fur of animals.

Life cycle: Annuals that reproduce by seed

Prevention: Sandburs are easy to dig or pull, especially when young. Do this before they set seed. To discourage this weed (and others) in lawns, fertilize and water properly to thicken the grass. Mulch around vegetables and ornamentals to prevent germination of seeds already in the soil. You can also use a pre-emergence herbicide containing pendimethalin (Halts), benefin (Balan), trifluralin (Treflan, Preen), or trifluralin and benefin (Team) to prevent the germination of sandbur seeds in the turf grasses and ornamentals listed on the product label.

Control: To kill established sandburs in lawns, apply imazaquin (Image) or calcium acid methanearsonate (Crabgrass Killer) according to label directions. Or spot-treat with herbicidal soap (Superfast, Scythe), glufosinate-ammonium (Finale), or glyphosate (Roundup).

SHEPHERD'S PURSE

CAPSELLA BURSA-PASTORIS (BRASSICACEAE)

BROAD-LEAFED ANNUAL

ZONES: ALL

Shepherd's purse, also called lady's purse or pepper plant, is a common winter annual weed in lawns and gardens. The seed germinates from November through March, producing a seedling with small, pale green seed leaves with tiny, glossy dots. Shepherd's purse grows 2–20 in. tall with slender, erect stems sprouting from the basal rosette (leaf whorl at base of plant). The deeply indented lower leaves grow on stalks; the upper leaves are without stalks and clasp the stem. Small white flowers with four petals appear in spring. Flowers alternate along the upper ends of the stems. The characteristic seedpods or capsules that follow are triangular or heart shaped—something like a little purse—and are attached by a stalk to the main stem. A multitude of tiny orange-brown or reddish seeds fill these capsules.

BABY GREENS FOR THE PICK-ING. *As with many members of the mustard family, the young leaves of shepherd's purse can be served in salads or cooked as greens. Best of all, they're free.*

Life cycle: Annual that reproduces by seed

Prevention: In lawns, dig out shepherd's purse early in the season, when the plants are young. Fertilize the lawn to thicken it and prevent the weed from establishing itself. In gardens, pull or hoe this weed when it is small, before seeds form. Kill seeds by solarizing the soil (see page 31) before planting winter vegetable crops. Mulch will prevent seeds already in the soil from growing.

Control: If chemical control is necessary in lawns, use a product containing dicamba, a selective herbicide for broad-leafed weeds. Spot-treat young plants with herbicidal soap (Superfast, Scythe), diquat dibromide, glufosinate-ammonium (Finale), or glyphosate (Roundup) according to label directions.

SMARTWEED

POLYGONUM (POLYGONACEAE)

BROAD-LEAFED, HERBACEOUS ANNUAL OR PERENNIAL

ZONES: ALL

Smartweeds aren't stupid. They hang out near drainage ditches, streamsides, and other poorly drained areas of your garden. Many species inhabit the South, ranging in height from ½–4 ft. tall. Their typically lance-shaped leaves alternate up the stem. At each swollen leaf joint, a papery, membranous covering called an ochea surrounds the stem. The branched stems are smooth and round and may be greenish to reddish. Spikes of greenish, white, pinkish, or red flowers appear from midsummer to early fall. These beadlike blooms are the hallmarks of smartweeds.

Life cycle: Seeds of both annual and perennial species germinate in spring and summer. Plants flower and drop seeds in summer and fall. Some perennial species, such as swamp smartweed (*Polygonum coccineum*), also spread by rhizomes (underground stems) and by rooting at leaf joints.

Prevention: Improve drainage in problem areas. Mulch garden beds to keep weed seeds from germinating. Place landscape fabric over the soil around desirable plants and cover it with mulch. Or apply a pre-emergence herbicide containing isoxaben (Portrait, Gallery) to garden beds in early spring according to label directions.

Control: Smartweeds are usually shallow rooted and easy to pull. Pull, hoe, cut, or mow plants before they flower and set seed. In lawns, spray with a selective, postemergence herbicide formulated for your type of grass. A blend of 2,4-D, MCPP, and dicamba (Weed-B-Gon, Weed-Stop) works for most grasses. If you have a centipede grass, St. Augustine, or zoysia lawn, you can also use a herbicide or weed-and-feed containing atrazine (Purge, Bonus S). Spot-treat weeds in garden beds with glufosinate-ammonium (Finale), diquat dibromide, herbicidal soap (Superfast, Scythe), or glyphosate (Roundup). Follow label directions carefully.

SORREL, RED

RUMEX ACETOSELLA (POLYGONACEAE)

BROAD-LEAFED PERENNIAL

✄ ZONES: ALL

Red sorrel, also known as sheep sorrel, occurs in lawns, gardens, and fields, and along roadsides. While common to areas with poorly drained, acidic soil, it also adapts to other soil types and to dry conditions. Young plants grow as a low rosette of leaves. As they mature, thin, upright, 4–16-in.-tall stems appear, branching near the top. Several stems may grow from a single crown; the plants spread by shallow but extensive woody, underground rootstocks to form clumps or patches. The arrow-shaped lower leaves are thick and 1–3 in. long. The upper leaves are usually thinner and smaller. Both the leaves and stems have a sour taste, something like that of cultivated sorrel. The flowers are carried on slender upright stalks near the top of the plants. Red sorrel is dioecious, meaning the orange-yellow male flowers and the red-orange female flowers are borne on separate plants. Red sorrel is related to curly dock (see page 275), a taller weed that grows from a thick taproot.

Life cycle: Perennial that reproduces by creeping rootstocks and by seed

Prevention: In lawns, pull or dig out red sorrel, removing as much of the shallow, spreading root system as possible. To help prevent the return of this weed, fertilize the lawn and aerate to improve drainage. Have the soil tested to determine its pH; if necessary, add lime to make the soil less acid. In gardens, hoe or pull red sorrel, taking care to get out the roots. If regrowth occurs from roots left behind, you will need to do more cutting and digging. After you clear an area, apply a thick mulch of landscape fabric or cardboard to smother the remaining roots and to prevent seeds already in the soil from germinating. You can also apply a pre-emergence herbicide containing isoxaben (Portrait, Gallery).

Control: For control of established plants in lawns, apply a herbicide containing dicamba. Or spot-treat red sorrel with glyphosate (Roundup), taking care not to get the chemical on desired plants. Always apply herbicides according to label directions.

SOW THISTLES

SONCHUS OLERACEUS, S. ASPER (ASTERACEAE)

BROAD-LEAFED ANNUALS

✄ ZONES: ALL

Sow thistles are common weeds in Southern gardens; they sometimes grow in lawns as well. They are summer annuals with stout taproots and hollow stems. Milky sap oozes out when a leaf or stem is broken. Yellow flower heads resemble dandelions; they are followed by fluffy seeds, spread by the wind. Annual sow thistle *(Sonchus oleraceus)*, shown above, also called colewort or hare's lettuce, grows 1–4 ft. tall. The lower leaves, attached to the stem by stalks, are 2–14 in. long. The upper leaves are smaller, lack stems, and clasp the stalk. Most of the bluish green leaves are deeply lobed with toothed margins; the terminal lobe is shaped like a broad arrow. Spiny sow thistle *(S. asper)* has upright stems 1–4 ft. high, with dark green leaves. The lower leaves are deeply lobed with spiny margins and short stalks. The upper leaves clasp the stem, without stalks; they are jagged, rather than lobed, and edged with sharp, stiff prickles. Stems and upper leaves may have a reddish tint, especially in areas of low moisture.

Life cycle: Annuals that reproduce by seed

Prevention: Pull sow thistle plants when they are young, making sure to remove them before they flower; sow thistle seeds may mature even after the plants have been pulled from the soil. When pulling larger plants, try to remove the taproot, as new shoots can grow from it. Mulching around vegetables and ornamentals will prevent sow thistle seeds already in the soil from germinating, as will soil solarization (see page 31) or applying a pre-emergence herbicide containing isoxaben (Portrait, Gallery), according to label directions.

Control: Spot-treat sow thistle plants with herbicidal soap (Superfast, Scythe), glyphosate (Roundup), diquat dibromide, or glufosinate-ammonium (Finale). Take care not to get these nonselective herbicides on desired plants.

SPEEDWELLS

VERONICA, VARIOUS SPECIES (*SCROPHULARIACEAE*)

BROAD-LEAFED ANNUALS

✎ ZONES: ALL

Speedwells are close relatives of veronicas, perennials prized for summer flowers. However, two annual speedwells can be pests, invading lawns and vegetable and ornamental beds. Persian speedwell *(Veronica persica)*, shown above, germinates in late winter or early spring, setting seed and dying by early summer. It is a branched plant with slender stems that spread over the ground, forming a low mat. The oval or rounded leaves are toothed around the edges. Pretty, four-petaled violet blue flowers with dark stripes and white centers appear on slender stalks in the leaf axils (the juncture of leaf and stem). Heart-shaped seed capsules follow the blooms. Purslane speedwell *(V. peregrina)* germinates in spring and matures by midsummer. An erect, branching plant 2–12 in. tall, this weed has narrow oblong leaves, ¼–1 in. long, rounded at the tip and usually with smooth margins. Minute, four-petaled white flowers are borne in the leaf axils. The seed capsule is similar to that of Persian speedwell.

Life cycle: Annuals that reproduce by seed

Prevention: Pull or hoe young plants before they set seed. A thick mulch will prevent seeds already in the soil from germinating. You can also solarize the soil (see page 31) or apply a pre-emergence product containing isoxaben (Portrait, Gallery) around the ornamentals listed on the label.

Control: Spot-treat speedwell in lawns with a product containing 2,4-D, MCPP, and dicamba (Weed-B-Gon, Weed-Stop), herbicidal soap (Superfast, Scythe), or glyphosate (Roundup). Do not get these chemicals on the surrounding grass.

SPURGES

CHAMAESYCE, VARIOUS SPECIES (*EUPHORBIACEAE*)

BROAD-LEAFED ANNUALS

✎ ZONES: ALL

Spotted spurge and prostrate spurge, sometimes listed as species of *Euphorbia*, are annual weeds whose stems exude a milky juice when cut. Spotted spurge *(Chamaesyce maculata)*, shown above, is particularly aggressive because it produces large quantities of seed within a few weeks of germination. Flourishing in hot weather, it grows from a shallow taproot, forming an upright, multi-branched plant 2–3 ft. tall in lawns, cracks in pavement, and gardens. The ¼–¾-in. oblong leaves have the characteristic reddish brown spot on the upper side. Clusters of tiny, pinkish brown flowers bloom at the base of the leafstalks, followed by seed capsules only ¹⁄₁₆ in. long. Prostrate spurge *(C. humistrata)* has smaller leaves with similar spots. It forms a creeping mat in lawns and gardens and roots at the nodes (places where leaves join the stems).

Life cycle: Annuals that reproduce by seed

Prevention: Keep lawns thick to crowd out spurge. Hoe or pull out plants early in the season, before they bloom and set seed. Mulch prevents seeds already in the soil from germinating. If chemical control is necessary, use a pre-emergence product containing isoxaben (Portrait, Gallery), benefin (Balan), dithiopyr (Dimension), or pendimethalin (Halts) in the lawn and around the ornamentals listed on the label.

Control: Spot-treat spurge plants with herbicidal soap when they are young. Use a selective herbicide for broad-leafed weeds containing 2,4-D, MCPP, and dicamba (Weed-B-Gon, Weed-Stop) to control spurge plants in lawns. For spurge growing in cracks in pavement, apply glyphosate (Roundup), diquat dibromide, or glufosinate-ammonium (Finale).

STRAWBERRY, WILD

DUCHESNEA INDICA (ROSACEAE)

BROAD-LEAFED, HERBACEOUS PERENNIAL

✏ ZONES: ALL

Don't go looking for a free meal from wild strawberry *(Duchesnea indica)*. Although its red, strawberrylike fruits look palatable, they have all the flavor of candle wax. But at least they aren't poisonous. Also called snakeberry, Indian strawberry, and mock strawberry, this creeping perennial can reach 6 in. tall. Leaves are composed of three leaflets, 1–3 in. long and less than 1½ in. wide, with rounded teeth on the margins. The true wild strawberry *(Fragaria virginiana)* isn't a weed. Its white flowers are followed by edible fruit.

Wild strawberry flower

The wild strawberry weed prefers moist, shady environments. Found in pastures and along roadsides, it often invades lawns and gardens. Plant runners root at the leaf joints to form new plants. Although some gardening books recommend using wild strawberry as a ground cover, in most gardens it is too rampant and has too little ornamental value to make this worthwhile.

Life cycle: Yellow, five-petaled flowers are produced from February through fall. They give rise to rounded, red, spongy, and flavorless fruits. Nondiscriminating birds and other wildlife eat the fruits and spread the seed. The plant also spreads by runners.

Prevention: Pull young plants before they can flower and set seed. Mulch garden beds to keep seeds from germinating.

Control: Pull, dig, or hoe plants when the soil is moist. To control wild strawberry in lawns, use a postemergence herbicide formulated for your type of grass. A combination of 2,4-D, MCPP, and dicamba (Weed-B-Gon, Weed-Stop) should work for most lawns. In garden beds, spot-treat plants with glyphosate (Roundup). Be sure to follow label directions carefully.

SUMAC

RHUS (ANACARDIACEAE)

DECIDUOUS OR EVERGREEN, WOODY TREE OR SHRUB

✏ ZONES: US, MS, LS, CS

Sumacs have a lot going for them. Few plants can match their brilliant fall colors of scarlet, crimson, orange, and yellow. Birds and other wildlife prize their reddish fruits. Sumacs also tolerate the worst, most barren, rockiest soils. Unfortunately, many species are extremely invasive, suckering at nearly the speed of light to form dense thickets. They're also erroneously accused of causing skin rashes, which should be rightfully blamed on a lookalike cousin called poison sumac *(Toxicodendron vernix)*.

Three deciduous species of sumac are common in the South. Smooth sumac *(Rhus glabra)* grows 10–20 ft. high and wide. Erect clusters of scarlet fruit are showy in fall and winter. Shining sumac *(R. copallina)* grows 10–25 ft. tall and wide. It has glossy leaves with winged stems and bears fuzzy, red fruit clusters. Staghorn sumac *(R. typhina)* is the easiest species to recognize. Growing 15–30 ft. tall and wide, it develops many-branched trunks covered with short, soft hairs that resemble the "velvet" on a deer's antlers. Its fuzzy crimson fruits last all winter. A cutleaf selection, 'Laciniata', is sometimes used as an ornamental.

Life cycle: Seeds germinate in spring after lying dormant in winter. Clusters of tiny, greenish or chartreuse flowers appear atop mature plants in early summer, followed by red fruits that ripen in early fall and last into winter. Birds and other animals eat the fruits and spread the seed. Most species also spread by suckering aggressively.

Prevention: In home gardens, plant sumacs in beds where their roots can be confined or in lawns where the suckers can be mowed.

Control: Spray with a nonselective herbicide containing glyphosate (Roundup) or triclopyr (Brush-B-Gon, Brush Killer) when plants are actively growing. Or cut trunks near the ground and paint triclopyr onto the cut surfaces. Be sure to follow label directions carefully.

THISTLES

CIRSIUM, CARDUUS (ASTERACEAE)

BROAD-LEAFED ANNUALS, BIENNIALS, AND PERENNIALS

ZONES: ALL

A number of thistles invade gardens, fields, meadows, and roadsides. Canada thistle *(Cirsium arvense)*, shown above, is a tough perennial that grows from deep, wide-spreading horizontal roots to form extensive colonies. Leaves are oblong or lance shaped, with spiny-toothed margins. The ridged stems, reaching from 1–4 ft. tall, branch near the top and bear clusters of ¾-in.-wide purple flower heads in summer and fall. Bull thistle *(Cirsium vulgare)* is a biennial that produces a rosette of deeply lobed and toothed leaves in the first year. The second year, flowering stems 2–5 ft. tall appear, bearing many spreading branches and topped with clusters of four or five showy rose purple flowers. Canada thistle leaves are smooth

Bull thistle flower

on top and smooth or hairy underneath; the leaves of bull thistle are prickly on top and cottony below. Musk thistle *(Carduus nutans)* is a biennial or winter annual with deep green, spiny-margined leaves that have lighter green midribs. The leafy stems grow up to 6 ft. tall, and carry solitary 1½–3-in.-wide dark rose or white flowers with distinctive bracts (small leaflike structures) at the base.

Life cycle: Annuals, biennials, and perennials that reproduce by seed; Canada thistle also reproduces by creeping roots

Prevention: Hoe or dig out thistles before they set seed, removing as much of the root system as possible. To weaken the roots, cut or mow new shoots as they appear. It may take several seasons to kill the roots of the perennial Canada thistle.

Control: For chemical control, use a selective herbicide for broadleafed weeds that contains 2,4-D, MCPP, and dicamba (Weed-B-Gon, Weed-Stop). Or use a nonselective herbicide containing glyphosate (Roundup). The best time to spray depends on the type of thistle, so check the herbicide label. Repeated treatment may be necessary.

THREE-SEEDED MERCURY

ACALYPHA VIRGINICA (EUPHORBIACEAE)

BROAD-LEAFED, HERBACEOUS ANNUAL

ZONES: ALL

Three-seeded mercury is one of those ubiquitous weeds you seldom notice in the home garden, because it grows happily among your good plants without taking over. It tolerates a wide variety of soils, from sandy to clay and from wet to dry. It also grows in either sun or shade. In the wild, you'll often find it along roadsides, stream banks, and drainage ditches. In home gardens, it inhabits both flower and vegetable gardens.

Growing 6–12 in. tall, three-seeded mercury develops a wiry main stem with thin, wide-spreading, ascending branches. The branches hold egg-shaped leaves with slightly toothed margins on long, hairy stems. Leaves are opposite on the lower stems and alternate near the top. When it grows in full sun, the plant's younger leaves often develop a coppery color, giving the weed its other common name of Virginia copperleaf. Many insects consider three-seeded mercury a tasty salad and riddle its leaves with holes.

Life cycle: Seeds germinate in spring and summer. From early summer to fall, seedlings produce clusters of tiny, greenish white flowers in the leaf joints up and down the stems. Three-lobed seedpods then develop. Each contains three, dull, reddish brown or gray, egg-shaped seeds. After dropping seeds, the plant dies with the frost.

Prevention: Three-seeded mercury is shallow rooted and easy to pull. Pull young plants before they have the chance to flower and set seed. Mulch garden beds to keep seeds from germinating.

Control: Hoe, dig, or pull young weeds when the soil is moist. In garden beds, spot-treat with glufosinate-ammonium (Finale), diquat dibromide, herbicidal soap (Superfast, Scythe), or glyphosate (Roundup). Keep these herbicides off desirable plants and follow label directions carefully.

TORPEDO GRASS

PANICUM REPENS (GRAMINEAE)

PERENNIAL GRASS

✎ ZONES: CS, TS

When torpedo grass takes aim at lawns, it's full speed ahead. This very aggressive, highly invasive grass grows 1–3 ft. high. Believed to have originated in Australia, it prefers moist, sandy soils near the coast. You'll often see it along canals, ditch banks, and lakeshores, where it grows out into the water to form floating mats. However, this erect, wiry creeper also grows on poorly drained, clay soils as well as sand dunes.

Torpedo grass invades lawns and gardens by producing creeping rhizomes that "torpedo" their way through the soil, sometimes traveling 20 ft. or more from the parent plant. Its narrow, flat or folded leaves are 2–10 in. long and about $\frac{1}{16}$–$\frac{1}{4}$-in. wide. Upper leaf surfaces are hairy, and edges are often rolled inward. Rigid stems bear flower heads composed of loose, open-branched clusters that are 3–9 in. long and angled upward.

Life cycle: This perennial grass reproduces primarily through an extensive network of wide-spreading rhizomes. It also spreads by seed.

Prevention: Improve drainage in lawn and garden areas. If possible, spray torpedo grass in unmanaged areas around your property with glyphosate (Roundup) or fluazifop-P-butyl (Fusilade, Grass-B-Gon), according to label directions, to prevent an invasion.

Control: Spot-treat torpedo grass in garden beds or lawns with a herbicide containing glyphosate (Roundup) or fluazifop-P-butyl (Fusilade, Grass-B-Gon) according to label directions, being careful to keep these herbicides off desired grass. Controlling torpedo grass in a heavily infested lawn is nearly impossible. You can either use glyphosate to kill the entire lawn and start over or learn to love torpedo grass.

VETCHES, COMMON AND HAIRY

VICIA SATIVA, V. VILLOSA (FABACEAE)

BROAD-LEAFED ANNUALS

✎ ZONES: ALL

These vetches are often planted as cover crops for their contribution of nitrogen to the soil and for erosion control on banks. However, they have escaped from cultivation and become weeds in gardens and along fences and roadsides. Common vetch *(Vicia sativa),* shown above, germinates in early winter and matures in spring. This branching, twining plant climbs on shrubs, trees, and fences and insinuates itself among perennials in flower beds. Growing 1–2½ ft. tall, it has compound leaves composed of five to seven pairs of oblong leaflets arranged on each side of a stalk. The stalk ends in a slender, coiling tendril that helps the plant climb. Showy pink or reddish flowers resembling sweet peas appear singly or in clusters of two in the leaf axils (the juncture of leaf and stem). Hairy, twisted, brown seedpods, 1½–3 in. long, follow; each contains 5 to 12 round seeds. Hairy vetch *(V. villosa)* has hairy stems to 6 ft. long, and hairy leaves. The compound leaves, which are smaller than those of common vetch, have 10 to 20 narrow leaflets and end in a tendril. Flower clusters are made up of 10 to 20 purplish red flowers, arranged on one side of the stalk. The seedpod is ¾–1 in. long.

Life cycle: Annuals that reproduce by seed

Prevention: Pull vetch before it sets seed. The stems twine around other plants and tend to break off when pulled, making it difficult to remove the whole weed at once. Landscape fabric or a thick mulch will help prevent seeds already in the soil from germinating.

Control: If chemical control is necessary, use a selective herbicide for broad-leafed weeds that contains 2,4-D, MCPP, and dicamba (Weed-B-Gon, Weed-Stop). Or spot-treat with glyphosate (Roundup). Always apply herbicides according to label directions.

KING OF THE WEEDS. *Crown vetch (Coronilla varia) is often touted as an attractive, carefree ground cover that tolerates poor, dry, rocky soil. But be warned: It seeds with abandon and quickly spreads to nearby fields, pastures, roadsides, and lawns.*

VIOLETS

VIOLA (VIOLACEAE)

BROAD-LEAFED ANNUALS AND PERENNIALS

 ZONES: ALL

Violets can be charming, but they can also become some of the worst, most intractable weeds. They are most likely to invade moist, shaded areas of the lawn or garden. Many different species inhabit the South, usually featuring heart-shaped leaves and purple or white spring flowers. Most grow from thick, spreading rhizomes (underground stems) that are resistant to herbicides. They also spread rapidly by seed.

Life cycle: Annuals and perennials that reproduce by seed; perennials that also reproduce by runners

Prevention: Dig up plants before they set seed, making sure to remove the entire rhizome.

Control: You can kill young plants in the lawn that haven't yet formed rhizomes by spraying them with a product containing 2,4-D, MCPP, and dicamba (Weed-B-Gon, Weed-Stop) or imazaquin (Image). To kill mature plants, spot-treat with triclopyr (Brush-B-Gon, Brush Killer) according to label directions.

CLEISTOGAMOUS RELATIONSHIPS. *One reason common violets spread so rapidly through the lawn is that the plants are cleistogamous. This means that their showy spring flowers aren't the only source of seed. Throughout the summer, inconspicuous, unopened, greenish-white flowers appear in the crowns of the plants. These self-pollinating blooms actually produce much more seed than their colorful counterparts.*

YARROW, COMMON

ACHILLEA MILLEFOLIUM (ASTERACEAE)

BROAD-LEAFED PERENNIAL

ZONES: ALL

Common yarrow, also known as milfoil, is a native found in the wild in fields and meadows. You'll often see some of its showy, pink-and-red-flowering selections in flower gardens. However, this tough plant sometimes invades lawns, as well as beds planted in more delicate perennials; its spreading rhizomes make it difficult to remove. The presence of yarrow in lawns may also indicate that the soil is acidic and infertile. Common yarrow grows 2–4 ft. tall if left unmowed; in lawns, it adapts to mowing and grows as low rosettes of foliage. The aromatic 2–6-in.-long leaves are lance shaped in outline and finely divided, giving the plant a feathery appearance. Fine hairs cover both stems and foliage. If yarrow is not mowed, flat-topped clusters made up of many individual flowers appear throughout the summer at the ends of the stems. The flowers are most often white in the wild, but pinkish or yellow forms may occur. Yarrow produces seed from late summer through fall.

Life cycle: Perennial that reproduces by seed and by spreading rhizomes

Prevention: In lawns, dig out yarrow, getting as much of the root system as possible, repeating if new growth appears. To help prevent reinfestation, have the soil tested; if it is overly acidic, add lime as recommended. Thicken the turf through fertilization and proper watering to help it compete with weeds.

Control: For chemical control, use a selective herbicide, labeled for broad-leafed weeds and containing dicamba. A nonselective herbicide containing glyphosate (Roundup) will kill yarrow, but take care not to get this chemical on desired plants. Always apply herbicides according to label directions.

Suppliers and EXPERT RESOURCES

*I*t seems there is nothing more dangerous than getting readers excited about a new plant or product, then failing to supply a source for it. Folks can get mighty peeved about that. So, to preserve your happiness and our health, the following pages contain all sorts of useful information including public gardens in your area, mail-order suppliers that specialize in beneficial insects and controls, organic gardening tools and supplies, pest-resistant plants, and telephone numbers for Cooperative Extension Offices across the South.

BOTANICAL GARDENS AND OTHER GARDENS OF NOTE

Take advantage of the public gardens near you. They are both inspiring and educational, and they often feature the newest plant introductions as well as tried-and-true plants that are adapted to your area. Many offer educational courses for both adults and children. Public gardens are a good place to get answers to your gardening questions. And, of course, there is hardly a better place for enjoying a leisurely stroll during a quiet spring morning or an autumn afternoon. Remember that addresses and phone numbers are subject to change.

Agecroft Hall Museum and Gardens
4305 Sulgrave Road
Richmond, VA 23221
(804) 353-4241
www.AgecroftHall.com

American Rose Society
P.O. Box 30000
8877 Jefferson Paige Road
Shreveport, LA 71130-0030
(318) 938-5402
www.ars.org

Arkansas State Capitol Rose Gardens
Office of Secretary of State
State Capitol
Little Rock, AR 72201-1094
(501) 682-1010
www.sosweb.state.ar.us

Asheville Botanical Gardens
151 W. T. Weaver Boulevard
Asheville, NC 28804
(828) 252-5190

Ashland, The Henry Clay Estate
120 Sycamore Road
Lexington, KY 40502
(606) 266-8581
www.henryclay.org

Atlanta Botanical Garden
1345 Piedmont Avenue
Atlanta, GA 30309
(404) 876-5859

Bayou Bend Collection and Gardens
1 Westcott Street
Houston, TX 77007
(713) 639-7750

Top left: *Tyler Rose Garden, Tyler, Texas;* below: *Birmingham Botanical Gardens, Alabama*

Bellingrath Gardens and Home
12401 Bellingrath Road
Theodore, AL 36582-9704
(800) 247-8420
www.bellingrath.org

Bernheim Arboretum and Research Forest
P.O. Box 130
Clermont, KY 40110
(502) 955-8512
www.win.net/bernheim

Birmingham Botanical Gardens
2612 Lane Park Road
Birmingham, AL 35223
(205) 879-1227
www.bbgardens.org

Bok Tower Gardens
1151 Tower Boulevard
Lake Wales, FL 33853-3412
(941) 676-1408

Briarwood, The Caroline Dormon Nature Preserve
P.O. Box 226
Natchitoches, LA 71458
(318) 576-3379

Brookgreen Gardens
Highway 17 South
Murrells Inlet, SC 29576
(843) 237-4218

Brookside Gardens
1500 Glenallen Avenue
Wheaton, MD 20902
(301) 949-8231

Callaway Gardens
Highway 27
Pine Mountain, GA 31822
(706) 663-2281
www.callawaygardens.com

Cheekwood, Nashville's Home of Art and Gardens
1200 Forrest Park Drive
Nashville, TN 37205
(615) 356-8000
www.cheekwood.org

Colonial Williamsburg
P.O. Box 1776
Williamsburg, VA 23187
(800) 447-8679
www.history.org

Bernheim Arboretum and Research Forest; Clermont, Kentucky

Core Arboretum
Department of Biology
P.O. Box 6057
West Virginia University
Morgantown, WV 26506-6057
(304) 293-5201, ext. 2547
www.as.wvu.edu/biology/

*Callaway Gardens;
Pine Mountain, Georgia*

Crosby Arboretum
Mississippi State University
P.O. Box 1639
370 Ridge Road
Picayune, MS 39466-1639
(601) 799-2311
www.crosbyarboretum.org

Cylburn Arboretum
4915 Greenspring Avenue
Baltimore, MD 21209
(410) 367-2217

Cypress Gardens
3030 Cypress Gardens Road
Moncks Corner, SC 29461
(843) 553-0515

Cypress Gardens
2641 South Lake Summit Drive
Winter Haven, FL 33884
(800) 282-2123

The Dallas Arboretum
8525 Garland Road
Dallas, TX 75218
(214) 327-8263

Dixon Gallery and Gardens
4339 Park Avenue
Memphis, TN 38117
(901) 761-5250
www.dixon.org

Dallas Arboretum; Dallas, Texas

Dothan Area Botanical Gardens
P.O. Box 5971
Dothan, AL 36302
(334) 793-3224
www.dabg.com

Sarah P. Duke Gardens
Duke University
Durham, NC 27708
(919) 684-3698
www.hr.duke.edu/dukegardens

Dumbarton Oaks
1703 32nd Street, NW
Washington, DC 20007
(202) 339-6401

Eureka Springs Gardens
Route 6
Eureka Springs, AR 72632
(501) 253-9244

Fairchild Tropical Garden
10901 Old Cutler Road
Miami, FL 33156
(305) 667-1651
www.ftg.org

Fort Worth Botanic Garden
3220 Botanic Garden Boulevard
Fort Worth, TX 76107
(817) 871-7686

Lewis Ginter Botanical Garden
1800 Lakeside Avenue
Richmond, VA 23228-4700
(804) 262-9887

Gunston Hall
10709 Gunston Road
Mason Neck, VA 22079
(703) 550-9220
www.gunstonhall.org

Hampton National Historic Site
535 Hampton Lane
Towson, MD 21286
(410) 823-1309

The Hermitage
4580 Rachel's Lane
Hermitage, TN 37076-1344
(615) 889-2941
www.thehermitage.com

Hillwood Museum and Gardens
4155 Linnean Avenue, NW
Washington, DC 20008
(202) 686-8500

Hodges Gardens
P.O. Box 900
Many, LA 71449
(318) 586-3523
www.hodgesgardens.qpg.com

Huntsville-Madison County Botanical Garden
4747 Bob Wallace Avenue
Huntsville, AL 35805
(256) 830-4447
www.hsvbg.org

Jasmine Hill Gardens and Outdoor Museum
3001 Jasmine Hill Road
Montgomery, AL 36093-1718
(334) 567-6463; fax (334) 567-6466
www.jasminehill.org

The Lady Bird Johnson Wildflower Center
4801 La Crosse Avenue
Austin, TX 78739
(512) 292-4200
www.wildflower.org

Ladew Topiary Gardens
3535 Jarrettesville Pike
Monkton, MD 21111
(410) 557-9466

Ladew Topiary Gardens; Monkton, Maryland

Maclay State Gardens; Tallahassee, Florida

Harry P. Leu Gardens
1920 North Forest Avenue
Orlando, FL 32803-1537
(407) 246-2620; fax (407) 246-2849
www.ci.orlando.fl.us/departments/
leu_gardens

Lilypons Water Gardens
6800 Lilypons Road
Buckeystown, MD 21717
(800) 999-5459

Lockerly Arboretum
1534 Irwinton Road
Milledgeville, GA 31061
(912) 452-2112

London Town House and Gardens
839 Londontown Road
Edgewater, MD 21037
(410) 222-1919

Longue Vue House and Gardens
7 Bamboo Road
New Orleans, LA 70124-1065
(504) 488-5488; fax (504) 487-7015
www.longuevue.com

Alfred B. Maclay State Gardens
3540 Thomasville Road
Tallahassee, FL 32308
(850) 487-4115
www.ssnow.com/maclay

Magnolia Plantation and Gardens
Route 4, Highway 61
Charleston, SC 29414
(843) 571-1266

Maymont
1700 Hampton Street
Richmond, VA 23220
(804) 358-7166

Memphis Botanic Garden
750 Cherry Road
Memphis, TN 38117
(901) 685-1566
www.intromemphis.com

Mercer Arboretum and Botanic Gardens
22306 Aldine Westfield Road
Humble, TX 77338
(281) 443-8731

Middleton Place
Highway 61
Charleston, SC 29407
(843) 556-6020

Minamac Wildflower Bog
13199 MacCartee Lane
Silverhill, AL 36576
(334) 945-6157

Missouri Botanical Garden
4344 Shaw Boulevard
St. Louis, MO 63110
(314) 577-9400; (800) 642-8842

Mobile Botanical Gardens
P.O. Box 8382
5151 Museum Drive
Mobile, AL 36689
(334) 342-0555

Monticello
Thomas Jefferson Memorial Foundation
P.O. Box 316
Charlottesville, VA 22902
(804) 984-9822
www.monticello.org

Mynelle Gardens
4736 Clinton Boulevard
Jackson, MS 39209-2402
(601) 960-1894; fax (601) 922-5759

Myriad Botanical Gardens
100 Myriad Gardens
Oklahoma City, OK 73102
(405) 297-3995

Norfolk Botanical Gardens
6700 Azalea Garden Road
Norfolk, VA 23518-5337
(757) 441-5830
www.communitylink.org/nbg

Magnolia Plantation and Gardens; Charleston, South Carolina

Monticello; Charlottesville, Virginia

North Carolina Botanical Garden
CB 3375, Totten Center
University of North Carolina at Chapel Hill
Chapel Hill, NC 27599-3375
(919) 962-0522

*The Lady Bird Johnson Wildflower Center;
Austin, Texas*

Oklahoma Botanical Garden and Arboretum
Oklahoma State University
Department of Horticulture and Landscape Architecture
360 Agriculture Hall
Stillwater, OK 74078-6027
(405) 744-6470
**home.okstate.edu/okstate/dasnr/hort/
hortlahome.nsf/toc/obga**

Orton Plantation Gardens
9149 Orton Road SE
Winnabow, NC 28479
(910) 371-6851

William Paca Garden
1 Martin Street
Annapolis, MD 21401
(410) 263-5553

JC Raulston Arboretum at North Carolina State University
Department of Horticultural Science
P.O. Box 7609
Raleigh, NC 27695-7609
(919) 515-3132
arb.ncsu.edu

Reynolda Gardens of Wake Forest University
100 Reynolda Village
Winston-Salem, NC 27106
(336) 758-5593
www.wfu.edu/gardens

Rip Van Winkle Gardens
5505 Rip Van Winkle Road
New Iberia, LA 70560
(318) 365-3332; (800) 375-3332

Rosedown Plantation and Historic Gardens
12501 Highway 10
St. Francisville, LA 70775
(225) 635-3332

San Antonio Botanical Gardens
555 Funston Place
San Antonio, TX 78209
(210) 207-3250
www.sabot.org/

Sandhills Horticultural Garden
Sandhills Community College
2200 Airport Road
Pinehurst, NC 28374
(910) 695-3882

George Washington's Mount Vernon: Estate and Gardens; Mount Vernon, Virginia

Marie Selby Botanical Gardens
811 South Palm Avenue
Sarasota, FL 34236-7726
(941) 366-5730
www.selby.org

The South Carolina Botanical Garden
Clemson University
Box 345215
Clemson, SC 29634-5215
(864) 656-3405

The State Botanical Garden of Georgia
2450 South Milledge Avenue
Athens, GA 30605
(706) 542-1244
www.uga.edu/~botgarden

Daniel Stowe Botanical Garden
6500 South New Hope Road
Belmont, NC 28012
(704) 825-4490
www.stowegarden.org

Tryon Palace Historic Sites and Gardens
P.O. Box 1007
610 Pollock Street
New Bern, NC 28563
(252) 514-4900; (800) 767-1560

Winterthur Museum, Garden, and Library; Winterthur, Delaware

Tyler Rose Garden
Tyler Parks Department
P.O. Box 7039
420 South Rose Park Drive
Tyler, TX 75702
(903) 531-1213

University of North Carolina at Charlotte Botanical Gardens
Biology Department, UNCC
9201 University City Boulevard
Charlotte, NC 28223-0007
(704) 547-2364

U.S. Botanic Garden
Maryland Ave. and First St., SW
Washington, DC 20024
(202) 225-8333

U.S. National Arboretum
3501 New York Avenue, NE
Washington, DC 20002
(202) 245-2726

George Washington's Mount Vernon: Estate and Gardens
Mount Vernon Ladies' Association
P.O. Box 110
Mount Vernon, VA 22121
(703) 780-2000
www.mountvernon.org

Winterthur Museum, Garden, and Library
Route 52
Winterthur, DE 19735
(800) 448-3883
www.winterthur.org

Woodlawn Plantation
P.O. Box 37
Mount Vernon, VA 22121
(703) 780-4000

MAIL-ORDER SUPPLIERS

Now that you've read about disease-resistant apples, tomatoes, roses, crepe myrtles, and other plants, you're probably wondering where you can get them. The mail-order nurseries listed on these pages can help. They are also sources for Southern native and organically grown plants, open-pollinated flower and vegetable seed, and gardening supplies. Call or write for current catalogs. Addresses and phone numbers are subject to change.

PLANT AND SEED SPECIALISTS

Ames Orchard and Nursery
18292 Wildlife Road
Fayetteville, AR 72701
(800) 443-0283
Disease-resistant fruit trees, grapes, and berries; pruning tools and orchard supplies

Antique Rose Emporium
9300 Lueckemeyer Road
Brenham, TX 77833-6453
(409) 836-9051; (800) 441-0002
Broad selection of own-root old roses

Barber Nursery
14282 Rogers Road
Willis, TX 77378
(409) 856-8074
Trees and shrubs grown from seed collected in Texas, Louisiana, and Arkansas

Brittingham Plant Farms
P.O. Box 2538
Salisbury, MD 21802-2538
**(410) 749-5153; fax (800) 749-5148
(Dept. SL99)**
Virus-free strawberry plants, as well as asparagus roots, raspberries, blackberries, blueberries, rhubarb, and grapes

Eco-Gardens
P.O. Box 1227
Decatur, GA 30031
(404) 294-6468
Native and exotic plants hardy in the Piedmont region including hellebores, trilliums, sedums, and asarums

Goodness Grows
P.O. Box 311
Lexington, GA 30648
(706) 743-5055; fax (706) 743-5112
Perennials and Southeastern native plants

Hidden Springs Nursery
170 Hidden Springs Lane
Cookeville, TN 38501
Contact by mail only. Disease-resistant antique apples, as well as apricots, grapes, mayhaws, hardy kiwis, medlars, quinces, pears, pawpaws, and plums

Holland Wildflower Farm
P.O. Box 328
Elkins, AR 72727
(800) 684-3734
www.hwildflower.com
Plants and seed of prairie wildflowers well suited to harsh winters and hot summers

Indigo Marsh
2513 West Lucas Street, B-6
Florence, SC 29501
(843) 679-0999
www.indigomarsh.com
Flowering shrubs and perennials, beneficial insects, and biological controls

Johnson Nursery, Inc.
5273 Highway. 52 E.
Ellijay, GA 30540
(888) 276-3187
www.johnsonnursery.com
Disease-resistant fruit trees including apples, peaches, pears, plums, cherries, and figs, as well as berries and grapes

Just Fruits and Exotics
30 St. Francis Street
Crawfordville, FL 32327
(850) 926-5644
justfruits@msn.com
Low-chill fruits including figs, kiwis, bananas, peaches, grapes, pears, mayhaws, apples, plums, and hardy citrus

Mail-Order Natives
P.O. Box 9366
Lee, FL 32059
(850) 973-4688
www.mindspring.com/~plants/natives.
catalogue.html
Trees and shrubs native to the Southeast region including pawpaws, hickories, oaks, and tupelos

Florida flame azalea

Native American Seed
127 N. 16th Street
Junction, TX 76849-0185
(800) 728-4043
www.seedsource.com
Seeds of Texas wildflowers and native grasses

Native Gardens
5737 Fisher Lane
Greenback, TN 37742
(423) 856-0220
Nursery-propagated native plants and seed for meadows and natural landscaping

Nature's Nook
1578 Marion Russell Road
Meridian, MS 39301-8807
(601) 485-5161
natures@cybertron.com
Tough perennials and small shrubs for harsh conditions in the Deep South

Niche Gardens
1111 Dawson Road
Chapel Hill, NC 27516
(919) 967-0078
www.nichegdn.com
Nursery-propagated Southeastern wildflowers and native trees and shrubs; perennials, ornamental grasses, and herbs

Pine Ridge Gardens
832 Sycamore Road
London, AR 72847-8767
(501) 293-4359
Native plants of the south central region including perennials, shrubs, hostas, and Japanese and Siberian irises

Seeds of Change
P.O. Box 15700
Santa Fe, NM 87506-5700
(888) 762-7333
www.seedsofchange.com
Organically grown, open-pollinated, and heirloom selections of vegetable and flower seed

Shooting Star Nursery
444 Bates Road
Frankfort, KY 40601
(502) 223-1679
Plant and seed natives east of the Rocky Mountains, as well as wildflower mixes. Consultation on habitat restoration

Cosmos

R. H. Shumway Seed Company
P.O. Box 10
Graniteville, SC 29829
(803) 663-9771
Open-pollinated vegetables, annuals, and perennials, as well as berries and green manure crops

Southern Exposure Seed Exchange
P.O. Box 170
Earlysville, VA 22936
(804) 973-4703
www.southernexposure.com
Heirloom and open-pollinated vegetables, annuals, herbs, grains, gourds; books and seed-saving supplies

Southern Perennials and Herbs
98 Bridges Road
Tylertown, MS 39667
(601) 684-1769
www.s-p-h.com/
Perennials, herbs, gingers, vines, grasses, as well as flowering shrubs adapted to the Deep South

Story House Herb Farm
587 Erwin Road
Murray, KY 42071
(502) 753-5928
storyhouseherbs@yahoo.com
Many varieties of organically grown herbs for the kitchen garden

Sunlight Gardens
174 Golden Lane
Andersonville, TN 37705
(423) 494-8237; (800) 272-7396
sungardens@aol.com
Nursery-propagated wildflowers for the Southeast and Northeast

Tomato Growers Supply Company
P.O. Box 2237
Fort Myers, FL 33902
(941) 768-1119; (888) 478-7333;
fax (888) 768-3476
www.tomatogrowers.com
Many selections of tomato seed; hot and sweet peppers; growing supplies and books

Wildseed Farms
425 Wildflower Hills
P.O. Box 3000
Fredericksburg, TX 78624-3000
(800) 848-0078
www.wildseedfarms.com/
Seed for several kinds of wildflowers, as well as regional mixes

Willhite Seed Inc.
P.O. Box 23
Poolville, TX 76487
(800) 828-1840
www.willhiteseed.com
Vegetables suited to the South including melons, corn, tomatoes, cowpeas, peppers, gourds, and squash

Woodlanders, Inc.
1128 Colleton Avenue
Aiken, SC 29801
(803) 648-7522
woodlanders@pop.duesouth.net
Southeastern native trees, vines, shrubs, ferns, ground covers, and perennials, as well as hard-to-find exotics

Louisiana iris

PRODUCTS AND SERVICES

A&L Eastern Agricultural Labs, Inc.
7621 Whitepine Road
Richmond, VA 23237
(804) 743-9401
Soil tests; analysis of plant tissue, water
and fertilizers for the East Coast

The Beneficial Insect Company
244 Forrest Street
Fort Mill, SC 20715-2325
(803) 547-2301
www.bugfarm.com
Beneficial insects; natural and biological
pest controls

Benner's Gardens
6974 Upper York Road
New Hope, PA 18938
(800) 753-4660
www.bennersgardens.com
Humane and environmentally safe deer
control products including mesh fencing

Biofac
P.O. Box 87
Mathis, TX 78368
(512) 547-3259; (800) 233-4914
Beneficial insects

Bio Ag Supply
710 S. Columbia
Plainview, TX 79072
(806) 293-5861; (800) 746-9900
wwinters@texasonline.net
Beneficial insects; organic products
including fish and seaweed fertilizer and
composting supplies

The Bug Store
113 W. Argonne
St. Louis, MO 63122
(800) 455-2847 (BUGS)
www.bugstore.com
Beneficial insects, natural and biological
pest controls, animal repellents, earthworms, and predator urine

Carolina Stalite Company
P.O. Box 1037
205 Klumac Road
Salisbury, NC 28145-1037
(877) 737-6284
www.stalite.com/
Expanded slate products to improve soil
drainage and reduce compaction (Perma-
Till) and to deter voles (VoleBloc)

DripWorks
190 Sanhedrin Circle
Willits, CA 95490
(707) 459-6323
www.dripworksusa.com
Drip irrigation supplies

Eden Organic Nursery Services
P.O. Box 4604
Hallandale, FL 33008
(954) 455-0229
www.eonseed.com
Organic seed of specialty vegetables,
herbs, and house plants; organic fertilizer
and pest control products

Gardener's Supply Company
128 Intervale Road
Burlington, VT 05401
(802) 863-1700
www.gardeners.com
Tools, fertilizers, greenhouses, floating
row covers, composters, as well as natural
pest controls

Gardens Alive!
5100 Schenley Place
Lawrenceburg, IN 47025
(812) 537-8651
gardener@gardens-alive.com
Soap Shield fungicidal soap, Scythe herbicidal soap, beneficial nematodes, organic
fertilizers, composting supplies, floating
row covers

Apple maggot trap

Harmony Farm Supply
P.O. Box 460
Graton, CA 95444
(707) 823-9125
www.harmonyfarm.com
Organic fertilizers, natural and biological pest controls, IPM monitoring tools, drip irrigation supplies, as well as seed for cover crops

Home Harvest Garden Supply
3712 Eastern Avenue
Baltimore, MD 21224
(800) 348-4769
www.homeharvest.com
Beneficial insects, natural and biological pest controls, organic fertilizers, hydroponic supplies, and grow lights

Integrated Fertility Management
333 Ohme Gardens Road
Wenatchee, WA 98801
(509) 662-3179; fax (509) 662-6594
Organic fertilizers, pest and disease controls; organic growing consultation; soil and plant tissue analysis

Natural Gardening Company
217 San Anselmo Avenue
San Anselmo, CA 94960
(415) 456-5060
www.naturalgardening.com
Organic gardening supplies and fertilizers, drip irrigation supplies, composters, as well as seed

Green lacewing

Nature's Control
P.O. Box 35
Medford, OR 97501
(541) 899-8318; fax 1-800-698-6250
bugsnc@teleport.com
Beneficial insects

Nitron Industries
P.O. Box 1447
Fayetteville, AR 72702-1447
(800) 835-0123
www.nitron.com
Organic fertilizers and Nitron A-35 for soil conditioning and detoxification

Peaceful Valley Farm Supply
P.O. Box 2209
Grass Valley, CA 95945
(530) 272-4769
www.groworganic.com
Organic gardening supplies, beneficial insects, natural pest controls, cover crops, bulbs, and wildflower seed

Rohde's Nursery and Nature Store
1651 Wall Street
Garland, TX 75041
(972) 864-1934; (800) 864-4445
www.beorganic.com
Native plants of Texas, organic fertilizers, natural and biological pest controls, bird and bat houses

Lacewing eggs encased in rice hulls.

The Urban Farmer Store
2833 Vicente Street
San Francisco, CA 94116
(415) 661-2204
Drip irrigation, lighting and pond supplies, and fertilizer systems

Worm's Way
7850 Highway 37 N
Bloomington, IN 47404-9477
(800) 274-9676
www.wormsway.com
Organic fertilizers, beneficial insects, composters, earthworms, hydroponic and indoor lighting equipment

Floating row cover protects these turnips from insect pests.

Fall color paints the hills of northeastern Alabama.

COOPERATIVE EXTENSION SERVICES

Have a question that this book doesn't answer? The horticultural specialists at your county Cooperative Extension Office are the folks to call. Phone numbers are subject to change.

ALABAMA

Baldwin (334) 937-7176
Bibb (205) 926-3117
Blount (205) 274-2129
Butler (334) 382-5111
Calhoun (256) 237-1621
Chilton (205) 755-3240
Colbert (256) 386-8570
Dekalb (256) 845-8595
Etowah (256) 547-7936
Hale (334) 624-8710
Houston (334) 794-4108
Jefferson (205) 325-5342
Lee (334) 749-3353
Limestone (256) 232-5510
Madison (256) 532-1577
Marion (205) 921-3551
Mobile (334) 690-8445
Montgomery (334) 265-0233
Morgan (256) 773-2549
St. Clair (205) 338-9416
Shelby (205) 669-6763
Talladega (256) 362-6187
Tuscaloosa (205) 349-3870, ext. 288
Walker (205) 221-3392

ARKANSAS

Benton (501) 271-1060
Cleburne (501) 362-2524
Craighead (870) 933-4565
Crittenden (870) 739-3239
Faulkner (501) 329-8344
Grant (870) 942-2231
Hot Spring (501) 332-5267
Jefferson (870) 534-1033
Miller (870) 779-3609
Ouachita (870) 837-2288
Perry (501) 889-2661
Sebastian (501) 782-4947
Washington (501) 444-1755

DELAWARE

Kent (302) 697-4000
New Castle (302) 831-2667
Sussex (302) 856-7303

DISTRICT OF COLUMBIA

Washington (202) 274-7115

FLORIDA

Alachua (904) 955-2402
Brevard (407) 633-1702
Broward (954) 370-3725
Charlotte (941) 639-6255
Dade (305) 248-3311
Duval (904) 387-8850
Flagler (904) 437-7464
Hillsborough (813) 744-5519
Lake (352) 343-4101
Lee (941) 338-3232
Leon (850) 487-3003
Manatee (941) 722-4524
Marion (352) 620-3440
Nassau (904) 879-1019
Orange (407) 836-7570
Pasco (352) 521-4288
Pinellas (727) 582-2100
Polk (941) 533-0765
St. Johns (904) 824-4564
Santa Rosa (850) 623-3868
Sarasota (941) 316-1000
Volusia (904) 822-5778

GEORGIA

Athens-Clarke (706) 613-3640
Augusta-Richmond (706) 821-2349
Bibb (912) 751-6338
Bulloch (912) 764-6101
Chatham (912) 652-7981
Cobb (707) 528-4070
Coweta (770) 254-2620
DeKalb (404) 371-2821
Dougherty (912) 436-7216
Douglas (770) 920-7225
Fayette (404) 461-6041, ext. 412

Southern magnolia

Floyd   (706) 295-6210
Fulton   (404) 730-7000
Glynn   (912) 267-5655
Gwinnett   (770) 822-7700
Hall   (404) 531-6988
Harris   (706) 628-4824
Lowndes   (912) 333-5185
Macon   (912) 472-7588
Pierce   (912) 449-2034
Pike   (770) 567-2010
Thomas   (912) 225-4130
Tift   (912) 386-7870
Walker   (706) 638-2548

KENTUCKY

Boone   (606) 586-6101
Bourbon   (606) 987-1895
Boyle   (606) 236-4484
Bullitt   (502) 543-2257
Christian   (502) 886-6328
Daviess   (502) 685-8480
Fayette   (606) 257-5582
Franklin   (502) 695-9035
Graves   (502) 247-2334
Hardin   (502) 765-4121
Jefferson   (502) 425-4482
Madison   (606) 623-4072
Simpson   (502) 586-4484
Warren   (502) 842-1681
Woodford   (606) 873-4601

LOUISIANA

Bossier   (318) 965-2326
Caddo   (318) 226-6805
Desoto   (318) 872-0533
East Baton Rouge   (225) 389-3056
Lincoln   (318) 251-5134
Morehouse   (318) 281-5741
Natchitoches   (318) 357-2224
Orleans   (504) 482-1107
Ouachita   (318) 323-2251
Rapides   (318) 473-6605
St. Charles   (504) 782-6231
St. John   (504) 497-3261
St. Landry   (318) 948-0561
St. Martin   (318) 332-2181
St. Tammany   (504) 892-2208
West Baton Rouge   (504) 336-2416
Winn   (318) 638-1014

MARYLAND

Home and Garden Information
Center (800) 342-2507
Toll free within Maryland

MISSISSIPPI

Adams   (601) 445-8201
Attala   (601) 289-1321
Desoto   (601) 429-1343
Forrest   (601) 545-6083
Harrison   (228) 865-4227
Hinds   (601) 372-1424
Holmes   (601) 834-2795
Jackson   (228) 769-3047
Lafayette   (601) 234-4451
Lamar   (601) 794-8504
Lauderdale   (601) 482-9764
Lee   (601) 841-9000
Leflore   (601) 453-6803
Lowndes   (601) 328-2111
Oktibbeha   (601) 323-5916
Pike   (601) 783-5321
Rankin   (601) 825-1461
Warren   (601) 636-5442
Washington   (601) 334-2669
Yazoo   (601) 746-2453

MISSOURI

Boone   (573) 445-9792
Butler   (573) 686-8064
Cape Girardeau   (573) 243-3581
Clay   (816) 792-7787
Cole   (573) 634-2824
Greene   (417) 862-9284
Jackson   (816) 252-5051

Jefferson   (314) 797-5391
Newton   (417) 455-9500
St. Charles   (314) 970-3000
St. Louis   (314) 889-2911

NORTH CAROLINA

Alamance   (336) 570-6740
Brunswick   (910) 253-2610
Buncombe   (828) 255-5522
Carteret   (252) 728-8421
Catawba   (828) 465-8240
Cumberland   (910) 484-7156
Davidson   (704) 242-2080
Durham   (919) 560-0525
Edgecombe   (252) 641-7815
Forsyth   (336) 767-8213
Gaston   (704) 922-0301
Guilford   (336) 375-5876
Henderson   (828) 697-4891
Lenoir   (252) 527-2191
Mecklenburg   (704) 336-2561
Moore   (910) 947-3188
Onslow   (910) 455-5873
Orange   (919) 732-8181, ext. 2050
Pamlico   (919) 745-4121
Pasquotank   (919) 338-3954
Pitt   (919) 757-2803
Randolph   (336) 318-6000
Wake   (919) 250-1100
Wayne   (919) 731-1520

Classically Southern: Azaleas bloom beneath a live oak.

Purple coneflowers, black-eyed Susans, and blazing star vie for attention.

OKLAHOMA

Choctaw (580) 326-3359
Cleveland (405) 321-4774
Comanche (580) 355-1176
Creek (918) 224-2192
Garfield (580) 237-1228
Kay (580) 362-3194
McClain (405) 527-2174
Muskogee (918) 687-2458
Oklahoma (405) 713-1125
Okmulgee (918) 756-1958
Osage (918) 287-4170
Payne (405) 747-8320
Rogers (918) 341-2736
Sequoyah (918) 775-4838
Tulsa (918) 746-3700
Wagoner (918) 486-4589
Washington (918) 534-2216

SOUTH CAROLINA

Aiken (803) 649-6297
Anderson (864) 226-1581
Beaufort (843) 470-3655
Charleston (843) 722-5940
Cherokee (864) 489-3141
Florence (843) 661-4800
Georgetown (843) 546-6421
Greenville (864) 232-4431
Greenwood (864) 229-6681
Kershaw (803) 432-9071
Lexington (803) 359-8515

Marion (843) 423-8285
Oconee (864) 638-5889
Orangeburg (803) 534-6280
Pickens (864) 868-2810
Richland (803) 929) 6030
Spartanburg (864) 596-2993
Sumter (803) 773-5561
York (803) 684-9919

'Ballerina', a disease-resistant rose

TENNESSEE

Anderson (423) 457-5400, ext. 246
Bradley (423) 476-4552
Campbell (423) 562-9474
Coffee (931) 723-5141
Davidson (615) 862-5995
Fayette (901) 465-5233
Franklin (931) 967-2741
Henry (901) 642-2941
Lawrence (931) 762-5506
Madison (901) 668-8543
Maury (931) 388-9557
Montgomery (913) 648-5725
Obion (901) 885-3742
Putnam (931) 526-4561
Rutherford (615) 898-7710
Sevier (423) 453-3695
Shelby (901) 544-0243
Warren (931) 473-8484
Washington (423) 753-1680
Williamson (615) 790-5721

TEXAS

Austin (409) 865-5911, ext. 170
Bastrop (512) 303-0187
Bell (254) 933-5305
Bexar (210) 467-6575
Brazoria (409) 849-5711
Brazos (409) 823-0129
Cameron (956) 399-7757
Chambers (409) 267-8347
Comal (830) 620-3440
Dallas (214) 904-3050
Denton (940) 565-5537
El Paso (915) 859-7725
Harris (281) 855-5600
Harrison (903) 935-4835
Jones (915) 823-2432
Lubbock (806) 767-1190
McLennan (254) 757-5180
McMullen (512) 274-3323
Midland (915) 687-1351
Nacogdoches (409) 560-7711
Nueces (512) 767-5223
Parker (817) 599-6591, ext. 168
Potter (806) 372-3829
San Patricio/Aransas
  (512) 790-0103
Smith (903) 535-0885
Tarrant (817) 884-1945
Taylor (915) 672-6048
Tom Green (915) 659-6524
Travis (512) 473-9600
Tyler (409) 283-8284
Val Verde (830) 774-7591
Victoria (512) 575-4581
Wichita (940) 716-5580

VIRGINIA

Albemarle   (804) 984-0727
Alexandria   (703) 519-3325
Appomattox   (804) 352-8244
Arlington   (703) 228-6400
Chesterfield   (804) 751-4401
Culpeper   (540) 727-3435
Fairfax   (703) 324-8556
Fauquier   (540) 341-7950
Frederick   (540) 665-5699
Giles   (540) 921-3455
Hanover   (804) 752-4310
Henrico   (804) 501-5160
Henry   (540) 634-4650
Loudoun   (703) 777-0373
Lynchburg   (804) 847-1585
Madison   (540) 948-6881
Newport News   (757) 591-4838
Norfolk   (757) 683-2816

Sugar maple in October

Northampton   (757) 414-0731
Orange   (540) 672-1361
Prince William   (703) 792-6285
Richmond   (804) 333-3420
Richmond City   (804) 786-4150
Rockingham   (540) 564-3080
Virginia Beach   (757) 427-4769
Warren   (540) 635-4549

WEST VIRGINIA

Berkeley   (304) 264-1936
Cabell   (304) 526-8676
Harrison   (304) 624-8650
Kanawha   (304) 768-1202
Ohio   (304) 234-3673
Preston   (304) 329-1391
Raleigh   (304) 255-9321

Bluebonnets and wildflowers, Texas Hill Country

SUPPLIERS AND EXPERT RESOURCES

INDEX

Note: Page references in **bold type** indicate main listings for garden plants, pests and beneficial insects, plant ailments, and weeds. Here you will find the most detailed information, including photographs or illustrations and chemical and other control methods. Page references in *italics* indicate other photographs or illustrations.

Photography Credits

For pages with six or fewer photographs, each image has been identified by its position on the page: Left (L), center (C), or right (R); top (T), middle (M), or bottom (B). On other pages, photographs are identified by their position in the grid (shown right). Photographs on the back cover are designated as "back."

L	LC	RC	R
1	1	1	1
2			
3			
4			

Ian Adams: 319. **William Adams:** 146 TR; 181 R; 215 L; 221 L; 272 L. **Henry C. Aldrich:** 269 R; 271 BR; 278 R; 283L. **Walt Anderson:** 176 R; 268 L; 291 BL. **Art Antonelli:** 171 BR, TR. **R.F. Ashely/Visuals Unlimited:** 199 T. **Max E. Badgley/Biological Photography:** 168 R; 177 M; 317 T. **Bill Beatty/Wild & Natural:** 201 R4; 299 TR; 301 R; 304 TL. **Bill Beatty/Visuals Unlimited:** 221 R; 241 L; 255 L; **Steve Bender:** 146 L. **Ronald F. Billings:** 151 R; 238 R. **Jack M. Bostrack/Visuals Unlimited:** 213 R. **Ralph S. Byther:** 188 R; 209 L; 211 L; 212 L; 216 L; 222 R; 226 R; 230 L; 232 TR; 243 L; 251 R; 252 R. **Gary W. Carter/Visuals Unlimited:** 142 BL; 182 BL; 202 L2; 281 TR. **James L. Castner:** back TR; 144 R4; 149 BR; 150 R; 163 L; 164 R; 166 R; 178 L, R; 179 L; 180 BL, TL; 181 L; 183 L; 191 BR; 192 L; 194 R; 195 L. **David Cavagnaro:** 33 T. **David Cavagnaro/Visuals Unlimited:** 154 R. **Dr. Pat Cobb:** 150 BL, TL. **Kevin & Betty Collins/ Visuals Unlimited:** 159 L. **Wendy W. Cortesi:** 260 BR. **Crandall & Crandall:** 33 BL; 79 B; 316 B. **Whitney Cranshaw:** 209 R; 259 R. **David Cudney:** 261. **John D. Cunningham/Visuals Unlimited:** 286 TR; 293 BR. **Alan & Linda Detrick:** back TL; 143 T; 152 L; 169 R. **J.F. Dill:** 144 L1, L2; 156 L; 160 TR; 188 L. **Robert W. Domm/Visuals Unlimited:** 199 BR. **Wally Eberhart/Visuals Unlimited:** 196 L. **Tom Edwards/ Visuals Unlimited:** 202 R2. **Clyde Elmore:** 270 BR; 273 L, TR; 274 BL; 277 L; 280 TR; 302 L. **R. Thomas E. Eltzroth:** 29 BR; 214 R; 217 R; 242 L. **Arlyn Evans/AgStock USA:** 160 L. **William E. Ferguson:** 29 T; 30 T; 149 L; 168 BL; 170 R; 174 L; 183 L; 185 L, R; 187 R; 201 R1, R3. **Charles Marden Fitch:** 169 L; 189 R; 190 L. **Galen D. Gates:** 320 T. **Susan M. Glascock:** 268 R; 284 R, TL; 286 BR; 290 R; 293 TR; 300 R; 304 BL. **David Goldberg:** 25 BL; 64 B; 72 B, M; 79 T; 228 L; 229 L; 246 L; 255 R; 258 L; 264 R; 266 R; 267 R; 273 BR; 282 TR; 283 TR; 286 L; 288 BL; 293 L; 297 R; 299 TL. **Harold Greer:** 244 L. **Austin Hagan:** 208 L, R; 210 L, R; 216 R; 218 BR; 224 L, R; 232 L; 237 L; 240 R; 249 L; 251 L; 253 L. **Ali Harivandi:** 235 L; 254 L; 265 TL; 274 L. **Jessie M. Harris:** 305 R. **Phil Harvey:** 50 BR; 231 L. **Larry Hodgson:** 82 B. **G.J. Holmes/North Carolina State University:** 213 BL. **Saxon Holt:** 67 TL; 215 R. **Jeffrey Howe/Visuals Unlimited:** 182 TL. **Tom Isakeit/Texas A&M University:** 253 BR, TR. **Richard C. Johnson/Visuals Unlimited:** 260 TR. **A.L. Jones/Visuals Unlimited:** 222 L. **Suzanne Kores/Fairchild Tropical Garden:** 70. **Dwight Kuhn:** 31. **Stephen J. Lang/Visuals Unlimited:** 203 B. **Magnolia Plantations:** 311 B. **Raymond R. Maleike:** 231 R; 235 R; 238 L; 257 R. **Charles Mann:** 315 B. **S. Maslowski/Visuals Unlimited:** 142 TR. **Joe McDonald/Visuals Unlimited:** 160 BR; 200 B; 202 L1. **Charles W. Melton:** 199 BL; 200 TL; 202 L3; 203 T. **William T. Molin:** 263 L; 285 L; 287 TR; 295 L. **Tim R. Murphy/University of Georgia:** 270 L; 278 L; 306 L.

D. Newman/Visuals Unlimited: 71. **M. Ober/Visuals Unlimited:** 260 TR. **Glenn M. Oliver/Visuals Unlimited:** 223 R. **Pamela K. Peirce:** 20 TL, TM; 23 TC; 29 BL; 34 B; 67 BR, TR; 162 TL; 167 TL; 173 BR; 177 R; 192 R; 196 TR; 213 TL; 220 R; 227 L, R; 229 R; 233 R; 247 L; 252 L; 263 R; 267 L; 270 TR; 279 L; 281 R; 285 R; 287 BR; 290 TL; 292 BL, R; 294 BR; 298 BR, TR; 301 L; 303 R; 306 R. **Rod Planck/Tom Stack & Associates:** 69 B. **Norman A. Plate:** 3; 27 TL; 36 TR; 37 TL, TR; 61 T; 65; 68 BC, BL. **James H. Robinson:** 196 BR; 202 R1. **James V. Robinson:** 148 R. **Henry W. Robison/Visuals Unlimited:** 151 TL. **Edward S. Ross:** 175 L. **Susan A. Roth:** 212 R; 321 B, T. **Janet Sanchez:** 291 TL; 303 L; 317 B. **Karen-Beth G. Scholthof:** 245 L. **Science VU/Visuals Unlimited:** 151 BL; 155 L; 214 L; 220 L; 239 L; 248 L. **Dave Shetlar:** 153 R; 154 L. **Richard Shiell:** 23 BL; 72 T; 201 L2; 202 L4; 245 R; 276 BL; 280 BR; 288 TR; 292 TL; 296 L; 305 BL, TL; 307 R. **Malcolm C. Shurtleff:** 207 L; 223 L; 240 L; 242 R; 243 L; 250 R. **Steve Sibbett:** 237 R. **Gary W. Simone:** 219 L, R; 225 L; 226 L; 228 R; 233 L; 254 R; 256 L, R. **Rob & Ann Simpson/Visuals Unlimited:** 201 L3. **John J. Smith:** 265 R; 269 L; 271 L; 272 R; 274 R; 279 R; 288 BR; 294 L; 300 L; 304 R. **J.G. Strauch, Jr.:** 204 TR; 244 R. **Dan Suzio:** 144 R1, R2, R3; 198 T; 282 BR. **Dean G. Swan:** 265 BL; 281 BR; 288 TL; 299 BL. **Gerald D. Tang:** 282 BL. **Richard Thom/Visuals Unlimited:** 198 B. **Michael S. Thompson:** 20 BL, M; 23 ML; 37 B; 204 BR. **Connie Toops:** 298 L. **Mark Turner:** 282 TL; 299 BR. **Larry Ulrich:** 318 T. **R. Valentine/Visuals Unlimited:** 225 R. **VISIONS-Holland:** 85 T. **Richard Walters/Visuals Unlimited:** 66; 193 R. **Washington State University:** 155 R. **Darrow M. Watt:** 68 M; 85 B. **William J. Weber/Visuals Unlimited:** 159 R; 162 BL; 191 TR; 201 L1; 277 R. **Ron West/Nature Photography:** 29 M; 36 TL; 68 TL, TR; 144 L3, L4; 145; 146 BR; 147 L, R; 148 L; 149 TR; 152 R; 153 L; 157 L, R; 158 L, R; 161 BL, R, TL; 162 L; 163 R; 164 L; 165 BR, L, TR; 166 BL, TL; 167 BL; 168 TL; 170 L; 171 L; 172 BR, R, TR; 173 L; 175 R; 177 L; 179 R; 180 R; 182 R; 184 BR, L, TR; 186 L, R; 187 BL, TL; 189 L; 190 BR, TR; 191 L; 193 L; 197 L, R; 198 M; 200 M; 201 R2; 211 R; 217 L; 232 BR; 239 L; 241 R; 250 L; 276 TL; 287 L; 291 R; 296 R. **Doug Wilson:** 23 BR; 50 BL. **Tom Woodward:** 7; 19 T; 83 TR; 84 R; 205 T. **Tom Wyatt:** 28 TR; 81 T; 318 B. **Peter F. Zika/Visuals Unlimited:** 284 BL. **Thomas A. Zitter:** 218 L; 230 R; 246 R; 257 BL, TL; 258 R.

Illustrators: Lois Lovejoy: 35. **Jane McCreary:** 24; 32. **Jenny Speckels:** 31; 42; 59; 78.

Acknowledgments

Our thanks to the following experts for their contributions to this book:

John Cisar (Professor, Environmental Horticulture, University of Florida); Patricia Cobb (Entomologist, Professor, Auburn University); Austin Hagan (Plant Pathologist, Professor, Auburn University)

Special thanks to John J. Arthur, American Cyanamid Company; Edgar Holcomb, University of Florida, IFAS (Institute of Food and Agricultural Sciences); Sally W. Smith; Britta Swartz